Troubleshooting and Configuring the Windows® NT®/95 Registry

201 West 103rd Street
Indianapolis, IN 46290-1097

To those who still believe, and those who help others to believe, in the good and in the power of the will. We can, because we try.

Copyright © 1997 by Sams Publishing

FIRST EDITION

International Standard Book Number: 0-672-31066-x

Library of Congress Catalog Card Number: 97-65464

2000 99 4

Interpretation of the printing code: the rightmost double-digit number is the year of the book's printing; the rightmost single-digit, the number of the book's printing. For example, a printing code of 97-1 shows that the first printing of the book occurred in 1997.

Composed in 2 Stone Sans, MCPdigital, Sabon, and Parisian by Macmillan Computer Publishing

Printed in the United States of America

Trademarks

Publisher and President *Richard K. Swadley*
Publishing Manager *Dean Miller*
Director of Editorial Services *Cindy Morrow*
Managing Editor *Mary Inderstrodt*
Director of Marketing *Kelli S. Spencer*
Assistant Marketing Managers *Kristina Perry*, *Rachel Wolfe*

Acquisitions Editor
Kim Spilker

Development Editor
Brian-Kent Proffitt

Software Development Specialist
Patricia J. Brooks

Production Editor
Brice P. Gosnell

Copy Editor
Margaret Bersen

Indexers
Johnna L. VanHoose
Bruce Clingaman

Technical Reviewer
Toby Tapp

Editorial Coordinator
Katie Wise

Technical Edit Coordinator
Lynette Quinn

Resource Coordinator
Deborah Frisby

Editorial Assistants
Carol Ackerman
Andi Richter
Rhonda Tinch-Mize

Cover Designer
Tim Amrhein

Book Designer
Louisa Klucznik

Copy Writer
David Reichwein

Production Team Supervisors
Brad Chinn
Charlotte Clapp

Production
Mona Brown
Deirdre Smith
Mary Ellen Stephenson
Becky Stutzman

Overview

Contents

Part III Making Changes to the Registry

Acknowledgments

I am amazed every day at the amount of work it takes to produce a book like this. I am grateful for the tremendous work of Kim Spilker, Brian Proffitt, Brice Gosnell, Patty Brooks, and Margaret Bersen at Sams Publishing, the technical editor Toby Tapp, and many others whose names I do not know. Without their help, I would be lost. I appreciate their boundless patience, their enormous effort, and their unwavering faith in me.

I am grateful to my friends at Mastering Computers, who gave me the opportunity to work with Windows NT, and the countless doors they have opened for me. I would particularly like to thank Chris, Frank, Dan, Lorrin, and Aaron for making learning more exciting, and for all their encouragement, friendship, and help, particularly with tips about System Policy Editor. I would also like to thank Kristen, Dave, Laurie, and Brittany for making the road more fun.

But mostly, I am grateful for my sweet wife, Kimbrey, who loves me in spite of me, who puts up with all my crazy hours and ideas, and waits until I leave to shake her head at the zany things I do. She spends all I earn, but gives to me more than I could ever express. To her, I am forever indebted.

About the Author

Clayton Johnson has been working with computers since 1983, and teaching about them since 1985. He has worked at all levels of the computer business from retail to manufacturing, with an emphasis on training. Since starting to teach seminars in 1991, he has taught over 900 seminars (and still counting). His seminars have taken him throughout the world, and his companies have had offices in the U.S., Australia, New Zealand, and the United Kingdom.

He has written and published three other books, *The Windows NT Registry*, *Trainers Hot Tips for WordPerfect 5.1*, and *Trainers Hot Tips for WordPerfect 6.0*, and is currently a contributor to *Windows NT Magazine*. He has also written 16 seminars on topics ranging from basic computer skills to WordPerfect to Microsoft Office to hardware troubleshooting to Windows NT.

His current company, Tip City, is dedicated to creating and producing innovative training materials for the corporate environment where conventional seminars, videotapes, and CDs may not meet the training needs of the organization. Feel free to contact Clayton via e-mail at `claytonj@registrymasters.com` or visit his Web site for more Registry hints and tips at `www.registrymasters.com`.

Tell Us What You Think!

As a reader, you are the most important critic and commentator of our books. We value your opinion and want to know what we're doing right, what we could do better, what areas you'd like to see us publish in, and any other words of wisdom you're willing to pass our way. You can help us make strong books that meet your needs and give you the computer guidance you require.

Do you have access to CompuServe or the World Wide Web? Then check out our CompuServe forum by typing `GO SAMS` at any prompt. If you prefer the World Wide Web, check out our site at `http://www.mcp.com`.

Note

If you have a technical question about this book, call the technical support line at 317-581-3833.

As the publishing manager of the group that created this book, I welcome your comments. You can fax, e-mail, or write me directly to let me know what you did or didn't like about this book—as well as what we can do to make our books stronger. Here's the information:

Fax: 317-581-4669

E-mail: `opsys_mgr@sams.samspublishing.com`

Mail: Dean Miller
Sams Publishing
201 W. 103rd Street
Indianapolis, IN 46290

Introduction

This book is designed to give administrators the tools they need to effectively manage, troubleshoot, and configure the Registry for both Windows NT and Windows 95 systems. Other books focus on the technical and programming aspects, which have limited value to the administrator needing to help the organization's users. This book is not really designed for programmers. It is designed for administrators and users to allow them to understand, use, and optimize the Registry. With this book, you will get the level of technical information required to administer all the systems in your organization.

Windows NT and Windows 95 Registries are both covered in *Troubleshooting and Configuring the Windows NT/95 Registry*. There are some differences, and even more similarities. The Windows NT Registry is not "compatible" with the Registry from Windows 95, and there is no easy upgrade from one to the other. The differences are based on feature differences, file structure, and locations of entries.

With such a difference, why have one book that covers both? The use, editing, and policies for both are almost exactly the same. As an administrator, nearly everything we do with the Registry is exactly the same in both NT 4.0 and 95. With the proliferation of Windows NT and Windows 95, you may have a combination of systems in your organization that includes both types of systems. The release of NT 4.0 brought the interface in line with Windows 95, and the user-level functions are almost identical. Virtually all of the things that are different between the two Registries are based on the differences in the file structure.

The file structure for the NT Registry is UNICODE, and the file structure for the 95 Registry is ASCII. This allows security features to be implemented for the NT Registry that are not available for the 95 Registry. So, even if the content and the locations were exactly the same, the two Registries still would not be compatible.

How to Read This Book

Obviously, you could read this book from cover to cover and learn nearly everything there is to know about the Registry. Alternatively, you can focus on information specific to NT or specific to 95. For a quick look at the common functions, see Table Intro.1. Table Intro.2 lists the functions, by chapter, that are specific to Windows NT, and Table Intro.3 lists the Windows 95–specific functions by chapter.

Table Intro.1. Common Registry functions.

Function	*Chapter Number*
The Role of the Registry	1
Registry Files	2
Registry Problems	3
Automatic Changes to the Registry	8
Making Manual Changes to the Registry Using `REGEDIT.EXE`	10
Remote Registry Editing	11

Function	*Chapter Number*
How the Registry Controls Hardware	12
Troubleshooting and Configuring Hardware Registry Settings	15
Q&A for Hardware and the Registry	16
How the Registry Controls Windows Networking	17
Troubleshooting and Configuring Networking Registry Settings	20
Q&A for Networking and the Registry	21
How the Registry Controls Windows Users	22
Troubleshooting and Configuring User Registry Settings	26
Q&A for Users and the Registry	27
System Policy Editor: Understanding Policy Files	28
System Policy Editor: Understanding Template Files	29
Managing the Local Registry with System Policy Editor	30
Creating Custom Policies	34

Table Intro.2. Windows NT–specific functions.

Function	*Chapter Number*
Protecting the NT Registry	4
Recovering from an NT Registry Failure	5
Making Manual Changes to the Registry with REGEDT32.EXE	9
Windows NT and the HAL	13
Windows NT Networking and the Registry	18
Windows NT 4.0 Users and the Registry	23
Windows NT 3.51 Users and the Registry	24
Managing Domain Computers with System Policy Editor	31
Managing Domain Users with System Policy Editor	32
Cloning Windows NT	35

Table Intro.3. Windows 95–specific functions.

Function	*Chapter Number*
Protecting the Windows 95 Registry	6
Recovering from a Windows 95 Registry Failure	7
Windows 95 and Plug and Play	14
Windows 95 Networking and the Registry	19
Windows 95 Users and the Registry	25
Managing Windows 95 Users with System Policy Editor	33
Cloning Windows 95	36

Sneak Peek at the Sections of the Book

The book is separated into sections that group common functions together. As an alternative to learning all the Windows 95 functions, for example, you could focus your efforts on System Policy Editor, in Part VII, "Advanced Registry Management." Whichever way you choose, there is much to learn and use in your organization.

Part I, "Registry Basics," gives the necessary information to get you started in understanding the Registry. What the Registry does, how it is organized, where the data is stored, and the terminology is discussed in detail.

Part II, "Protecting the Registry," gives hints, techniques, and step-by-step instructions so you can protect the Registries of your systems in your organization. The Registry can be fragile, and can easily be corrupted. Use the information in this section to ensure your Registries are secure.

Part III, "Making Changes to the Registry," explains and illustrates how the Registry is changed. Control Panel functions and the Registry editors are discussed in detail, allowing you to make the necessary changes to keep your system up to date and working in the optimum way.

Part IV, "Hardware Control and the Registry," focuses on the settings required to effectively control the hardware in your systems. Specific emphasis is placed on problem solving and troubleshooting, so that you can fix the hardware configuration problems that you are having.

Part V, "Networking Control and the Registry," is designed so you can control and troubleshoot networking challenges with NT and 95. Again, specific emphasis is placed on problem solving and troubleshooting, with network connectivity and configuration as major areas of concentration.

Part VI, "User Control and the Registry," will help you solve interface and usage problems that your users are having. It will allow you to change the nature of the interface, giving you choices and opportunities to reduce operator error and increase productivity and user satisfaction.

Part VII, "Advanced Registry Management," will take you beyond the normal editing and troubleshooting functions into the realm of organization-wide system and user management and control. The System Policy Editor can effectively make changes for every user on the network, if that is your choice. Cloning systems is also in this section, allowing you to quickly and effectively deploy standardized systems throughout your organization.

Part VIII, "Using Shareware Registry Tools," will introduce you to several shareware tools that can radically change your approach to the Registry. Step-by-step instructions will lead you through the process, and give you abilities not available in the standard offerings from Microsoft.

Conventions Used in This Book

Unless otherwise indicated, all of the information applies equally with Windows NT 4.0 and Windows 95. Rather than needing a separate volume that would have a significant overlap of information, they are all included together. When included information applies to both, Windows 95 and Windows NT 4.0 will be referred to as "Windows." Anytime Windows 3.x or Windows NT 3.5x are referred to, they will be named specifically, and unless named specifically, the term "Windows" will not include them.

Text Conventions

- New terms appear in *italics*.
- All code appears in `MONOSPACE`.
- Placeholders in text (words or text that are actually typed) are in *`monospace`* italics.
- Code that is too long to fit on one line will be broken, and a code continuation character (➥) will be inserted at the beginning of the second line. The text should actually be entered on one line without breakage.

Note

A Note box presents interesting pieces of information related to the surrounding discussion.

Tip

A Tip box offers advice or teaches an easier way to do something.

Caution

Caution boxes present warnings and describe the consequences of particular actions.

Warning

A Warning box advises you about potential problems and helps steer you clear of disaster.

Solutions

A special feature of this book are the Solutions. These special sections demonstrate how to solve tough problems with creative answers in a question and answer format. An index of Solutions can be found on the inside front cover of the book.

A Word About Editing the Registry

Because the Registry is so critical to NT and 95, any damage to the Registry can make the system unusable. Make sure the Registry has a good backup (using the detailed information in Chapters 4 and 6), and use extreme caution. With a secure backup, you can recover from nearly any failure.

I hope you enjoy it. Good luck on your journey.

Part I

Part I
Part I
Part I
Part I
Part I
Part I
Part I
Part I
Part I
Part I
Part I

Registry Basics

CHAPTER 1

The Role of the Registry

The Registry is a set of data files used to help Windows control hardware, software, the user's environment, and the "look and feel" of the Windows interface. Formerly, these functions were performed by `WIN.INI`, `SYSTEM.INI`, and `.INI` files that are associated with applications.

The evolution of application and operating system control has three distinct levels:

- In Legacy Windows systems, `SYSTEM.INI` and `WIN.INI` held all the control functions for the operating systems and applications. Essentially, `SYSTEM.INI` controlled the hardware while `WIN.INI` controlled the desktop and applications. All changes to drivers, fonts, settings, and preferences would be stored in the `.INI` files. Any new application that was installed added pointers to the `.INI` files. Those pointers would then be referenced in the application's code.
- Additional `.INI` files that controlled the applications were added by programmers who needed more control than was available because of the limited size of the `WIN.INI` and `SYSTEM.INI` files. For example, Microsoft included with Excel a file called `EXCEL.INI`, which held the options, settings, defaults, and other information critical to making Excel work correctly. The only pointer that was then required in `WIN.INI` was to the `EXCEL.INI` path and filename.
- The Registry was initially developed as a reference file for data-file associations to applications. It was expanded to include all functions for 32-bit operating systems and applications. Though some 32-bit applications still have `.INI` files, it is quite rare. The Registry has no absolute maximum size, but a setting controls the maximum size in the System section of the Control Panel. The larger size allows users to have more complex operating systems and more installed applications.

Originally, `SYSTEM.INI` and `WIN.INI` controlled all Windows and application features and access. It worked well when average users used only a few applications. As the number and complexity of applications grew, so did the number of entries to the `.INI` files. The downside of this approach, in a growing environment, is that everyone would make changes to the `.INI` files when applications were added to the system. However, no one ever removed references from their `.INI` files when they removed applications, so `SYSTEM.INI` and `WIN.INI` continued to get larger and larger. Each incremental size increase meant slower performance. Even upgrading applications presented its challenges. The upgrade would add entries but never take the old ones away, presumably to ensure compatibility if another program was to access the settings.

Because the maximum size of an `.INI` file is 64KB, an obvious problem arose. To counter the problem, vendors started supplying `.INI` files of their own, with just pointers to the specific `.INI` files in `WIN.INI` and `SYSTEM.INI`. The downside of this approach was the proliferation of `.INI` files throughout the system and the hierarchical nature of access. (If `WIN.INI` made a particular setting, and an application's `.INI` file overrode that setting, who was responsible and where should—or could—a system-wide setting that had priority be made?)

Another potential problem arose because of the `.INI` files. Because any user could easily edit the files with any text editor, the `.INI` files were always at risk. Users could try to edit the files and make mistakes, which might make the files useless, and the applications that they controlled non-functional. Also, there could also be a security problem because of the ease of access to the files and the information they contained.

The Registry is a set of files that control all aspects of the operating system and how it works with outside events. Those "events" range from accessing a hardware device directly to how the interface will react to a specific user to how an application will be run and much more. It was designed to work exclusively with 32-bit applications, and file size is limited to a whopping

40MB. That should be sufficient for most users, and usually the ones who do have a problem with it are only those with a very large number of users on an NT network. It would be nearly impossible to fill 40MB of Registry with application information alone. (Whenever you say something "is more than we'll ever need," just remember that IBM said that about the meager 16KB of RAM on the original IBM PC). Because Windows 95 networking is peer-to-peer, each system controls only itself, and has no Registry information on other systems. A Windows NT system may hold user information on thousands of people, dramatically increasing the Registry size.

Fortunately, if more space is required for the Registry because of the number of users, the network can be split up into multiple domains.

The Registry is complex by its very nature, and on purpose.

What the Registry Does

The Registry is the data file for all 32-bit hardware/driver combinations and 32-bit applications in both Windows NT and Windows 95. Sixteen-bit drivers do not work in NT, so all devices are controlled through the Registry, even those normally controlled by the BIOS. In Windows 95, 16-bit drivers will continue to work as real-mode devices, and they use `SYSTEM.INI` for control.

Sixteen-bit applications will work in either NT or 95, and the applications still refer to `WIN.INI` and `SYSTEM.INI` files for information and control.

Without the Registry, the operating system would not have the necessary information to run, to control attached devices, to launch and control applications, and to respond correctly to user input.

Data File for OS to Hardware/Drivers

The Registry is a database of all the settings and locations of 32-bit drivers in the system. Figure 1.1 illustrates the positioning of the Registry in relation to Windows NT and the drivers.

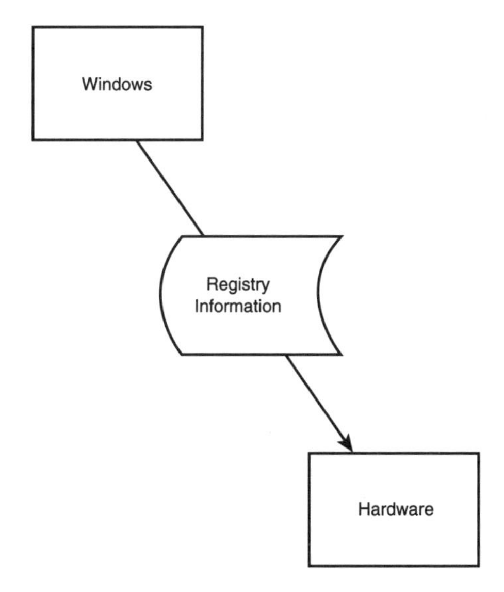

Figure 1.1.
Windows uses the Registry to control hardware.

When the OS needs to access hardware devices, it uses drivers, even if the device is a BIOS-supported device.

With Windows NT, the appropriate drivers are loaded, based on the information the BIOS supplies to NT. From that point on, NT never looks to the BIOS for information again, unless the system is restarted. Windows 95 also utilizes drivers for BIOS-supported devices, but continues to interact with the BIOS for some items.

Note

The utilization of BIOS information in Windows 95 allows greater backward compatibility with hardware than is available with Windows NT. Windows 95 has the capability to use both older and newer hardware than is usable with Windows NT, because new drivers are easier to write for 95, and 95 can still use real-mode drivers. This makes 95 more flexible than NT on the one hand, and more unstable on the other.

Non-BIOS–supported devices that are installed must also have a driver. The drivers are independent of the OS, but the OS needs to know where to find them, the filename, the version, and other settings and information. Depending on the device, the driver may be different for NT and 95. Some devices, like modems, use exactly the same drivers for both NT 4.0 and Windows 95. Without Registry entries for each of the devices, they would not be usable. Likewise, any problems with the Registry may also make them unusable. Obviously, if a programmer makes a mistake in the setup files that affect the Registry settings, the device may not work at all.

Solutions

If I have a bad driver, how can I get a new one?

If the driver you have is not working correctly, first try reinstalling the driver from the original disk. If the device still doesn't work, get a new driver from the manufacturer. Many times, the driver that ships with a device will be prepared before the final touches are made to the product. Inevitably, there will then be differences that may make the driver incompatible, or it may contain a bug.

The best place today to get a new driver from a manufacturer is to download it from the company's Internet Web site. Usually, the device documentation will contain the address to the site, and you can then download the driver directly.

Another alternative is to download it from the manufacturer's technical bulletin board (BBS) directly. Again, many manufacturers put a number in the documentation.

If you have no addresses available to get the file directly, call the technical support phone number and ask for a new driver. Most of the time, they will ask you for the date or version number of the driver, which you can get from the Control Panel, Windows NT Diagnostics, or other utilities such as Norton Utilities.

Data File for OS to Applications

When a user attempts to launch an application, the Registry supplies application information to the OS so the application can be found, the correct data file locations are set, and other settings are available. The relationship between Windows, the Registry, and applications is shown in Figure 1.2.

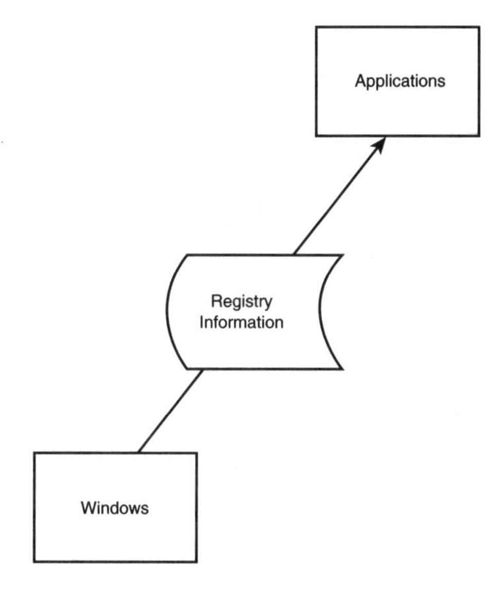

Figure 1.2.
Windows uses the Registry to control applications.

The Registry holds information about default data and auxiliary file locations, menus, button bars, window status, and other options. It also holds installation information such as the date of installation, the user who installed the software, the version number and date, and sometimes the serial number. Depending on the actual software installed, it may contain other application-specific information.

Two Types of Control

Although, in general, the Registry controls all 32-bit applications and drivers, the type of control it exercises is based on users and computers, not on applications or drivers. Every Registry entry controls a user function or a computer function. User functions would include the desktop appearance and home directory, for example. Computer functions are related to installed hardware and software, items that are common to all users.

Some application functions affect users, and others affect the computer and are not specifically set for an individual. Similarly, drivers may be user-specific, but, most of the time, they are for general use by the computer. All of the settings discussed in the rest of the book are separated by user and computer.

Some examples of user-type functions controlled by the Registry are

- Control Panel functions
- Desktop appearance and icons
- Network preferences
- Explorer functionality and features

Some of those functions are the same regardless of user; others are user-specific.

Computer-related control items are based on the computer name, without respect to the logged-in user. An example of this type of control would be installing an application. The availability and access to the application is constant, regardless of the user; however, icons to launch the application are dependent on the user logging in to the network. Network protocol availability and priority is based on the computer, but current connections are based on user information.

Here are some examples of computer-based control items in the Registry:

- Access control
- Login validation
- File and print sharing
- Network card settings and protocols
- System performance and virtual memory settings

Because every system has a set of Registry files for itself, any user who uses that machine will be bound by those settings. The settings are unique to that system. This is one of the reasons that every system should have its Registry protected through secure backups (see Chapter 4, "Protecting the NT Registry," and Chapter 6, "Protecting the Windows 95 Registry").

By default, Windows 95 user information is stored at each individual machine. Because Windows NT was designed as a network-connected (rather than a stand-alone) system, the Registry information for NT users can be stored in the domain controller (the primary information in the primary domain controller, and a copy of it in each of the backup domain controllers). Placing the user information in the domain controller for centralized use is called roaming profiles. If roaming profiles are used, as a user logs in to the network, the Registry settings for that user are transferred or *mapped* to the system where the user has logged in and are used there.

If the NT system is not part of a domain, but is used as a stand-alone system or part of a workgroup, the user's information is stored at the local machine (just as it is with 95), will not be transferred to another system, and is not available to any other system on the network. Each machine is fully independent of the others. If you created a "perfect" desktop setting on one system in the workgroup's network, it would not be available to any other system. On a domain, on the other hand, it is possible to transfer those settings from system to system.

Summary

Without the Registry, Windows 95 and Windows NT would not be possible. They are too complex to be controlled by the older .INI files, and their expansion capabilities allow almost unlimited installation and use of applications. The Registry is, however, much more complex than the .INI files, and understanding how it works, what it does, and how to work with it is critical for effective system administration.

The Registry controls all 32-bit applications and their functions on the system, plus the interaction between multiple applications, such as copying and pasting. It also controls all the hardware and drivers. Though most of the settings are made during installation and through the Control Panel, understanding the Registry is fundamental to reliable and capable management of Windows NT and Windows 95 systems.

CHAPTER 2

The Structure of the Registry

The Registry is a complex database of information that was built in a hierarchical fashion by the writers and programmers of Windows NT. Much like a community that is made of estates that are made of buildings that are made of walls that are made of bricks, the Registry has many components. Putting the bricks and walls and estates together differently creates a different view. Similarly, even though the Registry contains basically the same types of components on different systems, they will be brought together in a different way, creating an absolutely unique Registry.

Figure 2.1 shows the hierarchical levels of the Registry, and the building block nature of it.

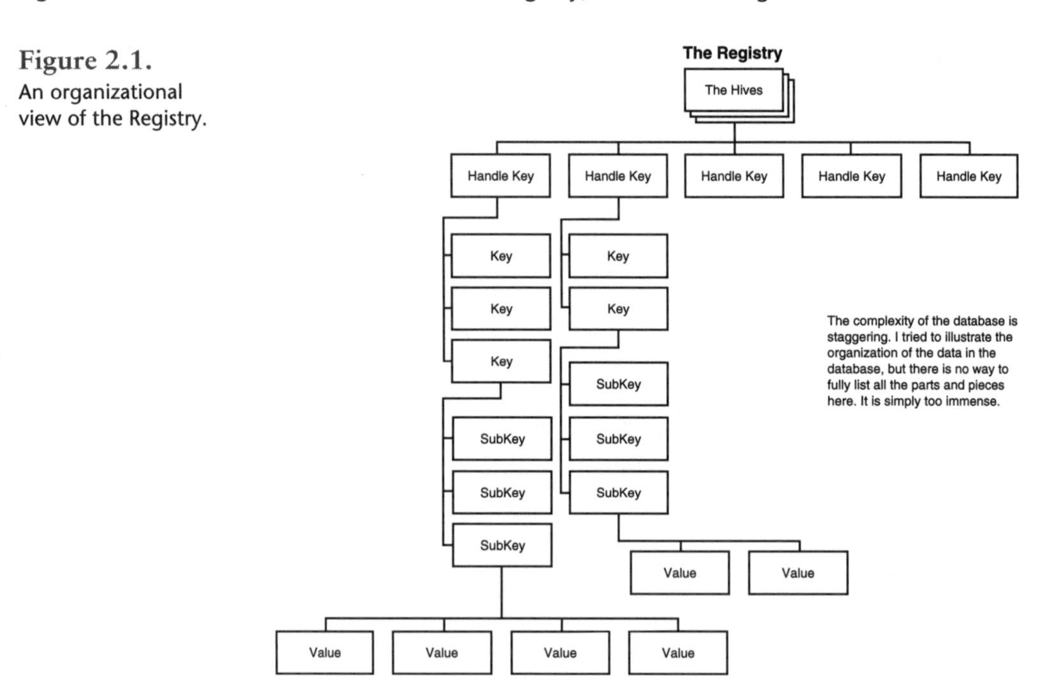

Figure 2.1.
An organizational view of the Registry.

Registry Files for Windows NT

Registry data for the computer settings and the default user settings is stored in five files in the `\WINNT\SYSTEM32\CONFIG` directory. (All references to the Windows NT system directory will be made as `\WINNT`, the default installation directory for the files. If your files are in a different location, use that directory name as a replacement for `\WINNT`.) Registry data for individual users in Windows NT is stored in the `\WINNT\Profiles\`*`username`*`\NTUSER.DAT` files. There is a profile and an `NTUSER.DAT` for every user who has logged on to that NT system. Additionally, there is a copy of that file on the Primary Domain Controller if the user is using a roaming profile. For more detail on roaming profiles, see Chapter 8, "Automatic Changes to the Registry."

The only users who have access to the Registry files are those in the Administrators or Power Users groups. Other users, although they can see the files, will not be able to edit, delete, or copy them. These files are often called the *hives*:

```
DEFAULT
SAM
SECURITY
SOFTWARE
SYSTEM
NTUSER.DAT
```

The other files in the `CONFIG` directory are auxiliary files for the Registry. Most of the auxiliary files have names that parallel the hive filenames, but with different extensions. The ones with the `.LOG` and `.EVT` extensions are event viewer files, and can be viewed with the Event Viewer. The ones with the `.SAV` extensions are files that were saved as part of the Last Known Good booting process (the last Registry that worked—these files won't change until your hardware changes and works correctly).

Registry Files for Windows 95

There are only two files that make up the hives in Windows 95, `SYSTEM.DAT` and `USER.DAT`.

All of the system Registry information for Windows 95 is stored in the system as `SYSTEM.DAT` in the Windows directory. All of the hardware settings and software information is stored in that file. It is much simpler than the NT Registry files, because there is not as much to control. Windows 95 was designed as a client to a network or as a stand-alone system, so there is not the same level of user control or security as in NT. That makes much of the work of the Registry easier, so the file is smaller.

Windows 95 Registry data for users is normally stored as `USER.DAT` in the Windows directory. If you set up the system through Control Panel | Passwords | User Profiles (as shown in Figure 2.2) to use more than one user profile, each user will have his own `USER.DAT` file stored as `\WINDOWS\Profiles\`*`username`*`\USER.DAT`. At startup, you would log on to the system, and the profile (`USER.DAT` information) from your directory would be loaded, maintaining your desktop and icons.

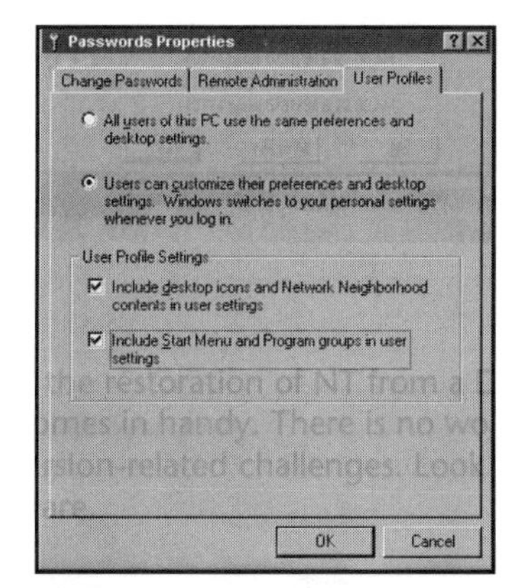

Figure 2.2.
Setting up the Windows 95 user profiles.

Handle Keys

All of the information is stored in the hives, but the Registry entries are displayed for review or editing in *handle keys* inside the Registry Editors. Handle keys are groupings of entries that are used to make finding and editing information easier. Because of this, the Registry is discussed in those terms here. There are six handle keys:

```
HKEY_LOCAL_MACHINE
HKEY_CLASSES_ROOT
HKEY_CURRENT_CONFIG
HKEY_DYN_DATA
HKEY_USERS
HKEY_CURRENT_USER
```

In NT 3.51 and earlier, there were only four handle keys; `HKEY_CURRENT_CONFIG` has been added in 95 and NT 4.0 to allow multiple hardware configurations. In Windows 95, there is yet another handle key, called `HKEY_DYN_DATA`, which holds all the Plug and Play information. Because NT 4.0 doesn't support Plug and Play, it does not use the `HKEY_DYN_DATA` handle key (even though you can see it with `REGEDIT.EXE`).

NT 4.0 has limited support for Plug and Play. It is limited to support for PCI devices that automatically determine their own port settings such as IRQs and I/O port addresses. NT 4.0 will not, however, override the settings of non-PCI hardware to bring it into compliance and ensure that the settings are not in conflict. NT 5.0/Cairo is supposed to implement those functions when it is released.

Note

The Registry in Windows NT is not compatible with the Windows 95 Registry. Upgrading from Windows 95 to Windows NT will require you to reinstall all 32-bit applications, re-create icons on the desktop, and re-create all of the user environment. This happens because, although the Registries look the same, some information is stored in different locations. This may contribute to application irregularities. Applications that work in Windows 95 may not work in NT. In order to get applications to work in NT, you will have to reinstall them (to the same directory, if desired, to save space). This also applies to Windows NT/ Windows 95 dual-boot environments.

Another reason the upgrade from Windows 95 to NT will not work is the difference in hardware control. The Windows 95 Plug and Play environment holds information differently than the HAL environment in NT, and the information cannot be transferred correctly. When both operating systems use a common hardware control scheme, there will be a seamless upgrade.

Handle keys simply make it easier to edit the Registry. Even though they are shown and edited as separate handle keys, `HKEY_CLASSES_ROOT` and `HKEY_CURRENT_CONFIG` are part of `HKEY_LOCAL_MACHINE`. (See Figure 2.3.) `HKEY_CURRENT_USER` is only a part of `HKEY_USERS`.

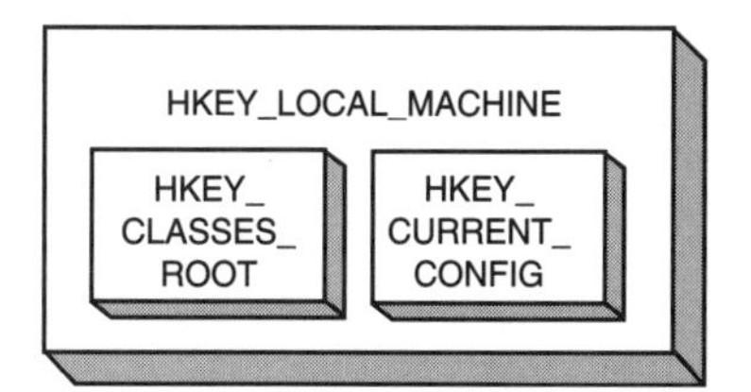

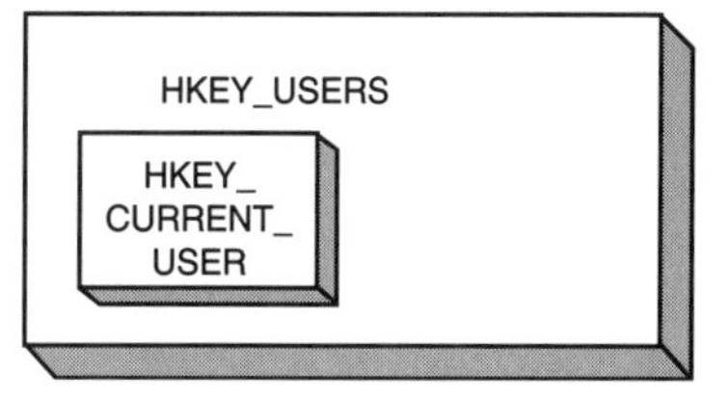

Figure 2.3.
All Registry entries are really part of two handle keys.

HKEY_LOCAL_MACHINE includes all of HKEY_CLASSES_ROOT and HKEY_CURRENT_CONFIG. Every time the computer is booted, the HKEY_CURRENT_CONFIG and HKEY_CLASSES_ROOT information is mapped and made available to view and edit.

HKEY_CLASSES_ROOT is actually HKEY_LOCAL_MACHINE\SOFTWARE\Classes, but editing it may be easier and less confusing in the HKEY_CLASSES_ROOT window. HKEY_CURRENT_CONFIG\SYSTEM\Current Control Set is the mapped information from HKEY\LOCAL_MACHINE\SYSTEM\Current Control Set.

HKEY_USERS includes the default user information and also the user information for whoever is currently logged in. When a domain member computer is started and a user logs in, the HKEY_CURRENT_USER information is automatically pulled from the domain controller, and the HKEY_CURRENT_USER information is mapped into the system's memory. The information about the rest of the users is not sent to the system, but is retained in the domain controller.

In a workgroup or a stand-alone computer, the information comes from the local hives because there is no domain controller.

Keys and Subkeys

The data is further divided into keys and subkeys, creating a hierarchical (Explorer-like) structure for easier editing, as shown in Figure 2.4. Each key has grouped information and is named based on the type of data in it. Every key that has a subkey is shown with a plus (+) sign in its folder icon to indicate that there is more below it. When opened, the folder's plus sign is replaced with a minus (-) sign, and the next level of subkeys is shown.

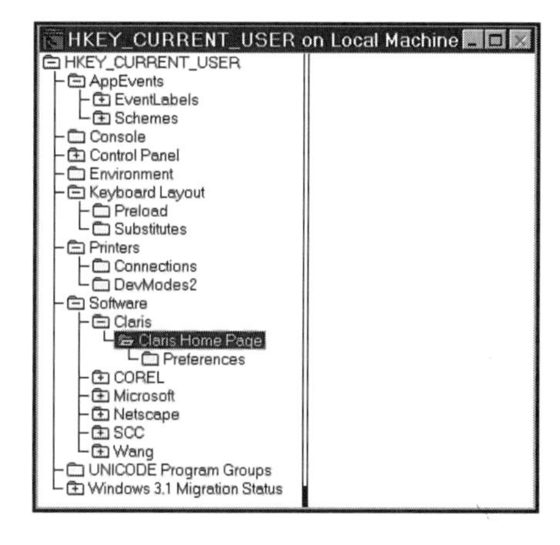

Figure 2.4.
The hierarchical structure makes it easier to find and edit necessary keys and values.

HKEY_LOCAL_MACHINE

All the settings to make software, hardware, and Windows work are in HKEY_LOCAL_MACHINE. All of the security, user rights, and sharing information is also included in this handle key, even though you cannot edit it here. User rights, security, and sharing information is edited through the Windows NT User Manager for Domains, the Explorer, and the Windows 95 Control Panel. The keys in HKEY_LOCAL_MACHINE in Windows NT are shown in Figure 2.5. Figure 2.6 shows the keys of HKEY_LOCAL_MACHINE for Windows 95.

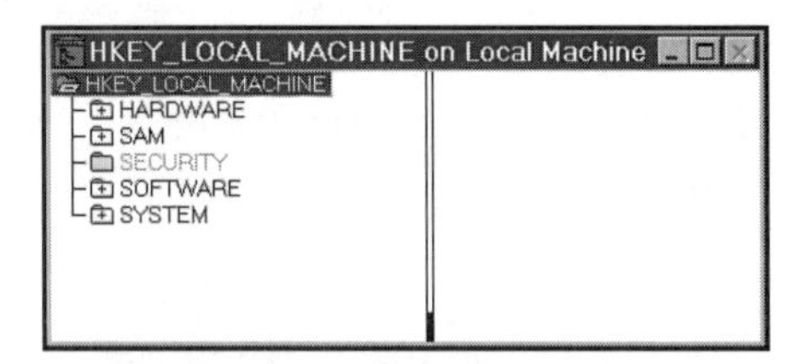

Figure 2.5.
HKEY_LOCAL_MACHINE keys in Windows NT.

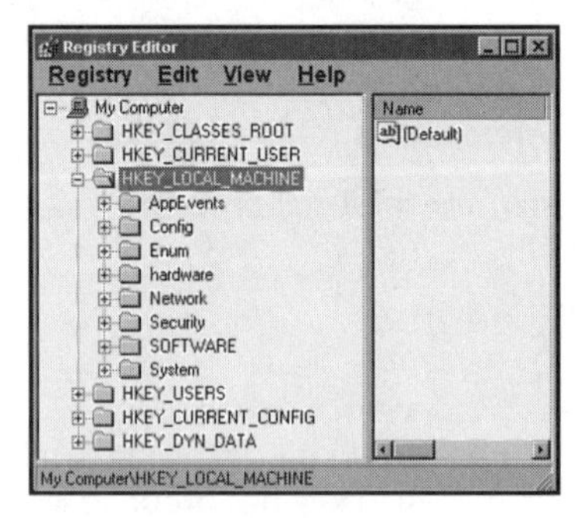

Figure 2.6.
HKEY_LOCAL_MACHINE keys in Windows 95.

For more detail on the individual keys, subkeys, and values contained in HKEY_LOCAL_MACHINE, see Appendix A, "A Closer Look at HKEY_LOCAL_MACHINE for Windows NT," or Appendix B, "A Closer Look at HKEY_LOCAL_MACHINE for Windows 95."

HKEY_CLASSES_ROOT

HKEY_CLASSES_ROOT contains all the information necessary to launch applications (see Figure 2.7):

- All the extensions and associations between applications and documents
- The names of all the drivers
- Strings used as pointers to the actual text they represent (for example, `aufile` actually represents `AU Format Sound`)
- Class ID numbers (the numbers used instead of names for accessing items)
- DDE and OLE information
- Icons used for applications and documents

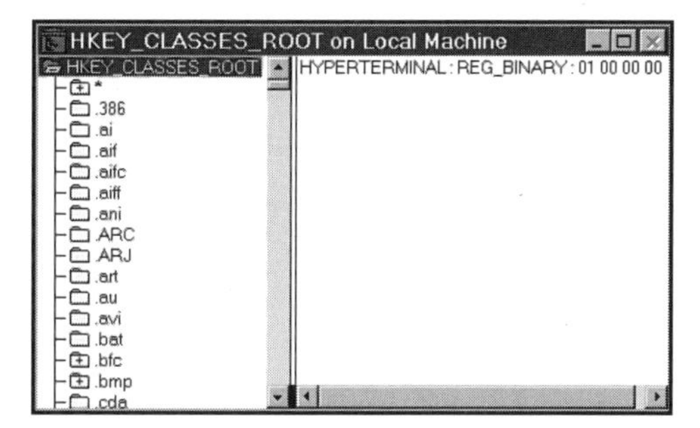

Figure 2.7.
HKEY_CLASSES_ROOT keys in Windows NT.

HKEY_CLASSES_ROOT in Windows 95 is shown in Figure 2.8, bearing a strong resemblance to the one in Windows NT. Because both share most of the same applications, the settings are almost identical.

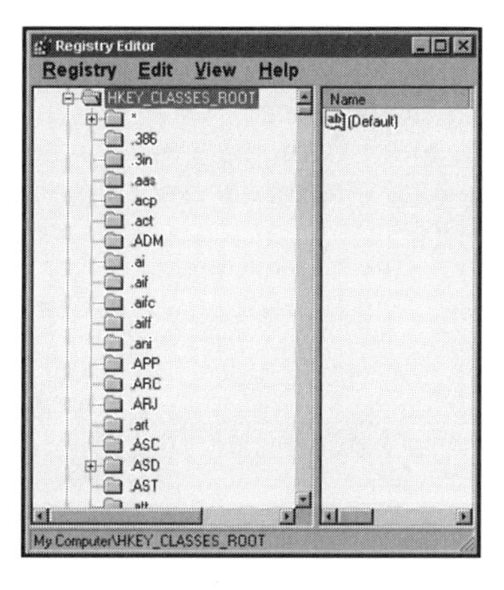

Figure 2.8.
HKEY_CLASSES_ROOT keys in Windows 95.

For more detail on the individual keys, subkeys, and values contained in HKEY_CLASSES_ROOT, see Appendix C, "A Closer Look at HKEY_CLASSES_ROOT."

Solutions

If the application control functions in the Registry and the interface are the same, why are there applications that work with Windows 95 that won't work with Windows NT?

Just because an application receives the "Windows 95 Compatible" logo from Microsoft, it doesn't mean that the program will also work with Windows NT. That was the original intention of Microsoft, but it turned out to be much more difficult than planned. When Microsoft determined that full compatibility would not be possible, they changed the standard, and decided that if the application was not compatible, it should at least be "graceful" in its refusal. Not all applications meet even that requirement.

continues

continued

The biggest difference between Windows 95 and NT has to do with control of hardware by applications. Windows 95 allows it, and Windows NT doesn't. So any application that will try to control hardware directly (instead of through operating system "calls") will fail in NT. That is the primary reason fax software for 95 will not work with NT. It is also the same reason that disk utilities, time clock programs, manufacturing control applications, and many others do not work in Windows NT.

HKEY_CURRENT_CONFIG

The mapping of `HKEY_LOCAL_MACHINE` for the current hardware configuration is in `HKEY_CURRENT_CONFIG`. If the system has only one configuration, the original configuration, the data will always be the same here. Creating an extra configuration in `Control Panel/System/Hardware Profiles` puts extra information in `HKEY_LOCAL_MACHINE`. With multiple configurations in Windows 95, you will be given a choice of profiles every time the computer is restarted. In Windows NT, you choose the hardware configuration in the Last Known Good menu by pressing the spacebar upon startup. Depending on which hardware profile is chosen, that specific information is mapped into `HKEY_CURRENT_CONFIG`. Figure 2.9 shows the `HKEY_CURRENT_CONFIG` keys in Windows NT, and Figure 2.10 shows the Windows 95 `HKEY_CURRENT_CONFIG` keys.

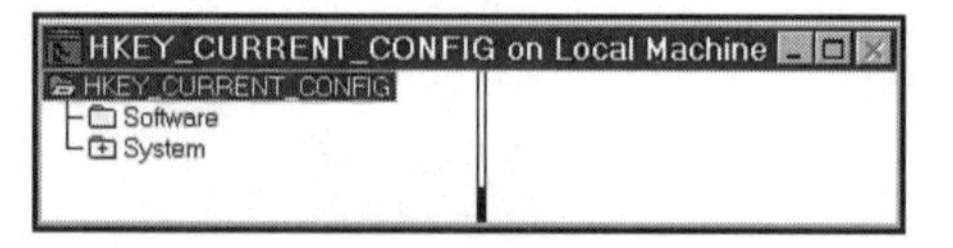

Figure 2.9.
`HKEY_CURRENT_CONFIG` keys in Windows NT.

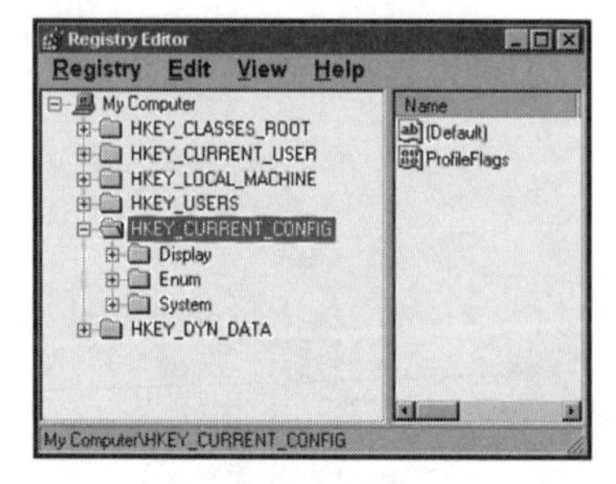

Figure 2.10.
`HKEY_CURRENT_CONFIG` keys in Windows 95.

For more detail on the individual keys, subkeys, and values contained in `HKEY_CURRENT_CONFIG`, see Appendix D, "A Closer Look at `HKEY_CURRENT_CONFIG` for Windows NT," or Appendix E, "A Closer Look at `HKEY_CURRENT_CONFIG` for Windows 95."

HKEY_DYN_DATA

HKEY_DYN_DATA is different from all the other Registry handle keys because it does not actually get written to the hard disk drive. A Windows 95 exclusive, HKEY_DYN_DATA is the handle key that stores Plug and Play information gathered and configured at startup. It is held in RAM and used by Windows 95 for hardware control. Because it is in RAM, and not pulled from the hard disk, every time you restart your machine, it is possible for the configuration to be different. There are over 1600 potential configurations that 95 must calculate at every startup. Of course, a potential problem may occur if the system changes critical settings and does not report that to Windows 95. It works well most of the time, but not always.

To turn off the Plug and Play configuration at startup, forcing Windows 95 to store the configuration settings, select the Resources tab in Control Panel | System after choosing the device. Some devices may also be controlled through their own applet, such as modems.

The keys in HKEY_DYN_DATA are shown in Figure 2.11. Depending on the system and installed features, there may be different keys in your system.

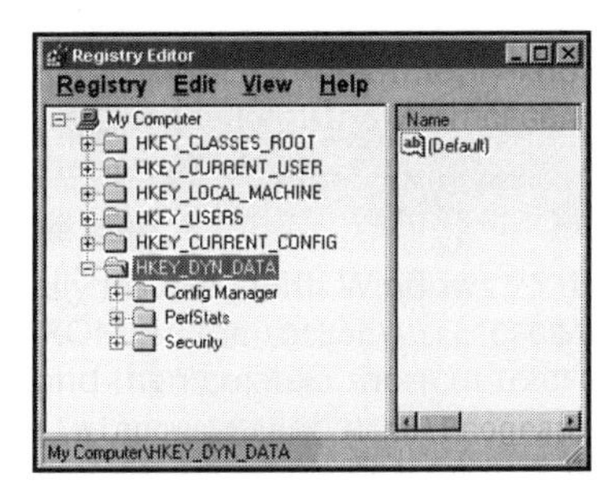

Figure 2.11. HKEY_DYN_DATA keys in Windows 95.

For more detail on the individual keys, subkeys, and values contained in HKEY_DYN_DATA, see Appendix F, "A Closer Look at HKEY_DYN_DATA."

HKEY_USERS

HKEY_USERS contains only information about the default user settings and the logged-in user. Although the hives contain settings for all the users individually, the user settings are normally inaccessible unless the user is actually logged in to the network. These settings tell the system which icons to use, what groups are available, which Start menu to use, what colors and fonts to use, and what Control Panel options and settings will be available. The associated keys are shown for Windows NT in Figure 2.12 and for Windows 95 in Figure 2.13.

Figure 2.12. HKEY_USERS keys in Windows NT.

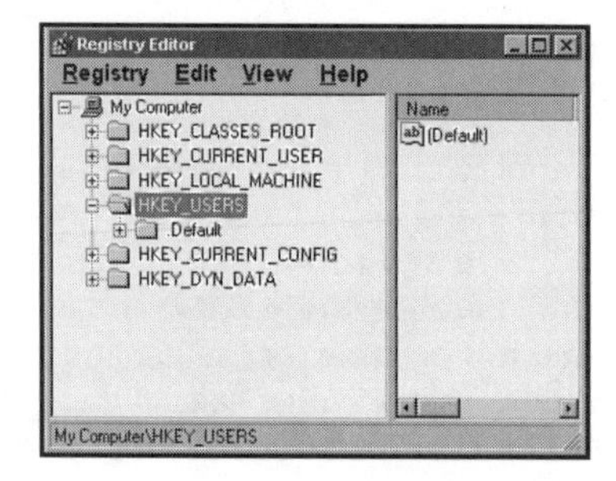

Figure 2.13.
HKEY_USERS keys in Windows 95.

For more detail on the individual keys, subkeys, and values contained in HKEY_USERS, see Appendix G, "A Closer Look at HKEY_USERS."

HKEY_CURRENT_USER

Instead of holding information for both the current user and the default users, HKEY_CURRENT_USER has mapped information only about the currently logged-in user. Notice the settings in Figure 2.14 for Windows NT, and the settings for Windows 95 in Figure 2.15.

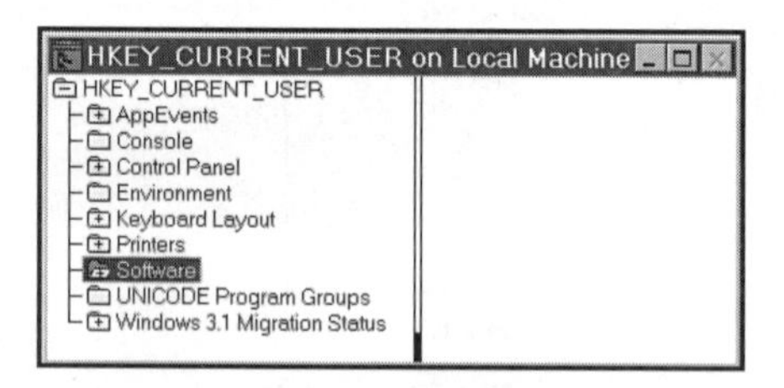

Figure 2.14.
HKEY_CURRENT_USER keys in Windows NT.

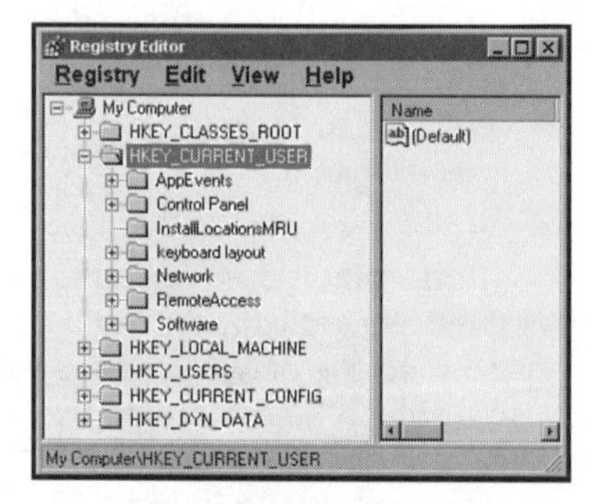

Figure 2.15.
HKEY_CURRENT_USER keys in Windows 95.

For more detail on the individual keys, subkeys, and values contained in HKEY_CURRENT_USER, see Appendix H, "A Closer Look at HKEY_CURRENT_USER."

Values

The actual settings in the Registry are in the values. These values and the resulting data are actually the controlling items, the most basic of all the building blocks of the Registry. There are six different types of data in the Registry, three of which are based on text strings, and three that are other data types.

String Values

In the Registry, a string is text information. It could be the text that is a description of a type of file, or a label on a hardware device, or even text that appears when you log on. It can be alpha or numeric information, usually with a maximum of 255 characters per string of text.

REG_SZ

REG_SZ stands for a simple text string. It is the most common type of value in the Registry, and many types of information can be entered into the NT String Editor dialog box, as shown in Figure 2.16. Descriptions, names, titles, paths, instructions, and other text items are examples of acceptable entries. The Windows 95 Edit String dialog box (shown in Figure 2.17) also shows the name of the value, but does not allow editing of the value name there.

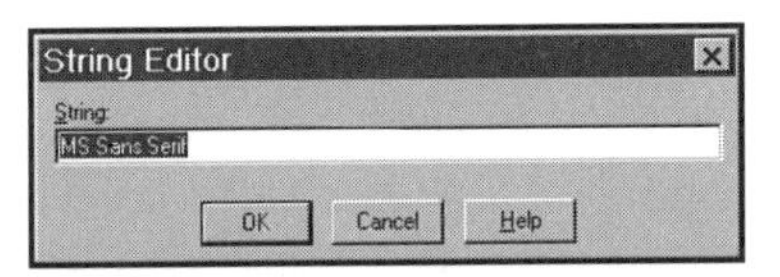

Figure 2.16. The String Editor dialog box in Windows NT.

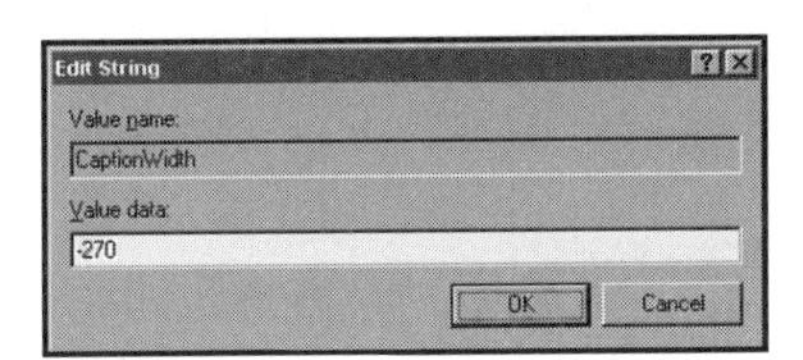

Figure 2.17. The Edit String dialog box in Windows 95.

A REG_SZ entry can also be a number. An example of the use of numbers in a REG_SZ entry is the entry of color saturation for RGB colors. In RGB color notation, white is listed as 255 255 255 (representing red, green, and blue saturation, respectively). White is full saturation. Red is 255 0 0 (full saturation of the red value and no others), green is 0 255 0, and blue is 0 0 255. All other colors are a combination of those. Light green is 192 220 192 and navy is 0 0 128. Dates, version numbers, and many other types of information are also represented as numeric information in a string entry.

REG_MULTI_SZ

A REG_MULTI_SZ entry allows the use of a list of items for a single value. Multiple network transport protocols, multiple items, lists of devices, and other similar list-entry items are examples of the use of a REG_MULTI_SZ entry. Figure 2.18 shows the dialog box used for data entry for a REG_MULTI_SZ value.

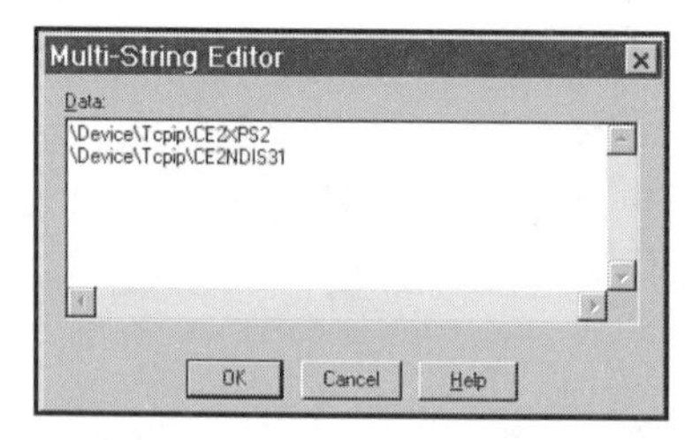

Figure 2.18. The Multi-String Editor dialog box.

Any items that would normally be in a list are examples of a REG_MULTI_SZ value. Items in a REG_MULTI_SZ value have multiple entries, each on its own line when more than one entry is used (such as multiple IP addresses for a single network card).

Windows 95 does not support REG_MULTI_SZ entries. Any items that are lists are entered as individual valuenames, or as comma-separated REG_SZ entries. The example shown in Figure 2.18, multiple IP addresses for a single network card, is not supported in Windows 95.

REG_EXPAND_SZ

REG_EXPAND_SZ is the notation for an expandable string. The editor, shown in Figure 2.19, looks exactly the same as the editor for a standard REG_SZ string. The difference is based on the use of variables. When a variable is typed into the REG_EXPAND_SZ editor, the system uses it as a variable, and replaces the variable with the proper text when activated.

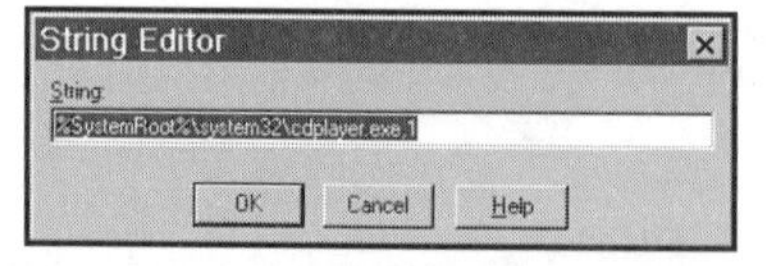

Figure 2.19. The String Editor dialog box.

An example would be the frequent use of %SYSTEMROOT%, which, when activated, would return the actual directory where the Windows NT files are located. %USERNAME% is used as a variable, and is replaced by the logged-on user's name. %PROCESSORFAMILY% would return Intel, Alpha, MIPS, or PowerPC when activated by the Registry.

Windows NT uses REG_EXPAND_SZ entries, but Windows 95 does not. That does not mean that 95 won't use variables. It does, but the 95 String Editor, used for editing REG_SZ entries, is intelligent enough to detect a variable and ensure that the system can use it.

Warning

If you use a REG_SZ string entry in Windows NT when a variable entry (REG_EXPAND_SZ) is required, the Registry will not replace the variable with the correct information. It will simply return the actual variable as text.

Other Data Types

The other three entries are numeric entries. REG_DWORD, REG_BINARY, and REG_RESOURCE_MAP allow numeric information to define settings for hardware and software items. Windows NT will use all three, but Windows 95 will only use REG_BINARY and REG_DWORD entries. Windows 95 still uses the same type of information, but always displays it as REG_BINARY entries in the Registry. In the Windows 95 Binary Editor, the data can be entered in binary code, using zeros and ones, or in hexadecimal. The actual numeric data for NT binary data can be entered in as Binary, Hexadecimal, or Decimal numeric entries. Those are three different ways to look at the same value, and depending on the type of data, one might be easier than the others. For example, the speed rating of a 100MHz processor might be listed as "1100011" in binary, "63" in hexadecimal, and "99" in decimal. In that circumstance, it is easier to work in decimal numbers. On the other hand, when you choose to disable the display of all the drives in the My Computer window, the decimal number is 67108863, but the binary equivalent is "11111111111111111111111111" (26 ones), each representing a drive letter to disable. In that case, editing in binary would be easier.

Warning

Even though the processor is labeled 100MHz by Intel, and actually shows up here as 99MHz, it is really the same. The difference is in the rounding. Intel rounds up (it sounds better), and the Registry rounds down. Don't change it.

REG_DWORD

REG_DWORD data is 32-bit information, always displayed as 4 bytes. It is useful for error-control functions, and may be viewed or edited in the DWORD Editor in the NT Registry in hexadecimal, binary, or decimal format. In the main windows of REGEDT32.EXE or REGEDIT.EXE, though, it will always show as hexadecimal. Figure 2.20 shows the DWORD Editor with the optional data display types for the numeric data entry.

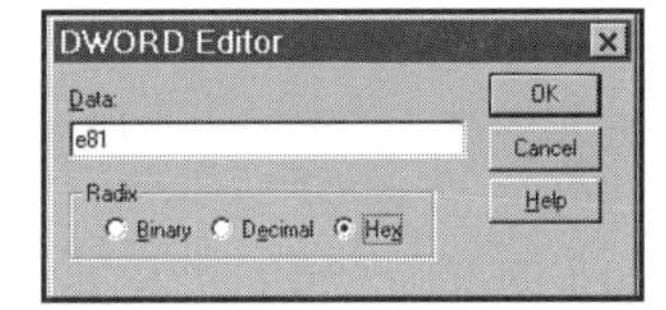

Figure 2.20.
The DWORD Editor dialog box.

The DWORD Editor is also used for the configuration of 32-bit components of application and operating-system software, for IRQ and other settings, and for dates.

REG_BINARY

REG_BINARY differs from REG_DWORD in that REG_BINARY can be any length, while REG_DWORD must be 32 bits in length. Most hardware-component information is stored in binary format (zeros and ones) and may be any length of bytes (each byte is represented by a two-digit number). This data can be displayed in either the standard binary format, in hexadecimal format, or in applications like Windows NT Diagnostics as easily readable data.

The way to edit NT REG_BINARY information is with the Binary Editor, as shown in Figure 2.21. Be very careful to enter the exact information. One misplaced 0 or 1 makes the entry completely wrong, and can have disastrous results.

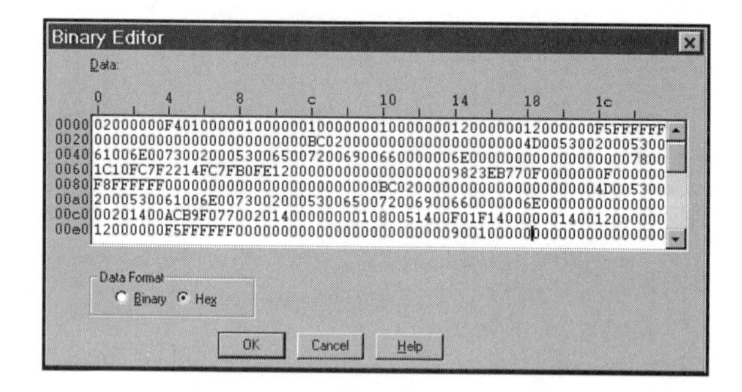

Figure 2.21.
The Binary Editor dialog box in Windows NT.

Notice in Figure 2.22, the Binary Editor for Windows 95, that there are no other listed options for data entry besides binary entries, and everything is shown as binary, with the hexadecimal equivalent showing at the right of the dialog box. You can enter data in hexadecimal on the right side, and the binary equivalent will be shown on the left, or the reverse.

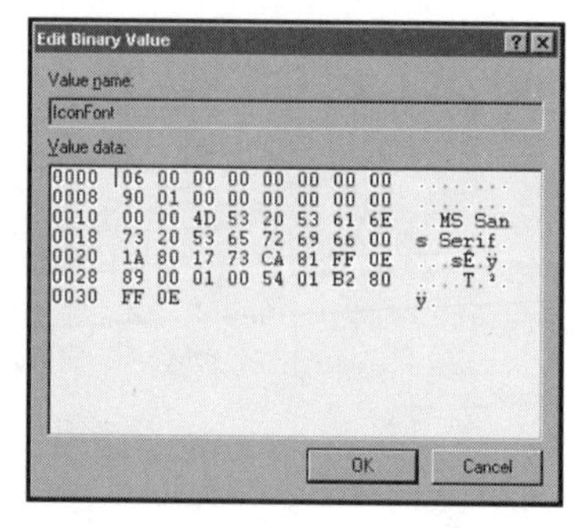

Figure 2.22.
The Edit Binary Value dialog box in Windows 95.

In Windows NT, REG_BINARY entries are quite rare. Most of the entries that are used in binary format are limited to 32 bits, and then are used as REG_DWORD entries. If a REG_DWORD entry were mistakenly entered as a REG_BINARY entry, it would still work without a problem. REG_BINARY entries simply have the flexibility to be longer.

In Windows 95, all 32-bit binary entries are shown as REG_BINARY, even though there is a REG_DWORD category. It's not until you actually edit the value that you can tell that it is a DWORD value.

Specialized System Entries

The REG_FULL_RESOURCE_DESCRIPTOR value entry in the Registry allows you to see and edit the actual settings that a hardware device is using. The data is pulled from many separate locations and is centralized for easy viewing. The most common place for this type of entry is the HKEY_LOCAL_MACHINE\HARDWARE\DESCRIPTION\System key and its enclosed values.

Figure 2.23 shows a full resource descriptor dialog box with its entries. The resources listed are the settings for a specific device, required for the system to configure it correctly.

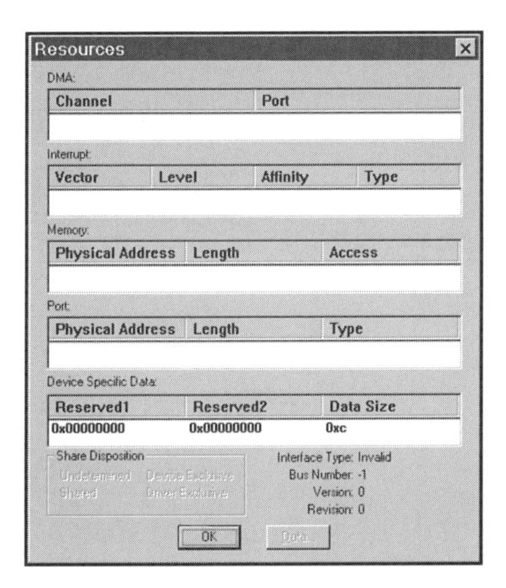

Figure 2.23.
A full resource descriptor dialog box in the Registry.

The Resource Lists value entry in the Registry is used when there is more than one set of full resource descriptors for a specific hardware device such as memory or network cards. The Resource Lists dialog box appears, as shown in Figure 2.24, allowing you to choose the type of resource list you want to see, and then the resource descriptor dialog box appears, allowing you to see and edit the entries.

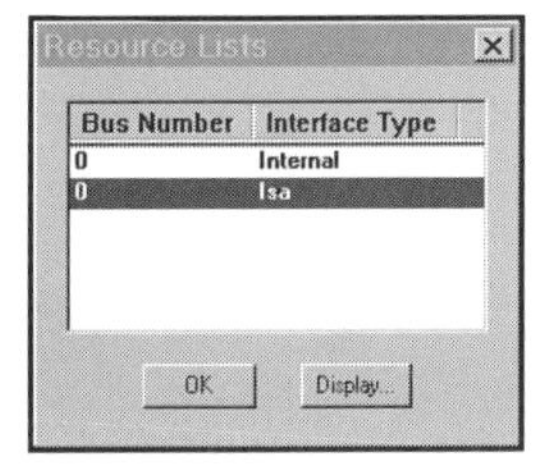

Figure 2.24.
A Resource Lists dialog box in the Registry.

Summary

The structure of the Registry is based on a hierarchical database of information that the operating system uses to configure itself, to activate and use hardware and software, and to present an acceptable interface to the user.

Windows 95 and Windows NT show the data in the Registry in different ways, but the same type of data is available. Characteristically, Windows 95 entries are easier to read, using `REGEDIT.EXE`, but Windows NT entries, shown in this chapter in `REGEDT32.EXE`, allow for more detail, which leads to greater control and easier editing.

Part II

Part II
Part II
Part II
Part II
Part II
Part II
Part II
Part II
Part II
Part II
Part II

Protecting the Registry

CHAPTER 3

Potential Registry Problems

If the Registry is severely damaged, access to hardware and software may be drastically limited, and the system may not even boot. Even in a case of a minor problem, an application may not work as it was designed, or may perform erratically.

Although Registry problems are rare, when they occur it can be devastating to the system, to applications, or even to data. The Registry is protected while it is running, so it is not possible to copy, delete, or change the contents, except through a "certified" program (installation programs, registry editing tools, and security changes through User Manager for Domains and the Explorer). Because of this protection, the Registry is quite secure—but it is not bulletproof. Problems can and do occur, and you need to be prepared to recognize them so you can fix them.

How to Recognize When You Have a Registry Problem

Most of us have heard of or felt the following symptoms, all of them characteristic of Registry problems:

- "It worked yesterday, but it won't work today."
- "It worked until I added this software/hardware, and now I can't use it."
- "My system doesn't work the way it used to."
- "When I try to shut down the computer, it just keeps beeping and beeping."
- "My computer won't start up."
- "Eeeeeek! It's the dreaded Blue Screen of Death!" (See Figure 3.1.)

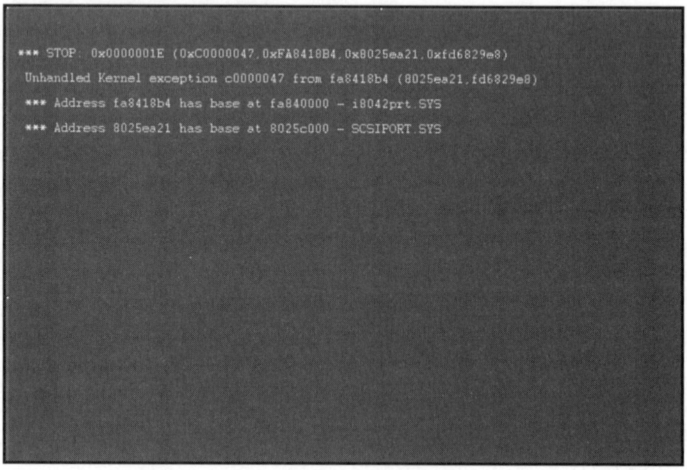

```
*** STOP: 0x0000001E (0xC0000047,0xFA8418B4,0x8025ea21,0xfd6829e8)
Unhandled Kernel exception c0000047 from fa8418b4 (8025ea21,fd6829e8)
*** Address fa8418b4 has base at fa840000 - i8042prt.SYS
*** Address 8025ea21 has base at 8025c000 - SCSIPORT.SYS
```

Figure 3.1.
An example of the Blue Screen of Death in Windows NT.

Note

The STOP message in Windows NT (lovingly called the Blue Screen of Death) identifies the type of exception. The second line qualifies the exception, showing whether it was *user mode* (involving user-mode operating system software) or *kernel mode* (involving the operating system or third-party drivers or hardware). The third and fourth lines describe which components were actually involved and at what addresses. The error in Figure 3.1 shows that it was a SCSI driver that failed. Check for compatibility and be sure you have the correct driver. It could also be that the settings were in error, meaning either they were wrong when they were added, or the Registry got corrupted and reported them incorrectly.

Each one of the symptoms or complaints listed is serious, although the seriousness of the problems varies. In any case, Registry problems will force you to take the time for repair, wasting precious productivity for your organization.

Recognizing the actual problem may not be as easy as recognizing the symptom. When problems occur, you generally assume, rightly or not, that it was something you did. That seems to be ingrained in us from our youth. For example, if a program starts acting strangely, we try to retrace our keystrokes to determine our mistakes. This is reinforced by the first question that comes from the mouths of support staff: "What did you do?" (with emphasis placed on different words based on their disposition at the time).

It might not even have anything to do with user mistakes. Problems in the Registry occur for various reasons, and often the symptoms mask the real nature of the problem.

Registry Problems

Rather than dealing with the symptoms, deal with the problems that can occur. With every type of control available through the Registry, there is a corresponding potential problem, as illustrated in Figure 3.2.

Sometimes, it feels like a whole set of dominoes falling down. One problem affects another, which limits the use of another item, and so on. An example would be the effect of a Registry error in the configuration of a network card. Without the correct information, the card cannot be activated. Without the card activated, no data can be transferred on the network, the server cannot be contacted for logon, and no user validation is possible. The user gets an error message that no domain controller can be found, and network resources may not be available. Is it really a problem with the server? Not at all.

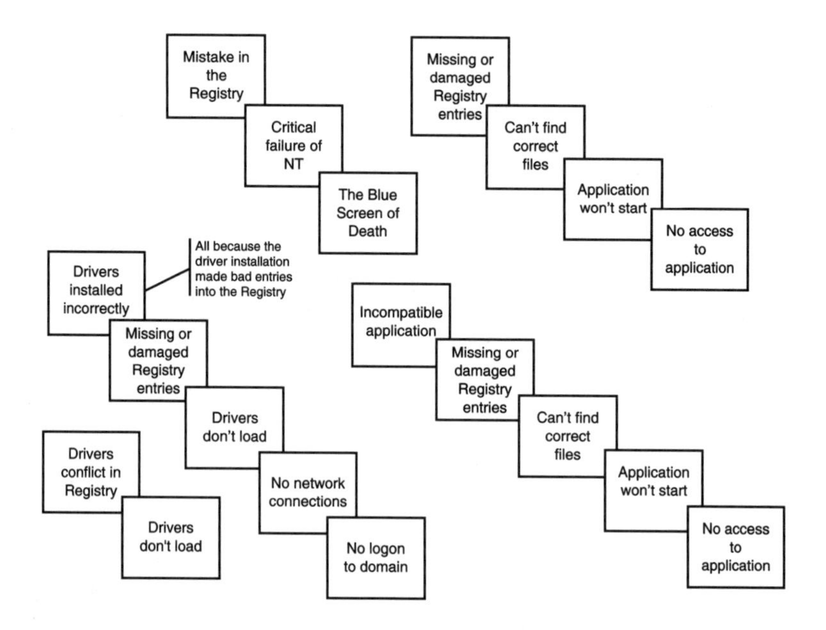

Figure 3.2.
The cascading effects of errors in the Registry.

The process can be difficult to stop, and often it is difficult to determine exactly what caused it and where it started.

It is obvious, however, where it ends: a loss of productivity for the organization, wasted time, and possibly even severe financial losses.

If the Registry gets corrupted for any reason, system or application functions may fail, and a support technician must isolate the problem and repair it.

The Registry normally works, most of the time, without any problems. It can, however, get corrupted in many ways. Programs that you add to the system, system changes and problems, and manual changes are the three main ways that errors are introduced. Of course, the results of these errors can vary in their scope and seriousness.

The three most common ways the Registry gets corrupted are

- Applications and drivers are added to the system
- Hardware changes from settings or failure
- Users make changes to the Registry

It is impossible to prevent all errors from happening. If you know what can happen, it is easier to troubleshoot errors. By protecting the Registry (as outlined in Chapter 4, "Protecting the NT Registry," and Chapter 6, "Protecting the Windows 95 Registry"), you always have a safety net. By using the tools and procedures discussed in Chapter 5, "Recovering from an NT Registry Failure," and in Chapter 7, "Recovering from a Windows 95 Registry Failure," you can recover from even the most severe problems. Take a look at each of the types of problems in more depth.

Program Errors

Adding and removing programs account for the majority of errors found in the Registry. Most users add between six and seven applications, and add or upgrade drivers, four or five times per year. During initial installation and setup, the numbers are even greater.

Warning

One of the original requirements for programs to receive the "Designed for Windows 95" logo was that the application is also compatible with Windows NT. That requirement has been reduced to "tested on Windows NT." At the very worst, if the application doesn't work with NT, it is supposed to "degrade gracefully," which means it will not damage NT. Unfortunately, that is not always the case, particularly with applications that use Plug and Play. With no support from NT for Plug and Play, many applications make unfortunate assumptions that create serious problems in the Registry. To their credit, Microsoft shipped a Software Compatibility List with the early betas of NT 4.0. Unfortunately, they did not continue that with the shipping version, assuming that all the applications in the Windows 95 list would work.

Here are the most common reasons that applications cause problems with the Registry:

- **Poorly written application (bugs)**—There are no applications without bugs or errors. In the best case, the errors that are there are minor, esoteric problems that you may never see, which were left alone because of time and money constraints. To a programmer, a problem may be minor, but it becomes a major problem to you if it crashes your system. With the current pace of operating-system and application-version changes and updates, it is nearly impossible to ensure that everything will work together correctly. Also, today's common practice of releasing "beta" software to allow programmers and users to prepare adequately is a two-edged sword. As an example, with NT 4.0 beta 2, Microsoft released features that did not make the final release and significantly changed other features. Applications that expected or required certain elements may not work as well as planned.

  The widespread lack of flowcharting program logic and using only pseudo-code to program may also create severe problems. The logic may simply be flawed. A programmer may have inadvertently hit an uppercase O when a zero was called for. Many software vendors have been forced to severely slash their development budgets, and users often face the brunt of errors.

Note

It sounds as if I don't appreciate programmers. Actually, I do. I believe they do a tremendous job, even when faced with unbelievable deadlines, massive budget cuts, incredible hours, and more tedium than most people could ever live through. I am amazed daily that computers and software can do what is considered commonplace. Keep it up.

- **Driver incompatibility**—Most drivers are tested in as many environments as possible before being shipped to the general public. The open architecture of the PC world creates significant risk because any type of eclectic combination of parts and pieces is possible. Testing all combinations and ensuring the compatibility of all the devices is impossible. The other challenge arises when drivers for Windows 95 are used for Windows NT. In all but one type of driver, the drivers are unique between the platforms. Windows 95 drivers may directly access the hardware they control, and Windows NT drivers are prohibited from doing that. The exception to the rule of unique drivers is modem drivers. The same drivers that are written for Windows 95 will work with Windows NT. NT 4.0 modem drivers will also work with Windows 95. However, NT 3.5*x* drivers will not.
- **Incorrect drivers used**—If an incorrect driver is used to activate a device, that device may not work as designed. For example, Xircom has a great PCMCIA modem for laptop computers. It uses a specific driver that is on the manufacturer's driver diskette, and the driver also ships with NT. However, depending on the firmware version on the card, the driver may not work. There is an old version and a new version of the card, and each requires a specific driver to work correctly.

Note

Because of the relationship between Windows 95 and Plug and Play, drivers in Windows 95 normally do not have the same problem as in Windows NT. If a driver is replaced on the hard disk by accident, or if the firmware changes, Windows 95 will simply install a new driver.

- **Incorrect entries added to the Registry by the application during installation**—During installation, most applications use a file called `SETUP.INF` for detailed information about what disks are required, which directories should be created, where to copy files, and Registry entries that need to be made to make the application work correctly. If there is a mistake in the `SETUP.INF` file, the change will still be made, and there may be serious problems.
- **Incorrect associations set between applications and file types by an application**—When an application is installed, default document types are recorded in the Registry. A user can then double-click to start the application and load the document. Many times, other applications use the same extension. For example, the last graphics program loaded will be the one launched when a TIF graphic is activated based on the settings in the Registry. Occasionally, completely different, non-compatible applications will use the same extensions on their document files, and the document-loading shortcut won't work. In the best of cases, you may still have to change the associated application to another.
- **Errors created during the uninstall process**—Whether you remove applications through Add/Remove programs in the Control Panel, through a proprietary uninstall feature of the application, or through a third-party utility, you run a risk of damaging the Registry. Besides taking out the program, auxiliary, and data files, an uninstall routine may attempt to remove Registry entries as well. It may inadvertently remove required entries for other applications because it is nearly impossible for the system to know all the entries accessed by an application.

- **Errors in fonts**—When the font ID in the Registry gets corrupted, you will see a different font than the one listed in the application. It can be annoying and may require you to remove some or all of your fonts and replace them. For an example, see Figure 3.3.

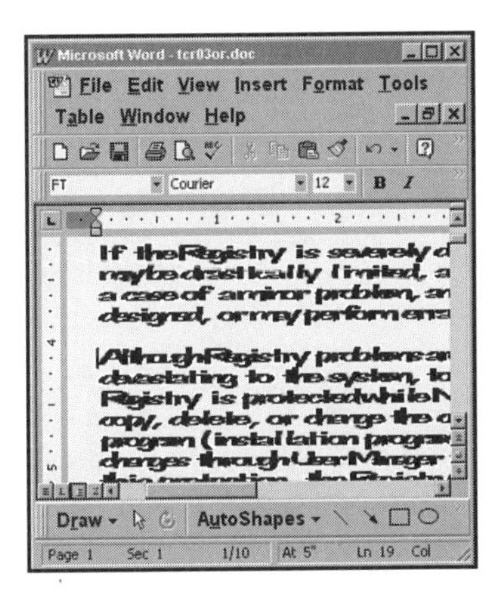

Figure 3.3.
The actual font does not match the name of the font.

Unfortunately, you may find out about these problems too late, after you have lost time, money, and/or data. Also, you are almost powerless to truly solve them, because someone else wrote the program, and most people do not have the expertise required to change the application itself. The best you can do as an administrator is to repair the Registry and look for an update or replacement.

Do you really want bug-free applications?

The term "bug-free applications" means that the program will work, as promised, the first time and each and every time. In order to have that, everyone would either have to have systems that are all exactly alike, or wait for every possible bug to be worked out before we got the programs. I am not sure we would like either.

On the other hand, do we have to put up with error-prone, buggy, poorly designed, and poorly executed programs? No! Even the software behemoths have learned the hard way that they need to have well-designed, well-written, and extremely well-tested software to compete.

Vote with your feet, and with your pen. Let them know how you feel, and then always get the best software and drivers you can. If the software and hardware/driver companies want to stay in the business, they will have to continually strive to do better.

System Problems

If the computer system itself has a problem, the Registry can become corrupted. Usually, these errors can be prevented with proper system care and management.

- **Virus**—Viruses are an insidious attempt to affect our systems by changing the nature of files. Much as viruses attack the human body by replacing good cells with bad, or damaging the cells that are there, computer viruses do the same thing with files on disk drives. You get them the same way, too. Contact with infected drives allows the viruses to migrate to a clean disk. Normally, you get them from floppies that have been infected by another system, from files downloaded from online and Internet services, and very occasionally, from application installation disks.

Tip

Windows NT is actually quite resistant to most strains of computer viruses. For example, it will not allow viruses to invade the boot sector. Some of the new viruses, such as Word macro viruses, can be devastating to the Registry. A simple virus-checking program, such as those from Symantec/Norton Utilities and McAfee and Associates, works very well.

- **The actual NT Registry size is greater than the Maximum Registry Size in the Control Panel**—The maximum Registry size is directly related to the size of the maximum paging file. Although it cannot get larger than 12MB, if your system has only 32MB of RAM, the maximum Registry size is 8MB. If the size of the Registry hits or tries to exceed the maximum Registry size, it will no longer be usable, and may cause a STOP error.

  What you can do about this problem is to change the maximum Registry size with the System functions in the Control Panel. Select the Virtual Memory button in the Performance tab, and set the Maximum Registry Size as shown in Figure 3.4. If the paging file size needs to be adjusted, you will be prompted automatically.

Figure 3.4. Changing the Maximum Registry Size.

Virtual Memory
Drive [Volume Label] Paging File Size (MB)
C: 51 - 101
OK
Cancel
Help
Paging File Size for Selected Drive
Drive: C:
Space Available: 245 MB
Initial Size (MB): 51
Maximum Size (MB): 101
Set
Total Paging File Size for All Drives
Minimum Allowed: 2 MB
Recommended: 43 MB
Currently Allocated: 51 MB
Registry Size
Current Registry Size: 4 MB
Maximum Registry Size (MB): 8

Warning

Reducing the size of the paging file in the Virtual Memory portion of the System section of the Control Panel in NT may reduce the maximum Registry size. Even though the system will warn you, some of those warnings go unheeded, and the Registry may be in peril. It is highly recommended that you make sure the maximum Registry size is at least 2MB larger than the current size. If you are going to be adding hardware or several new user accounts, check this before proceeding.

This is not a problem in Windows 95; it always has a variable size for the Registry.

- **Electrical surges, spikes, or brownouts**—Nearly all power problems can be easily avoided with good surge protectors and UPS devices (uninterruptible power supplies). Starting at less than $50 for good surge devices and less than $100 for UPS devices, it's cheap insurance against error. Not only will a UPS make your hardware last longer, but if anything is being written to or read from the hard disk at the time of the power problem, it is most likely that information will be damaged or destroyed unless a UPS keeps the system running, even without normal power.
- **Disk problems**—Most of the time you will replace hard disks because of capacity limitations far sooner than you would because of hardware failure. If the whole hard drive fails, of course, you will have to restore your Registry from a backup. The other concern is the failure of individual sectors or clusters on the drive. Although it is highly unlikely with today's systems, a fault in the surface of the drive media may make parts of the disk unreadable, including those where the Registry files are located. Regular maintenance is critical, and a good backup is vital.

Tip

Windows NT file systems include the capability to hot-fix the drive (that is, repair errors on the fly) most of the time without your even being aware that there was a problem. If you have a Registry problem resulting in the Blue Screen of Death, it may help to run `CHKDSK.EXE` from the `\WINNT\SYSTEM32` directory.

Manual Changes

When people manually edit the Registry, they are prone to make errors because of the complexity of the data, and the errors may be significant enough to cause the system to quit working. It is very unfortunate that Microsoft has chosen to deal with the Registry and Registry editing as a "black art," leaving many people in the dark as to the real uses of all the settings in the systems.

Microsoft's refusal to adequately, and publicly, supply information about the correct settings is extremely frustrating to system administrators. Certainly, more damage has and will be done because of lack of knowledge than because of too much information. Most of the actual edited changes that are made by users are done with the Registry editors.

Copying Another System's Registry

Copying other Registries is a very serious mistake many users make. Just because it works on the other machine doesn't mean it will automatically work on this one. Much of what is in the Registry is specific to the individual system, even if the hardware is the same. Copying the files that make up the Registry to another system will not work. Characteristically, if another system's Registry is used, most of the hardware will not work, and user and security issues may make the data and application information inaccessible.

There are some parts of the Registry items that can be used for another system, however, and the special procedure for doing that is shown in Chapter 11, "Remote Registry Editing."

Summary

If you could eliminate all the problems listed in this chapter, Windows NT and 95 would run without failure almost indefinitely. That is probably not realistic. However, knowing how the Registry can get corrupted can help you use better system-management techniques and may prompt you to take better care of it.

CHAPTER 4

Protecting the NT Registry

The Registry is a precious and important part of the Windows NT system. Because so many things can go wrong with the Registry, and because such dire consequences are associated with its failure, it's imperative that you protect the Registry as much as possible. To protect against a failure of the Registry, there needs to be an additional copy to replace the corrupted one.

Tip

Motto: planning before prevention, prevention before anticipation, and anticipation before crisis.

Dealing with the Registry is a perfect example of this motto in action. Mistakes with the Registry can turn into crises, so you must plan, prevent, and anticipate problems to avoid crises.

When discussing Registry protection, you might wonder whether you can copy and save the files to another disk, or whether you can copy the files from another system. The answer to both is a resounding *no*! Registry files are locked when NT is running, and only a special program can copy them to another location. This chapter presents four ways to protect the Registry:

- The Repair Disk Utility
- Using NT Backup to protect the Registry
- Third-party applications to back up the Registry
- Special options for multiboot systems and FAT volumes

Each Registry-protection strategy has its benefits and limitations. But whatever method you choose, *back it up*! Decreases in productivity because of Registry losses are shameful. It's no fun at all to get your system running after a disaster without a good backup. After you read this chapter, you'll know how to keep that from happening to you.

The Repair Disk Utility

The Repair Disk Utility, `RDISK.EXE`, is the first step in protecting your Registry. It will create a partial copy of the Registry. Having that copy on the local computer's hard disk is a fast and easy way to recover from minor errors. This cannot be a regular copy from Explorer or File Manager, but must be created with `RDISK.EXE`. You can also create a disk copy of the information with it. Then, even if the system's hard disk is unusable, and the hard disk cannot read the repair data, there is still a way to recover the Registry. (This will be explained in detail in Chapter 5, "Recovering from an NT Registry Failure.")

When you installed Windows NT, you were prompted to create an Emergency Repair Disk, or *ERD*. You were also given an option to do it later. By the time you got to that point in the installation, you were probably tired of sitting there and chose not to create the disk. Unfortunately, that decision may come back to haunt you.

Tip

You should create an Emergency Repair Disk when you are prompted for it during installation.

However, you must do more than simply create an ERD. You must also maintain a current copy. The ERD holds the system section of the Registry. It includes the pointers to the drivers that are used to control the hardware and the settings for each of those drivers. Imagine the problems you would face if, after you changed or added a device (like a disk-drive controller), the Registry failed. If you repaired the current Registry with a Registry that has other settings or devices, the system might not work. Unfortunately, that has led to many a reinstallation of NT. So, you should update your Emergency Repair Disk every time you make a significant hardware or software change to the system.

Creating a Safe Copy of the Registry and an Emergency Repair Disk

To update the safe copy of the Registry, create a new ERD. To update your current safe copy, run RDISK.EXE from the command prompt. That safe copy of the Registry is saved in a different location, and is not changed by editing or application installation. It is a snapshot copy of part of the Registry taken for later use. Running RDISK.EXE will bring up the dialog box shown in Figure 4.1. Select the Update Repair Info button to copy the Registry to a safe place on the hard disk drive, and the Create Repair Disk button to copy it onto a floppy disk.

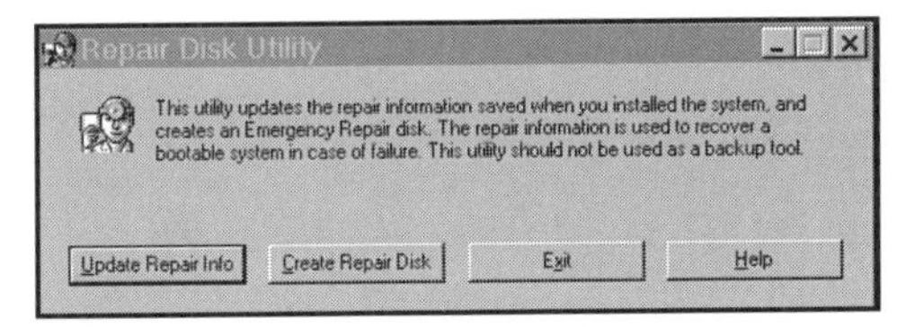

Figure 4.1. Opening dialog box for the Repair Disk Utility, RDISK.EXE.

Click the Update Repair Info button to change the system information in the \WINNT\REPAIR directory (shown in Figure 4.2).

RDISK.EXE replaces selected files that are saved in the \REPAIR directory with new files that contain updated information about the system configuration. As Figure 4.2 illustrates, not all Registry files are saved, so running the Repair Disk Utility is not all that you should do to protect your systems. The files are saved in a compressed format, so they can fit on a high-density disk.

To copy the files to the disk, choose Create Repair Disk from the options shown in Figure 4.1. The Repair Disk Utility will format the disk before saving the configuration files, so any data currently on the disk will be lost.

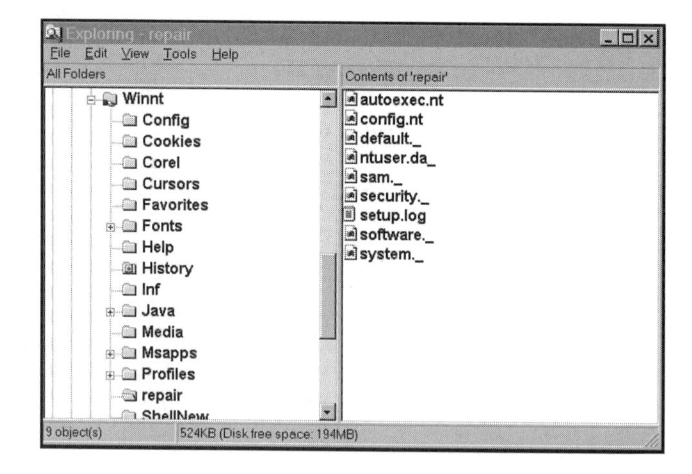

Figure 4.2.
Files in the `\WINNT\REPAIR` directory.

Tip

Label the disk with the computer name (the one it uses in NT) and date it. For example, if you make a new ERD for the system called `SALES1` on January 12, 1997, create a label that includes that information, plus your name, so others can talk with you if there are problems. That will make it easier to select the correct disk for repairs, and help the user get back up and running sooner.

Note

Running `RDISK.EXE -S` will automatically save the repair information to the hard disk. After that information is saved, you will be prompted to create a repair disk, which will be an additional safety net. The information saved to the hard disk is actually the data used to restore the Registry with Last Known Good, as described in Chapter 5. The ERD is used in conjunction with the installation program to repair the system. It will also be explained in Chapter 5.

Last Known Good relies on the information stored on the hard disk for its repair functions. If you don't save the information to the hard disk, Last Known Good restores old information, possibly causing the system to fail. Run `RDISK.EXE` regularly to ensure that your Registry is protected, both on the hard disk and on the Emergency Repair Disk.

Using NT Backup to Protect the Registry

Microsoft includes a utility to back up files, including Registry files, called NT Backup. It requires a supported tape drive, and can back up and restore files from any drives on the local system, as well as from any network-connected drives. It can back up those drives whether they use the Windows NT file system (NTFS) or the file allocation table (FAT) file system. It is powerful, very fast, and fully integrated into Windows NT.

To launch NT Backup, select Start | Programs | Administrative Tools and click Backup. The opening window (shown in Figure 4.3) shows the available drives on the system, plus any that are mapped from other systems on the network. It's possible to back up and restore local and remote files on any NTFS or FAT volumes from your own computer using an attached tape drive.

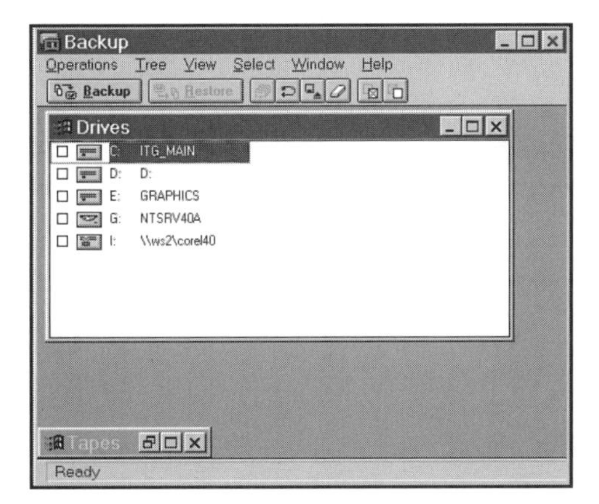

Figure 4.3.
Select the drives to back up with NT Backup.

Choosing a drive automatically selects all the directories and files on the drive. Double-click the drive letter, and the files that are in the directory are shown. Figure 4.4 shows the list of the files. Deselect any that you do not want to back up. Most of the time, the only reason not to back up information is if there is a limited amount of space on the tape. Then you could choose not to back up something that you already had a good copy of.

Warning

Some people mistakenly believe that if they have the software on disk, they don't need to back it up. If you don't back up the software as well as the data, it may take days to get all the software correctly installed again.

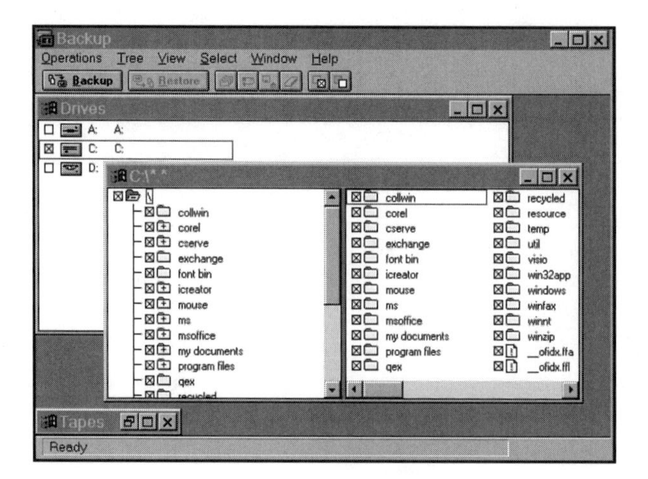

Figure 4.4.
NT Backup offers an easy way to back up the Registry.

Tip

Deselect the paging file (in the `\WINNT` directory) so it will not be backed up. There is no need to back it up because NT will recreate it if it is missing. Deselecting it will save a lot of tape space and boost your backup performance.

The files can be backed up by individual files (including hidden files), directories, whole volumes, or multiple volumes. Verification is available to ensure reliable backups or restorations, and access can be limited to the owner or administrator. However, the Registry is not automatically backed up. Without a backup of the Registry, even if the files are restored to a new system, the applications won't work. On the other hand, restoring a Registry over a new system with different hardware could make the hardware inaccessible.

Tip

If you are backing up your system for protection against disaster, make sure the Registry is fully backed up. If you are going to move the data to another system, use the advanced features in Chapter 10, "Making Manual Changes to the Registry Using `REGEDIT.EXE`," to copy only portions of the `HKEY_LOCAL_MACHINE/Software` keys to the new system.

To add a copy of your registry to the backup set, choose Operations | Backup and select the local drive where the Registry is stored. Then select the Backup Local Registry check box, as shown in Figure 4.5.

There is no option to include the Registries of the other computers, however. That must be done from the local machine only, and is one of the major limitations of NT Backup. For an alternative choice of programs, see the "Professional Backup Programs for Windows NT" section near the end of this chapter.

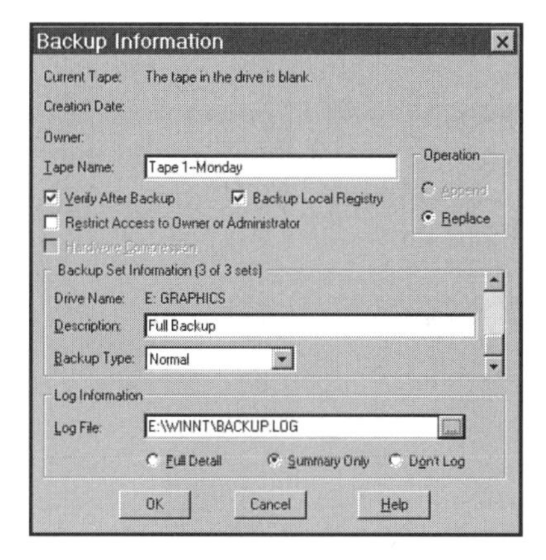

Figure 4.5.
Choosing to include the local Registry in the backup.

After the drives are selected and you choose to continue to back up the drive, NT Backup prompts you for information about the tape. If you are using a new tape, you will be asked to supply a name for it. If you have inserted a tape that has been used previously, you will be given the choice to retain the name or to rename the tape, as shown in Figure 4.6.

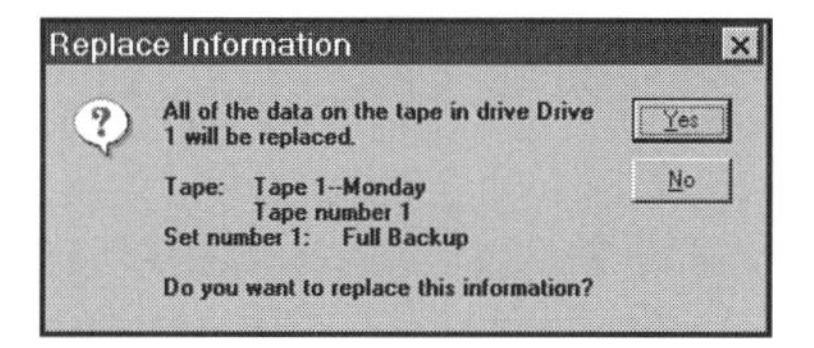

Figure 4.6.
Tape information is critical for later backup.

When the backup is completed, a notice similar to the one shown in Figure 4.7 appears on-screen. It is then okay to remove and secure the tape in a safe place for use in case of disaster.

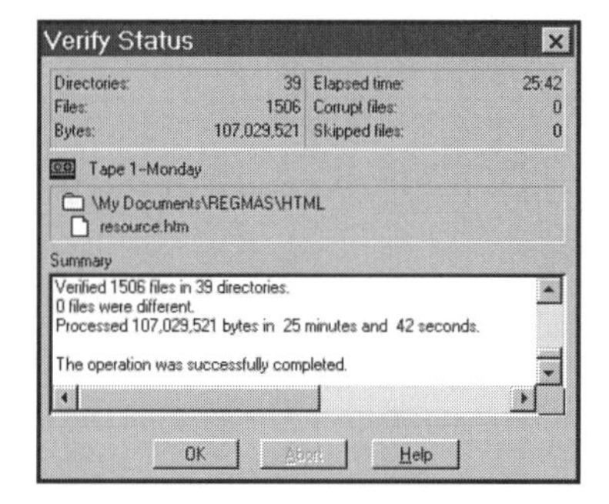

Figure 4.7.
The Verify Status screen, shown after a successful backup.

Warning

Never remove the tape until NT Backup indicates that it is safe to do so. The only times it will tell you to do that is when the backup is finished, another tape is required to finish the backup, or if the tape is defective.

To get all of the data back into the system, you need to restore it using NT Backup. Windows NT must be running with a supported tape drive installed. The restoration process is discussed in greater detail in Chapter 5. Just as a note, though, you can restore the Registry files by selecting Operations | Restore and checking the Restore Local Registry check box. You will also be given the opportunity to restore file permissions, which is critical. Figure 4.8 shows the screen that gives you that option.

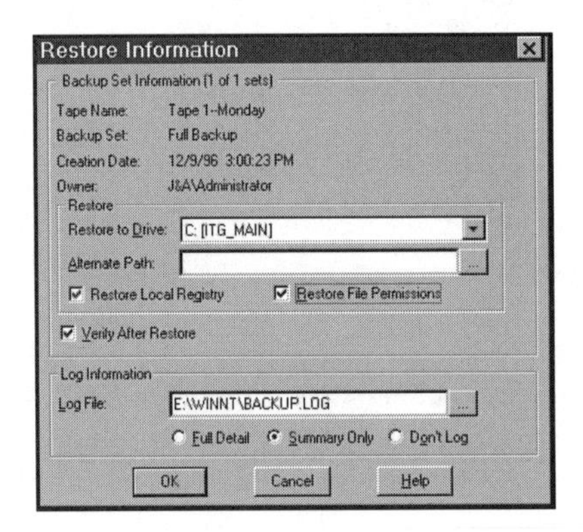

Figure 4.8.
Don't forget to restore the Registry if necessary.

Using Options with NT Backup for More Versatility

NT Backup can also be run from the command line, which allows any desired options to be activated with a single command. When NT Backup is then launched, no additional user input is required. Choosing the `/b` command-line option backs up the local Registry.

Other options that can be used on the command line are shown in Table 4.1.

Table 4.1. Command-line backup options.

Option	*Description*
`backup`	Sets the system to back up the drives.
`restore`	Sets the system to restore the data.
`/t` (type)	Specifies the type of backup (`normal` backs up all files; `incremental` only backs up files that changed since the last backup).
`/a`	Appends the new backup at the end of the current data on the tape. If this option is not selected, the data currently on the tape will be overwritten.
`/v`	Verifies the backup operation to ensure it went as planned.
`/r`	Restricts file access to the owner or administrator. The Backup operators can still back up and restore, but they cannot read the files.
`/d` *`text`*	Sets a description of the backup contents.
`/hc:on` or `/hc:off`	Turns on or off hardware compression.

With these options, you can create a batch file to automate repeated backups of drives. These are the most commonly used options, but there are other options available. Those options and more details are shown in the help file for NT Backup.

Warning

Just because you chose the Verify option and it finished with no errors doesn't mean that your backup is error-free. The only way to ensure that your data will be available is to use multiple tapes, rotating them daily. Use a Monday tape set, a separate set for Tuesday, and so on. Then make an extra set for the weekend. Also, keep them off-site for protection against damage and theft.

Tip

Backup tapes will not last forever. Replace them annually to ensure correct backups.

Examples of NT Backup Command Lines

If you wanted to back up all the files on your local drives (`C:` and `D:`), back up the Registry, verify the operation, and name the backup `"Full Monthly Backup"`, the command line would be

```
ntbackup backup C: D: /t normal /v /d "Full Monthly Backup"
```

If you wanted to back up only the files that have changed on drives `M:` and `N:` (mapped from other systems on the network), verify the backup, and name it `"3/12/97 Changes"`, the command line would be

```
ntbackup backup M: N: /t incremental /v /d "3/12/97 Changes"
```

Whatever your choices, it would be very easy to add that line to a batch file, making it simpler to activate the backup process.

Limitations of NT Backup

The three most pressing limitations of NT Backup are

- NT Backup will not back up files (including hidden files) or directories that you do not own or whose access has been restricted. To ensure a full backup, make sure you are a member of the Backup Operators group. Members of this group can back up items even if they do not have direct ownership or the other specific permissions. They cannot read the files, but they can back them up.

The best and most important example of this is home directories for users on the network. Access to those directories is restricted to every user (including the network administrator) except the owner of the directory. Unless the user who is logged on is a member of the Backup Operators group, only the directories will be backed up, not the files inside.

Ensure that the user who will be backing up the files is added (by the network administrator) to the Backup Operators group in User Manager for Domains.

- NT Backup cannot be used to back up registries on remote computers.
- NT Backup has no scheduling capabilities of its own. It has to be run from the command prompt unless an outside scheduler is used. With an outside scheduler, it only launches the application or batch file. Even if there is a problem or failure during the backup, the schedule has already been completed just by the launch of the application. With an internal scheduler, the schedule is reset only when the application completes its task. Imagine your chagrin if you assumed the backup went as planned, but it had failed. You might get a message in the Event Viewer, but you might not.

Using the NT Schedule Service and the AT Command to Automate Backups

The AT command sets up a schedule to run programs at a specified time and date. It can run on your own computer, or you can schedule it to run on another. The Schedule service must be running for the AT command to work. To activate the Schedule service, select Services in the Control Panel. Scroll to find Schedule and change the Startup options. If you will be using the AT command, you must set the Schedule service startup option to Automatic.

After the AT command puts the command into the Schedule service, the service takes over and launches the application at the appointed time.

Note

Because scheduled commands are stored in the Registry, scheduled tasks are not lost if you have to restart the Schedule service or your computer.

To back up all the files on the C: drive and in the Registry on the server called BACKSERV every night at 10:00 p.m., use the following command:

```
AT \\BACKSERV 22:00 /every: M,T,W,Th,F "ntbackup.exe backup c:\ /b"
```

Tip

Without any parameters listed, AT lists currently scheduled commands in the queue. After you queue your command, run AT without any parameters to see if it's actually listed in the schedule.

Note

To use the AT command, you must be a member of the local administrators group. If you are not a member, you will receive an error, and the command will not be put in the Schedule queue.

Unfortunately, the AT command is not particularly reliable. Sometimes it works, and sometimes it doesn't. The Schedule service does its job very well, and as long as the command is queued correctly, it will work. Unfortunately, the reliability of the AT command to get the command queued is questionable.

Even if the command is used correctly with no syntax errors, it will not always work. In fact, there are times when a batch file will work, and other times when the same file will not. Because of this, it is not recommended.

Using Third-Party Applications

Microsoft, by its own admission, does not offer the best in system utilities. It focuses on the core operating system, and depends on third-party companies to fill in when NT utilities need extra help. In many cases, shareware applications can adequately meet the needs of most users. Unfortunately, no shareware backup programs are currently available. The amount of effort involved to create and maintain a top-quality program requires it to be a commercial product. Third-party backup programs can even be quite expensive. However, for the money, the programs listed here do an outstanding job of maintaining a backup for nearly any size organization. For that reason, most system administrators go to a professional-level backup program and use one of the following programs.

Professional Backup Programs for Windows NT

Table 4.2 lists the programs that are currently considered to be the best professional backup programs for Windows NT. Each has its benefits and shortcomings, and some are better at certain tasks than others. You can find reviews of these products in computer magazines and at Internet sites (such as `www.winntmag.com`).

Table 4.2. Professional backup programs for Windows NT.

Product	*Company*	*Phone Number*
ARCServe	Cheyenne Software	800-243-9462
NetWorker	Legato	415-812-6000
Backup Exec	Seagate Software	800-327-2232
Storage Manager	Seagate Software	800-327-2232
Backup Director	Seagate Software	800-327-2232
UltraBac	Barratt Edwards Intl	206-644-6000

Whichever program you choose, make sure you back up regularly, rotate your tapes, and store tapes off-site for optimum protection.

Tip

Cheyenne ARCServe, version 6, allows you to restore a full Windows NT system to a completely bare drive. It comes with a DOS command-line utility that allows the restoration without NT already running. As of this writing, it is the only product on the market that allows that. However, other products will soon catch up and include that feature.

If at all possible, get software with that feature. Not only will it save you time, but it will also ensure that your entire system gets restored. In the Advanced Registry Editing section of Chapter 7, "Recovering from a Windows 95 Registry Failure," you'll find a tip urging you to restore shares to an existing Windows NT system because a restore from tape will not do it.

By using ARCServe version 6, or others that have the same feature, you will eliminate that requirement.

Types of Backups

No matter what type of program you use, you can make different types of backups depending on the type of data to be backed up, tape capacity, and personal preference. The type of backup you perform also affects your restoration process (as shown in Chapter 5). The two most common types are full backups and incremental (or differential) backups.

Full Backup

As the name implies, a full backup backs up everything on the hard drives. Full backups offer the best protection and the easiest restoration; they also require the most tape capacity. Without sufficient capacity, you might have to use additional tapes, which eliminates the possibility of performing unattended backups in the middle of the night. However, full backups make the most sense for a data server, where most of the files change every day anyway.

Incremental Backups

By reducing the backup to only the files that have changed, the tape capacity can be significantly reduced. The tape backup program examines the attributes of the files on the hard drive to determine whether they have changed. If they have changed, they are backed up.

An effective backup strategy is to perform a full backup once a week or once a month. In between the full backups, simply back up any files that have changed. Every backup program mentioned in Table 4.2 is capable of performing both types of backups.

Note

Microsoft recommends that you create a 300–500MB boot and system volume so that you can easily recover from a Registry or disk-drive disaster. By having that volume and booting to a DOS-based operating system, the Registry files are no longer locked and can be copied without limitation. Applications and data files can be put on an NTFS volume using RAID 5 (striping with parity), ensuring their availability (even in the case of a disk-drive failure).

The only problem with this is that FAT volumes offer none of the protection or fault tolerance offered by NTFS volumes. In essence, you must choose between easy copying and restoration versus fault tolerance and security.

One solution to this dilemma is to use hardware RAID instead of the software RAID included in Windows NT. Then, you would get optimum protection and still have the ability to boot to DOS and copy or restore the Registry easily.

The disadvantage of an incremental backup strategy is in its restoration after a crash. The restoration process requires that you go back to the full backup and restore it, then restore every incremental backup in order (without skipping any). Skipping is dangerous because the skipped backup may contain a file that was never changed (and hence, was never backed up) on any of the other tapes.

Special Options for Dual-Boot Systems

Hives are only locked from use when NT is running. If you boot to another system, DOS, Windows 95, or even another copy of Windows NT, you can easily copy all the files in the `\WINNT\SYSTEM32\CONFIG` directory to another drive (even to a removable media drive like the ZIP or JAZ drives from Iomega). It's a fast and easy way to copy files, and it's also very easy to restore them. Simply highlight the files in File Manager (Windows 3.x) or Explorer (Windows 95) and copy them to another location.

If the system volume (where NT is stored) is a FAT volume, any other operating system can see and copy the files. If the system volume is NTFS, only NT, Linux, and utilities such as `NTFSDOS.EXE` can read and copy them.

Note

Beware of the potential security problems associated with Linux and `NTFSDOS.EXE`. If you can copy the files, so can others. The only real protection you have for your files is physical security: locking them behind closed doors, forcing others to access them through the network.

Summary

No matter how you decide to back up the Registry, it's crucial that you do it. It's recommended that you perform more than one backup, using the RDISK.EXE utility for immediate help, and using a backup program as a part of your everyday routine as insurance against other crashes.

Protect your backups and your repair disks, and be diligent about maintaining your Last Known Good information. Maybe you will be one of the rare people who never need it, but at least you will sleep better knowing you are well protected.

CHAPTER 5

Recovering from an NT Registry Failure

The worst has happened: The Registry has crashed, and you can't get into your computer. Work still has to get done, and deadlines are looming. Don't you wish you could just press Ctrl+Z and make it all come back?

Unfortunately, there isn't an Undo for Registry changes, whether they are made manually or generated by the installation of hardware, drivers, or software. But having a good backup and a good plan for restoration is the next best thing. If you wait until the crisis hits to decide what to do, it may make you feel old way too early.

If your Registry is gone, it's gone. But this chapter shows you how to get your system going again.

Using the Last Known Good Configuration

Most Registry crashes occur because of something you do: You make a Registry change, you add a driver for hardware, you add software, and so on. The fastest way to recover from a change-induced crash is to return to the last Registry that worked. Every time you boot Windows NT, you are presented with the option of selecting the Last Known Good menu by pressing the spacebar. (See Figure 5.1.)

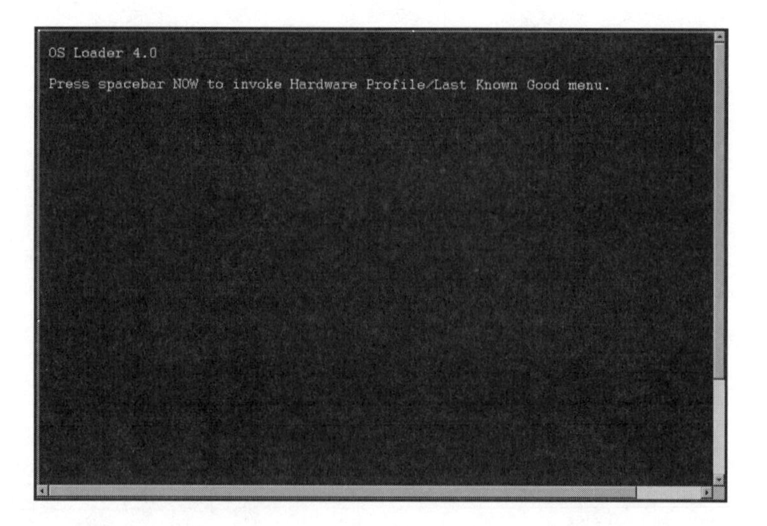

OS Loader 4.0
Press spacebar NOW to invoke Hardware Profile/Last Known Good menu.

Figure 5.1.
The OS 4.0 Loader screen.

The Last Known Good menu (shown in Figure 5.2) gives you two options for recovery in addition to choosing a hardware profile. You can choose the Last Known Good settings (created the last time NT started correctly), or you can return to the last configuration you saved.

Some people have asked whether there is a way to eliminate the Last Known Good menu at startup. Though it may seem like a hassle today, imagine the repercussions of its demise. If you couldn't get to the last saved or last correctly configured Registry, you would have to go to much greater lengths to fix the Registry.

Figure 5.2.
The Last Known Good menu.

```
Hardware Profile/Configuration Recovery Menu

This menu allows you to select a hardware profile
to be used when Windows NT is started.

If your system is not starting correctly, then you may switch to a previous
system configuration, which may overcome startup problems.
IMPORTANT: System configuration changes made since the last successful
startup will be discarded.

Original Configuration
Configuration 2



Use the up and down arrow keys to move the highlight
to the selection you want. Then press ENTER.
To switch to the Last Known Good configuration, press 'L'.
To Exit this menu and restart your computer, press F3.

Seconds until highlighted choice will be started automatically: 30
```

If you switch to the Last Known Good configuration, you are given the option of returning to the default configuration by pressing the D key.

There is an important difference between choosing the default configuration and choosing Last Known Good. If you choose the default configuration, you are returned to the last saved Registry and given options for the hardware profiles. If you choose Last Known Good, you get the Registry that was copied during the last startup for each of the profiles that was used. Your original configuration profile might be from yesterday, but your other Last Known Good profiles might be from some time ago!

Warning

The Last Known Good may not be as good as you think. Just because the Registry worked for startup doesn't mean it will work for everything. Data is saved at startup, but the error(s) that caused the system crash might not have taken effect until *after* the system started and wrote new data to the disk.

Tip

Save your Registry often to prevent problems.

Generally, Last Known Good takes care of your problem. You can run your system again, fix the problem, and save the configuration in the `\REPAIR` directory with `RDISK.EXE`.

Using the Emergency Repair Disk

If Last Known Good doesn't work, the next line of defense is to use the Emergency Repair Disk (ERD) that you created at installation or with `RDISK.EXE`. It is critical that an ERD is created for every system in the organization, and that it is updated regularly.

Tip

I update the ERD every time I make significant changes to the system, be they hardware or software. I install the new item, test it to make sure it works correctly, then I update the ERD. I even include a line on my installation checklist to make sure everyone else does, too. (I include software installations as well, because the software installation may change hardware settings.)

Using the ERD is simple, but it requires the three Windows NT installation floppies.

Tip

If you don't have the installation floppies, create them from the Windows NT CD-ROM using the command `WINNT32 /OX` or `WINNT /OX`. This will create floppies, but will not actually perform the installation. `WINNT.EXE` can be executed from any system, but `WINNT32.EXE` requires Windows NT.

Reboot the system with disk 1 in the floppy drive. It will load many drivers and prompt you for disk 2. Disk 2 reads the hard disk drives for any currently installed instance of Windows NT. If it finds your installation, it prompts you to reinstall, upgrade, or repair the NT version it found.

Note

Because the installation routine used drivers from the Windows NT CD-ROM that were copied to the floppies, even if your drive controller driver was corrupted, you could still run this repair routine.

If you choose to repair the NT version, you must decide which sections of the system to test. Testing options include

- Inspecting the Registry files
- Inspecting the startup environment
- Verifying Windows NT System files
- Inspecting the boot sector

You might as well test all of these and fully check your system. Sometimes, the problem is not what you assumed. After you choose to continue, the system detects any mass storage devices (disk drives and controllers), prompts for disk 3, then for the ERD.

If you have an ERD, the process is easy. You can restore any or all of the following Registry files, but you might lose configuration data entered since the last update of the ERD.

You can restore any of the following Registry files (hives):

- `SYSTEM` (system configuration)
- `SOFTWARE` (software information)
- `DEFAULT` (default user profile)
- `NTUSER.DAT` (new user profile)
- `SECURITY` (security policy) and `SAM` (user account database)

After you choose which Registry files you want restored, you'll be prompted to match the files and settings on the ERD with the ones on the hard disk. If files are missing or have different dates or sizes, you'll be notified and prompted to update or skip the files.

Tip

Check the files one by one rather than choosing to fix all of the files. There may be files that are of no use to you, perhaps from devices that you have removed from the system. Replacing those files may cause errors in your system.

If you don't have an ERD, the system must find the files on original media (the location that you installed from). At best, you'll lose all configuration information, meaning you must reconfigure all your devices. It's possible that you'll have to reinstall all your devices. The worst-case scenario is you'll have to reinstall NT from scratch.

A Registry restoration through the Repair utility and the ERD will restore most critical settings to your computer. The limitation of the ERD is that it does not cover the full Registry. It does not contain, and therefore cannot restore, all the user settings, file security settings, and shares. Most of the time, though, those are not affected by crashes.

Full Registry Restoration

A full Registry restoration is dependent on what type of backup you made, what condition the rest of NT is in, and what type of file system you are using. If the system is completely down, the process of getting everything working can be more difficult than if the system is operable but in need of repair.

Table 5.1 lists the restoration requirements as they relate to the state of the system, the file system employed, and the backup type.

Table 5.1. Registry restoration options.

System Condition	*File System*	*Backup Type*	*Restoration*
Running	NTFS or FAT	Full backup	Restore all or part from backup
Running	NTFS or FAT	Incremental backup	Restore full, then all incrementals to ensure that all of the Registry is copied
Running	NTFS	Full copy	Not available
Running	FAT	Full copy	Start other OS, copy files from source
Not running	NTFS	Full backup	Reinstall NT, restore all or part from backup
Not running	NTFS	Incremental backup	Reinstall NT, then restore full, then restore all incrementals to ensure that all of the Registry is copied
Not running	FAT	Full	Restore all or part from backup, if a restore application is available from DOS
Not running	FAT	Incremental	Restore full, then all incrementals to ensure that all of the Registry is copied, if a restore application is available from DOS
Not running	FAT	Full copy	Start other OS, copy files from source
Running	FAT or NTFS	None	Reinstall applications, configure settings, manually change Registry

System Condition	*File System*	*Backup Type*	*Restoration*
Not running	FAT or NTFS	None	Reinstall NT, applications, configure all settings, manually change Registry

Obviously, the best option is to have a full backup available, whether it be a backup (FAT or NTFS) or a copy (FAT only). Any other option means a lot of work, and potentially reinstalling NT.

Note

As you can see from Table 5.1, FAT volumes make the restoration of a destroyed system much easier. The only disadvantages are FAT volumes' lack of security and fault tolerance. The lack of security can be overcome by putting all applications and data files on a separate volume from the system volume (where NT and the Registry are held). Make the extra volume NTFS, and then apply necessary security as desired.

Fault tolerance is another issue. NTFS allows you to mirror or duplex the system volume, so even if there is a hard-drive crash, the system won't go down. There is no loss of use of the system from the console or by network users. That same capability can be obtained with hardware functions called hardware RAID, which adds the capability of hot-swapping the drives so that the system never has to be taken down.

Hardware RAID uses a specialized controller card and specially designed hard disk drives (usually in an external cabinet) to allow the fault tolerance. Windows NT looks to it as a single device, even though there may be four, six, or even more hard drives in the cabinet. It uses its own functions to maintain drive performance and reliability.

Software RAID is a function in Windows NT, using Disk Administrator, that allows similar redundancy and reliability. It uses off-the-shelf disk drives and controllers, and relies on Windows NT to supply the necessary software to produce a fault-tolerant system.

The best choice, then, is FAT with hardware RAID (and copy or back up the Registry), or NTFS with software RAID (and a little longer restoration cycle).

Whatever method you choose to protect your Registry, protect it so you don't have to reconstruct your system from scratch.

Note

Even after 13 years of experience with computers and their users, it still amazes me how many people never back up. Who does? Usually, they are the ones who have had a serious crash without a backup, and had no other choice but to rebuild their systems from scratch. Don't be one of the statistics. Even if the system crashes, you can feel confident with your restoration options.

Restoring Your System with NT Backup

In the previous chapter, you saw how to back up the system using NT Backup. Restoring the system is also very easy. The only caveat is that NT must be installed, the system files must be in the same directory as the original (such as `C:\WINNT`), and a supported tape drive must be running.

After launching NT Backup with Start | Programs | Administrative Tools | Backup, select the Tapes window (as shown in Figure 5.3). Select the tape and tape set you would like to use.

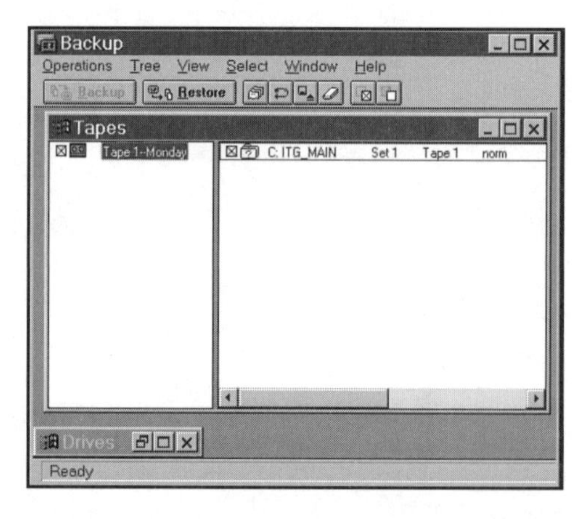

Figure 5.3. Select the tape and set to Restore.

If you want to restore only part of the current tape set (only some of the directories or files), double-click the tape-set name. NT Backup performs a Catalog Status procedure to list all the files that are contained on the tape. This procedure is very similar to a `DIR` command in DOS, except that it takes longer. Select and deselect files as necessary (as Figure 5.4 illustrates).

After you choose the files and directories, confirm the options for the restoration with Operations | Restore. If you want the Registry to be restored to the local system, you must select it in the dialog box shown in Figure 5.5. Selecting the files in the catalog is not enough. If you do not select Restore Local Registry from the Restore Information dialog box, you will receive a File in Use error, and the files will not be restored.

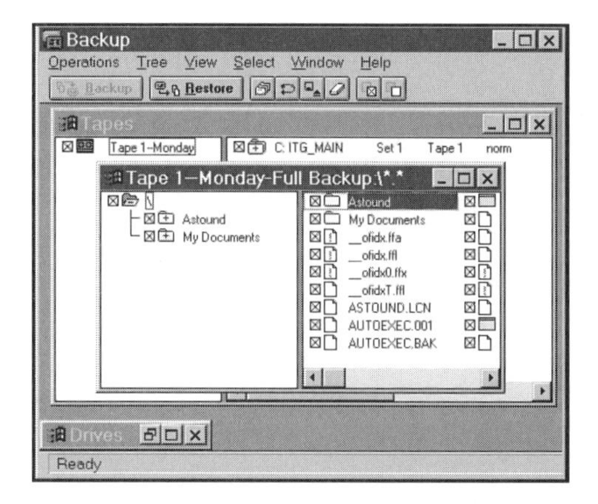

Figure 5.4.
Choose which directories and files will be restored.

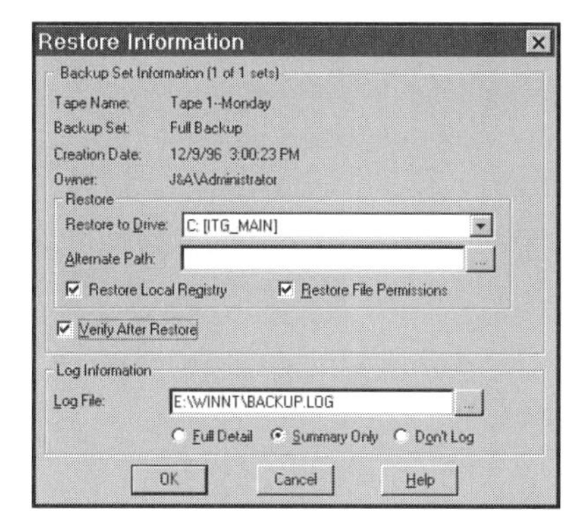

Figure 5.5.
The Restore Information dialog box.

NT Backup prompts you if any files will be overwritten, as shown by the dialog box in Figure 5.6. Be very careful about overwriting files that are on your system. Selecting Yes to All restores all the backed-up files and replaces any that are currently there, regardless of the date of the files.

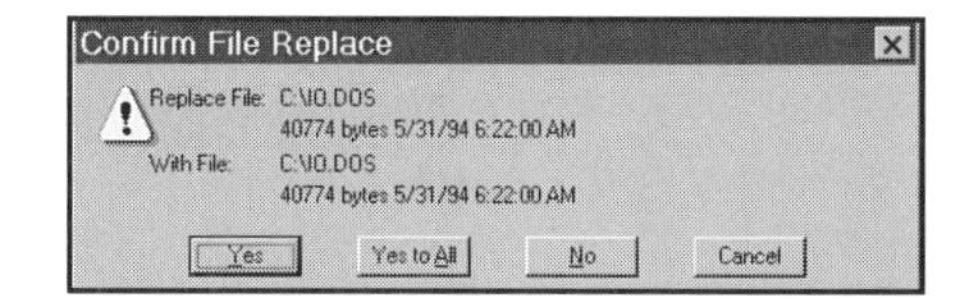

Figure 5.6.
The choice to overwrite is yours.

Tip

This is where the restoration of NT from a DOS application to a completely bare drive really comes in handy. There is no worry about overwriting files, which may cause version-related challenges. Look for that feature when evaluating backup software.

Summary

Your ability to recover from a disastrous system crash is fully dependent on the quality of your backup. Without a conscientious effort to protect your information, you will spend too many hours trying to recover, only to find that full recovery is impossible.

After you have created good backups, protect them well. With that backup information, you can then quickly recover, regardless of the level of problem. If the problem is minor, use Last Known Good. If it is a little more serious, you can probably recover with your Emergency Repair Disk. If neither of those will restore the required information, use the backups created with your backup software.

CHAPTER 6

Protecting the Windows 95 Registry

The Windows 95 Registry is susceptible to the same types of problems as the Windows NT Registry. The requirement for protection is just as great, but some of the tools are different. With no security settings available, the possibility of user error is also greater. Fortunately, there are several ways to protect the Windows 95 Registry, all of them associated with having extra copies in case of failure.

Windows 95 Backup Software

A tape backup program is included with Windows 95. It is an option to install if you choose "Custom" during the Windows 95 installation, or you can install it later with Add/Remove Programs from the Control Panel. Once you've installed the backup program, activate it with Start | Programs | Accessories | System Tools | Backup. Upon startup, the program informs you that it will create a Full System Backup set for you, as shown in Figure 6.1.

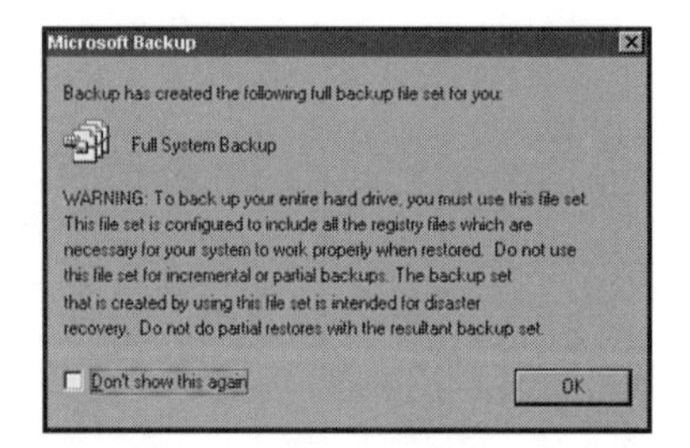

Figure 6.1.
Windows 95 Backup defaults to maximum protection.

The process shown in Figure 6.2 will create a file in the Accessories folder called `Full System Backup.Set` and it will tag, for backup, all the files on all the drives, plus the Registry. The backup file set will not be completed until all of the Registry is reviewed and the listing of all drives is completed.

The `Full System Backup.Set` is not automatically loaded at startup (after the very first time the software is run), even though the system tells you about it every time the software loads. If you want to use the `Full System Backup.Set`, you must open it with File | Open File Set.

Alternatively, you can choose just the drives, folders, and files that you would like to use. Select the drive letter, and the system will review the contents of the drive, as shown in Figure 6.3, and calculate the amount of tape space required to back up the files.

The next step is to choose the location where the backup will go. You have the choice of hard disk drives, floppy disks, or detected tape drives. If the system does not detect the presence of a tape drive, you will not be given that option. Many people also are using the new high capacity removable drives, such as the ZIP and JAZ drives from Iomega or the Syquest 135MB drive. They make very good, fast backup devices. See Figure 6.4 for details of the drive selection.

After selecting the target location, you will be prompted for a label of the backup. (See Figure 6.5.) After you supply the label, the backup will begin streaming onto the target drive.

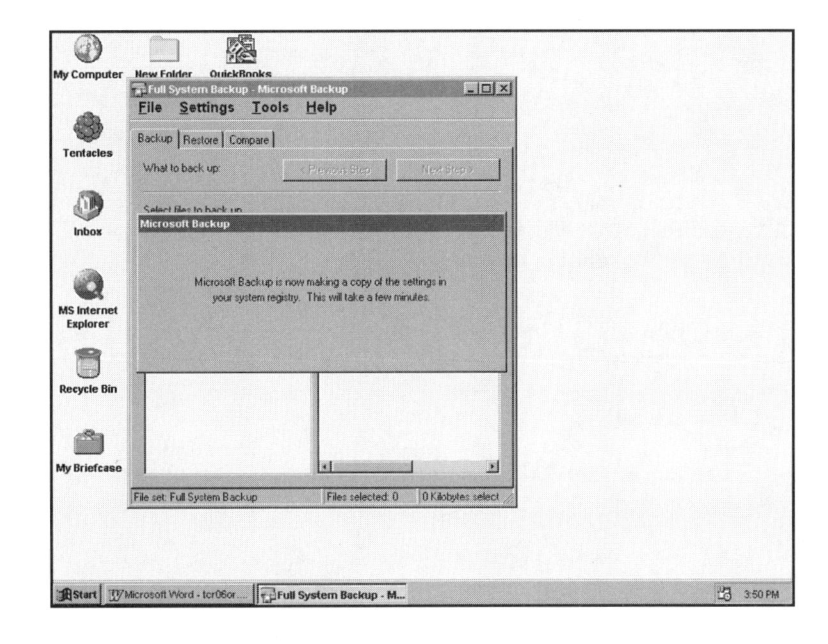

Figure 6.2.
Activation of the backup set starts the copying of Registry files.

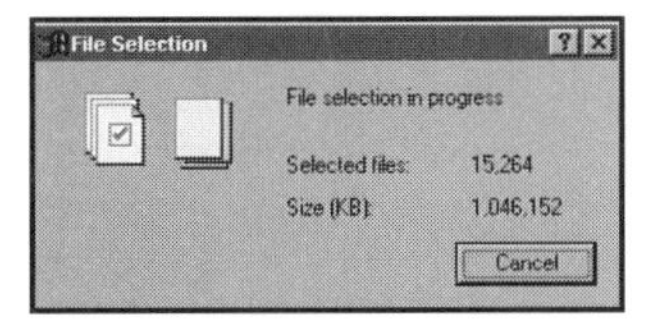

Figure 6.3.
Select the drives to back up.

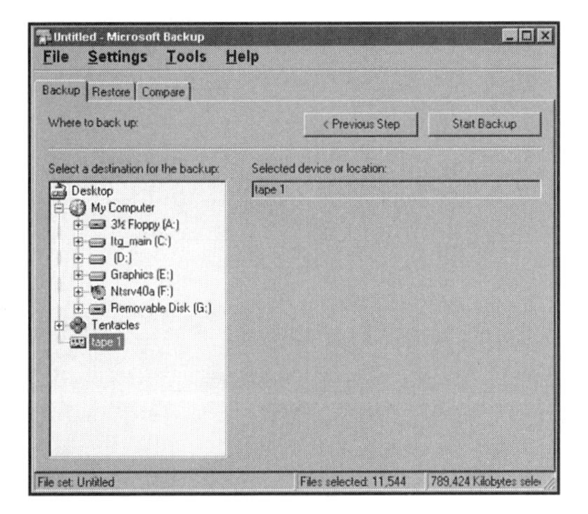

Figure 6.4.
Select the device where the backup will be stored.

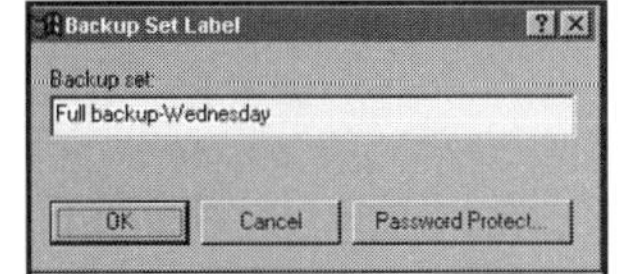

Figure 6.5.
Supplying an appropriate label for the backup.

Limitations of Windows 95 Backup

The Windows 95 Backup allows no specification settings for the tape drive. There is also no choice on compression. The filtering to choose the types of files to back up is pulled from the HKEY_CLASSES_ROOT, and the only options are to exclude all the types you do not want to back up. Also, the number and type of tape drives supported is quite limited. Obviously, there are better programs that allow more flexibility and choice. However, it is better to back up using a less-than-perfect solution than not at all.

Using a Tape Drive with Third-Party Software

Many tape drives come with their own software, or bundled with another company's backup software. Generally, these applications give better options than Windows 95 Backup.

Solutions

Why doesn't Microsoft create better utility software?

Microsoft's goal is to create fabulous operating systems, desktop applications, and to rule the whole world of computers. Dominance in the utility market would seem to be a likely companion, but they choose not to produce cutting-edge utility products. Whether that is to remain friends with the FTC, or to take advantage of the other talent in the business, or to narrow their focus, I am not sure. But Microsoft has stated publicly that they are not going to play a dominant role in the utility business.

The biggest concern is that the software is Windows 95 software. Windows 95 software is unique in its management of files, long filenames, and writing data to the disk. If you try to use Windows 3.x or Windows NT software to drive your tape drive, it will fail miserably, and it may destroy all your data.

Tip

When evaluating backup software, look for a software package that also includes a DOS-based restoration program. Without that, you would have to reinstall Windows 95 before you could restore all of your data. With it, you may be able to restore all of your OS, applications, and data to a bare hard drive.

As part of your disaster recovery preparation, create a diskette that has the correct software on it, and keep it in a safe and protected place.

Copy the Registry Files in Safe Mode

When Windows 95 is running, the Registry files are locked from access except through a Registry editor or the system itself, and the files cannot be copied to another location. If you start Windows 95 in Safe Mode, the Registry does not get loaded in the same way, and SYSTEM.DAT and USER.DAT are available for copying. It is actually the files protected from the system in Safe Mode.

Enter Safe Mode by pressing F8 when the computer says Starting Windows 95... during bootup. Change the attributes of SYSTEM.DAT and USER.DAT to change them from their hidden and read-only state to one where they can be seen and copied. After copying the Registry files, don't forget to change them back again to read-only and hidden.

Use Microsoft Configuration Backup to Back Up Your Registry Files

Microsoft supplies Configuration Backup (commonly known as CFGBACK) with Windows 95 as an alternative backup source for the Registry. With CFGBACK, you back up only the Registry, not any of the other files on the system. The benefit of using CFGBACK is the opportunity to create historical backups and choose any of them to restore.

CFGBACK.EXE is not normally installed with Windows 95. It is not even on the installation diskettes, just on the CD-ROM, in the \Other\Misc\CFGBACK directory. Copy all the files to any directory on the system, and then create a shortcut to CFGBACK.EXE on the desktop. If you create the shortcut in the \Windows\Start Menu\Programs\Accessories\System Tools, it will show up in the menu for you.

To create a backup of the Registry, start CFGBACK and supply a unique name in the Selected Backup Name slot, as shown in Figure 6.6, and click Backup to continue.

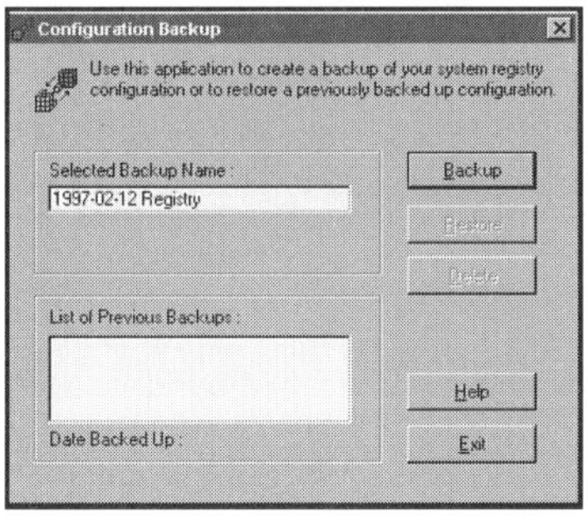

Figure 6.6.
Enter the name of the Registry backup.

Warning

Make sure you have closed all programs prior to using CFGBACK. If there are applications open, the use of CFGBACK may cause the system to crash, data to be lost, and an incomplete backup to be stored.

You may create up to nine copies of the Registry with CFGBACK. If you want to replace one of the currently saved Registries, highlight it in the List of Previous Backups, and click Backup. It will create a new copy over the old one, keeping the same name. It is not necessary to delete the old file first.

Export the Registry to a Text File

Another alternative to a standard backup is the option in REGEDIT.EXE to export the Registry to text. Normally used as a comparison tool, the Export option can also be used as a way to preserve and protect the Registry information.

To export any key in the Registry, highlight the key and select Registry | Export Registry File. It will copy the key, prompt you for the name and location to store the file, and save the data there with a .REG extension. Figure 6.7 shows the Export Registry File dialog box, with an option at the bottom to include the entire Registry. Select that, and all the Registry will be saved to the hard disk drive.

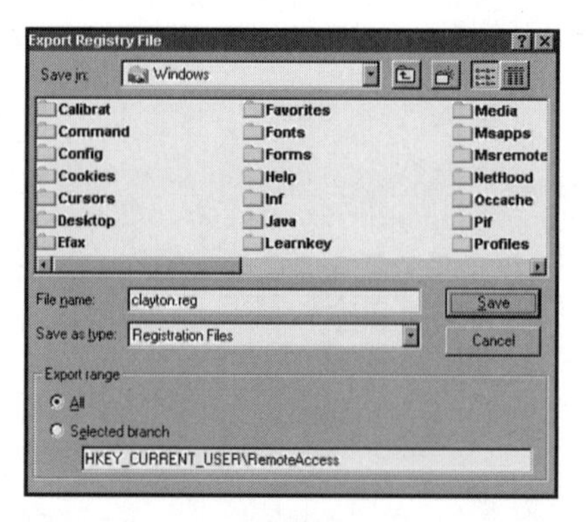

Figure 6.7.
Export the Registry to a text file.

Once the file is exported, you can read the contents with any text editor, as shown in Figure 6.8.

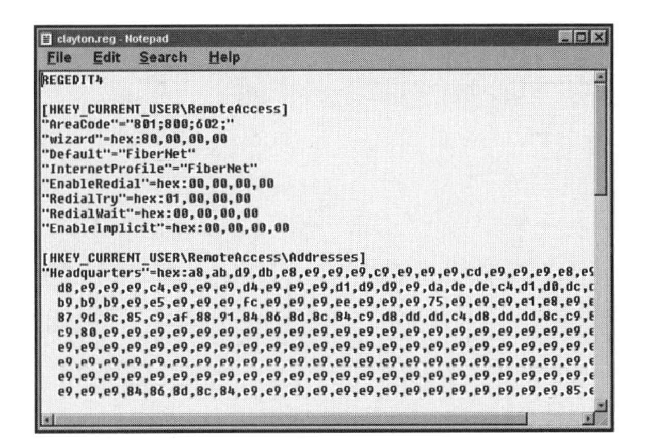

Figure 6.8.
The contents of the exported Registry.

Warning

When you want to look at the contents of an exported Registry (with a `.REG` extension), *do not* double-click on the file. The `.REG` extension is associated with `REGEDIT.EXE`, and will automatically import the data into the Registry without waiting for confirmation. If it is not the correct data, it can be devastating to the Registry.

To edit the file, highlight it, and then right-click and choose Edit.

Summary

Whichever way you choose to back up the Registry, just do it. It is too fragile to take chances with, and good management sense dictates that you have several copies of the Registry on hand in case of emergency.

CHAPTER 7

Recovering from a Windows 95 Registry Failure

A Registry failure in Windows 95 isn't quite as dramatic as it is in Windows NT. Even though both have their own version of the Blue Screen of Death, Windows 95 is generally more forgiving when it fails.

Warning
Restoring the Registry will overwrite the Registry that is there. For example, if you have a key that has five values in it, and overwrite the Registry with a key that only has four, only the four will be retained. Be very careful.

There are four levels of recovery from a Windows 95 Registry failure, and each has its own types of problems that it fixes:

Restart
Redetect
Restore
Reinstall

Let's look at each one individually to determine the most appropriate times to use it, and what types of problems are solved.

Restart the System

Much of the Windows 95 Registry is stored in RAM. If that information gets corrupted, it must be re-read in order to get correct information. When you restart the system, the Registry pulls the data off the hard drive into RAM where it will be used by the system.

An example of this problem is font IDs. Every font is known to the system with an ID number. When a font is used in a document, the font is stored by that number and labeled with a name. Figure 3.3 in Chapter 3, "Potential Registry Problems," is a perfect example of this problem. The font IDs got corrupted, and the font displayed and printed was not the one listed.

Restarting the system refreshes the data from the hard disk, the fixed font ID numbers are generated, and the fonts displayed and printed correctly.

An alternative would be to remove and reinstall all of the fonts on the system, but that would take much more time.

Redetect the Devices

If a device is acting inconsistently, the Registry settings that control the device may be corrupted. In order to reset the Registry, you could remove and reinstall the drivers, or you could ask Windows 95 to redetect them.

Many times, when a device is not working correctly, there will be a notification in the Device Manager. Figure 7.1 shows Device Manager with a device that is either in conflict with other devices or not working correctly.

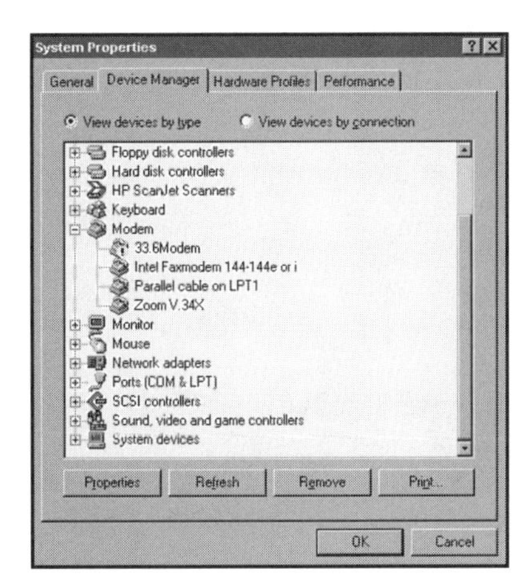

Figure 7.1.
The modem Registry information is incorrect.

Note

Obviously, if the device never worked, there can be other problems. But if the device was working, and now it is not, the Registry needs to be restored.

To redetect an item, select Add New Hardware in the Control Panel. The first question asked is "Do you want Windows to search for your new hardware?" as shown in Figure 7.2. If you choose Yes, Windows 95 will do an exhaustive search for "new" devices.

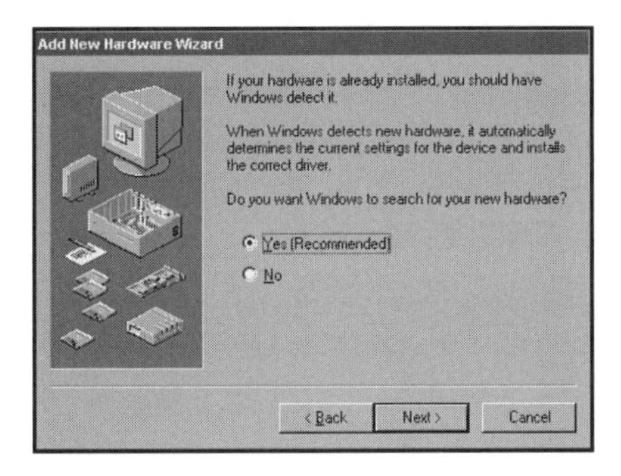

Figure 7.2.
Device detection in the Control Panel.

Any device that is incorrectly configured, or whose driver is not found, will be detected and displayed.

Remove the old device and let Windows 95 use the new one.

Restore the Registry from a Backup

Depending on how you backed up the Registry, you can use many options to restore it.

Restore from Tape

Regardless of the program you used to back up the data to a tape drive, the procedure to restore it is the same. Figure 7.3 shows an example from Windows 95 Backup.

1. Open the program.
2. Select the backup set.
3. Choose Restore.

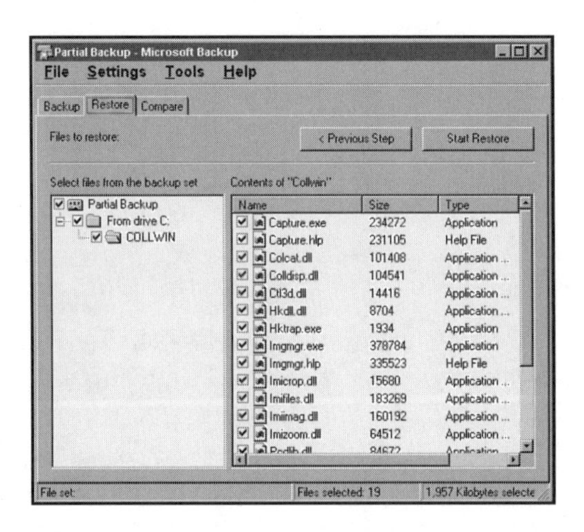

Figure 7.3.
Restoring data from Windows 95 Backup.

Depending on the program, you may be given options regarding overwriting files that are newer, overwriting files that have not changed, and selecting individual files and file types that should not be overwritten. As you can see in Figure 7.3, these options do not exist in Windows 95 Backup.

Restore from CFGBACK

Restoring the Registry from CFGBACK has many benefits. If you have created several backups, you can choose the precise one to use for the restoration. You can surgically place Registry entries, going back to a Registry that you know works well.

To restore from CFGBACK, highlight the backup you want to restore in the List of Previous Backups (as shown in Figure 7.4), and select Restore.

CFGBACK will overwrite the existing Registry. Be cautious in choosing the Registry that you want to use.

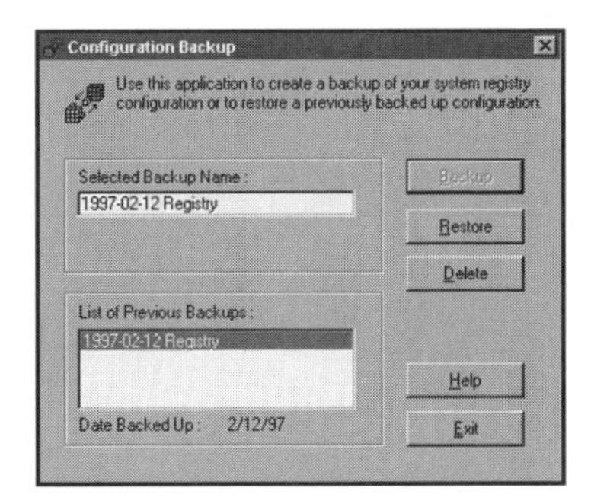

Figure 7.4.
Restoring the Registry from CFGBACK.

Import Registry File

An alternative to using a "backup" is importing a .REG file that was exported earlier. The .REG file includes the location of the data, so simply double-clicking on the file will enter the data in the Registry. It is the simplest of all the restoration procedures, but also the one most prone to error. The error doesn't come from the data being written into the wrong place by REGEDIT.EXE; it comes from users double-clicking when they shouldn't.

Warning

When you want to look at the contents of an exported Registry (with a .REG extension), *do not* double-click on the file. The .REG extension is associated with REGEDIT.EXE, and it will automatically import the data into the Registry without waiting for confirmation. If it is not the correct data, it can be devastating to the Registry.

To edit the file, highlight it, and then right-click and choose Edit.

Solutions

How can I protect myself from someone accidentally overwriting my Registry by double-clicking on a .REG file?

With most data files, when you want to change the association between the file and an application, you can hold the Shift key down, right-click on the data file, and choose Open With... to make the change. With a .REG file, you can do the same thing. As shown in Figure 7.5, highlight a .REG file, Shift+double-click, select Notepad to use to open the file, and click the option setting Always use this program to open this type of file.

continues

continued

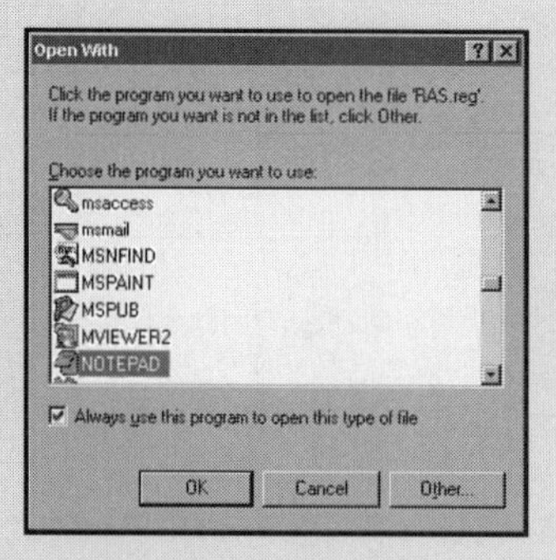

Figure 7.5. Changing the default double-click action for a `.REG` file.

Then, if anyone double-clicks the `.REG` file, it will open into Notepad instead of automatically updating the Registry.

You can still import the `.REG` file. Open `REGEDIT.EXE`, select Registry | Import Registry File, select the file and click Open, as shown in Figure 7.6.

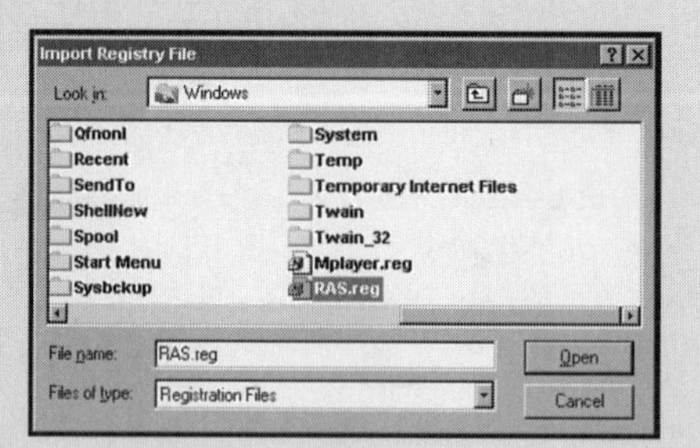

Figure 7.6. Importing a `.REG` file in `REGEDIT.EXE`.

This change will protect your system from mistakes and allow more security.

Reinstall

The last resort is to reinstall the driver, application, or Windows 95. Usually, it only takes about an hour or so to reinstall just about anything. If you reinstall it over the current files, much of the configuration information would stay the same. In the case of drivers, you would need to reenter the configuration data.

Actually finding the cause and fixing it may take even longer than reinstallation, which is why reinstallation is a fairly common "solution" used by technical support. The main question is, "Do you want to find out what went wrong, or do you just want to make it work?" The answer to that may very well depend on who is asking the question, the frequency of the problem, and the availability of the software for reinstallation.

Tip

In most circumstances, you would remove drivers in the Control Panel. When you remove a driver in the Control Panel to reinstall it, do not click OK and exit between the processes of deleting the driver and reinstalling it. If you do, you will need to restart the system and reload the drivers from disk.

If you simply take out the old driver and then add it back immediately (without leaving the dialog box), Windows 95 will reconfigure the settings and reload the information into the Registry without having to reinstall the driver.

Summary

There are several tools that allow you to restore the Registry in case of a failure. Your data will probably be safe, regardless of the method you use, with the exception of reformatting the drive. The best way to feel confident about recovering your system Registry is to have good backups.

Part III

Part III
Part III
Part III
Part III
Part III
Part III
Part III
Part III
Part III
Part III
Part III

Making Changes to the Registry

CHAPTER 8

Automatic Changes to the Registry

Instead of being a static file that never changes, the Registry is always changing. Although this constant change requires you to properly back up your system, it also allows you to have systems that react (at least somewhat) to your wishes instead of forcing you to change. Windows 95 systems check the hardware configuration every time they boot. Plug and Play functions then automatically set configuration settings in the Registry for every device. Unlike Windows 95, Windows NT does not support Plug and Play hardware configuration, except for PCI devices. All other device settings in Windows NT must conform to the actual hardware settings. Even so, the changes that the Registry undergoes are significant.

Most users will never use an editor to change the Registry, so for the system to react to the user, it must be changed in other ways. Actually, you should be glad that users don't normally make edit changes. Edit changes by nontechnical, untrained personnel frequently end up in error.

Other than manual changes, most changes made to the Registry are made from three different actions:

- Making changes to the Control Panel changes the Registry settings for both the user and the system.
- The installation of software and drivers for hardware add Registry entries and make settings in them.
- System policies and profile changes from the server update the Registry on individual systems on the network.

Figure 8.1 illustrates many of the ways in which the Registry can be changed.

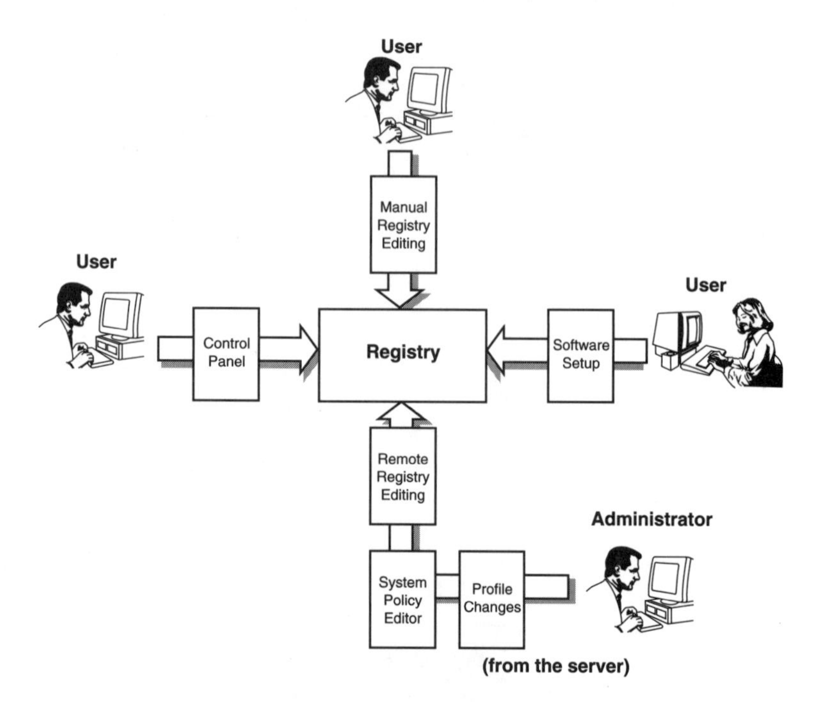

Figure 8.1. Changes to the Registry are made in many ways.

How to go about directly editing the Registry is covered in Chapters 9 through 11.

The Connection Between the Control Panel and the Registry

Every change made in the Control Panel has a corresponding entry in the Registry. Making changes in the Control Panel applets is easier than manually editing the Registry because of the graphical nature of the programs, and results in fewer mistakes as well as fewer Registry problems.

Tip

Whenever possible, make changes to the local system with the Control Panel to reduce errors and administrative overhead.

Tables 8.1–8.3 list the applets in the Control Panel and the corresponding key that is affected by changes made in each of the applets. When changes to the configuration information managed by an applet affect more than one key, *Multiple locations* is listed.

Table 8.1. Control Panel applets and corresponding Registry keys available in both Windows NT and Windows 95.

Control Panel Applet	*Associated Registry Key*
Add/Remove Software	`HKEY_CURRENT_USER\Console\Application Console`
Date/Time	`HKEY_LOCAL_MACHINE\System\CurrentControlSet\Control\TimeZoneInformation`
Display (User settings)	`HKEY_CURRENT_USER\Control Panel\Desktop`
Display (Computer settings)	`HKEY_LOCAL_MACHINE\Hardware\ResourceMap\Video`
Find Fast	`HKEY_LOCAL_MACHINE\Software\Microsoft\Shared Tools\Find Fast`
Fonts	`HKEY_LOCAL_MACHINE\Software\Microsoft\Windows NT\CurrentVersion\Fonts`
Internet	`HKEY_LOCAL_MACHINE\Software\Microsoft\Windows\CurrentVersion\Internet Settings`
Keyboard	`HKEY_CURRENT_USER\Control Panel\Desktop`
Mail	Multiple locations
Modems	`HKEY_LOCAL_MACHINE\Software\Microsoft\Windows\CurrentVersion\Unimodem`
Mouse	`HKEY_CURRENT_USER\Control Panel\Mouse`
Multimedia	`HKEY_LOCAL_MACHINE\Software\Microsoft\Multimedia`

continues

Table 8.1. continued

Control Panel Applet	*Associated Registry Key*
Network	Multiple locations
Ports	`HKEY_LOCAL_MACHINE\Hardware\ResourceMap`
Printers	`HKEY_CURRENT_USER\Printers`
Regional Settings	`HKEY_CURRENT_USER\Control Panel\International`
Sounds	`HKEY_CURRENT_USER\AppEvent\Schemes\Apps\Default`
System	Multiple locations

Table 8.2. Control Panel applets and corresponding Registry keys available only in Windows NT.

Control Panel Applet	*Associated Registry Key*
Accessibility Options	`HKEY_CURRENT_USER\Control Panel\Accessibility`
Devices	`KEY_LOCAL_MACHINE\System\CurrentControlSet\Services`
PC Card	`HKEY_LOCAL_MACHINE\Hardware\Description\System\PCMCIA PCCARDs`
SCSI Adapters	`HKEY_LOCAL_MACHINE\Hardware\ResourceMap\ScsiAdapter`
Server	Multiple locations
Services	`KEY_LOCAL_MACHINE\System\CurrentControlSet\Services`
Tape Devices	`HKEY_LOCAL_MACHINE\Hardware\ResourceMap\OtherDrivers\TapeDevices`
Telephony	`HKEY_LOCAL_MACHINE\Software\Microsoft\Windows\CurrentVersion\Telephony`
UPS	`HKEY_LOCAL_MACHINE\System\CurrentControlSet\Service\UPS`

Table 8.3. Control Panel applets and corresponding Registry keys available only in Windows 95.

Control Panel Applet	*Associated Registry Key*
Add New Hardware	`HKEY_CURRENT_USER\Control`
Desktop Themes (Plus Pack)	`HKEY_CURRENT_USER\Software\Microsoft\Plus!\Themes`
Joystick	`KEY_LOCAL_MACHINE\System\CurrentControlSet\Control\MediaProperties\PrivateProperties\Joystick`
Passwords	`KEY_LOCAL_MACHINE\System\CurrentControlSet\Control\PwdProvider\MSNP32`

One Control Panel applet, Add/Remove Programs, does not actually have specific pointers to the Registry, but launches other applications that put information there. Some actually put information in multiple locations, such as Mail, Network, Server, and System. Most of them restrict their activities to the particular locations listed in Tables 8.1 through 8.3.

Changes to the Registry—Activating the Screen Saver

To illustrate the changes that are made to the Registry, you will change the Screen Saver in the Control Panel's Display applet. The initial dialog of this applet is shown in Figure 8.2.

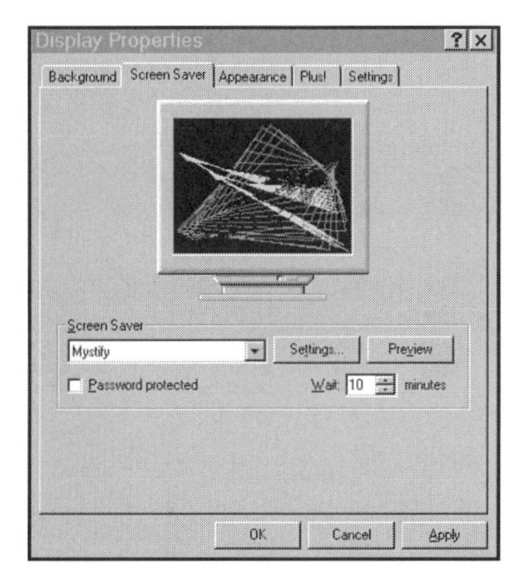

Figure 8.2.
Changing the screen saver in the Control Panel.

The Control Panel gives you the option of choosing your screen saver from a list. The name and details are entered into the Registry in `HKEY_CURRENT_USER\Control Panel\Desktop`. The values affected are the name (`SCRNSAVE.EXE`), the on/off status (`ScreenSaveActive`), and the number of seconds until it is activated (`ScreenSaveTimeout`). Additionally, if you want to require the use of your password to reenter the system, another on/off change is made (`ScreenSaverIsSecure`).

The unchanged Registry is shown in Figure 8.3. After the changes are made in the Control Panel, they show up in the Registry. The changes are immediate and permanent. Although it might not take effect until the next logon, they are made immediately to the Registry. You can change them back, but there is no undo feature. The changed Registry is shown in Figure 8.4.

Without question, it is easier to activate the screen saver with the Control Panel than it is to edit the Registry directly. Activating the screen saver through the Control Panel automatically updates the Registry for you.

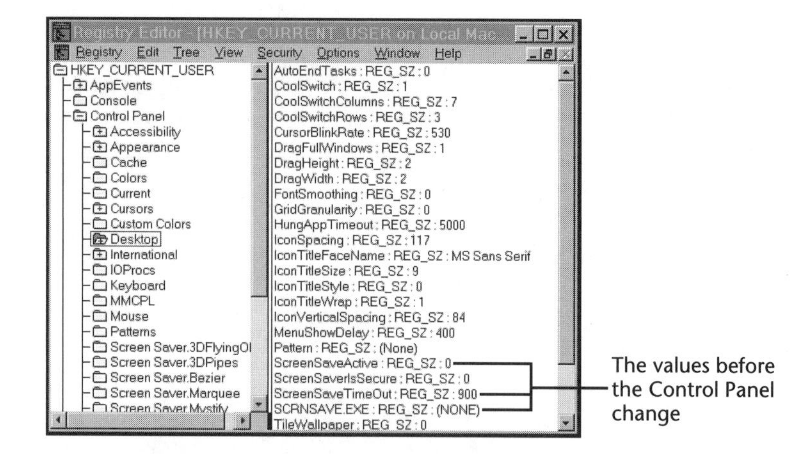

Figure 8.3.
The Registry before the changes.

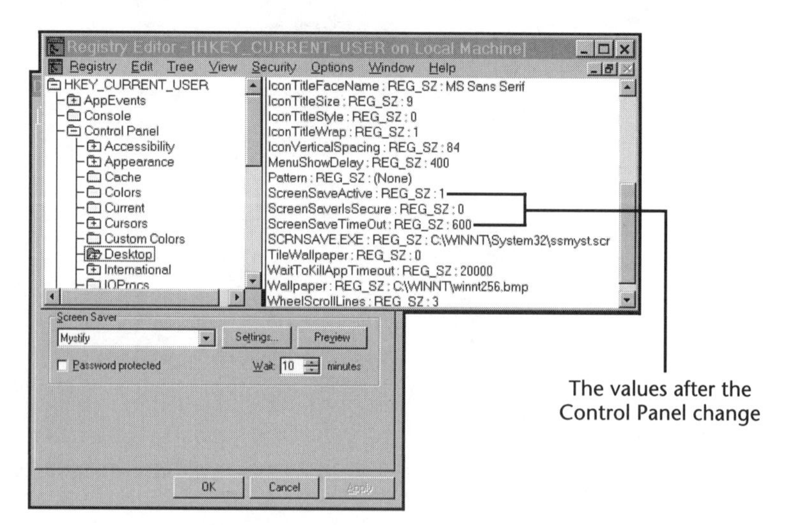

Figure 8.4.
The Registry after the screen saver is activated.

Changes to the Registry—Activating DHCP Requests in Windows NT

Changes to the Registry are not limited to user functions. Because the Control Panel is where the networking functions are set up, the resulting settings are also in the Registry. DHCP settings are located in `HKEY_LOCAL_MACHINE\System\CurrentControlSet\Services\CE2NDIS31\Parameters\Tcpip` (my TCP/IP transport protocol is `CE2NDIS31`). Insert your driver name to see your parameters. To find your transport protocol driver, use Windows NT Diagnostics | Network | Transports to see the available transports. Your card driver used for TCP/IP is the entry with the prefix `NetBT`. (See Figure 8.5.)

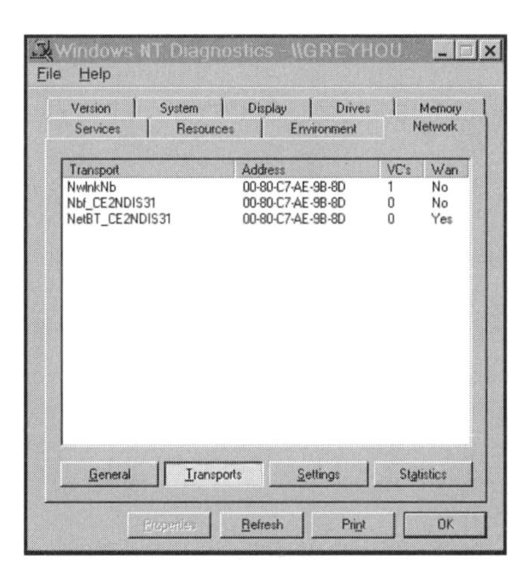

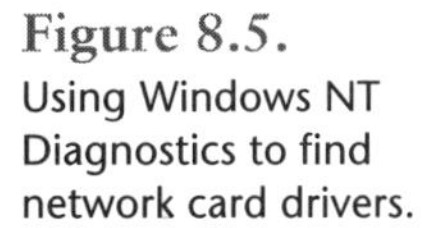

Figure 8.5.
Using Windows NT Diagnostics to find network card drivers.

Note

DHCP allows the dynamic allocation of IP addresses and subnet masks for TCP/IP network protocols. If DHCP is turned off, you must go to every machine on the network and set the address and subnet mask for the system to use. If there is a duplicate address given or if an incorrect mask is used, the system is not able to communicate with the server for logon and file usage.

If it is enabled, DHCP supplies addresses and the subnet mask from the server, so only one set of addresses and one subnet mask has to be entered.

Using DHCP reduces administration time, increases accuracy of IP-address allocation, and eases troubleshooting. It is a real time-saver, and one that should be used.

If your user has a fixed IP address and you need to change it, select Control Panel | Network | Protocols | TCP/IP Protocol | Properties, as shown in Figure 8.6.

The Registry in Figure 8.7 shows a fixed IP address with DHCP allocation disabled. The actual IP address is shown in the `IPAddress` value, and the subnet mask is shown in the `SubnetMask` value.

If you enable the Obtain an IP address from a DHCP server radio button in the Control Panel, the `IPAddress` and `SubnetMask` values are blank. The `EnableDHCP` value is activated (set to `1`), and the IP address and the subnet mask are in the `DhcpIPAddress` and `DhcpSubnetMask` values, respectively. (See Figure 8.8.)

Obviously, it's best to make the change with the Control Panel, if possible.

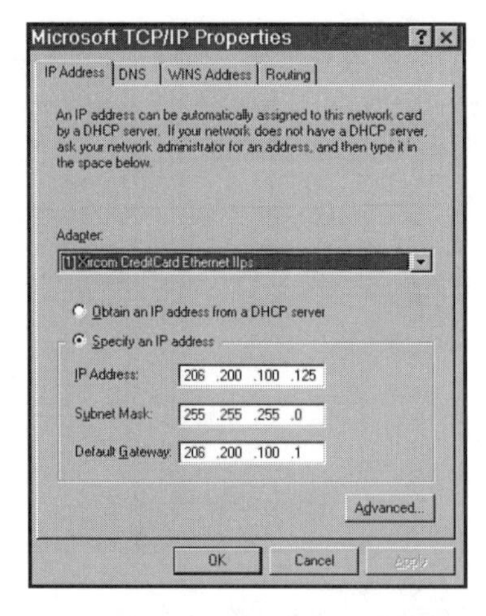

Figure 8.6.
Changing the allocation of IP addresses in NT.

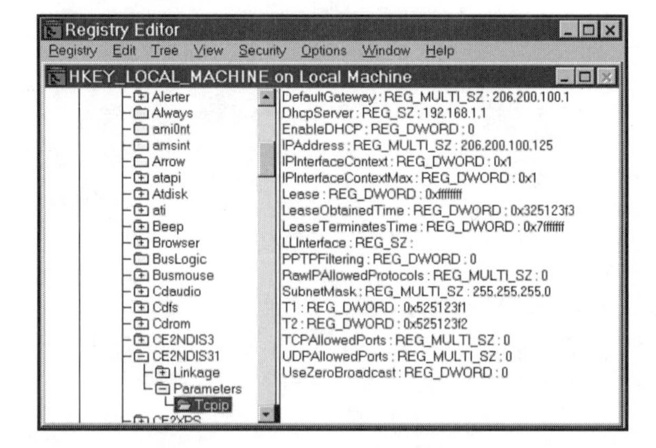

Figure 8.7.
The Registry entry for fixed IP address `206.200.100.125`.

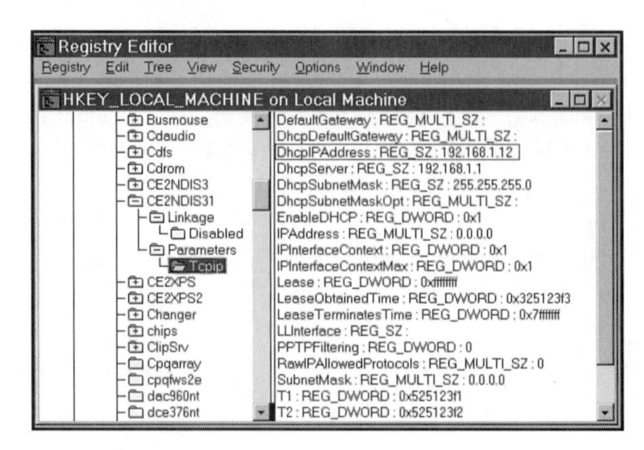

Figure 8.8.
The Registry entry for DHCP-allocated IP address `192.168.1.12`.

Software Installation Changes

When software is installed, it usually changes the Registry. Usually, software engineers use files with specific entries called .INF files to make those changes. If the item is included with Windows NT, it might have a specific named .INF file, like the CHIPS.INF file, a configuration file for Chips & Technologies video cards. Most of the time, though, the file is called OEMSETUP.INF and set into individual directories based on the type of driver it is. In fact, on the NT Workstation installation CD-ROM, 136 of the 182 .INF files in the \DRVLIB directory tree are labeled OEMSETUP.INF.

Every time you select the option to install from disk, NT looks for a file called OEMSETUP.INF. Of course, there is more to that .INF than just Registry entries. Figure 8.9 shows part of the CHIPS.INF file, which is used to install a Chips & Technologies video card driver. Notice the entries that indicate the location of the files, and the entries in the Registry that point to the file locations.

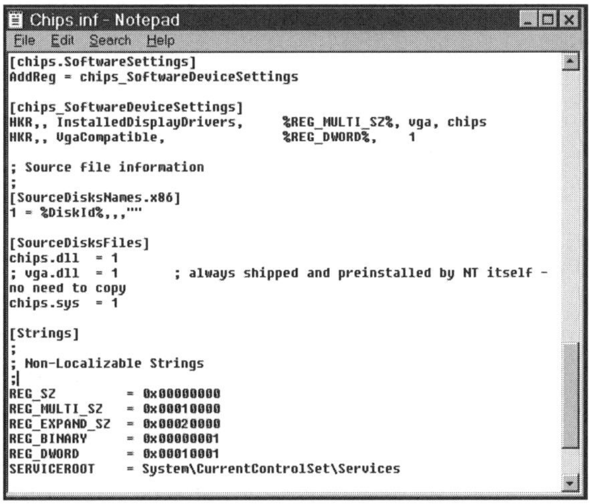

```
[chips.SoftwareSettings]
AddReg = chips_SoftwareDeviceSettings

[chips_SoftwareDeviceSettings]
HKR,, InstalledDisplayDrivers,     %REG_MULTI_SZ%, vga, chips
HKR,, VgaCompatible,               %REG_DWORD%,    1

; Source file information
;
[SourceDisksNames.x86]
1 = %DiskId%,,,""

[SourceDisksFiles]
chips.dll  = 1
; vga.dll  = 1       ; always shipped and preinstalled by NT itself -
no need to copy
chips.sys  = 1

[Strings]
;
; Non-Localizable Strings
;
REG_SZ         = 0x00000000
REG_MULTI_SZ   = 0x00010000
REG_EXPAND_SZ  = 0x00020000
REG_BINARY     = 0x00000001
REG_DWORD      = 0x00010001
SERVICEROOT    = System\CurrentControlSet\Services
```

Figure 8.9. Part of the CHIPS.INF file for a Chips & Technologies video card.

The actual installation of the video driver is performed by selecting Control Panel | Desktop | Settings | Display Type | Change, as shown in Figure 8.10. Choose the driver from the lists provided by Microsoft (not all drivers are supplied by Microsoft, though) and click OK. The Control Panel copies the driver to the correct location and makes the Registry entries for you, resulting in the entries shown in Figure 8.11.

If your driver is not listed or if you have an updated driver, simply click Have Disk and specify the location of the file. It looks for the OEMSETUP.INF file and uses it to install the driver.

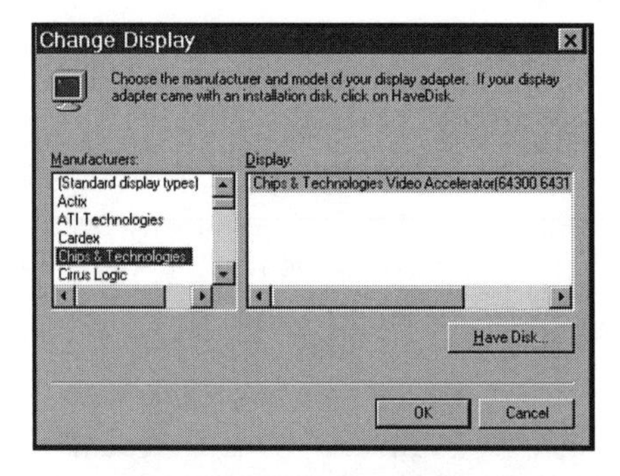

Figure 8.10.
Installing the Chips & Technology video driver.

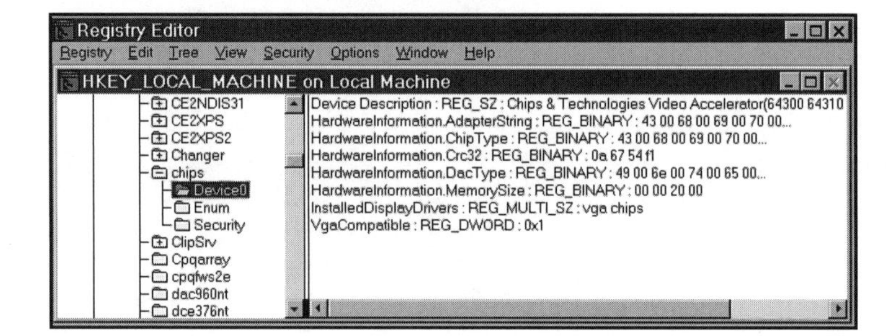

Figure 8.11.
Video-driver entries in the Registry.

Roaming Profiles

Each user who has logged on to a system has a local profile on that system. When any changes are made to the desktop, they are saved in that local system's profile for that user. If that user goes to another system and logs on there, none of the changes follow from the original machine. He must re-create all the icons, menu items, wallpaper settings, and so on for the new machine.

Roaming profiles allow a user to have a consistent desktop, regardless of which system he logs on to. All user settings are on any system the user logs on to, without requiring the user to reconfigure the desktop. In Windows NT, the information for a roaming profile is stored in the Primary Domain Controller (PDC) in `\WINNT\PROFILES\username\NTUSER.DAT`. In Windows 95, the profiles are stored at the local machine in `\Windows\Profiles\username\USER.DAT`.

Note

Windows NT 4.0 profiles are different than those of Windows 95, and also different than those of Windows NT 3.5*x*. Because of those differences, each user will have to have a profile for each of the operating systems he uses.

When the user logs on, the profile is brought to the individual machine, and entries are made into the Registry, overriding the locally stored profile for the user. It is impossible to read the profiles with any sort of text editor, so it is impossible to see the exact contents of the file. However, the profile affects all the desktop entries, so it's safe to say that it changes the entries in the following keys in `HKEY_CURRENT_USER`:

- `AppEvents`
- `Control Panel`
- `Environment`
- `Printers`
- `Software`

System Policy Editor Preview

System Policy Editor (SPE) has taken the place of the User Profile Editor that was available with NT 3.5*x*. With much more capability, SPE can make changes to registries for any computer or user on the domain, or all of them at once.

There is a System Policy Editor for Windows 95, and a separate one for Windows NT. Originally, Microsoft planned to have them work together, but a last-minute change was made that made the policy files they create incompatible. The actual work done and all of the processes are the same—just the final policy file is different. For more detail on the differences, see Chapter 28, "System Policy Editor: Understanding Policy Files."

The system administrator chooses policies to implement, and whether those policies will be for individuals, groups, or all users. When the policies are activated, they change user information in the Registry. Similarly, you can apply changes to computers, which updates `HKEY_LOCAL_MACHINE`.

After the policy changes are made, the user cannot avoid them. As soon as a user logs on to the network, the policy is implemented, and the Registry is updated. The policy overwrites any Registry change the user makes. Even if the user makes subsequent changes, they are changed back to the policy entries.

Though that might seem overly restrictive to some, it allows you to effectively manage the network from a single location.

The files that SPE uses to update the Registry entries are templates, files with an `.ADM` extension. A sample is shown in Figure 8.12.

The actual change illustrated in Figure 8.12 determines whether the user can update the Registry manually using any type of Registry editor.

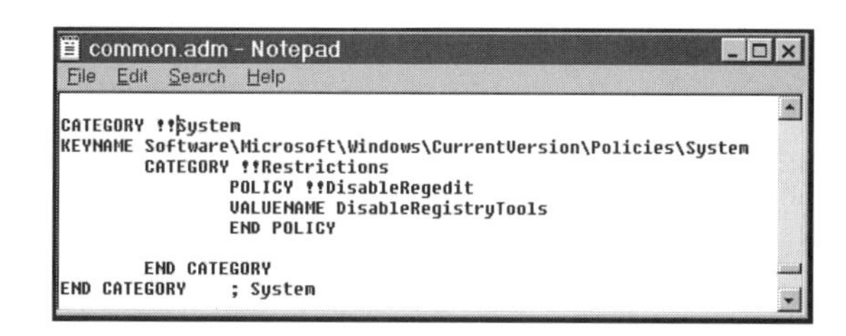

Figure 8.12.
A portion of the `COMMON.ADM` file, which can update the Registry.

The System Policy Editor will be discussed in greater detail in Chapters 28 through 34. The important thing to note now is that the Registry gets changed without user intervention. It is you who intervenes on behalf of the organization.

Summary

Because you have several outside influences affecting and changing the Registry, it is important to understand the order in which those changes are made, which indicates the priority of those changes. The order is as follows:

1. At logon, the Registry for the current user is loaded (HKEY_CURRENT_USER).
2. Next come any changes based on the logon script (they are very rare, but occasionally they happen).
3. The local profile overrides the current user's Registry.
4. The roaming profile overrides the local profile.
5. Policies implemented by you are loaded last, and have ultimate priority.

Wherever the changes come from, it is easy to see the dynamic changes to the Registry, and how they affect your system use.

CHAPTER 9

Making Manual Changes to the Registry Using REGEDT32.EXE

You just got off the phone with Microsoft technical support, having waited on hold for what seemed like an eternity. The support representative referenced a KnowledgeBase article Q-seven million or something like that, and told you that you need to edit the Registry and make a change to one of the keys.

In every instance when Microsoft recommends editing the Registry, they put in a warning/disclaimer reminding you of the fragile nature of the Registry, and urge you to back it up before continuing.

So, before you continue, back up the Registry now!

Editing the Registry

The Windows NT Registry Editor is `REGEDT32.EXE`, located in the `\WINNT\SYSTEM32` directory. There is no icon or menu item in the Start menus on purpose. With an icon or a menu item, users would be more likely to edit the Registry, creating significantly more work for the administrators of the network.

The limitations of who can use the Registry Editor are different, depending on whether you are connected to a domain. If you are not connected to a domain, logging on as Administrator to your local machine will allow you to edit the Registry.

To edit the Registry of a domain-connected NT system, you must be a member of either the Administrators or Power Users group, or from a trusted domain who has been granted access to those groups.

Starting the Registry Editor

Usually, the easiest way to start the Registry Editor is to launch it from the Start-Run dialog box. Simply type **`REGEDT32`** and press Enter. There is no need to enter the directory path because the directory is automatically in the environment variables.

At launch, you'll see the screen shown in Figure 9.1.

For a quick review of the structure of the Registry, see Chapter 2, "The Structure of the Registry."

For each handle key window, the left pane in the screen shown in Figure 9.2 shows the keys and subkeys (considered the same for this discussion). They are organized in expandable branches. Any branch that has subkeys is shown with a plus (+) sign in the folder icon. Double-clicking the folder expands the branch. After the branch has been expanded, the plus sign is replaced with a minus (-) sign, indicating that the branch may be collapsed.

Tip

Before you edit and change the look of the windows, panes, and branches in the editor, deselect the Save Settings on Exit option in the Options menu. The next time (and every time) you start the editor, it will have the same clean look.

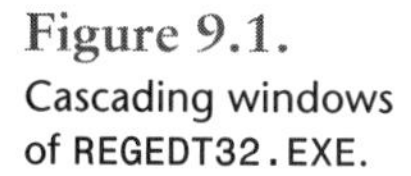

Figure 9.1.
Cascading windows of `REGEDT32.EXE`.

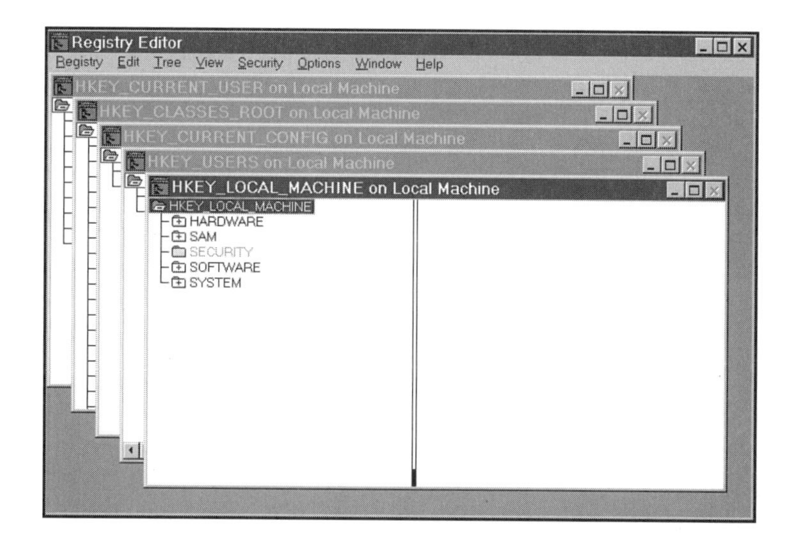

Figure 9.2.
`REGEDT32.EXE` with expanded and collapsed folders.

The right pane of Figure 9.3 shows all the values in the key that are highlighted in the left pane. If no values are shown, that means that values exist only in the subkeys. The syntax for a value is `ValueName:ValueType:Data`.

Start with the most common function in Registry editing: editing a current entry in the Registry.

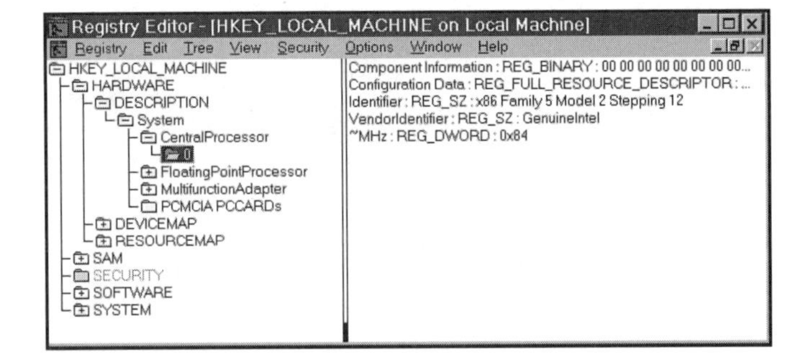

Figure 9.3.
`REGEDT32.EXE` value syntax.

Warning

Whoa! Back up the ponies! Before you continue, you need to know the most important menu option there is: Read Only Mode. As discussed earlier, any entry in the Registry is immediate and permanent. One mistake and boom! You may have made an error that will test the validity of your backup.

To protect yourself while you are looking around, go to the Options menu and select Read Only Mode. It is a toggle switch, allowing you to go back and forth quickly and easily. A warning dialog (in many cases, a welcome sight) tells you when you are in Read Only Mode. (See Figure 9.4.)

With the editor in Read Only Mode, changes are preceded with a warning that you are working in Read Only Mode. None of the changes you make take effect.

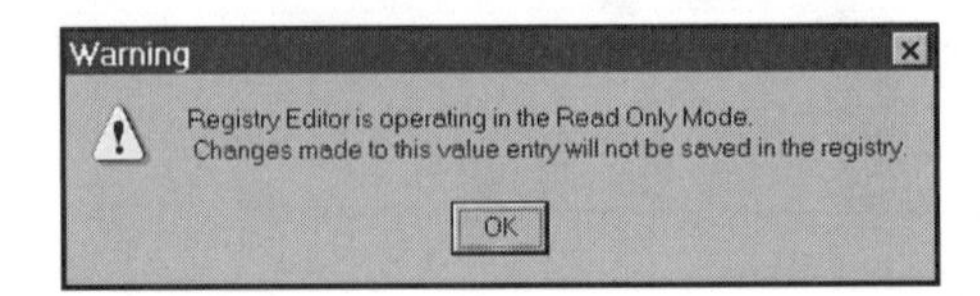

Figure 9.4.
Read Only Mode warning in `REGEDT32.EXE`.

Tip

If your Registry Editor is set in the Options menu to Save Settings on Exit and also to Read Only Mode, `REGEDT32.EXE` will be in Read Only Mode as an added safety belt for the user the next time you start it.

Editing Registry Values

To edit a value, double-click it. Double-clicking invokes the proper editor. There is a separate editor for strings, including expandable strings (see Figure 9.5), multiple strings (see Figure 9.6), binary data (see Figure 9.7), and DWORD (see Figure 9.8). When you edit DWORD and binary information, you have additional choices to work in binary, hexadecimal, or decimal format.

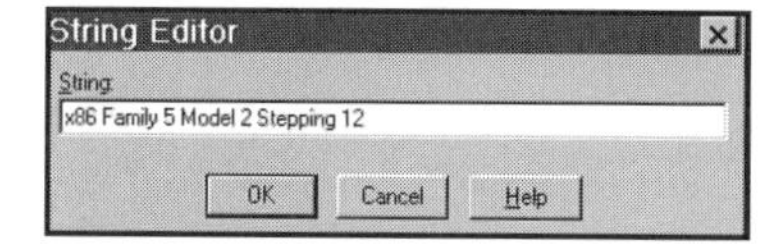

Figure 9.5.
Editing data with the String Editor.

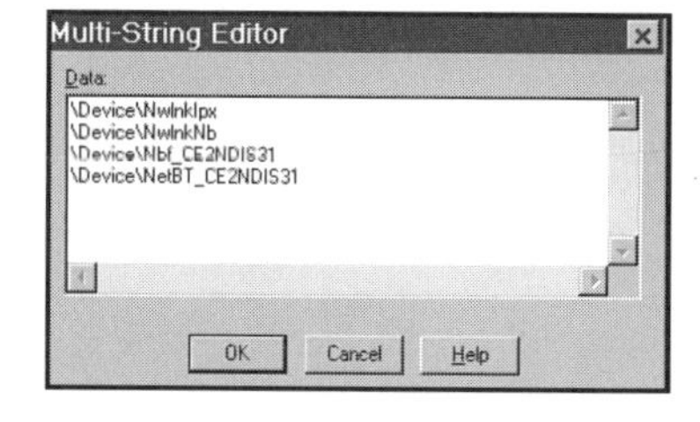

Figure 9.6.
Editing data with the Multi-String Editor.

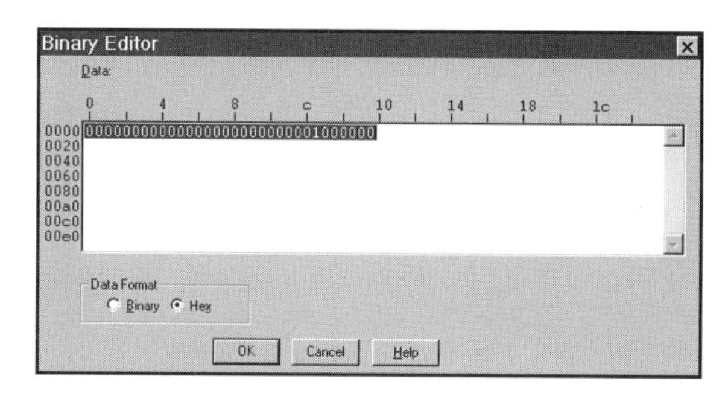

Figure 9.7.
Editing data with the Binary Editor.

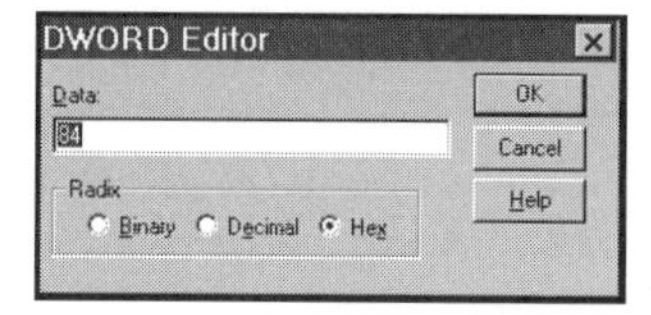

Figure 9.8.
Editing data with the DWORD Editor.

Enter the information, watch the system save it automatically (by watching the hourglass light up), and you can exit safely. The update is automatic, but depending on the type of information you changed, it may not take effect immediately. Changes to some types of information take effect immediately. Others wait until you log off and back on, and others wait until you restart your system.

Note

Determining when Registry information gets used can help you determine what actions are required to activate the update. If you have updated software, drivers, settings for hardware, or similar information, a restart is normally required because the information is used at startup. If the information is user-based, you'll usually be required to log off and back on again. Sometimes, the update takes effect immediately, allowing you to continue working; unfortunately, that is quite rare indeed.

Quick Steps to Edit the Registry

For easy reference, here is a list of steps to edit a value in the Registry:

- Select the correct handle key.
- Find the key.
- Double-click the value to be changed.
- Enter the correct value.
- Exit the Registry Editor and restart or log off if necessary.

Adding a Value to a Current Key

If the value you need is not currently present, you can easily add one. All values are listed in alphabetical order, so it makes it easy to find them.

Warning

If you add a key or value that is not understood by Windows NT because of spelling errors or because it is not a recognizable entry, nothing happens in most cases. I have experimented many times by adding entries similar to those found in Windows 95 without damaging the system. If Windows NT cannot use the information, it simply ignores it.

To add a value to a key, highlight the key, and select Edit | Add Value. Figure 9.9 shows the Add Value dialog box. You are prompted for the value name and data type.

Figure 9.9.
The Add Value dialog box in `REGEDT32.EXE`.

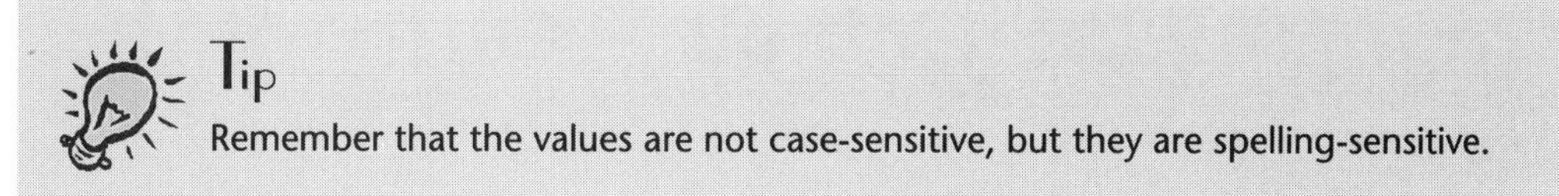

Tip

Remember that the values are not case-sensitive, but they are spelling-sensitive.

Most of the new entries you create are regular string values unless you specifically direct them to be otherwise.

Finding a Key

If you are not sure where the key is, you can locate it using View | Find Key. (See Figure 9.10.) The editor searches the Registry for the key name and moves your highlight there. However, it searches only in the current handle key, and only in the order listed in the dialog box.

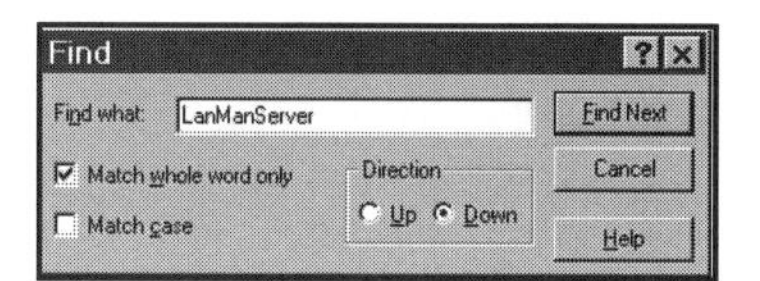

Figure 9.10.
Finding a key with REGEDT32.EXE.

The search starts at the key that is currently highlighted and goes up or down from there. If a match is found, your highlight moves there. The Find Key dialog box remains open, giving you an opportunity to continue your search by clicking the Find Next button. If another match is found, the tree expands as necessary and highlights the next match. If there is no match to your request, you are then informed by an error dialog box. (See Figure 9.11.)

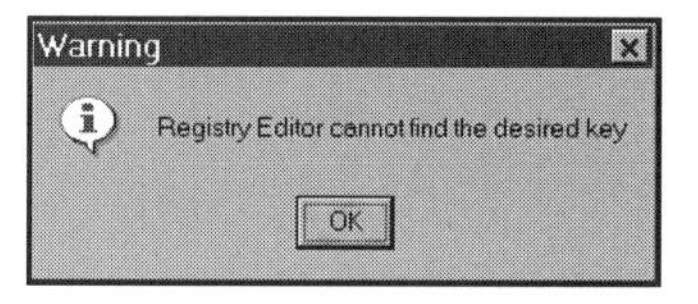

Figure 9.11.
Unable to find a key with REGEDT32.EXE.

Unfortunately, the search capabilities of REGEDT32.EXE are extremely limited. If you don't start from the right place or search in the right direction, your search is unsuccessful. Searching only for keys is also very limiting. To ensure the best results, start from the handle key (such as HKEY_CURRENT_USER), and use wildcard characters (* or ?) to extend your search through the entire key.

To extend the search capabilities of REGEDT32.EXE, use the shareware program REGSRCH.EXE, included on the CD-ROM with this book.

Changing the Default Security of the Registry

By default, the Registry can be edited only by members of the Administrators or Power Users groups. Each user in those groups, however, has equal access.

To add users or groups, highlight the key and select Security | Permissions. Current permissions are shown in the resulting dialog box. (See Figure 9.12.) To change the current permissions of the groups or individual users, highlight the name and select the type of access in the dialog shown in Figure 9.13.

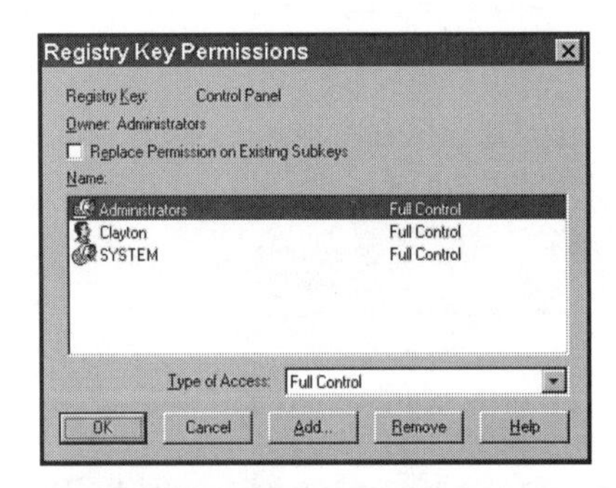

Figure 9.12.
Setting permissions with `REGEDT32.EXE`.

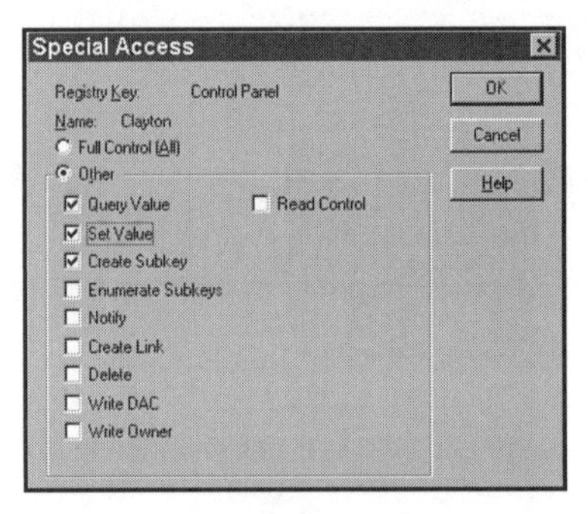

Figure 9.13.
Special access options with `REGEDT32.EXE`.

To add others so they can also participate in Registry security, click Add and choose from the list of groups and users. Then determine the level of permissions they will receive. The permission changes will take effect immediately.

Registry Permissions

`REGEDT32.EXE` allows you to set permissions for individual users or groups to restrict access to the Registry. The standard permissions are Read and Full Control. Read access allows users to see the Registry entries, but not to change them. It is the default setting for the Everyone group. Full Control allows the user to read and change entries, including editing, adding, and deleting entries. It also includes permission to restrict other users from editing the Registry, and to take ownership of keys and subkeys. By taking ownership of a key with the Write Owner permission (included in Full Control), it is possible to determine who will be able to access the Registry, and in which way.

For more specific settings and permissions, select Special Access as shown in Figure 9.13. Table 9.1 shows the permissions and what they allow a user to do.

Table 9.1. Special access permissions.

Permissions	*Allowed function*
Query Value	Read a value entry from a Registry key
Set Value	Set a value entry in a Registry key
Create Subkey	Create a subkey on a selected Registry key
Enumerate Subkeys	Identify the subkeys of a Registry key, such as by expanding the tree view
Notify	Notify events from a key in the Registry
Create Link	Create a symbolic link in a particular key
Delete	Delete a Registry object
Write DAC	Change the security permissions of a key
Write Owner	Take ownership of a key
Read Control	Read the security permissions of a key

Warning

Always remove the Everyone group from any permission settings to increase security. It is not related to any domain, and any user who can get into your system in any way is part of the Everyone group. If you want your domain users to be able to read the Registry but not edit it, set the Read permission for the Domain Users group. Then, unless the user is part of the domain, he cannot even see it.

Determine what the security should be on keys and subkeys according to your organization's security policy. Then set those settings on the system through Security | Permissions.

Tip

Users who log directly on to their own systems (locally, not as a member of the domain) as Administrator can make any desired changes to their local Registry. This produces a significant security and administrative risk. To prevent the user

continues

continued

from logging on locally, change the Administrator password at every machine. Even though this is time-consuming, it provides a level of security that is worth the effort.

Auditing Registry Usage, or "Who's Been Eating My Porridge?"

The three bears wouldn't have wondered if they had auditing in place. With auditing, you can tell who has been editing the Registry, and whether those edits occurred locally or from a remote location.

The person editing the Registry has no idea that he is being audited. There is no noticeable overhead or warning. Though you may have chosen the Everyone group to audit, the reporting of the audit is done individually. All results of the audit are posted in the security log in Event Viewer.

Note

User rights and auditing can be a very sensitive issue. Auditing someone's activities without notification may violate individual rights. Inclusion of the phrase "We reserve the right to restrict access and audit usage of files, directories, and the Registry without subsequent notice" (or similar language) in your security policy is important. Consult your attorney for exact language and restrictions.

To activate auditing, select Security | Auditing, and add the groups or individuals to be audited with the Add button. Then choose the success or failure of the action to report. Figure 9.14 shows the Auditing dialog box, and Table 9.2 contains the events that may be audited, and a short description of each.

Table 9.2. Events that can be audited.

Events to Audit	*Description*
Query Value	Reads a value entry from a Registry key
Set Value	Sets value entries in a Registry key
Create Subkey	Creates subkeys on a selected Registry key
Enumerate Subkeys	Audits events that attempt to identify the subkeys of a Registry key, such as expanding the tree view
Notify	Notifies events from a key in the Registry

Events to Audit	*Description*
Create Link	Creates a symbolic link in a particular key
Delete	Deletes a Registry object
Write DAC	Changes security permissions of a key
Read Control	Reads the security permissions of a key

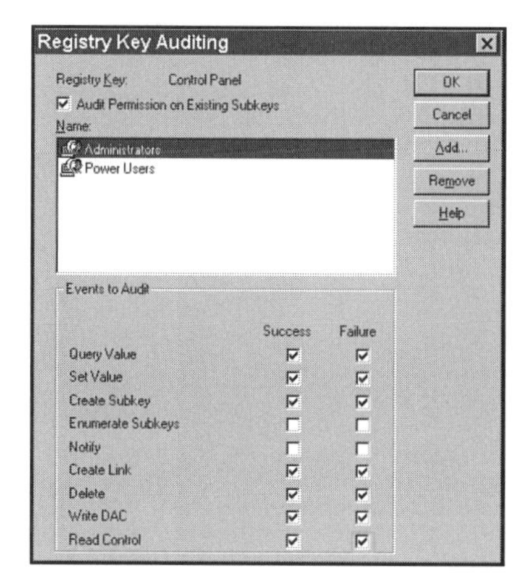

Figure 9.14.
Auditing access with REGEDT32.EXE.

These events can also be performed by the user called SYSTEM, but that usually happens during installation or modification of software and changes in Control Panel. A user would never log on as SYSTEM; it is reserved for the operating system internal functions.

Warning

NEVER remove SYSTEM as a qualified user in the permissions. Doing so may make the changing of the Registry with the Control Panel or software installation impossible. Changes will not take effect, and the software may be unusable.

Note

Auditing the failure of access to the Registry is as important as auditing the successful editing. Knowing that a restricted user gained access to information is critical, and immediate action is required. However, it is equally important and more timely to know whether a restricted user is trying to access restricted information. Sometimes, learning about and trying to recover from inappropriate access is like recovering all the feathers in the wind. Keeping them protected in the first place is a much better use of time and resources.

The reporting of auditing results is done in the security log of the Event Viewer. Choose Event Viewer from the Administrative Tools menu, and select Log | Security. (See Figure 9.15.) Any successful items are shown with a key, and unsuccessful attempts are shown with a lock. Double-click the report line for additional details. (See Figure 9.16.)

Event Viewer - Security Log on \\WS2

Log View Options Help

Date	Time	Source	Category	Event	User	Computer
10/8/96	1:43:35 PM	Security	Privilege Use	576	Administrator	WS2
10/8/96	1:43:35 PM	Security	Privilege Use	576	Administrator	WS2
10/8/96	1:43:19 PM	Security	Privilege Use	578	Bob	WS2
10/8/96	1:43:08 PM	Security	Object Access	560	Bob	WS2
10/8/96	1:43:08 PM	Security	Object Access	562	Bob	WS2
10/8/96	1:43:08 PM	Security	Object Access	560	Bob	WS2
10/8/96	1:43:02 PM	Security	Object Access	562	Bob	WS2
10/8/96	1:43:02 PM	Security	Object Access	560	Bob	WS2

Figure 9.15. Results of auditing control in Event Viewer.

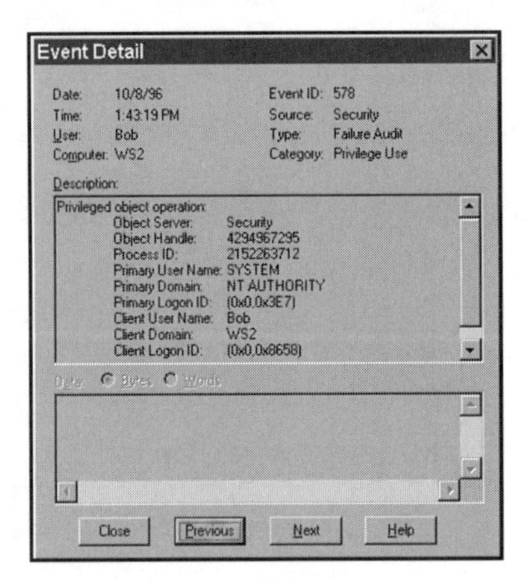

Figure 9.16. Detail from an audit failure provides important security information.

Even though this is not one of the more enjoyable functions of an administrator, it may be necessary to protect your organization's information and the integrity of the systems. The information you get from auditing can also be printed for future reference by saving it as a text file with Log | Save As and printing the text file.

Ownership of the Registry Keys

All Registry entries are owned by the Administrators group. The only reason to own a key or subkey is to select who can or cannot access the Registry. The critical reason that ownership transfer is available is to thwart damage, whether intentional or not, caused by the owner leaving the organization.

If a user takes ownership of a key and its subkeys, that person has the right to determine who has access to it. Conceivably, that user could restrict all access to the key prior to leaving the organization. If no others had access to the data, reinstallation might be required to restore the capability to edit the data. However, regardless of the user, regardless of the restriction (even if the Administrator was given the No Access permission), it is impossible to prevent Administrator from taking ownership. That ability is fundamental in maintaining system security. The

Administrator is the only one who can keep the data from going into a black hole, a location from which there is no return.

Warning

Be careful to whom you give the Administrator password. It's almost always impossible to restrict the Administrator. He has access to any files on the network, in any directory, plus access to the Registry for any user/computer on the network. He cannot be restricted.

That is why you also need to secure your Administrator password, and only give it to a few trusted people. Widespread use of the Administrator user name and password seriously compromises the security of the network.

To take ownership of a key, highlight the key, select Security | Owner, and click Take Ownership. At that point, you have Full Control permissions and can choose to whom you want to grant or restrict access.

Exporting the Registry

Occasionally, it would be nice to have the data in the Registry in a text format. You might use it to determine changes that are made that may not be easily found.

For example, if you want to see the changes made when Control Panel options are exercised, you can take a snapshot of the current Registry using Registry | Save Subtree As and selecting the location and the file name. The data is then written into the file, and it can be read with any text editor or word processor. (See Figure 9.17.)

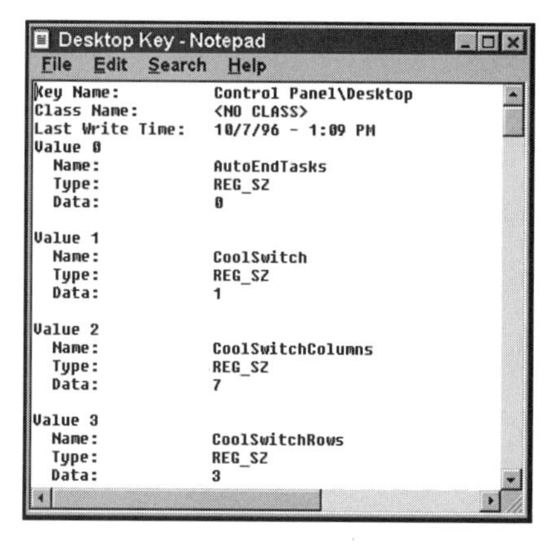

Figure 9.17.
Exported data from `HKEY_CURRENT_USER\Control Panel`.

After you make the changes, you can export the data into a second text file. Using your word processor, you can compare the two documents to see the actual changes. The Registry changes can be used later to customize the Registry as needed.

Alternately, if two systems perform differently but are said to be set up in exactly the same way, you can use this tool to find out whether that is really the case. Usually, there are differences in the Registry that make the two systems work differently.

Advanced Registry Editing Options

Although Microsoft does not support it, they still include in `REGEDT32.EXE` the capability to export a section of the Registry to a file, edit the file, and put it back into the Registry. Generally, this is used by programmers to test the viability of proposed changes.

Similarly, you can take a slice of a Registry from one machine and put it into another, overwriting the current Registry entries. I think it is obvious why this is not supported or encouraged by Microsoft. The misuse of this tool can be disastrous. Hardware information and software settings nearly always vary from system to system. However, if you are careful, you can use this to fix a system that is not currently correct. Be very careful. Proceed with extreme caution, and at your own risk.

An example of when this tool would be very helpful is in the restoration of shares on the network after a server has crashed. Performing a full restore on top of a currently installed NT system restores the applications, data, and the file and directory permissions to a new server (in the same domain), but not the shares. Re-creating the shares manually may take a long time, and any errors mean the system is down even longer than anticipated. Rather than doing that, use the steps shown in the next section to restore the shares. (See Figure 9.18.)

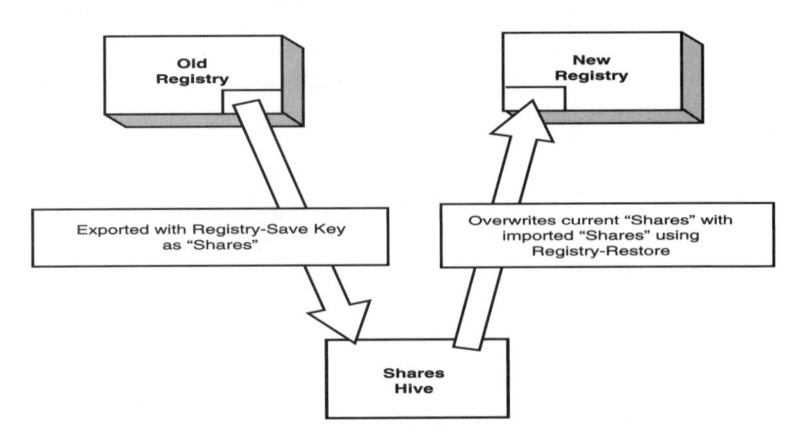

Figure 9.18. Using part of an old Registry to fix a new one.

Tip

Another example of using the Save Key/Restore Key function would be the copying of Program Manager icons and groups from one machine to another, rather than re-creating them. Use the following procedure and use `HKEY_CURRENT_USER\`*`User SID`*`\UNICODE Program Groups` as the key to restore.

Pulling the Shares from Another System

The step-by-step procedure for restoring the shares from another system is listed here for your convenience.

1. Restore the Registry from the crashed computer's backup to a temporary directory on the new computer (such as `C:\OLD_REG`).
2. Start the Registry Editor.
3. In the `HKEY_LOCAL_MACHINE` window, highlight the handle key, select Registry | Load Hive to open the old Registry, and access the files in the temporary directory listed in Step 1.
4. Select and open the `SYSTEM` hive (see Figure 9.19), and give it a name (like `Old`) when it prompts you for the name for the new key (see Figures 9.20 and 9.21).

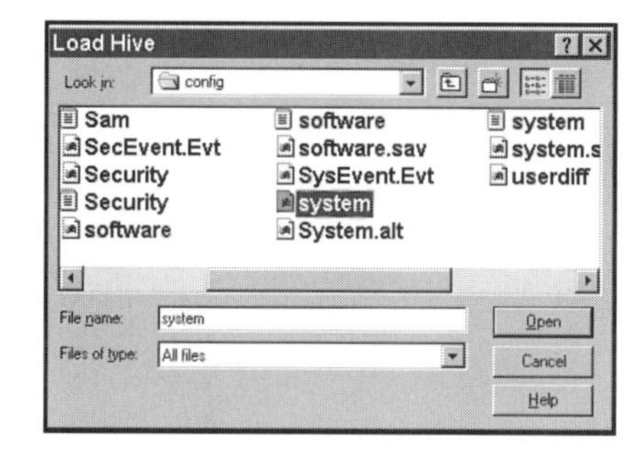

Figure 9.19. Accessing the `SYSTEM` hive from the old Registry.

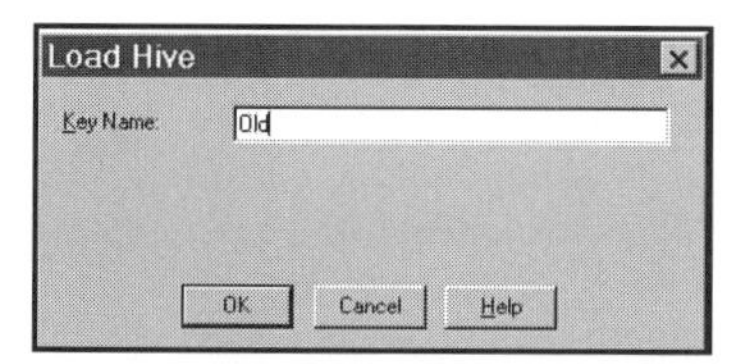

Figure 9.20. Loading `Old` hive with `REGEDT32.EXE`.

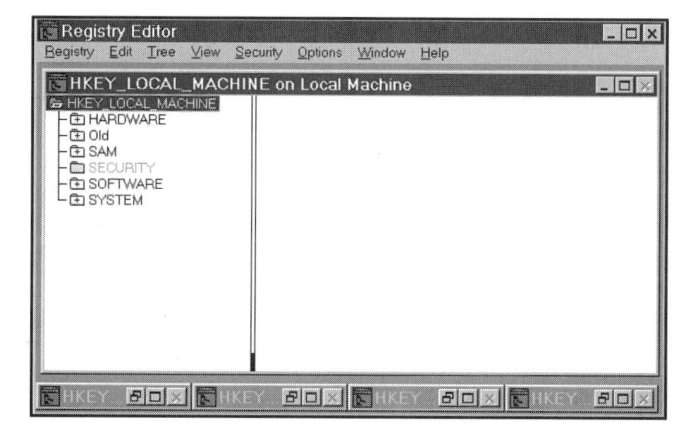

Figure 9.21. `HKEY_LOCAL_MACHINE` with `Old` hive loaded.

5. Open the Old key and go to `System\CurrentControlSet\Services\LanManServer\Shares`. These are the shares your system had previously, and the success of this procedure depends on having the data in the correct locations, and the same partitions and drive letters available.
6. Choose Registry | Save Key and save the key as `Shares` or another appropriate name. (See Figure 9.22.)

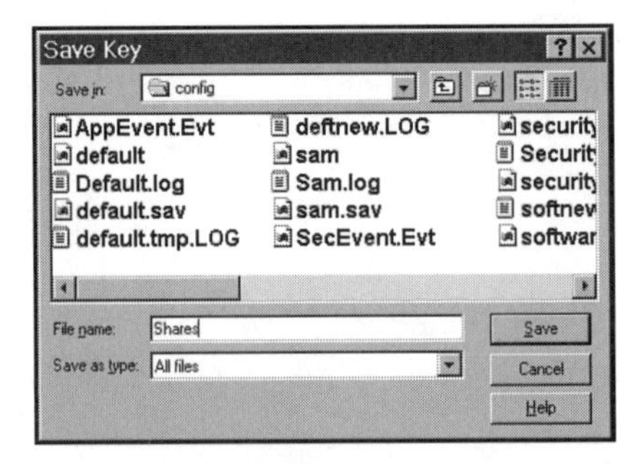

Figure 9.22.
Saving part of the `Old` key as `Shares`.

7. Open the `HKEY_LOCAL_MACHINE\SYSTEM\CurrentControlSet\Services\LanManServer` key and highlight `Shares`. (See Figure 9.23.)

Figure 9.23.
Restoring the `Shares` hive over the original.

8. Select Registry | Restore, then highlight the `Shares` file and click Open.
9. Confirm the overwriting of the keys, subkeys, values, and data on the screen shown in Figure 9.24.

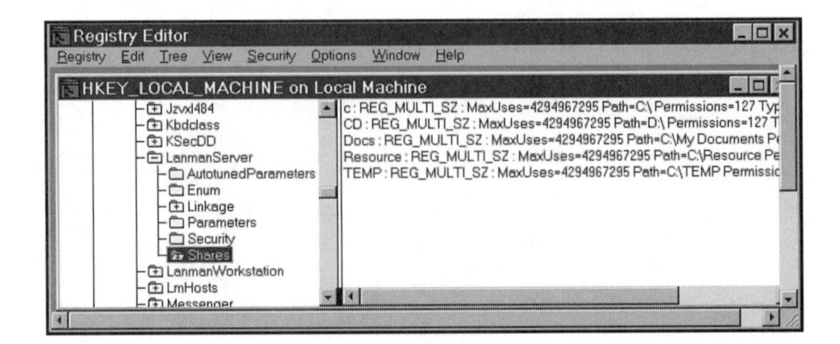

Figure 9.24.
The updated `Shares` key, showing the new shares available.

10. After you restart your system, the shares will be available on that new server.

Editing *Any* User's Settings

Occasionally, it is necessary to load a Registry hive that is not normally opened in order to edit it. Such is the case with user settings, so you can edit the settings for any user even if he is not logged on to the network.

1. Start the Registry Editor.
2. In HKEY_USERS, highlight the handle key, select Registry | Load Hive to go to the profile location for the desired user (\WINNT\Profiles*Username*), and select NTUSER.DAT. (See Figure 9.25.)

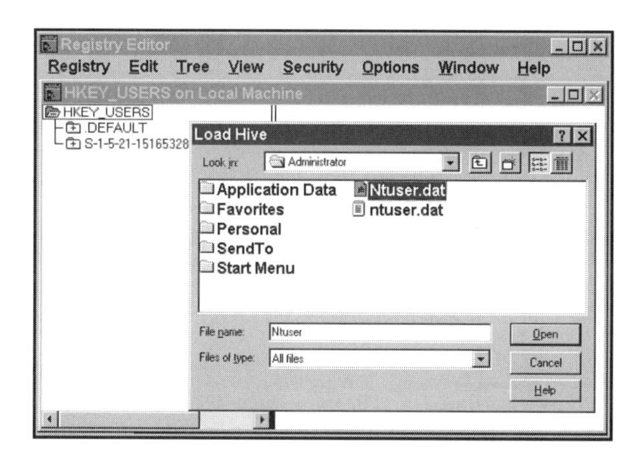

Figure 9.25.
Opening another user's NTUSER.DAT for editing.

Note

Load Hive only works on HKEY_USERS and HKEY_LOCAL_MACHINE.

3. When prompted for the name of the key, put in the user's name. After entering the user's name, REGEDIT.EXE will insert the user's Registry data into HKEY_USERS under the user's name. (See Figure 9.26.)
4. Edit any of the entries for the user.
5. Save the key using Registry | Save Key.
6. Save the key as NTUSER.DAT in the \WINNT\Profiles*Username* directory, replacing the one that is currently there.

The next time the user logs on, those settings will take effect.

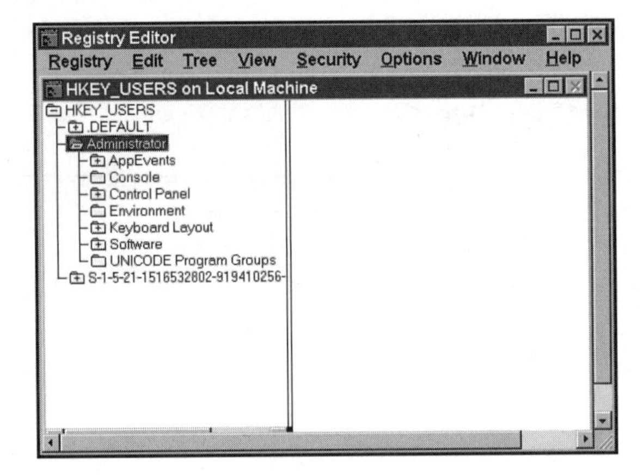

Figure 9.26.
The Administrator's user settings are available for editing.

Summary

REGEDT32.EXE is an extremely powerful editor of the Registry. It provides required security, performance, and ease-of-use features that make it very popular. With proper use, you can edit any of the Registry safely, quickly, and effectively. You can use REGEDT32.EXE to make the everyday changes necessary for maintenance on your own system, and on others throughout the network. The features of security, loading additional hives, and saving and restoring keys makes it a particularly good choice for advanced system administrators.

CHAPTER 10

Making Manual Changes to the Registry Using REGEDIT.EXE

Most users who have been using Windows NT for a long time have used `REGEDT32.EXE`, the Windows NT Registry Editor. Windows 95 users, or NT users coming from a Windows 95 background, however, have always used `REGEDIT.EXE`. The good news is that both are included with Windows NT 4.0, and you can use either. Windows 95 users don't have a choice.

There are significant differences, however, in the features that each possesses. Each has its strengths and weaknesses, and most NT users will end up using both. Table 10.1 compares `REGEDT32` with `REGEDIT`.

Table 10.1. Comparison of `REGEDT32` and `REGEDIT`.

Feature	*REGEDT32*	*REGEDIT*
All handle keys available	X	X
Edit current Registry	X	X
Edit local NT Registry	X	X
Edit local 95 Registry		X
Remotely edit other NT Registries	X	X
Remotely edit other 95 Registries		X
Export and import hives	X	X
Export hives as text	X	X
Tiled view of multiple handle keys	X	
Copy key name available		X
Right mouse button support		X
Single-click cascading of folders		X
Print contents	X	X
Edit multiple string entries	X	
Security available on keys and values	X	
Auditing available on keys and values	X	
Search for keys	X	X
Search for values		X
Search for data strings		X
Read-only mode	X	
Change screen font	X	
Resource list entries as window	X	binary only

`REGEDT32.EXE` focuses more on the high-security, hardware-level editing, whereas `REGEDIT.EXE` is designed for ease of use and broad appeal. Most tasks you perform can be done in `REGEDIT.EXE` with no problem, and, in many cases, it can be done more easily and quickly than with `REGEDT32.EXE`.

Note

REGEDIT.EXE and Explorer are very similar, much as REGEDT32.EXE and File Manager are similar.

With REGEDIT.EXE and Explorer, all items are shown on one screen in one window, cascading with the plus signs outside the folder. Right mouse button support is extensive, and almost makes the inclusion of the menus redundant. The speed and ease of use are paramount, and features not considered crucial are not included.

REGEDT32.EXE and File Manager both use multiple windows, allowing the cascading, tiling, and minimizing of windows to customize the look of the data. The folders look the same, the menus are more extensive than their newer counterparts, and they are feature-laden. Unfortunately, there is no right mouse button support. Security is a premium function and is prominently presented in the menus.

Whatever your choice, both are outstanding editors. The inclusion of both indicates Microsoft's willingness to allow different work styles with NT.

Protecting the Registry with REGEDIT.EXE

The Registry is no less vulnerable with REGEDIT.EXE than with REGEDT32.EXE. Indeed, it may be more vulnerable because there is no read-only mode. Without a read-only mode, utmost care must be taken to protect the Registry from damage.

Back up the Registry with the tools listed in Chapter 4, "Protecting the NT Registry," and Chapter 6, "Protecting the Windows 95 Registry," or use the export features in REGEDIT.EXE as discussed later in this chapter.

Editing the Registry with REGEDIT.EXE

Run REGEDIT.EXE from the Start | Run menu. You will see all the handle keys represented on one screen. (See Figure 10.1.) Similar to the Explorer interface, REGEDIT.EXE is easy to use and straightforward in its procedures, and it's easy to understand the relationships between keys.

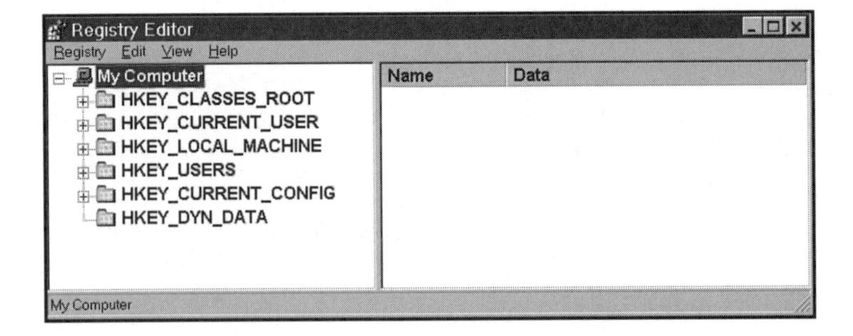

Figure 10.1.
The interface of `REGEDIT.EXE`.

Note

Even though `HKEY_DYN_DATA` is shown, there is no configurable Plug and Play support in Windows NT 4.0. The handle key is inaccessible, but is included to maintain visual continuity with the editing of Windows 95 Registries.

The folders cascade and consolidate with a single-click on the plus (+) and minus (-) signs to the left of the key names. You don't even have to wait for the display of all the values in the key. To open the key and see inside, a single-click on the key name is required, as shown in Figure 10.2.

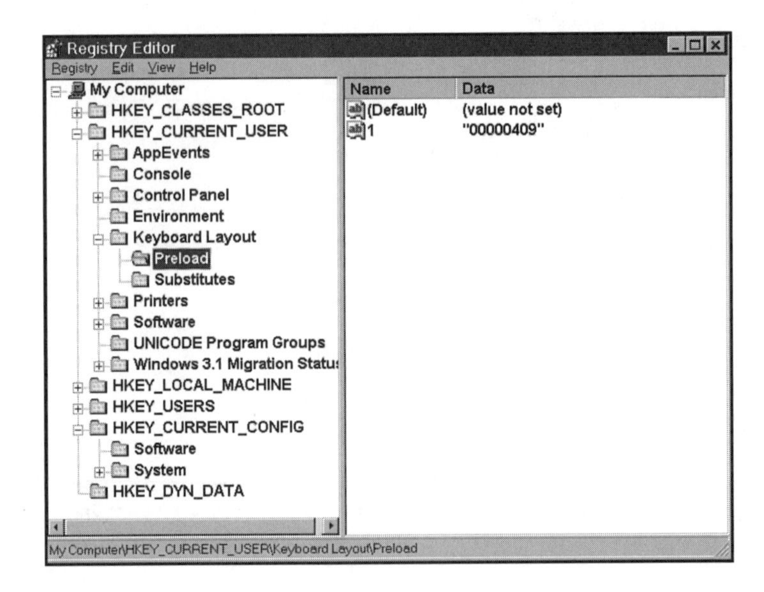

Figure 10.2.
Cascaded folders in `REGEDIT.EXE`.

Tip

The full path to the key is shown in the status line at the bottom of the REGEDIT.EXE window. Having it there is handy; you don't have to remember the actual path.

If you create documentation, use Edit | Copy Key Name rather than typing the whole name into text. Imagine the difference between typing HKEY_LOCAL_MACHINE\SOFTWARE\Microsoft\Windows NT\CurrentVersion\Winlogon and just copying it.

Also, when you start creating your own custom policies for System Policy Editor (see Chapter 34, "Creating Custom Policies"), copying the key name will reduce errors and improve performance.

Shortcut for Faster Collapsing of the Registry View

When the Registry is expanded, the connection to the parent key is shown with a dotted line, as illustrated in Figure 10.3. Although you can scroll up until you find the Collapse button, or you can collapse individual sections, it is faster to collapse entire trees.

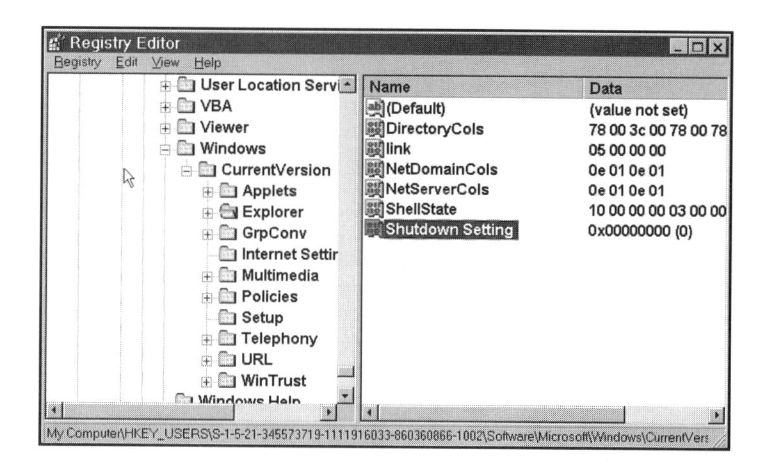

Figure 10.3. Double-click the vertical line to collapse the tree.

Adding Keys to the Registry

Additional keys can be added to the Registry by application installation routines, driver installation, or manually. To manually add a key below another, highlight the current key, select Edit | New | Key, and type the name. The new key will be cascaded below the current key, and a plus sign will be added to the left of the key name, as shown in Figure 10.4.

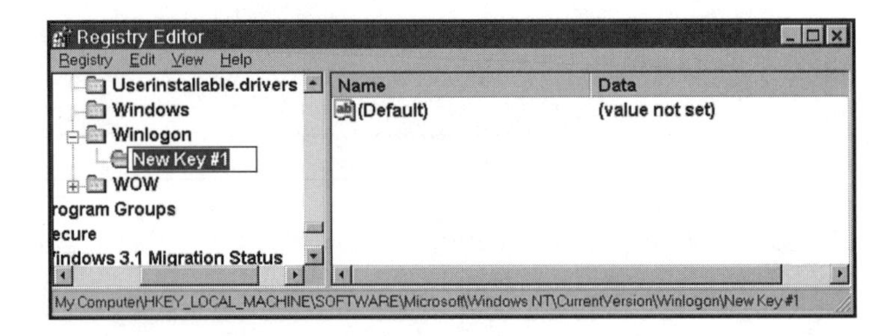

Figure 10.4.
Adding a new key in `REGEDIT.EXE`.

Tip

As in Explorer, right mouse button support is extensive in `REGEDIT.EXE`. Virtually all menu items can be accessed though the context-sensitive menus available when you right-click items in the window.

Right-click the title bar for window options. (See Figure 10.5.) Right-click a key for options to expand or collapse the key view, create a new key, create new values in the key, delete or rename the key, copy the key name, or search for keys, values, or data. (See Figure 10.6.)

Right-click a value to modify the data, or delete or rename the value name. (See Figure 10.7.) Right-click an open space in the right pane to make a new key, a new string value, a new binary value, or a new DWORD value. (See Figure 10.8.)

The context-sensitive menus are an intuitive, fast, and easy-to-use alternative to wading through the pull-down menus.

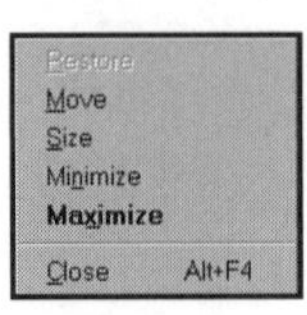

Figure 10.5.
Pop-up menu for the Registry Editor title bar.

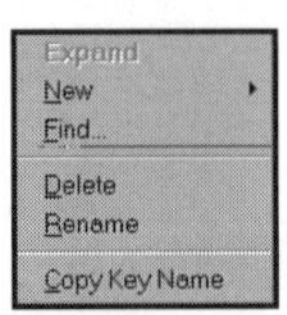

Figure 10.6.
Pop-up menu for a Registry key.

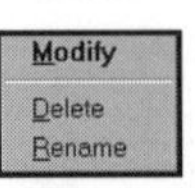

Figure 10.7.
Pop-up menu for a Registry value.

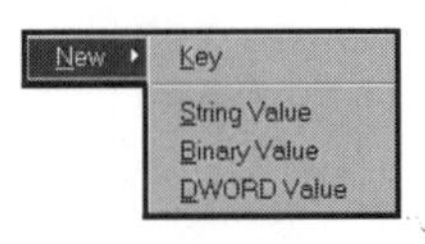

Figure 10.8.
The general pop-up menu for the Registry Editor.

If the key or value name that you add is not supported in the Registry, it will not be activated even though it is present. The key names are not case-sensitive, but they are spelling-sensitive.

Values in REGEDIT.EXE

The values in the `REGEDIT.EXE` window are in the right pane, listed in alphabetical order, as shown in Figure 10.9.

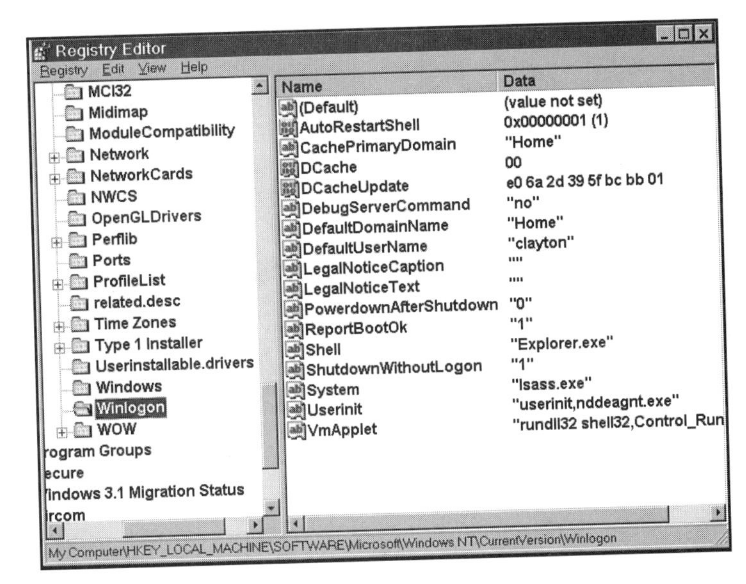

Figure 10.9. Values in the `Winlogon` key.

Tip

If the column of value names is too narrow to read effectively, position your cursor on the line between Name and Data. The cursor will change to a vertical line with a two-headed horizontal arrow. Grab the line and move it to the right to expand the column width.

`REGEDIT.EXE` only shows two value types: string and binary. String values include standard strings as well as expandable strings. Any variable (such as `%systemroot%`) is automatically considered expandable, so an additional editor is not required. Binary entries include both binary and DWORD entries, with binary being variable-length values, and DWORD being fixed-length 32-bit values. For more detail on value types, see Chapter 2, "The Structure of the Registry."

Adding Values to the Registry with `REGEDIT.EXE`

To add a new value to a key, right-click in any empty space in the right pane in the `REGEDIT.EXE` window. The right mouse button click brings up a menu choice to add either a string, binary, or DWORD value (refer to Figure 10.8).

Notice that the options do not include a multistring editor. That makes adding a multistring virtually impossible. There is also no specific entry for a variable string, assuming that a normal string editor will work the same. Any variable will automatically expand or contract the size of the string as necessary when replaced with the variable.

When you select the option to create a string value, `REGEDIT.EXE` responds with a new value, as shown in Figure 10.10.

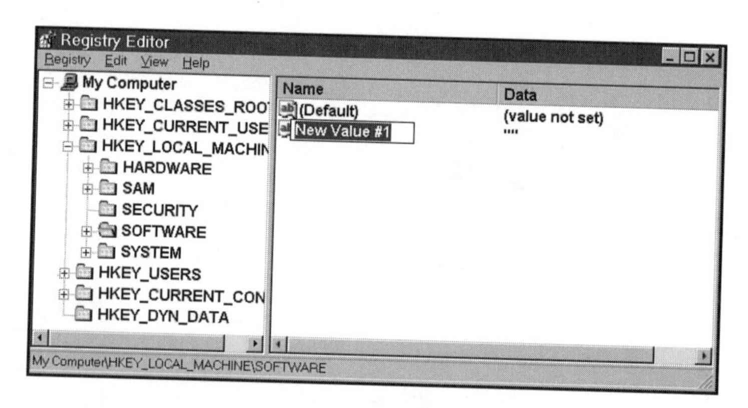

Figure 10.10.
A new value created with `REGEDIT.EXE`.

If you had chosen a binary or DWORD value instead, you would also have been prompted for the value name. Only the representative icon and the underlying type would be different. Type the name of the value and press Enter. The actual data in the value is empty, requiring you to edit the new value entry. Double-click the new value to edit it.

Solutions

How can I change the key name if I misspell it?

If you misspell the key name, right-click it, select Modify, and correct the spelling.

Occasionally, you will be asked to add a default value for a key. A default value cannot be added to an existing key, but one is created with every new key.

Warning

Never create a value without a name. A value without a name cannot be renamed or deleted. It should not create any problems to have it there, but it might.

Editing Values

To edit a value, double-click the value name or right-click it and choose Modify. (See Figure 10.11.) Choosing Modify allows you to change the data, not the name of the value.

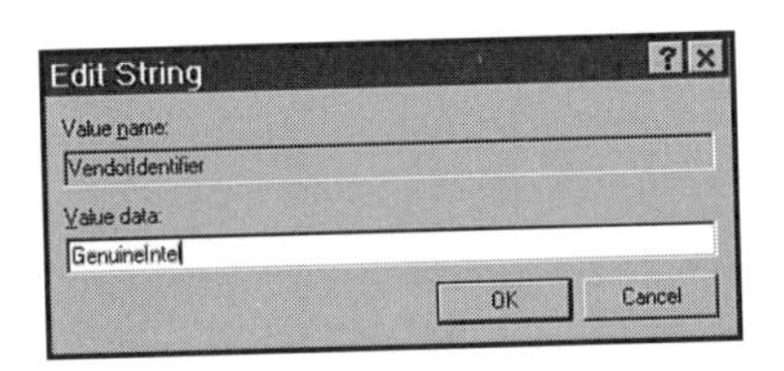

Figure 10.11.
Editing a string value.

Enter the desired information in the Value data area. Text data is not case-sensitive. For binary data, it is important to ensure the correct spacing and completeness of the data. Incorrect data can cause the value to be ignored, or worse yet, can cause the system or application to become unstable. Figures 10.12 and 10.13 show the Binary and DWORD editors, respectively.

To edit an expandable string, use the standard string editor and put your variables in as required. `REGEDIT.EXE` assumes any variable that is put into a string is going to be replaced by data, not used as literal text.

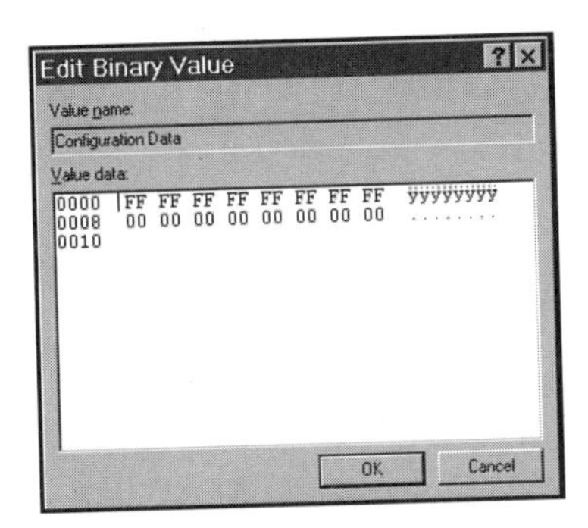

Figure 10.12.
Editing a binary value.

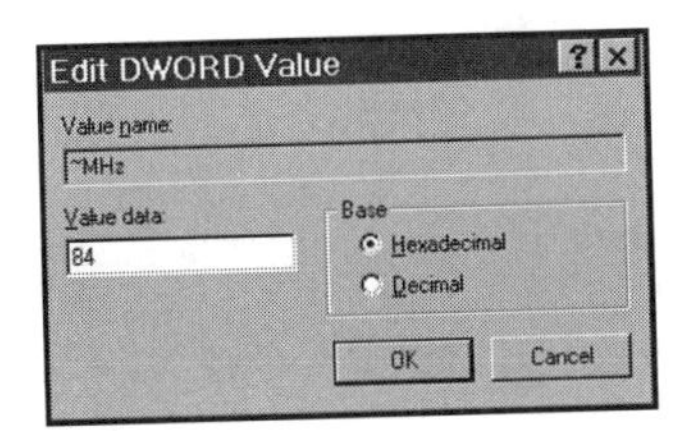

Figure 10.13.
Editing a DWORD value.

Warning

All changes to the Registry are immediate and permanent. There is no Undo feature, no discarding of changes at exit, and no temporary modifications. Any reconstruction of entries required because of mistakes must be done manually, or through the restoration of the Registry from a backup.

Finding Specific Entries in the Registries

Searching the Registry with `REGEDIT.EXE` is very powerful, much stronger than the search capabilities of `REGEDT32.EXE`. In `REGEDIT.EXE`, you can search for keys, value names, data, or any combination of the three.

To search the Registry, select Edit | Find, press Ctrl+F, or right-click the left pane. Select the type of data to search for, whether to restrict the search to the full string, and the string to be found.

For example, if you want to find the Shutdown options, type the word **`shutdown`** in the Find what field of the Find dialog box. (See Figure 10.14.) Select Find Next or press Enter to start the search. If the search is successful, it highlights the found string. (See Figure 10.15.)

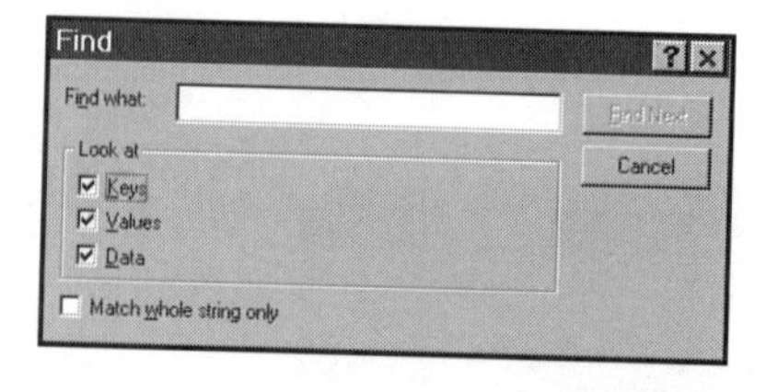

Figure 10.14.
Searching the Registry by keys, values, or data.

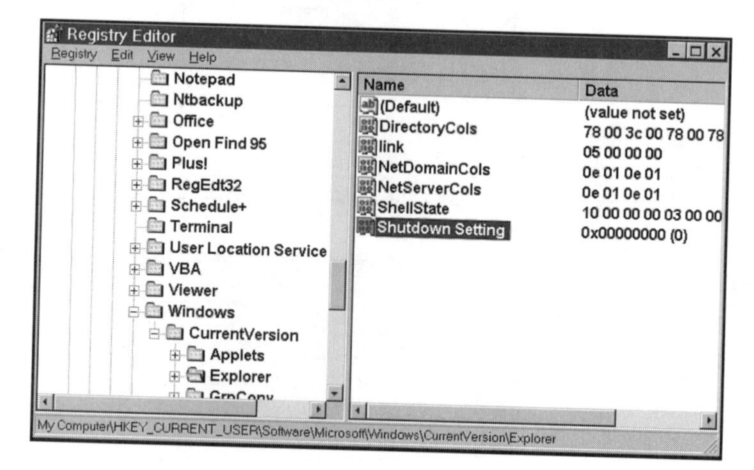

Figure 10.15.
Search results.

If that is not the entry you seek, press F3 to continue the search.

Tip

The Find feature in REGEDIT.EXE only goes down the Registry. It will not search above the current location. Before you start the search, make sure you are where you want to start. If you want to search the entire Registry, start at My Computer. If you want to search from another location (to restrict the scope of the search), highlight that location prior to starting the process.

If the search is unsuccessful, the dialog box in Figure 10.16 appears, indicating that the search has been completed. Upon confirmation, REGEDIT.EXE returns you to the last highlighted location.

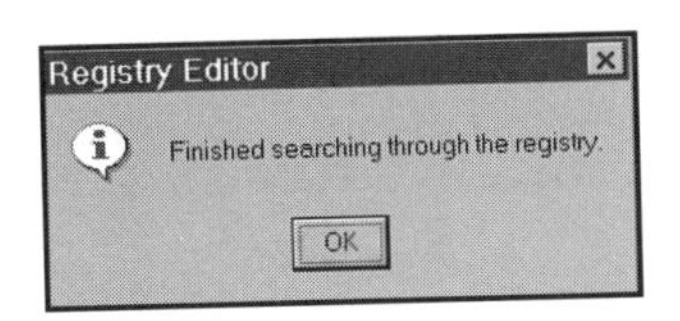

Figure 10.16.
Unable to find data in the Registry.

Exporting Registry Data

With REGEDIT.EXE, it is easy to export a key, handle key, or even the whole Registry to a file that can be edited with a text editor. To export the Registry as a text file, select the key and use Registry | Export Registry File, which invokes the dialog box shown in Figure 10.17.

Having this data as a text file makes it easier to troubleshoot. You can open a broken Registry and use a document-comparison feature of a word processor to compare it with a working Registry.

Additionally, you can export the software key in HKEY_LOCAL_MACHINE, add new software, and compare the current settings with the previous settings to determine what the software installation did.

Figure 10.17.
Exporting the Registry with REGEDIT.EXE.

The filename entered automatically has an `.REG` extension and can be easily edited. You can use a word processor, Notepad, WordPad, or any other editor you choose. The contents of the file are illustrated in Figure 10.18. Notice the `.REG` extension (in the title bar) that was added by `REGEDIT.EXE`.

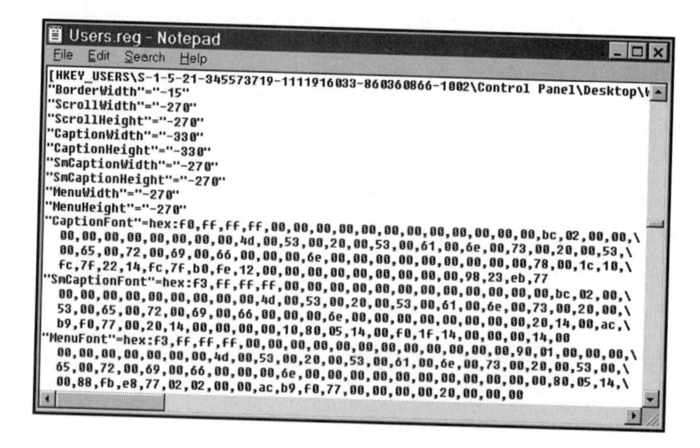

Figure 10.18.
The contents of the exported Registry key.

Of course, because this data is shown and edited as text, it is possible to use common word-processing techniques (cut/copy and paste) to update the values and data. You can use the document-compare feature to compare the Registries, and easily change the one with differences.

The exported data can be confusing to read. As you can see in Figure 10.18, every alphanumeric text string is contained in quotes. Table 10.2 is a legend of the other conventions used by the document.

Table 10.2. `.REG` legend.

Convention	*Description*
[Keyname]	Handle key, key, and subkeys
"Valuename"=	Value Name
@=	Default value for key
="data"	String data
=hex:	Binary data in hexadecimal format

With the information in this table, you should be easily able to browse, read, understand, and edit the Registry with an exported text file.

Warning

Be careful. Just because something is easy doesn't mean you should do it. Incorrect entries in the Registry can make it unstable or unusable. Be very careful about editing the text file and importing it back into the Registry.

Importing a Registry File

After the .REG file has been edited or updated, it can be swiftly imported into the Registry. Select the key where the file will be imported, and using the Registry | Import Registry File menu item, select the new file. It overwrites all the current entries and updates the Registry. If this action is successful, you will see the dialog shown in Figure 10.19.

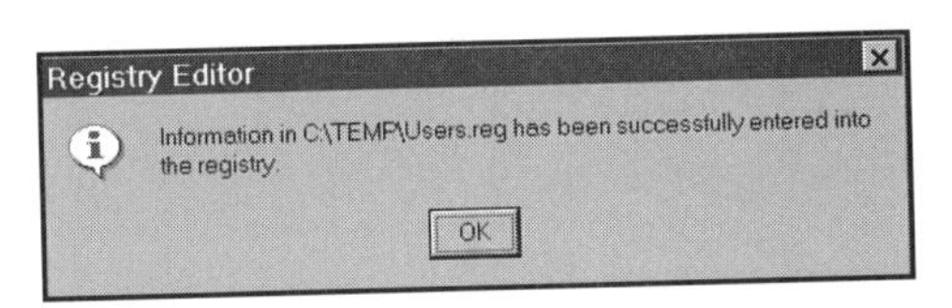

Figure 10.19.
The Registry is updated with the imported .REG file.

When would you use the Export and Import Registry File functions?

- As a rudimentary backup procedure—It allows you to back up the entire Registry to a text-based file that you can easily transport to a new system.
- To duplicate entries from one system to another—Be very careful; some entries are user- or machine-specific, and if they are copied to another system, the system might become unstable or unusable.
- Making the same change for many people—Rather than manually entering the same information over and over, import a .REG file. This is faster and results in fewer errors. Just make sure the information is correct before you duplicate it.

Warning

Another way to import the data from a .REG file into the Registry is to double-click it. If you double-click a .REG file, it will immediately write the data into the currently open Registry. That may have disastrous results.

An unsuspecting user may double-click the file as a means of opening it for editing. Upon doing so, the Registry is currently updated, with no option for undoing the process.

continues

continued

As a safeguard, consider removing the association between the .REG file and the REGEDIT.EXE. When you right-click the .REG file, it gives you an option to merge the file (into the Registry), but none to "Open with..."

To remove the association, search the HKEY_CLASSES_ROOT for "regfile." Expand the key (as shown in Figure 10.20), and remove the "open" key from the "shell" key. By doing this, you will restrict the user from importing the .REG file with the context-sensitive menu or by double-clicking the .REG file. The user will still have the opportunity to merge the data using the menus inside REGEDIT.EXE, but will be protected from making a mistake with the file.

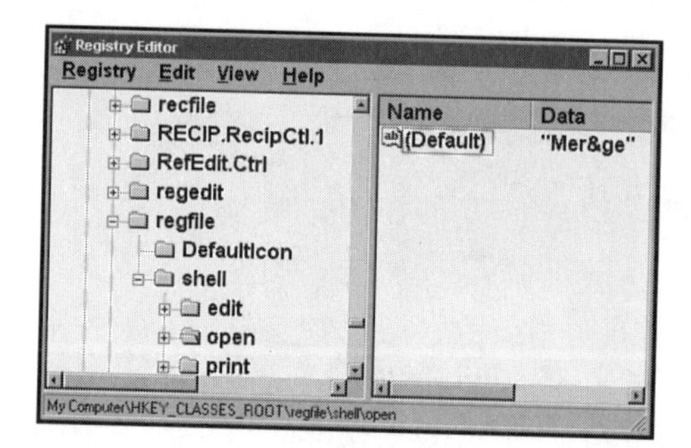

Figure 10.20.
The association for a .REG file is in the Registry.

Summary

REGEDIT.EXE will do most of the editing functions necessary to most people. Its easy-to-use features, speed, and convenience make it a great choice for anyone needing to edit the Registry.

If you could use it to edit REG_MULTI_SZ entries and REG_FULL_DESCRIPTOR entries, and had the read-only mode and security of REGEDT32.EXE, REGEDIT.EXE would probably be the choice of most system administrators.

Because of the feature mix between REGEDT32.EXE and REGEDIT.EXE, most administrators will use both, and you should, too.

CHAPTER 11

Remote Registry Editing

Because most changes made to the system are made through means other than direct editing, you don't actually have to edit your own system very often. However, to make changes to another system, you might think you'd need to get up, go to the other system, and use the Control Panel.

Luckily, you don't need to do that. Instead, you can use either of the Registry Editors to make the changes remotely. Making a remote Registry change requires knowing where to find the settings, and what the values are supposed to be. Table 8.1 in Chapter 8, "Automatic Changes to the Registry," shows where the Control Panel makes changes to the Registry. Additional settings for remote changes are included in Chapters 12 through 27.

By using the remote Registry editing functions, you can save a tremendous amount of time in system administration. Be careful, though, because editing another system's Registry can be as dangerous as editing your own. Take the normal precautions of creating backups before making any changes to the Registry.

Remote Windows NT Registry Editing

You can only edit a Windows NT system from another Windows NT system. Windows 95 will not edit an NT system. The only effective way to edit any system from NT is by using `REGEDT32.EXE`.

Connecting to a Remote NT Computer Using `REGEDT32.EXE`

To open another computer's Registry with `REGEDT32.EXE`, choose Registry | Select Computer. The system automatically browses the network for computers that qualify for editing. (See Figure 11.1.) A system automatically qualifies if it is running Windows NT Server or Workstation and is a member of the domain. If you can see the target computer in the browse list, you should be able to edit it unless security permissions have been set to restrict the process. If you cannot see it in the browse list, you can still enter the computer name using the UNC (universal naming convention) name, allowing you to edit the Registry on that machine. That would be particularly useful in editing a system in a trusting domain, or those connected only as a member of a workgroup. To edit a machine called `SERVER1`, type `\\SERVER1` in the blank.

After connecting to the remote computer, `REGEDT32.EXE` opens two additional windows: `HKEY_USERS` on *system name* and `HKEY_LOCAL_MACHINE` on *system name*. (See Figure 11.2.)

The AutoRefresh is not available for remote registries message indicates that any changes that the user makes to his own Registry while you are editing it are not shown to you, and any changes you make are not shown to the remote user. The main reason for this is to boost performance. Of course, none of the changes take effect until the user logs off and logs back on or restarts the system.

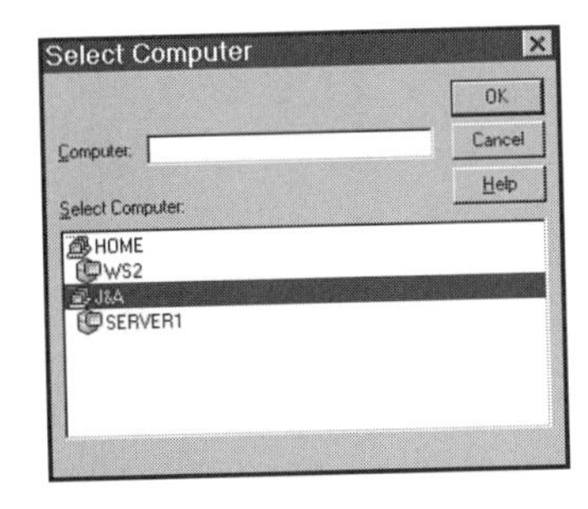

Figure 11.1.
Browsing for available computers for remote Registry editing.

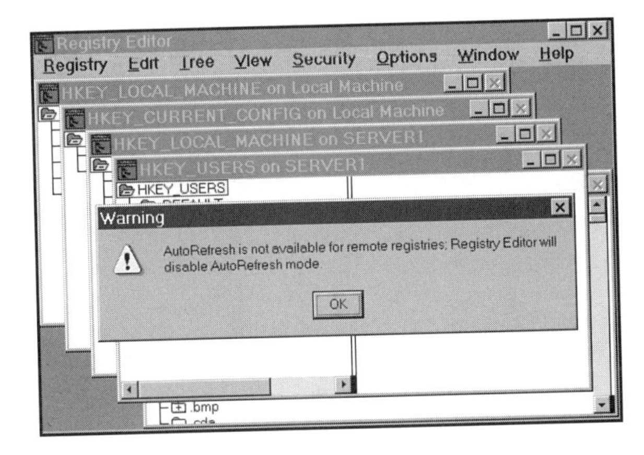

Figure 11.2.
Available windows for editing on a remote computer—and a warning.

Because the other handle keys are simply mapped portions of `HKEY_USERS` and `HKEY_LOCAL_MACHINE`, they are not shown. All editing must be done through `HKEY_USERS` and `HKEY_LOCAL_MACHINE`.

The locations of the other handle keys are shown in Table 11.1.

Table 11.1. Handle keys and their respective locations.

Mapped Handle Key	*Actual Location*
`HKEY_CLASSES_ROOT`	`HKEY_LOCAL_MACHINE\Software\Classes`
`HKEY_CURRENT_CONFIG`	`HKEY_LOCAL_MACHINE\SYSTEM\CurrentControlSet\Hardware Profiles\`*`Profile Number`*
`HKEY_CURRENT_USER`	`HKEY_USERS\`*`User SID`* (Security ID number)

With the connection in place, changes are made to the remote computer in exactly the same way as changes are made to your own systems.

Editing a Non-Domain NT Computer's Registry Remotely

Unless a user is a member of the Administrator's local group or the Domain Admin global group, he cannot edit a remote Registry. If you are a member of the Administrator's local group of a domain, you can edit any member of the domain, any member of a trusting domain, and any workgroup-connected NT computer on the network. The rights assigned to the Administrator's local group pass to the other machines.

If you are logged on as Administrator on a non-domain–connected computer, you can browse for, specify, and connect to any computer's Registry on the physical network, including those systems that are members of a domain.

Warning

Security Breach! If anyone can log on to his local machine and edit any other Registry on the network, you have a major hole in your security. To partially plug that hole, use the Hide your server from the browser Registry change discussed in Chapter 18, "Windows NT Networking and the Registry." You would need to know the exact name of the server to edit its Registry. That name may be very easily obtained, however, by looking at any shortcut or printer share that uses the server.

To increase security, *never* give users the administrator password to the local machine.

In addition, Microsoft will patch this hole, at least partially, with the introduction of DFS (Distributed File Services) late in 1997. No longer will the actual server name be shown in the shortcuts and shares. By removing that information, it will be much more difficult to obtain the server name, and therefore, security will be increased.

Editing NT User Settings with `NTUSER.DAT` and `REGEDT32.EXE`

To remotely edit another NT user's Registry, that user must be logged on to the network, and you must know which machine that user is currently using. Then, you can edit the user information that is loaded there. Or, rather than editing the information that way, you can simply load the information directly from the user's `NTUSER.DAT` file in his profile directory, shown in Figure 11.3, which is where the system gets all the user information for a domain-connected user. The system shows this information in the `HKEY_CURRENT_USER` handle key. The information is also listed by the SID in the `HKEY_USERS` on the system where the user is logged on.

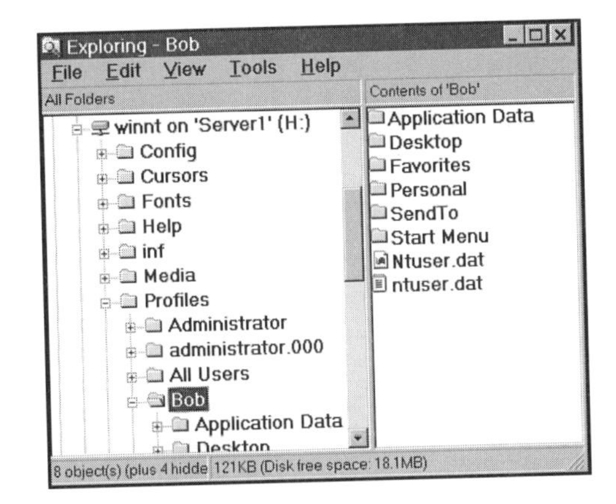

Figure 11.3.
Each user has a profile directory where his personal data is held.

To open Bob's `NTUSER.DAT` file, perform the following steps:

1. Open `REGEDT32.EXE`.
2. Highlight the handle key `HKEY_USERS`.
3. Select Registry | Load Hive.
4. Go to `\WINNT\Profiles\Bob` on a domain controller's hard drive.
5. Select `NTUSER.DAT`. (See Figure 11.4.)

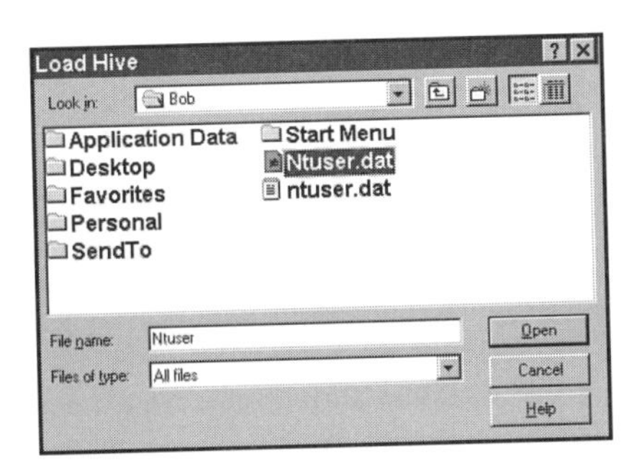

Figure 11.4.
Loading `NTUSER.DAT` for Bob.

When prompted for the key name, as shown in Figure 11.5, put in the user's name. (Actually, any name can be used. The user's name is simply a placeholder.) Then edit the user's information. (See Figure 11.6.)

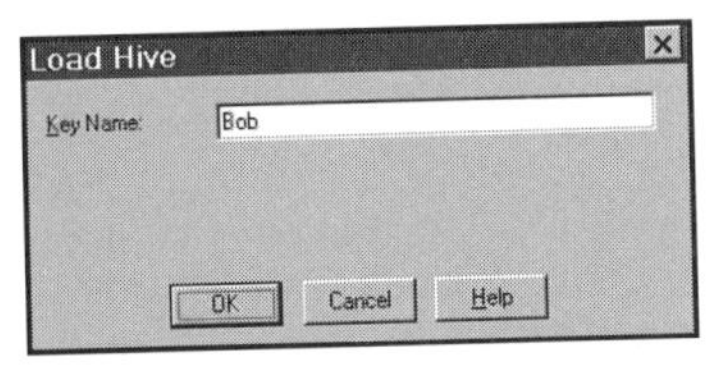

Figure 11.5.
Assigning a name for the `NTUSER.DAT` information.

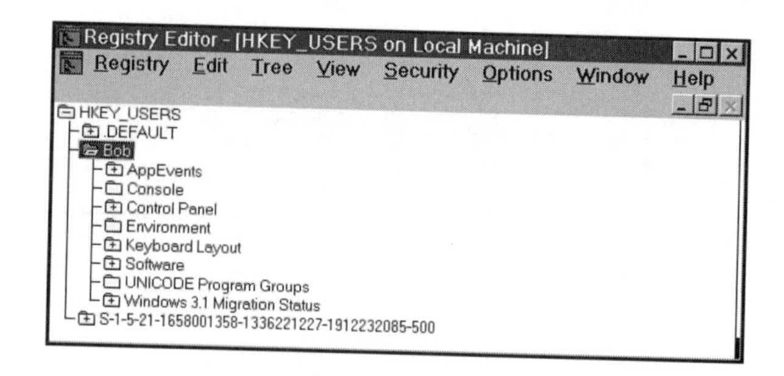

Figure 11.6.
HKEY_USERS with Bob's user information.

Make any necessary changes to the user's Registry settings, and then unload the hive using Registry | Unload Hive. A warning dialog gives you one last chance to make sure all your changes are correct. (See Figure 11.7.) All data is saved for that user. The next time the user logs on, those settings take effect.

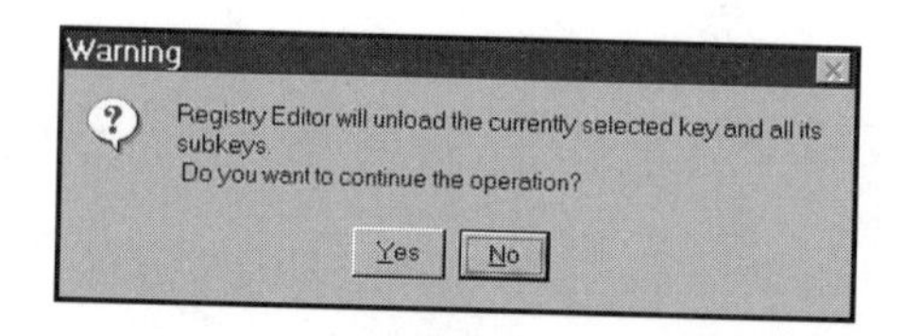

Figure 11.7.
Unloading the edited hive.

Using the Load Hive function makes it extremely easy to remotely edit any user's information, whether he is logged on to the domain or not. It is also very useful for editing the user information for a user who is not a member of the domain.

Remote Windows 95 Registry Editing

For a Windows 95 system's Registry to be edited remotely, it must have remote administration enabled, and it must be running the remote Registry service. Windows NT automatically runs a remote Registry service, so you are required to make no changes at the NT system.

Setting Up the Windows 95 System

Remote registry service is not automatically installed with Windows 95. To install the service, which is only available on the CD-ROM, perform the following steps:

1. Go to Control Panel | Network and choose Add.
2. Select Service and click Add.
3. Instead of using any services listed, choose Have Disk and browse for the `\Admin\Nettools\Remotreg` directory.
4. Confirm the location and choose OK to select the remote registry service. (See Figure 11.8.)
5. Restart your system.

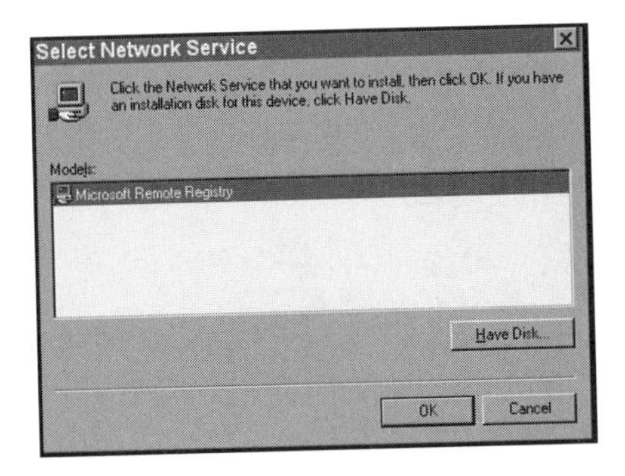

Figure 11.8.
Setting up the remote registry service.

After you install the remote registry service, the User-level access control radio button must be enabled. Open the Network section of Control Panel. On the Access Control tab (see Figure 11.9), select User-level access control, and supply the name of the domain where the administrators are located. (This is where you'll find the list of groups and users for the remote administration service.)

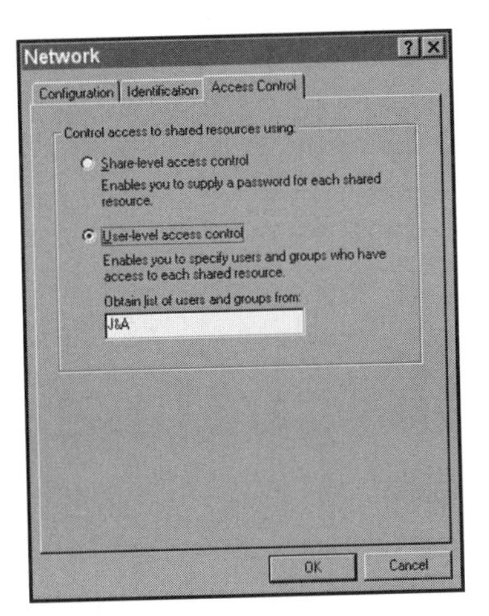

Figure 11.9.
Setting the User-level access control radio button.

Warning

A change in the access control source in Windows 95 forces all shares to be lost. All shares in that system must be recreated. Share-level security information is stored only at the local system, but user-level information is stored in the domain controller.

To start the remote administration service on the Windows 95 system, go to the Passwords section of the Control Panel. Select the Remote Administration tab (as shown in Figure 11.10) and click the Enable Remote Administration of this server radio button.

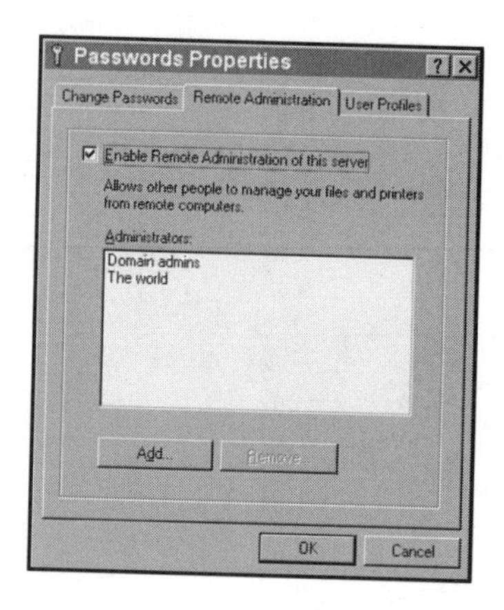

Figure 11.10.
Setting up remote administration on a Windows 95 system.

Note

Even though the dialog box says "server," any Windows 95 system can be edited this way. When remote functions are allowed, the system is working as a "server" to the other system.

Add the users and groups who will be allowed to edit the Registry. After confirmation, the system must be restarted; it then allows remote editing.

Remote Registry Editing with `REGEDT32.EXE` and Windows NT

The only way to open a Windows 95 system's Registry with an NT system is, surprisingly, to use `REGEDT32.EXE`. Use Registry | Select Computer to open the Registry. (See Figure 11.11.)

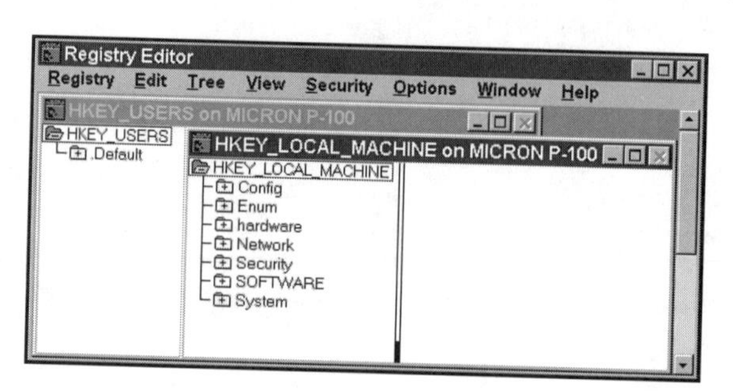

Figure 11.11.
Editing the Windows 95 Registry with `REGEDT32.EXE`.

The difference between the Windows 95 Registry and the Windows NT Registry is quickly evident with the rearrangement of the location of many of the keys in `HKEY_LOCAL MACHINE` and the missing SID-identified user in `HKEY_USERS`. All security-based items (the keys named SAM and Security) in `HKEY_LOCAL_MACHINE` are also missing in the Windows 95 Registry.

Note

When the Registries are set side by side, it's really no wonder that some applications written for Windows 95 are not compatible with Windows NT. Everything seems to be in a different place. In fact, it is actually quite amazing that any of it works. You will hail the day when the Registries have exactly the same structure, with the only differences being the extent of the features represented by the keys.

It is not possible to edit the individual user information for Windows 95 users from within Windows NT. The logged-on user is not shown, and the `USER.DAT` files created for each are not readable with NT. The only ways to edit and maintain them are with the System Policy Editor, or to edit the files in Windows 95.

Remote Registry Editing with `REGEDIT.EXE` and Windows NT

The process appears to be exactly the same for remote editing of a Windows 95 system in Windows NT and Windows 95. The main difference is that `REGEDIT.EXE` in Windows NT does not do remote Registry editing for either Windows NT systems or Windows 95 systems.

The menus indicate that it will, using the Registry | Connect Network Registry menu choice. It even prompts you to browse or type Computer name to select the system. (See Figure 11.12.) But it will not work.

However, you can edit the remote 95 Registry from another Windows 95 system.

Solutions

I'm confused. Which system and which editor can edit which type of system? Why can't I do all my work from one system?

Table 11.2 shows which editors on which platforms can edit remote systems.

Again, the differences and incompatibilities between the Windows 95 and Windows NT systems rear their ugly heads. Those incompatibilities make it impossible for all to work together correctly. Only when the Registries are merged will there be complete compatibility.

Table 11.2. Remote Registry editing tool comparison.

Platform/Program	*95 Remote?*	*NT Remote?*
Windows NT/`REGEDT32.EXE`	System only	YES
Windows NT/`REGEDIT.EXE`	NO	NO
Windows 95/`REGEDIT.EXE`	YES	NO

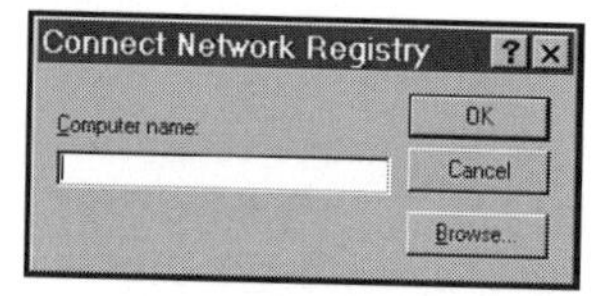

Figure 11.12.
Connecting to another system's Registry using REGEDIT.EXE.

When REGEDIT.EXE pulls in the Registry for a Windows NT computer, it indicates by an error message that it couldn't connect to all hives. (See Figure 11.13.) Even though it says to disconnect and try again, connecting to a remote system will always bring up the same results. REGEDIT.EXE cannot edit the remote NT Registry.

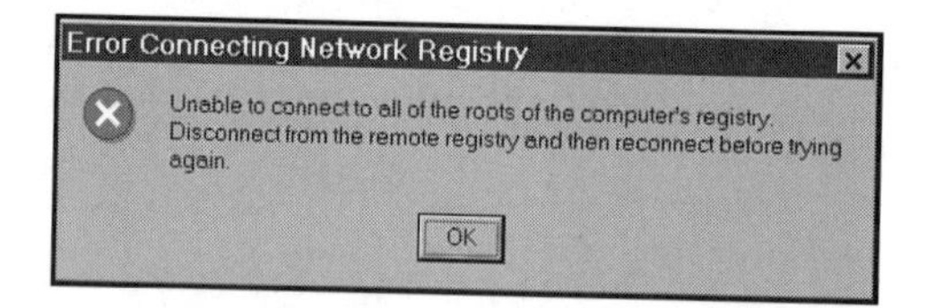

Figure 11.13.
The Windows NT hives are not available for editing remotely with REGEDIT.EXE.

When you try to edit a Windows 95 system from REGEDIT.EXE in NT, you get the error message shown in Figure 11.14.

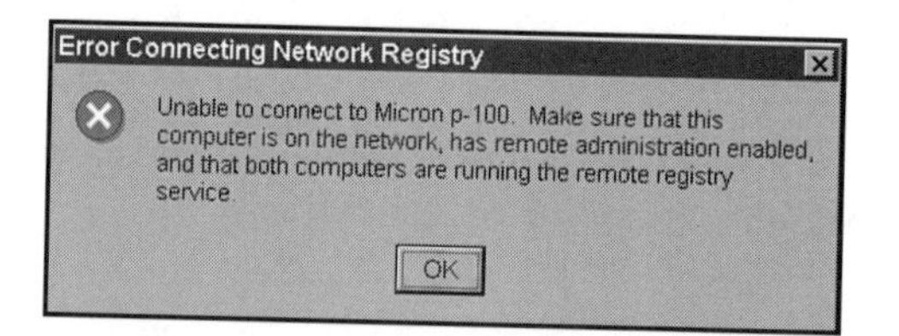

Figure 11.14.
Windows NT's REGEDIT.EXE does not allow editing of a Windows 95 Registry.

Warning

It doesn't help to try to run the REGEDIT.EXE file in your Windows 95 directory (if you have one) under NT. It still launches the one installed with NT.

To remotely edit Windows 95 systems, you must use REGEDT32.EXE from Windows NT, or use REGEDIT.EXE while running a Windows 95 system.

Remote Registry Editing with REGEDIT.EXE and Windows 95

The process for remote editing of a Windows 95 Registry is exactly the same as it is in Windows NT, with one big difference: It works! Inside Windows 95, if you are listed on the remote system as an authorized user, you can edit another 95 system's Registry quickly and easily.

To connect to the remote system, select the Registry | Connect Network Registry menu choice in `REGEDIT.EXE`. You can browse for the name of the computer, or type it in directly. Once it is connected, the remote system will show all of its handle keys, as shown in Figure 11.15.

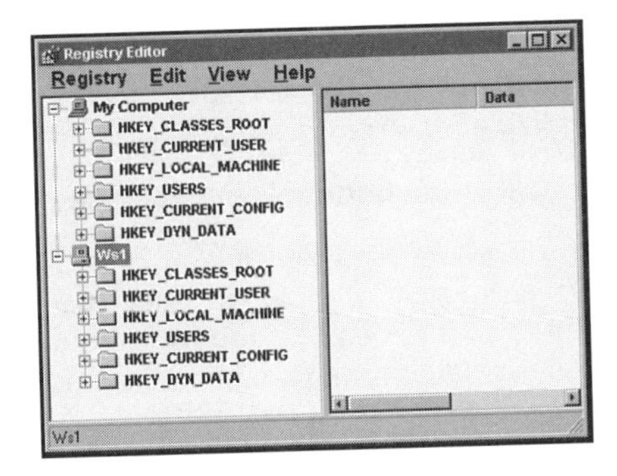

Figure 11.15. Remote editing of another Windows 95 system.

When you are finished with the editing of the remote system, highlight the name of the remote system, and select Registry | Disconnect Network Registry. Select the system whose Registry you would like to disconnect, and then click OK, as shown in Figure 11.16. The display in `REGEDIT.EXE` will return to normal, with only the local system's Registry displayed.

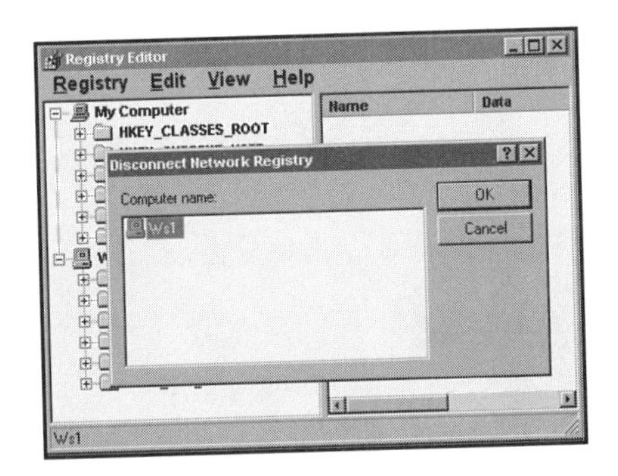

Figure 11.16. Disconnecting from another Windows 95 system's Registry.

Summary

Someday, perhaps in the near future, you can have one editor with all the features of `REGEDT32.EXE` and `REGEDIT.EXE`. That one editor will be able to edit all the Registries (because they will be the same), and will be available to both local and remote systems.

Until then, anything that can be edited locally can be edited remotely, provided the correct editor is used. `REGEDT32.EXE` can remotely edit the system and user Registry information for NT systems and the system Registry information for Windows 95 systems. `REGEDIT.EXE` for Windows NT has no remote editing capabilities as of this writing. For full editing of system and user functions for Windows 95 systems, use `REGEDIT.EXE` on a Windows 95 system.

Common functions that are easily understood by even novice users can be directed from afar. You can simply explain the changes to the user and direct him to make those changes. However, if either you or the user is uncomfortable with the user making modifications in the Control Panel, or if he is restricted from the Control Panel, you can easily make the changes remotely.

If the remote system starts but logon functions are unavailable, the individual can't make the changes, but the Registry is still available for a remote connection.

If the desired changes are not available in the Control Panel, the only option is to edit the Registry remotely or in person.

Once again, be careful about making remote changes to the Registry. Mistakes may not show up immediately, so all remote changes should be preceded by thorough testing on local systems. Also, allowing systems to be updated remotely, particularly Windows 95 systems, opens them up to significant security risks. Proceed with caution and care.

Part IV

Part IV
Part IV
Part IV
Part IV
Part IV
Part IV
Part IV
Part IV
Part IV
Part IV
Part IV

Hardware Control and the Registry

CHAPTER 12

How the Registry Controls Hardware

In Windows NT and Windows 95, 32-bit functions never access hardware directly. In every case, there is a driver or API (application programming interface) that actually communicates with the hardware. Microsoft provides the APIs, or hooks, to make the process easier for the software vendor, and distributes the technical information through the Software Developer's Kit (SDK). With that information, the programmer need only connect to the hook, and Microsoft will do the rest. NT or 95 will then make the procedure call, utilize the system resources, and communicate with the hardware device.

In DOS and 16-bit operating systems, programmers could bypass the operating system and write information directly to the hardware. The hardware would have to be very specific, and different routines would have to be written for each type of hardware.

Windows 95 allows both types of hardware access and control. Programmers can choose which type of function they will use. Windows NT does not allow any direct hardware access because any access may open the door for security challenges and instability. In Windows NT, every 16-bit function is translated (or "thunked") into a 32-bit request, and then used by NT. NT then sends 32-bit code to control access to the device.

The downside of the NT approach is the problem that Windows NT has with some Windows 95 and DOS applications. Certain applications, like fax and backup applications, try to work directly with the hardware in the system. There are a great number of 95 applications that use fax cards and tape drives, and a very small number for Windows NT. Those written for 95 will not work at all in NT.

The Role of the Registry

In order for all the communication to happen between the hardware and the OS, the Registry needs to provide the information to the operating system. The Registry holds, at a minimum, basic settings that allow communication. Some of those settings are described in Table 12.1.

Table 12.1. Hardware settings controlled by the Registry.

Setting	*Description*
IRQ (interrupt request)	Alerts the CPU to request CPU intervention
I/O port address	Indicates which device is sending information (stored in RAM in first 4KB)
RAM address	Where the device's BIOS information is to be stored in system RAM
DMA channel	Used to transfer information directly to RAM

In most cases, the hardware settings are the same on the physical device as they are in the Registry. With Windows 95, if there is a difference, or if there is a conflict between what is set and what the system needs to use to ensure coexistence, Windows 95 will change the Registry setting through Plug and Play. Figure 12.1 illustrates the startup and setting resolution process in Windows 95.

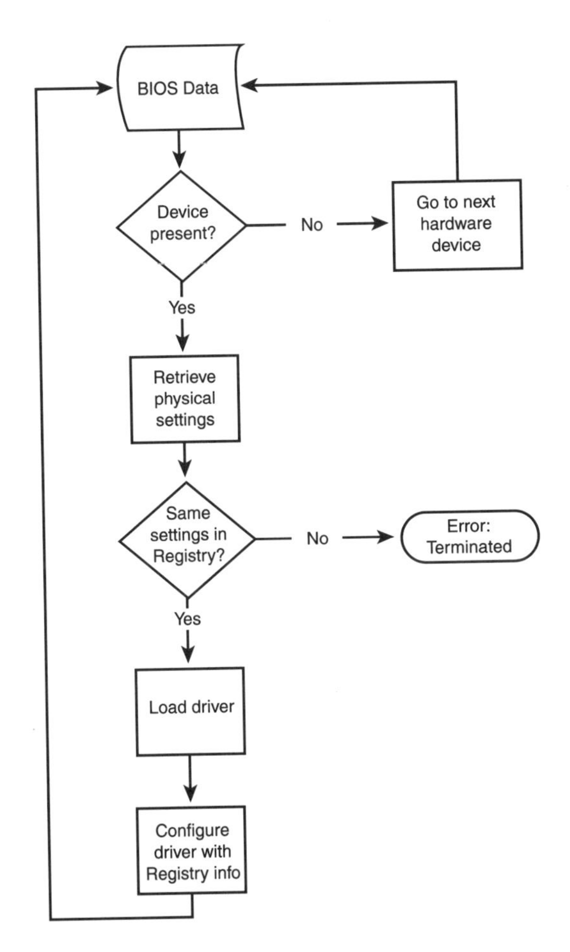

Figure 12.1. Windows 95 hardware settings resolution process.

Windows NT does not have the same level of Plug and Play that is available in Windows 95. With the exception of PCI devices, all hardware settings on devices must match the settings in the Registry. If the settings are not the same, the device driver will not load, and the device will not work. Figure 12.2 shows the startup process for hardware and its settings resolution in Windows NT.

The Registry plays a key role in making all the devices work. If the Registry is corrupted, and the settings are not available, the device will not work.

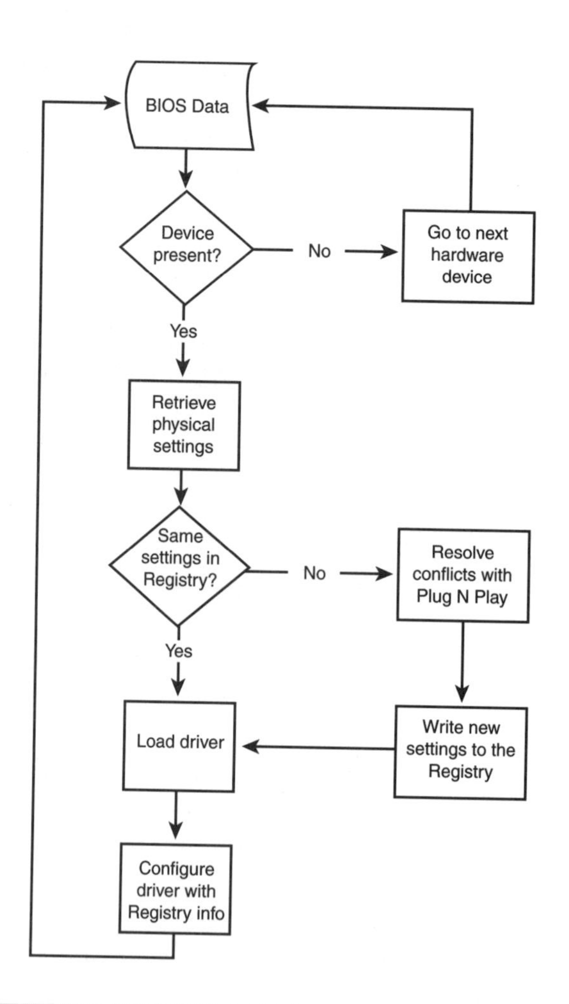

Figure 12.2.
Windows NT hardware settings resolution process.

Solutions

Why doesn't Windows NT support Plug and Play?

Windows NT does support Plug and Play, but it is very limited. All devices that use the PCI bus are automatically configured at startup. Characteristically, they use an IRQ in a completely separate range (32-36), and the IRQ, I/O port address, and other settings are set automatically. Once the device is configured, it will normally not change those settings, unless there is a specific change to devices on the PCI bus. Even then, new devices introduced to the bus will normally choose a different setting than that of the cards already present.

continues

If there is a change to the setting on the card, Windows NT may not recognize the card, and any devices attached to it will not work. The only time NT will adjust the settings in the Registry is when there is a difference in the number or type of cards on the PCI bus.

Although dynamic addressing of devices would be handy, and might reduce setup and configuration challenges, Microsoft engineers sacrificed it for stability. In order to allow dynamic addressing, the driver software would have to have direct access to the hardware. Then, if the driver had a significant problem, it could crash the hardware and bring down the entire system. To protect the stability of the system, Microsoft chose to limit the degree of Plug and Play support.

Hardware Registry Settings in Windows NT

All the settings and controls for hardware for Windows NT are in HKEY_LOCAL_MACHINE. There are several subkeys that hold the information required by Windows NT for operations.

Note

Windows NT reads BIOS information and other information from devices in the system only one time. After startup, all device control is done through the drivers and the Registry. NT never makes a BIOS call again.

Figure 12.3 shows a cascading view of HKEY_LOCAL_MACHINE with DESCRIPTION, DEVICEMAP, and RESOURCEMAP open. These three subkeys hold the settings and control information for the hardware. DESCRIPTION supplies data to NT about the system board, the processors, and the bus. DEVICEMAP either directly holds data and settings about the devices connected to the bus or supplies a description and location of a driver. RESOURCEMAP holds settings for many of the drivers for the devices.

Seldom would you ever make settings here. Instead, you would make all the settings in Control Panel, and then Control Panel would store them in these keys for use by Windows NT, and for viewing by Windows NT Diagnostics.

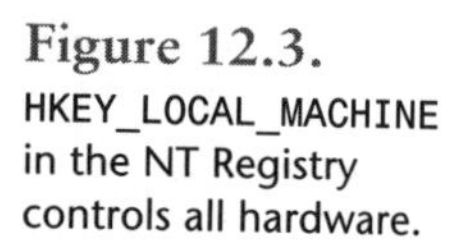

Figure 12.3.
HKEY_LOCAL_MACHINE in the NT Registry controls all hardware.

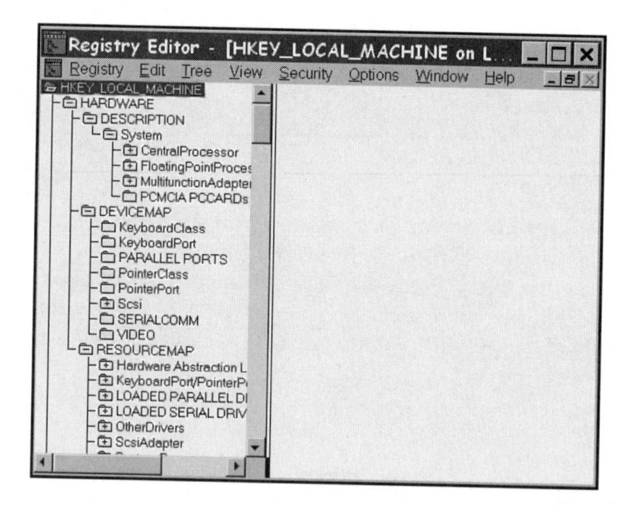

Hardware Registry Settings in Windows 95

All the settings and controls for hardware in Windows 95 are in `HKEY_LOCAL_MACHINE`. The `Enum` key holds information on every BIOS-supported device that is used in the system, as shown in Figure 12.4.

Figure 12.4.
The HKEY_LOCAL_MACHINE\Enum key in Windows 95.

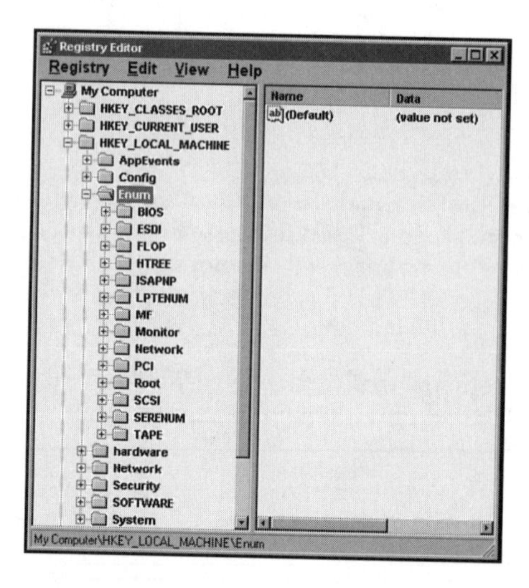

Non-BIOS-supported devices have their own key under `HKEY_LOCAL_MACHINE` that allows for setup and support. There are three types of settings in the Registry for devices:

- Standard configuration through Plug and Play

- Forced configuration through Device Manager
- Configuration at boot from `CONFIG.SYS`

When Plug and Play sets the configuration, it is stored in `HKEY_DYN_DATA` and then copied to `HKEY_LOCAL_MACHINE` as a backup. In `HKEY_LOCAL_MACHINE`, the configuration information is held in `HKEY_LOCAL_MACHINE\Enum\Root` for most devices. Figure 12.5 shows the binary `Settings` value, indicating that it has been set through Plug and Play.

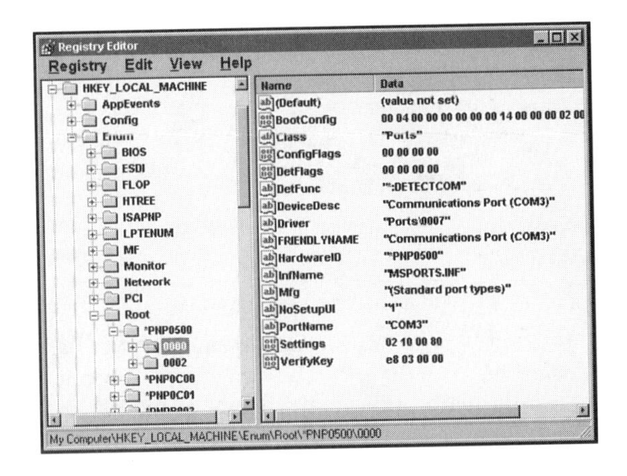

Figure 12.5. Binary `Settings` information for COM3.

The SCSI adapter in my system has a forced configuration, ensuring that the configuration used in Device Manager is the same as the hardware configuration. Figure 12.6 shows a `ForcedConfig` setting that cannot be changed at startup.

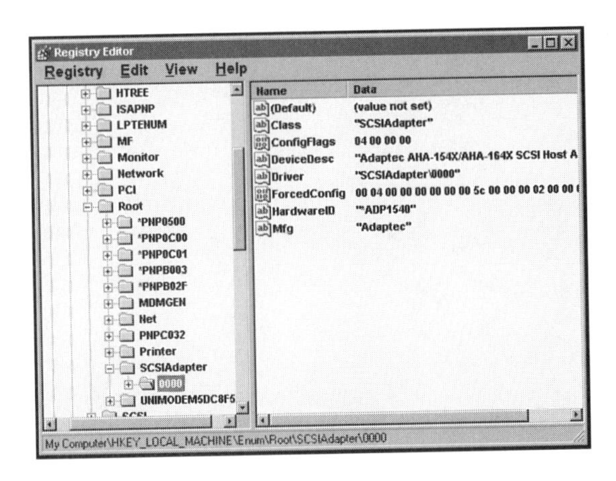

Figure 12.6. Binary `ForcedConfig` information for the Adaptec 1542C SCSI Host Adapter.

My sound card uses a driver in `CONFIG.SYS` for its initial support. The entry in the Registry, `BootConfig`, ensures that the system will point to the 16-bit driver for its configuration settings, as shown in Figure 12.7. It actually loads a 32-bit driver after Windows 95 starts, and uses it for all the rest of the sound during the session.

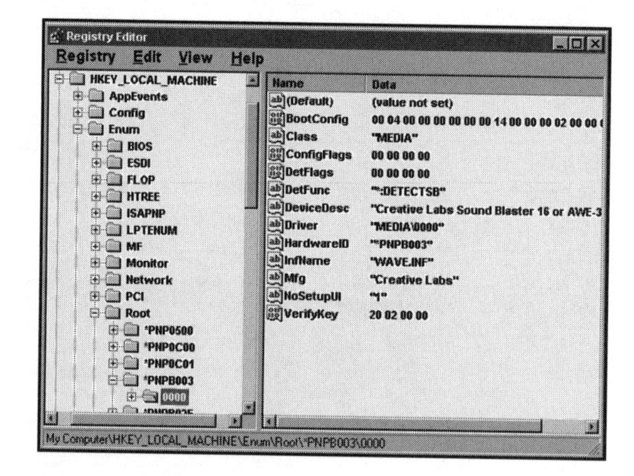

Figure 12.7.
Binary `BootConfig` information for the SoundBlaster Sound Card.

Summary

With all the settings and configuration information in the Registry, hardware in Windows 95 and NT can be controlled easily. The Registry also contains the location of each of the drivers used for control, and any information specific to the use of the hardware by the operating system.

CHAPTER 13

Windows NT and the HAL

Windows NT uses a Hardware Abstraction Layer (HAL) to allow NT to communicate correctly with the hardware on the system. The HAL is actually a `.DLL` (dynamically linked library) file that creates "hooks" so the operating system and the drivers do not have to know anything about the processor, the BIOS, or the system board. When NT wants to send something to the processor, it uses a driver, Registry information, and an API (application programming interface) built into NT, and loaded during installation.

By using the HAL, Windows NT is scalable, meaning that the same operating system can be used on different platforms. There are two HALs for each of the following platforms listed, one for single processor systems and one for multiple processor systems (up to four processors). If you will be using more than four processors, you can get an alternative HAL from the manufacturers for up to 32 processors.

Intel

COMPAQ

DEC Alpha

PowerPC (Motorola and/or IBM)

MIPS (to be discontinued after NT 4.0)

Not only can Windows NT install on any of those platforms, it can also be transported between them. Because the kernel of the operating system only talks to the HAL, you simply need to change the HAL. For example, if you had a current Windows NT Server running as a Domain Controller (holding all the security information) and it had several applications installed, you wouldn't want to start from scratch and start over again. If you started over, you would have to recreate all your usernames, security information, and applications. Instead of doing that, you could simply move all the files to the new machine by restoring a backup there, and then change the HAL.

Solutions

Why does COMPAQ have its own HAL? Why doesn't it just use the same Intel HAL that everybody else does?

The HAL is designed to allow processor and system board independence from Windows NT. NT only talks to a virtual processor, as an example. As long as the hardware presents itself to the HAL in the same way, then you could easily use the same HAL. COMPAQ chooses to use a BIOS that is not compatible with other Intel system boards, and its system board circuitry is also different. Rather than change its systems, COMPAQ simply created a new HAL.

A HAL is similar to a language translator. Imagine that you know how to speak only English. If someone who spoke only Spanish needed to talk to you, you would need a translator. He could translate your words into Spanish, and your

continues

friend's words into English. That is equivalent to the role of the HAL. If your friend spoke only Latin American Spanish, and your translator spoke European Spanish, most of the words would work just fine, but there might be some words that would not be understood. That is why COMPAQ chose to create its own HAL. Most things are the same, but there is enough difference that a new HAL was the best answer.

If your friend spoke only Russian, you would need a completely different translator. That is the reason for so many types of HALs.

The other benefit directly related to the HAL is stability. If the hardware and applications have to go through the HAL, there is an extra layer of protection. It is not that NT cannot crash—it is just extremely rare.

A byproduct of the use of the HAL is the inability of NT to use some Windows 95 drivers, and all 16-bit real-mode drivers. Normally, in Windows 3.*x* or Windows 95, those real-mode drivers get loaded through `CONFIG.SYS`. Because the drivers are not written to use NT APIs, they will not work in NT at all. Only 32-bit drivers that are written to conform to NT specifications will work. Some drivers that are written for Windows 95 will work, and others won't.

Changing the HAL

If you will be moving NT from one type of system to another, and you need to change the HAL, you can do that quite simply with the installation diskettes and CD-ROM. Start the system with the diskettes. When the system finds a copy of Windows NT on the hard disk drive, it will ask you whether you would like to install a new instance of NT, upgrade the current one, or repair the system. Tell NT you want to repair the system. When it examines the HAL, and compares it to the one it loaded during startup, it will ask you if you would like to change the HAL. Confirm the change, and your HAL will be changed, and the rest of the NT files for the new system will be copied, if necessary.

The HAL and the Registry

Information about the HAL is stored in the Registry in `HKEY_LOCAL_MACHINE\RESOURCEMAP\Hardware Abstraction Layer`. Below that key is a key that shows the actual HAL that is installed. Figure 13.1 shows the location of the HAL in the Registry.

The Registry supplies the information necessary for uninterrupted usage, and can be changed when necessary.

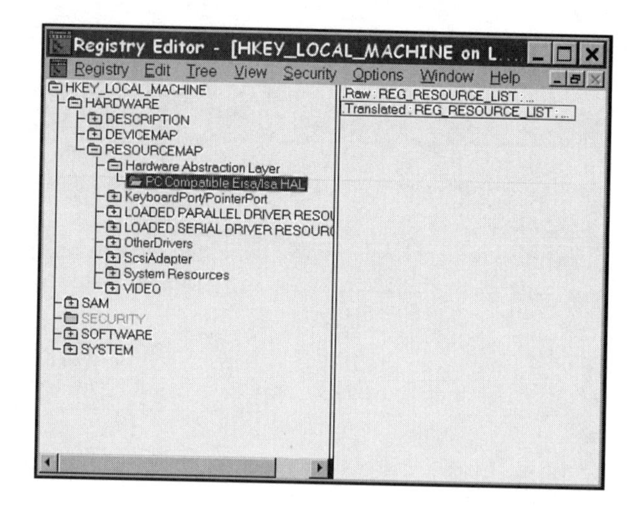

Figure 13.1.
HAL information and settings are stored in the Registry.

Summary

Though not like HAL from *2001: A Space Odyssey*, the HAL in NT can also make your work easier. Using a HAL means that NT will be able to work across multiple platforms, protect the hardware from accidental or malicious interference from rogue applications or drivers, and be able to use standardized driver models. The challenge comes with DOS and 16-bit applications that normally communicate directly with the hardware. In many cases, they do not work at all, and, in other cases, the performance and stability are compromised.

CHAPTER 14

Windows 95 and Plug and Play

Windows 95 also uses a HAL (Hardware Abstraction Layer), but it is quite different from the one in Windows NT. Instead of being the absolute solution to hardware access as in NT, in Windows 95, the HAL is a recommended solution. Every time Windows 95 loads, a new HAL is created, based on the actual hardware present. The hooks for applications and drivers are still there, but they are an optional item. If software vendors want to write information directly to the hardware device, they can do so. That helps software to have more of an operating system-independent nature, although all drivers for supported hardware would have to be included in the application.

Games are a common example of writing directly to the hardware. The number of supported devices is very small, and, in many cases, there is a performance benefit derived from direct access. Fax modems and tape drives are also examples of using built-in drivers and bypassing the HAL. Most applications prefer to use the HAL and drivers that support it. One exception, in the past, was WordPerfect software. You had the choice of using Windows drivers for printing, or using WordPerfect printer drivers. Those included with WordPerfect were extremely fast, and had many benefits over Windows printer drivers, but the maintenance of them was too time-consuming and difficult.

Another huge difference in the HAL between Windows 95 and Windows NT is its construction. The Windows 95 HAL is assembled at startup with Plug and Play. For optimum performance and reliability, there are several items necessary. If any of the following items is missing, there are limitations on how well Plug and Play can work:

- Plug and Play BIOS on the system board
- Plug and Play BIOS on the interface cards
- Plug and Play functions in Windows 95

The goal of all three is to create easier-to-use configuration procedures and to eliminate conflicts in the settings of devices. The conflict resolution is done by changing one or more settings on devices or in the Windows 95 Registry.

Plug and Play BIOS on the System Board

Normally, the BIOS on a system board is configurable only through an on-board setup program. By standardizing the procedure for setting the BIOS data and allowing an outside program to make the settings, Phoenix Technologies made Plug and Play a reality for the system BIOS. Now, Windows 95 can change the BIOS settings for any BIOS-supported device as necessary to remove conflicts.

Windows 95 will continue to make BIOS calls for some devices, even though most BIOS-supported devices are driven directly through 32-bit drivers. By actually changing the settings in the BIOS, the system does not need to go through a conflict resolution every time 95 loads.

If there is no Plug and Play BIOS on the system board, Windows 95 will translate the settings that are present and use its own settings. Then, every time that device is activated, there will be a translation. That slows access to the devices and hurts overall performance.

Plug and Play BIOS on Interface Cards

A Plug and Play BIOS on an interface card allows the card settings to be made with software. That software may be supplied with the card, or the card may be configurable with Windows 95 Plug and Play functions. By allowing the card to be set with software after the physical installation, it can streamline troubleshooting and maintenance. If the card was incorrectly configured with hardware settings, it would be necessary to open the case, remove the cards, and change the settings. If the card is configured with software, the settings are changed, and the system will normally need to be restarted to activate the new settings.

Plug and Play Functions in Windows 95

The Plug and Play function inside Windows 95 reports its findings to the Registry, and the data is held in `HKEY_DYN_DATA`. It is the only handle key that is not stored on the hard disk. All of its functions start with Windows 95, and are discarded at shutdown. In between, part of the data is written into `HKEY_LOCAL_MACHINE\Config`. Whenever the system needs information about the settings of a device, it will look to `HKEY_DYN_DATA` for it. Each of the subkeys under Config Manager, shown in Figure 14.1, holds information about a specific device, including the settings and configuration.

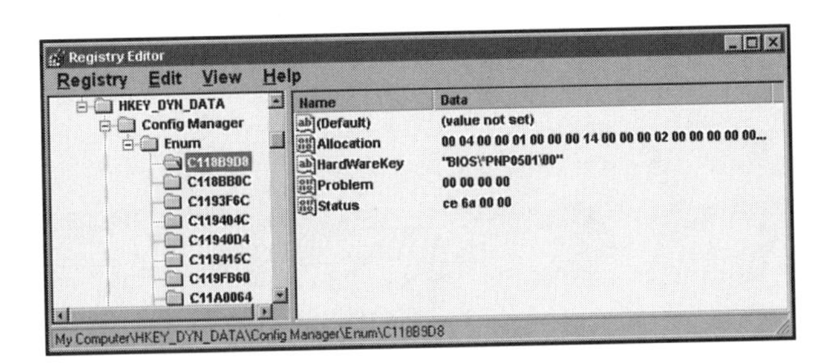

Figure 14.1.
Device configuration and control in HKEY_DYN_DATA.

The highlighted key is the one that controls the COM1 serial port, as shown in the `HKEY_LOCAL_MACHINE\Enum\BIOS\PNP0501\00` key. The key from `HKEY_LOCAL_MACHINE` tells the system where to find the actual configuration data in `HKEY_DYN_DATA`. If the system loses information about any of the hardware, and things don't seem to be working correctly, the first thing to do is to restart Windows 95. At restart, Windows 95 will examine the device and set the device settings dynamically.

Putting It All Together

If your system has all three Plug and Play components, it is extremely easy to set up and configure. Figure 14.2 illustrates a system where IRQ settings need to be matched for the device to work.

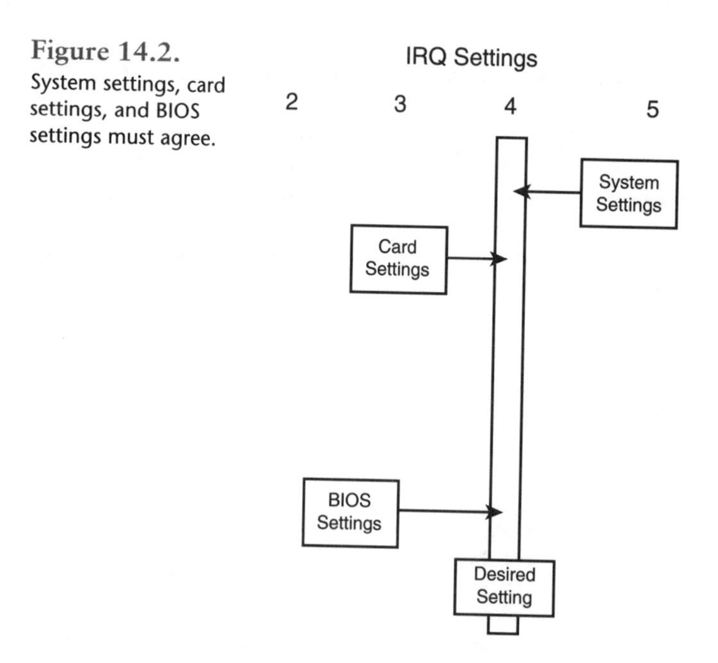

Figure 14.2.
System settings, card settings, and BIOS settings must agree.

If all the devices are Plug and Play, during setup, the settings would be changed by Windows 95, and they would all be set correctly. Figure 14.3 shows the result of changed settings, where the settings have all changed to match.

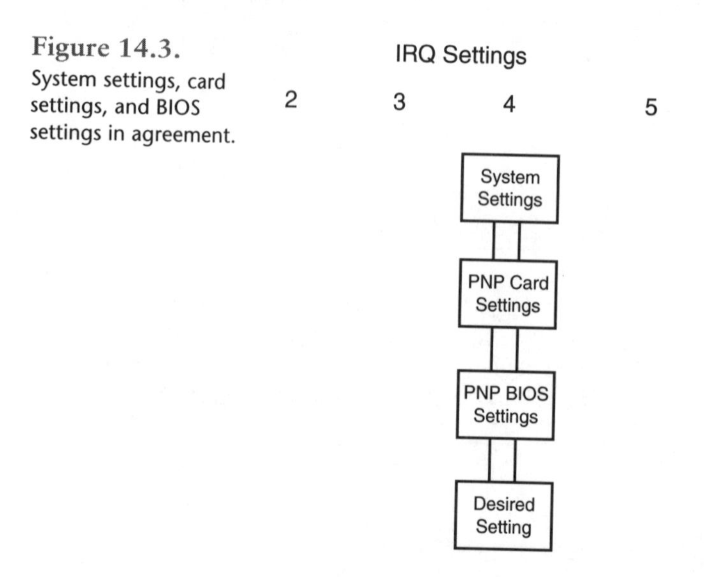

Figure 14.3.
System settings, card settings, and BIOS settings in agreement.

If one or more of the devices is not compliant with Plug and Play, Windows 95 will set what it can, and then translate to that which it cannot change. Figure 14.4 shows the translation for the card settings, because the card was not Plug and Play.

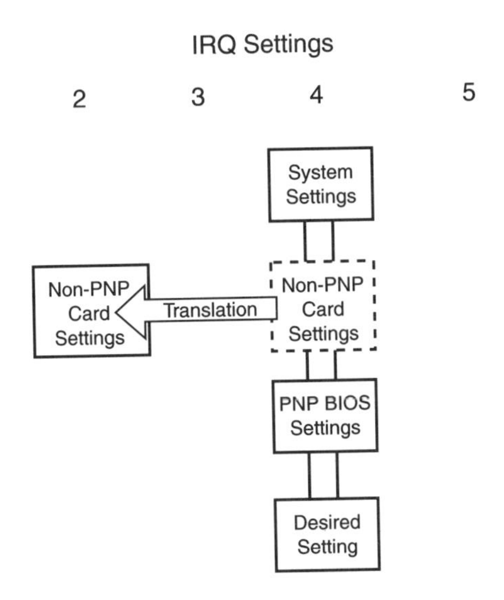

Figure 14.4.
Card settings cannot be changed, so the data is translated.

Obviously, the system will be slowed because of the translation. The card will still work at IRQ 4, but it will not work as fast. There are also some cards that will not work at all this way. The best configuration is to have all Plug and Play devices, if possible.

Making the Settings in Windows 95

Start Windows 95 and go to the System applet in the Control Panel. At the Device Manager tab, select each item to look for any item where there is a red X, which indicates that the device has been found, but it is not working at all. If you see a yellow circle with an exclamation point, as shown in Figure 14.5, it means that the device has not been configured correctly.

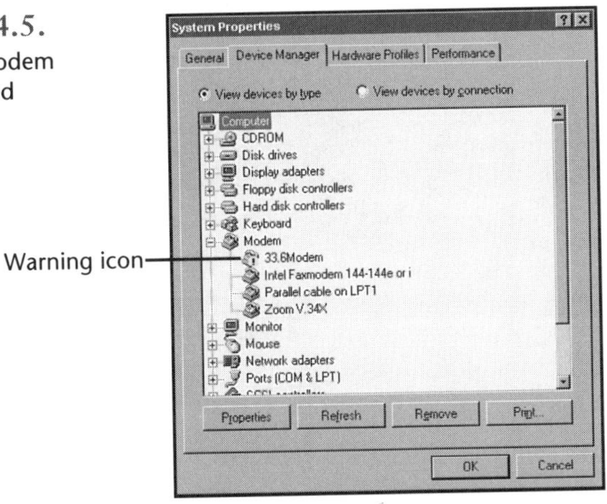

Figure 14.5.
The 33.6Modem is configured incorrectly.

Double-click on the device, and the system may tell you the problem, and how to correct it. Figure 14.6 gives you the instructions to solve the problem.

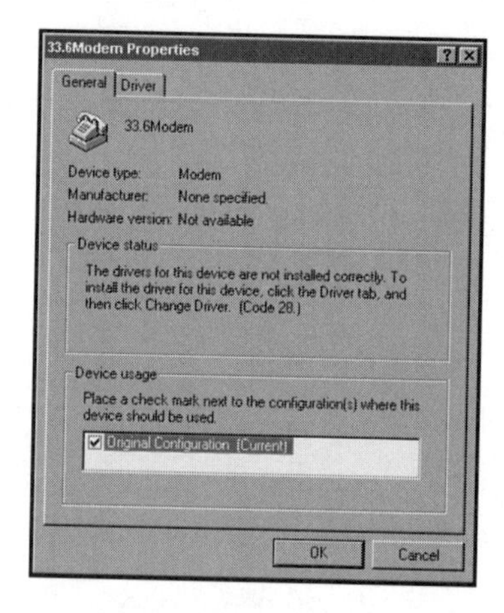

Figure 14.6.
33.6Modem Properties screen gives instructions for eliminating conflict.

If the instructions are not sufficient to allow you to troubleshoot and configure the device correctly, you will need to try to isolate the problem manually. First, you should ensure that the physical installation of the device was done correctly. Next, you should check the settings on the device and see if they are set to available settings in the system. Finally, you need to confirm that the driver that was installed is the proper one and is set up correctly.

Once the configuration is established, the data is written into `HKEY_LOCAL_MACHINE` and then used at subsequent startups. The system will find out what the device is set to, read the Registry to see if it is supposed to be set to another setting, and then the final setting is written into `HKEY_DYN_DATA`. Every time the device is used, the information comes out of `HKEY_DYN_DATA`.

Summary

The dynamic nature of Plug and Play allows easy configuration of most devices in Windows 95. Nearly all new devices can be configured dynamically, and they work extremely well. Most devices, even those that do not support Plug and Play, can still be dynamically configured, but the performance suffers. In some situations, translation will not work, and the setting will have to be made manually.

All of the settings are stored in the Registry for Windows 95 to use to start and operate the devices.

CHAPTER 15

Troubleshooting and Configuring Hardware Registry Settings

Because the Registry is such an integral part of how hardware works in Windows NT and 95, there may be times when you need to change it to make different functions work. This chapter shows several of those options. Microsoft has to put out their operating system according to their best guess of how everyone would like it. If you try to do something they didn't anticipate, you can get errors. Those errors may require a change to the Registry.

Troubleshooting Hardware Settings

The key to all troubleshooting is isolation. You need to isolate the problem to be able to fix it.

Most of the time, when you get a hardware problem in NT or 95, you get an error message. Some of the error messages are easier to decipher than others, and sometimes they give you no clue at all. Normally, though, at least the error message tells you what didn't work.

In Windows 95, the first thing to do is to restart the system. In many cases, restarting the system will reconfigure the Registry for you, and the problem may go away. Restarting is particularly helpful if you leave your system running all the time. It seems as if some of the challenges are cumulative, and the longer you leave your system running, the worse it gets. Restarting your system is a little like slapping it around to wake it up and take notice of what it is supposed to do.

After restarting, check the Device Manager in Control Panel | System. All of the hardware devices are there, and the configurations are accessible. If the configuration seems OK, check to see if the hardware is working correctly with its diagnostic program, or use a third-party diagnostic program to test it.

Some Hardware Problems Associated with the Registry

This section examines some problems that are associated with the Registry and its data. Each problem is in the form of a question, with its answer specified. In many cases, the answer can also be applied to other similar circumstances. Each question also indicates whether the problem is from Windows 95, NT, or both.

Solutions

When I start Windows 95, I get a strange error message that looks for a device file. It doesn't list a file, so I can't tell which file to replace. What do I do?

If you have ever seen this error message, you've probably been bewildered:

```
Cannot find a device file that may be needed to run Windows or a Windows
application.
The Windows registry or SYSTEM.INI file refers to this device file, but
the device file no longer exists.
```

continues

```
If you deleted this file on purpose, try uninstalling the associated
application using its uninstall program or setup program.
If you still want to use the application associated with this device
file, try reinstalling that application to replace the missing file.
```

It would be easier if the file were listed. Because there is not one listed, it means that one of the `StaticVxD` (virtual device driver) values in the Registry is blank, contains only spaces, or contains corrupted information. The `StaticVxD` values are in `HKEY_LOCAL_MACHINE\System\CurrentControlSet\Services\VxD` key, as shown in Figure 15.1.

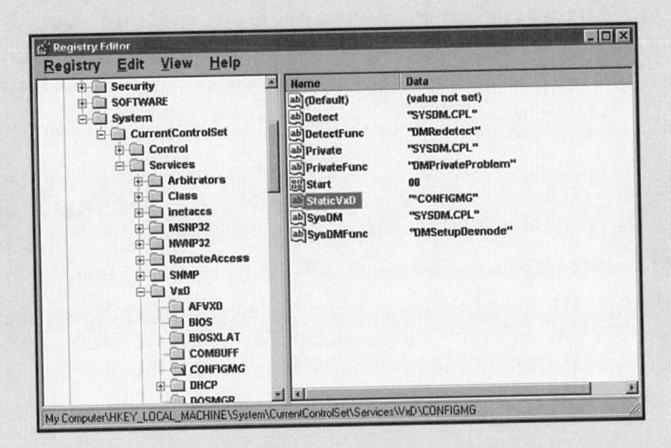

Figure 15.1. The `StaticVxD` values in the Registry of Windows 95.

The asterisk in front of the name means it is part of the `VMM32.VXD` file. Without one, it would be a regular file copied to the hard disk. If the problem entry is part of `VMM32.VXD`, you will need to replace the whole file.

Remember that information in the Registry can be corrupted, and the best way to protect yourself is to have a backup of the Registry, as outlined in Chapter 4, "Protecting the NT Registry," and Chapter 6, "Protecting the Windows 95 Registry."

Solutions

How do I fix a Registry access failed message?

When Windows 95 is detecting hardware in Control Panel/Add New Hardware, I get the following error message:

```
SDMErr(80000003): Registry access failed.
```

To fix that Registry problem, you will need to use `REGEDIT.EXE` in real mode. Don't worry; it's not as bad as it seems. Restart your computer, and while it is booting, at the Starting Windows 95 message, press F8, and choose Safe Mode Command Prompt Only from the menu.

continues

continued

At the DOS prompt, type REGEDIT /E REG.TXT and press Enter. Ignore any messages. At the next DOS prompt, type REGEDIT /C REG.TXT and press Enter. Restart your computer, and the Registry file data structures will have been regenerated, the Registry should work fine, and you will be able to detect new hardware.

REGEDIT.EXE in Windows 95 can also be run for other functions in real mode. For more options and instructions for its use in real mode, restart the system to Safe Mode Command Prompt Only and type REGEDIT /?. The help file will review all of the command-line options.

Solutions

I changed the role of my system in the File System section of the Performance section in the System applet in the Control panel, and my performance went down. What did I do wrong?

Assuming that you chose a value that reflected the actual nature of the work you do, it wasn't you. To choose a performance profile, select Control Panel | System | Performance | Advanced settings | Typical role of this machine, and you will see the dialog box pictured in Figure 15.2.

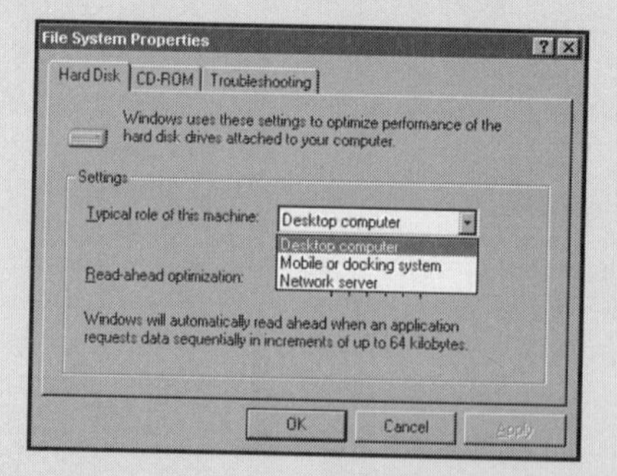

Figure 15.2. Changing the performance characteristics of your Windows 95 system.

If that doesn't change the performance of your system, there is probably a corrupted value in the Registry. The NameCache and PathCache values in the HKEY_LOCAL_MACHINE\Software\Microsoft\Windows\CurrentVersion\FS Templates key control how the performance functions work. The keys Desktop, Mobile, and Server hold the necessary information. Desktop shows no values for NameCache or PathCache because the default performance characteristics are set for a desktop system. For a Mobile or docking system profile, use the following data in the Mobile key.

continues

Value Name	Value Data
NameCache	51 01 00 00
PathCache	10 00 00 00

In the Server key, the data for the Network Server profile should be the following.

Value Name	Value Data
NameCache	a9 0a 00 00
PathCache	40 00 00 00

If any of the settings are not correct in your system, your performance will suffer greatly.

Setting the performance options will greatly affect your system performance, and then you can be sure that your settings are correct and you are actually getting the performance you requested. Another performance tip is to use a logon script to map all of your network drives and printers to drive letters and printer ports. Occasionally, there are problems with how the requests are handled.

Solutions

When my logon script in Windows 95 tries to set up my printers on the network with a `NET USE LPT2: \\Server1\Laser` command, I get an error that says the device does not exist on the network. I know it does, because it works from other machines. What can I do?

This error happens when you use a port that is not actually on your system. Of course, having additional printers other than what you have the capacity for is part of why we have networks. A simple change will make it so your system can use any virtual port for assignment to a network printer.

To fix the error condition, you could either change each printer in the Control Panel | Printers | File | Properties | Details | Port Settings and deselect the Spool MS-DOS Print Jobs option, or you could change the Registry one time for all printers on that system.

The Registry change is in `HKEY_LOCAL_MACHINE\System\CurrentControlSet\control\Print\Printers`. Add two `DWORD` values, and set them both to `0` to disable the spooling of MS-DOS print jobs.

- `DOSSpoolMask`
- `PrintersMask`

Even though you may use your printers only for Windows print jobs, this will make your system recognize them when they are set up in your logon script. If you connect to your printers through the Control Panel function for printers, you will not need to do this.

Most of the time, servers are not used to run applications. In some circumstances, however, it is necessary to use them as a workstation. It may be that you have a very small network and cannot dedicate a system exclusively to the network, or maybe you need to run applications at the server occasionally because of its location or connections. NT Server is tuned differently than Workstation to handle its role more effectively. That tuning may make the system behave a little differently than you might expect. The next Solution shows that.

Solutions

Why does it take so long to launch my 16-bit Windows applications on my server?

By default, the Windows-on-Windows (WOW) function does not start on a server until an application that is using it starts. Then, after it starts, it will stay in memory ready to be used until the system is restarted. On a Workstation, the WOW files are automatically launched at startup.

If you are going to be using 16-bit Windows applications at your server, and you want them to launch faster, change the Registry. The value to change is in `HKEY_LOCAL_MACHINE\SOFTWARE\Microsoft\Windows NT\CurrentVersion\WinLogon`. In the `Userinit` value, add the following text to the rest of the data.

```
,win.com wowexec
```

With the data in the value, it will look like Figure 15.3, and the server will start your 16-bit Windows applications faster.

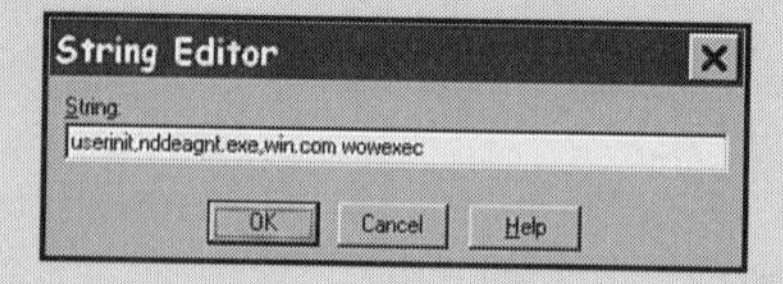

Figure 15.3. The server will automatically start the WOW executables.

Just because you are upgrading your operating system software, that doesn't mean you want to change all of the other application software or your hardware. Backward compatibility is a two-edged sword. You always limit performance when you ensure that older devices and software will work. On the other hand, if your current investment in hardware and software will not work on the new OS, it might not be a wise decision to upgrade. Here is another example of making backward compatibility work.

Solutions

I want to use my old modem with NT 4.0, but it says it is not supported. It worked in NT 3.51, so what do I need to do to make it work?

continues

NT 4.0 uses the UNIMODEM driver for all the modems it supports. Those are the same drivers that work for Windows 95. If you have a Windows 95 driver for your modem, you could just use that, or you can make a change to the Registry that will allow you to use the older modem.

In `HKEY_LOCAL_MACHINE\SOFTWARE\Microsoft\RAS\Protocols`, add a new `REG_DWORD` value called `EnableUnimodem`. Set it to 0 to turn off the UNIMODEM driver requirement, and restart your system. After restarting your system, install the driver for your modem.

Fonts in Windows 95 and in NT 4.0 are stored in the Fonts folder and registered for use in the Registry. If the Font ID gets corrupted in the Registry, you can restart your system, as illustrated in Chapter 3, "Potential Registry Problems." The next question is also related to fonts, but is associated with font entries in the Registry.

Solutions

On my Windows 95 system, and also on my NT 4.0 system, I try to add TrueType fonts, and I get an error message that says they are already installed, and that I need to remove the old ones first. I checked in the folder, and they are not there and do not show up when I try to use the fonts in my applications. What should I do?

You will need to fix the Registry. The `fonts` key is either missing or damaged.

Before working on the Registry, move all the font files to another location (an empty folder is the easiest). If the `fonts` key is in the Registry, remove it and then add it again. If it is not there, then add it.

Add the `fonts` key to `HKEY_LOCAL_MACHINE\SOFTWARE\Microsoft\Windows\CurrentVersion` in Windows 95. In Windows NT 4.0, add the `fonts` key to `HKEY_LOCAL_MACHINE\SOFTWARE\Microsoft\Windows NT\CurrentVersion`.

Install all of the fonts that you moved, and the system will rebuild all the values for you. Make sure you have the `Copy fonts to Fonts` folder selected. Then you can remove all the fonts in the temporary folder.

Summary

By fixing the Registry, changing entries, and adding keys and values as needed, you can change the way Windows NT and Windows 95 work. You will be able to improve performance, add options, correct errors, and eliminate pesky problems.

CHAPTER 16

Questions and Answers for Hardware and the Registry

Sometimes the information you need isn't really an error or a problem, but you want to be able to do something that isn't normally allowed, or maybe something that Microsoft didn't even dream of. Exceptional performance comes from being able to add 2 plus 2 and get 8, or even 10. The standard answer will always be four, but if you can take options in the Registry and make them give you extra, unplanned capabilities, you will always succeed in getting optimum usability from your systems. It is the "art" of computing, added on top of the science.

Solutions

I have a communications program that is supposed to be compatible with NT and 95, but it doesn't allow the use of COM3 or COM4. I don't have COM1 or COM2 available. Can I make the software use COM3 or COM4?

Windows NT does not allow the use of COM3 or COM4 for modems, so its software isn't written for it. If you change the Registry, it will work. The key to change is `HKEY_LOCAL_MACHINE\HARDWARE\DEVICEMAP\serialcomm`. Add a string value called `COM3` if you want to add COM3, or `COM4` if you need to use COM4. The text string is the same as the value name (`com3=com3`). Restart the system, and you will be able to use the software with COM3 or COM4.

Hardware settings are one of the most critical functions in working with the Registry. The Registry can also control the software that works with the hardware, as the next question illustrates.

Solutions

When ScanDisk runs through the System Agent inside Windows 95, it always pauses for me to select the drives. Isn't it supposed to run unattended?

Yes, all of the tools in System Agent are supposed to run unattended, if the Registry settings are correct. In the `HKEY_LOCAL_MACHINE\SOFTWARE\Microsoft\Plus!\System Agent\SAGE` key, there are subkeys for each of the four tools in the System Agent.

- `Compression Agent`
- `Disk Defragmenter`
- `Low disk space notification`
- `ScanDisk for Windows`

Each of the subkeys should have a value called `Settings` with a binary value of `01`. If the `Settings` value is set to `00`, or if it is not there, the program will ask the user for input.

Plug and Play is a fantastic feature, and it has saved literally thousands of hours of fiddling with settings on devices and trying to match them with the software configuration. One of the downsides, though, is that it never seems to know when to stop. The next question is a common one that makes administrators crazy.

Solutions

Even though I installed a printer driver for my LaserJet 4L, every time I restart my system, I get a message that Windows 95 has found new hardware and is installing the software for it. I already have it, so why does it keep doing it again?

The HP LaserJet 4L and other Plug and Play devices may have this problem if the Registry is damaged. `HKEY_LOCAL_MACHINE\Enum` holds the information about devices configured with Plug and Play. The common keys to look at are listed in Table 16.1.

If Windows 95 tries to keep installing the device, remove the key, and let Windows 95 reinstall it when you restart the system.

Table 16.1. Common Plug and Play keys.

Key	*Type of Device*
ISAPNP	ISA devices (sound cards, video cards, and so on)
LPTENUM	Parallel devices (printers, ZIP drives, and so on)
PCI	PCI devices (video cards, network cards, and so on)
SCSI	SCSI host adapters
SERENUM	Serial port devices (modems, ports)
TAPE	Tape drives

Yes, it is an old cliché to "just reinstall Windows." Actually, it's quite rare to need to do that, but it is not uncommon to need to reinstall parts and pieces. Reinstalling is one of the easy ways to get back to a known state. Be careful about reinstalling too much, though, because you may create a tremendous amount of extra work for yourself.

Solutions

I got an error that said I couldn't install any more fonts in my system. It says in the Windows 95 Resource Kit that there is no limit to the number of fonts I can have in Windows 95. What did I do wrong? Is it the same in NT?

continues

continued

You have that many fonts? There is actually a limit on the number of fonts, based on the maximum size of a key in the Registry. In both 95 and NT, a Registry key cannot be larger than 64KB, not including subkeys. Considering average filename length, you could get somewhere between 1,000 and 1,500 fonts in your system before it ran out of space in the Registry.

The entry in the Registry also contains the path if it is different than the Fonts folder. In Figure 16.1, the Animations font and the Arquitectura Regular font are in a different directory, as shown by the shortcut arrow.

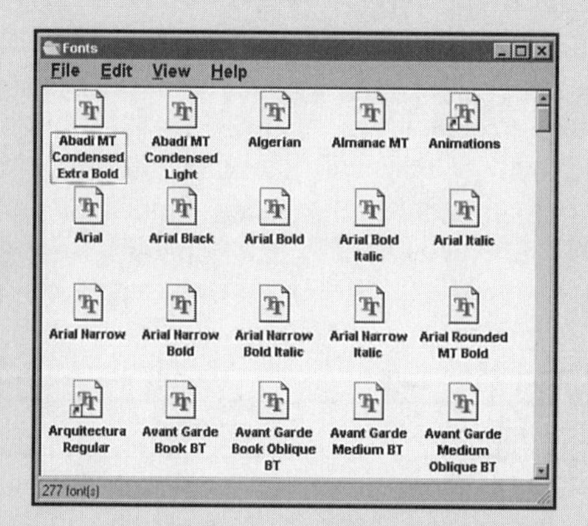

Figure 16.1. Fonts in the Fonts folder.

If you need more room, copy any of the fonts that are in another directory into the Fonts folder, and you will have even more room. Then you can add more fonts.

As soon as some people hear that there are no limits, they *have* to find out for sure. On the other hand, that "Oh, I bet I can find the limit!" mentality is what propels us forward in this technology age.

Sometimes people just want to be left alone, though, as the next question illustrates.

Solutions

How can I ensure that no one can come across the network and make changes to my Registry in Windows NT?

You cannot take away all rights to access your Registry without removing yourself from the network. If you want to limit access to only the members of the Administrators group, then you need to make your system look like a Server to Registry editors.

continues

By default, NT Server Registries can only be remotely edited by members of the Administrators group, but NT Workstation can be edited remotely by any user who is attached to the network, even if she has not logged onto the domain.

To restrict access, add a new key to `HKEY_LOCAL_MACHINE\SYSTEM\CurrentControlSet\Control\SecurePipeServers` on your Workstation. The new key is `WinReg`, a `REG_SZ` class entry. In the new key, add a value named `Description`, a `REG_SZ` entry. Edit the `Description` value, and type in `Registry Server`. When you restart the Workstation, everyone but members of the Administrators group will be restricted from accessing your Registry.

Restricting users from the Registry is particularly important. Imagine the potential damage if someone tried to edit your Registry and was unfamiliar with the correct procedures. That's another reason to have a good backup.

Solutions

I have a ZIP drive that I use with my notebook that is running NT 4.0. Whenever I do not have it connected, I get error messages, and errors show up in the event log. How can I make it stop? I know it is not connected.

You can turn off the error reporting in the Registry. Change the value called `ErrorControl` in `HKEY_LOCAL_MACHINE\SYSTEM\CurrentControlSet\Services\`*`device driver`*. By default, it is set to `1`, so if you change it to `0`, the device driver will no longer report errors.

Be careful turning off error control, however, because if something is truly wrong, you won't know that either.

It seems as if every day our computers get slower and slower. (That's actually good, because we must be getting better.) Here's a question that illustrates the problem, and a possible solution.

Solutions

Can I make my NT server faster? Sometimes, it just feels slow.

Hardware is the real key to making your server faster, but you can set your server priorities to give the most performance to server functions. Then, all that you do have will be given to the server functions.

By default, all server functions in both Server and Workstation have the same priority in NT 4.0 as foreground applications. To boost the priority so that it is greater than any foreground application, change the `HKEY_LOCAL_MACHINE\SYSTEM\CurrentControlSet\Services\LanmanServer\Parameters` key. Add a

continues

continued

REG_DWORD value called ThreadPriority, and set the value to 2. If you set it to 0, it would run at the priority of background applications. Setting it to 1 is the same as not having a value at all because it would set the priority of server threads the same as for foreground applications.

This Solution won't necessarily speed up your server, but it will ensure that the server functions are running as fast as they can.

If you've ever done too much, gone too far, or changed something you shouldn't have, this next Solution is for you.

Solutions

I messed up my NT server by changing a number of variables, and it works worse now than when I started. Help!

If you had a backup of your Registry, you could simply restore that. In the absence of a backup, you can remove a few values in one key, and Windows NT will reconfigure itself, and return its parameters.

In HKEY_LOCAL_MACHINE\SYSTEM\CurrentControlSet\Services\LanmanServer\Parameters, there are several values. Remove all of them *except*:

- EnableSharedNetDrives
- LMAnnounce
- NullSessionPipes
- NullSessionShares
- Size

When NT Server is restarted, it will automatically reconfigure its server service and optimize it with Microsoft's parameters.

Disk space limitations can cause all types of problems. Getting new disk drives opens up all sorts of new opportunities, or extra performance.

Solutions

I have a new disk drive, and my C: drive is getting very full. Can I set it so my printer will spool to another directory on another drive?

Yes, you can, and it only takes a simple Registry entry. Add a REG_SZ value called DefaultSpoolDirectory to HKEY_LOCAL_MACHINE\SYSTEM\CurrentControlSet\Control\Print\Printers. Set the value to be the name of any current directory on a local physical drive. If you are going to put the directory on an NTFS partition, the Everyone group must be given full control.

continues

Restart your system, and when you send a job to print, it will be spooled at the new location.

In many cases, you need to just change the way things work. Someone else makes software decisions for your organization, and you would like it to work differently. That is the case with the previous Solution, and the next one, too.

Solutions

I don't like having a little message pop up on my screen every time I send something to print to my NT Server. We are all in the same room. How can I get rid of the annoying messages?

You could turn off the print notification at the server, and then you would only know if the print job finished by looking at it. `HKEY_LOCAL_MACHINE\SYSTEM\CurrentControlSet\Control\Print\Providers` is the key where you need to add a new `DWORD` value called `NetPopup`. Set the `NetPopup` value to `0`, and the system will no longer bother you with the messages.

The paging file not only makes your systems work better, by allowing you to use hard disk space as if it were RAM, but it also gives you a safety net for the system. If your NT system crashes, the paging file can hold the entire contents of RAM for investigative purposes. You need to make sure the paging file is at least as large as RAM. Some applications want it extremely large. If your application is particularly sluggish, consider expanding the size of your paging file.

Solutions

I got a warning that my maximum Registry size needed to be expanded. When I went to change it, NT said I needed to expand my paging file space to do that. Isn't there any other way?

Windows NT sets the maximum Registry size limit by default to 25 percent of the *page pool* (all of the paging files added together). If you go past that, you will need to expand the page pool or expand the percentage for calculating the maximum Registry size.

To change the percentage, add a key named `RegistrySizeLimit` to `HKEY_LOCAL_MACHINE\SYSTEM\CurrentControlSet\Control`. Then add a `REG_DWORD` value with the same name, `RegistrySizeLimit`, to that key. Set the value to the maximum, `0xffffffff`, and you should be OK.

It shouldn't bother you again. With the price of hard disk space today, though, you really ought to consider getting more space and just expanding your paging file space.

When upgrading from NT 3.51 to 4.0, put in the CD, use the Run command, and, at the `\i386` directory, run `WINNT32 /u`. That will save all your settings, users, groups, and replace your current drivers with NT 4.0 drivers. It is fast, easy, and very efficient.

Solutions

I want to upgrade to NT 4.0, but I have HPFS volumes, and the NT documentation says they are not supported in 4.0. Are there any workarounds to allow me to still use them?

If we didn't have one, you can bet that the question would not be listed here. You will need to copy a file, `PINBALL.SYS`, from an NT 3.51 system, and then make some changes to the Registry. Copy `PINBALL.SYS` to `%systemroot%\System32\Drivers`.

At the `Pinball` key, add the values shown in Table 16.2. These are case-sensitive!

When you restart your system, you will be able to use the HPFS volumes in NT 4.0.

Table 16.2. Add a value to the `Pinball` key.

New Values	*Type*	*Data*
`ErrorControl`	`REG_DWORD`	0x1
`Group`	`REG_SZ`	Boot file system
`Start`	`REG_DWORD`	0x1
`Type`	`REG_DWORD`	0x2

Speaking of pinball, have you tried `PINBALL.EXE` yet? It is available for both Windows 95 and for NT 4.0, and brings a new level of gaming to PCs. No more 320×200. This is full-sound, full-motion, high-intensity Super VGA gaming.

Windows NT can run DOS, 16-bit Windows, 32-bit Windows, OS/2, and POSIX applications. It can also understand most UNIX commands as well. If you run OS/2 applications, this next Solution may make them work better.

Solutions

How can I get better performance for my OS/2 applications in Windows NT?

I can't guarantee it, but many applications written for OS/2 will run faster if you disable the OS/2 subsystem. The applications will still work, but they will run under a Virtual DOS Machine (VDM). NT gives more resources to the application in the VDM than it does in the OS/2 subsystem. You won't have to do

continues

anything different to run your applications; you just need to make a simple Registry change.

In `HKEY_LOCAL_MACHINE\SYSTEM\CurrentControlSet\Control\SessionManager`, change the `GlobalFlag` value from `0` to `20100000`. Once you restart your system, all of your OS/2 applications will use a VDM when they start.

An earlier Solution in this chapter turned off logging. Now you'll learn how to turn it on for a service that normally doesn't report its errors.

Solutions

I am having some challenges with RAS on my NT Server, but there aren't any errors shown in Event Viewer. Can I make it log the errors there?

You can make RAS errors show in the Event Viewer by telling the system to log them. By default, RAS error logging is turned off. To turn it on, change the `Logging` value in `HKEY_LOCAL_MACHINE\SYSTEM\CurrentControlSet\Services\RasMan\Parameters` to `1`. After restarting RAS, any errors will automatically be logged to Event Viewer.

Sometimes it seems that there are annoyances in software that just bug you. Most of the time, they are the product of a great idea, but sometimes there isn't enough thought as to how this will feel after the hundredth time it happens. Such is the case with this next Solution.

Solutions

How can I get my system *not* to automatically start CD-ROMs when I put them in my system?

That really depends on whether you are running Windows 95 or Windows NT. There is an option in the interface for disabling the Autorun feature in Windows 95. In NT, you will need to change the Registry.

In Windows 95, to disable both the CD-ROM and audio CD Autorun feature, follow the steps shown here.

1. Go to Control Panel | System | Device Manager | CD-ROM.
2. Open the CD-ROM branch and then go to the properties of the CD-ROM driver.
3. At the Settings tab, clear the Auto Insert Notification box.

When you restart your system, CDs will not automatically play in Windows 95.

continues

continued

To remove the Autorun feature in Windows NT, edit the `HKEY_LOCAL_MACHINE\System\CurrentControlSet\Services\CDRom` key. Change the `Autorun` value to `0`.

In either of these instances, it will not affect how your CDs will run—just when. It does get annoying when you insert a CD-ROM to give the system a file it needs, and it starts up automatically. It is even more annoying when you have a CD tower, and when you change one, it will start all of the CDs currently in the tower.

There is a difference between a CD tower and a CD jukebox. The tower has multiple drives, each with a CD in it. All of the data is online simultaneously. It works great as a lookup/database function. A jukebox has many CDs, but only one plays at a time. If a different CD is needed, the system goes out, finds it, and then plays it. A tower is a great option for a network, but using a jukebox on a network might not be the best solution. If multiple users are trying to access different CDs on the same machine, that machine would spend most of its time switching between the two.

Solutions

Windows 95 was installed on my system with a CD-ROM, so whenever I need to make changes to my system, it always prompts me for a CD, which I don't have at my desk. All of the files have been copied to the server, and I want it to automatically go there for the files. Is that possible?

It is not only possible, it may be the best way to do it. A change in the Registry will change where it looks for your Windows 95 files. You could also do this for Windows NT, but the Registry change is in a different location.

To change the Registry for Windows 95 systems, edit the `HKEY_LOCAL_MACHINE\Software\Microsoft\Windows\CurrentVersion\Setup` key. Change the path in the `SourcePath` value to the new location. That location can either be a local directory, a UNC to a shared directory on the network, or a mapped drive letter.

In Windows NT, the Registry key is `HKEY_LOCAL_MACHINE\Software\Microsoft\Windows NT\CurrentVersion`. The `SourcePath` value is the same, and the limitations are the same.

That should make it a lot easier to change your system.

Summary

Without a doubt, one of the most important things you can do as administrators is to optimize the performance of your systems. That has almost as much to do with keeping them working as it does with smoothing out the rough spots that get in the way of optimum performance. This chapter demonstrates how to do both.

Part V

Part V
Part V
Part V
Part V
Part V
Part V
Part V
Part V
Part V
Part V
Part V

Networking Control and the Registry

CHAPTER 17

How the Registry Controls Windows Networking

The term "Windows networking" refers to any system that has a native client or server function that will work with Windows 3.1, Windows for Workgroups, Windows 95, Windows NT, and DOS. It is based on a set of rules developed by Microsoft and modified as the need has arisen. There are specific functions, features, and quirks that are unique to the networking world. All of the networking functions are controlled by the Registry when you are working with Windows 95 and Windows NT.

The basic concept of networking is that you share expensive devices and data among several people to reduce cost and increase efficiency. The management of the devices was discussed in earlier chapters. All of the sharing of the devices and data and the management of the traffic are dependent on the Registry and will be covered in Chapters 18 through 21. For example, when you share a folder or printer in Windows 95 or NT, it stores the share information in `HKEY_LOCAL_MACHINE\System\CurrentControlSet\Services\LanmanServer\Shares`. If that information is changed in the Registry, or if the Registry becomes corrupted, the nature of the share will change.

In order for a system to be able to work on a network, it must have several components installed. For all but NT Server, these are optional items. Though they come with the software, you do not have to install them to make the software work. You would only install the networking components to get network capabilities on the system. Windows NT Server will not install if the following networking components are not installed:

- Server capabilities
- Client capabilities
- Network card or modem
- Protocols
- Security

When you install these components, pointers are set in the Registry for locations of files, settings are set for the configuration of those files, and networking services are installed.

Data Transfer in a Network Setting

Data that transfers from one computer to another is controlled by software and settings that adhere to rules called the OSI model. OSI (Open Systems Interconnection) was developed in 1977 so computers could easily talk with one another, and a set of rules was given to all manufacturers to ease the interconnection. It's a complex set of rules, but the bottom line is that all data that needs to get from one computer to another uses many layers of functions to get there.

Microsoft uses the OSI model as the foundation for its NDIS driver functions. OSI sets the standards, and then other companies determine how those will actually be implemented in their network tools. Novell has its own opinions about how the OSI model should be implemented, and they have done that in their own client software and drivers. Microsoft has chosen a different path for its NDIS drivers and the Windows networking client. Sun has also chosen a different path.

The key to making networking work in a cross-platform setting is that, eventually, the data gets to a format that can be transferred from one card to another. There can be no worry about how one 10BASE-2 Ethernet card will transfer information to another.

Figure 17.1 is a simplified model that shows the layers of steps that data has to go through to get from one user to another.

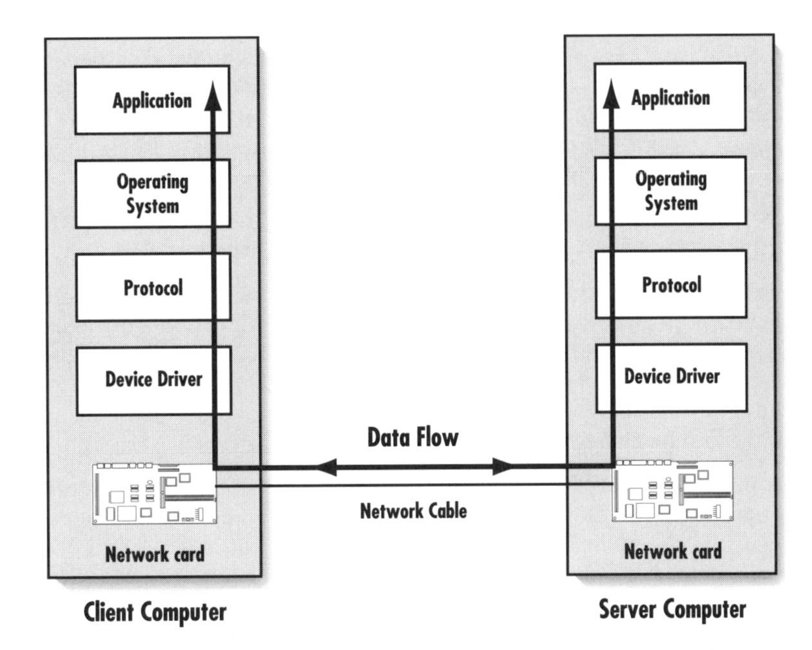

Figure 17.1. Layers of steps for data transfer on a network.

Every layer has settings, which are held in the Registry. Every layer adds information based on those settings to the actual data that goes across the network. When that information is received on the other end, it tells the receiving computer how to deal with the data.

If any of the data that the computer sends across the network is incomplete or incorrect, the data transmission will not be complete, and errors will occur.

Most of the time, the error messages will tell you that the data did not transfer, and you will need to investigate to determine the reason. The error could be practically anywhere in the settings.

Troubleshooting a network and determining the causes of a misconnection reminds me of the "Man of a Thousand Disguises." There are so many variables that the errors you receive may point to dozens of potential problems. For more network troubleshooting with the Registry, see Chapter 20, "Troubleshooting and Configuring Networking Registry Settings."

Server Capabilities

Working as a server means that you share access to your disk drives, printers, and other devices with other users who connect with your system. The user will not have access to items that you have not shared. Users can connect to you through network cabling, modem, or other transmission opportunities such as radio waves, microwave relay, or direct digital connection.

In order to set up a system to work as a server on the network, it needs to have a network card or other connection device enabled. A network card is inserted, and the system needs a driver. This file, or set of files, controls the physical access into and out of the card. Normal settings include IRQ and I/O port address settings. Those settings must be unique inside the PC, or conflicts will keep the system from transferring information to or from the card.

The driver information and settings will be stored in `HKEY_LOCAL_MACHINE\Enum` for Windows 95 systems and in `HKEY_LOCAL_MACHINE\SYSTEM\CurrentControlSet\Services` for Windows NT.

For example, you have installed a network card in your NT system with the IRQ set to 10 and the I/O port address set to 300 with jumpers on the card. When you install the card driver in Windows, you would use the same settings. After completion of the driver setup, you close the Network Control Panel applet, and you will be prompted to restart the system. When you restart, you try to find the server, but you cannot log onto the domain because the system says there is no machine with that name on the network.

Normally, you would then check the cable and the domain name to see if the card was started. If the driver loaded, the card must have been able to be seen by the system. This indicates that the I/O port address is not the problem. If the I/O port address was in conflict, the card driver would not have loaded, and you would have gotten an error in the Event Viewer.

Because the driver loaded, the I/O port address is OK, and the system thinks there is a network. The IRQ is the setting that allows the system to communicate with the network card. With an incorrect IRQ, the driver loads, but there are no systems on the network, not even yours. Not being able to see any systems on the network is indicative of an IRQ problem. You then need to use another IRQ setting that is not in use by any other card in the system. If you can see your system, but no others, that may be a connection problem.

The other part of the server function that is critical in the server settings is the computer name. All access to shares is through a name in a UNC (Universal Naming Conventions) format. A share called `LASER1` on a system named `SERVER1` would be listed as `\\SERVER1\LASER1`. The name for the computer, the names of the shares, and all of the settings for the shares are in the Registry.

Client Component

Just as the server functions need a network card/connection device, the client also requires one. All of the settings for the card and the driver are in exactly the same locations as they would be for a machine acting as a server. Most systems can act as both.

In addition to the device entries, the client computer must also have a redirector. To connect to a Windows NT, Windows 95, or Workgroups machine, you must have the Microsoft client.

To connect to a NetWare server, you would need a NetWare client. You can get that client software from Microsoft or from Novell. Either way, the settings for the client are in the Registry. Client software is also available that can be added to Windows 95 and Windows NT to allow them to connect to Banyan VINES, UNIX, AS/400, and other network servers.

Protocols

The three standard protocols are TCP/IP, NetBEUI, and NWLink (IPX/SPX). All three are supported in Windows networking, and in 95 and NT they can all be present at the same time. The computer needs information about each protocol so the computers can talk to each other.

In terms of the settings the user needs to make, NetBEUI is the simplest protocol. Some people wrongly assume that there are no settings in the Registry for NetBEUI. There are several, but they are configured automatically, and the user does not need to set any of them. In the Registry, NetBEUI settings are in keys with an NBF designator.

The next protocol, in order of difficulty of setup, is NWLink. NWLink is Microsoft's implementation of Novell's IPX/SPX protocol. It is the most commonly used protocol in local area networks, because of Novell's dominance in the market. NWLink is also automatically configured to defaults, and for most networks, that is enough. Occasionally, there is a need to modify the settings for a more advanced or complicated networking environment. All of the settings for NWLink in the Registry use the NwlnkIpx label.

TCP/IP is the most difficult and most configurable of the protocols. It is commonly used as the protocol to connect different types of systems together so they can transfer information. Because TCP/IP has so many items that need to be set, it is very easy to make a little mistake that will keep the systems from communicating with each other. In the Registry, all generic TCP/IP protocol settings will be under the `Tcpip` key, and all card-specific settings will have the NetBT label.

Security

Every network has the ability to implement security features. How much security you implement and enforce depends on the number of people on the network, how much of a security risk the people are, and how sensitive the data is on the network.

Security features in the Registry are in many different locations. In Windows NT, there is a complete hive for just security settings that can be implemented through NTFS security, and another that holds all the user names, passwords, and access rights. They are not accessible through the Registry editors, but all of the data is managed through the Registry.

Other security features are based on the interface, logon, and information stored in easily accessible locations. By changing the settings in the Registry, you limit access and reduce your risk exposure. Individually, the settings may not create a positive security environment, but together, they can lock down the network and make it very difficult to penetrate.

Summary

The Registry is an integral part of making networking work in Windows 95 and Windows NT. The settings for all the devices, protocols, redirectors, and shares are stored in the Registry. By making sure that the information for each part is correct, you can make the whole network work. It may be tedious to ensure that all the settings are correct, but it is the only way to isolate problems in the Registry associated with networking.

CHAPTER 18

Windows NT Networking and the Registry

Networking is at the core of NT. Unlike other Windows products, networking is so critical to how NT works that it was designed into all of its inner workings. It has been designed so that premium security on the network is possible, and high network performance is expected.

NT Server and Workstation differ, but not in the way most people expect. The kernel of the software is exactly the same. Both use the same `.DLL` files, the same drivers, the same components, and the same Registry entries. The difference is in the tuning and the settings. Because NT Server's main duty is to allow access to files and to transfer them quickly, the system is tuned for that. NT Workstation is designed as a system where local application performance is at a premium, so the system resources are tuned for that.

The other main difference is in the included software. NT Server includes additional software such as Internet Information Server, DHCP Server, WINS Server, DNS Server, Migration Tool for NetWare, Network Client Administrator, Server Manager, and others. All of those are not found by default on the Workstation, although you can load management software for many of them on the Workstation platform. Additionally, there are features that you get on NT Server that you don't get on Workstation. The most noticeable is the lack of fault tolerance in Disk Administrator in NT Workstation.

None of the items listed can be loaded into NT Workstation, because of two Registry entries. If those two entries were to be changed, Workstation would tell software that it is Server, and so it is OK to load the software.

One of the Registry entries is hidden and unchangeable by the Registry editors. The other setting is easy to change, but may cause disastrous results if not used very carefully. Because it is not possible to make both changes, you can only change the system temporarily, allowing you to change system features or install software.

The changeable setting is in the `HKEY_LOCAL_MACHINE\SYSTEM\CurrentControlSet\Control\ProductOptions` key. The value name is `ProductType`. To indicate that it is NT Server, the value is `LanmanNT`. To indicate that it is NT Workstation, the value is `WinNT`.

Warning

The `ProductType` Registry change will cause a fatal system error if the data is different than the hidden entry during startup. If you reboot your system before changing the value back to the original, you will get the Blue Screen of Death, and you will have to restore your old Registry to be able to use your system again.

To allow NT Workstation to use fault tolerance functions in disk Administrator, do the following:

1. Change the value to `LanmanNT` in the Registry.

Warning

Microsoft has decided that this is a violation of the license agreement, and, with Service Pack 2, has disabled the change of the `ProductType` value in `REGEDT32.EXE`. However, you can still make the change in `REGEDIT.EXE`.

2. Exit the Registry, but do not restart the system. You will get an error message that says you are in violation of your software license. Figure 18.1 shows the error you will get.

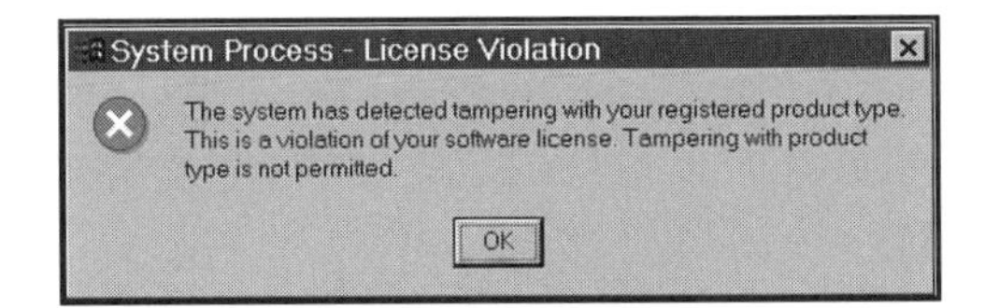

Figure 18.1. License agreement warning.

3. Use Disk Administrator to implement fault tolerance on your disk drives.
4. When you are finished, you will be prompted to restart your system. Do not restart it yet.
5. Change the Registry back to WinNT.
6. Restart your system.

Even though the system will restart as Workstation, the fault tolerance will work perfectly. You can do the same thing to allow the installation of Internet Information Server or SQL Server on a Workstation.

The difference between NT Server and NT Workstation is really only one of focus. The underlying functions are identical.

This chapter divides the Registry information for Windows NT into common settings, NT Server networking settings, and NT Workstation settings. Obviously, if you are going to use your server as a non-dedicated server to run applications locally, you may want to implement more of the Workstation settings than normal. Likewise, if you are going to use your workstation as a server, either in a workgroup or a domain, you may want to change the tuning.

Common Settings

The settings that are common to both NT Workstation and NT Server deal mostly with the drivers and the protocols.

Driver Settings

The network card driver information in the Registry in Windows NT is in `HKEY_LOCAL_MACHINE\System\CurrentControlSet\Services`. My driver for my CreditCard Ethernet Adapter IIps from Xircom uses a driver named `CE2XPS.SYS`. In the Registry, as shown in Figure 18.2, there are two entries for the driver.

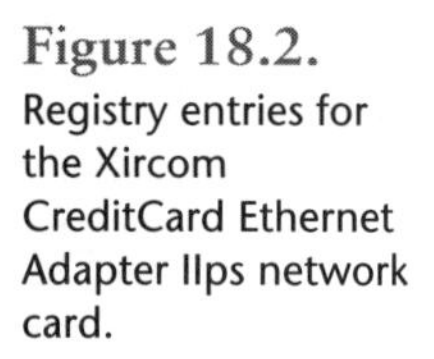

Figure 18.2. Registry entries for the Xircom CreditCard Ethernet Adapter IIps network card.

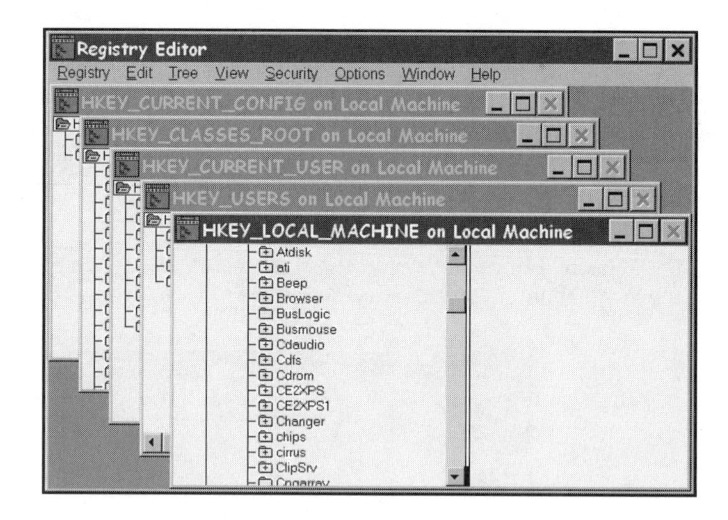

The entry with the card driver name is the settings for the driver, including the location of the driver, the labels, and other parameters. Figure 18.3 shows the expanded tree of keys below the driver listing.

Figure 18.3. Driver settings in the Registry.

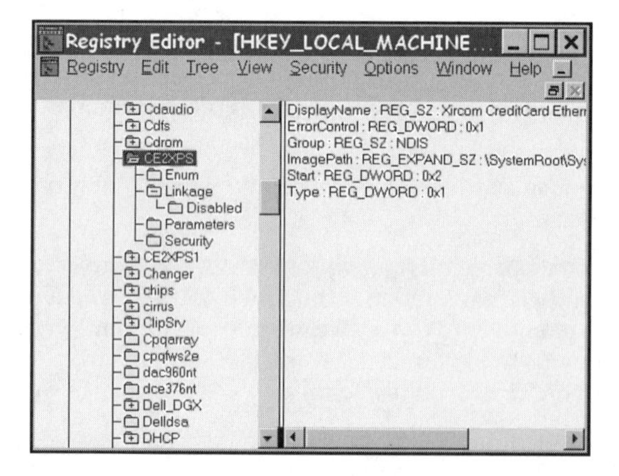

The network driver entry that has a number at the end of it is the instance of the network card. With only one Xircom adapter in the system, the entry ends with a 1. If there had been a second card, the Registry key would have been labeled `CE2XPS2`, and so on, incrementing the numbers for additional installed adapters. If you had a second adapter, but it used a different driver, it would have that driver listed, and the card settings entry would still have a 1 at the end. It is the first instance of that card. Figure 18.4 shows the Registry with 2 Xircom adapters loaded into the system.

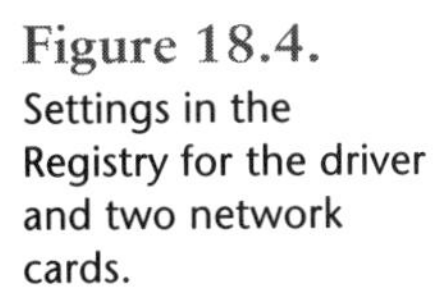

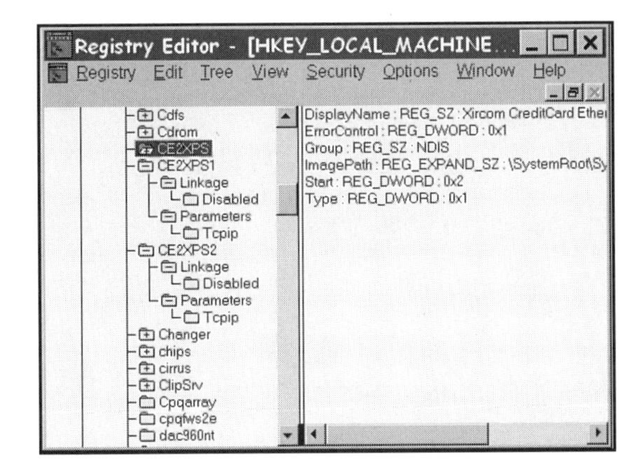

Figure 18.4.
Settings in the Registry for the driver and two network cards.

The settings for each of the cards must be unique, or the resulting conflicts would mean that data could not be transferred to the cards or accepted by the cards.

Each of the card settings must be different, or the cards would not work correctly. The card settings are in the `Parameters` key, and the TCP/IP settings for the individual cards are in the `Parameters\Tcpip` key.

Protocols

Some protocol settings are set for the individual card, and others are set for the system as a whole. The settings that are unique to the card are set in `HKEY_LOCAL_MACHINE\System\CurrentControlSet\Services\`*`card driver`*`\Parameters\Tcpip`. The settings that are generic to the card are usually settings for all systems on this network. Those settings are in `HKEY_LOCAL_MACHINE\System\CurrentControlSet\Services\Tcpip\Parameters`. Figure 18.5 shows the parameters that need to be set for TCP/IP to work in the network. The most important settings are the domain name, the name server address, the host name, and whether IP routing has been enabled. All of those settings are normally made in the Control Panel, but could be made with a Registry editor, either locally or remotely.

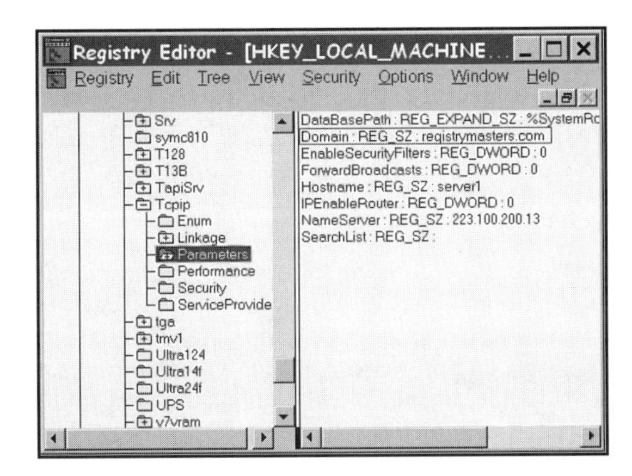

Figure 18.5.
General TCP/IP settings in the Registry.

Regardless of the type of driver, the type of card, or the number of cards in the system, this information is critical.

NT Server-Specific Settings

The four main functions unique to NT Server are

- Shares
- Server performance
- Security
- Network management (DNS, WINS, DHCP)

Each is recorded in a different location in the Registry. Because all the information is in the Registry, the system can access it equally whether at the interface, through networking functions, and directly from an application.

Shares

The information about shares is stored in `HKEY_LOCAL_MACHINE\System\CurrentControlSet\Services\LanmanServer\Shares`. All of the shares created are stored here, each using a single `REG_MULTI_SZ` entry. All of the information about the name, the maximum number of users, the security permissions, and other functions is stored in each value.

Through remote Registry editing, you can add or remove shares from a machine, if you know the syntax of the data in the value.

Server Performance

Windows NT tunes itself for optimum performance. You have some choices in the `HKEY_LOCAL_MACHINE\Software\Microsoft\Windows` key and also in the `HKEY_LOCAL_MACHINE\Software\Microsoft\Windows NT` key.

The Control Panel System Properties has a Performance tab that allows you to select a performance boost for the Server service. Even if you move the slider all the way to maximum, it will not change the server performance. It is basically a non-feature, and it just doesn't work.

For optimum performance, adjust the settings about the paging files, the caching, and the hardware. Together, little changes add up to better performance.

Security

Besides the NTFS security and the user rights information that each have their own hives, there is much more regarding security and Windows NT Server. Most risks are isolated to people trying to get access to unauthorized locations on the network. That all starts with a password. A user may have certain rights and privileges with his own user name and password, and want more. Other individuals may not currently have access, and want to get it. Whichever the case, access to the system is limited to those who have the correct rights.

In order to make it more difficult for unauthorized users to get access, you can do several things. An example would be to not show the last user name that was logged on. Then the user would have to guess the name and the password, making it more difficult. That setting and almost all other settings regarding logon to the network are in `HKEY_LOCAL_MACHINE\Software\Microsoft\Windows NT\CurrentVersion\WinLogon`.

Network Management

DNS, WINS, and DHCP management allow a server to communicate with other computers through TCP/IP. Because it is the most complex, there is more in the Registry about TCP/IP than both of the other protocols combined. Servers manage the settings, and allocate information to other systems on the network. All of the settings such as IP addresses, host names, and NetBIOS names are managed by servers on the network.

The settings are in several keys in `HKEY_LOCAL_MACHINE\SYSTEM\CurrentControlSet\Services`, and the configuration of the managers are there also.

NT Workstation-Specific Settings

In addition to the functions that are common to both Server and Workstation, there are settings that affect the performance of a Workstation. Specifically, working as a client is fundamental to connecting to a server.

Connecting as a Client to NT

The client connections to Microsoft networks have settings in `HKEY_LOCAL_MACHINE\SYSTEM\CurrentControlSet\Services\Rdr`. The settings are normally made in the Control Panel, but may be done in the Registry as well. Settings that control the connection can be added also, and some of those are in Chapter 20, "Troubleshooting and Configuring Networking Registry Settings" and Chapter 21, "Questions and Answers for Networking and the Registry."

Connecting as a Client to NetWare

You can easily add a connection to NetWare servers with a client for NetWare, included with NT Workstation. Once installed, the client has settings in the `HKEY_LOCAL_MACHINE\SYSTEM\CurrentControlSet\Services\NwRdr` key. The client then reads information from the Registry and uses it to control the connection. If there are any errors in the settings, usually connections will be impossible.

Connecting to Other Servers

There are client connections available for NFS (UNIX), Banyan VINES, IBM's AS/400, and others. If the client connection installs as a service, the settings will be in `HKEY_LOCAL_MACHINE\SYSTEM\CurrentControlSet\Services`. If the client does not install as a service, but rather as an application that runs at startup, the settings will be in `HKEY_LOCAL_MACHINE\Software` with a key assigned to it.

Summary

All of the settings for networking are in the Registry. Most are set in the Control Panel, but they can also be set directly with a Registry editor, or with remote editing or System Policy Editor. Most of the settings are in the `HKEY_LOCAL_MACHINE\SYSTEM\CurrentControlSet\Services` key or in the `HKEY_LOCAL_MACHINE\Software` key.

CHAPTER 19

Windows 95 Networking and the Registry

Windows 95 treats networking very differently than Windows NT. In relative terms, compared to the security and integration of networking with NT, Windows 95 networking feels "tacked on." Windows 95 was designed as a desktop operating system, with networking added. Security features are not as strong, but then again, Windows 95 works as a desktop system with fewer hardware requirements, and it has more backward compatibility than Windows NT.

Networking functions in 95 are very similar in components to NT Workstation, where the focus is on local applications, then client connections to servers, and then sharing disk drives and printers with others.

Network Cards and Drivers

Because Windows 95 has Plug and Play, it automatically detects new network cards that have been inserted into the system and loads the drivers for them. The driver information will be in `HKEY_LOCAL_MACHINE\Enum\PCI` for PCI-based cards or `HKEY_LOCAL_MACHINE\Enum\ISAPNP` for all ISA-based cards or `HKEY_LOCAL_MACHINE\Enum\PCMCIA` for PCMCIA network cards. There will be a code for the vendor of the network card, and under it, a code for the card will be listed. The settings for the card are in binary code, so it makes it very difficult to set the cards through the Registry.

Details for the drivers are in `HKEY_LOCAL_MACHINE\System\CurrentControlSet\Services\Class\Net`, with each adapter having a key under Net. My modem is used as a dial-up adapter, so it uses the `0000` key, and my normal network card uses `0001`. Figure 19.1 shows the contents of the key for the network card. Additional adapters would be listed as `0002`, `0003`, and so on.

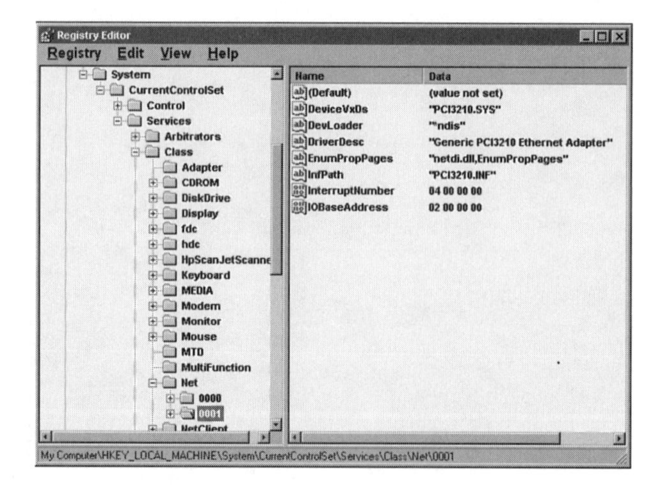

Figure 19.1.
Settings for the 3210 Generic PCI Network Adapter.

Client Connections

As in Windows NT, you can have multiple client connections simultaneously to different networks. The two that are the most common are clients for Microsoft networks and clients for NetWare networks. The NetWare client will support both bindery services (NetWare 3.12 and earlier) and NDS (NetWare 4.0 and later).

Information about the Microsoft client is in `HKEY_LOCAL_MACHINE\Enum\Network\Vredir`, and information about the NetWare client is in `HKEY_LOCAL_MACHINE\Enum\Network\NWRedir`. The settings for the clients are also in binary code, making it very difficult to edit here.

Specific details of the clients are in `HKEY_LOCAL_MACHINE\System\CurrentControlSet\Services\Class\NetClient`, with the individual clients listed with `0000` and `0001` keys. The values in those keys name the exact location of the driver files. In my system, the client for Microsoft networks is `0000`, and the client for NetWare is `0001`.

One of the most important settings is the default client. Figure 19.2 shows that `0000`, or the Microsoft client, is the default. You can also set that in the Control Panel. It is critical because it determines which network will be logged onto first, and which logon script will have precedence.

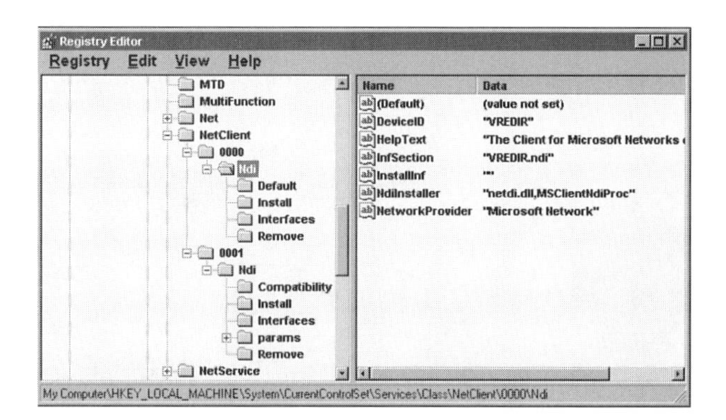

Figure 19.2.
Settings for the clients in the Registry.

Protocols

The protocol bindings are easily found in the Registry, and there are separate keys for each adapter or modem used as a dial-up adapter. The protocol bindings are listed in `HKEY_LOCAL_MACHINE\Enum\Network`. Table 19.1 lists the keys and their protocols.

Table 19.1. Protocols in Windows 95.

Registry Keys	*Protocols*
`MSTCP`	TCP/IP
`NETBEUI`	NetBEUI
`NWLINK`	NWLink
`NWNBLINK`	NWLink with NetBIOS

The settings for the protocols are in `HKEY_LOCAL_MACHINE\System\CurrentControlSet\Services\Class\NetTrans`, for network transport. That is where the IP addresses are held for TCP/IP, the frame types for NetWare networking, and other details about the transport protocols. Figure 19.3 shows the TCP/IP settings, which are in the `0009` key.

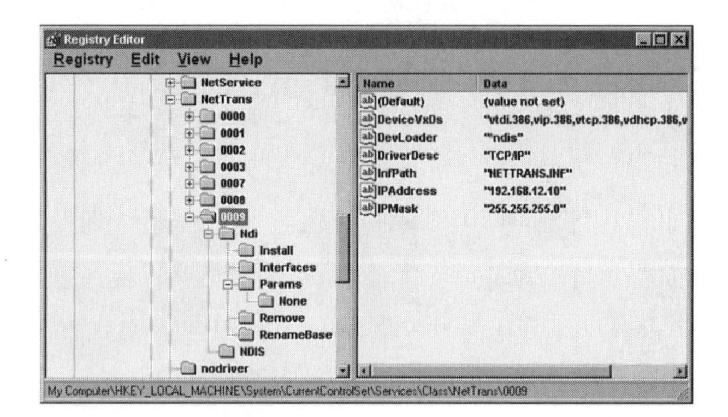

Figure 19.3.
TCP/IP settings in the Windows 95 Registry.

File and Print Sharing

You can set up file and printer sharing easily in the Control Panel, in the Networking applet. In the Configuration tab, if you don't have it listed, you can add the service. When it is added, you will get entries in the Registry in the `HKEY_LOCAL_MACHINE\System\CurrentControlSet\Services\Class\NetService` key. It lists the drivers and the controls necessary for the file and print sharing to work.

Summary

Information that is required for Windows 95 systems to connect to a network is contained in the Registry and in auxiliary files on the hard disk. Because of the limitations associated with protecting files and the Registry in Windows 95, it is not as secure as Windows NT, but the benefits of performance and the use of older devices outweigh that for many people. The ease of use, of setting up cards and drivers, and of sharing files and printers has made Windows 95 the most networked of all operating systems, and brought networking to countless thousands who would never have ventured forth before.

CHAPTER 20

Troubleshooting and Configuring Networking Registry Settings

Making networking work well is one of the most difficult functions in the realm of computing. Most of the time, the difficulty is due to the sheer number of variables. The problems are usually related to difficulty in getting connected, or the lack of performance, but the symptoms may mask the real problems. Many times, the error indicates that the domain controller cannot be found or a timeout error has occurred in accessing files on the network.

The biggest challenge, then, is isolating the actual problem, and then fixing it. At times, that is "easier said than done." Some of the problems and their fixes are described in this chapter.

Solutions

In Windows 95, when I set my system to use User Level access, and I log on to the NT domain, it still comes up and asks me what my Windows password is. Isn't one enough?

If you set the system right, it is. You can quickly set the system so it will use the password you gave for domain logon for Windows logon as well. To set that, you will need to disable the password caching for Windows 95. In `HKEY_LOCAL_MACHINE\Software\Microsoft\Windows\CurrentVersion\Policies\Network`, add a new `DWORD` value called `DisablePwdCaching`, and set it to `1`.

This will also work if the user is logging on to a NetWare network. Then the network logon function will relay the password to Windows 95 for its logon.

Solutions

I recently upgraded from Windows for Workgroups to Windows 95. I use only TCP/IP protocols, and my system hangs every time I try to connect to another computer. What is wrong?

Upgrading from WFW running the 32-bit TCP/IP stack adds an unsupported value to the Registry. Remove the value, and your system should work just fine. When you upgraded, an entry in the `SYSTEM.INI` file created the `EnableRouting` value in `HKEY_LOCAL_MACHINE\System\CurrentControlSet\Services\VxD\MSTCP` key. Remove the value, remove the line `EnableRouting=1` in the `SYSTEM.INI` file, and restart your system. It should give you TCP/IP access then.

As you can see, the situations can get quite complex. Making systems connect, particularly when different types of networks are involved, can be very challenging.

Solutions

We merged two NetWare networks together and I want to connect to both, but I cannot see the systems that are from the old network. What should I do?

If you connect your NT Workstation to more than one NetWare network, each using a different frame type, or if the one NetWare network is bound to more than one frame type, your system may not see all the systems on the network. To see all the systems on the network, your card must be set to more than one frame type. You may enter as many types as are currently on your networks.

Change the `PKType` value in `HKEY_LOCAL_MACHINE\SYSTEM\CurrentControlSet\Services\NWLinkIpx\NetConfig\`*`network_card`*.

`PKType` is a `REG_MULTI_SZ` entry, and the possible values for `PKType` are shown in Table 20.1. Check with your administrator for the correct frame types.

Table 20.1. Possible values for `PKTType`.

Value	*Frame Type*
`0`	Ethernet II
`1`	Ethernet 802.2
`2`	Ethernet 802.3
`3`	Ethernet SNAP
`4`	ARCnet
`ff`	Auto Detect

If the value is set to `ff`, as shown in Figure 20.1, remove the `ff` setting. If `ff` is left in the Registry, it ignores all the specified settings, and the change is ineffective.

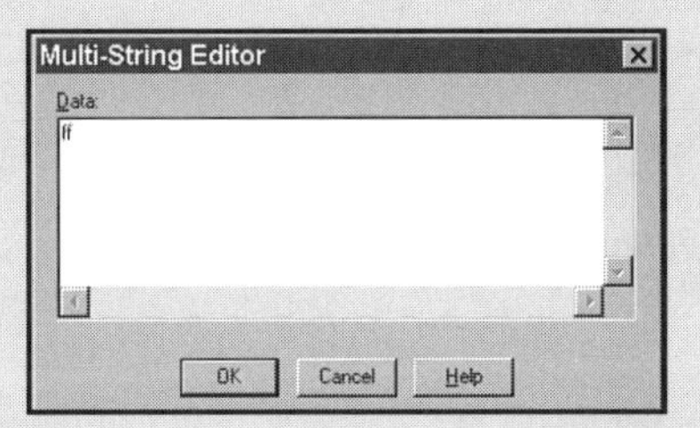

Figure 20.1. The Multi-String Editor with automatic frame type set for `NWLink`.

Because it is a multiple string value, you can set the `PKType` parameter to as many values as necessary. (See Figure 20.2.) Each of the entries for a frame type should be on its own line in the Multi-String Editor dialog box.

continues

continued

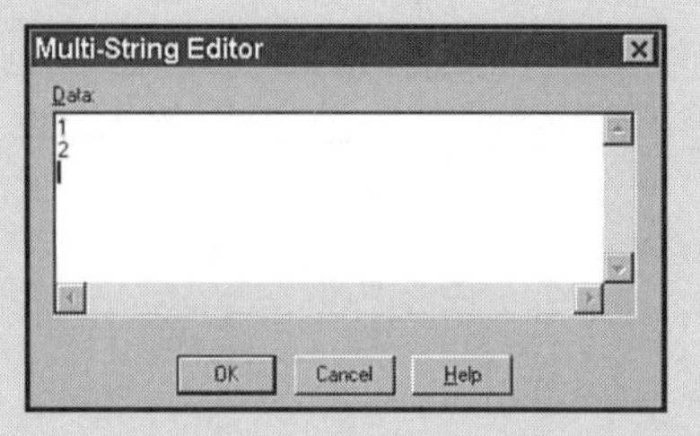

Figure 20.2.
Enter each of the types on a separate line.

Don't use REGEDIT.EXE to make this change because it involves a REG_MULTI_SZ entry.

To activate this change, restart the system. The Workstation looks for all of the listed frame types and responds to systems that are using them.

Using a TCP/IP network involves many components. If any of those components doesn't work correctly, you will have problems. In all cases, compromises must be made. Microsoft attempts to make the systems meet the needs of the widest audience. Those choices might not be the ones you would make. Some of those standard functions, even working correctly, will cause problems in a non-standard environment. Such is the case with the next question.

Solutions

When I am not connected to my network, my notebook always seems to take extra time to boot. Any ideas why?

If your system uses WINS for name resolution, every system that boots needs to find the WINS server. If your laptop is not connected to the network, it will not find the WINS server, and will time out eventually.

The WinsDownTimeout parameter sets the amount of time NBT waits before trying to use another WINS server. Most networks using WINS have two WINS servers, a primary and a secondary, that keep track of computer names on the network. If a system cannot find the primary WINS server, it searches for the secondary one. If it cannot find that, it does not use any name-recognition functions, and TCP/IP networking is significantly hampered. Luckily, that's OK when you're not connected, and the default is much more than enough in most cases if you are connected.

The value name to add is WinsDownTimeout, a REG_DWORD entry, in the HKEY_LOCAL_MACHINE\SYSTEM\CurrentControlSet\Services\NetBT\Parameters key.

The data is time in milliseconds, and the range of the data is 1000–0xFFFFFFFF, with a default of 15,000 (15 seconds). Set it lower, and the logon process when the laptop is not connected to the network is much faster.

One of the great misconceptions in the computer business is that of "unlimited." There are only a very, very few times when that is actually true. Normally, when the term unlimited is used to describe functions, it means that the numbers are so great that you would normally never hit them. The next situation is an example of the unlimited term being used a little too loosely. It is, in fact, nowhere near unlimited.

Solutions

I got an error that there were not enough connections at the server for me to connect. I didn't know there was a limit.

If you get an error that says the system was unable to find a free connection and couldn't connect to another system, you may need to expand the number of connections available at the server to each user.

In the `HKEY_LOCAL_MACHINE\SYSTEM\CurrentControlSet\Services\LanmanServer\Parameters` key, add a new value name called `MaxFreeConnections`, a `REG_DWORD` entry.

The range of the data is from `2` to `8`. Normally, it is between `2` and `4` as the default, depending on the configuration of the system. Set it to `8` to provide the best connection performance.

Connection challenges seem to go up even more radically when you add in the phone lines and RAS. There are additional functions in the software that need to be set correctly, and also you have to deal with other outside influences related to line quality and connections.

Add the Internet, and then you get even more variables. The Internet is a great tool, but the same factors that make it great, make it uncontrollable and more difficult to use. No one has complete control, and though there are a significant number of "standards," there is still a lot of room for difference. The next problem is an illustration of that.

Solutions

I seem to be having more and more trouble connecting to sites on the Internet from my NT Workstation. Is it just traffic, or am I doing something wrong?

With the Internet getting more and more congested, you may receive timeout errors if the time it takes to connect to the target system is too long, or if the number of hops is too great. To increase the number of hops available or to increase the time before error, make this Registry change.

Edit the `HKEY_LOCAL_MACHINE\SYSTEM\CurrentControlSet\Services\Tcpip\Parameters` key, and change the data in the value called `DefaultTTL`.

continues

continued

The range of entries is 1–255 with the default at `32`. If you are experiencing a significant number of timeout errors while connected to servers in the Internet, increase this number. `64` should be sufficient to eliminate nearly all the errors you have.

Dial-Up Networking is a fabulous tool that greatly standardized the way people connect with Windows 95 and NT. Prior to that, using communications programs was cumbersome at best. DUN isn't perfect now either, but it is a lot easier than the alternatives used to be. Getting the actual connection is also not the only problem you might encounter.

Solutions

I am dialing into my office network from my home, and I am having trouble getting a logon completed. The RAS server is on a different segment than my Domain controller. Do I need to move my domain controller or my RAS server?

You don't need to move either; you can just make a Registry change to the RAS server. Because the amount of time it takes to connect to the network through a dial-up router is longer than the time `NetLogon` will wait, the user often gets an error message that says he has been logged on using cached account information. He can still connect to his shares and the printers, but it takes extra time to regenerate the connection the first time each is used. If he is able to connect normally, he is lucky. The router must have had an open line ready and waiting.

By default, `NetLogon` sends out three broadcast/multicast `<1C>` frames looking for the PDC or BDC at five-second intervals. That adds up to only about 15 seconds, but the dial-up router may take as long as 30–60 seconds, sometimes more. If the dial-up router cannot make the connection before `NetLogon` times out, the system must use cached information for validation.

Fix this by extending the delay. This does not affect normal performance; it simply extends the `NetLogon` wait time if necessary.

In the `HKEY_LOCAL_MACHINE\SYSTEM\CurrentControlSet\Services\NetLogon\Parameters` key, edit the `ExpectedDialupDelay` value. Enter the data in total seconds, and each of the three frames will be broadcast in about one-third of the time. The recommended value to enter is `60`. If you find that it still doesn't connect, you can extend it.

A dial-up connection is actually no different than any other network connection in the way that systems are addressed. It is simply another network connection. It has all the same requirements as any other connection, with logon, authorization, security, and so on. Some of the functions that might happen to the client may be different, based on the location of the client. For example, not all messages and all broadcasts will go to a client connected by modem. This is set up that way to preserve bandwidth on the modem connection.

Solutions

Every time I dial into my RAS server, I get the error `No logon server was available to validate your password. One or more services may not be available across the network.` Why can't I log on to my NT domain?

If you use NWLink as your primary protocol to dial in to an NT network with RAS, you may not be able to be validated because the NetBIOS broadcasting functions are disabled by default. The logon request is not broadcast, and no logon is available.

The only functions available to you are those from Workgroup-connected machines not participating in the domain security. Other functions also may not be available, even if you are connected.

The real culprit is the forwarding of IPX type 20 packets between the remote RAS client through the RAS server to other servers on the network that use NetBIOS functions.

At the RAS server, change the `HKEY_LOCAL_MACHINE\SYSTEM\CurrentControlSet\Services\NwlnkIpx\Parameters` key by editing the `DisableDialinNetbios` value. Table 20.2 shows the options available.

Table 20.2. Broadcast options using RAS and `DisableDialinNetbios`.

Settings	*Broadcasts*
0	Client to RAS server to network and back
1 (default)	Client to RAS server only
2	Network to RAS server to client only
3	All IPX type 20 broadcasts disabled

Set this to zero (0), and you can easily connect to the network. The only downside to this setting is that other broadcasts from the network go down your connection as well.

More challenges come up because of the limitations imposed on Dial-Up Networking. Making the correct settings to create a workable, balanced environment can be a real challenge.

Solutions

How can I make my browsing better when I dial in to the network?

With a dial-up connection, if you are having difficulty seeing computer names, network shares, or printers during browsing, you may need to change this

continues

continued

parameter. This tip extends the routing of broadcasts from remote clients across routers, extending throughout the entire network. It also allows broadcasts to extend to the remote client from the network. Without this, browsing may not work.

Change the `NetBiosRouting` value in the `HKEY_LOCAL_MACHINE\SYSTEM\CurrentControlSet\Services\NWlnkRip\Parameters` key.

The default is `0` to reduce traffic. That is like turning off someone's drinking water so they don't drown. Some traffic is necessary to make networking work. Table 20.3 shows the other available values.

Table 20.3. `NetBiosRouting` possibilities.

Settings	*Results*
0	Do not forward broadcasts
2	Forward NetBIOS packets from remote client to LAN
4	Forward NetBIOS packets from LAN to remote client
6	Two-way forwarding of NetBIOS packets

Change the data, and choose `2`, `4`, or `6`, depending on your needs.

Traffic is another consideration in connecting to a network by modem. The bandwidth issue is always present, and until that's solved, we will have to deal with challenges like the next one.

Solutions

Why do I keep getting errors when I am copying data from my server across my dial-up connection?

Moving data from the very fast LAN to the relatively (and sometimes horribly) slow RAS-connected client can force a number of problems. If the RAS client cannot keep up, the packets are discarded and must be re-transmitted.

To solve the problem, RAS uses some physical memory (about 64KB per client) and also part of its paging file as a buffer. Unless the paging file and the amount of space allocated for RAS are sufficient, there will be errors. Reliability is also a concern. If the sender on the LAN sends more data than can be buffered, RAS kicks in with a NetBIOS flow control. This can cause communication errors to occur.

continues

Expand the size of the buffer on the RAS server to improve performance and increase reliability. To expand the size, change the `MaxDynMem` value in the `HKEY_LOCAL_MACHINE\SYSTEM\CurrentControlSet\Services\RemoteAccess\Parameters\NetbiosGateway` key.

The range of the data is 131,072–4,294,967,295 bytes. The default value is `655350` (640KB) per client connection. The minimum (128KB) is ridiculously small, and 4GB may be just a bit excessive. Choose something in between, and type it as bytes.

After you restart the RAS service, have the clients reconnect, and their data transfer performance will be better.

There are only so many connections you can make to one NT server with RAS. The actual maximum is 256 connections. Unfortunately, there are not that many that you can use. The next question relates to that very problem.

Solutions

When I dial in to my network, and try to connect to all the shares I need, I get error messages that say I cannot connect because there are no more available connections. What should I do?

All RAS clients together can have a total of 255 simultaneous NetBIOS sessions. Each client has a maximum number of sessions, but the active number is what is calculated in that 255. For example, if 10 remote clients connected and each one was using 25 sessions, the eleventh would only be able to use five sessions. Each session may be a connection to a printer, a share, and so on.

To correct this problem, you can have some of the clients connect to another RAS server, or you can limit the number of sessions available to each user. If you want to limit the number of connections each user can have, you can change `HKEY_LOCAL_MACHINE\SYSTEM\CurrentControlSet\Services\RemoteAccess\Parameters\NetbiosGateway`.

The value to edit is `MaxSessions`, and the range of the data is 1–255 sessions per connected client, with the default at `255`. Set it at `16`, and 16 users can simultaneously be connected, never running into the limit.

One easy way to calculate the value is to divide 255 by the number of available RAS connections and set that as the maximum. Past the maximum, new sessions temporarily disconnect the oldest sessions. The oldest item would still show in the lists, but when activated, it would take a little longer to actually connect.

If you had the maximum 256 connections to the network, none of the clients could actually connect to printers or shares. All of the connections would be taken just by connecting to the server.

Solutions

When I dial in to my RAS server, I hear the modem make all the funny sounds it makes during the connection, I log on, and then I get an error, `Unable to connect to shares.`

When you are connecting over a dial-up router or RAS server, the time required to connect is often more than the system can wait for. Increasing the `NetLogon` parameter was discussed earlier in this chapter. Use `ConnectMaxTimeout` to change the timeout for connections to shares.

Increase the value, and the system pauses to overcome delays in connecting to shares across the remote connection.

In the `HKEY_LOCAL_MACHINE\SYSTEM\CurrentControlSet\Services\Rdr\Parameters` key, the timeout value is entered in `ConnectMaxTimeout` as a number of seconds. The default is `45` (seconds), and you can set it anywhere from 0–400.

The expansion of your business sometimes requires you to have multiple connections to the Internet. Those connections each need their own IP address and domain name. Getting those names is critical to multiple Internet domain functions and success on the Internet as a server.

Solutions

I want to allow multiple domain names on my Internet Information Server. The names are set with the IP addresses in the DNS server, the IP addresses are set on the cards, and yet I still cannot get connections to it other than the first domain name I set. Did I miss something?

Yes, you did. You need to make a Registry change on top of the other things you did. Your ISP may assign multiple domain names in the DNS (Domain Name Service) server to connect to your server. Each of those domain names has an independent IP address. You can have all of those addresses on the same card, using the same outside connection, simultaneously. This enables your single Web server to service multiple companies or domain names, looking like separate servers to each.

Set up RAS to connect to your ISP with one of the IP addresses. Add all the other IP addresses to your network adapter. Set up the first address, including the subnet mask, with Control Panel | Network | Protocols | TCP/IP. Select Advanced to add the remaining IP addresses and corresponding subnet masks.

Then, change the Registry to allow all packets to come through the RAS connection. When a packet has the correct IP address in the header, the client connects to the Web server.

continues

Find HKEY_LOCAL_MACHINE\SYSTEM\CurrentControlSet\Services\RasArp\Parameters. Add a value named DisableOtherSrcPackets, as a REG_DWORD value, and set this at 0 to allow the connections.

In addition to Windows and DOS machines, you can also have Macintosh systems connect to your NT server, and participate in the network. However, there is no native NT client for the Macintosh, so the normal Macintosh client is used, and the information is translated at the NT server. The Services for Macintosh are included with NT Server, and expand the capabilities of your network. If there were a native NT client that could be loaded onto the Macintosh client, the built-in challenges in Services for Macintosh would just go away. Hopefully, Apple will release it soon. Unfortunately, even though the native client performed well during Beta testing, the release date is unknown.

Solutions

I connect to a Windows NT network with my Macintosh, and when I do a File Find command on my system, looking for a file on the server, my system seems to hang, and everyone else's does, too. When the search is done, everything goes back to normal. Do I just have to live with this?

No, you don't just have to live with it. Macintosh computers use a special command called CatSearch to do the File Find. That CatSearch may make all the systems appear to hang if there are a lot of Macintosh clients on the network, or there are a lot of files the search has to go through.

Support for the AFP CatSearch command was added in Windows NT 3.51. This command is used so the Macintosh client asks the server to do the search, instead of performing the search of the Macintosh volume itself. CatSearch instructs Windows NT to look through all directories and files, based on the specified search parameters.

When the search is performed at the root of a Macintosh volume with many directories, subdirectories, and files, it can delay the processing of requests from other Macintosh clients and the Macintosh clients will appear to stop responding while they wait for their request to be processed.

You can disable the CatSearch function for a particular Macintosh volume on the NT Server by adding Service Pack 2 (or higher), and then make a Registry change.

The key to change is in HKEY_LOCAL_MACHINE\SYSTEM\CurrentControlSet\Services\MacFile\Parameters\Volumes. Edit the value for the volume where you want to disable CatSearch (each volume has a value). Add DisableCatsearch=1 to the end of the list, as shown in Figure 20.3. Exit the Registry editor, and then stop and restart Services for Macintosh.

continues

continued

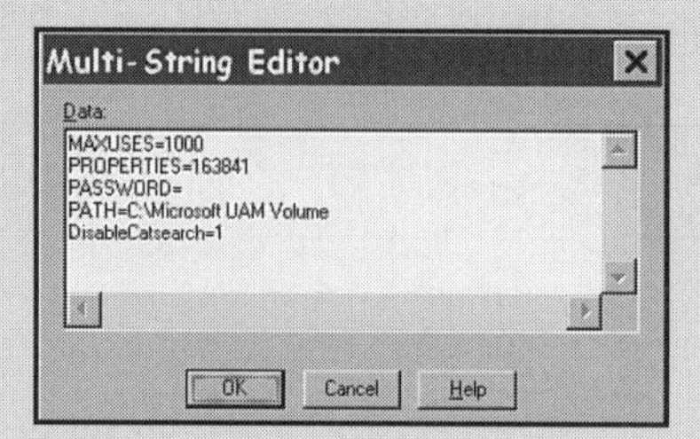

Figure 20.3. Removing the CatSearch function for a particular Macintosh volume.

Be aware that disabling may make your searches even slower, if you are not careful with your requests. Instead of searching everything on the entire volume, you may want to narrow your search. The search will be faster, and everyone's performance will go up.

Sometimes things just bug you, and they feel like a little pebble in your shoe. The passwords for Dial-Up Networking are just like that. No matter how many times you enter the password, and tell DUN to save it, it never seems to be saved. It's frustrating.

Solutions

I hate it. No matter how many times I tell my system to save my password when I am making a Dial-Up Networking connection from Windows 95, it doesn't save it. Why not?

I can appreciate your feelings, because it drives a lot of people crazy. The problem can be caused by any of the following situations:

- Password caching is disabled.
- One or more of the files associated with Dial-Up Networking is missing or damaged (you would get an error if this was the case).
- Your password list (`.PWL`) file is damaged.
- The `RNA.PWL` file (if it exists) is damaged.

This can easily happen after making a change to your Access Control functions in the Networking Control Panel applet, or if you change the name of the workgroup, or if you log on to a different domain.

Ensure that password caching is enabled in the `HKEY_LOCAL_MACHINE\Software\Microsoft\Windows\CurrentVersion\Policies\Network` key. If password caching is disabled, the `DisablePwdCaching` value will be set to `1`.

If the key was not there, or was set to `0`, remove Dial-Up Networking, and then reinstall it.

continues

Create a new password (`.PWL`) file by deleting the one based on your username (*`username`*`.PWL`). Also delete the `RNA.PWL` file if it is on your computer and then restart your computer.

When the Enter Network Password or Welcome To Windows dialog box appears, type the password that you normally use, and then click OK. When you are prompted to confirm the password that you entered, type the password again in the Confirm New Password box, and then click OK.

The password list for your username and the `RNA.PWL` file will be recreated on your system. Then, Dial-Up Networking should remember your password correctly.

Summary

The Registry controls all of the devices that are used in networking, and all the settings for Windows NT and 95 to use features and functions of many different types of networks. With the correct settings, it should work just as Microsoft designed it. With the extra options in this chapter, you can make it work the way you want it to.

CHAPTER 21

Questions and Answers for Networking and the Registry

Some people have characterized networking as "magic," or "smoke and mirrors." Actually, it is really neither. It is complex, and every network ends up being quite different. This chapter will give you more insights into how things work, and some options for customizing the network to more closely meet your needs.

Solutions

How can I set the minimum password length for Windows 95?

Having a password of more than four characters strengthens your security. In fact, the longer the password is, the more difficult it is to break. Set the minimum password length in the `HKEY_LOCAL_MACHINE\Software\Microsoft\Windows\CurrentVersion\Policies\Network` key. Add a `DWORD` value called `MinPwdLen` and set it to the number of characters you would like, in decimal format.

Security is a huge issue to deal with. Using the maximum password length will make your work a little easier. In Windows NT, you can set the password length in User Manager for Domains, in the Policies | Account Policies section.

Solutions

Normally, I log on to an NT domain from a Windows 95 system. Can I get a confirmation that it actually let me log on?

Normally, you would only know if it didn't work. If you need to get a confirmation, a simple change to the Registry will do that for you. Add a `REG_DWORD` value called `DomainLogonMessage` to the `HKEY_LOCAL_MACHINE\Network\Logon` key. Set the value of the `DomainLogonMessage` to `1`, and every time you log on to the domain, you will get a message similar to the one in Figure 21.1.

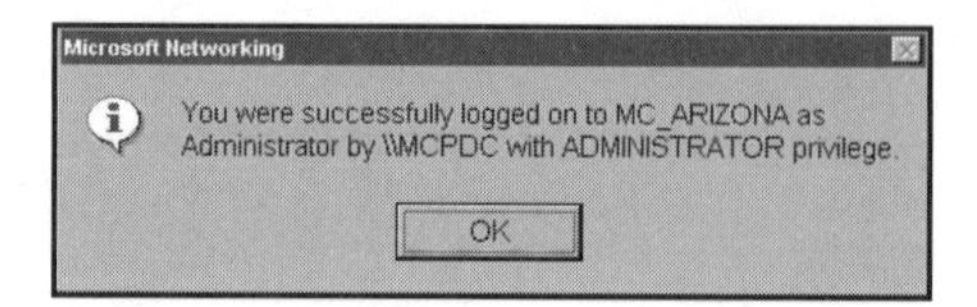

Figure 21.1. Domain logon confirmation.

Because networking is not as fundamental to Windows 95 as it is to Windows NT, some features are not included in the interface. In an effort to make it as powerful as possible, Microsoft did include many options that make 95 a much better client on the network.

Solutions

Windows NT allows me to easily set multiple IP addresses to a single network card. Can I do the same thing with Windows 95?

Yes, you can; it just isn't part of the interface. Maybe Microsoft didn't think anyone would want to do it. The IP address information is stored in the Registry in the `HKEY_LOCAL_MACHINE\System\CurrentControlSet\Services\Class\NetTrans` key. Find the subkey that holds the IP address. Figure 21.2 shows the key with the correct IP addresses set.

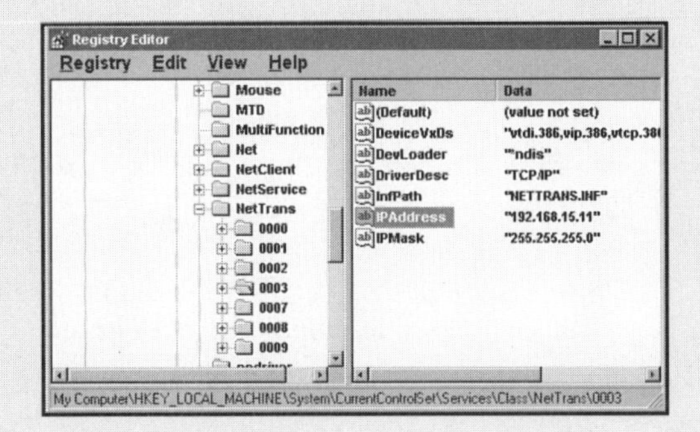

Figure 21.2. Location of the IP addresses in the Windows 95 Registry.

If you want to add another IP address to the network card, edit the `IPAddress` value, and add another IP address to the end of the string, separated by a comma, but no spaces. Figure 21.3 shows the correct format of the text.

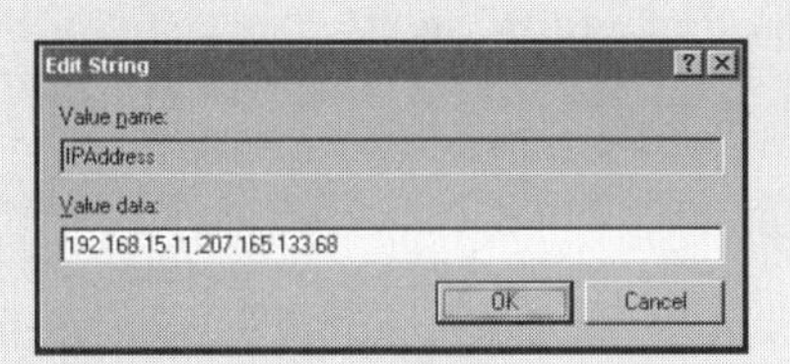

Figure 21.3. Adding an additional IP address to a network card.

Whenever you add an IP address, you must also add the corresponding subnet mask for that address in the `IPMask` value. Figure 21.4 shows the key with the correct values for two IP addresses attached to the same card.

continues

continued

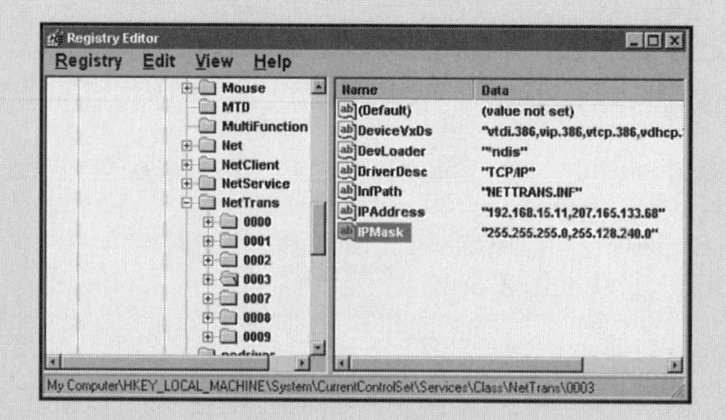

Figure 21.4. Multiple IP addresses assigned to the same network card.

You can add as many addresses as will fit within the limitation of 255 characters of the String entry.

A cache normally holds the last information given it. If the cache fills up, the first item is expelled, and the next is taken in. Sometimes, a function that looks exactly like a cache doesn't perform the same way. The next problem is an indication of that.

Solutions

I use Windows 95 on my notebook, and I connect to several different networks using TCP/IP. Because each one uses a different set of IP addresses, I have the server assign me an IP address through DHCP. I have used several different PCMCIA network cards, and several docking stations, and even modems to connect, and now, all of a sudden, I am not getting an IP address, and I cannot get onto the network. What went wrong?

The Windows 95 Registry stores information about every network card and modem used for Dial-Up Networking. The information, called a MAC address, is unique for every network card in the world. Once Windows 95 gets to eight cards listed, it will not list any more. If you were to go back to one of the cards you had used previously, you would probably get an address. Once past eight, you will never get another.

Figure 21.5 shows the location of the storage of the MAC addresses. The Registry will create a new `DhcpInfo0x` key for every new network card it finds, plus one for any modem used to dial into a network where the server will provide an IP address (such as an Internet service provider).

continues

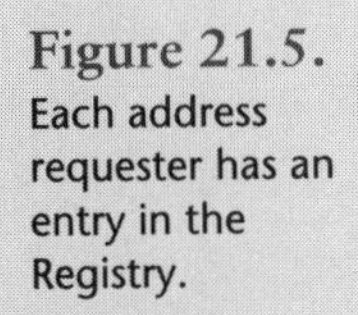

Figure 21.5.
Each address requester has an entry in the Registry.

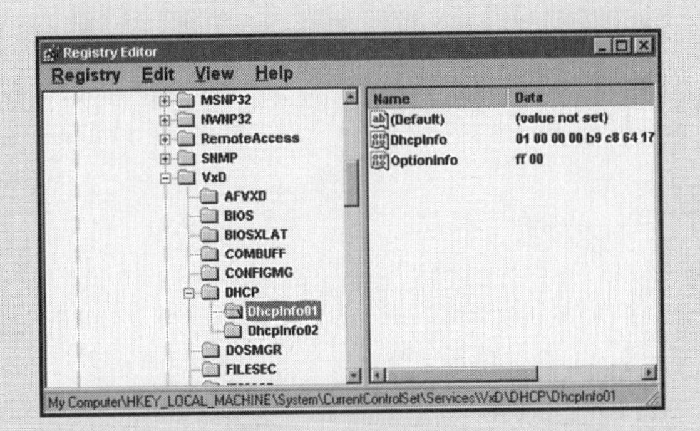

Because the system will automatically put an entry for each DHCP address requester, you can simply remove all of the subkeys below `Dhcp` except `DhcpInfo00`, if it exists. The necessary ones will be re-created as necessary. Then, as you connect to the network, a DHCP request will be given, and you will get a dynamically assigned IP address.

Remotely editing the Registry is a powerful function. If you can edit another system's Registry from your desktop, it will save you time, effort, and give you freedom from explaining more than you actually want to. You should train your users as much as possible, but explaining IP addresses and DNS servers may not really help them, anyway.

Solutions

I need to change the IP address, the subnet mask, the DNS host name, and DNS server on several NT systems on my network. Do I have to go to each one and run the Control Panel options, or can I do it remotely with a Registry editor?

Making all the TCP/IP settings on a remote machine is quite simple, if you know where the Registry entries are. All TCP/IP functions are separated into two categories: general settings and card-specific settings. The card-specific settings require you to know the network card driver, but the general settings just use the `Tcpip` key in `HKEY_LOCAL_MACHINE\SYSTEM\CurrentControlSet\Services\Tcpip\Parameters`. The TCP/IP settings that use the general settings are listed in Table 21.1, with the values that are associated with them.

continues

continued

Table 21.1. Generic TCP/IP settings.

TCP/IP Function	*Registry Value*
Domain name	`Domain`
Host name	`Hostname`
IP Routing	`IPEnableRouter`
DNS Server	`NameServer`

The TCP/IP settings that use the network card driver information use `HKEY_LOCAL_MACHINE\SYSTEM\CurrentControlSet\Services\`*`Adapter Name`*`\Parameters\Tcpip`, and are listed in Table 21.2, with their values.

Table 21.2. Card-specific TCP/IP settings.

TCP/IP Function	*Registry Value*
DHCP	`EnableDHCP`
IP Address	`IPAddress`
Subnet Mask	`SubnetMask`
Default Gateway	`DefaultGateway`

With this information, you can easily find the correct location to make any TCP/IP setting you need on a remote system, without having to go there and use the Control Panel. You also won't have to try to explain it to your users, so they can be your fingers for you.

Another way to quickly set the TCP/IP information across the network would be to create a custom template file for System Policy Editor, as outlined in Chapter 34, "Creating Custom Policies."

Solutions

My NT system can't find the files it needs to run TCP/IP correctly. Where are they? What are they?

For TCP/IP to work properly, the system needs access to several files, including `HOSTS`, `LMHOSTS`, `NETWORKS`, and `PROTOCOLS`. Normally, those files are in `%SYSTEMROOT%\SYSTEM32\DRIVERS\ETC`. If they are going to be stored in any other location, that location needs to be specified in the Registry.

In `HKEY_LOCAL_MACHINE\SYSTEM\CurrentControlSet\Services\Tcpip\Parameters`, edit the value named `DatabasePath`. It is a `REG_EXPAND_SZ` entry, which means that you can enter a variable, and it will be replaced with the actual data when read. Enter the location of the files.

Until there is a better way, you will have to continue to use all the settings, files, and options created for the Internet when it was still quite small. Now that it is huge, with nearly 20 million hosts (at the time of this writing), some of the functions are a little dated. The fact that it still works at all is amazing, but the challenges of using the Internet effectively are sometimes daunting.

Solutions

Our network has a gateway setup to give us access to the Internet, but sometimes it doesn't work. Then I can't get the information I need. What can I do to make it work better?

A gateway allows access to the Internet from your network. It is essentially the connecting point to the Internet. Sometimes it gets too busy to allow all the traffic to pass through. Other times, it may not be able to transmit data because its line to the Internet is down. Whatever the case, there is not much you can do, except to have a backup gateway in place.

If a system cannot transmit data through a gateway, even after several tries, the Transport Control Protocol (TCP) asks the IP portion to switch to a backup gateway if one has been specified, and this Registry change has been made. The address for the backup gateway is set in Control Panel | Network | Protocol | TCP/IP Protocol | Properties | Advanced. But that is not enough; you also need to make a change to the Registry.

The value name to add is `EnableDeadGWDetect`, a `REG_DWORD` value, in the `HKEY_LOCAL_MACHINE\SYSTEM\CurrentControlSet\Services\Tcpip\Parameters` key. Set the value to `1`, and if the first gateway does not respond, it will switch to the second.

The Internet is a very flexible network, sometimes to its detriment. Because information may be transferred over many lines, go through many routers, and be handled by so many servers, the security of the information may be compromised. The sensitivity of the data will determine what level of security is required, and, fortunately, there are many options that allow you to increase that security.

Solutions

I am concerned about sending private data over the Internet. Do I have any options that will give me more security than PPP or SLIP?

Certainly, PPP and SLIP are good protocols for transferring data over the Internet, but they are not very secure.

PPTP (Point to Point Tunneling Protocol) is designed to allow secure, authenticated connections to a server. NT 4.0 is the first Windows NT server to support it, and it ushers in a breakthrough in security across phone lines. It basically creates a secure tunnel through which all the data goes. None can get in, and

continues

continued

none can get out, until the data hits the end. Unauthorized users are not welcome.

The PPTP functions in NT 4.0 are in the `HKEY_LOCAL_MACHINE\SYSTEM\Services\RASPPTPE\Parameters\Configuration` key.

In order to enable PPTP, there are two values that need to be changed.

The value name `AuthenticateIncomingCalls` turns on the authentication procedure so only listed IP addresses can connect. It is a `REG_DWORD` entry. Set it to `1`, and only PPTP connections can be made, and only from the IP addresses in the next value.

`PeerClientIPAddresses` is a `REG_MULTI_SZ` value that lists all authenticated addresses for PPTP connection.

The format of `PeerClientIPAddresses` is a valid IP address *`xxx.xxx.xxx.xxx`* with each entry on an separate line. The entries are the only IP addresses of PPTP clients from which this server will accept PPTP calls.

Both values must be set. If one is not set, PPTP will not work.

Browsing is another great challenge in a Windows network. Browsing is the function that lets you see what you can connect to, either as a printer client or a server's share client. If you don't have the list, you need to know exactly the name of the server and the name of the shared device. If you want to choose from a list, browsing has to be working on the network. It's interesting to see how some of the things that Microsoft says are so, just aren't. Browsing is one of the tools that you must take control of, or it may not work as expected.

Solutions

Who should be my master browser? How can I choose?

Windows networking uses a master browser and a browse server. The browse server holds a list of all the shares on the network. The master browser answers requests for the list. They can be separate machines or the same machine. Set systems that have the highest performance/lowest demand combination to be your browse servers (2 per segment), and your domain controller to be your master browser.

Whatever you do, do not let your Windows 95 systems be your browse servers. There is a bug in the server list maintenance function of Windows 95 that will make it so no one can browse the network. Turn it off in Windows 95 with Control Panel | Network | File and Printer Sharing for Microsoft Networks.

On the NT system you would like to be a browse server, edit the `MaintainServerList` value in the `HKEY_LOCAL_MACHINE\SYSTEM\CurrentControlSet\Services\Browser\Parameters` key. Set the `MaintainServerList` value to YES, and the system will be a browse server.

continues

On the NT system that you would like to be the master browser, set the `IsDomainMaster` in the `HKEY_LOCAL_MACHINE\SYSTEM\CurrentControlSet\Services\Browser\Parameters` to `1`.

Internal security comes from limiting choices that users have on the network. If you limit the number of options a user has at his disposal, you can reduce the risk exposure. Forcing the users to know share names and server names can certainly hinder their progress in breaking your security.

Solutions

I don't want everyone to be able to see my NT system on the network. Is there any way that I can hide it?

You can hide it by adding a single Registry change. It will hide the system from Network Neighborhood, My Computer, and Open/Save dialog boxes.

To hide it, add a new `REG_DWORD` value called `Hidden` to the `HKEY_LOCAL_MACHINE\SYSTEM\CurrentControlSet\Services\LanmanServer\Parameters` key. Set the value to `1` to hide the system from the browse list.

Even though the system is hidden from the browse list, you can still connect to it with a UNC name.

Managing the browse lists and determining what users are going to see on the network really comes down to restricting what will be shown, or expanding what will be shown.

Solutions

I want to be able to browse all the shares on the network, even though they are on a different segment. Can I do that with NT?

Configure your network with your NT server so it functions as a multihomed router, with two or more network cards, each connected to a separate segment. Then you can add a new Registry value, and the systems on any segment can browse all of the shares on any other segment.

By default, each segment will have its own browse list, and the users will only be able to see the rest of the browse list that they belong to. What you will do is disable one of the browse lists so everyone will be part of the same browse list, and they will get to see all of the shares on both segments.

continues

continued

The new value will be entered in the HKEY_LOCAL_MACHINE\SYSTEM\CurrentControlSet\Services\Browser\Parameters key. The value name is UnboundBindings, a REG_MULTI_SZ entry. In the value, enter the name of one of the network cards. You can find the name of your network card in the HKEY_LOCAL_MACHINE\SYSTEM\CurrentControlSet\Services key. There will be two names for each card, one with a number at the end. For example, the driver for a Xircom Creditcard Ethernet Adapter IIps is CE2XPS. In the Registry, you would find CE2XPS and CE2XPS1 keys. If you had more than one of the same network card, the second would end in a 2. Use the name with the number on the end.

You should only put one of the network card names in the list if you only have two network cards in the server. If you have three, you would put in two names. The idea is to remove all but one browse list.

How much of a remote system's shares can be seen by the rest of the network is also configurable in the Registry. The setting is actually at the server, not at the workstation.

Solutions

I can't see the shares of any systems that are connected to my NT Server with RAS. Is that normal?

Yes, it is, but you can change it, if you would like. At the server, add a REG_DWORD value called RemoteListen to the HKEY_LOCAL_MACHINE\SYSTEM\CurrentControlSet\Services\RemoteAccess\Parameters\NetBIOSGateway key. If you set this value to 2, remote clients look just like those connected directly to the network.

Warning

If you have several systems connected to the RAS server at once, the traffic associated with this procedure may be overwhelming. Also, the resources required to manage those connections may be significant. Limiting the number of connections reduces the overhead.

Traffic on a network is always a concern. If there is too much traffic, the normal packets to be transferred will be extremely slow. You can watch your traffic with Network Monitor, SMS, or other tools from third-party vendors.

Solutions

When I connect to my server from NT Workstation, I don't always get my share connections. When I browse, I can find them, and when I activate the programs that use the connections, they work, but they are slow. Why?

Even if you select to reconnect at logon, the network shares are sometimes not available. The system that is sharing them might be busy. The browse server might be busy, and the browse master wouldn't be able to give them to you. You should consider adding another browser server, if it happens too often. As an added help, you can force your system to keep trying.

Instead of making a cursory attempt at finding the shares, it will keep trying until it either verifies the shares, or verifies that the shares are not available.

In `HKEY_LOCAL_MACHINE\SYSTEM\CurrentControlSet\Control\NetworkProvider`, there should be a `REG_DWORD` value called `RestoreConnection`. If it is not there, add it.

Set the `RestoreConnection` value to `1` to ensure the connections are restored.

If it seems that your connections take too long, you could set `RestoreConnection` to `0`, and then it would ghost the connections and only actually connect when they are needed.

Some of the entries that are in the Registry are designed for specific uses. In some cases, there are ways to use a change in the Registry to achieve a particular function that it was not necessarily designed for. The next tip is one of those.

Solutions

I need to do some maintenance on the servers. Can I disconnect my network users so it forces them to log off the network?

There is an option to force users off the network after a preset time of no activity, and you could possibly use that as an alternative.

If a user is connected to your network without activity for too long, this can indicate a potential security threat. Other users can use the system without the logon requirement. A good way to ensure that users log off their systems when they leave them is to set up automatic disconnection. The system recognizes the idle time and, after a preset period, disconnects the idle user.

Another circumstance in which this Solution becomes handy is in an environment where you have more users than IP addresses in your DHCP server. Users get an IP address from DHCP only when they connect to the network. When a user disconnects, the IP address goes back into the pool to be allocated to another. If someone forgets to disconnect, the IP address is used for an idle system, and thus is essentially wasted.

continues

continued

Add a new value to `HKEY_LOCAL_MACHINE\System\CurrentControlSet\Services\LanmanServer\Parameters` to the server. The new value name is `AutoDisconnect`, a `REG_SZ` entry.

The range of the data is 0–4294967295 (`0xffffffff`) in minutes. That is over 4 *billion* minutes, or over 8,171 years! If a user hasn't disconnected by then, he probably won't notice if you do it for him.

Setting `AutoDisconnect` to `0` does not turn it off, but rather it sets the disconnect for 0 minutes. As soon as you log on and take a deep breath, you get disconnected. If you need to make sure everyone is off the system, you could set it to 0. Then, to activate the setting, you need to restart the server. As soon as it restarts, every user would be disconnected.

Some may say that idleness is a curse. Of course, there are reasons to be idle on the network, and that is OK. It is when the connection is taken and not being used that it is frustrating for the technical support staff. On the other hand, getting disconnected because of no traffic is a real hassle if you are doing so many things at once that you miss using a connection because you took a moment too long to return to the dial-up connection.

Solutions

How can I change the amount of time my RAS server waits before disconnecting idle users?

It is important to remove idle users from RAS connections so others can use the connections. The waiting time is set in `HKEY_LOCAL_MACHINE\SYSTEM\CurrentControlSet\Services\RemoteAccess\Parameters`, in the `AutoDisconnect` value.

The range is 0–60000 minutes, with the default of 20 (minutes). Setting it to 0 disables `AutoDisconnect`.

Netware IPX and Microsoft NWLink use three different types of identification numbers to allow communication across the network. The IPX/NWLink client uses its MAC address (the physical address of the network card) so others can communicate with it. The server uses two different types of addresses, an internal network number (also called a virtual network number), and an external network number. There has been a great amount of confusion regarding this.

The internal, or virtual, network number is a number assigned to a server that uses IPX/SPX or NWLink as a communications protocol. It's basically the identifier or address of that server that makes it unique in a multiple-server environment. That address is how the rest of the systems know which server sent the information.

The external network number is the network or segment number. Each segment on a multisegment network has its own external network number. In a server with multiple network cards attached to different segments, each card is assigned its own external network number.

The next three questions reference these numbers.

Solutions

I am having trouble seeing my NetWare servers during a browse from Windows NT. What's going on?

Windows NT automatically sets the internal network number for NWLink. Set to zero, the system generates a unique, random number to use as its internal network number. The setting in the Control Panel to change the number is available only if more than one network card is installed.

Setting the number manually may be required if the system cannot see the server during a browse. It may also be required if you choose to use multiple frame types on a single adapter, if you have bound NWLink to multiple adapters on your system, or if your computer is acting as a Windows NT server for an application that uses the NetWare Service Advertising Protocol (SAP), such as SQL Server or Systems Network Architecture (SNA) Server.

Manually set the number in `HKEY_LOCAL_MACHINE\SYSTEM\CurrentControlSet\Services\NwlnkIpx\Parameters`. The value name is `VirtualNetworkNumber`.

Use the number that the NetWare network administrator creates. The number must be an 8-digit hexadecimal number, for example, `abcd1234`. (It can actually be any 8-digit hexadecimal number, as long as it is the same at the workstation as it is at the NetWare server.) When using the DWORD Editor, make sure that Hex is selected as the data type, and type the new number. The only time to manually set the internal network number is if the system cannot automatically do so itself.

Warning

After you set the number in the Registry, return to the Control Panel. If the NWLink IPX/SPX Protocol Configuration dialog box is opened and if you click on OK to confirm, the number resets to zero. If you cancel, the number is left alone.

Here is another question that is closely related.

Solutions

I am running Windows NT, connected to a NetWare server. I can send data to everyone on my segment, but I cannot send anything to the other segment. What should I do?

When there is more than one segment on a network running NWLink, each segment must have a unique external network number, or number for that segment. When traffic moves from one segment to the other, this number, which identifies where the data came from, is part of the header in the packet.

The key where the changes will take place is `HKEY_LOCAL_MACHINE\SYSTEM\CurrentControlSet\Services\NWLnkIPX\NetConfig\`*`adapter name`*.

Because each segment could be using a different frame type, you must set two values, `NetworkNumber` and `PktType`, for each frame type.

The `PktType` settings are listed in Table 21.3 for your convenience.

Table 21.3. Possible values for `PktType`.

Value	*Frame Type*
`0`	Ethernet II
`1`	Ethernet 802.2
`2`	Ethernet 802.3
`3`	Ethernet SNAP
`4`	Arcnet
`ff`	Auto Detect

`NetworkNumber` is a `REG_MULTI_SZ` entry, and the numbers correspond with the values in `PktType`.

Enter an 8-digit hexadecimal number as a `NetworkNumber` value for each corresponding `PktType`. To obtain the number entered as a `NetworkNumber`, run the `IPXROUTE CONFIG` command from the command prompt on a working system, or look in the `Autoexec.ncf` file at a NetWare server that is on the same segment.

The next question is very similar, except that the two networks are connected to two separate network cards.

Solutions

I am trying to access two different IPX networks on two different network adapters from my NT Server. I can't seem to get the systems on both segments to communicate with each other. What should I do?

If you are running more than one segment, and if each segment is attached to its own network card, you can make them all communicate with each other by changing the Registry. Each card shows under `NWLink\NetConfig` independently. Using the preceding same functions (`NetworkNumber` and `PktType`), you can set the external network number for each card.

By default, both networks would use the same frame type. Change the frame types as required, as shown in Table 21.3, and enter the corresponding network numbers.

Directory Services Manager for NetWare allows you to manage all of the NetWare servers in a network from a Windows NT domain. The users and groups all get centralized into one list, and it is extremely easy to manage. The next question relates to setting it up correctly.

Solutions

How do I add NetWare 4.*x* servers to Directory Services Manager for NetWare?

Directory Service Manager for NetWare (DSMN) enables NT to pull NetWare servers into the NT domain. All the users and groups become part of the domain, and the server stays running, but no NetWare client is required. A simple logon from the NT PDC allows access. With NT 4.0, the client (CSNW) and gateway (GSNW) support NetWare 4.*x* servers directly. DSMN talks to them only if they are running in bindery emulation (making them look like a 3.*x* server).

However, when you try to connect to a NetWare 4.*x* server, even if you are running them in bindery emulation, you will get an error that prevents you from connecting. Make this change to make the connection work:

In `HKEY_LOCAL_MACHINE\SYSTEM\CurrentControlSet\Services\MSSYNC\Parameters`, add a value named `Allow4X`, as a `REG_DWORD` value.

Set the `Allow4X` value to `1`, and the system running DSMN will recognize NetWare 4.*x* servers running in bindery emulation.

Because Macintosh clients do not have a native client for Windows networking, all the translation must be done at the server. This may put a tremendous load on the server. If you are going to use Macintosh clients, consider dedicating a server on the NT network just for them. Then make the settings necessary to make the Macintosh clients perform as well as they can.

Solutions

How can I boost the performance for my Macintosh clients?

When the server is set up to use services for Macintosh, those Mac clients can use an NTFS volume (or part of one) as a network share. The shared directories are still available to the standard Windows and DOS clients, which allows for easy sharing of data.

The biggest challenge is the performance of the client functions for the Macintosh. Extending the amount of RAM and the amount of paging file space allocated for the Macintosh services is a tremendous boon to performance.

Be aware, though, that whenever more resources are allocated to a particular service, they are removed from another. Make sure you have enough RAM and paging file space to accommodate all requirements.

In `HKEY_LOCAL_MACHINE\SYSTEM\CurrentControlSet\Services\MacFile\Parameters`, add the value name `PagedMemLimit`, a `REG_DWORD` entry, to extend the default size of the paging file allocated to Macintosh services.

To extend the amount of RAM allocated, add the `REG_DWORD` value named `NonPagedMemLimit`.

The default for `PagedMemLimit` is `20000` kilobytes (about 20MB). It can be set to any amount from 1000–256000 (kilobytes, in decimal).

The default for `NonPagedMemLimit` is `4000` (approximately 4MB of RAM). Allocate any amount from 256–16000 (256KB–16MB).

If you extend the amount of the paging file and RAM, your Macintosh performance should go up.

Summary

Customization is simply making things work the way you want them to. There are many options in Windows 95 and Windows NT to make them perform the way you would like them to, either as a server or as a client. To go beyond that, you will need to edit the Registry to create the optimum networking environment.

Part VI

Part VI
Part VI
Part VI
Part VI
Part VI
Part VI
Part VI
Part VI
Part VI
Part VI
Part VI

User Control and the Registry

CHAPTER 22

How the Registry Controls Windows Users

The Registry plays a critical role in how a networked user can access Windows 95 and Windows NT. It controls who has access to the system, how the process works, the automation of the logon process, and the connection to other systems on a network. The Registry also controls the interface, what it looks like, which icons are used, the fonts, the colors, the toolbars, the menus, and even the responsiveness of the windows. It even controls the applications, access to those applications, and how the applications will work.

The Registry is like the hand in a glove. Without the hand, the glove does have some definition, some form. Depending on the hand that is in the glove, however, it can be radically different. Not only will the Registry bring life to the system, but how you modify and customize the Registry is what brings art to the process. Your systems can be as radical or as conservative as you want them to be. Given time, our systems mirror our attitudes and outlooks on life.

Controlling Access to the System

Earlier chapters discussed the process of networking and how it requires the Registry for network access and security. You get to choose whether you will set up the system for a single user or for multiple users, and how much security you will have toward this local machine.

The choices regarding network access are covered in previous chapters, but they are similar to the challenge of access to a single machine. In Windows NT, for example, a logon is required. The logon can be to the network, or just to the local machine. In either case, a user name and password are required. The settings in the Registry are in hidden hives that cannot be accessed through the Registry, but access to the system is controlled by it.

In Windows 95, you have the choice of setting up your system so it requires a logon to access the system. Unfortunately, this safeguard is easily defeated because of virtually unpluggable holes in the Registry.

Controlling the Interface

The Windows interface is what you see when you start Windows. It may be as simple as the default Explorer icons and menus, or as different as Program Manager in its new clothes. It can be as simple as the DOS prompt or as advanced as Norton NT Tools. Whatever the case, you use the interface to interact with the computer, and it is your responsibility to make it reflect, as much as possible, who you are and how you like to work.

You can do that by choosing all of the following:

- Interface application
- Icons
- Fonts
- Colors
- Window properties
- Toolbars
- Menus

Nearly all of the choices you make are in the Control Panel, with a few reserved exclusively for the Registry. Even when the choices are made in the Control Panel, they end up in the Registry. Some take effect immediately upon application, such as icon fonts in Explorer, and others require logoff and logon to activate. The icon fonts in Program Manager work that way. The greater complexity of the Registry allows greater customization than was possible with the `.INI` files.

Microsoft refers to the current level of interface as the "WIMP" interface, an acronym (of course!) that stands for Windows, Icons, Mouse, and Pointer. They are working on new options for the interface that will make it even easier, more secure, and faster. All of those, regardless of the nature of the interface, will also be controlled by the Registry. Though the current interface would have been possible, though difficult, using `WIN.INI`, voice activation wouldn't, and neither would some other systems that simply use hand movement without touching the screen. Voice activation, for example, is currently done with Windows 3.x by using its own `.INI` files (which are limited to 64KB each), limiting the scope and the integration of the operations. With a hierarchical database of extremely large capacity, voice activation could be integrated more fully into the operating system and security, have a broader vocabulary, and allow for more performance.

Note

NT 5.0 will be available in beta within a very short time. One of the most widely speculated portions of it has to do with the interface. The new interface is called "Active Desktop," where there is a seamless integration between the information on the local disk drives, the network drives, and the Internet. After all, do we really care where it is, as long as we can get to it?

Well, actually, yes we do. It all comes down to a question of trust. Do I trust someone whom I have never met, someone who may have different goals, values and agendas, someone who can destroy with one keystroke all of my information? If we do not care if our sensitive data is out of our control, it means that the data is actually not very sensitive at all. When it comes to programs, I also care where they are, and I want them local as much as possible. Until data transfer rates get much faster than they are now, I have no desire to launch Excel across the Internet with my current telephone line connection.

As for the look and feel, many remark as to the "dumbing down" of the interface. It will be very similar to a Web browser. The buttons across the top help us navigate the functions we need to use. The address space allows us to jump to any location, whether local, on our network, or across the Internet. It will also allow us to search all of our files from one location, regardless of the file's location.

Will you like it? I can't say. Some of you will, some won't, and some will avoid the issue altogether.

Application Access and Use

Using applications in Windows is easier and faster than ever before. Basic functions haven't changed much, but the amount and scope of things we ask the computer to do would have crippled systems just a few years ago. The complexity of the applications has brought features that we only dreamt of in the past. Now our dreams are a little different. We not only want the power, but we want it to be extremely fast and reliable.

The sheer number of entries that new applications make in the Registry is staggering, and unfortunately, the law of averages quickly catches up, and we have more errors than we should. Even if the entries are correct on a basic system, how does the programmer know they will be right on a highly modified system? Many times, he or she has to assume, and an assumption that makes perfect sense in a cubicle in Redmond or San Jose or Boston may not work at all in the rest of the country, much less the rest of the world.

The problem, then, becomes not one of making assumptions and setting entries into the Registry, but one of the lack of documentation and distribution of those entries. You either need to make installation programs take twice as long because of the surveying required, or you need to have the ability to change the settings after the application is installed, or preferably both.

Without adequate documentation into the Registry changes an application makes, you can only hope to do the best you can.

Another challenge associated with the Registry and the installation and use of applications today is who gets to use the program after it is installed. If you install an application under a specific user, will others also get to use it? If you set it so everyone can use it, do you have the ability to restrict access to it if you need to?

Summary

There is still much that could be done to make user functions better. Fortunately, the Registry composition and design allow for the kind of changes that are necessary. The next five chapters discuss the Registry's role in the interface in significant detail. If you apply the information that is in them to your system, not only will it work better, but it will more closely reflect your personality as well.

CHAPTER 23

Windows NT 4 Users and the Registry

Windows NT 4.0 users are controlled through the Registry and through user profiles. User information in the Registry is stored in the NTUSER.DAT file in the user's profile folder.

User Profiles

User profile information is stored in %systemroot%\profiles\%username%. The menu information is held there, as well as options and desktop icons. Inside each profile are the startup applications, the folders for Network Neighborhood, and other lists of information.

The most important ones to notice are the Default User profile and the All Users profile. The Default User profile is the template for all new users. Whatever is set there will be duplicated when a new user logs onto the system. If you want to give every new user the same Send To menu, you could change it in the Default User profile folder. Any changes to the .DEFAULT user in HKEY_CURRENT_USERS in the Registry get saved in the NTUSER.DAT file in the Default User profile folder.

The All Users profile is new to NT 4.0. It doesn't have an NTUSER.DAT file, so the only information that can be used for all users is the menu and folder information. The real benefit of the All Users profile is in the installation of software. Previously, any software that was installed worked only for the user who installed it, but now programmers can set their applications so the installation will update the All Users profile. When a user logs onto Windows NT, it pulls the information from the user's profile, plus all the information from the All Users profile.

Registry Settings

There are several locations that control how the user will work in Windows NT 4.0. Software that is installed changes HKEY_LOCAL_MACHINE and may also affect HKEY_CURRENT_USER. Operating system installation and features affect HKEY_LOCAL_MACHINE, but the settings for the desktop affect HKEY_CURRENT_USER. The entries in this chapter are categorized into the following sections.

Operating system basic functions
Connections
Generic Windows functions
User preferences on the desktop
Software settings in HKEY_CURRENT_USER

By looking in each of the sections, you will get a good idea how Microsoft designed the user functions in the Registry, and where you will need to look to aid in your troubleshooting.

Operating System Basic Functions

The settings for Windows NT basic functions are in HKEY_LOCAL_MACHINE\SOFTWARE\Microsoft\Windows NT\CurrentVersion. It covers all the settings necessary for NT to work on this system. Even though none of the settings are user-dependent, many of them still affect the users and how they work.

One of the most important functions to see is the HKEY_LOCAL_MACHINE\SOFTWARE\Microsoft\Windows NT\CurrentVersion\Fonts key. In the Fonts key, Microsoft lists all the fonts that are available to the user. Normally, you would make changes in the Fonts applet in the Control Panel. However, if you lose your font metrics, which match the screen font to the printer font, you might need to restore this key. Also, it is a good place to look to see where the actual font file is located. Putting the font in the actual Fonts folder instead of making a shortcut there saves space in the Registry, speeds up the performance of the system, and reduces errors.

Another function that is closely related to fonts is Font Substitution. There is no function in NT to specify font substitution if a font that is specified is not available. Suppose you receive a document from a friend who uses a font you do not have. NT will try to determine whether the font specified is a serif or sans-serif font, and then change the screen font to MS Serif or MS Sans Serif, respectively. If you know the problem is going to happen, you could change the font by adding a substitution yourself in HKEY_LOCAL_MACHINE\SOFTWARE\Microsoft\Windows NT\CurrentVersion\FontSubstitutes.

Tip

One day I was presented with a problem that I needed to fix in a hurry. I had a CorelDRAW! document, a form, that had 185 separate boxes with text in them. The text was 5-point Palatino, a TrueType font. When I printed it, it looked terrible, even though it looked great on the screen.

When TrueType fonts are used below 6 points, they do not align well unless the font is installed in the printer as a built-in font. I knew Times New Roman was a built-in font in the HP LaserJet, so all I needed to do was replace the Palatino font with the Times New Roman. But there were 185 instances. Currently, CorelDRAW! allows a font substitution function in its versions, but it did not in that version. There were no styles to work with, as in my word processor.

To fix the problem, I added a value to my HKEY_LOCAL_MACHINE\SOFTWARE\Microsoft\Windows NT\CurrentVersion\FontSubstitutes key, replacing Palatino with Times New Roman, and then I removed Palatino from the Fonts folder. When I logged off and back on again, Palatino was replaced, and the document printed perfectly. It took less than five minutes to fix a problem that could have taken hours to change in the document.

For 16-bit Windows compatibility and for other .INI file connections, see HKEY_LOCAL_MACHINE\SOFTWARE\Microsoft\Windows NT\CurrentVersion\IniFileMapping. If there is a problem with an application that is a 16-bit Windows application, you may be able to trace it with the information here. If you make a change in the Registry for a specific application, and the change doesn't stick, you might look here to see if there is an .INI file also. In many cases, .INI files write information into the Registry. You need to make the change in both places, if that is the case.

Other functions related to the use of NT are also in the `Windows NT\CurrentVersion` key. Familiarize yourself with the key, so if you have problems to solve, you will know where to look.

Connections

Functions relating to logging on to Windows NT and connecting to the network are located in `HKEY_LOCAL_MACHINE\SOFTWARE\Microsoft\Windows NT\CurrentVersion\Winlogon`. This key stores the current user name, the domain or workgroup name, the shell name, and much more. If the problem is in logging on, this is the first place to look.

Tip

If you have logged onto a domain, and then switched to another domain, there may be some confusion as people look in the domain name section in the logon screen. Both domain names will show, along with the machine name. If you no longer want the original domain name to show, remove it from the value named `DCache` in the `HKEY_LOCAL_MACHINE\SOFTWARE\Microsoft\Windows NT\CurrentVersion\Winlogon` key.

Generic Windows Functions

How the Windows functions will work are in the `HKEY_LOCAL_MACHINE\SOFTWARE\Microsoft\Windows\CurrentVersion` key. This key is the same in Windows NT 4.0 as it is in Windows 95. Applications can use this key to set up how the windows in their applications will work.

Tip

Want to get rid of the Inbox from your desktop? You can do it by removing the key that is used to tell Explorer to put it there. The key that controls the icon is in `HKEY_LOCAL_MACHINE\SOFTWARE\Microsoft\Windows\CurrentVersion\Explorer\Desktop\NameSpace`. There are actually three keys there, one for the Inbox, one for the Recycle Bin, and one for the Internet. Removing the icon only changes how the system looks. The Inbox icon just allows you to install the Windows Messaging System, the Recycle Bin icon allows you to easily undelete files you have sent there, and the Internet icon allows you to install Internet Explorer. Once the Internet Explorer is installed, the icon changes, as does the Inbox function. I would be very hesitant to delete the Recycle bin. You can still delete things to the bin, but you must go to the Recycler directory in `Explorer.exe` to retrieve files. Also, all the files are shown in a bin named after the SID of the user.

A great key in the HKEY_LOCAL_MACHINE\SOFTWARE\Microsoft\Windows\CurrentVersion is Run. When an application is loaded there, it will start during the startup of the system. The difference between this and using the Startup folder in the user profile is that this works for anyone using the system, and it requires a Registry change to take it out.

If the data you seek isn't in the Windows NT key, check here, in the HKEY_LOCAL_MACHINE\SOFTWARE\Microsoft\Windows\CurrentVersion key, particularly if the same function works in both NT and 95.

User Preferences on the Desktop

The icon font, the wallpaper, the screen saver, and other preferences are stored on a user-by-user basis in HKEY_CURRENT_USER\Control Panel\Desktop. Though most are normally changed through the Control Panel, you can easily use the location for remote editing and for custom templates in System Policy Editor.

Software Settings in HKEY_CURRENT_USER

The Software key in HKEY_CURRENT_USER is used as a registration function for the software. It provides information for the application to use for the user who has logged onto the network or the local system. If you want an application to work for a user, in many cases, it will require a listing in this key. The difference between the information in this key and that in the HKEY_LOCAL_MACHINE\Software key is that the information HKEY_CURRENT_USER is specific to the user who is going to use the application. In the case of Pinball, for example, there are user options in the program for customization of the table, the keys, and so on. Those are only for the current user. If someone else logs on, the options will return to the default.

Summary

The functions that control and enable users in Windows NT are extensive and complex. By understanding the locations of the Registry entries, and the types of information in each, you can better troubleshoot the problems users might have in working with NT, applications, and system preferences.

CHAPTER 24

Windows NT 3.51 Users and the Registry

The Control Panel was one of the biggest changes in the move from NT 3.51 to NT 4.0. With NT 3.51, most of the user changes to the desktop had to be made in the Registry because there wasn't the level of control in Control Panel. Nearly all of the functions in HKEY_LOCAL_MACHINE, HKEY_CLASSES_ROOT, HKEY_USERS, and HKEY_CURRENT_USER are exactly the same in both versions. Nearly all the Registry changes that can be made to the system in NT 4.0 can also be made in NT 3.51, and the opposite is also true. The biggest difference in the versions is the Explorer interface. When it comes to the Registry, though, most is the same.

The biggest difference is in HKEY_CURRENT_USER\Control Panel\Desktop. Rather than having a location in the Control Panel Desktop applet for changing the fonts, for example, you need to do it directly in the Registry. The same is true for many other items as well.

Because NT 3.51 also does not accept policies, if you want to change things like the Legal Notice Caption and Text in HKEY_LOCAL_MACHINE\Software\Microsoft\CurrentVersion\Winlogon, you must do it manually.

Also, because NT 3.51 uses Program Manager and File Manager, the settings relating to Explorer do not apply.

Display Attributes

Changing the display attributes in the Windows NT 3.51 Control Panel is very limited. In the Display applet, the only things you can change are the display drivers, resolution, and the number of colors. In the Desktop applet, you have more choices, but still there are limitations. In the Desktop applet, you can change the wallpaper, background patterns, screen savers, and horizontal icon spacing. In the Colors applet, you can change the colors of many of the desktop items, but not all of them.

But what if you want to change the icon font, or even the icon vertical spacing? In order to make those changes, you would need to edit the Registry directly.

The icon font characteristics are set in HKEY_CURRENT_USER\Control Panel\Desktop. Figure 24.1 shows the Desktop key. The font name is in the IconTitleFaceName value.

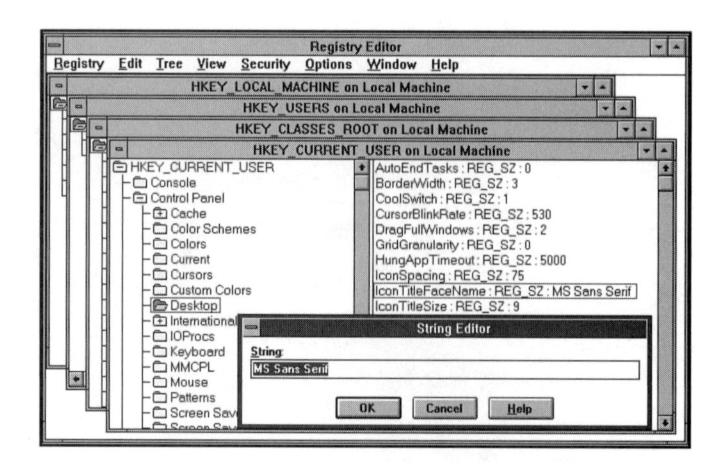

Figure 24.1.
The Desktop key holds the values for icon fonts.

By changing the IconTitleFaceName value in the Registry, you can choose whichever font you would like.

Warning

If you misspell the name of the font, or the font is not available in your system, the system will revert back to MS Sans Serif. Use caution when entering the font name.

You can also change the size of the font with IconTitleSize. The entry is in points. Each point is one-twelfth of an inch. If the current size is too small, experiment with larger values. This is particularly helpful when using screen resolutions of 800x600 and larger.

If you want to change the vertical spacing of the icons, add the value IconVerticalSpacing (a REG_SZ entry) and experiment with numbers. The current spacing, by default, is 75 pixels.

Should I Stay with NT 3.51?

Are there features that would make me want to upgrade to NT 4.0? Absolutely, but they are mostly related to the interface, as a user. The estimates that Microsoft has touted concerning productivity gains seem a little inflated, but only a little. Printing in a multiple-platform environment is also greatly enhanced.

Stability is the main reason to stay with NT 3.51. It is very stable and will almost never crash. A rogue video driver can kill an NT 4.0 machine, but will hardly cause a ripple in the performance and stability of a 3.51 machine.

Tip

A great value to add to the Registry is in the HKEY_LOCAL_MACHINE\Software\Microsoft\Windows NT\CurrentVersion\Winlogon key. Add the value AutoRestartShell as a DWORD value, and set the value to 1.

Occasionally, the Program Manager fails, leaving Windows NT running, with no way to access it. The background remains with no icons or windows. There is no way to restart Program Manager except to log off and log back on again. With the AutoRestartShell entry, it will automatically restart if it ever happens to your system.

Summary

Use the hardware settings, the network settings, and the non–Explorer-based settings that are given for NT 4.0, and for NT 3.51. By editing the Registry, you won't get the flash, but you can make your system work better and have more control over how it will work.

CHAPTER 25

Windows 95 Users and the Registry

Knowing the locations of the Registry settings for users is the most critical part of troubleshooting user problems in the Registry. Windows 95 still uses the `WIN.INI` and `SYSTEM.INI` files for information, even for 32-bit functions. You will need to familiarize yourself with the Registry locations as well. As an upgrade to Windows for Workgroups, Windows 95 is fabulous, the administrator has many more options for control, and the user has countless options for customization.

Operating System Basic Functions

The settings for Windows 95 basic functions are in `HKEY_LOCAL_MACHINE\SOFTWARE\Microsoft\Windows\CurrentVersion`. Many system-specific settings required for 95 are also there. These settings are not usually user-dependent, but even so, much of it still affects the users and how they work.

Like NT, the `HKEY_LOCAL_MACHINE\SOFTWARE\Microsoft\Windows\CurrentVersion\Fonts` key is one of the most important keys in the system. In the `Fonts` key, Microsoft lists all the fonts that are available to the user. Normally, you would make changes in the Fonts applet in the Control Panel. However, if you lose your font metrics, which matches the screen font to the printer font, you might need to restore this key. Also, it is a good place to look to see where the actual font file is located. Putting the font in the actual Fonts folder, instead of making a shortcut, saves space in the Registry, speeds up the performance of the system, and reduces errors.

Applications

The Registry in Windows 95 is very similar in structure to the Windows NT Registry. One of the main differences is in the location of entries. Of course, one of the main reasons to have `HKEY_CLASSES_ROOT` and `HKEY_CURRENT_USER` is to make the process of hitting the correct entries easier for developers. It doesn't really matter where the actual entry is as long as there is a pointer to it in `HKEY_CLASSES_ROOT` and `HKEY_CURRENT_USER`. The developers only point to `HKEY_CLASSES_ROOT` and `HKEY_CURRENT_USER`.

Nearly all of the application functions are there; therefore, preparing applications for users is extremely easy. The only other component that is used in most cases is `HKEY_LOCAL_MACHINE\Software`. Because of this component, there is a demand to make it the same in both 95 and NT, in order to achieve compatibility for software. Because of these requirements, it also makes it easier for the administrator and technical support staff.

Every application that will be controlled by the Registry needs to put information into `HKEY_LOCAL_MACHINE\Software`. Normally, the installation will add a key under Software for the manufacturer. Additional keys can also be installed for the software title, the version, and any other information required to make the software work correctly.

The new keys will point to the executable files, the `.DLL` files, the settings, and the user-definable options in the applications. If you have an application that has been moved on the system to a different location other than the original installation, the pointers in the Registry will be wrong.

User Profiles

For the user, Windows 95 normally stores information in the current user's profile, the USER.DAT in the \Windows\Profiles directory. The \Windows\Profiles directory is maintained if there are multiple profiles set up, or if the user logs onto a domain for user validation. If there is only one user, the USER.DAT file will be stored in the \Windows directory.

Inside the USER.DAT file, there are settings for the user to be able to customize the interface, select the keyboard layout, and many other options. That information is accessed through the HKEY_CURRENT_USER handle key in the Registry. Figure 25.1 shows the keys in HKEY_CURRENT_USER in REGEDIT.EXE.

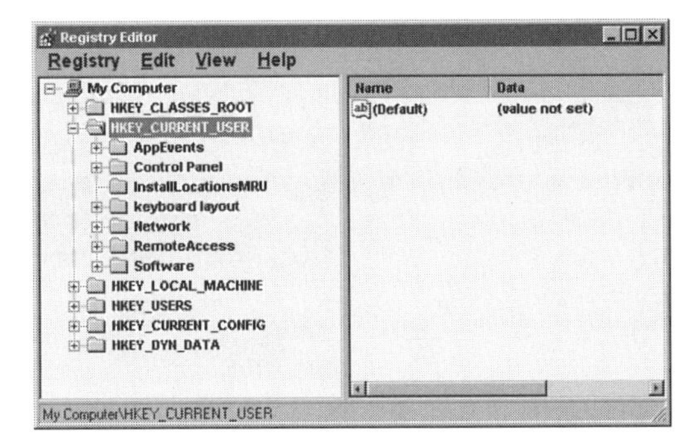

Figure 25.1.
User functions in HKEY_CURRENT_USER.

Connections

Functions relating to logging on to Windows 95 or to the network are located in the HKEY_LOCAL_MACHINE\SYSTEM\CurrentControlSet\Services\MSNP32\NetworkProvider and HKEY_LOCAL_MACHINE\Network\Logon keys. These keys store the current username, the domain or workgroup name, the shell name, and much more. If the problem is in logging on, this is the first place to look. There is still a HKEY_LOCAL_MACHINE\SOFTWARE\Microsoft\Windows\CurrentVersion\Winlogon key, but it doesn't have any values in it, and it doesn't do anything.

Generic Windows Functions

How Windows functions will work are in the HKEY_LOCAL_MACHINE\SOFTWARE\Microsoft\Windows\CurrentVersion key. This key is the same in Windows NT 4.0 as it is in Windows 95. Applications can use this key to set up how the windows in their applications will work.

Just like in Windows NT, you can get rid of the Inbox from your desktop by removing the key that is used to tell Explorer to put it there. The key is in HKEY_LOCAL_MACHINE\SOFTWARE\Microsoft\Windows\CurrentVersion\Explorer\Desktop\NameSpace. There are actually four keys there in Windows 95: one for the Inbox, one for the Recycle Bin, one for the Internet, and one for the Microsoft Network. Removing the icon only changes how the system looks. The Inbox button allows you to install the Windows Messaging System, the Recycle Bin allows you to easily undelete files you have sent there, and the Internet button allows you to install Internet

Explorer. Once Internet Explorer is installed, the icon changes, as does the Inbox function. Be very careful about deleting the Recycle bin. You can still delete things to the bin, but you must go to the Recycler directory in `Explorer.exe` to retrieve files. Also, all the files are shown in a bin named after the SID of the user.

Another great key in the `HKEY_LOCAL_MACHINE\SOFTWARE\Microsoft\Windows\CurrentVersion` is `Run`. When an application is loaded there, it will start during the startup of the system. The difference between this and using the Startup folder in the user profile is that this works for anyone using the system, and it requires a Registry change to take it out.

Windows 95 has a key that is very different from the ones in Windows NT. In the `HKEY_LOCAL_MACHINE\SOFTWARE\Microsoft\Windows\CurrentVersion\RunServices` key, you can set up services to run at startup that are not normally part of the system. In Windows NT, the services are all loaded the same way, at startup, so there is no need for this key.

User Preferences on the Desktop

The icon font, the wallpaper, the screen saver, and other preferences are stored on a user-by-user basis in `HKEY_CURRENT_USER\Control Panel\Desktop`. Though these are normally changed through the Control Panel, you can easily use the location for remote editing and for custom templates in System Policy Editor.

Summary

Working with Windows 95 users can be complex, because of the myriad of locations that store the entries. If you know where to look, you can certainly find the settings. Remember, though, that some information is still stored in `WIN.INI` and `SYSTEM.INI`. Use the Find command to help you troubleshoot the challenges users might run into working with Windows 95, applications, and system preferences.

CHAPTER 26

Troubleshooting and Configuring User Registry Settings

If no one ever touched computers after they were set up, they would probably never fail. Then again, not much work would get done. That user component makes the computer work, but it can also cause problems. Some of the changes users make are accidental, and occasionally, some are malicious. Most of the time the changes are based on doing things the users think will be beneficial, and then they find out later that there are side effects that no one warned them about.

Even though there are many settings for users in the Registry, not many of them are so critical to the workings of the system that you cannot keep the system going. Most of the changes that you need to make are based on preferences.

User settings are in separate files from the rest of the Registry. In Windows 95, the settings are stored in `C:\Windows\USER.DAT` if User Profiles are not set up. If they are, the user settings will be unique for every user who logs onto the machine, and each will have a `USER.DAT` file in `C:\Windows\Profiles\`*`username`*.

Setting User Preferences in the Registry

Most user settings are done through the Control Panel on a local system, and they focus on the Display and Sounds applets. The other settings nearly always come down to hardware, drivers, and applications. The display settings for both Windows 95 and Windows NT are in the `HKEY_CURRENT_USER\Control Panel\Desktop` and the `HKEY_CURRENT_USER\Control Panel\Desktop\WindowMetrics` keys. You would seldom need to edit the Registry directly, because the Control Panel gives you much more flexibility than in Windows 3.x.

Sound functions for both 95 and NT are in the `HKEY_CURRENT_USER\Control Panel\Sound` and `HKEY_CURRENT_USER\Control Panel\Sounds` keys. The `Sound` key controls some of the device options specific to users, and the `Sounds` key lists the settings for the sounds. The other place where sounds are specified are in the `HKEY_CURRENT_USER\Software\Microsoft\Plus!\Themes`.

One of the locations that has made the most improvement from Windows 3.x and Windows NT 3.51 to the present interface is the Appearance tab in the Display applet in the Control Panel. In prior versions, it was necessary to make most of the interface appearance changes in the `.INI` files or in the Registry. Now you can do it with a graphic interface, both speeding up the process but also making it more reliable.

If there is a problem with user functions, they can nearly always be fixed through the conventional methods of Control Panel and User Manager for Domains (in Windows NT). The few options that lie outside the included applications require Registry changes.

Solutions

I used the NameNumericTail value, and now I can't find Exchange. What did I do wrong?

The side effect of using `NameNumericTail` is that some programs may not be able to find all of their parts and pieces and will give your errors. Windows 95 actually stores the filenames in 8.3 format, with the long filename as a comment. Some applications look for only the long filename, others only the short names.

The problem usually happens only when you use the `Program Files` location for your applications. If you install your applications in another location, it usually doesn't create a problem. The short name for `Program Files` is normally `Progra~1`. With `NameNumericTail` turned off, the name would be `Programf`. If the application looks only for `Progra~1`, then `NameNumericTail` will not work for you.

`NameNumericTail` is in the `Hkey_Local_Machine\System\CurrentControlSet\Control\FileSystem` key. If your application doesn't work now, you will need to disable or delete `NameNumericTail`, and fix the `Program Files` folder.

Rename the `Program files` folder to any name (such as "test"), and then rename it back to `Program Files`. That will restore the original `Progra~1` short filename for it.

Changing the way that Windows works may have alternative consequences that you didn't foresee. Be careful in making changes to too many systems at once. If the change becomes a problem, then you will have a great number of changes to make.

Solutions

I had shortcuts built into my SendTo folder in Windows 95. When I changed to User Profiles, all I get is the one for all users. If I change it, then all users would get the changes, and I don't want that to happen. How can I get my own SendTo folder again?

1. Create a `SendTo` folder in each user's personal folder.
2. Edit the Registry for each user to change the `SENDTO` value to point to the `SendTo` folder you created for each user. The key is `HKEY_USERS\`*`username`*`\SOFTWARE\Microsoft\Windows\CurrentVersion\Explorer\Shell Folders`.
3. Add a `SENDTO` string in the `HKEY_USERS\`*`username`*`\SOFTWARE\Microsoft\Windows\CurrentVersion\Explorer\User Shell Folders`, and then have it also point to the `SendTo` folder you created for each user.
4. Add any shortcuts you would like to that folder.

It isn't particularly difficult; it will just take a little extra time.

Sometimes, it would be nice to get to do what you want with the Explorer interface. Unfortunately, Microsoft has embedded the settings into the Registry that would be nice to change.

Solutions

When I double-click on My Computer, I want it to launch Explorer instead. How can I make it do that?

You will need to change your Registry. The function of My Computer, and all of the other icons on the desktop, is controlled by the Registry.

In either Windows 95 or Windows NT, you would do the following:

1. Open `HKEY_CLASSES_ROOT\CLSID\20D04FE0-3AEA-1069-A2D8-08002B30309D\Shell`.
2. Add a new key called `Open`.
3. In the `Open` key, add a new key called `Command`.
4. Add a value to the `Command` key as a regular string value, with no name.
5. As the string, enter `Explorer.exe`.

The next time you double-click My Computer, it will launch Explorer, and not My Computer.

If you want to make the system use My Computer again, take out the two values listed.

Explorer gives you tremendous options to work within your systems. However, it has some quirks and some characteristics that annoy many people.

Solutions

Whenever I create a new file or folder and Explorer is open, I need to either go to the end of the list of the contents to see it, or I have to press F5 to refresh. Is there a way to automatically refresh the contents of my folders?

A simple Registry change will make it happen.

Open `HKEY_LOCAL_MACHINE\System\CurrentControlSet\Control\Update`.

Edit the `UpdateMode` value, and change it to 0 in Windows NT or 00 in Windows 95.

The next time you make changes in Explorer, they will be immediate.

In Explorer, all of the icons show the applications with which they are associated. It makes it easy to differentiate different types of files, even without extensions. Some flexibility would be nice.

Solutions

How can I make the icons in Explorer for the .BMP files show a thumbnail of the file, instead of the Paint file icon?

You can change the Registry to change how the system shows icons.

1. In either 95 or NT 4.0, open `HKEY_CLASSES_ROOT\Paint.Picture\DefaultIcon`.
2. Edit the default value, and change it to `%1`.
3. Choosing Large icon in the View menu will make them easier to read.

I am not exactly sure why Microsoft didn't make the bitmap thumbnail the default, except that on an 800×600 or higher resolution, anything other than large icons is almost impossible to read.

Solutions

I removed some programs from my system, but their names still show up in the Add/Remove Programs list in Control Panel. Do I have to reinstall them, and then remove them again in order for it to remove them from the list?

No. You can edit the Registry and take them out of the list. The list is actually several keys under `HKEY_LOCAL_MACHINE\Software\Microsoft\Windows\CurrentVersion\Uninstall`. If you remove the key, you cannot use the Add/Remove Programs to uninstall the applications. I would only recommend this if, for some reason, it left the item there. Don't assume that this solution will protect you against people uninstalling applications because the application isn't there. If uninstallation is not done through Control Panel, it could cause serious damage to the system by deleting files that are in use by other programs.

This solution is exactly the same for Windows 95 and Windows NT 4.0.

Removing entries in the Registry is a little risky. You should always make a backup of the Registry before proceeding.

Solutions

In Internet Explorer, when I download things from the Internet, it asks whether I should save the .EXE file to disk or if it should just run it. There is also a selection for it not to ask me again. I told it to open the file, and never to ask me again, but I have changed my mind. How do I get the dialog box back?

continues

continued

The setting is in `HKEY_CLASSES_ROOT\Exefile` for either Windows NT or Windows 95. Change the `EditFlags` value from `d8 07 01 00` (don't ask any more) to `d8 07 00 00` (ask every time). Figure 26.1 shows the dialog box.

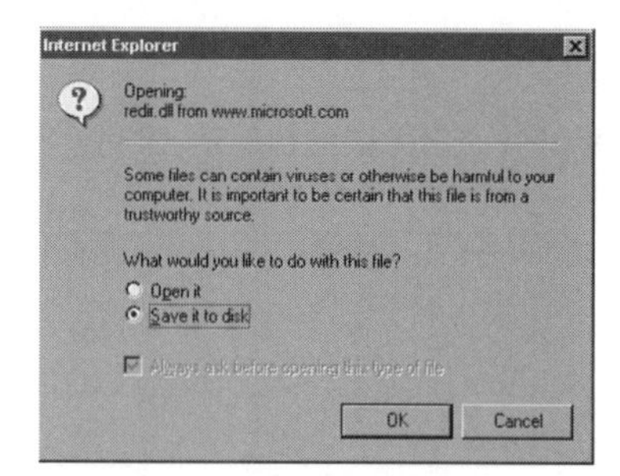

Figure 26.1.
Choosing how Internet Explorer will handle downloaded files.

Some of what you do on the Desktop is based on the Registry, and some is based on the User Profile. The next Solution is part of the Registry, whereas changing the Send To options is part of the User Profile.

Solutions

The context-sensitive menu that opens when I right-click on the Desktop or in Explorer and select New is becoming very long. I hardly ever use those functions, and I would like to get rid of them. How can I do that?

`HKEY_CLASSES_ROOT` controls all the 32-bit applications in your system. During installation, many applications add to the New menu by changing the Registry. If you don't want items in the New menu, you will need to do a little surgery on the Registry yourself.

If there is an association between a file type and an application, the Registry shows a plus sign in the folder next to the extension. Figure 26.2 shows the Registry folders indicating an association to a file type.

continues

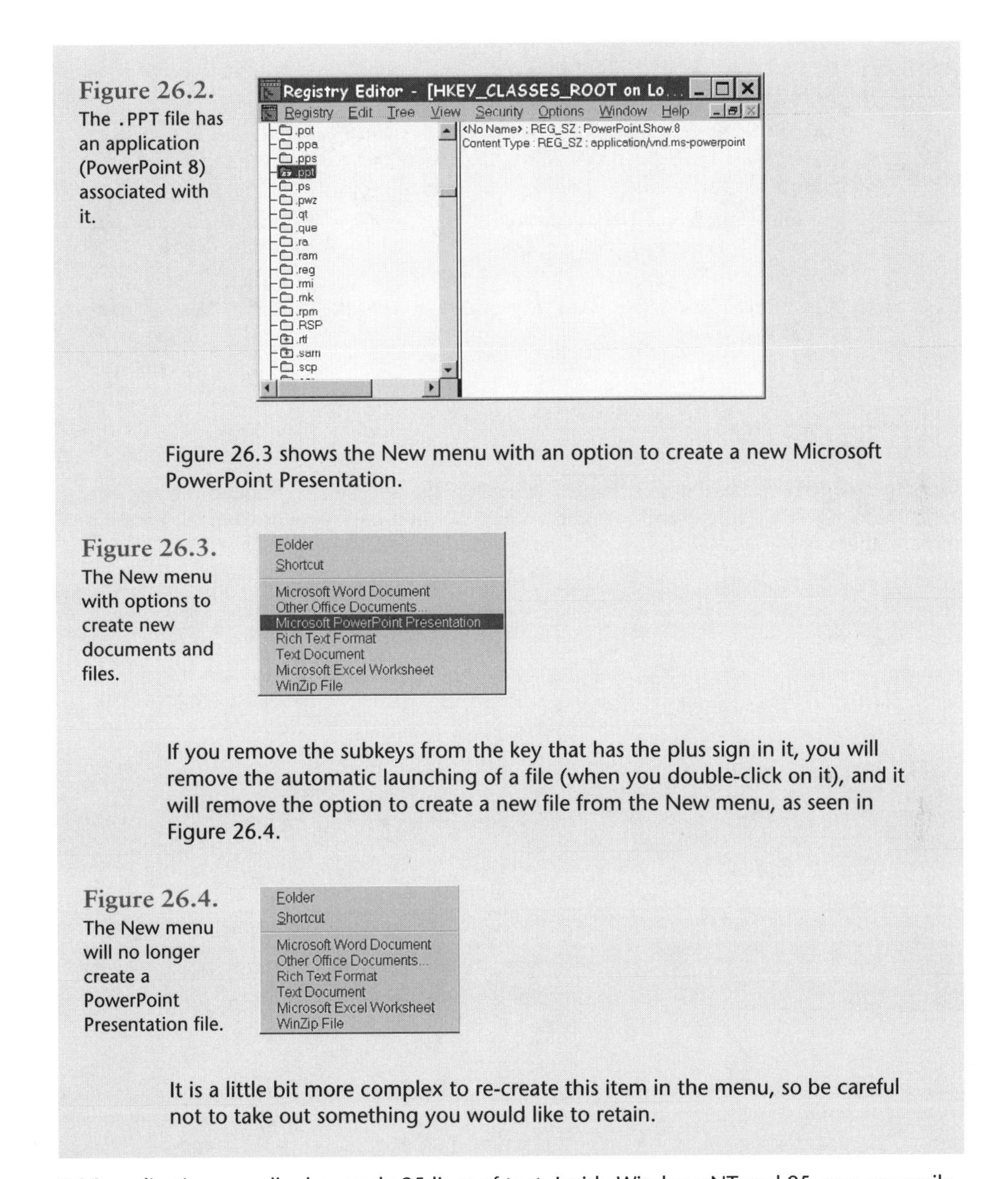

Figure 26.2.
The .PPT file has an application (PowerPoint 8) associated with it.

Figure 26.3 shows the New menu with an option to create a new Microsoft PowerPoint Presentation.

Figure 26.3.
The New menu with options to create new documents and files.

If you remove the subkeys from the key that has the plus sign in it, you will remove the automatic launching of a file (when you double-click on it), and it will remove the option to create a new file from the New menu, as seen in Figure 26.4.

Figure 26.4.
The New menu will no longer create a PowerPoint Presentation file.

It is a little bit more complex to re-create this item in the menu, so be careful not to take out something you would like to retain.

DOS applications usually show only 25 lines of text. Inside Windows NT and 95, you can easily change that with a menu option. Others aren't so nicely done.

Solutions

I want to see more lines in my Telnet session than it lets me. I also want to set it so I can see more than the 25 lines above the one I am using when I scroll up. How can I make the change?

The Telnet scroll-back buffer controls the size, and it is set to 25 lines. You need to change that, and you can set it for as many lines as you would like.

Open the Registry, and edit the `HKEY_CURRENT_USER\Software\Microsoft\Telnet` key. Edit the `Rows` value, and change it from the default of 25 to as many lines as you would like.

Summary

With the changes described in this chapter, you can make your system respond the way you expect it to. If you are careful and use wisdom, you can take back your desktop, and make it respond the way you want it to.

CHAPTER 27

Questions and Answers for Users and the Registry

The Explorer interface and user options hold one of the largest sections of things you can do with the Registry. Many items will work for both Windows 95 and Windows NT 4.0. It's like a new car. As soon as you get it, there are little things you want to do to personalize it. Some people even go wild and change it completely. You have the same options here.

Solutions

I don't really like the look of Windows 95 or NT 4.0. Can I just go back to Program Manager?

Using Program Manager in Windows 95 isn't a very good solution, because it is the 16-bit version that came in Windows for Workgroups. It does not support long filenames, and it has other serious limitations, too.

In Windows NT, though, Program Manager is the 32-bit version that came with NT 3.51. It has all the support you need and is very popular. Some users just don't like the Explorer interface. (See Figure 27.1.) Rather than stay with Windows 3.*x* or NT 3.51, simply use Program Manager. (See Figure 27.2.) It is an updated 32-bit version with the same features and an updated look. Still, it requires no additional training, and it will feel like a new pair of Hush Puppies.

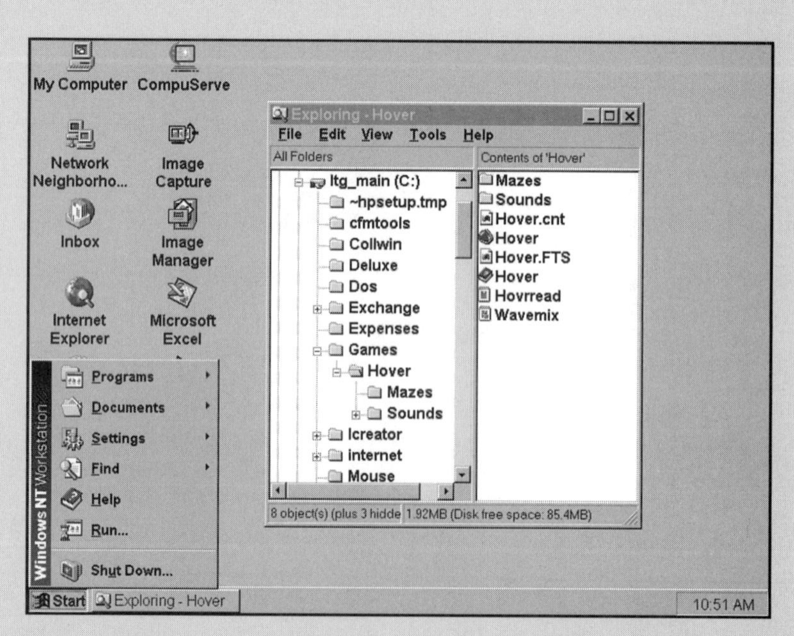

Figure 27.1. Before: The Explorer interface in Windows NT Workstation.

To change to Program Manager, open the `HKEY_LOCAL_MACHINE\SOFTWARE\Microsoft\Windows NT\CurrentVersion\Winlogon` key, and edit the `Shell` value. Enter `PROGMAN.EXE` and restart the system. Then, every time NT starts, it will use the Program Manager interface.

continues

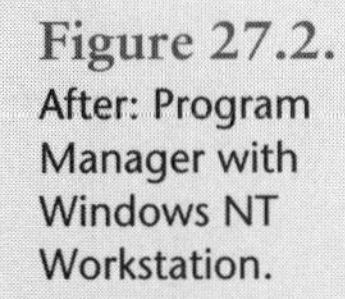

Figure 27.2.
After: Program Manager with Windows NT Workstation.

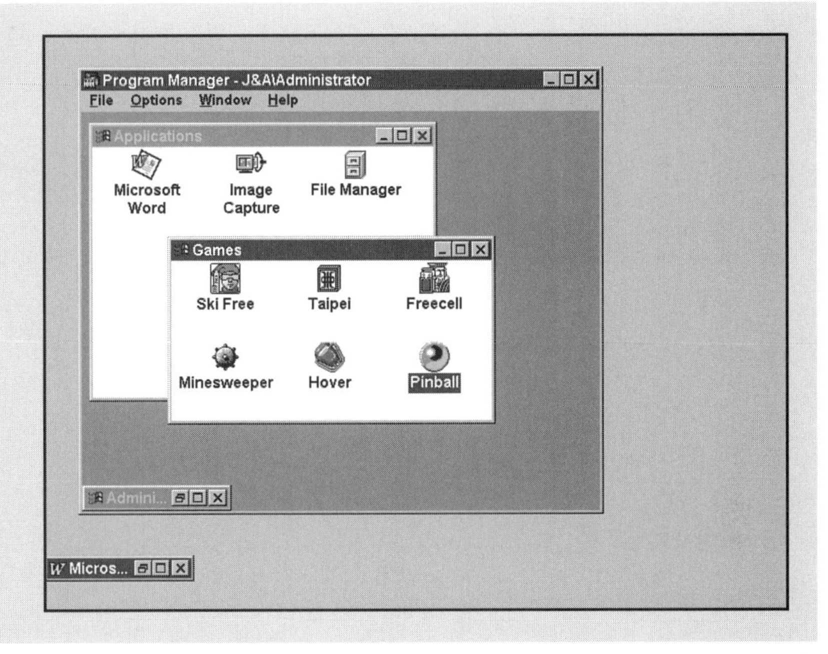

Whether they run Program Manager or Explorer, many people like to use File Manager. File Manager still ships with NT 4.0, and it is the 32-bit version, so it is powerful, stable, and easy to use. Unfortunately, it will not work on Windows 95.

Solutions

I like the new NT interface enough; I just wish I could get the old Task List back. Can I?

The Task List that you've used for years with Windows isn't anything special; it's just small, easy, and fast.

If you change to Program Manager and press Ctrl+Esc, the old Task List pops up. If you are in Explorer and you press Ctrl+Esc, you get the Start menu (as shown in Figure 27.1). But many of you already have a single key (the Windows key) that launches the Start menu.

The new Task Manager in NT 4.0 also includes a mini-Performance Monitor, statistical information, and a task list. (See Figure 27.3.)

To get the old Task List with NT 4.0, add the `TaskMan` value to `HKEY_LOCAL_MACHINE\SOFTWARE\Microsoft\Windows NT\CurrentVersion\Winlogon`. The `TaskMan` value is a `REG_SZ` entry. The data is `TASKMAN.EXE`. It is included with NT 4.0, so you don't have to copy anything.

continues

continued

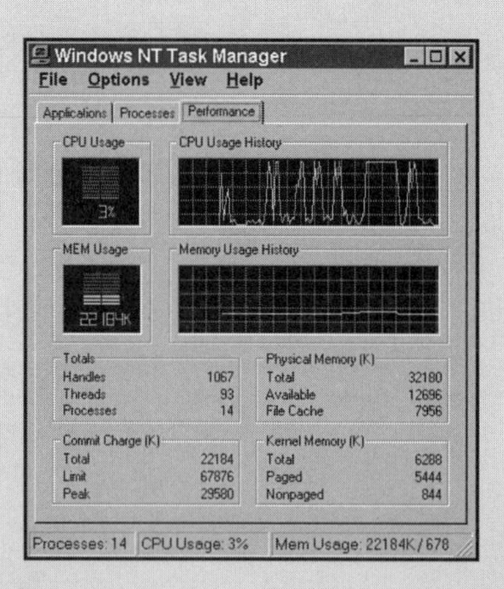

Figure 27.3. The new Task Manager showing the performance characteristics of the system.

To activate this change, log off and log on again. After logon, launch the Task List with Ctrl+Esc. (See Figure 27.4.)

Figure 27.4. The old Task List with Windows NT 4.0.

To launch Windows NT 4.0 Task Manager, with all its features, hold the Shift key down, and then press Ctrl+Esc.

Solutions

Can I change my wallpaper that shows on my logon screen in Windows NT?

Every individual gets a choice of wallpapers in the Control Panel, which updates the `NTUSER.DAT` file. By changing the wallpaper in the default section of `HKEY_USERS`, the logon wallpaper is changed.

continues

Add the name of the wallpaper to the `Wallpaper` value in `HKEY_USERS\.DEFAULT\Control Panel\Desktop`. It will show when you log off the next time.

Consider putting your company logo as the wallpaper that starts up, as shown in this Solution. Then, let your users select the one that they want to use the rest of the time.

Solutions

Can I change where my wallpaper is on the screen?

Yes. It's easy, and it works in both NT 4.0 and in Windows 95. In the Control Panel, you only have the options of having your wallpaper centered (see Figure 27.5) or tiled (so it fills the whole screen). If you want it somewhere else, so it doesn't get covered by your icons, you need to make a Registry change.

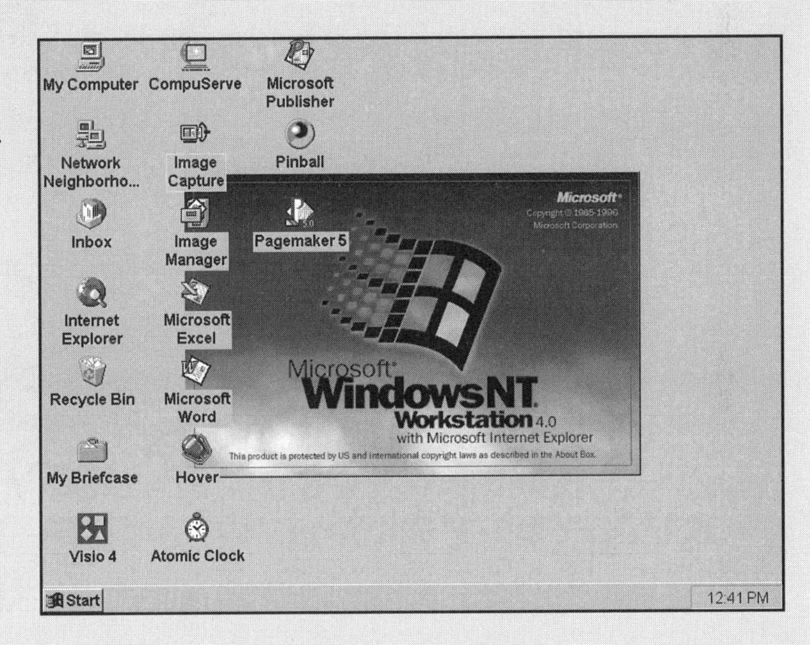

Figure 27.5. A centered wallpaper with the icons on top.

Make the change in `HKEY_CURRENT_USER\Control Panel\Desktop`.

By the way, using this Solution will also move the wallpaper for the previous Solution if you put it in `HKEY_USERS\.DEFAULT\Control Panel\Desktop`.

continues

continued

Two values must be added to the key (with Edit | Add Value in `REGEDT32.EXE`):

- `WallpaperOriginX` sets the horizontal location of the left side of the graphic.
- `WallpaperOriginY` sets the vertical location of the top of the graphic.

The value is in pixels. A value of `100` for `WallpaperOriginX` specifies that the wallpaper image is 100 pixels from the left of the screen. A value of `275` for `WallpaperOriginY` makes the graphic start 275 pixels from the top.

Obviously, your screen's resolution affects the actual location. A pixel in a 640×480 screen is much larger than one in a 1024×768 screen. Try different values for different effects.

When you log off and log on again, the wallpaper will be in the new location. (See Figure 27.6.)

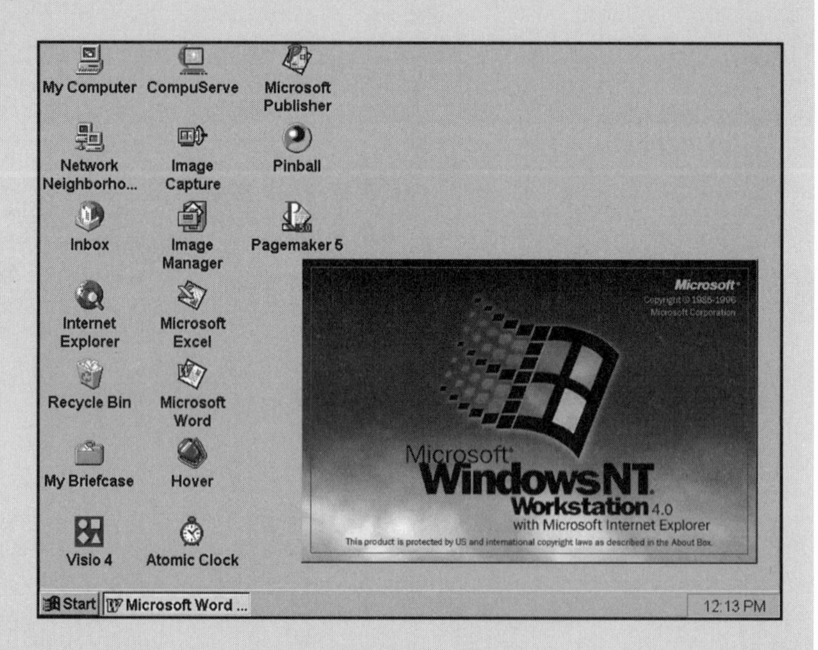

Figure 27.6. The wallpaper moved to the right and down.

The values for the graphic in Figure 27.6 are

Resolution	800×600
`WallpaperOriginX`	285
`WallpaperOriginY`	225

Other resolutions and different size graphics require different values. Experiment with yours and place the wallpaper anywhere you choose. Set your icons in place, and use the next Solution to make sure they stay there.

Here are several more Solutions that work in both NT and 95.

Solutions

I've got a really fast machine, but it doesn't feel any faster than my old one. Why not?

Much of what the performance characteristics of hardware do is related to the applications you use. The demand for calculations, the need for hard disk performance, and other factors are critical, but they are not as noticeable.

Make your menus faster by changing the amount of time the system waits before having a menu appear when your mouse floats over a pop-up location. Those locations are indicated on the menus with a right triangle. If you're having trouble keeping up, or your mouse actions are not precise, and you keep getting menus you don't want, you can increase the delay.

To change the menu speeds, edit the `MenuShowDelay` value in `HKEY_CURRENT_USER\Control Panel\Desktop`. (This will also work with Windows 95, but the value name must be added.)

The range for this value is 1–10,000 (milliseconds). The higher the number, the longer the wait. The default value of `400` is for novice mouseketeers, whereas lower values appeal to speed rats.

To activate `MenuShowDelay`, log off and log on again.

Another way to boost the performance of the system is to change the way the windows fly out of the Taskbar and minimize back in. Watching the default animation for the windows reminds me of the genie in the bottle. My one wish is that it could be faster. So, here's how to make a wish come true.

Add a new `REG_SZ` value called `MinAnimate` to the `HKEY_CURRENT_USER\Control Panel\Desktop\WindowMetrics` key.

Animation is either on or off. To enable animation on, use `1`; use `0` to disable it.

To activate `MinAnimate`, log off and log on again. Then, minimize a window. Boom! It's gone! It's going to feel a lot faster.

Animation and the menu speeds make the most difference on a slow machine. On a Pentium Pro 200, you won't see as much of a difference as you will on a 486 running at 33MHz.

Solutions

How can I get rid of the shortcut arrows on my icons?

Do you really want to do that? They are there to show which icons are duplicates, and which icons actually represent files. If you are careful, you can remove the arrows, but double-check before removing any icons.

continues

continued

Every time you make a shortcut, either for the desktop or for Explorer, NT or 95 puts a little arrow in the lower-left corner and describes the icon as Shortcut to .... (See Figure 27.7.) It's easy to edit the name, but you must use this Solution to get rid of the arrow. All shortcuts then appear with the same icons as the main application. It makes the desktop cleaner but can also help users who feel they can delete anything with an arrow attached.

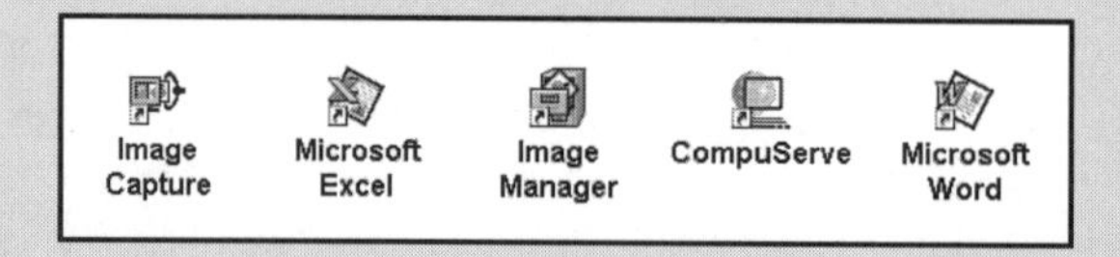

Figure 27.7. Icons with the shortcut arrow.

In `HKEY_CLASSES_ROOT\Lnkfile`, the value name that creates the arrow is called `IsShortcut`. Remove the value and the arrows go away (see Figure 27.8), not just for the new icons, but also for all other shortcuts in the system (see Figure 27.9).

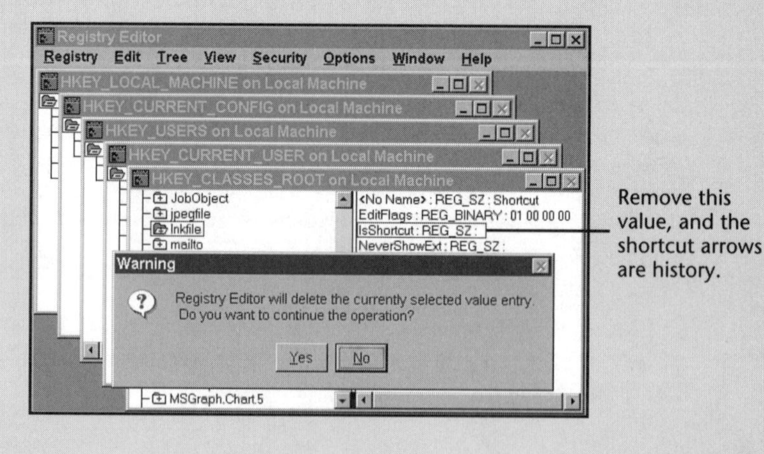

Figure 27.8. Removing the `IsShortcut` value.

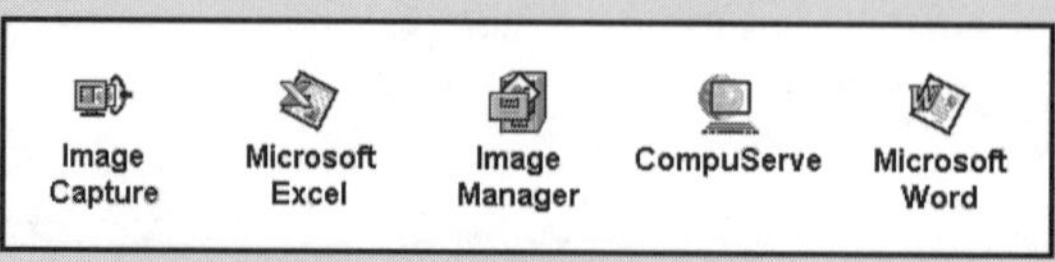

Figure 27.9. Icons without the shortcut arrow.

To activate this change, log off and log on again. Your arrows will be gone.

If you use this Solution, right-click the icon and check the properties before you delete it. You don't want to delete an application inadvertently.

Warning

One of the greatest challenges for technical support is the cavalier deletion of items on the desktop. Many users just assume that everything is just an icon that points to something else. That was the case in Windows 3.x, but not in Windows 95 or NT. With the Explorer interface, what you see on the desktop may be a shortcut to something else or it may be the actual file. Use the Recycle Bin as a way to restore deleted files, if necessary.

Solutions

Why don't my icons stay where I put them?

By default, Windows NT and Windows 95 save the settings on the desktop when the session ends. Essentially, it is the same as Save Settings on Exit options in NT 3.5*x* and Windows for Workgroups. There is no way to turn that off from the interface, so you need to do it in the Registry. Then, even if you change them during the session, the icon locations are always the same.

In `HKEY_CURRENT_USER\Software\Microsoft\Windows\CurrentVersion\Policies\Explorer`, change the `NoSaveSettings` value.

The setting is either turned on (`1`) or off (`0`). To save the settings every time you log off, remove the value or set it to `0`. To ensure that your desktop looks exactly the same every time you log on, follow these steps:

1. Set your desktop exactly as you want it.
2. Log off and on again.
3. Add the value and set it to `1`.
4. Log off and log on again.

I call this the maid feature. Once I set all my windows and icons in place and turn this on, it will always be the same when I start up the system. It's just as if a maid came in and cleaned it up for you.

Solutions

Can I choose my screen saver and set how long the screen saver will wait before starting if no one logs onto my NT system?

The timeout setting for a screen saver determines how long the system waits before the screen saver starts if there is no activity. Setting it for the default user

continues

continued

in HKEY_USERS sets it for the logon screen if no one logs on immediately. Also, set ScreenSaveTimeOut (in seconds) in the same key.

In HKEY_USERS\.DEFAULT\Control Panel\Desktop, in the SCRNSAVE.EXE value, enter the name of the screen saver. It must be in the Windows NT directory, in the System32 directory below it, or the full path must be listed.

Do not use one of the OpenGL Screen savers on Windows NT Server. They will eat up all of your CPU time and make the server performance much worse. Most of the others should be OK, but as an alternative, press Ctrl+Alt+Del and lock the Workstation. You will have to supply the original user's password or the Administrator password to get in. Because it blanks out the contents of the screen, it is an effective deterrent to prying eyes.

Solutions

Every time I leave NT, it seems my shutdown option is different. Can I set it so it will always be the same?

Not really. Each time you leave NT, it sets in the Registry the option that was used. You can set your choice in the Registry, but it is overwritten by the system as soon as you leave your current session.

If this Registry change is made as part of System Policy Editor, it will set the Registry each time you log on. For more details about using one of these Solutions as a policy in System Policy Editor, see Chapter 34, "Creating Custom Policies."

For example, if you want the default choice when leaving to be to close all programs and log on as a different user, you can set a policy to do that. Then, every time you select Start | Shut Down, your preferred choice will be selected.

The Registry location is HKEY_CURRENT_USER\Software\Microsoft\Windows\CurrentVersion\Explorer, and the value name is Shutdown Setting.

Table 27.1 shows the possible settings for this Solution. Select the shutdown option desired, and enter the setting in the string editor.

Table 27.1. Shut-down options for Windows NT.

Setting	*Option*
1	Shut down the computer?
2	Restart the computer?
3	Close all programs and log on as a different user?

Using System Policy Editor would be a great option for this Solution. Regardless of what the user did the last time, it would always stay the same. See more about creating custom templates to implement Registry changes in Chapter 34.

Solutions

I use Windows NT Workstation as a stand-alone system, and I am the only one who ever uses it. Do I have to log on every time?

Windows NT requires a logon, but it is possible to automate it. To set it so the system will automatically log on, you will need to make four Registry changes. All of the values are in `HKEY_LOCAL_MACHINE\SOFTWARE\Microsoft\Windows NT\CurrentVersion\Winlogon`.

The value names required are

- `AutoAdminLogon`
- `DefaultDomainName`
- `DefaultUserName`
- `DefaultPassword`

If any are missing, add them with Edit | Add Value. Each is a `REG_SZ` value.

Set `AutoAdminLogon` to `1` to turn it on, and `0` to disable it. The `DefaultUser name` contains the name of the last user who logged on to the network. Change it to the user name you plan to use. The `DefaultDomainName` is normally there, but the `DefaultPassword` is usually not. Adding the value is easy, but be aware that the string for the password is clear text (unencrypted) and can be read by any user who has access to the Registry.

To activate this change, restart the system.

Warning

To override the automatic logon procedure, hold the Shift key down during logoff and until the logon dialog box appears. When you log on as another user, the system resets the `AutoAdminLogon` to `0` and changes the default name and password to the ones you just used.

After you work on the system, make sure you change all the settings back so the automatic logon works.

Tip

Use the System Policy Editor to set these values. As long as the policy is in force, the system automatically changes the settings to the desired ones even if they have changed after manual editing.

See the System Policy Editor details in Chapter 31, "Managing Domain Computers with System Policy Editor."

Solutions

How can I remove all the names from the Start | Documents menu?

You can remove the document names easily by going to the Start | Settings | Taskbar | Start Menu Programs | Documents Menu and clicking the Clear button. All of the document names are stored in the Registry, as are other settings of Most Recently Used (MRU) lists. Even though you can clear out the documents list, there is not an easy way to remove the rest of the MRU lists. Even though there may be more MRU settings in your computer, Table 27.2 shows the three most commonly used.

Table 27.2. Most commonly used lists in the Registry.

Registry Key	*Description*
`DocFindSpecMRU`	MRU for the Find Files command
`FindComputerMRU`	MRU for the Find Computer command
`RunMRU`	MRU for the Run command

The keys are in the `HKEY_CURRENT_USER\Software\Microsoft\Windows\CurrentVersion\Explorer` key, in both Windows 95 and in Windows NT 4.0.

To clear the lists, delete every value in the key, except Default.

Be careful deleting anything from the Registry. The changes are immediate and permanent. One false move, and you're dead. Back it up regularly, especially before removing entries.

Solutions

I don't like the way Windows 95 gives me short filenames. Can I change it?

You can change it, with a change in the Registry. The key is `HKEY_CURRENT_USER\Software\Microsoft\Windows\CurrentVersion\Explorer`, and the value to add is `NameNumericTail`. Set it to `0` and you won't get names that end in ~1 or ~2. The shortened names will take the first four characters from the first word of the long filename, and the first four characters from the second word.

continues

Be careful, though, because installing Windows 95 components, Plus! Components, or applications through the Add/Remove Programs tool in Control Panel may corrupt your files. If you are going to add a new program or feature, edit the Registry first, and change the `NameNumericTail` to `1` before you do. Then you can change it back later.

Summary

With these Solutions, you can change the way Windows NT looks and feels. The Solutions in this chapter allow you to use the old-style functions and interface for easy transition to NT 4.0, to boost the performance of the Explorer interface, and to customize the desktop. Use them freely to improve your comfort level and enjoyment of Windows NT.

Part VII

Part VII
Part VII
Part VII
Part VII
Part VII
Part VII
Part VII
Part VII
Part VII
Part VII
Part VII

Advanced Registry Management

CHAPTER 28

System Policy Editor: Understanding Policy Files

In an organization with tens, hundreds, or even thousands of users, the effective and efficient management of all of these Registries can be unwieldy, if not impossible. Up to this point in the book, all of the changes to the Registry have been made one system at a time. Imagine making all (or even half!) of the changes discussed in this book for 100 systems. The time to do that would be much too great. System Policy Editor allows you to make changes for all the systems on your network at one time. It also allows you to make changes to an individual system. User management is also easier with System Policy Editor. User-based changes can be made for an individual, for groups of users, or for all users on the network. These changes are made from an individual system, an NT server or a Windows 95 system, and then distributed to all the systems at logon.

The changes to be made to the Registries of the systems on the network fall into four categories:

- Restrictions on users
- System-wide updates/standardization
- Permanent changes to the system
- Overcoming limitations/bugs

This section will introduce you to one of the most powerful ways to perform system-wide management of the Registries: the System Policy Editor. This allows you to impose updates on systems for user-level and computer-level changes. It requires no user input, and the user has no choice to accept or reject the settings, because the policy automatically overrides any changes the user makes.

Understanding Policy Files

The Latin root of *policy* is the same as for *police* (*politia*). Webster's Dictionary defines policy as a "high-level overall plan embracing the general goals and acceptable procedures of a government body." A policy in Windows NT or 95 is exactly the same. As an administrator, you must impose procedures and maybe even restrictions on users on the network. From the System Policy Editor in Windows NT Server 4.0, you can set policies for NT 4.0 systems only. It will not set policies for Windows 95 systems or NT 3.5*x* systems. The System Policy Editor in Windows 95 will only create policies for Windows 95 systems.

The System Policy Editor for Windows NT is installed during the Server installation. The System Policy Editor for Windows 95 on the Windows 95 installation CD-ROM, and can be run directly from the CD or copied onto the hard disk. The menus, interface, and all functions are the same as the Policy Editor in NT, but the policy file created by the Windows 95 Policy Editor is saved in ASCII, while the policy file created by the NT Policy Editor is saved in Unicode. The two policy files are completely incompatible. The System Policy Editor in Windows 95 can create policies only for systems running Windows 95, and the System Policy Editor for NT can create policies only for NT 4.0. And, unlike Windows 95, the System Policy Editor for Windows NT also allows the use of multiple template files, making the addition of policies very simple.

Even though many of the system settings for NT 4.0 are exactly the same, Windows NT 3.5*x* doesn't even look for a policy at logon. The existence of a policy file has no impact on NT 3.5*x*.

Note

System Policy Editor does not actually *provide* policy for the users. It simply is the tool to help you implement the policies you currently have. If you impose a policy that has not been agreed upon, you'll encounter upset people, maybe even an uprising. On the other hand, if policies for your organization are well-defined, implementation is easy, and users accept them. Discuss the policies first, and then implement them.

Because of their similarity, this book will deal with both editors together. Only during the template file discussion will they be separated.

Any policy that you implement updates the Registry automatically at logon. Types of changes include user-specific and computer-specific changes. User-specific changes affect `HKEY_USERS`, and computer-specific changes update `HKEY_LOCAL_COMPUTER`.

Examples of user-specific changes include

- Desktop look, feel, and sound
- Menu options
- Application restrictions
- Performance functions
- Available Control Panel options

These settings can be implemented for a specific user, all users, or by groups (as set up in User Manager for Domains).

Examples of computer-specific changes include

- Logon settings
- Networking
- Connections
- Startup options
- Remote Access
- Printers

Computer-level policies can be set for all systems in general or for specific systems only.

Policies implemented on the system override all other settings that conflict, as illustrated in Figure 28.1. For example, you could set a policy demanding that the wallpaper be the company logo. If a user changed it during a session (using Control Panel | Display | Background), the company logo would reappear as soon as he logged off and back on again.

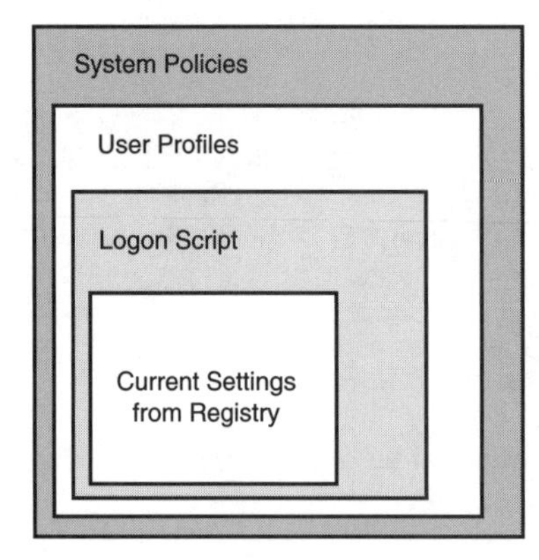

Figure 28.1.
Policies override all other settings at logon.

Policies override all other settings at logon, and I want to indicate a layering effect. It overrides the settings, but not all the settings that are in the Registry will be affected by the logon script. Similarly, the User Profiles will not override everything that is set by the first two. Policies have ultimate priority. Anything they change will overwrite any other settings in the system.

Warning

One upset user at a seminar asked me if this is where administrators learn to be God. I hope that is not the case. Excess restrictions on users only make adversaries of them, and productivity suffers.

Not all settings in the Registry are affected by the implementation of a logon script. Similarly, User Profiles do not override everything set by the Registry and the logon script. Policies have ultimate priority. Anything they change overwrites any other settings in the system.

Creating a Policy File

Open System Policy Editor in NT with Start | Programs | Administrative Tools | System Policy Editor. Start the Windows 95 editor by activating `POLEDIT.EXE`, which is on the Windows 95 installation CD, in the `\ADMIN\APPTOOLS\POLEDIT` directory. After opening the editor, select File | New Policy, and you will be presented with the screen shown in Figure 28.2. Notice that there is an icon for default computer and another for default user. Any policy settings created for the default computer automatically affect every NT 4.0 or Windows 95 system on the network. Any policy created for default user likewise affects every user on the network that is running NT 4.0 or Windows 95.

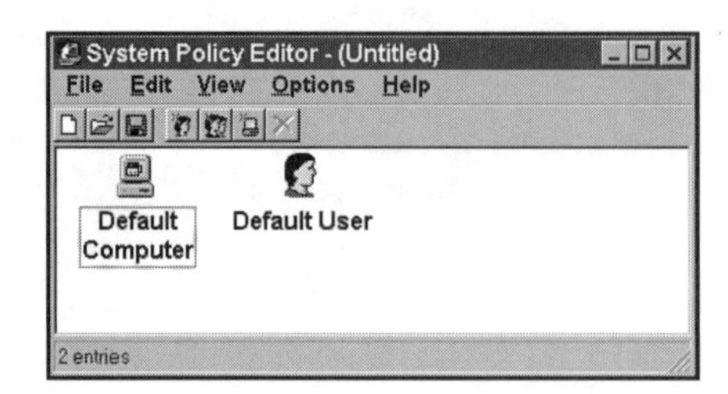

Figure 28.2.
System Policy Editor in Windows NT 4.0 server.

To create specific policies for individual systems, click the Add Computer button or select Edit | Add Computer. Provide the name of the system in the dialog box and click OK to continue. More detail about working with policies for systems is included in Chapter 31, "Managing Domain Computers with System Policy Editor" and Chapter 33, "Managing Windows 95 Users with System Policy Editor." Adding a computer to the policy creates an icon as shown in Figure 28.3.

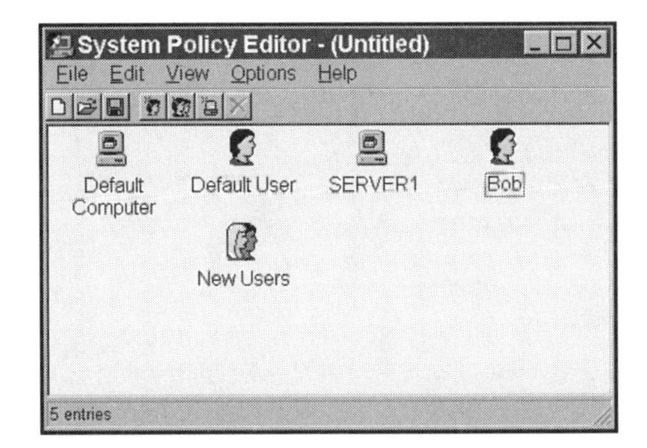

Figure 28.3. Creating a policy specifically for `SERVER1`, `Bob`, and the `New Users` group.

To create policies for individual users or groups, click the Add User button or the Add Group button respectively, then supply the name and choose OK to continue. More detail about working with policies for users and groups is included in Chapter 32, "Managing Domain Users with System Policy Editor" and also in Chapter 33, "Managing Windows 95 Users with System Policy Editor." Adding a user and a group to the policy creates an icon as shown in Figure 28.3.

Unlike the Registry Editor, the System Policy Editor does not automatically save changes. If you do not save them, changes are lost at exit. To save the policy, select File | Save.

Policy files are stored in the `NETLOGON` share in a Windows NT network, so all users logging on to the system have immediate access to them. The actual path to the `NETLOGON` share is `%systemroot%\system32\Repl\import\scripts`. Any changes to the NT policy are saved there as `NTCONFIG.POL` for NT systems. NT always looks for a policy named `NTCONFIG.POL` at logon. If it is not there, no change to the Registry occurs. As long as they are present, any changes activated in the policy overwrite any Registry settings, as shown in Figure 28.4. Likewise, Windows 95 looks for a policy file called `CONFIG.POL` in the `NETLOGON` share.

Tip

System Policy Editor also works with networks other than Windows NT networks. In a Novell network, save the policy file in the `PUBLIC` directory. For Banyan, Pathworks, and other networks, you must specify for each system where the file is to be found. For stand-alone Windows NT and Windows 95 systems, you must also specify the location. After you set that, all the systems look to that point for the information.

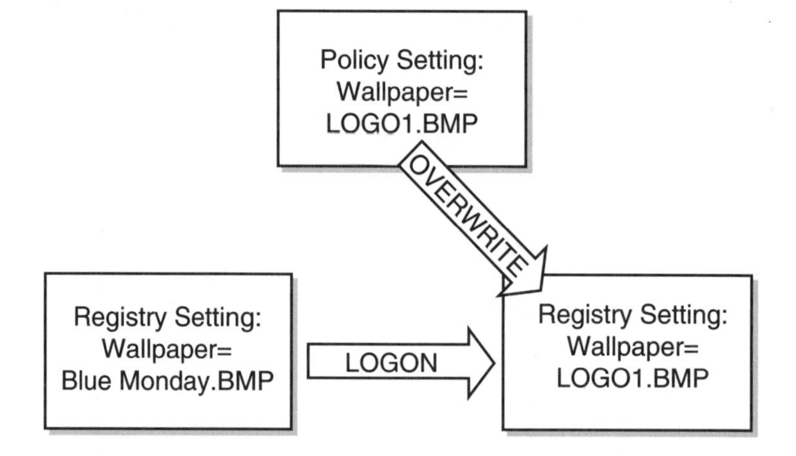

Figure 28.4.
Policies overwrite Registry settings at logon.

The policy updates the Registry at logon. Any time the Registry is manually changed, the policy overwrites the Registry at logon. Regardless of the number of times the change is made, as long as the policy is in effect, it forces specific Registry settings.

If, after the change is made, the policy file is removed or the policy is no longer specified, the user can change the setting in his personal Registry without it being overwritten. Returning to the wallpaper example discussed previously, if the user changes his wallpaper and no policy maintains the setting of the logo wallpaper, the wallpaper is not changed back.

Policies that restrict users should be present at all times, regardless of the preferences of the user or any change made by software. An example of such a case is the restriction on common groups. If you disable access to common groups for a particular user, that user can enable access to the groups if he knows where the Registry change is for that setting. Likewise, any Registry change that can be implemented through the Registry is a perfect candidate for a permanent policy.

Tip

A good idea for administrators using the System Policy Editor tool is to always create some way to get back to normal in the event of a mistake. If you ever need to remove all of the settings you have created for users, it's wise to have a backup file that returns all the systems to normal. If you have created a policy file that has all settings specifically turned off, you could simply copy the backup file over the current policy file, and order everyone to log off and log on again to return the settings to their original state.

Tip

I keep a backup that I know functions properly of my last favorite policy file. If I need to return to that point, I copy the file to the `NETLOGON` share, log off, and log back on again.

After certain policies have written to the Registry, they no longer need to be in effect. An example of such a policy is one that changes IP address settings for the network: After everyone has logged on to the network, that policy need not remain in effect. Another example of such a policy is one that restricts a user from editing the Registry: The user cannot undo such a change, so there is no reason for the policy to remain in effect.

If the setting can change during the session, and if the policy is no longer in place, the policy is defeated by a Registry change.

Warning

If your NT system uses the FAT file system for your System volume, you may be putting your policy files and logon scripts in jeopardy. The default permissions for the `NETLOGON` share give everybody Read access. If you share the `\WINNT` directory or any other in the `\WINNT\SYSTEM32\Repl\Import\Scripts` tree giving Full Control to everyone, access extends through all subdirectories and files as well as the original shared directory. That means that any user can get to that directory and delete files, including policy files.

The best security is with the NTFS file system. With it, you can set specific permissions on individual files, giving everyone but the administrators (who require Full Control) Read access to the policy file and logon scripts.

Summary

System Policy Editor allows an administrator to effectively manage a large number of users and systems in an organization from a single location. The opportunities for the direction of change are significant and far-reaching. Used wisely, System Policy Editor can save huge amounts of time and effort in training, troubleshooting, management, standardization, and administration of a network. Used unwisely as a tool for domination and user restriction, it may cause a revolt among your users.

Use caution, concern, and communication, along with training, to implement policies in your organization to meet the organization's needs and agendas.

CHAPTER 29

System Policy Editor: Understanding Template Files

Whereas a policy file includes the actual implemented changes for systems and users on the network, template files include the possible changes to be made. Each Registry change is listed in the file with the same information you would need to edit the Registry directly. System Policy Editor reads the template and translates the difficult language into a Windows-based, Explorer-like list of changes that can be made.

The templates for Windows NT are located in the `\WINNT\Inf` directory and all have an `.ADM` extension. (See Figure 29.1.) They are text files that can be viewed and edited with Notepad or WordPad.

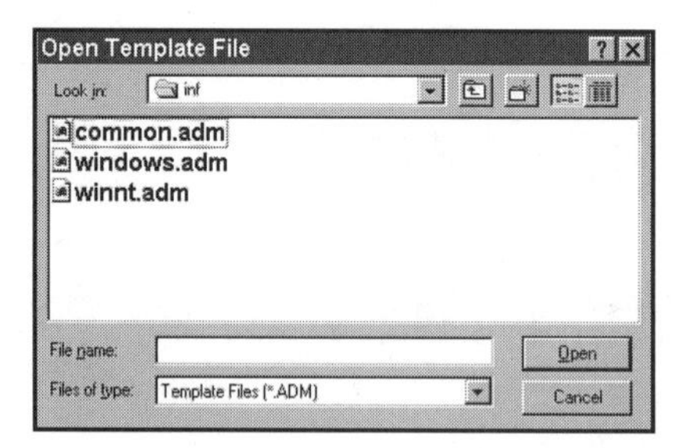

Figure 29.1.
The `.ADM` files in the `\WINNT\Inf` directory.

In Windows 95, the System Policy Editor uses the template called `ADMIN.ADM` by default. Any additions or changes are normally made to that file. It is a little more difficult to troubleshoot if there are any errors because all settings are in one file, and it is quite lengthy. You may use any template file with the 95 System Policy Editor, but you can only use one file. To change the template file, select Options | Template | Open template, and browse for the desired file.

Tip

The option to use a different template file is a great help in preparing template files for use in Windows 95. Rather than putting all the new settings directly into `ADMIN.ADM` and having to edit a large file, simply put the settings in a new small file. Open the template, test it, and when it is exactly correct, append it to the `ADMIN.ADM` file.

Windows NT System Policy Editor seems to have learned from that limitation, because it allows you to use as many templates as you like, and they can be named anything you desire. That seemingly small difference makes a huge difference in actual day-to-day use.

Tip

When you create your own template files, make them as small as possible. Small template files load more quickly and are easier to troubleshoot. If you are going to use Windows 95, append the small file onto the end of the current `ADMIN.ADM` file.

By default, NT looks for `.ADM` files in the `\WINNT\Inf` directory. If you put them elsewhere, it may take you longer to find them, particularly if you have to go to multiple places to retrieve them.

Importing Templates into System Policy Editor

To import a template file into System Policy Editor, select Options | Policy Template. In Windows NT, the dialog box shown in Figure 29.2 appears, giving you options to add or remove templates from the list of currently loading templates.

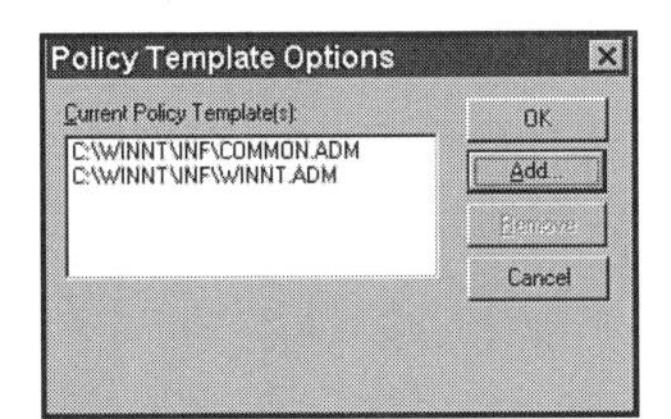

Figure 29.2.
The Policy Template Options dialog box in Windows NT.

You can add as many files as you like. Even if the files you add are not valid template files, they will show in the list.

In Windows 95, with its limitation of a single template file, the dialog box is slightly different, as shown in Figure 29.3.

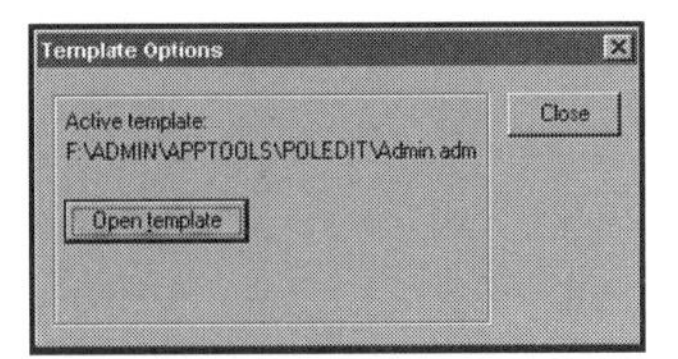

Figure 29.3.
The Template Options dialog box in Windows 95.

When you click OK at the Policy Template Options dialog box, System Policy Editor imports the template file. If the syntax is correct in the entries, System Policy Editor imports them, showing you the status of the file update on the status line. (See Figure 29.4.)

The template files are not case-sensitive, but it is critical to have the correct syntax, or structure. Incorrect syntax prevents the file from loading (as shown in Figure 29.5) and returns an error message regarding the type of error and the line on which it occurred.

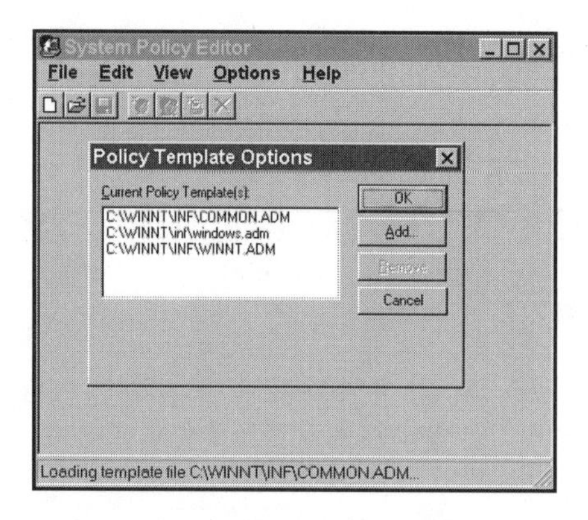

Figure 29.4.
The template files loading into System Policy Editor.

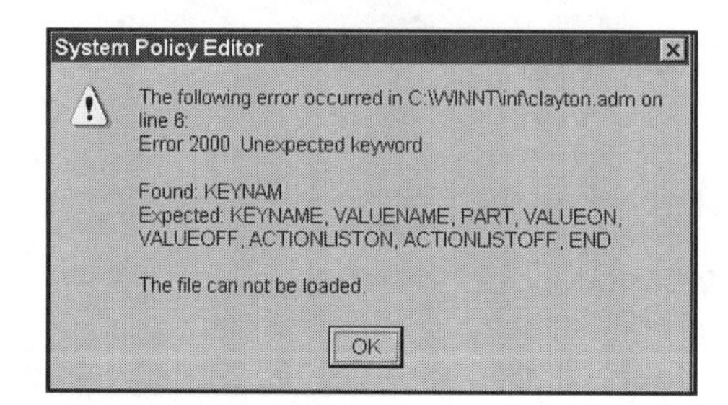

Figure 29.5.
Faulty template files do not load into System Policy Editor.

Tip

Imagine the challenge associated with finding an error on line 126. Make short template files for easier editing

The template file loads into System Policy Editor if the syntax is correct. If the keys or values are not in the Registry when System Policy Editor updates it, they are created. If the entries have no validity for the operating system, they are ignored by the Registry.

After the templates are loaded, you can use them by opening a current policy file or by creating a new one. The only available entries are those that are from the template. When you save the policy file over the top of an existing file, it does not save all the entries, just the ones that relate to the current template file.

Tip

To ensure that your policy will always be in place, add template files but don't remove them. If you remove a template file, the settings associated with that template are not saved.

Default Templates in Windows NT 4.0

Three default templates come with Windows NT 4.0: COMMON.ADM, WINNT.ADM, and WINDOWS.ADM. Because the System Policy Editor does not work with Windows 95 systems, the WINDOWS.ADM file will not be discussed in depth here. It was developed so it could be used in creating a single policy for both NT and 95. It actually has no value now because the policies are not compatible.

Solutions

If the policy files in Windows NT and Windows 95 are not compatible, why did Microsoft supply us with the WINDOWS.ADM file?

I am sure it was the original intent of the developers to make one System Policy Editor (the one released with NT 4.0) that could manage all the policies for NT and 95. It appears as though they finished the project, and then someone else came in and imposed changes on them. It would be just as easy as forcing the policies to be in Unicode.

Unicode policies could be used in a multilanguage environment and are also more difficult to edit directly, giving a tiny bit of additional security. If the policies could have been retained as ASCII, one editor and one policy file could have done it all.

Using COMMON.ADM

COMMON.ADM is the template file for Registry entries that are the same for Windows NT 4.0 and Windows 95. Placing these entries in a single file reduces the likelihood of error and duplication. In the System Policy Editor, these entries are shown with no designation for the operating system.

The entries in COMMON.ADM (shown in Figure 29.6) that affect the computer system settings are limited to the location of the policy file, SNMP (Simple Network Management Protocol), and executable files to run at startup.

Note

Even though the COMMON.ADM file includes settings that would work for Windows 95, the policy files created by System Policy Editor in NT 4.0 are not compatible with Windows 95.

As you can see in Figures 29.7 and 29.8, many more entries are associated with users than with the computers in COMMON.ADM. Most of the system-specific entries are also associated directly with the operating system.

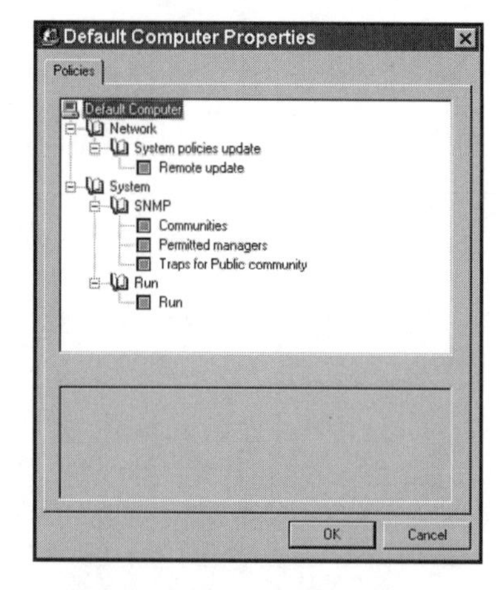

Figure 29.6. System-specific entries in `COMMON.ADM`.

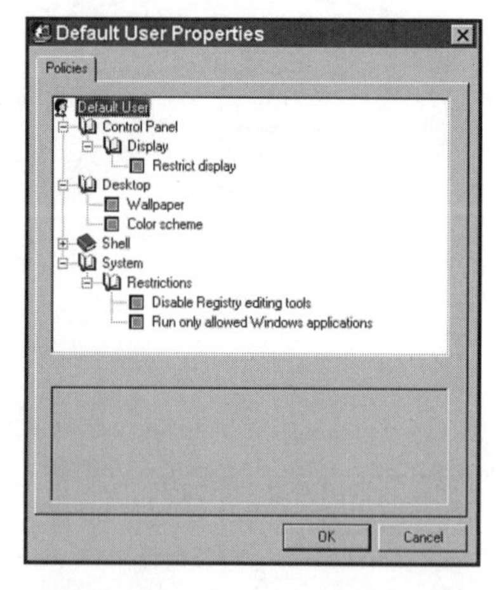

Figure 29.7. User-specific entries in `COMMON.ADM`.

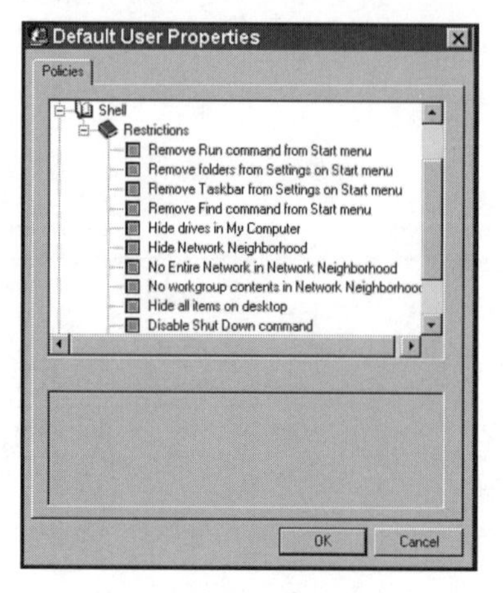

Figure 29.8. User-specific Shell Restriction entries in `COMMON.ADM`.

The common entries in the user-specific listing illustrate the great similarity of the user interfaces for NT 4.0 and 95. Most of these entries deal with restrictions placed on users. Of course, how completely you implement these restrictions depends on the experience level of users in your organization.

Using WINNT.ADM

WINNT.ADM is the template file that holds the Windows NT–specific entries for users and computer systems. These entries, even if written into the Windows 95 Registry, would have no effect on the Windows 95 Registry. Certainly, the requirement for separate files, and differences in the locations and types of entries in the files, indicate that there are still many significant differences between the operating systems and Registries. The focus and implementation of NT 4.0 and 95 are significantly different even though, from the outside, NT 4.0 and 95 look the same. Also, notice that the number of system-specific entries far outpaces the user options. (See Figures 29.9 through 29.11.)

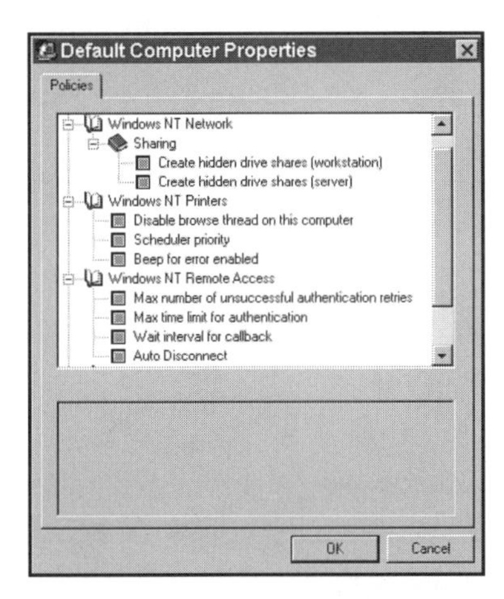

Figure 29.9. Some system-specific entries in WINNT.ADM.

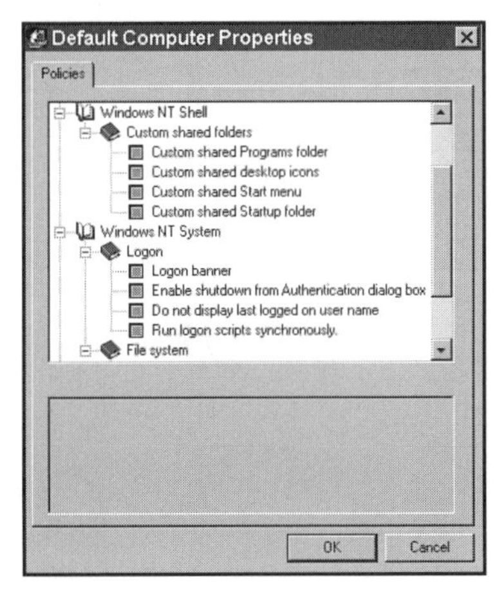

Figure 29.10. More system-specific entries in WINNT.ADM.

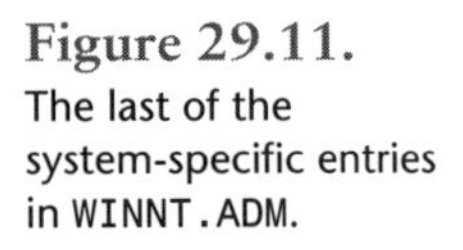

Figure 29.11.
The last of the system-specific entries in `WINNT.ADM`.

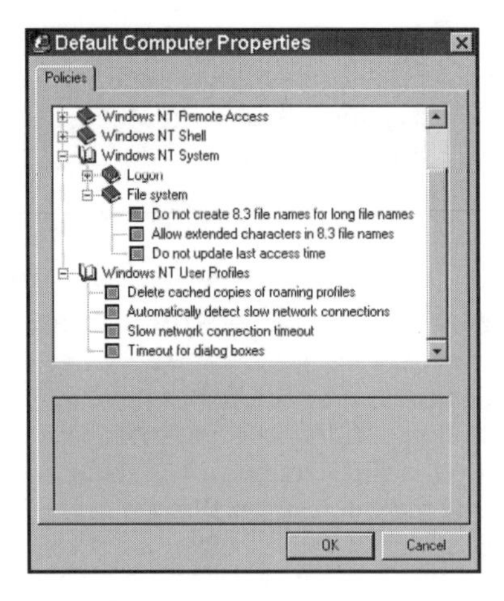

The ability to customize the NT systems on your network is fabulous. Compared to the customization options available in NT 3.5*x*, you have tremendous control. The best part is that it all comes in System Policy Editor, allowing you to make all these network-system changes from one location.

The options for managing and restricting users through System Policy Editor are shown in Figures 29.12 and 29.13.

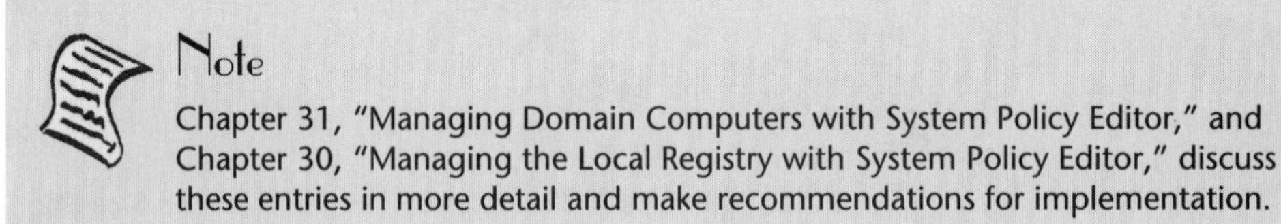

Note

Chapter 31, "Managing Domain Computers with System Policy Editor," and Chapter 30, "Managing the Local Registry with System Policy Editor," discuss these entries in more detail and make recommendations for implementation.

Together, `COMMON.ADM` and `WINNT.ADM` provide the framework for settings for system and user restrictions with System Policy Editor.

Figure 29.12.
User options in `WINNT.ADM`.

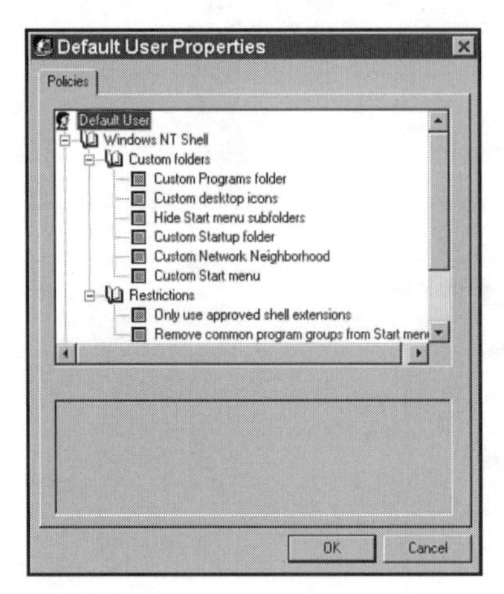

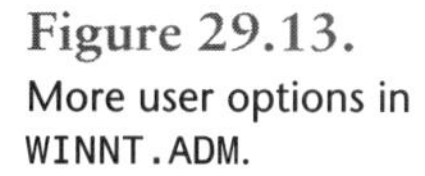

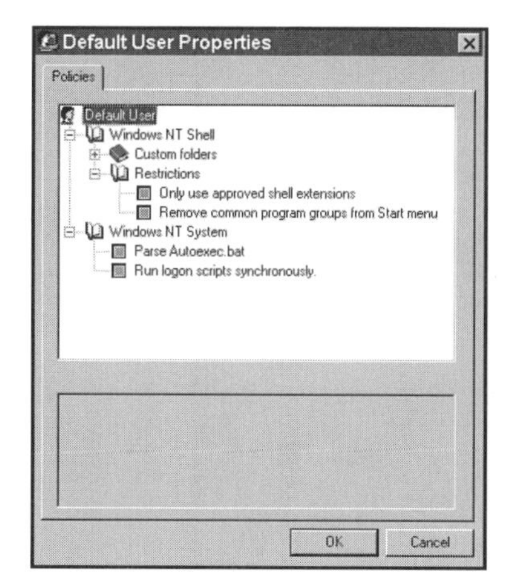

Figure 29.13.
More user options in `WINNT.ADM`.

Default Template in Windows 95

Windows 95 uses the template called `ADMIN.ADM`. It has the same entries as `COMMON.ADM` in Windows NT, plus more. Those additional entries were included in Windows NT as `WINDOWS.ADM`. Like the template files in NT, `ADMIN.ADM` contains settings for both system and user Registries.

Using `ADMIN.ADM`

`ADMIN.ADM` was the first of the template files for the System Policy Editor. It is exclusive to Windows 95, although there are some overlapping entries with the `COMMON.ADM` template in NT 4.0. This template is critical to proper management of Windows 95 systems in organizations where any sort of standardization and security is required. Without the imposition of a policy, Windows 95 users can do nearly anything they want to, much to the chagrin of system administrators and technical support.

The options for computer-based system policies are illustrated in Figures 29.14 through Figure 29.17. Additional detail about each of the settings is in Chapter 33, "Managing Windows 95 Users with System Policy Editor." Figure 29.14 shows the available policies for Network access control, logon functions, and the NetWare client.

Figure 29.15 shows the Microsoft client policy options, plus the options for File and Print sharing for NetWare networking, passwords, and dial-up network restrictions.

Sharing functions in Microsoft networking, SNMP, and policy file location (Remote Update) functions are shown in Figure 29.16.

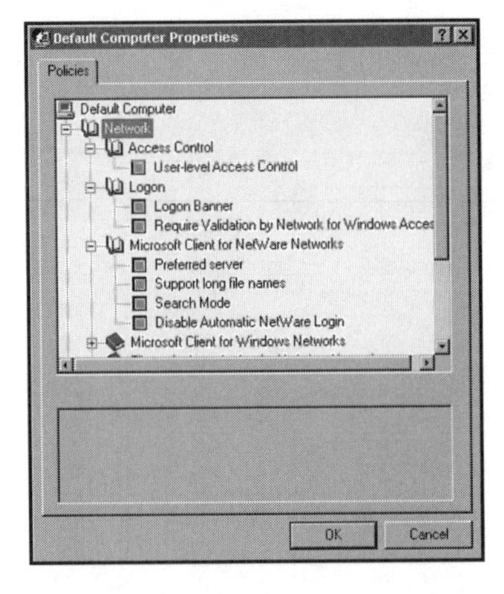

Figure 29.14. Some of the computer policies in ADMIN.ADM.

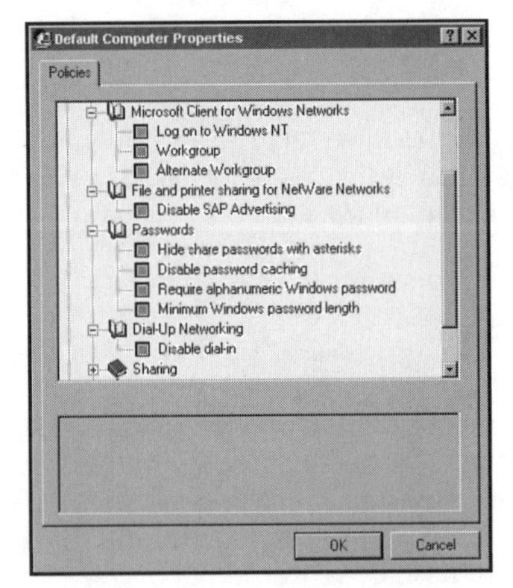

Figure 29.15. Computer policies in ADMIN.ADM affect client policy options.

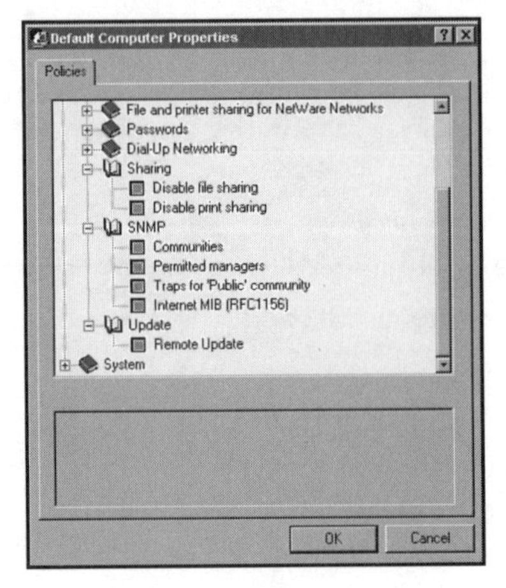

Figure 29.16. Computer policies in ADMIN.ADM affect sharing and SNMP.

System policy modifications are shown in Figure 29.17.

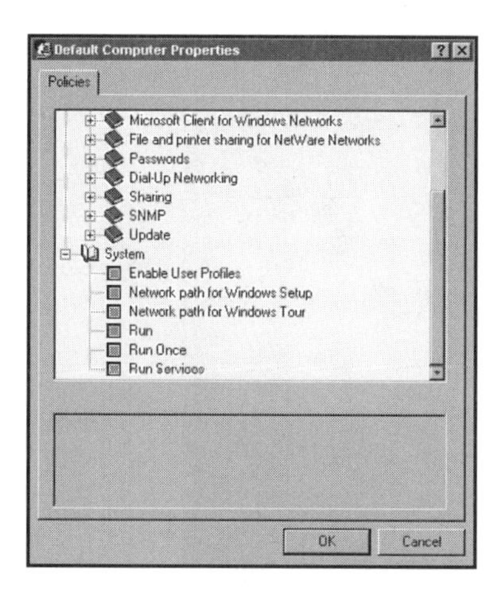

Figure 29.17.
System options from ADMIN.ADM computer policies .

The basic premise of user-based settings in the policies for Windows 95 is restrictions. As a stand-alone system, if the user takes liberties with his system, it may mean that the user is down, if the system crashes. Attach that same system to a network, and the potential problems are magnified. Figure 29.18 shows some of the restrictions that could be imposed on users with System Policy Editor. Additional detail is available in Chapter 33.

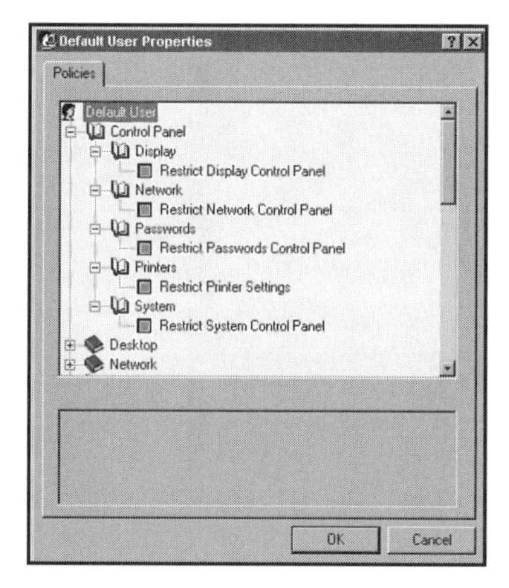

Figure 29.18.
Some of the user restriction policies in ADMIN.ADM.

Figure 29.19 shows the desktop and network sharing restrictions in the ADMIN.ADM template and System Policy Editor.

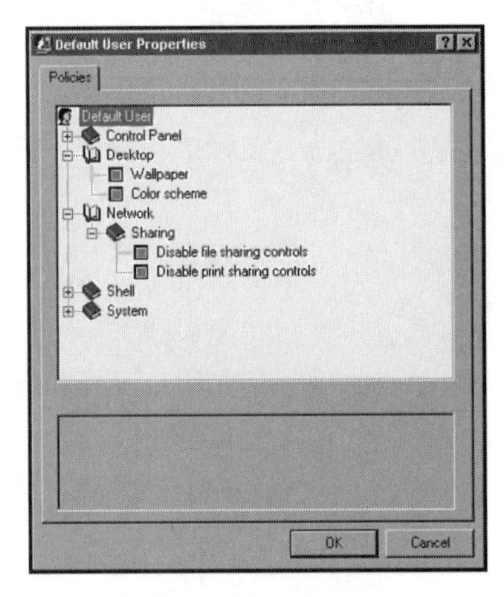

Figure 29.19. Additional user restriction policies in ADMIN.ADM.

Changing what the users will see in their Windows 95 desktop is the purpose of the template options in Figure 29.20.

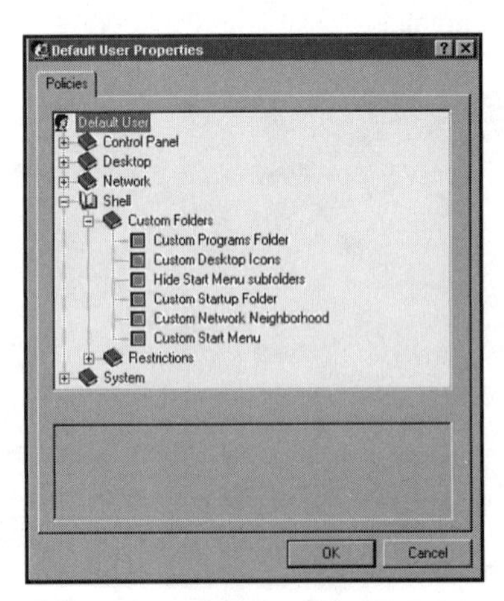

Figure 29.20. Customization options in ADMIN.ADM.

Shell restrictions (shown in Figure 29.21) can radically change the available options for the Windows 95 user.

Some of the harsher restrictions are shown in Figure 29.22 as the administrator can remove many options from the user with System Policy Editor.

Together, the policies available for Windows 95 systems and users can create quite a tight policy, and make 95 systems very acceptable systems for working on a network as part of a standards-based organization.

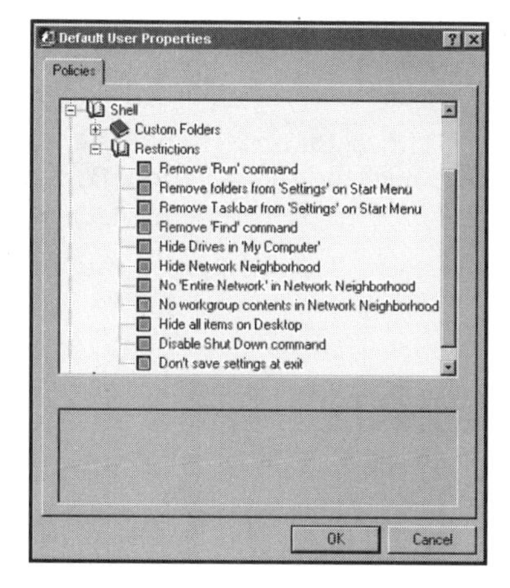

Figure 29.21. Shell restriction policies in `ADMIN.ADM`.

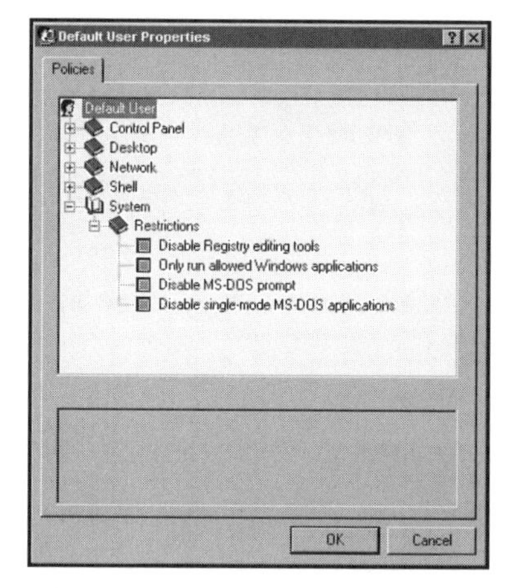

Figure 29.22. Additional restriction policies in `ADMIN.ADM`.

Solutions

Why are there so many more policies for Windows 95 systems than for Windows NT systems? I thought they were almost the same thing.

Windows NT systems were designed from the ground up with the capability for system administrators to manage and control them. Windows 95 was designed as a single-user system, with networking and standards compliance features "tacked on." In order to effectively manage Windows 95 systems in an organization, more is required, hence the greater number of policies available.

ADM File Structure

The required syntax for a template file is critical for understanding current files and for creating new files. CLASS, KEYNAME, and VALUENAME hold the actual information that will change the Registry. CATEGORY, POLICY, and PART are used to create the interface of the System Policy Editor.

CLASS

This setting determines whether the change affects HKEY_LOCAL_MACHINE or HKEY_CURRENT_USER (for the named user). As many categories as desired can be under this heading.

CATEGORY

This setting sets the text for initial headings and groups multiple policies for ease of use and editing. CATEGORY settings are shown in the System Policy Editor as a book. There can be as many layers of categories as desired, because they are used to create the hierarchical structure in the interface. An END CATEGORY entry is required to close the CATEGORY.

POLICY

POLICY entries are the actual selections that you can choose. They are shown with a check box. An END POLICY entry is required to close the POLICY.

KEYNAME

For each of the policies, there needs to be a key name and at least one value. The KEYNAME entry does not include the handle key name.

Tip

Do not start the KEYNAME with a backslash (\). Instead, start with the key below the handle key. If you start with a backslash, the setting will not be recognized in the Registry even though an error will not occur in the importing of the file.

VALUENAME

The VALUENAME is the same as in the Registry.

PART

The data for the values and the type of System Policy Editor entry desired are listed in `PART`. An `END PART` entry is required to close the `PART`.

Strings

Strings are shown in the `.ADM` file starting with a double exclamation (`!!`). The text following the double exclamation cannot include a space. The text listed in the `[Strings]` section replaces the entry in System Policy Editor. An alternative is to simply put the text in quotation marks.

Figure 29.23 shows all the syntax components of a template file. Note that the `CATEGORY`, `POLICY`, and `PART` entries all have a corresponding `END` component as well.

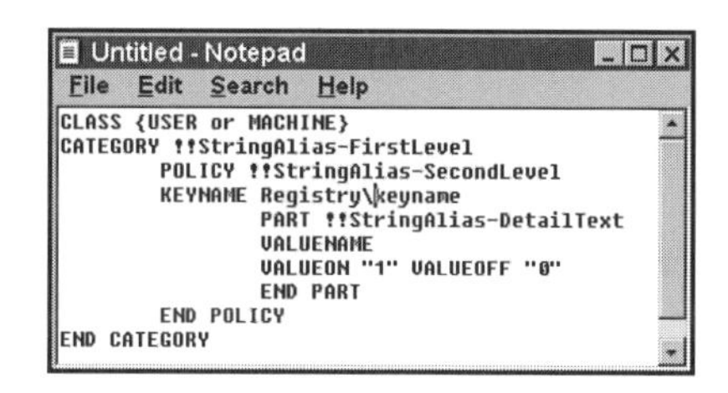

Figure 29.23.
Syntax for `.ADM` files.

Each of the corresponding parts of the System Policy Editor screen is generated by the `.ADM` file. An example from the `WINNT.ADM` file is shown in Figure 29.24.

Tip

One of the most common mistakes for creators of template files is the omission of the closing entry. For every `CATEGORY`, there must be an `END CATEGORY`. For every `POLICY`, there must be an `END POLICY`. For every `PART`, there must be an `END PART`.

Figure 29.24.
Each section of the .ADM file affects the System Policy Editor screen.

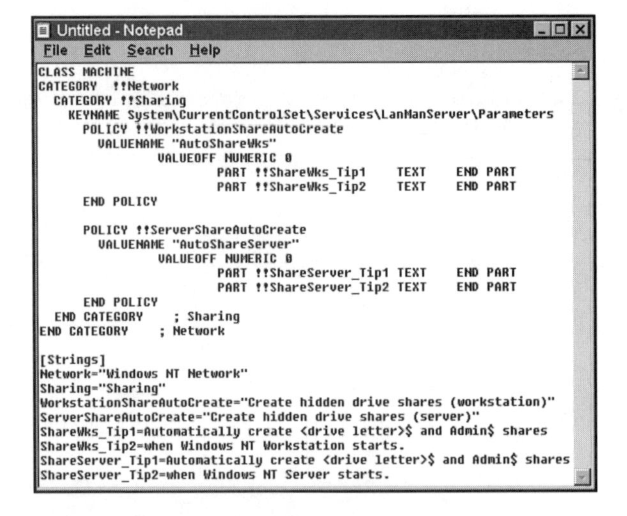

```
CLASS MACHINE
CATEGORY  !!Network
  CATEGORY !!Sharing
    KEYNAME System\CurrentControlSet\Services\LanManServer\Parameters
      POLICY !!WorkstationShareAutoCreate
        VALUENAME "AutoShareWks"
                VALUEOFF NUMERIC 0
                        PART !!ShareWks_Tip1     TEXT    END PART
                        PART !!ShareWks_Tip2     TEXT    END PART
      END POLICY

      POLICY !!ServerShareAutoCreate
        VALUENAME "AutoShareServer"
                VALUEOFF NUMERIC 0
                        PART !!ShareServer_Tip1 TEXT    END PART
                        PART !!ShareServer_Tip2 TEXT    END PART
      END POLICY
  END CATEGORY    ; Sharing
END CATEGORY    ; Network

[Strings]
Network="Windows NT Network"
Sharing="Sharing"
WorkstationShareAutoCreate="Create hidden drive shares (workstation)"
ServerShareAutoCreate="Create hidden drive shares (server)"
ShareWks_Tip1=Automatically create <drive letter>$ and Admin$ shares
ShareWks_Tip2=when Windows NT Workstation starts.
ShareServer_Tip1=Automatically create <drive letter>$ and Admin$ shares
ShareServer_Tip2=when Windows NT Server starts.
```

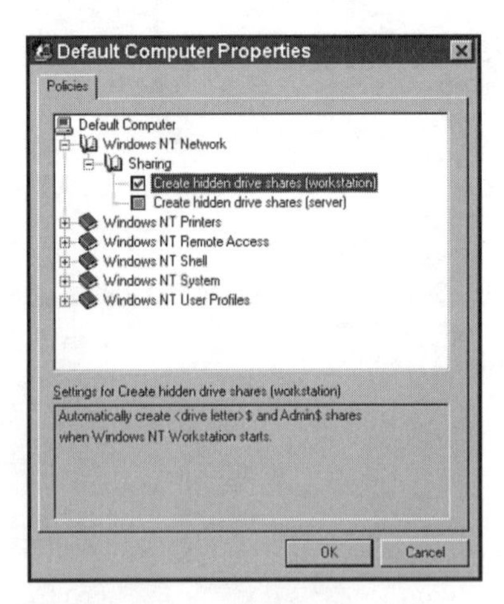

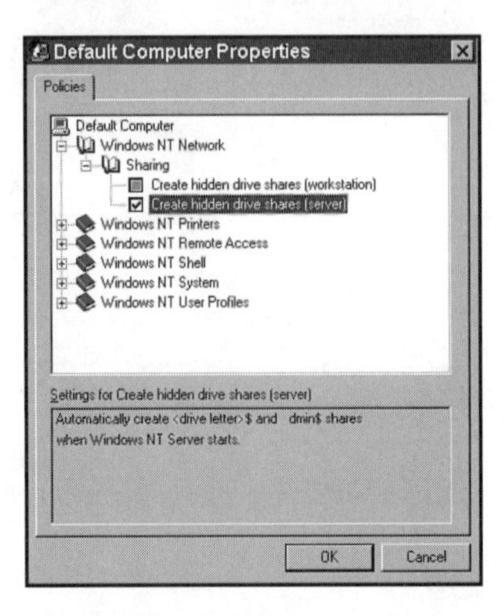

Contents of COMMON.ADM

With these standard template files, it is possible to learn a great deal about the Registry and entries that can be made. Use these steps to find the actual Registry setting being made by the System Policy Editor.

1. Open .ADM file.
2. Search for text from System Policy Editor screen.
3. If it is in [Strings], search for string text.

Tip

The text around the found text is the actual change in the Registry.

After the desired policy has been found, note the KEYNAME, the VALUENAME, and the action that will happen when the policy is activated.

COMMON.ADM has just a few settings for the computer. Because these functions were designed to work with both Windows NT and Windows 95, the criteria for inclusion in COMMON.ADM are stringent. Only functions that both can use and only Registry settings that are exactly the same can be included.

Note

The fact that the System Policy Editor for NT cannot prepare or edit policies for Windows 95 makes COMMON.ADM peculiar. Obviously, in the design phase of System Policy Editor, there was the full intention of making the policies compatible. Somewhere along the line, a decision was made to change the policy file to Unicode, and all the collaboration and partnership work was for naught.

There are many more settings in COMMON.ADM for the user because of the shared interface with Windows NT and Windows 95. Note that many of the Registry changes simply add values. Those values are just some of the undocumented items that can be placed in the Registry.

Of course, one of the most important parts of the policies is the restrictions that can be placed on users. In Listing 29.1, all the Registry locations and values are listed. If a restricted user was to get access to this file, he could read the entries, and make changes to remove restrictions. The .ADM files are stored in the \WINNT\INF folder. Restrict access to increase security.

Listing 29.1. COMMON.ADM.

```
CLASS MACHINE
CATEGORY !!Network
     CATEGORY !!Update
          POLICY !!RemoteUpdate
```

continues

Listing 29.1. continued

```
            KEYNAME System\CurrentControlSet\Control\Update
            ACTIONLISTOFF
                VALUENAME "UpdateMode"          VALUE NUMERIC 0
            END ACTIONLISTOFF
                PART !!UpdateMode               DROPDOWNLIST REQUIRED
                VALUENAME "UpdateMode"
                ITEMLIST
                    NAME !!UM_Automatic         VALUE NUMERIC 1
                    NAME !!UM_Manual            VALUE NUMERIC 2
                END ITEMLIST
                END PART
                PART !!UM_Manual_Path           EDITTEXT
                VALUENAME "NetworkPath"
                END PART
                PART !!DisplayErrors            CHECKBOX
                VALUENAME "Verbose"
                END PART
                PART !!LoadBalance              CHECKBOX
                VALUENAME "LoadBalance"
                END PART
            END POLICY
        END CATEGORY     ; Update
    END CATEGORY     ; Network
    CATEGORY !!System
        CATEGORY !!SNMP
            POLICY !!Communities
            KEYNAME System\CurrentControlSet\Services\SNMP
            ➥\Parameters\ValidCommunities
                PART !!CommunitiesListbox       LISTBOX
                    VALUEPREFIX ""
                END PART
            END POLICY
            POLICY !!PermittedManagers
            KEYNAME System\CurrentControlSet\Services\SNMP
            ➥\Parameters\PermittedManagers
                PART !!PermittedManagersListbox    LISTBOX
                    VALUEPREFIX ""
                END PART
            END POLICY
            POLICY !!Traps_Public
            KEYNAME System\CurrentControlSet\Services\SNMP
            ➥\Parameters\TrapConfiguration\Public
                PART !!Traps_PublicListbox      LISTBOX
                    VALUEPREFIX ""
                END PART
            END POLICY
        END CATEGORY     ; SNMP
        CATEGORY !!Run
            POLICY !!Run
            KEYNAME Software\Microsoft\Windows\CurrentVersion\Run
                PART !!RunListbox               LISTBOX EXPLICITVALUE
                END PART
            END POLICY
        END CATEGORY
    END CATEGORY     ; System
    CLASS USER
    CATEGORY !!ControlPanel
```

```
    CATEGORY !!CPL_Display
        POLICY !!CPL_Display_Restrict
        KEYNAME Software\Microsoft\Windows\CurrentVersion\Policies\System
            PART !!CPL_Display_Disable     CHECKBOX
            VALUENAME NoDispCPL
            END PART
            PART !!CPL_Display_HideBkgnd   CHECKBOX
            VALUENAME NoDispBackgroundPage
            END PART
            PART !!CPL_Display_HideScrsav  CHECKBOX
            VALUENAME NoDispScrSavPage
            END PART
            PART !!CPL_Display_HideAppearance CHECKBOX
            VALUENAME NoDispAppearancePage
            END PART
            PART !!CPL_Display_HideSettings   CHECKBOX
            VALUENAME NoDispSettingsPage
            END PART
        END POLICY
    END CATEGORY     ; Display
END CATEGORY     ; Control Panel
CATEGORY !!Desktop
    KEYNAME "Control Panel\Desktop"
    POLICY !!Wallpaper
             PART !!WallpaperName           EDITTEXT
             VALUENAME "Wallpaper"
             END PART
             PART !!WALLPAPER_TIP1          TEXT    END PART
             PART !!WALLPAPER_TIP2          TEXT    END PART
        PART !!TileWallpaper                CHECKBOX DEFCHECKED
        VALUENAME "TileWallpaper"
        VALUEON "1" VALUEOFF "0"
        END PART
    END POLICY
    POLICY !!ColorScheme
        PART !!SchemeName                   DROPDOWNLIST
        KEYNAME "Control Panel\Appearance"
        VALUENAME Current                   REQUIRED
        ITEMLIST
            NAME !!Lavender VALUE !!Lavender
            ACTIONLIST
                KEYNAME "Control Panel\Colors"
                VALUENAME ActiveBorder     VALUE "174 168 217"
                VALUENAME ActiveTitle      VALUE "128 128 128"
                VALUENAME AppWorkspace     VALUE "90 78 177"
                VALUENAME Background       VALUE "128 128 192"
                VALUENAME ButtonDkShadow   VALUE "0 0 0"
                VALUENAME ButtonFace       VALUE "174 168 217"
                VALUENAME ButtonHilight    VALUE "216 213 236"
                VALUENAME ButtonLight      VALUE "174 168 217"
                VALUENAME ButtonShadow     VALUE "90 78 177"
                VALUENAME ButtonText       VALUE "0 0 0"
                VALUENAME GrayText         VALUE "90 78 177"
                VALUENAME Hilight          VALUE "128 128 128"
                VALUENAME HilightText      VALUE "255 255 255"
                VALUENAME InactiveBorder   VALUE "174 168 217"
                VALUENAME InactiveTitle    VALUE "90 78 177"
                VALUENAME InactiveTitleText     VALUE "0 0 0"
```

continues

Listing 29.1. continued

```
          VALUENAME Menu            VALUE "174 168 217"
          VALUENAME MenuText        VALUE "0 0 0"
          VALUENAME InfoText        VALUE "174 168 217"
          VALUENAME InfoWindow      VALUE "0 0 0"
          VALUENAME Scrollbar       VALUE "174 168 217"
          VALUENAME TitleText       VALUE "255 255 255"
          VALUENAME Window          VALUE "255 255 255"
          VALUENAME WindowFrame     VALUE "0 0 0"
          VALUENAME WindowText      VALUE "0 0 0"
     END ACTIONLIST
     NAME !!Tan256 VALUE !!Tan256
     ACTIONLIST
          KEYNAME "Control Panel\Colors"
          VALUENAME ActiveBorder    VALUE "202 184 149"
          VALUENAME ActiveTitle     VALUE "0 0 0"
          VALUENAME AppWorkspace    VALUE "156 129 78"
          VALUENAME Background      VALUE "128 64 64"
          VALUENAME ButtonDkShadow  VALUE "0 0 0"
          VALUENAME ButtonFace      VALUE "202 184 149"
          VALUENAME ButtonHilight   VALUE "228 220 203"
          VALUENAME ButtonLight     VALUE "202 184 149"
          VALUENAME ButtonShadow    VALUE "156 129 78"
          VALUENAME ButtonText      VALUE "0 0 0"
          VALUENAME GrayText        VALUE "156 129 78"
          VALUENAME Hilight         VALUE "0 0 0"
          VALUENAME HilightText     VALUE "255 255 255"
          VALUENAME InactiveBorder  VALUE "202 184 149"
          VALUENAME InactiveTitle   VALUE "156 129 78"
          VALUENAME InactiveTitleText      VALUE "0 0 0"
          VALUENAME Menu            VALUE "202 184 149"
          VALUENAME MenuText        VALUE "0 0 0"
          VALUENAME InfoText        VALUE "202 184 149"
          VALUENAME InfoWindow      VALUE "0 0 0"
          VALUENAME Scrollbar       VALUE "202 184 149"
          VALUENAME TitleText       VALUE "255 255 255"
          VALUENAME Window          VALUE "255 255 255"
          VALUENAME WindowFrame     VALUE "0 0 0"
          VALUENAME WindowText      VALUE "0 0 0"
     END ACTIONLIST
     NAME !!Wheat256 VALUE !!Wheat256
     ACTIONLIST
          KEYNAME "Control Panel\Colors"
          VALUENAME ActiveBorder    VALUE "215 213 170"
          VALUENAME ActiveTitle     VALUE "0 0 0"
          VALUENAME AppWorkspace    VALUE "173 169 82"
          VALUENAME Background      VALUE "0 64 64"
          VALUENAME ButtonDkShadow  VALUE "0 0 0"
          VALUENAME ButtonFace      VALUE "215 213 170"
          VALUENAME ButtonHilight   VALUE "235 234 214"
          VALUENAME ButtonLight     VALUE "215 213 170"
          VALUENAME ButtonShadow    VALUE "173 169 82"
          VALUENAME ButtonText      VALUE "0 0 0"
          VALUENAME GrayText        VALUE "173 169 82"
          VALUENAME Hilight         VALUE "0 0 0"
          VALUENAME HilightText     VALUE "255 255 255"
          VALUENAME InactiveBorder  VALUE "215 213 170"
          VALUENAME InactiveTitle   VALUE "173 169 82"
```

```
     VALUENAME InactiveTitleText     VALUE "0 0 0"
     VALUENAME Menu               VALUE "215 213 170"
     VALUENAME MenuText           VALUE "0 0 0"
     VALUENAME InfoText           VALUE "215 213 170"
     VALUENAME InfoWindow         VALUE "0 0 0"
     VALUENAME Scrollbar          VALUE "215 213 170"
     VALUENAME TitleText          VALUE "255 255 255"
     VALUENAME Window             VALUE "255 255 255"
     VALUENAME WindowFrame        VALUE "0 0 0"
     VALUENAME WindowText         VALUE "0 0 0"
END ACTIONLIST
NAME !!Celery VALUE !!Celery
ACTIONLIST
     KEYNAME "Control Panel\Colors"
     VALUENAME ActiveBorder       VALUE "168 215 170"
     VALUENAME ActiveTitle        VALUE "0 0 0"
     VALUENAME AppWorkspace       VALUE "80 175 85"
     VALUENAME Background         VALUE "32 18 46"
     VALUENAME ButtonDkShadow     VALUE "0 0 0"
     VALUENAME ButtonFace         VALUE "168 215 170"
     VALUENAME ButtonHilight      VALUE "211 235 213"
     VALUENAME ButtonLight        VALUE "168 215 170"
     VALUENAME ButtonShadow       VALUE "85 175 85"
     VALUENAME ButtonText         VALUE "0 0 0"
     VALUENAME GrayText           VALUE "80 175 85"
     VALUENAME Hilight            VALUE "0 0 0"
     VALUENAME HilightText        VALUE "255 255 255"
     VALUENAME InactiveBorder     VALUE "168 215 170"
     VALUENAME InactiveTitle      VALUE "80 175 75"
     VALUENAME InactiveTitleText      VALUE "0 0 0"
     VALUENAME Menu               VALUE "168 215 170"
     VALUENAME MenuText           VALUE "0 0 0"
     VALUENAME InfoText           VALUE "168 215 170"
     VALUENAME InfoWindow         VALUE "0 0 0"
     VALUENAME Scrollbar          VALUE "168 215 170"
     VALUENAME TitleText          VALUE "255 255 255"
     VALUENAME Window             VALUE "255 255 255"
     VALUENAME WindowFrame        VALUE "0 0 0"
     VALUENAME WindowText         VALUE "0 0 0"
END ACTIONLIST
NAME !!Rose VALUE !!Rose
ACTIONLIST
     KEYNAME "Control Panel\Colors"
     VALUENAME ActiveBorder       VALUE "207 175 183"
     VALUENAME ActiveTitle        VALUE "128 128 128"
     VALUENAME AppWorkspace       VALUE "159 96 112"
     VALUENAME Background         VALUE "128 64 64"
     VALUENAME ButtonDkShadow     VALUE "0 0 0"
     VALUENAME ButtonFace         VALUE "207 175 183"
     VALUENAME ButtonHilight      VALUE "231 216 220"
     VALUENAME ButtonLight        VALUE "207 175 183"
     VALUENAME ButtonShadow       VALUE "159 96 112"
     VALUENAME ButtonText         VALUE "0 0 0"
     VALUENAME GrayText           VALUE "159 96 112"
     VALUENAME Hilight            VALUE "128 128 128"
     VALUENAME HilightText        VALUE "255 255 255"
     VALUENAME InactiveBorder     VALUE "207 175 183"
     VALUENAME InactiveTitle      VALUE "159 96 112"
```

continues

Listing 29.1. continued

```
          VALUENAME InactiveTitleText      VALUE "0 0 0"
          VALUENAME Menu              VALUE "207 175 183"
          VALUENAME MenuText          VALUE "0 0 0"
          VALUENAME InfoText          VALUE "207 175 183"
          VALUENAME InfoWindow        VALUE "0 0 0"
          VALUENAME Scrollbar         VALUE "207 175 183"
          VALUENAME TitleText         VALUE "255 255 255"
          VALUENAME Window            VALUE "255 255 255"
          VALUENAME WindowFrame       VALUE "0 0 0"
          VALUENAME WindowText        VALUE "0 0 0"
     END ACTIONLIST
     NAME !!Evergreen VALUE !!Evergreen
     ACTIONLIST
          KEYNAME "Control Panel\Colors"
          VALUENAME ActiveBorder      VALUE "47 151 109"
          VALUENAME ActiveTitle       VALUE "0 0 0"
          VALUENAME AppWorkspace      VALUE "31 101 73"
          VALUENAME Background        VALUE "48 63 48"
          VALUENAME ButtonDkShadow    VALUE "0 0 0"
          VALUENAME ButtonFace        VALUE "47 151 109"
          VALUENAME ButtonHilight     VALUE "137 218 186"
          VALUENAME ButtonLight       VALUE "47 151 109"
          VALUENAME ButtonShadow      VALUE "31 101 73"
          VALUENAME ButtonText        VALUE "0 0 0"
          VALUENAME GrayText          VALUE "31 101 73"
          VALUENAME Hilight           VALUE "0 0 0"
          VALUENAME HilightText       VALUE "255 255 255"
          VALUENAME InactiveBorder    VALUE "47 151 109"
          VALUENAME InactiveTitle     VALUE "31 101 73"
          VALUENAME InactiveTitleText        VALUE "0 0 0"
          VALUENAME Menu              VALUE "47 151 109"
          VALUENAME MenuText          VALUE "0 0 0"
          VALUENAME InfoText          VALUE "47 151 109"
          VALUENAME InfoWindow        VALUE "0 0 0"
          VALUENAME Scrollbar         VALUE "47 151 109"
          VALUENAME TitleText         VALUE "255 255 255"
          VALUENAME Window            VALUE "255 255 255"
          VALUENAME WindowFrame       VALUE "0 0 0"
          VALUENAME WindowText        VALUE "0 0 0"
     END ACTIONLIST
     NAME !!Blues VALUE !!Blues
     ACTIONLIST
          KEYNAME "Control Panel\Colors"
          VALUENAME ActiveBorder      VALUE "161 198 221"
          VALUENAME ActiveTitle       VALUE "0 0 0"
          VALUENAME AppWorkspace      VALUE "69 139 186"
          VALUENAME Background        VALUE "0 0 64"
          VALUENAME ButtonDkShadow    VALUE "0 0 0"
          VALUENAME ButtonFace        VALUE "164 198 221"
          VALUENAME ButtonHilight     VALUE "210 227 238"
          VALUENAME ButtonLight       VALUE "164 198 221"
          VALUENAME ButtonShadow      VALUE "69 139 186"
          VALUENAME ButtonText        VALUE "0 0 0"
          VALUENAME GrayText          VALUE "69 139 186"
          VALUENAME Hilight           VALUE "0 0 0"
          VALUENAME HilightText       VALUE "255 255 255"
          VALUENAME InactiveBorder    VALUE "164 198 221"
```

```
        VALUENAME InactiveTitle    VALUE "69 139 186"
        VALUENAME InactiveTitleText         VALUE "0 0 0"
        VALUENAME Menu             VALUE "164 198 221"
        VALUENAME MenuText         VALUE "0 0 0"
        VALUENAME InfoText         VALUE "164 198 221"
        VALUENAME InfoWindow       VALUE "0 0 0"
        VALUENAME Scrollbar        VALUE "164 198 221"
        VALUENAME TitleText        VALUE "255 255 255"
        VALUENAME Window           VALUE "255 255 255"
        VALUENAME WindowFrame      VALUE "0 0 0"
        VALUENAME WindowText       VALUE "0 0 0"
   END ACTIONLIST
   NAME !!Teal VALUE !!Teal
   ACTIONLIST
        KEYNAME "Control Panel\Colors"
        VALUENAME ActiveBorder     VALUE "192 192 192"
        VALUENAME ActiveTitle      VALUE "0 128 128"
        VALUENAME AppWorkspace     VALUE "128 128 128"
        VALUENAME Background       VALUE "0 64 64"
        VALUENAME ButtonDkShadow   VALUE "0 0 0"
        VALUENAME ButtonFace       VALUE "192 192 192"
        VALUENAME ButtonHilight    VALUE "255 255 255"
        VALUENAME ButtonLight      VALUE "192 192 192"
        VALUENAME ButtonShadow     VALUE "128 128 128"
        VALUENAME ButtonText       VALUE "0 0 0"
        VALUENAME GrayText         VALUE "128 128 128"
        VALUENAME Hilight          VALUE "0 128 128"
        VALUENAME HilightText      VALUE "255 255 255"
        VALUENAME InactiveBorder   VALUE "192 192 192"
        VALUENAME InactiveTitle    VALUE "192 192 192"
        VALUENAME InactiveTitleText         VALUE "0 0 0"
        VALUENAME Menu             VALUE "192 192 192"
        VALUENAME MenuText         VALUE "0 0 0"
        VALUENAME InfoText         VALUE "192 192 192"
        VALUENAME InfoWindow       VALUE "0 0 0"
        VALUENAME Scrollbar        VALUE "192 192 192"
        VALUENAME TitleText        VALUE "0 0 0"
        VALUENAME Window           VALUE "255 255 255"
        VALUENAME WindowFrame      VALUE "0 0 0"
        VALUENAME WindowText       VALUE "0 0 0"
   END ACTIONLIST
   NAME !!TheReds VALUE !!TheReds
   ACTIONLIST
        KEYNAME "Control Panel\Colors"
        VALUENAME ActiveBorder     VALUE "192 192 192"
        VALUENAME ActiveTitle      VALUE "128 0 0"
        VALUENAME AppWorkspace     VALUE "128 128 128"
        VALUENAME Background       VALUE "64 0 0"
        VALUENAME ButtonDkShadow   VALUE "0 0 0"
        VALUENAME ButtonFace       VALUE "192 192 192"
        VALUENAME ButtonHilight    VALUE "255 255 255"
        VALUENAME ButtonLight      VALUE "192 192 192"
        VALUENAME ButtonShadow     VALUE "128 128 128"
        VALUENAME ButtonText       VALUE "0 0 0"
        VALUENAME GrayText         VALUE "128 128 128"
        VALUENAME Hilight          VALUE "128 0 0"
        VALUENAME HilightText      VALUE "255 255 255"
        VALUENAME InactiveBorder   VALUE "192 192 192"
```

continues

Listing 29.1. continued

```
          VALUENAME InactiveTitle   VALUE "192 192 192"
          VALUENAME InactiveTitleText        VALUE "0 0 0"
          VALUENAME Menu            VALUE "192 192 192"
          VALUENAME MenuText        VALUE "0 0 0"
          VALUENAME InfoText        VALUE "192 192 192"
          VALUENAME InfoWindow      VALUE "0 0 0"
          VALUENAME Scrollbar       VALUE "192 192 192"
          VALUENAME TitleText       VALUE "255 255 255"
          VALUENAME Window          VALUE "255 255 255"
          VALUENAME WindowFrame     VALUE "0 0 0"
          VALUENAME WindowText      VALUE "0 0 0"
     END ACTIONLIST
     NAME !!WindowsDefault VALUE !!WindowsDefault
     ACTIONLIST
          KEYNAME "Control Panel\Colors"
          VALUENAME ActiveBorder    VALUE "192 192 192"
          VALUENAME ActiveTitle     VALUE "0 0 128"
          VALUENAME AppWorkspace    VALUE "128 128 128"
          VALUENAME Background      VALUE "0 128 128"
          VALUENAME ButtonDkShadow  VALUE "0 0 0"
          VALUENAME ButtonFace      VALUE "192 192 192"
          VALUENAME ButtonHilight   VALUE "255 255 255"
          VALUENAME ButtonLight     VALUE "192 192 192"
          VALUENAME ButtonShadow    VALUE "128 128 128"
          VALUENAME ButtonText      VALUE "0 0 0"
          VALUENAME GrayText        VALUE "128 128 128"
          VALUENAME Hilight         VALUE "0 0 128"
          VALUENAME HilightText     VALUE "255 255 255"
          VALUENAME InactiveBorder  VALUE "192 192 192"
          VALUENAME InactiveTitle   VALUE "192 192 192"
          VALUENAME InactiveTitleText        VALUE "0 0 0"
          VALUENAME Menu            VALUE "192 192 192"
          VALUENAME MenuText        VALUE "0 0 0"
          VALUENAME InfoText        VALUE "192 192 192"
          VALUENAME InfoWindow      VALUE "0 0 0"
          VALUENAME Scrollbar       VALUE "192 192 192"
          VALUENAME TitleText       VALUE "255 255 255"
          VALUENAME Window          VALUE "255 255 255"
          VALUENAME WindowFrame     VALUE "0 0 0"
          VALUENAME WindowText      VALUE "0 0 0"
     END ACTIONLIST
     NAME !!BlueAndBlack VALUE !!BlueAndBlack
     ACTIONLIST
          KEYNAME "Control Panel\Colors"
          VALUENAME ActiveBorder    VALUE "192 192 192"
          VALUENAME ActiveTitle     VALUE "0 0 0"
          VALUENAME AppWorkspace    VALUE "128 128 128"
          VALUENAME Background      VALUE "0 0 128"
          VALUENAME ButtonDkShadow  VALUE "0 0 0"
          VALUENAME ButtonFace      VALUE "192 192 192"
          VALUENAME ButtonHilight   VALUE "255 255 255"
          VALUENAME ButtonLight     VALUE "192 192 192"
          VALUENAME ButtonShadow    VALUE "128 128 128"
          VALUENAME ButtonText      VALUE "0 0 0"
          VALUENAME GrayText        VALUE "128 128 128"
          VALUENAME Hilight         VALUE "255 255 0"
          VALUENAME HilightText     VALUE "0 0 0"
```

```
                    VALUENAME InactiveBorder  VALUE "192 192 192"
                    VALUENAME InactiveTitle   VALUE "192 192 192"
                    VALUENAME InactiveTitleText         VALUE "0 0 0"
                    VALUENAME Menu            VALUE "192 192 192"
                    VALUENAME MenuText        VALUE "0 0 0"
                    VALUENAME InfoText        VALUE "192 192 192"
                    VALUENAME InfoWindow      VALUE "0 0 0"
                    VALUENAME Scrollbar       VALUE "192 192 192"
                    VALUENAME TitleText       VALUE "255 255 255"
                    VALUENAME Window          VALUE "255 255 255"
                    VALUENAME WindowFrame     VALUE "0 0 0"
                    VALUENAME WindowText      VALUE "0 0 0"
               END ACTIONLIST
               NAME !!Wheat VALUE !!Wheat
               ACTIONLIST
                    KEYNAME "Control Panel\Colors"
                    VALUENAME ActiveBorder    VALUE "192 192 192"
                    VALUENAME ActiveTitle     VALUE "128 128 0"
                    VALUENAME AppWorkspace    VALUE "128 128 128"
                    VALUENAME Background      VALUE "128 128 64"
                    VALUENAME ButtonDkShadow  VALUE "0 0 0"
                    VALUENAME ButtonFace      VALUE "192 192 192"
                    VALUENAME ButtonHilight   VALUE "255 255 255"
                    VALUENAME ButtonLight     VALUE "192 192 192"
                    VALUENAME ButtonShadow    VALUE "128 128 128"
                    VALUENAME ButtonText      VALUE "0 0 0"
                    VALUENAME GrayText        VALUE "128 128 128"
                    VALUENAME Hilight         VALUE "128 128 0"
                    VALUENAME HilightText     VALUE "0 0 0"
                    VALUENAME InactiveBorder  VALUE "192 192 192"
                    VALUENAME InactiveTitle   VALUE "192 192 192"
                    VALUENAME InactiveTitleText         VALUE "0 0 0"
                    VALUENAME Menu            VALUE "192 192 192"
                    VALUENAME MenuText        VALUE "0 0 0"
                    VALUENAME InfoText        VALUE "192 192 192"
                    VALUENAME InfoWindow      VALUE "0 0 0"
                    VALUENAME Scrollbar       VALUE "192 192 192"
                    VALUENAME TitleText       VALUE "0 0 0"
                    VALUENAME Window          VALUE "255 255 255"
                    VALUENAME WindowFrame     VALUE "0 0 0"
                    VALUENAME WindowText      VALUE "0 0 0"
               END ACTIONLIST
          END ITEMLIST
          END PART
     END POLICY
 END CATEGORY     ; Desktop
CATEGORY !!Shell
     CATEGORY !!Restrictions
          KEYNAME Software\Microsoft\Windows\CurrentVersion\Policies\Explorer
               POLICY !!RemoveRun
               VALUENAME "NoRun"
               END POLICY
               POLICY !!RemoveFolders
               VALUENAME "NoSetFolders"
               END POLICY
               POLICY !!RemoveTaskbar
               VALUENAME "NoSetTaskbar"
               END POLICY
```

continues

Listing 29.1. continued

```
                  POLICY !!RemoveFind
                  VALUENAME "NoFind"
                  END POLICY
                  POLICY !!HideDrives
                  VALUENAME "NoDrives"
                  VALUEON NUMERIC 67108863     ; low 26 bits on (1 bit per drive)
                  END POLICY
                  POLICY !!HideNetHood
                  VALUENAME "NoNetHood"
                  END POLICY
                  POLICY !!NoEntireNetwork
                  KEYNAME Software\Microsoft\Windows\CurrentVersion\
➥Policies\Network
                  VALUENAME "NoEntireNetwork"
                  END POLICY
                  POLICY !!NoWorkgroupContents
                  KEYNAME Software\Microsoft\Windows\CurrentVersion\
➥Policies\Network
                  VALUENAME "NoWorkgroupContents"
                  END POLICY
                  POLICY !!HideDesktop
                  VALUENAME "NoDesktop"
                  END POLICY
                  POLICY !!DisableClose
                  VALUENAME "NoClose"
                  END POLICY
                  POLICY !!NoSaveSettings
                  VALUENAME "NoSaveSettings"
                  END POLICY
      END CATEGORY
END CATEGORY     ; Shell
CATEGORY !!System
KEYNAME Software\Microsoft\Windows\CurrentVersion\Policies\System
      CATEGORY !!Restrictions
            POLICY !!DisableRegedit
            VALUENAME DisableRegistryTools
            END POLICY
            POLICY !!RestrictApps
            KEYNAME Software\Microsoft\Windows\CurrentVersion\Policies\Explorer
            VALUENAME RestrictRun
            PART !!RestrictAppsList LISTBOX
            KEYNAME Software\Microsoft\Windows\CurrentVersion\Policies
            ➥\Explorer\RestrictRun
            VALUEPREFIX ""
            END PART
            PART !!RestrictApps_Tip1              TEXT     END PART
            PART !!RestrictApps_Tip2              TEXT     END PART
            PART !!RestrictApps_Tip3              TEXT     END PART
            PART !!RestrictApps_Tip4              TEXT     END PART
            END POLICY
      END CATEGORY
END CATEGORY     ; System
[strings]
Network="Network"
Update="System policies update"
RemoteUpdate="Remote update"
UpdateMode="Update mode"
```

```
UM_Automatic="Automatic (use default path)"
UM_Manual="Manual (use specific path)"
UM_Manual_Path="Path for manual update"
DisplayErrors="Display error messages"
LoadBalance="Load balancing"
System="System"
DisableFileSharing="Disable file sharing"
DisablePrintSharing="Disable print sharing"
ControlPanel="Control Panel"
CPL_Display="Display"
CPL_Display_Restrict="Restrict display"
CPL_Display_Disable="Deny access to display icon"
CPL_Display_HideBkgnd="Hide Background tab"
CPL_Display_HideScrsav="Hide Screen Saver tab"
CPL_Display_HideAppearance="Hide Appearance tab"
CPL_Display_HideSettings="Hide Settings tab"
Desktop="Desktop"
Wallpaper="Wallpaper"
WallpaperName="Wallpaper Name"
TileWallpaper="Tile Wallpaper"
Wallpaper_Tip1="Specifiy location and name (e.g.  c:\winnt\winnt256.bmp)"
Wallpaper_Tip2="  "
ColorScheme="Color scheme"
SchemeName="Scheme name"
Lavender="Lavender 256"
Celery="Celery 256"
Rose="Rose 256"
Evergreen="Evergreen 256"
Blues="Blues 256"
WindowsDefault="Windows Default"
BlueAndBlack="Blue and Black"
Teal="Teal"
TheReds="The Reds"
Wheat="Wheat"
Wheat256="Wheat 256"
Tan256="Tan 256"
Shell="Shell"
RemoveRun="Remove Run command from Start menu"
RemoveFolders="Remove folders from Settings on Start menu"
RemoveTaskbar="Remove Taskbar from Settings on Start menu"
RemoveFind="Remove Find command from Start menu"
HideDrives="Hide drives in My Computer"
HideNetHood="Hide Network Neighborhood"
NoEntireNetwork="No Entire Network in Network Neighborhood"
HideDesktop="Hide all items on desktop"
DisableClose="Disable Shut Down command"
NoSaveSettings="Don't save settings at exit"
SNMP="SNMP"
Communities="Communities"
CommunitiesListbox="Communities"
PermittedManagers="Permitted managers"
PermittedManagersListbox="Permitted managers"
Traps_Public="Traps for Public community"
Traps_PublicListbox="Trap configuration"
Restrictions="Restrictions"
DisableRegedit="Disable Registry editing tools"
Run="Run"
RunServices="Run services"
```

continues

Listing 29.1. continued

```
RunListbox="Items to run at startup"
RunServicesListbox="Services to run at startup"
NoWorkgroupContents="No workgroup contents in Network Neighborhood"
RestrictApps="Run only allowed Windows applications"
RestrictAppsList="List of allowed applications"
RestrictApps_Tip1="     "
RestrictApps_Tip2="To create a list of allowed applications, click Show,"
RestrictApps_Tip3="then Add, and enter the application executable name"
RestrictApps_Tip4="(e.g., Winword.exe, Poledit.exe, Powerpnt.exe)."
DomainLogonConfirmation="Display domain logon confirmation"
NoDomainPwdCaching="Disable caching of domain password"
```

Contents of WINNT.ADM

The policies in WINNT.ADM are specific to Windows NT 4.0. Even though many of the actual Registry settings under the CLASS MACHINE section are also usable under NT 3.5*x*, NT 3.5*x* does not look for or use policies. You can, however, use many of the Registry settings directly and modify your 3.5*x* environment.

Most of the entries in WINNT.ADM (shown in Listing 29.2) are associated with system functions because most of the interface/user functions are included with COMMON.ADM. Using the system functions can significantly increase security by limiting access to sensitive areas of Windows NT.

Listing 29.2. WINNT.ADM.

```
CLASS MACHINE
CATEGORY  !!Network
        CATEGORY !!Sharing
                KEYNAME System\CurrentControlSet\Services\
➥LanManServer\Parameters
                POLICY !!WorkstationShareAutoCreate
                          VALUENAME "AutoShareWks"
               VALUEOFF NUMERIC 0
                          PART !!ShareWks_Tip1          TEXT    END PART
                          PART !!ShareWks_Tip2          TEXT    END PART
                END POLICY
                POLICY !!ServerShareAutoCreate
                          VALUENAME "AutoShareServer"
               VALUEOFF NUMERIC 0
                          PART !!ShareServer_Tip1       TEXT    END PART
                          PART !!ShareServer_Tip2       TEXT    END PART
                END POLICY
        END CATEGORY    ; Sharing
END CATEGORY    ; Network
CATEGORY  !!Printers
KEYNAME System\CurrentControlSet\Control\Print
          POLICY !!PrintManager_Browser_Restrict
          VALUENAME  DisableServerThread
          PART !!Disable_Server_Tip1                    TEXT
          END PART
          PART !!Disable_Server_Tip2                    TEXT
          END PART
```

```
        END POLICY
        POLICY !!Scheduler_Thread_Priority
        PART !!Scheduler_Priority                  DROPDOWNLIST
        VALUENAME SchedulerThreadPriority
             ITEMLIST
                  NAME "Above Normal"  VALUE NUMERIC  1
                  NAME "Normal"        VALUE NUMERIC  0
                  NAME "Below Normal"  VALUE NUMERIC  -1
             END ITEMLIST
        END PART
        END POLICY
        POLICY !!Beep_Enabled
        VALUENAME BeepEnabled
              VALUEOFF NUMERIC 0
        PART !!Beep_Tip1                       TEXT     END PART
        PART !!Beep_Tip2                       TEXT     END PART
        END POLICY
END CATEGORY
CATEGORY  !!RemoteAccess
KEYNAME System\CurrentControlSet\Services\RemoteAccess\Parameters
        POLICY !!MaximumRetries
             PART !!RAS_Length                 NUMERIC REQUIRED
             MIN 1 MAX 10 DEFAULT 2
             VALUENAME AuthenticateRetries
             END PART
        END POLICY
        POLICY !!MaximumTime
             PART !!RAS_Time                       NUMERIC REQUIRED
             MIN 20  MAX 600 DEFAULT 120
             VALUENAME AuthenticateTime
             END PART
        END POLICY
        POLICY !!CallBackTime
             PART !!INT_Time                       NUMERIC REQUIRED
             MIN 2 MAX 12 DEFAULT 2
             VALUENAME CallbackTime
             END PART
        END POLICY
        POLICY !!Auto_Disconnect
             PART !!Autodisconnect_Time             NUMERIC REQUIRED
             MIN 0  DEFAULT 20
             VALUENAME AutoDisconnect
             END PART
        END POLICY
END CATEGORY
CATEGORY !!Shell
      CATEGORY !!CustomSharedFolders
              KEYNAME "Software\Microsoft\Windows\CurrentVersion
              ➥\Explorer\User Shell Folders"
              POLICY !!CustomFolders_SharedPrograms
                      PART !!CustomFolders_SharedProgramsPath
                      EDITTEXT REQUIRED  EXPANDABLETEXT
                      DEFAULT !!CustomFolders_SharedProgramsDefault
                      VALUENAME "Common Programs"
                      END PART
              END POLICY
              POLICY !!CustomFolders_SharedDesktop
                      PART !!CustomFolders_SharedDesktopPath
```

continues

Listing 29.2. continued

```
                EDITTEXT REQUIRED  EXPANDABLETEXT
                DEFAULT !!CustomFolders_SharedDesktopDefault
                VALUENAME "Common Desktop"
                END PART
            END POLICY
            POLICY !!CustomFolders_SharedStartMenu
                PART !!CustomFolders_SharedStartMenuPath
                EDITTEXT REQUIRED  EXPANDABLETEXT
                DEFAULT !!CustomFolders_SharedStartMenuDefault
                VALUENAME "Common Start Menu"
                END PART
            END POLICY
            POLICY !!CustomFolders_SharedStartup
                PART !!CustomFolders_SharedStartupPath
                EDITTEXT REQUIRED  EXPANDABLETEXT
                DEFAULT !!CustomFolders_SharedStartupDefault
                VALUENAME "Common Startup"
                END PART
            END POLICY
        END CATEGORY
END CATEGORY    ; Shell
CATEGORY  !!System
        CATEGORY !!Login_Policies
            POLICY !!LogonBanner
            KEYNAME "Software\Microsoft\Windows NT\CurrentVersion\Winlogon"
                PART !!LogonBanner_Caption          EDITTEXT
                VALUENAME "LegalNoticeCaption"
                MAXLEN 255
                DEFAULT !!LogonBanner_DefCaption
                END PART
                PART !!LogonBanner_Text             EDITTEXT
                VALUENAME "LegalNoticeText"
                MAXLEN 255
                DEFAULT !!LogonBanner_DefText
                END PART
            END POLICY
            POLICY !!Shutdown_Restrict
            KEYNAME "Software\Microsoft\Windows NT\CurrentVersion\Winlogon"
                VALUENAME  ShutdownWithoutLogon
                VALUEON "1"  VALUEOFF "0"
                PART !!Shutd_Tip1     TEXT    END PART
                PART !!Shutd_Tip2     TEXT    END PART
                PART !!Shutd_Tip3     TEXT    END PART
            END POLICY
            POLICY !!LastUserName_Restrict
            KEYNAME "Software\Microsoft\Windows NT\CurrentVersion\Winlogon"
                VALUENAME DontDisplayLastUserName
                VALUEON "1"  VALUEOFF "0"
                PART !!Dont_Display_Tip1      TEXT    END PART
                PART !!Dont_Display_Tip2      TEXT    END PART
                PART !!Dont_Display_Tip3      TEXT    END PART
            END POLICY
            POLICY !!Run_Logon_Script_Sync
            KEYNAME "Software\Microsoft\Windows NT\CurrentVersion\Winlogon"
                VALUENAME RunLogonScriptSync
                PART !!Script_Tip1    TEXT    END PART
                PART !!Script_Tip2    TEXT    END PART
```

```
                        PART !!Script_Tip4    TEXT    END PART
                END POLICY
        END CATEGORY    ; Login Policies
        CATEGORY !!FileSystem
                KEYNAME System\CurrentControlSet\Control\FileSystem
                POLICY !!Disable8dot3Names
                VALUENAME "NtfsDisable8dot3NameCreation"
                END POLICY
                POLICY !!AllowExtCharsIn8dot3
                        VALUENAME "NtfsAllowExtendedCharacterIn8dot3Name"
                        PART !!ExtChars_Tip1  TEXT    END PART
                        PART !!ExtChars_Tip2  TEXT    END PART
                END POLICY
                POLICY !!DisableLastUpdate
                        VALUENAME "NtfsDisableLastAccessUpdate"
                        PART !!LastAccess_Tip1   TEXT    END PART
                        PART !!LastAccess_Tip2   TEXT    END PART
                END POLICY
        END CATEGORY    ;  File system
END CATEGORY    ; System
CATEGORY  !!UserProfiles
KEYNAME "Software\Microsoft\Windows NT\CurrentVersion\winlogon"
                POLICY !!DeleteRoamingCachedProfiles
                VALUENAME "DeleteRoamingCache"
                PART !!DeleteCache_Tip1         TEXT  END PART
                PART !!DeleteCache_Tip2         TEXT  END PART
                END POLICY
                POLICY !!EnableSlowLinkDetect
                VALUENAME "SlowLinkDetectEnabled"
                END POLICY
                POLICY !!SlowLinkTimeOut
                        PART !!SlowLinkWaitInterval  NUMERIC REQUIRED
                        MIN 1 MAX 20000 DEFAULT 2000
                        VALUENAME SlowLinkTimeOut
                        END PART
                END POLICY
                POLICY !!ProfileDlgTimeOut
                        PART !!ProfileDlgWaitInterval  NUMERIC REQUIRED
                        MIN 0 MAX 600 DEFAULT 30
                        VALUENAME ProfileDlgTimeOut
                        END PART
                END POLICY
END CATEGORY
CLASS USER
CATEGORY !!Shell
        CATEGORY !!CustomFolders
                KEYNAME "Software\Microsoft\Windows\CurrentVersion
                ➥\Explorer\User Shell Folders"
                POLICY !!CustomFolders_Programs
                        PART !!CustomFolders_ProgramsPath
                        EDITTEXT REQUIRED EXPANDABLETEXT
                        DEFAULT !!CustomFolders_ProgramsDefault
                        VALUENAME "Programs"
                        END PART
                END POLICY
                POLICY !!CustomFolders_Desktop
                        PART !!CustomFolders_DesktopPath
                        EDITTEXT REQUIRED  EXPANDABLETEXT
```

continues

Listing 29.2. continued

```
                    DEFAULT !!CustomFolders_DesktopDefault
                    VALUENAME "Desktop"
                    END PART
            END POLICY
            POLICY !!HideStartMenuSubfolders
                    KEYNAME Software\Microsoft\Windows
                    ➥\CurrentVersion\Policies\Explorer
                    VALUENAME NoStartMenuSubFolders
                    PART !!HideStartMenuSubfolders_Tip1  TEXT  END PART
                    PART !!HideStartMenuSubfolders_Tip2  TEXT  END PART
            END POLICY
            POLICY !!CustomFolders_Startup
                    PART !!CustomFolders_StartupPath
                    EDITTEXT REQUIRED  EXPANDABLETEXT
                    DEFAULT !!CustomFolders_StartupDefault
                    VALUENAME "Startup"
                    END PART
            END POLICY
            POLICY !!CustomFolders_NetHood
                    PART !!CustomFolders_NetHoodPath
                    EDITTEXT REQUIRED  EXPANDABLETEXT
                    DEFAULT !!CustomFolders_NetHoodDefault
                    VALUENAME "NetHood"
                    END PART
            END POLICY
            POLICY !!CustomFolders_StartMenu
                    PART !!CustomFolders_StartMenuPath
                    EDITTEXT REQUIRED  EXPANDABLETEXT
                    DEFAULT !!CustomFolders_StartMenuDefault
                    VALUENAME "Start Menu"
                    END PART
            END POLICY
        END CATEGORY
        CATEGORY !!Restrictions
                KEYNAME Software\Microsoft\Windows
                ➥\CurrentVersion\Policies\Explorer
                        POLICY !!ApprovedShellExt
                        VALUENAME "EnforceShellExtensionSecurity"
                        END POLICY
                        POLICY !!NoCommonGroups
                        VALUENAME "NoCommonGroups"
                        END POLICY
        END CATEGORY
END CATEGORY    ; Shell
CATEGORY  !!System
     POLICY !!Parse_Autoexec
     KEYNAME "Software\Microsoft\Windows NT\CurrentVersion\Winlogon"
          VALUENAME ParseAutoexec
          VALUEON "1"  VALUEOFF "0"
          PART !!Parse_Tip1                  TEXT     END PART
          PART !!Parse_Tip2                  TEXT     END PART
     END POLICY
        POLICY !!Run_Logon_Script_Sync
        KEYNAME "Software\Microsoft\Windows NT\CurrentVersion\Winlogon"
                VALUENAME RunLogonScriptSync
                VALUEOFF NUMERIC 0
                PART !!Script_Tip1          TEXT    END PART
```

```
                PART !!Script_Tip2              TEXT    END PART
                PART !!Script_Tip3              TEXT    END PART
        END POLICY
END CATEGORY
[strings]
Network="Windows NT Network"
Sharing="Sharing"
WorkstationShareAutoCreate="Create hidden drive shares (workstation)"
ServerShareAutoCreate="Create hidden drive shares (server)"
ShareWks_Tip1=Automatically create <drive letter>$ and Admin$ shares
ShareWks_Tip2=when Windows NT Workstation starts.
ShareServer_Tip1=Automatically create <drive letter>$ and Admin$ shares
ShareServer_Tip2=when Windows NT Server starts.
System="Windows NT System"
Login_Policies="Logon"
LogonBanner="Logon banner"
LogonBanner_Caption="Caption"
LogonBanner_Text="Text"
LogonBanner_DefCaption="Important Notice:"
LogonBanner_DefText="Do not attempt to log on unless
➥you are an authorized user."
Shutdown_Restrict="Enable shutdown from Authentication dialog box"
Shutd_Tip1="When this box is checked, you can click Shut Down"
Shutd_Tip2="in the Authentication dialog box to select options."
Shutd_Tip3="Default: NT Server = Off, NT Workstation = On"
LastUserName_Restrict="Do not display last logged on user name"
Dont_Display_Tip1="When this box is checked, Windows NT does not"
Dont_Display_Tip2="automatically display the user name of the last person"
Dont_Display_Tip3="to log on in the Authentication dialog box."
Printers="Windows NT Printers"
PrintManager_Browser_Restrict="Disable browse thread on this computer"
Disable_Server_Tip1="When this box is checked, the print spooler does not"
Disable_Server_Tip2="send shared printer information to other print servers."
Scheduler_Thread_Priority="Scheduler priority"
Scheduler_Priority="Priority"
Thread_Priority_Above_Normal="Scheduler priority above normal"
Thread_Priority_Below_Normal="Scheduler priority below normal"
Thread_Priority_Normal="Scheduler priority normal"
Beep_Enabled="Beep for error enabled"
Beep_Tip1="A check in this box enables beeping (every 10 seconds) when a remote"
Beep_Tip2="job error occurs on a print server."
RemoteAccess="Windows NT Remote Access"
MaximumRetries="Max number of unsuccessful authentication retries"
RAS_Length="Number of retries"
MaximumTime="Max time limit for authentication"
RAS_Time="Length in seconds"
CallBackTime="Wait interval for callback"
INT_Time="Length in seconds"
Auto_Disconnect="Auto Disconnect"
Autodisconnect_Time="Disconnect after (minutes)"
UserProfiles="Windows NT User Profiles"
DeleteRoamingCachedProfiles="Delete cached copies of roaming profiles"
DeleteCache_Tip1="When users with roaming profiles log off,"
DeleteCache_Tip2="delete the locally cached profile (to save disk space)."
EnableSlowLinkDetect="Automatically detect slow network connections"
SlowLinkTimeOut="Slow network connection timeout"
SlowLinkWaitInterval="Time (milliseconds)"
ProfileDlgTimeOut="Timeout for dialog boxes"
```

continues

Listing 29.2. continued

```
ProfileDlgWaitInterval="Time (seconds)"
Parse_Autoexec="Parse Autoexec.bat"
Parse_Tip1="When this box is checked, environment variables declared"
Parse_Tip2="in autoexec.bat are included in the users environment."
Shell="Windows NT Shell"
CustomFolders="Custom folders"
CustomFolders_Programs="Custom Programs folder"
CustomFolders_ProgramsPath="Path to location of Programs items"
CustomFolders_ProgramsDefault="%USERPROFILE%\Start Menu\Programs"
CustomFolders_Desktop="Custom desktop icons"
CustomFolders_DesktopPath="Path to location of desktop icons"
CustomFolders_DesktopDefault="%USERPROFILE%\Desktop"
HideStartMenuSubfolders="Hide Start menu subfolders"
HideStartMenuSubfolders_Tip1="Check this if you use a custom Programs folder"
HideStartMenuSubfolders_Tip2="or custom desktop icons."
CustomFolders_Startup="Custom Startup folder"
CustomFolders_StartupPath="Path to location of Startup items"
CustomFolders_StartupDefault="%USERPROFILE%\Start Menu\Programs\Startup"
CustomFolders_NetHood="Custom Network Neighborhood"
CustomFolders_NetHoodPath="Path to location of Network Neighborhood items"
CustomFolders_NetHoodDefault="%USERPROFILE%\NetHood"
CustomFolders_StartMenu="Custom Start menu"
CustomFolders_StartMenuPath="Path to location of Start menu items"
CustomFolders_StartMenuDefault="%USERPROFILE%\Start Menu"
CustomSharedFolders="Custom shared folders"
CustomFolders_SharedPrograms="Custom shared Programs folder"
CustomFolders_SharedProgramsPath="Path to location of shared Programs items"
CustomFolders_SharedProgramsDefault="%SystemRoot%\Profiles
➥\All Users\Start Menu\Programs"
CustomFolders_SharedDesktop="Custom shared desktop icons"
CustomFolders_SharedDesktopPath="Path to location of shared desktop icons"
CustomFolders_SharedDesktopDefault="%SystemRoot%\Profiles\All Users\Desktop"
CustomFolders_SharedStartMenu="Custom shared Start menu"
CustomFolders_SharedStartMenuPath="Path to location of shared Start menu items"
CustomFolders_SharedStartMenuDefault="%SystemRoot%\Profiles\
➥All Users\Start Menu"
CustomFolders_SharedStartup="Custom shared Startup folder"
CustomFolders_SharedStartupPath="Path to location of shared Startup items"
CustomFolders_SharedStartupDefault="%SystemRoot%\Profiles
➥\All Users\Start Menu\Programs\Startup"
Restrictions="Restrictions"
ApprovedShellExt="Only use approved shell extensions"
NoCommonGroups="Remove common program groups from Start menu"
FileSystem="File system"
Disable8dot3Names="Do not create 8.3 file names for long file names"
AllowExtCharsIn8dot3="Allow extended characters in 8.3 file names"
ExtChars_Tip1="Short file names with extended characters may not be viewable"
ExtChars_Tip2="on computers that do not have same character code page."
DisableLastUpdate="Do not update last access time"
LastAccess_Tip1="For files that are only being read, do not update the last"
LastAccess_Tip2="access time.  This will increase the
➥file system's performance."
Run_Logon_Script_Sync="Run logon scripts synchronously."
Script_Tip1="Wait for the logon scripts to complete before starting"
Script_Tip2="the users's shell.  If this value is also set in the"
Script_Tip3="Computer section, that value takes precedence."
Script_Tip4="User section, this value takes precedence."
```

Contents of ADMIN.ADM

The policies in ADMIN.ADM are for use in Windows 95. Most of the entries in ADMIN.ADM are associated with user functions because that is where most of the benefit comes in creating policies for Windows 95. Listing 29.3 shows the entire contents of ADMIN.ADM.

Listing 29.3. Contents of ADMIN.ADM.

```
CLASS MACHINE
CATEGORY !!Network
KEYNAME Software\Microsoft\Windows\CurrentVersion\Policies\Network
    CATEGORY !!AccessControl
        POLICY !!AccessControl_User
        KEYNAME System\CurrentControlSet\Services\VxD\FILESEC
        VALUENAME Start
        VALUEON NUMERIC 0 VALUEOFF DELETE
        ACTIONLISTON
            KEYNAME System\CurrentControlSet\Services\VxD\FILESEC
            VALUENAME StaticVxD VALUE filesec.vxd
        END ACTIONLISTON
        ACTIONLISTOFF
            KEYNAME Security\Provider
            VALUENAME Platform_Type  VALUE NUMERIC 0
            KEYNAME System\CurrentControlSet\Services\VxD\FILESEC
            VALUENAME StaticVxD VALUE DELETE
            KEYNAME System\CurrentControlSet\Services\VxD\NWSP
            VALUENAME Start        VALUE DELETE
            VALUENAME StaticVxD VALUE DELETE
            KEYNAME System\CurrentControlSet\Services\VxD\MSSP
            VALUENAME Start        VALUE DELETE
            VALUENAME StaticVxD VALUE DELETE
        END ACTIONLISTOFF
            PART !!AuthenticatorName EDITTEXT
            KEYNAME Security\Provider
            VALUENAME Container
            END PART
            PART !!AuthenticatorType DROPDOWNLIST
            KEYNAME Security\Provider
            VALUENAME Platform_Type REQUIRED
            ITEMLIST
                NAME !!AT_NetWare VALUE NUMERIC 3
                ACTIONLIST
                    KEYNAME System\CurrentControlSet\Services\VxD\NWSP
                    VALUENAME StaticVxD VALUE nwsp.vxd
                    VALUENAME Start        VALUE NUMERIC 0
                    KEYNAME Security\Provider
                    VALUENAME Address_Book  VALUE nwab32.dll
                END ACTIONLIST
                NAME !!AT_NTAS  VALUE NUMERIC 2
                ACTIONLIST
                    KEYNAME System\CurrentControlSet\Services\VxD\MSSP
                    VALUENAME StaticVxD VALUE mssp.vxd
                    VALUENAME Start        VALUE NUMERIC 0
                    KEYNAME Security\Provider
                    VALUENAME Address_Book  VALUE msab32.dll
                END ACTIONLIST
```

continues

Listing 29.3. continued

```
                NAME !!AT_NT  VALUE NUMERIC 1
                ACTIONLIST
                    KEYNAME System\CurrentControlSet\Services\VxD\MSSP
                    VALUENAME StaticVxD VALUE mssp.vxd
                    VALUENAME Start        VALUE NUMERIC 0
                    KEYNAME Security\Provider
                    VALUENAME Address_Book  VALUE msab32.dll
                END ACTIONLIST
            END ITEMLIST
            END PART
        END POLICY
    END CATEGORY  ; User-Level Security
    CATEGORY !!Logon
        POLICY !!LogonBanner
        KEYNAME Software\Microsoft\Windows\CurrentVersion\Winlogon
            PART !!LogonBanner_Caption EDITTEXT
            VALUENAME "LegalNoticeCaption"
            MAXLEN 255
            DEFAULT !!LogonBanner_DefCaption
            END PART
            PART !!LogonBanner_Text EDITTEXT
            VALUENAME "LegalNoticeText"
             MAXLEN 255
            DEFAULT !!LogonBanner_DefText
            END PART
        END POLICY
        POLICY !!ValidatedLogon
        KEYNAME Network\Logon
        VALUENAME "MustBeValidated"
        END POLICY
    END CATEGORY
    CATEGORY !!NWClient
    KEYNAME System\CurrentControlSet\Services\VxD\NWREDIR
        POLICY !!PrefServer
        KEYNAME System\CurrentControlSet\Services\NWNP32\NetworkProvider
            PART !!PrefServerName EDITTEXT REQUIRED
            VALUENAME "AuthenticatingAgent"
            MAXLEN 48
            END PART
        END POLICY
        POLICY !!SupportLFN
            PART !!SupportLFNsOn DROPDOWNLIST REQUIRED
            VALUENAME "SupportLFN"
            ITEMLIST
                NAME !!LFN_No311     VALUE NUMERIC 1
                NAME !!LFN_All         VALUE NUMERIC 2
            END ITEMLIST
            END PART
        END POLICY
        POLICY !!SearchMode
            PART !!SearchMode1 NUMERIC
            VALUENAME SearchMode
            MIN 0 MAX 7 DEFAULT 0
            END PART
        END POLICY
        POLICY !!DisableAutoNWLogin
            KEYNAME System\CurrentControlSet\Services\NWNP32\NetworkProvider
```

```
            VALUENAME DisableDefaultPasswords
        END POLICY
    END CATEGORY    ; Microsoft Netware-Compatible Network
    CATEGORY !!MSClient
        POLICY !!LogonDomain
        KEYNAME Network\Logon
        VALUENAME "LMLogon"
            PART !!DomainName    EDITTEXT REQUIRED
            MAXLEN 15
            KEYNAME System\CurrentControlSet\Services\MSNP32\NetworkProvider
            VALUENAME AuthenticatingAgent
            END PART
            PART !!DomainLogonConfirmation CHECKBOX
            KEYNAME Network\Logon
            VALUENAME DomainLogonMessage
            END PART
            PART !!NoDomainPwdCaching CHECKBOX
            KEYNAME Network\Logon
            VALUENAME NoDomainPwdCaching
            END PART
        END POLICY
        POLICY !!Workgroup
        KEYNAME System\CurrentControlSet\Services\VxD\VNETSUP
            PART !!WorkgroupName EDITTEXT REQUIRED
            VALUENAME "Workgroup"
            MAXLEN 15
            END PART
        END POLICY
        POLICY !!AlternateWorkgroup
        KEYNAME System\CurrentControlSet\Services\VxD\VREDIR
            PART !!WorkgroupName EDITTEXT REQUIRED
            VALUENAME "Workgroup"
            MAXLEN 15
            END PART
        END POLICY
    END CATEGORY    ; Microsoft Network
    CATEGORY !!NWServer
        POLICY !!DisableSAP
            KEYNAME System\CurrentControlSet\Services\NcpServer\Parameters
            VALUENAME Use_Sap
            VALUEON "0" VALUEOFF "1"
            ACTIONLISTON
                KEYNAME System\CurrentControlSet\Services\NcpServer\Parameters\
➥Ndi\Params\Use_Sap
                VALUENAME "" VALUE "0"
            END ACTIONLISTON
            ACTIONLISTOFF
                KEYNAME System\CurrentControlSet\Services\NcpServer\Parameters\
➥Ndi\Params\Use_Sap
                VALUENAME "" VALUE "1"
            END ACTIONLISTOFF
        END POLICY
    END CATEGORY
    CATEGORY !!Passwords
        POLICY !!HideSharePasswords
        VALUENAME "HideSharePwds"
        END POLICY
        POLICY !!DisablePasswordCaching
```

continues

Listing 29.3. continued

```
        VALUENAME "DisablePwdCaching"
        END POLICY
        POLICY !!RequireAlphaNum
        VALUENAME "AlphanumPwds"
        END POLICY
        POLICY !!MinimumPwdLen
            PART !!MPL_Length NUMERIC REQUIRED
            MIN 1 MAX 8 DEFAULT 3
            VALUENAME MinPwdLen
            END PART
        END POLICY
    END CATEGORY    ; Passwords
    CATEGORY !!RemoteAccess
        POLICY !!RemoteAccess_Disable
        VALUENAME "NoDialIn"
        END POLICY
    END CATEGORY    ; Remote Access
    CATEGORY !!Sharing
        POLICY !!DisableFileSharing
        VALUENAME "NoFileSharing"
        END POLICY
        POLICY !!DisablePrintSharing
        VALUENAME "NoPrintSharing"
        END POLICY
    END CATEGORY
    CATEGORY !!SNMP
        POLICY !!Communities
        KEYNAME System\CurrentControlSet\Services\SNMP\
➥Parameters\ValidCommunities
            PART !!CommunitiesListbox LISTBOX
                VALUEPREFIX ""
            END PART
        END POLICY
        POLICY !!PermittedManagers
        KEYNAME System\CurrentControlSet\Services\SNMP\
➥Parameters\PermittedManagers
            PART !!PermittedManagersListbox LISTBOX
                VALUEPREFIX ""
            END PART
        END POLICY
        POLICY !!Traps_Public
        KEYNAME System\CurrentControlSet\Services\SNMP\
➥Parameters\TrapConfiguration\Public
            PART !!Traps_PublicListbox LISTBOX
                VALUEPREFIX ""
            END PART
        END POLICY
        POLICY !!InternetMIB
        KEYNAME System\CurrentControlSet\Services\SNMP\Parameters\RFC1156Agent
            PART !!ContactName EDITTEXT REQUIRED
            VALUENAME sysContact
            END PART
            PART !!Location EDITTEXT REQUIRED
            VALUENAME sysLocation
            END PART
        END POLICY
    END CATEGORY
```

```
    CATEGORY !!Update
        POLICY !!RemoteUpdate
        KEYNAME System\CurrentControlSet\Control\Update
        ACTIONLISTOFF
            VALUENAME "UpdateMode" VALUE NUMERIC 0
        END ACTIONLISTOFF
            PART !!UpdateMode DROPDOWNLIST REQUIRED
            VALUENAME "UpdateMode"
            ITEMLIST
                NAME !!UM_Automatic VALUE NUMERIC 1
                NAME !!UM_Manual    VALUE NUMERIC 2
            END ITEMLIST
            END PART
            PART !!UM_Manual_Path EDITTEXT
            VALUENAME "NetworkPath"
            END PART
            PART !!DisplayErrors CHECKBOX
            VALUENAME "Verbose"
            END PART
            PART !!LoadBalance CHECKBOX
            VALUENAME "LoadBalance"
            END PART
        END POLICY
    END CATEGORY    ; Update
END CATEGORY    ; Network
CATEGORY !!System
KEYNAME Software\Microsoft\Windows\CurrentVersion\Setup
    POLICY !!EnableUserProfiles
        KEYNAME Network\Logon
        VALUENAME UserProfiles
    END POLICY
    POLICY !!NetworkSetupPath
        PART !!NetworkSetupPath_Path EDITTEXT REQUIRED
        VALUENAME "SourcePath"
        END PART
    END POLICY
    POLICY !!NetworkTourPath
        PART !!NetworkTourPath_Path EDITTEXT REQUIRED
        VALUENAME "TourPath"
        END PART
        PART !!NetworkTourPath_TIP TEXT END PART
    END POLICY
    POLICY !!Run
        KEYNAME Software\Microsoft\Windows\CurrentVersion\Run
        PART !!RunListbox LISTBOX EXPLICITVALUE
        END PART
    END POLICY
    POLICY !!RunOnce
        KEYNAME Software\Microsoft\Windows\CurrentVersion\RunOnce
        PART !!RunOnceListbox LISTBOX EXPLICITVALUE
        END PART
    END POLICY
    POLICY !!RunServices
        KEYNAME Software\Microsoft\Windows\CurrentVersion\RunServices
        PART !!RunServicesListbox LISTBOX EXPLICITVALUE
        END PART
    END POLICY
END CATEGORY
```

continues

Listing 29.3. continued

```
CLASS USER
CATEGORY !!ControlPanel
    CATEGORY !!CPL_Display
        POLICY !!CPL_Display_Restrict
        KEYNAME Software\Microsoft\Windows\CurrentVersion\Policies\System
            PART !!CPL_Display_Disable CHECKBOX
            VALUENAME NoDispCPL
            END PART
            PART !!CPL_Display_HideBkgnd CHECKBOX
            VALUENAME NoDispBackgroundPage
            END PART
            PART !!CPL_Display_HideScrsav CHECKBOX
            VALUENAME NoDispScrSavPage
            END PART
            PART !!CPL_Display_HideAppearance CHECKBOX
            VALUENAME NoDispAppearancePage
            END PART
            PART !!CPL_Display_HideSettings CHECKBOX
            VALUENAME NoDispSettingsPage
            END PART
        END POLICY
    END CATEGORY    ; Display
    CATEGORY !!CPL_Network
        POLICY !!CPL_Network_Restrict
        KEYNAME Software\Microsoft\Windows\CurrentVersion\Policies\Network
            PART !!CPL_Network_Disable CHECKBOX
            VALUENAME NoNetSetup
            END PART
            PART !!CPL_Network_HideID CHECKBOX
            VALUENAME NoNetSetupIDPage
            END PART
            PART !!CPL_Network_HideAccessCtrl CHECKBOX
            VALUENAME NoNetSetupSecurityPage
            END PART
        END POLICY
    END CATEGORY    ; Network
    CATEGORY !!CPL_Security
        POLICY !!CPL_Security_Restrict
        KEYNAME Software\Microsoft\Windows\CurrentVersion\Policies\System
            PART !!CPL_Security_Disable CHECKBOX
            VALUENAME NoSecCPL
            END PART
            PART !!CPL_Security_HideSetPwds CHECKBOX
            VALUENAME NoPwdPage
            END PART
            PART !!CPL_Security_HideRemoteAdmin CHECKBOX
            VALUENAME NoAdminPage
            END PART
            PART !!CPL_Security_HideProfiles CHECKBOX
            VALUENAME NoProfilePage
            END PART
        END POLICY
    END CATEGORY    ; Security
    CATEGORY !!CPL_Printers
        POLICY !!CPL_Printers_Restrict
        KEYNAME Software\Microsoft\Windows\CurrentVersion\Policies\Explorer
            PART !!CPL_Printers_HidePages CHECKBOX
```

```
            VALUENAME NoPrinterTabs
            END PART
            PART !!CPL_Printers_DisableRemoval CHECKBOX
            VALUENAME NoDeletePrinter
            END PART
            PART !!CPL_Printers_DisableAdd CHECKBOX
            VALUENAME NoAddPrinter
            END PART
        END POLICY
    END CATEGORY    ; Printers
    CATEGORY !!CPL_System
        POLICY !!CPL_System_Restrict
        KEYNAME Software\Microsoft\Windows\CurrentVersion\Policies\System
            PART !!CPL_System_HideDevMgr CHECKBOX
            VALUENAME NoDcvMgrPage
            END PART
            PART !!CPL_System_HideConfig CHECKBOX
            VALUENAME NoConfigPage
            END PART
            PART !!CPL_System_NoFileSys CHECKBOX
            VALUENAME NoFileSysPage
            END PART
            PART !!CPL_System_NoVirtMem CHECKBOX
            VALUENAME NoVirtMemPage
            END PART
        END POLICY
    END CATEGORY    ; System
END CATEGORY    ; Control Panel
CATEGORY !!Desktop
KEYNAME "Control Panel\Desktop"
    POLICY !!Wallpaper
        PART !!WallpaperName COMBOBOX REQUIRED
        SUGGESTIONS
            !!Wallpaper1 !!Wallpaper2 !!Wallpaper3 !!Wallpaper4 !!Wallpaper5
            !!Wallpaper6 !!Wallpaper7 !!Wallpaper8 !!Wallpaper9 !!Wallpaper10
        END SUGGESTIONS
        VALUENAME "Wallpaper"
        END PART
        PART !!TileWallpaper CHECKBOX DEFCHECKED
        VALUENAME "TileWallpaper"
        VALUEON "1" VALUEOFF "0"
        END PART
    END POLICY
    POLICY !!ColorScheme
        PART !!SchemeName DROPDOWNLIST
        KEYNAME "Control Panel\Appearance"
        VALUENAME Current REQUIRED
        ITEMLIST
            NAME !!Lavender VALUE !!Lavender
            ACTIONLIST
                KEYNAME "Control Panel\Colors"
                VALUENAME ActiveBorder   VALUE "174 168 217"
                VALUENAME ActiveTitle    VALUE "128 128 128"
                VALUENAME AppWorkspace   VALUE "90 78 177"
                VALUENAME Background     VALUE "128 128 192"
                VALUENAME ButtonDkShadow VALUE "0 0 0"
                VALUENAME ButtonFace     VALUE "174 168 217"
                VALUENAME ButtonHilight  VALUE "216 213 236"
```

continues

Listing 29.3. continued

```
        VALUENAME ButtonLight     VALUE "174 168 217"
        VALUENAME ButtonShadow    VALUE "90 78 177"
        VALUENAME ButtonText      VALUE "0 0 0"
        VALUENAME GrayText        VALUE "90 78 177"
        VALUENAME Hilight         VALUE "128 128 128"
        VALUENAME HilightText     VALUE "255 255 255"
        VALUENAME InactiveBorder  VALUE "174 168 217"
        VALUENAME InactiveTitle   VALUE "90 78 177"
        VALUENAME InactiveTitleText VALUE "0 0 0"
        VALUENAME Menu            VALUE "174 168 217"
        VALUENAME MenuText        VALUE "0 0 0"
        VALUENAME InfoText        VALUE "174 168 217"
        VALUENAME InfoWindow      VALUE "0 0 0"
        VALUENAME Scrollbar       VALUE "174 168 217"
        VALUENAME TitleText       VALUE "255 255 255"
        VALUENAME Window          VALUE "255 255 255"
        VALUENAME WindowFrame     VALUE "0 0 0"
        VALUENAME WindowText      VALUE "0 0 0"
    END ACTIONLIST
    NAME !!Tan256 VALUE !!Tan256
    ACTIONLIST
        KEYNAME "Control Panel\Colors"
        VALUENAME ActiveBorder    VALUE "202 184 149"
        VALUENAME ActiveTitle     VALUE "0 0 0"
        VALUENAME AppWorkspace    VALUE "156 129 78"
        VALUENAME Background      VALUE "128 64 64"
        VALUENAME ButtonDkShadow  VALUE "0 0 0"
        VALUENAME ButtonFace      VALUE "202 184 149"
        VALUENAME ButtonHilight   VALUE "228 220 203"
        VALUENAME ButtonLight     VALUE "202 184 149"
        VALUENAME ButtonShadow    VALUE "156 129 78"
        VALUENAME ButtonText      VALUE "0 0 0"
        VALUENAME GrayText        VALUE "156 129 78"
        VALUENAME Hilight         VALUE "0 0 0"
        VALUENAME HilightText     VALUE "255 255 255"
        VALUENAME InactiveBorder  VALUE "202 184 149"
        VALUENAME InactiveTitle   VALUE "156 129 78"
        VALUENAME InactiveTitleText VALUE "0 0 0"
        VALUENAME Menu            VALUE "202 184 149"
        VALUENAME MenuText        VALUE "0 0 0"
        VALUENAME InfoText        VALUE "202 184 149"
        VALUENAME InfoWindow      VALUE "0 0 0"
        VALUENAME Scrollbar       VALUE "202 184 149"
        VALUENAME TitleText       VALUE "255 255 255"
        VALUENAME Window          VALUE "255 255 255"
        VALUENAME WindowFrame     VALUE "0 0 0"
        VALUENAME WindowText      VALUE "0 0 0"
    END ACTIONLIST
    NAME !!Wheat256 VALUE !!Wheat256
    ACTIONLIST
        KEYNAME "Control Panel\Colors"
        VALUENAME ActiveBorder    VALUE "215 213 170"
        VALUENAME ActiveTitle     VALUE "0 0 0"
        VALUENAME AppWorkspace    VALUE "173 169 82"
        VALUENAME Background      VALUE "0 64 64"
        VALUENAME ButtonDkShadow  VALUE "0 0 0"
        VALUENAME ButtonFace      VALUE "215 213 170"
```

```
    VALUENAME ButtonHilight  VALUE "235 234 214"
    VALUENAME ButtonLight     VALUE "215 213 170"
    VALUENAME ButtonShadow   VALUE "173 169 82"
    VALUENAME ButtonText     VALUE "0 0 0"
    VALUENAME GrayText       VALUE "173 169 82"
    VALUENAME Hilight        VALUE "0 0 0"
    VALUENAME HilightText    VALUE "255 255 255"
    VALUENAME InactiveBorder VALUE "215 213 170"
    VALUENAME InactiveTitle  VALUE "173 169 82"
    VALUENAME InactiveTitleText VALUE "0 0 0"
    VALUENAME Menu           VALUE "215 213 170"
    VALUENAME MenuText       VALUE "0 0 0"
    VALUENAME InfoText       VALUE "215 213 170"
    VALUENAME InfoWindow     VALUE "0 0 0"
    VALUENAME Scrollbar      VALUE "215 213 170"
    VALUENAME TitleText      VALUE "255 255 255"
    VALUENAME Window         VALUE "255 255 255"
    VALUENAME WindowFrame    VALUE "0 0 0"
    VALUENAME WindowText     VALUE "0 0 0"
END ACTIONLIST
NAME !!Celery VALUE !!Celery
ACTIONLIST
    KEYNAME "Control Panel\Colors"
    VALUENAME ActiveBorder   VALUE "168 215 170"
    VALUENAME ActiveTitle    VALUE "0 0 0"
    VALUENAME AppWorkspace   VALUE "80 175 85"
    VALUENAME Background     VALUE "32 18 46"
    VALUENAME ButtonDkShadow VALUE "0 0 0"
    VALUENAME ButtonFace     VALUE "168 215 170"
    VALUENAME ButtonHilight  VALUE "211 235 213"
    VALUENAME ButtonLight     VALUE "168 215 170"
    VALUENAME ButtonShadow   VALUE "85 175 85"
    VALUENAME ButtonText     VALUE "0 0 0"
    VALUENAME GrayText       VALUE "80 175 85"
    VALUENAME Hilight        VALUE "0 0 0"
    VALUENAME HilightText    VALUE "255 255 255"
    VALUENAME InactiveBorder VALUE "168 215 170"
    VALUENAME InactiveTitle  VALUE "80 175 75"
    VALUENAME InactiveTitleText VALUE "0 0 0"
    VALUENAME Menu           VALUE "168 215 170"
    VALUENAME MenuText       VALUE "0 0 0"
    VALUENAME InfoText       VALUE "168 215 170"
    VALUENAME InfoWindow     VALUE "0 0 0"
    VALUENAME Scrollbar      VALUE "168 215 170"
    VALUENAME TitleText      VALUE "255 255 255"
    VALUENAME Window         VALUE "255 255 255"
    VALUENAME WindowFrame    VALUE "0 0 0"
    VALUENAME WindowText     VALUE "0 0 0"
END ACTIONLIST
NAME !!Rose VALUE !!Rose
ACTIONLIST
    KEYNAME "Control Panel\Colors"
    VALUENAME ActiveBorder   VALUE "207 175 183"
    VALUENAME ActiveTitle    VALUE "128 128 128"
    VALUENAME AppWorkspace   VALUE "159 96 112"
    VALUENAME Background     VALUE "128 64 64"
    VALUENAME ButtonDkShadow VALUE "0 0 0"
    VALUENAME ButtonFace     VALUE "207 175 183"
```

continues

Listing 29.3. continued

```
        VALUENAME ButtonHilight  VALUE "231 216 220"
        VALUENAME ButtonLight     VALUE "207 175 183"
        VALUENAME ButtonShadow   VALUE "159 96 112"
        VALUENAME ButtonText     VALUE "0 0 0"
        VALUENAME GrayText       VALUE "159 96 112"
        VALUENAME Hilight        VALUE "128 128 128"
        VALUENAME HilightText    VALUE "255 255 255"
        VALUENAME InactiveBorder VALUE "207 175 183"
        VALUENAME InactiveTitle  VALUE "159 96 112"
        VALUENAME InactiveTitleText VALUE "0 0 0"
        VALUENAME Menu           VALUE "207 175 183"
        VALUENAME MenuText       VALUE "0 0 0"
        VALUENAME InfoText       VALUE "207 175 183"
        VALUENAME InfoWindow     VALUE "0 0 0"
        VALUENAME Scrollbar      VALUE "207 175 183"
        VALUENAME TitleText      VALUE "255 255 255"
        VALUENAME Window         VALUE "255 255 255"
        VALUENAME WindowFrame    VALUE "0 0 0"
        VALUENAME WindowText     VALUE "0 0 0"
    END ACTIONLIST
    NAME !!Evergreen VALUE !!Evergreen
    ACTIONLIST
        KEYNAME "Control Panel\Colors"
        VALUENAME ActiveBorder   VALUE "47 151 109"
        VALUENAME ActiveTitle    VALUE "0 0 0"
        VALUENAME AppWorkspace   VALUE "31 101 73"
        VALUENAME Background     VALUE "48 63 48"
        VALUENAME ButtonDkShadow VALUE "0 0 0"
        VALUENAME ButtonFace     VALUE "47 151 109"
        VALUENAME ButtonHilight  VALUE "137 218 186"
        VALUENAME ButtonLight     VALUE "47 151 109"
        VALUENAME ButtonShadow   VALUE "31 101 73"
        VALUENAME ButtonText     VALUE "0 0 0"
        VALUENAME GrayText       VALUE "31 101 73"
        VALUENAME Hilight        VALUE "0 0 0"
        VALUENAME HilightText    VALUE "255 255 255"
        VALUENAME InactiveBorder VALUE "47 151 109"
        VALUENAME InactiveTitle  VALUE "31 101 73"
        VALUENAME InactiveTitleText VALUE "0 0 0"
        VALUENAME Menu           VALUE "47 151 109"
        VALUENAME MenuText       VALUE "0 0 0"
        VALUENAME InfoText       VALUE "47 151 109"
        VALUENAME InfoWindow     VALUE "0 0 0"
        VALUENAME Scrollbar      VALUE "47 151 109"
        VALUENAME TitleText      VALUE "255 255 255"
        VALUENAME Window         VALUE "255 255 255"
        VALUENAME WindowFrame    VALUE "0 0 0"
        VALUENAME WindowText     VALUE "0 0 0"
    END ACTIONLIST
    NAME !!Blues VALUE !!Blues
    ACTIONLIST
        KEYNAME "Control Panel\Colors"
        VALUENAME ActiveBorder   VALUE "161 198 221"
        VALUENAME ActiveTitle    VALUE "0 0 0"
        VALUENAME AppWorkspace   VALUE "69 139 186"
        VALUENAME Background     VALUE "0 0 64"
        VALUENAME ButtonDkShadow VALUE "0 0 0"
```

```
        VALUENAME ButtonFace      VALUE "164 198 221"
        VALUENAME ButtonHilight   VALUE "210 227 238"
        VALUENAME ButtonLight      VALUE "164 198 221"
        VALUENAME ButtonShadow    VALUE "69 139 186"
        VALUENAME ButtonText      VALUE "0 0 0"
        VALUENAME GrayText        VALUE "69 139 186"
        VALUENAME Hilight         VALUE "0 0 0"
        VALUENAME HilightText     VALUE "255 255 255"
        VALUENAME InactiveBorder VALUE "164 198 221"
        VALUENAME InactiveTitle   VALUE "69 139 186"
        VALUENAME InactiveTitleText VALUE "0 0 0"
        VALUENAME Menu            VALUE "164 198 221"
        VALUENAME MenuText        VALUE "0 0 0"
        VALUENAME InfoText        VALUE "164 198 221"
        VALUENAME InfoWindow      VALUE "0 0 0"
        VALUENAME Scrollbar       VALUE "164 198 221"
        VALUENAME TitleText       VALUE "255 255 255"
        VALUENAME Window          VALUE "255 255 255"
        VALUENAME WindowFrame     VALUE "0 0 0"
        VALUENAME WindowText      VALUE "0 0 0"
    END ACTIONLIST
    NAME !!Teal VALUE !!Teal
    ACTIONLIST
        KEYNAME "Control Panel\Colors"
        VALUENAME ActiveBorder    VALUE "192 192 192"
        VALUENAME ActiveTitle     VALUE "0 128 128"
        VALUENAME AppWorkspace    VALUE "128 128 128"
        VALUENAME Background      VALUE "0 64 64"
        VALUENAME ButtonDkShadow VALUE "0 0 0"
        VALUENAME ButtonFace      VALUE "192 192 192"
        VALUENAME ButtonHilight   VALUE "255 255 255"
        VALUENAME ButtonLight      VALUE "192 192 192"
        VALUENAME ButtonShadow    VALUE "128 128 128"
        VALUENAME ButtonText      VALUE "0 0 0"
        VALUENAME GrayText        VALUE "128 128 128"
        VALUENAME Hilight         VALUE "0 128 128"
        VALUENAME HilightText     VALUE "255 255 255"
        VALUENAME InactiveBorder VALUE "192 192 192"
        VALUENAME InactiveTitle   VALUE "192 192 192"
        VALUENAME InactiveTitleText VALUE "0 0 0"
        VALUENAME Menu            VALUE "192 192 192"
        VALUENAME MenuText        VALUE "0 0 0"
        VALUENAME InfoText        VALUE "192 192 192"
        VALUENAME InfoWindow      VALUE "0 0 0"
        VALUENAME Scrollbar       VALUE "192 192 192"
        VALUENAME TitleText       VALUE "0 0 0"
        VALUENAME Window          VALUE "255 255 255"
        VALUENAME WindowFrame     VALUE "0 0 0"
        VALUENAME WindowText      VALUE "0 0 0"
    END ACTIONLIST
    NAME !!TheReds VALUE !!TheReds
    ACTIONLIST
        KEYNAME "Control Panel\Colors"
        VALUENAME ActiveBorder    VALUE "192 192 192"
        VALUENAME ActiveTitle     VALUE "128 0 0"
        VALUENAME AppWorkspace    VALUE "128 128 128"
        VALUENAME Background      VALUE "64 0 0"
        VALUENAME ButtonDkShadow VALUE "0 0 0"
```

continues

Listing 29.3. continued

```
        VALUENAME ButtonFace     VALUE "192 192 192"
        VALUENAME ButtonHilight  VALUE "255 255 255"
        VALUENAME ButtonLight     VALUE "192 192 192"
        VALUENAME ButtonShadow   VALUE "128 128 128"
        VALUENAME ButtonText     VALUE "0 0 0"
        VALUENAME GrayText       VALUE "128 128 128"
        VALUENAME Hilight        VALUE "128 0 0"
        VALUENAME HilightText    VALUE "255 255 255"
        VALUENAME InactiveBorder VALUE "192 192 192"
        VALUENAME InactiveTitle  VALUE "192 192 192"
        VALUENAME InactiveTitleText VALUE "0 0 0"
        VALUENAME Menu           VALUE "192 192 192"
        VALUENAME MenuText       VALUE "0 0 0"
        VALUENAME InfoText       VALUE "192 192 192"
        VALUENAME InfoWindow     VALUE "0 0 0"
        VALUENAME Scrollbar      VALUE "192 192 192"
        VALUENAME TitleText      VALUE "255 255 255"
        VALUENAME Window         VALUE "255 255 255"
        VALUENAME WindowFrame    VALUE "0 0 0"
        VALUENAME WindowText     VALUE "0 0 0"
    END ACTIONLIST
    NAME !!WindowsDefault VALUE !!WindowsDefault
    ACTIONLIST
        KEYNAME "Control Panel\Colors"
        VALUENAME ActiveBorder   VALUE "192 192 192"
        VALUENAME ActiveTitle    VALUE "0 0 128"
        VALUENAME AppWorkspace   VALUE "128 128 128"
        VALUENAME Background     VALUE "0 128 128"
        VALUENAME ButtonDkShadow VALUE "0 0 0"
        VALUENAME ButtonFace     VALUE "192 192 192"
        VALUENAME ButtonHilight  VALUE "255 255 255"
        VALUENAME ButtonLight     VALUE "192 192 192"
        VALUENAME ButtonShadow   VALUE "128 128 128"
        VALUENAME ButtonText     VALUE "0 0 0"
        VALUENAME GrayText       VALUE "128 128 128"
        VALUENAME Hilight        VALUE "0 0 128"
        VALUENAME HilightText    VALUE "255 255 255"
        VALUENAME InactiveBorder VALUE "192 192 192"
        VALUENAME InactiveTitle  VALUE "192 192 192"
        VALUENAME InactiveTitleText VALUE "0 0 0"
        VALUENAME Menu           VALUE "192 192 192"
        VALUENAME MenuText       VALUE "0 0 0"
        VALUENAME InfoText       VALUE "192 192 192"
        VALUENAME InfoWindow     VALUE "0 0 0"
        VALUENAME Scrollbar      VALUE "192 192 192"
        VALUENAME TitleText      VALUE "255 255 255"
        VALUENAME Window         VALUE "255 255 255"
        VALUENAME WindowFrame    VALUE "0 0 0"
        VALUENAME WindowText     VALUE "0 0 0"
    END ACTIONLIST
    NAME !!BlueAndBlack VALUE !!BlueAndBlack
    ACTIONLIST
        KEYNAME "Control Panel\Colors"
        VALUENAME ActiveBorder   VALUE "192 192 192"
        VALUENAME ActiveTitle    VALUE "0 0 0"
        VALUENAME AppWorkspace   VALUE "128 128 128"
        VALUENAME Background     VALUE "0 0 128"
```

```
            VALUENAME ButtonDkShadow VALUE "0 0 0"
            VALUENAME ButtonFace     VALUE "192 192 192"
            VALUENAME ButtonHilight  VALUE "255 255 255"
            VALUENAME ButtonLight     VALUE "192 192 192"
            VALUENAME ButtonShadow   VALUE "128 128 128"
            VALUENAME ButtonText     VALUE "0 0 0"
            VALUENAME GrayText       VALUE "128 128 128"
            VALUENAME Hilight        VALUE "255 255 0"
            VALUENAME HilightText    VALUE "0 0 0"
            VALUENAME InactiveBorder VALUE "192 192 192"
            VALUENAME InactiveTitle  VALUE "192 192 192"
            VALUENAME InactiveTitleText VALUE "0 0 0"
            VALUENAME Menu           VALUE "192 192 192"
            VALUENAME MenuText       VALUE "0 0 0"
            VALUENAME InfoText       VALUE "192 192 192"
            VALUENAME InfoWindow     VALUE "0 0 0"
            VALUENAME Scrollbar      VALUE "192 192 192"
            VALUENAME TitleText      VALUE "255 255 255"
            VALUENAME Window         VALUE "255 255 255"
            VALUENAME WindowFrame    VALUE "0 0 0"
            VALUENAME WindowText     VALUE "0 0 0"
        END ACTIONLIST
        NAME !!Wheat VALUE !!Wheat
        ACTIONLIST
            KEYNAME "Control Panel\Colors"
            VALUENAME ActiveBorder   VALUE "192 192 192"
            VALUENAME ActiveTitle    VALUE "128 128 0"
            VALUENAME AppWorkspace   VALUE "128 128 128"
            VALUENAME Background     VALUE "128 128 64"
            VALUENAME ButtonDkShadow VALUE "0 0 0"
            VALUENAME ButtonFace     VALUE "192 192 192"
            VALUENAME ButtonHilight  VALUE "255 255 255"
            VALUENAME ButtonLight     VALUE "192 192 192"
            VALUENAME ButtonShadow   VALUE "128 128 128"
            VALUENAME ButtonText     VALUE "0 0 0"
            VALUENAME GrayText       VALUE "128 128 128"
            VALUENAME Hilight        VALUE "128 128 0"
            VALUENAME HilightText    VALUE "0 0 0"
            VALUENAME InactiveBorder VALUE "192 192 192"
            VALUENAME InactiveTitle  VALUE "192 192 192"
            VALUENAME InactiveTitleText VALUE "0 0 0"
            VALUENAME Menu           VALUE "192 192 192"
            VALUENAME MenuText       VALUE "0 0 0"
            VALUENAME InfoText       VALUE "192 192 192"
            VALUENAME InfoWindow     VALUE "0 0 0"
            VALUENAME Scrollbar      VALUE "192 192 192"
            VALUENAME TitleText      VALUE "0 0 0"
            VALUENAME Window         VALUE "255 255 255"
            VALUENAME WindowFrame    VALUE "0 0 0"
            VALUENAME WindowText     VALUE "0 0 0"
        END ACTIONLIST
    END ITEMLIST
    END PART
  END POLICY
END CATEGORY    ; desktop
CATEGORY !!Network
KEYNAME Software\Microsoft\Windows\CurrentVersion\Policies\Network
  CATEGORY !!Sharing
```

continues

Listing 29.3. continued

```
            POLICY !!DisableFileSharingCtrl
            VALUENAME NoFileSharingControl
            END POLICY
            POLICY !!DisablePrintSharingCtrl
            VALUENAME NoPrintSharingControl
            END POLICY
        END CATEGORY  ; Sharing
    END CATEGORY  ; Network
    CATEGORY !!Shell
    KEYNAME "Software\Microsoft\Windows\CurrentVersion\Explorer\User Shell Folders"
        CATEGORY !!CustomFolders
            POLICY !!CustomFolders_Programs
                PART !!CustomFolders_ProgramsPath EDITTEXT REQUIRED
                VALUENAME "Programs"
                END PART
            END POLICY
            POLICY !!CustomFolders_Desktop
                PART !!CustomFolders_DesktopPath EDITTEXT REQUIRED
                VALUENAME "Desktop"
                END PART
            END POLICY
            POLICY !!HideStartMenuSubfolders
                KEYNAME Software\Microsoft\Windows\CurrentVersion\Policies\Explorer
                VALUENAME NoStartMenuSubFolders
                PART !!HideStartMenuSubfolders_Tip1 TEXT  END PART
                PART !!HideStartMenuSubfolders_Tip2 TEXT  END PART
            END POLICY
            POLICY !!CustomFolders_Startup
                PART !!CustomFolders_StartupPath EDITTEXT REQUIRED
                VALUENAME "Startup"
                END PART
        END POLICY
                PART !!CustomFolders_NetHoodPath EDITTEXT REQUIRED
                VALUENAME "NetHood"
                END PART
            END POLICY
            POLICY !!CustomFolders_StartMenu
                PART !!CustomFolders_StartMenuPath EDITTEXT REQUIRED
                VALUENAME "Start Menu"
                END PART
            END POLICY
        END CATEGORY
        CATEGORY !!Restrictions
            KEYNAME Software\Microsoft\Windows\CurrentVersion\Policies\Explorer
                POLICY !!RemoveRun
                VALUENAME "NoRun"
                END POLICY
                POLICY !!RemoveFolders
                VALUENAME "NoSetFolders"
                END POLICY
                POLICY !!RemoveTaskbar
                VALUENAME "NoSetTaskbar"
                END POLICY
                POLICY !!RemoveFind
                VALUENAME "NoFind"
                END POLICY
                POLICY !!HideDrives
```

```
            VALUENAME "NoDrives"
            VALUEON NUMERIC 67108863    ; low 26 bits on (1 bit per drive)
            END POLICY
            POLICY !!HideNetHood
            VALUENAME "NoNetHood"
            END POLICY
            POLICY !!NoEntireNetwork
                KEYNAME Software\Microsoft\Windows\CurrentVersion\
➥Policies\Network
                VALUENAME "NoEntireNetwork"
            END POLICY
            POLICY !!NoWorkgroupContents
                KEYNAME Software\Microsoft\Windows\CurrentVersion\
➥Policies\Network
                VALUENAME "NoWorkgroupContents"
            END POLICY
            POLICY !!HideDesktop
            VALUENAME "NoDesktop"
            END POLICY
            POLICY !!DisableClose
            VALUENAME "NoClose"
            END POLICY
            POLICY !!NoSaveSettings
            VALUENAME "NoSaveSettings"
            END POLICY
    END CATEGORY
END CATEGORY    ; Shell
CATEGORY !!System
KEYNAME Software\Microsoft\Windows\CurrentVersion\Policies\System
    CATEGORY !!Restrictions
           POLICY !!DisableRegedit
        VALUENAME DisableRegistryTools
        END POLICY
        POLICY !!RestrictApps
        KEYNAME Software\Microsoft\Windows\CurrentVersion\Policies\Explorer
        VALUENAME RestrictRun
            PART !!RestrictAppsList LISTBOX
            KEYNAME Software\Microsoft\Windows\CurrentVersion\
➥Policies\Explorer\RestrictRun
                VALUEPREFIX ""
            END PART
        END POLICY
        POLICY !!DisableMSDOS
        KEYNAME Software\Microsoft\Windows\CurrentVersion\Policies\WinOldApp
        VALUENAME Disabled
        END POLICY
        POLICY !!DisableSingleMSDOS
        KEYNAME Software\Microsoft\Windows\CurrentVersion\Policies\WinOldApp
        VALUENAME NoRealMode
        END POLICY
    END CATEGORY
END CATEGORY
[strings]
System="System"
NetworkSetupPath="Network path for Windows Setup"
NetworkSetupPath_Path="Path:"
NetworkTourPath="Network path for Windows Tour"
NetworkTourPath_Path="Path:"
```

continues

Listing 29.3. continued

```
NetworkTourPath_Tip="Note: the path must end in TOUR.EXE"
EnableUserProfiles="Enable User Profiles"
Network="Network"
Logon="Logon"
LogonBanner="Logon Banner"
LogonBanner_Caption="Caption:"
LogonBanner_Text="Text:"
LogonBanner_DefCaption="Important Notice:"
LogonBanner_DefText="Do not attempt to log on unless
➥you are an authorized user."
ValidatedLogon="Require Validation by Network for Windows Access"
Sharing="Sharing"
DisableFileSharing="Disable file sharing"
DisablePrintSharing="Disable print sharing"
AccessControl="Access Control"
AccessControl_User="User-level Access Control"
AuthenticatorName="Authenticator Name:"
AuthenticatorType="Authenticator Type:"
AT_NetWare="NetWare 3.x or 4.x"
AT_NT="Windows NT Server or Workstation"
AT_NTAS="Windows NT Domain"
Passwords="Passwords"
HideSharePasswords="Hide share passwords with asterisks"
DisablePasswordCaching="Disable password caching"
RequireAlphaNum="Require alphanumeric Windows password"
MinimumPwdLen="Minimum Windows password length"
MPL_Length="Length:"
RemoteAccess="Dial-Up Networking"
RemoteAccess_Disable="Disable dial-in"
Update="Update"
RemoteUpdate="Remote Update"
UpdateMode="Update Mode:"
UM_Automatic="Automatic (use default path)"
UM_Manual="Manual (use specific path)"
UM_Manual_Path="Path for manual update:"
DisplayErrors="Display error messages"
LoadBalance="Load-balance"
MSClient="Microsoft Client for Windows Networks"
NWServer="File and printer sharing for NetWare Networks"
LogonDomain="Log on to Windows NT"
DomainName="Domain name:"
Workgroup="Workgroup"
AlternateWorkgroup="Alternate Workgroup"
WorkgroupName="Workgroup name:"
NWClient="Microsoft Client for NetWare Networks"
PrefServer="Preferred server"
PrefServerName="Server name:"
SupportLFN="Support long file names"
SupportLFNsOn="Support long file names on:"
LFN_No311="NetWare 3.12 and above"
LFN_All="All NetWare servers that support LFNs"
SearchMode="Search Mode"
SearchMode1="Search Mode:"
DisableAutoNWLogin="Disable Automatic NetWare Login"
DisableSAP="Disable SAP Advertising"
ControlPanel="Control Panel"
CPL_Display="Display"
```

```
CPL_Display_Restrict="Restrict Display Control Panel"
CPL_Display_Disable="Disable Display Control Panel"
CPL_Display_HideBkgnd="Hide Background page"
CPL_Display_HideScrsav="Hide Screen Saver page"
CPL_Display_HideAppearance="Hide Appearance page"
CPL_Display_HideSettings="Hide Settings page"
CPL_Network="Network"
CPL_Network_Restrict="Restrict Network Control Panel"
CPL_Network_Disable="Disable Network Control Panel"
CPL_Network_HideID="Hide Identification Page"
CPL_Network_HideAccessCtrl="Hide Access Control Page"
CPL_Printers="Printers"
CPL_Printers_Restrict="Restrict Printer Settings"
CPL_Printers_HidePages="Hide General and Details pages"
CPL_Printers_DisableRemoval="Disable Deletion of Printers"
CPL_Printers_DisableAdd="Disable Addition of Printers"
CPL_System="System"
CPL_System_Restrict="Restrict System Control Panel"
CPL_System_HideDevMgr="Hide Device Manager page"
CPL_System_HideConfig="Hide Hardware Profiles Page"
CPL_System_NoFileSys="Hide File System button"
CPL_System_NoVirtMem="Hide Virtual Memory button"
CPL_Security="Passwords"
CPL_Security_Restrict="Restrict Passwords Control Panel"
CPL_Security_Disable="Disable Passwords Control Panel"
CPL_Security_HideSetPwds="Hide Change Passwords page"
CPL_Security_HideRemoteAdmin="Hide Remote Administration page"
CPL_Security_HideProfiles="Hide User Profiles page"
Desktop="Desktop"
Wallpaper="Wallpaper"
WallpaperName="Wallpaper name:"
Wallpaper1="Black Thatch.bmp"
Wallpaper2="Blue Rivets.bmp"
Wallpaper3="Bubbles.bmp"
Wallpaper4="Circles.bmp"
Wallpaper5="Egypt.bmp"
Wallpaper6="Houndstooth.bmp"
Wallpaper7="Pinstripe.bmp"
Wallpaper8="Straw Mat.bmp"
Wallpaper9="Tiles.bmp"
Wallpaper10="Triangles.bmp"
TileWallpaper="Tile wallpaper"
ColorScheme="Color scheme"
SchemeName="Scheme name:"
Lavender="Lavender 256"
Celery="Celery 256"
Rose="Rose 256"
Evergreen="Evergreen 256"
Blues="Blues 256"
WindowsDefault="Windows Default"
BlueAndBlack="Blue and Black"
Teal="Teal"
TheReds="The Reds"
Wheat="Wheat"
Wheat256="Wheat 256"
Tan256="Tan 256"
DisableFileSharingCtrl="Disable file sharing controls"
DisablePrintSharingCtrl="Disable print sharing controls"
```

continues

Listing 29.3. continued

```
Shell="Shell"
CustomFolders="Custom Folders"
CustomFolders_Programs="Custom Programs Folder"
CustomFolders_ProgramsPath="Path to get Programs items from:"
CustomFolders_Desktop="Custom Desktop Icons"
CustomFolders_DesktopPath="Path to get Desktop icons from:"
HideStartMenuSubfolders="Hide Start Menu subfolders"
HideStartMenuSubfolders_Tip1="Check this if you use a custom Programs Folder or"
HideStartMenuSubfolders_Tip2="custom Desktop icons."
CustomFolders_Startup="Custom Startup Folder"
CustomFolders_StartupPath="Path to get Startup items from:"
CustomFolders_NetHood="Custom Network Neighborhood"
CustomFolders_NetHoodPath="Path to get Network Neighborhood items from:"
CustomFolders_StartMenu="Custom Start Menu"
CustomFolders_StartMenuPath="Path to get Start Menu items from:"
Restrictions="Restrictions"
RemoveRun="Remove 'Run' command"
RemoveFolders="Remove folders from 'Settings' on Start Menu"
RemoveTaskbar="Remove Taskbar from 'Settings' on Start Menu"
RemoveFind="Remove 'Find' command"
HideDrives="Hide Drives in 'My Computer'"
HideNetHood="Hide Network Neighborhood"
HideDesktop="Hide all items on Desktop"
DisableClose="Disable Shut Down command"
NoSaveSettings="Don't save settings at exit"
DisableRegedit="Disable Registry editing tools"
DisableMSDOS="Disable MS-DOS prompt"
DisableSingleMSDOS="Disable single-mode MS-DOS applications"
Run="Run"
RunOnce="Run Once"
RunServices="Run Services"
RunListbox="Items to run at startup:"
RunOnceListbox="Items to run once at startup:"
RunServicesListbox="Services to run at startup:"
SNMP="SNMP"
Communities="Communities"
CommunitiesListbox="Communities:"
PermittedManagers="Permitted managers"
PermittedManagersListbox="Permitted managers:"
Traps_Public="Traps for 'Public' community"
Traps_PublicListbox="Trap configuration:"
NoEntireNetwork="No 'Entire Network' in Network Neighborhood"
NoWorkgroupContents="No workgroup contents in Network Neighborhood"
RestrictApps="Only run allowed Windows applications"
RestrictAppsList="List of allowed applications:"
DomainLogonConfirmation="Display domain logon confirmation"
InternetMIB="Internet MIB (RFC1156)"
ContactName="Contact Name:"
Location="Location:"
NoDomainPwdCaching="Disable caching of domain password"
```

Summary

Template files give you the settings possible for the policy. Windows NT System Policy Editor allows you to use multiple template files, and modify the current files, or even to add your own (see Chapter 34, "Creating Custom Policies"). Its capability to use multiple template files makes the System Policy Editor stand out in its ease of use and performance. Understanding what changes you want to make and the effect those changes will have is critical; otherwise, you may damage the systems, and the troubleshooting may be difficult.

CHAPTER 30

Managing the Local Registry with System Policy Editor

When you want to edit the Registry of your own system or another system on the network, you use REGEDT32.EXE or REGEDIT.EXE to make necessary changes. You can use these programs to edit system Registries whether the systems are members of the domain or not, and whether they are even peer-to-peer systems on a simple network.

System Policy Editor was designed for the editing of members of the network. The policy gets implemented only when the user logs on to the domain. However, it is possible to edit the Registry directly, not waiting for a logoff/logon to update, and also to make changes to workgroups-connected systems.

The only limitation to editing those systems through System Policy Editor is that the only available options for changes are those included in the loaded templates.

Tip

Another great benefit of editing the Registry using System Policy Editor is the ability to make a large number of changes, and then choose to save them or not. Unlike REGEDT32.EXE and REGEDIT.EXE, System Policy Editor does not automatically update the Registry with each individual change.

Opening the Registry for Editing

To open the Registry for the local system, select File | Open Registry. Figure 30.1 shows that the labels are Local Computer and Local User instead of Default Computer and Default User.

Figure 30.1.
Direct Registry editing with System Policy Editor.

When you open the template for the local computer or local user, you will see their actual settings instead of their policies. Notice in Figure 30.2 that there are no grayed boxes, only blank or checked boxes. This makes it easy to check the current status of a policy and to assertively set Registry changes.

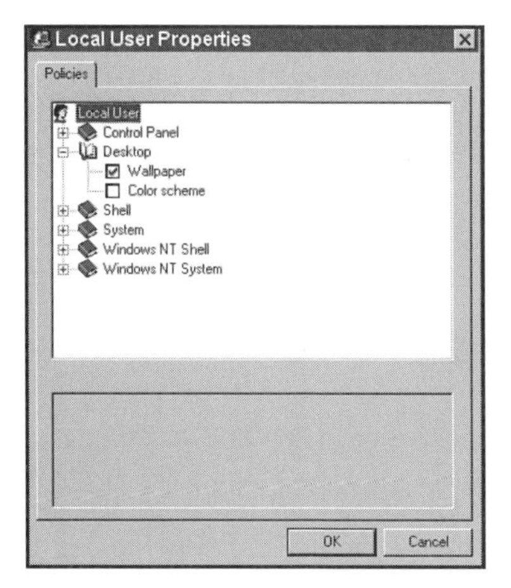

Figure 30.2.
Actual Registry settings shown for Local User Properties.

Any changes made are only for that computer and user, and cannot be applied to multiple computers or users. When you finish the changes in System Policy Editor, save the information with File | Save. If you choose to close the Registry without saving, the system prompts you to save it, as shown in Figure 30.3.

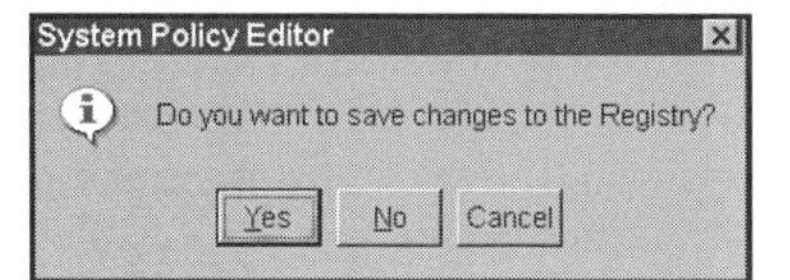

Figure 30.3.
Changes prompt an opportunity to save the Registry.

Editing Another System's Registry with System Policy Editor

Unlike policy editing with System Policy Editor, direct Registry editing can only be done one system at a time. To open another system's Registry, choose File | Connect. You can then choose to browse for a computer, or type the computer's name.

Tip

Even if the computer you need is not in the browse list, you can type the name for any Windows NT or Windows 95 system (with Remote Registry Editing enabled) on the physical network. It does not need to be a member of the domain.

When you select a computer, you are also prompted to choose which user account on the system to modify. Figure 30.4 illustrates this dialog box.

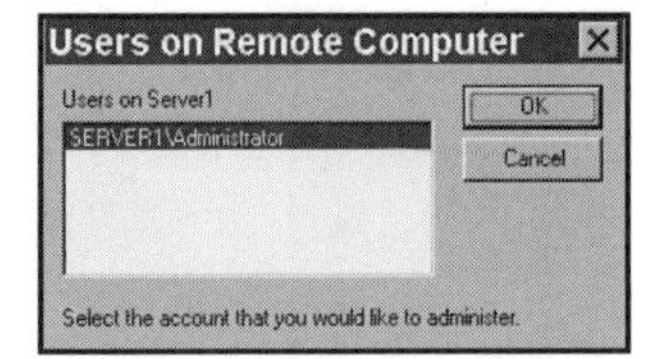

Figure 30.4.
Choose the user profile you want to edit.

Even though you are given a choice of users, you can only access the user (and his policy) that is currently active. If no one is currently logged on, you are not given an opportunity to select any user. However, information about who is logged on can be valuable; not knowing what user is active could mean that you edit information incorrectly.

Directly Editing the Registry for Specific Changes

One of the most powerful ways to use direct editing is to make surgically placed changes to the Registry. Editing the Registry with System Policy Editor can be used for making specific one-time changes to domain-connected systems. In the policy file, users may be specified as a member of one or more groups (groups from the User Manager for Domains), or specified individually. If a user is specified as a member of a group, but not as an individual, only the group's policies take effect. If you want to isolate that user for a specific change without making him an individual in the policy file and without making that change a part of the group's policy file, you can choose to edit his Registry directly.

For example, Bill is a member of the Accounting group in User Manager for Domains. You choose to implement a policy for that group, and make several settings. Those settings apply for all members of the group and any new members put into that group as long as the policy stays in effect. If you want to change the Registry for Bill, but not the rest of the Accounting group, you can connect to his Registry and make the necessary changes.

Note

If you take someone out of a domain group, any policies already set and activated for the group will still be in effect. Policies update the Registry, and the policy-based Registry changes remain even if the policy is no longer in effect.

Changing the Location/Name of the Active Policy File

To allow Windows NT or Windows 95 systems to use a different policy file than the one in the `NETLOGON` share, you must make a change to the Registry. To change the location and/or the name of the file to look to for policies, change the local Registry of each of the Windows 95 systems with System Policy Editor. Follow these steps:

1. Add the template `COMMON.ADM`.
2. Open the local Registry with File | Open Registry.
3. Double-click the local computer.
4. As shown in Figure 30.5, expand the Network and System policies update options.

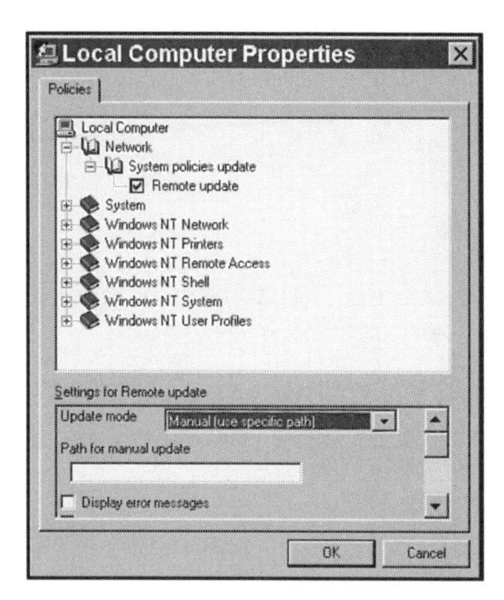

Figure 30.5.
Setting a location for the policy file.

5. Select Remote update.
6. Choose Manual from the drop-down list for the Update mode.

Note

The setting is a little deceptive, in that it says Manual in the Update mode. There is nothing manual about the update. The Registry is automatically updated at logon; it just uses a different path.

7. Enter the path for the policy file (`\\`*`servername`*`\NETLOGON\NTCONFIG.POL` or `\\`*`servername`*`\NETLOGON\CONFIG.POL`).

Warning

Unless you insert the name of the file, the system will not recognize it. Be very specific.

8. Select OK.
9. Save the changes.

Tip

If you are an advanced user, manager, or technical support technician, and you don't want another person determining policy for your system, you could change the location of your policy file to your local machine, and any policy changes made for the network would not affect your system or user Registry files.

Summary

Though a small part of the System Policy Editor, direct Registry editing is very powerful and important. The three most important ways to use this feature are

- To make changes for an individual, even without an individual policy;
- To edit Registries of systems so they can find the policy file, if it is in a location different than the default location;
- To make changes with System Policy Editor for computers and users that are not members of the domain.

CHAPTER 31

Managing Domain Computers with System Policy Editor

It has never been easier to manage hundreds of computers. System Policy Editor allows you to configure settings for individual computers or for every computer in your entire network. System Policy Editor focuses primarily on performance and security.

In this section, you will look at all of the possible settings in System Policy Editor in `COMMON.ADM` and `WINNT.ADM`. After that, you will look at the conflict between named computers and the default computer's settings. Then comes the best part: You will learn about what settings you should use.

The settings are listed with the categories, policies, and parts for each separated by a forward slash, like this: Network/System Policies Update/Remote Update.

Note

Notice the explanations for each of the settings. This embedded information makes implementing policies much easier. It is what you hoped for in `REGEDT32.EXE`, but did not receive.

For every item in System Policy Editor, there are three possible settings (see Figure 31.1): Ignore, Activate, and Deactivate.

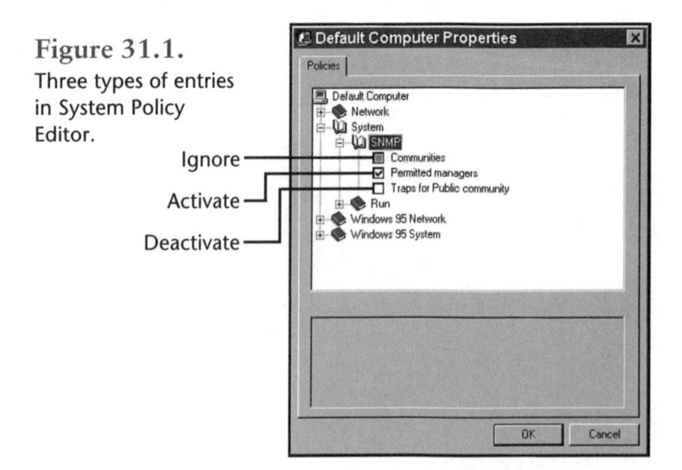

Figure 31.1.
Three types of entries in System Policy Editor.

If the check box is gray, as the Communities check box appears in Figure 31.1, the setting is ignored and the Registry for that item is untouched. Whatever the current setting is, it remains. If the value or key is not currently in the Registry, it will not be inserted. This setting may also be called inactive.

If the check box is checked, as the Permitted managers check box appears in Figure 31.1, the setting is activated and the necessary keys and/or values are added if required.

If the check box is cleared, as the Traps for Public community check box appears in Figure 31.1, the setting is deactivated regardless of the previous setting. Keys and/or values may be added to force the settings to an off position.

Tip

In a new policy, all of the items are set to gray (ignore). Whatever is currently set in the Registry will remain. Before you make any changes to the default computer or to any other named computer, create a specific policy for your own system (or the server on which you are running System Policy Editor). In that policy, deactivate every item. Then, if you configure settings that turn out to be disastrous, you will have at least one system that is unaffected.

Note

Opening a current policy or the local Registry allows you to see which items are currently selected. Some of the settings may be different, based on whether the system is a server or a workstation, and whether it is a domain controller.

Computer Policies in COMMON.ADM

Computer-related policies in COMMON.ADM are relatively few because the underlying functions of Windows NT and Windows 95 are very different. Many more of the computer-related items are in the named template files for NT and 95.

Network/System Policies Update/Remote Update

The ability to set a specific location and policy filename is critical in three different cases:

- In the case of a multiple platform that normally needs to use differently named files
- In the case of a Workgroups-connected system, where there is no NETLOGON share
- In the case of a special policy for an individual user

Windows NT looks in the NETLOGON share for NTCONFIG.POL. Windows 95, on the other hand, looks in NETLOGON for CONFIG.POL. If the policy file will have a different name or be in a different location, you can change the location where Windows NT looks and the filename for which it searches.

Tip

Can you use a common name for the policy file, or should you have separate files? The benefits are obvious for having a single file to manage. However, because Windows 95 cannot use the NT policy file (it is Unicode, and 95 requires a policy file in ASCII), you really have no choice. In the future, a consistent structure will allow you to make a single file and a consolidated policy.

The Remote Update setting is a little deceptive, in that it says `Manual` in the Update mode. There is nothing manual about the update. The Registry is automatically updated at logon, but it just uses a different path. Enter the path as shown in Figure 31.2.

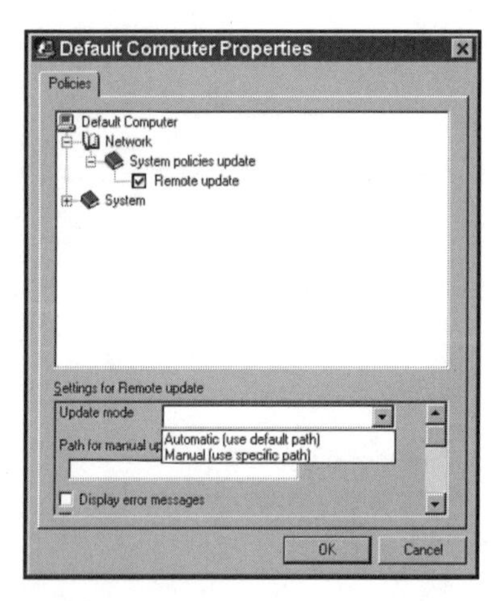

Figure 31.2.
Setting a location for `NTCONFIG.POL`.

The check box in Figure 31.3 may also be important. It allows you to select the Load Balancing option. If the location you choose to set is `\\Server1\Policies\MISCONFIG.POL` and `SERVER1` is extremely busy, NT looks for the same path and file on other logon servers (domain controllers).

Warning

Unless you insert the name of the file, the system will not recognize it. Be very specific.

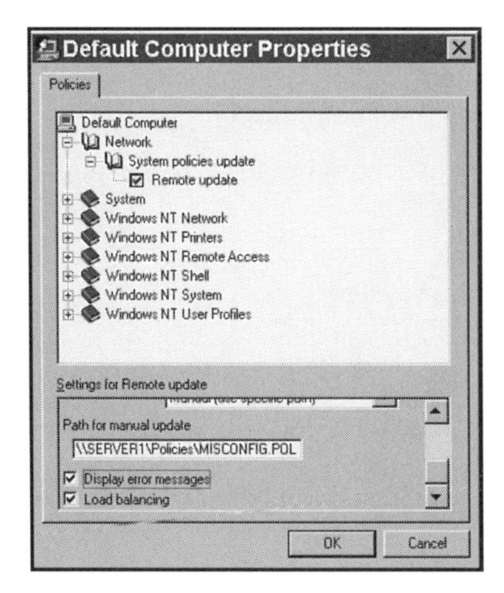

Figure 31.3.
Enabling load balancing for better performance.

Tip

You can choose any name you want for this `.POL` file. Put the file name in the path, and NT will use it. The only computers that will use the specified file are the ones set with an option to do so.

System/SNMP/Communities

SNMP (Simple Network Management Protocol) is used to get and set status information about a host on a TCP/IP network, including data about the user, the physical location of the host computer, and different services running on the host. (See Figure 31.4.)

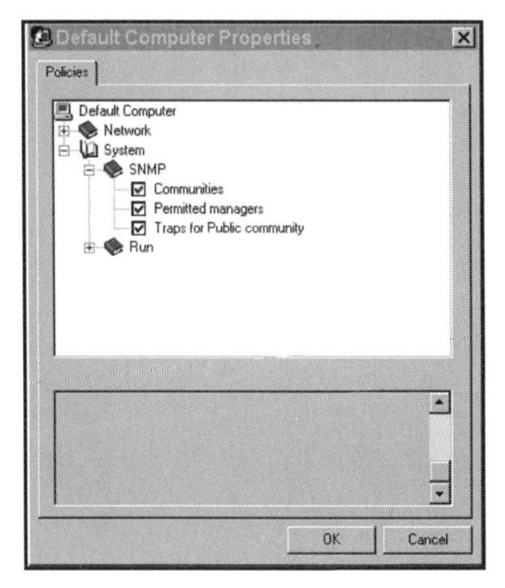

Figure 31.4.
SNMP options in `COMMON.ADM`.

A *community* is a group of hosts, all running the SNMP service. The community name is placed in the SNMP packet when the trap is sent. In nearly every instance, all hosts belong to Public, which is the standard name for the common community.

This setting allows you to list the additional communities to which you want the server to belong. You may list as many as you want.

System/SNMP/Permitted Managers

You can list all the managers in your system who can both change settings and generate errors for SNMP items. Valid entries include IP addresses of systems and host names.

System/SNMP/Traps for Public Community

A trap in SNMP is a block of data that indicates the failure of a request across the TCP/IP network, usually because of authentication. This can occur when the correct community name is not listed, when the host name does not match the IP address, or in other situations in which there is a failure to communicate.

Add the names of traps to use for testing authentication across the TCP/IP network.

System/Run/Run

The Run function is used to set items to be run at startup. It's better to use the Run function than to use the Startup group because the Run function requires a Registry change for the user to disable it. Most users are not able to make those changes, so the likelihood of the application running as intended is much higher.

The value name (as shown in Figure 31.5) is just text information. The only time you see the value name is if the program remains in memory. In that case, the value name text is displayed in the Taskbar. The actual program is the value. After the policy is in place, the Registry for that system is updated, as shown in Figure 31.6.

Tip

Always use the full path to the application listed in the value. If the application location isn't in the path, the function will fail.

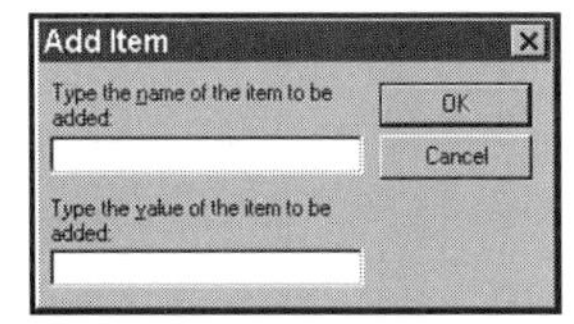

Figure 31.5.
Adding items to be run at startup.

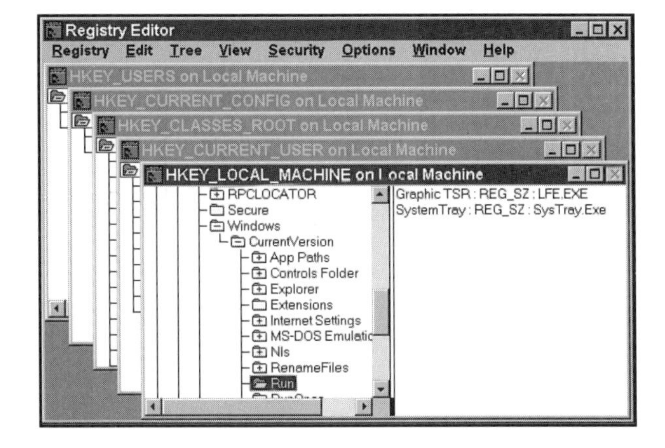

Figure 31.6.
Items entered in the System Policy Editor Run function update the Registry.

Computer Policies in `WINNT.ADM`

The policies in `WINNT.ADM` are much more specific than those in `COMMON.ADM`. Some of the policies in `WINNT.ADM` are very similar to those in `WINDOWS.ADM`; the main difference between the two is the location of the Registry entry.

Windows NT Network/Sharing/Create Hidden Drives Shares (Workstation or Server)

By default, NT creates hidden shares (also called *administrative shares*) for all fixed disk drives on all NT systems. (See Figure 31.7.) These shares are accessible (without a password) only by Administrator from the machine he has logged on to. Other users can access them with the correct password using Map Network Drive (seen in Figure 31.8), typing in the name of the share (`\\SERVER1\C$`, for instance).

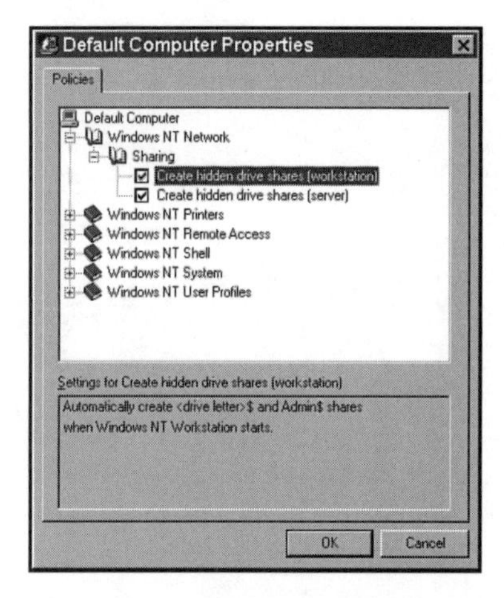

Figure 31.7.
Changing administrative share status.

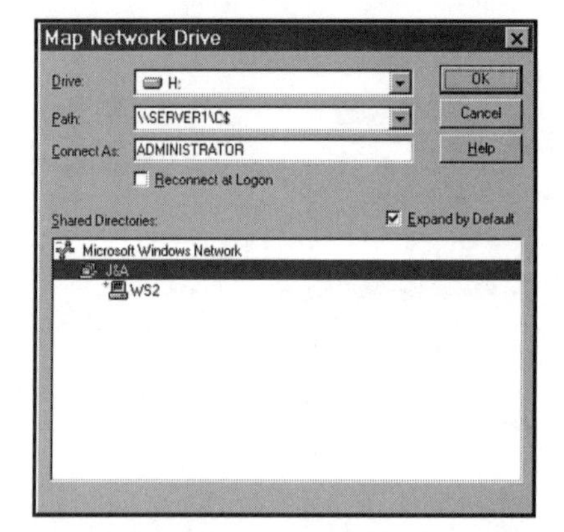

Figure 31.8.
Using an administrative share to gain access to a nonshared resource.

Only members of the Domain Admin global group or the local Administrators group have access to hidden shares. If any other user is logged on to the system, it is not necessary to log him off, but you will need to connect to the share as an administrator, supplying the correct password.

After the correct password is supplied, the root directory and all subdirectories and files are accessible even if they have not been shared in the normal way.

The default for NT is always to create these shares. This entry is used in System Policy Editor to disable the creation of these shares. That requires you to clear the check box.

Tip

You can manually create administrative, or hidden, shares for floppy drives, CD-ROM drives, and other removable media devices. They are not automatically created, even if this setting is turned on.

To create the share, there must be a diskette or other appropriate medium in the drive. You are sharing the drive, not the medium, but the system needs access to the drive to complete the sharing process. After the share is created, any medium can be in the drive, and it can be accessed in the same way as shares on a network.

This is particularly helpful if you need to use someone else's CD-ROM drive, or if you have no 5-1/4" floppy to use. NT 4.0 doesn't support older floppies anyway, but you can access that 5-1/4" floppy when it is on 3.5*x* on another machine on the network. You can then use it from another system across the network.

Windows NT Printers/Disable Browse Thread on this Computer

By enabling this setting at a specific system, that computer's printer shares no longer appear in the browse list in Connect Network Printer. The printers may still be accessed, but the name of the printer must be entered in order to do so. (See Figure 31.9.)

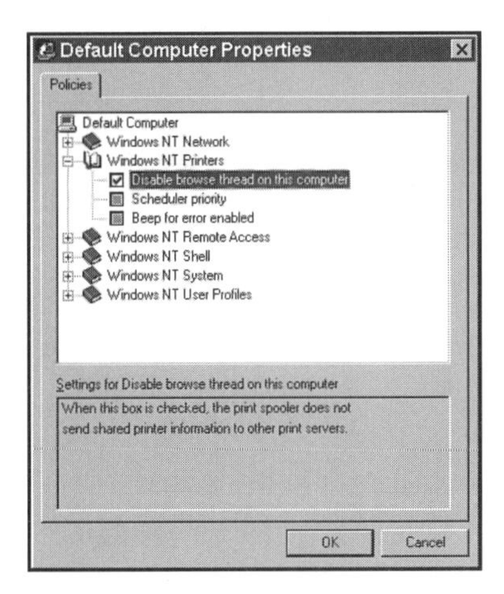

Figure 31.9.
Removing the printer name from other browse lists.

Windows NT Printers/Scheduler Priority

Set this printer's priority above or below normal with this setting. When set above normal, print jobs have a higher priority in combination with foreground and background application threads. Each thread gets a priority between 1 and 14. The higher the number, the sooner the thread gets processed. Boosting this number gets print jobs done faster, but application performance may suffer. (See Figure 31.10.)

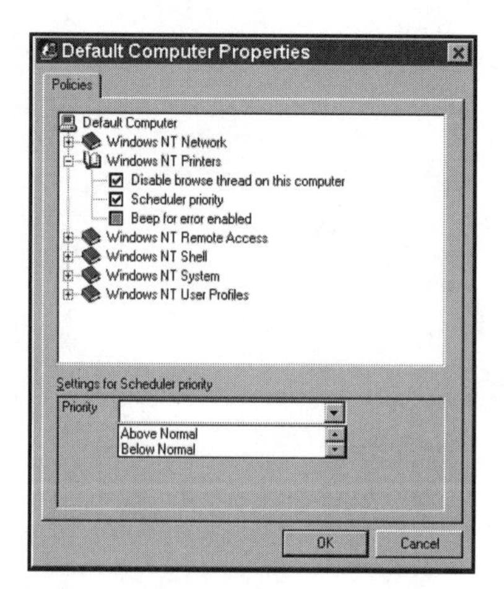

Figure 31.10.
Priority scheduling for print processes.

Windows NT Printers/Beep for Error Enabled

What an annoying thought: Every time there is an error, even a simple timeout error, the system beeps at you. In that case, you might not want the system to beep at you for print errors. On the other hand, if you are not sitting at the location of the print queue, you might not know there is a problem. Your user would wonder why the print job didn't work, and send another, and another, and another, assuming that he must have done something wrong in the way it was sent. Figure 31.11 shows the setting to turn the error beep on.

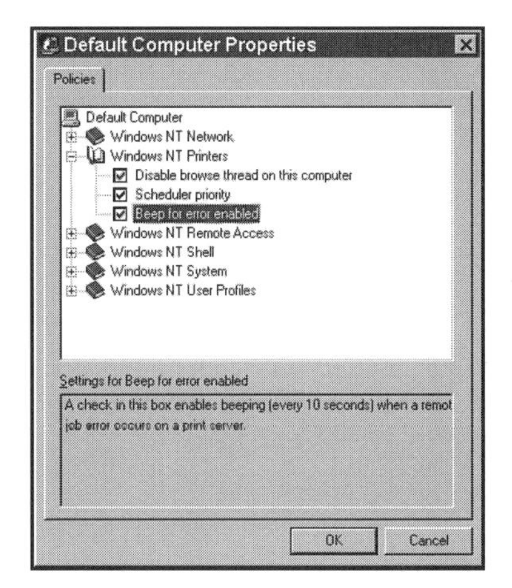

Figure 31.11.
Turn on the error beeping at an unmanned print server.

Windows NT Remote Access/Max Number of Unsuccessful Authentication Retries

This is one of the best ways to keep hackers out of your network. If they don't type the password correctly in the specified number of tries, they will be disconnected. This setting is made at the RAS server only. (See Figure 31.12.)

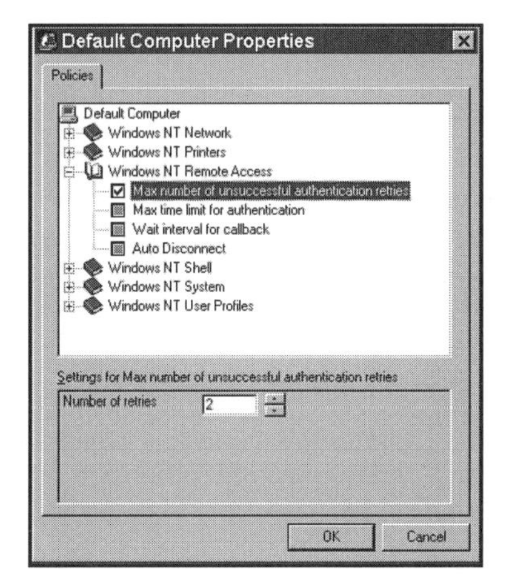

Figure 31.12.
How many times will it take to get it right?

Windows NT Remote Access/Max Time Limit for Authentication

When set at the RAS Server, this setting determines how long the user can wait before entering a password and attempting a logon. It can be a valuable security item because a user who knows his password is more likely to enter it quickly than one who is guessing. The default time is 20 (seconds), but don't set it below 7, or your user may not be able to respond in time. (See Figure 31.13.)

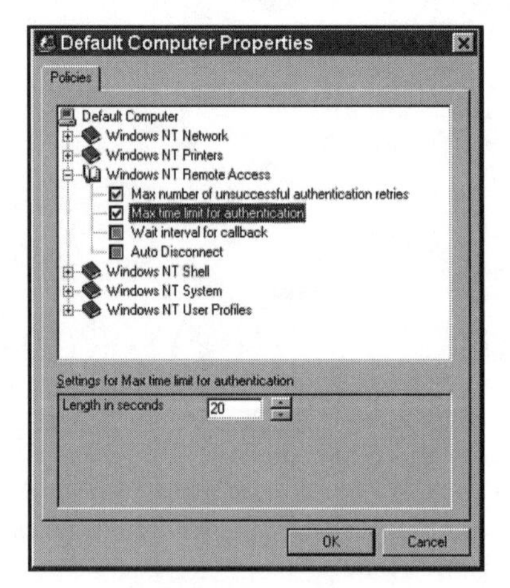

Figure 31.13.
Setting the maximum time for user input at logon.

Windows NT Remote Access/Wait Interval for Callback

One security option is to have the server call the client back. If the user is not at the correct number, he won't be able to connect. Callback can be set up on a user-by-user basis in User Manager for Domains. This is set only on the RAS Server, and the default setting of 2 (seconds) is usually sufficient except when the delay in resetting the modem after disconnection is too long. In that case, increase this number. (See Figure 31.14.)

The autodisconnect is critical for freeing incoming telephone lines. If there is no activity across the lines for 20 minutes, RAS hangs up. Change this value to increase or decrease this amount of time. In a high-demand environment, you may want to decrease it. (See Figure 31.15.)

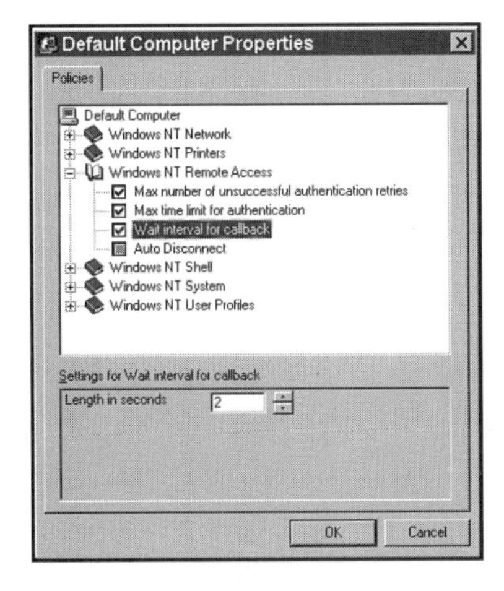

Figure 31.14.
How long should I wait before calling back?

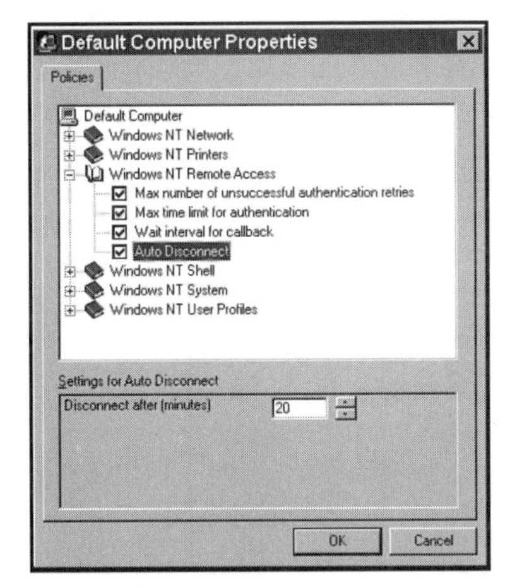

Figure 31.15.
If there is no active traffic, end the connection.

Windows NT Shell/Custom Shared Folders/Custom Shared Programs Folders

If you want all users to be able to access the same applications, you must install the applications and put shortcuts to each in the folder specified in this setting. (See Figure 31.16.)

Windows NT Shell/Custom Shared Folders/Custom Shared Desktop Icons

Some people want to use icons other than the ones that come with NT. Copy the files to the location specified in this tip to give users access to them. (See Figure 31.17.)

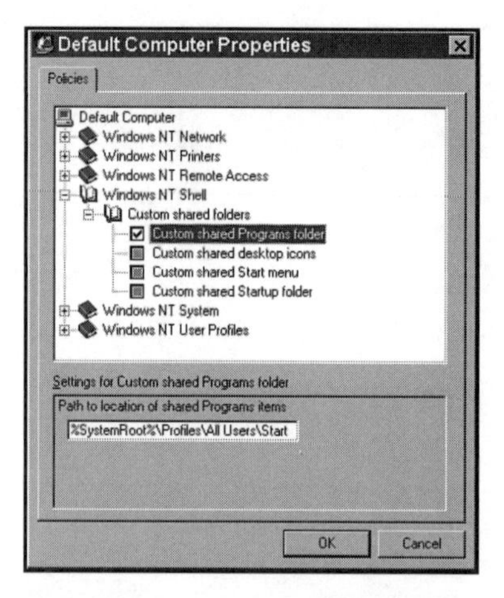

Figure 31.16.
Setting the location for shared application shortcuts.

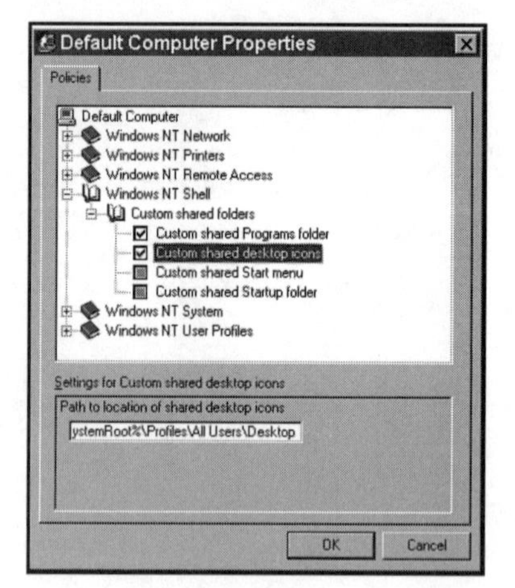

Figure 31.17.
Setting the location for custom folder icons.

Windows NT Shell/Custom Shared Folders/Custom Shared Start Menu

Want everyone's Start menu to have the same items? Copy shortcuts of those items to this location and change the Registry with this tip. (See Figure 31.18.)

Windows NT Shell/Custom Shared Folders/Custom Shared Startup Folder

If you want to easily specify what items load at startup, you can place shortcuts in here. These programs run after Explorer launches, and appear on the Taskbar. Those that you put in the Run section in COMMON.ADM do not show on the Taskbar, and launch prior to Explorer. (See Figure 31.19.)

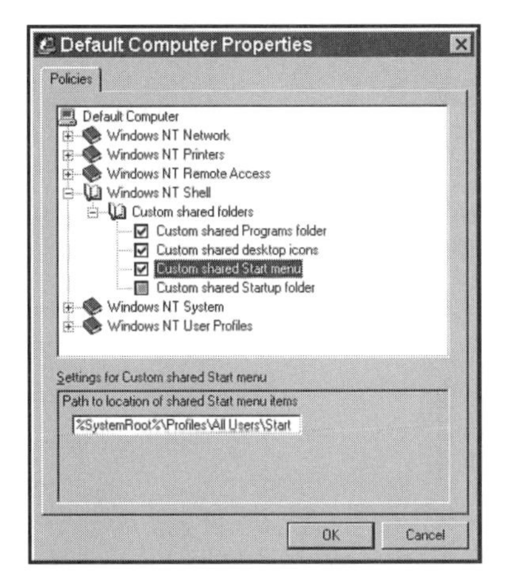

Figure 31.18. The correct location for a standardized Start menu.

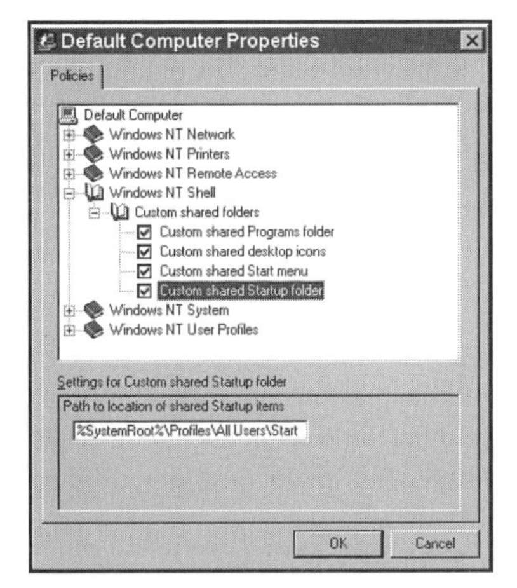

Figure 31.19. Startup items go here.

Windows NT System/Logon/Logon Banner

Originally, this setting was used to inform users of legal rights during logon. Now, however, this setting changes `HKEY_LOCAL_COMPUTER` and has no bearing on the user. The caption is the text in the title bar, and the other text is the data in the dialog box. (See Figure 31.20.)

Tip

Use this setting to notify users of specific information regarding the system to which they are logging on. For example, you might warn the user to never shut down the system because it is a server and others need access to it.

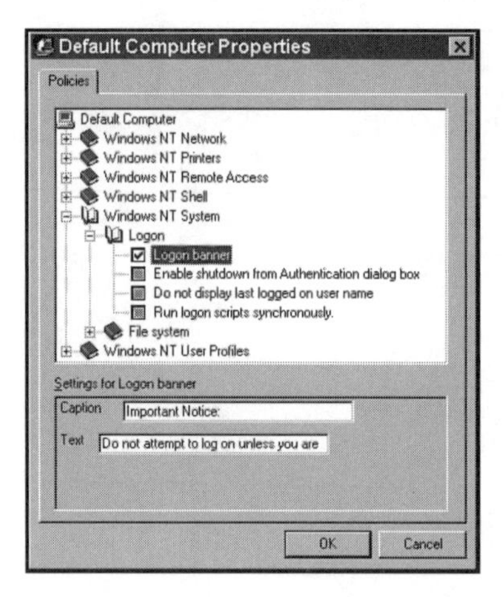

Figure 31.20.
Special information for your users at logon.

Windows NT System/Logon/Enable Shutdown from Authentication Dialog Box

After the system has started, you may want to require the user to log on before shutting down the system. Turning off this setting requires a logon before shutdown. Requiring the user to log on before shutting down the system can be a minor security feature if you combine it with disabling the reset and power buttons or restricting physical access to them. Then, the user must log on before he can shut the system down and restart the computer into another operating system or to a diskette-based OS that has less security. (See Figure 31.21.)

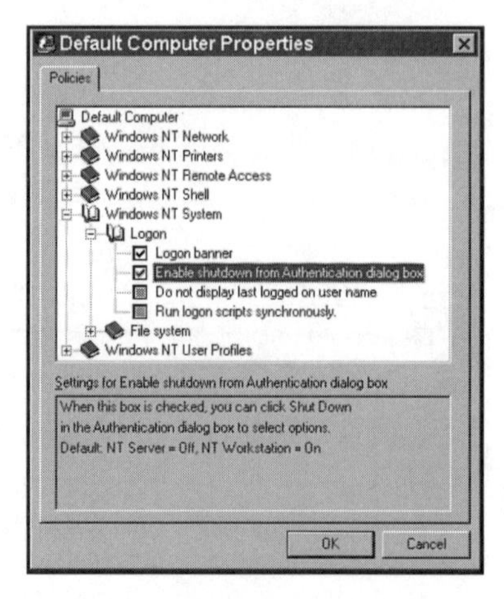

Figure 31.21.
Enable shutdown from the Authentication dialog box.

Windows NT System/Logon/Do Not Display Last Logged On User Name

Normally, when you get to the logon dialog box, the only information required is the password. However, if you require a hacker to guess the user name also, it may be more difficult to break into the domain. Combine that with a complex naming scheme, and security is much stronger. (See Figure 31.22.)

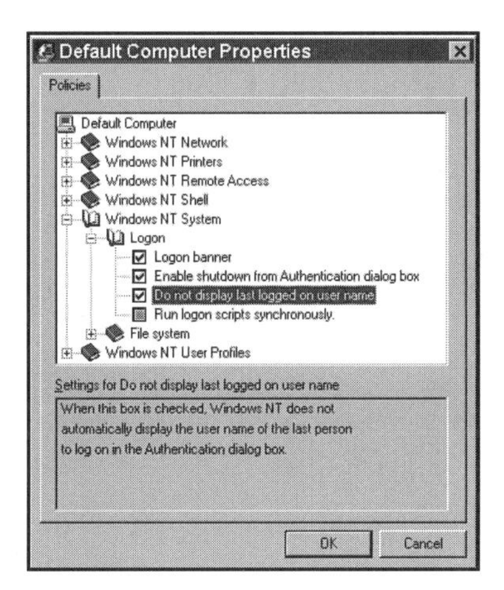

Figure 31.22.
Improve security by showing less at logon.

Windows NT System/Logon/Run Logon Scripts Synchronously

If this setting is disabled, some shortcuts in the startup group may start before their required drive mapping is completed. That causes errors and makes the startup process incorrect. (See Figure 31.23.)

Warning

If your logon script calls another batch file at the end, it may not complete before the shell starts. To ensure that the shell waits for all of the commands, put them directly in the logon script file.

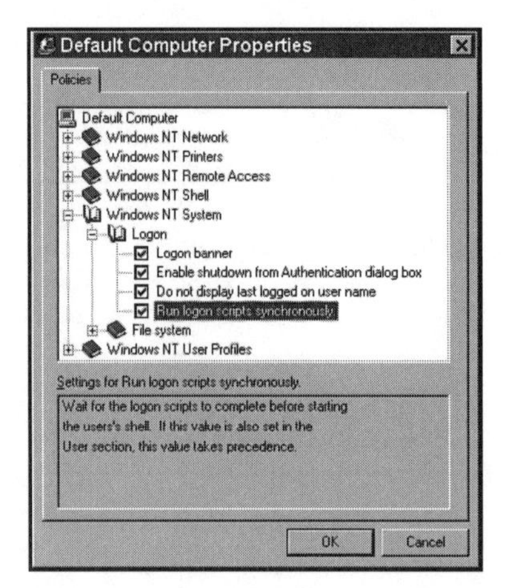

Figure 31.23.
Make the shell wait its turn.

Tip

There is already a small delay between the time when the logon script starts and the time when the Startup group starts. You may be able to achieve the necessary results by putting all drive mapping at the very beginning of the logon script. Doing so makes your startup process faster.

Windows NT System/File System/Do Not Create 8.3 Filenames for Long Filenames

The only time an 8.3 filename (the original DOS file naming rule, with an 8-character filename and an optional 3-character extension) is required is in operating systems that cannot recognize the long filenames. The use of 16-bit Windows or DOS applications inside Windows NT is not affected by this setting. They do not use it. They get truncated filenames from the operating system on the fly. Disabling the creation of the 8.3 filenames improves performance in writing to the disk drive by eliminating the duplication of effort. (See Figure 31.24.)

Tip

Always disable the writing of 8.3 filenames for dedicated servers for SQL, Exchange, Internet Information Server, and others that will not be running any other OS or applications.

Another potential benefit is that DOS versions prior to 7.0 cannot read those long filenames. If someone gains access to your server and boots to DOS, he can't read much of what is written there.

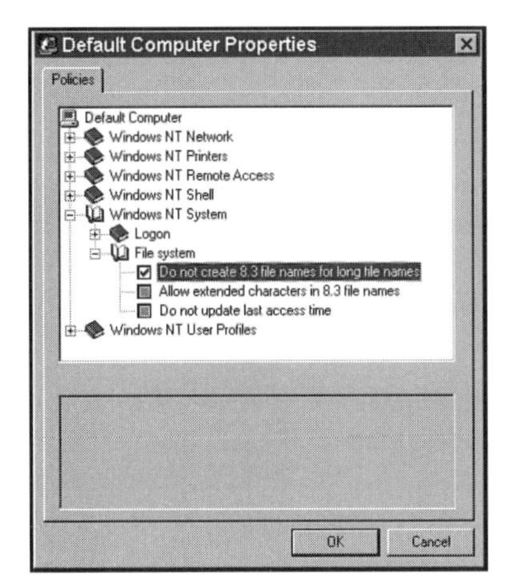

Figure 31.24.
Get rid of the past.

Windows NT System/File System/Allow Extended Characters in 8.3 Filenames

Extended characters are available in long filenames in Windows NT and Windows 95. Adding this setting allows you to use them when 8.3 filenames are created in 16-bit Windows or DOS applications. (See Figure 31.25.)

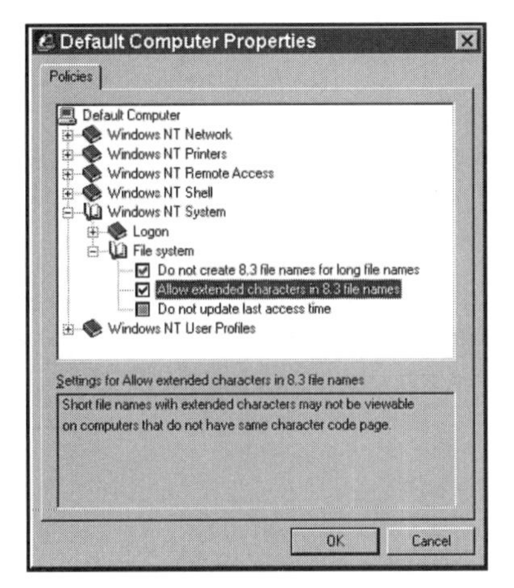

Figure 31.25.
Extended characters in an 8.3 filename.

Tip

Have you ever had a file that was corrupted and you could never delete it, even though the directory seemed empty? Allowing extended characters may let you see that file and delete it, and then you can clean up your hard drive without a reformat.

Windows NT System/File System/Do Not Update Last Access Time

Even read-only files have access flags on them that indicates the last time the file was accessed. Enabling this setting shortens the writing time to the disk drive and boosts performance. It still updates the access information if the file is changed. (See Figure 31.26.)

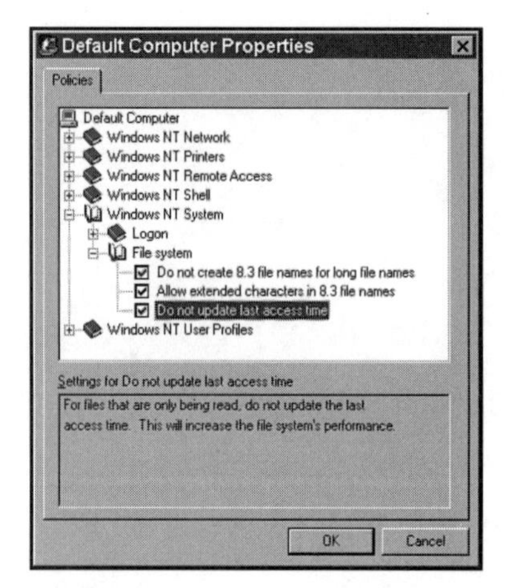

Figure 31.26.
Boost your disk drive performance.

Windows NT System/Windows NT User Profiles/Delete Cached Copies of Roaming Profiles

Roaming user profiles are stored on the domain controller. When the user logs on to the system, the user profile is loaded across the network. All the information is also cached to allow that profile to be used, even if the connection to the network is slow or does not work. The user's desktop, icons, and other environment data does not have to be re-created if the system cannot connect to the domain controller.

Delete the cached profiles only if your network is very stable and the connections are sure. (See Figure 31.27.)

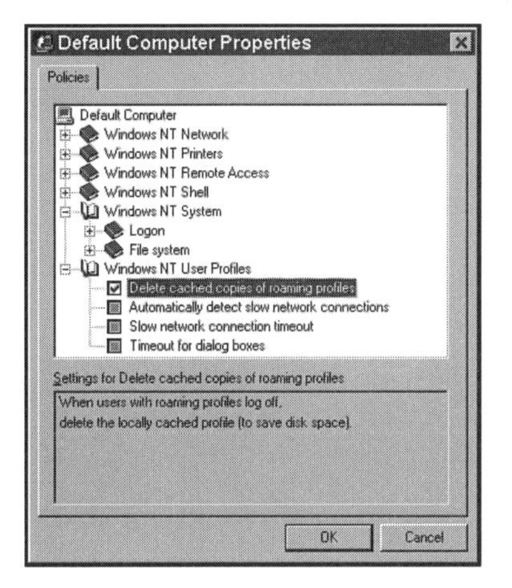

Figure 31.27.
Delete cached profile information.

Windows NT System/Windows NT User Profiles/Automatically Detect Slow Network Connections

The default for this setting is on even without this setting. Slow network connections affect the loading of profiles, the error messaging system, and many other communication functions.

Note

The phrase *slow network connection* does not refer to ARCNet, LANTastic, or AT&T StarLAN. It refers to remote connections through routers, switches, gateways, and modems that do not respond quickly enough. After a specific threshold of time is passed, it is considered a slow network connection.

If you want the remote system to work exactly like a locally connected system, disable this setting. (See Figure 31.28.)

Windows NT System/Windows NT User Profiles/Slow Network Connection Timeout

How long is too long? How slow is too slow? You get to determine that here. The default is `2000` (milliseconds), or 2 seconds. Increase that time to cut your system a little slack. (See Figure 31.29.)

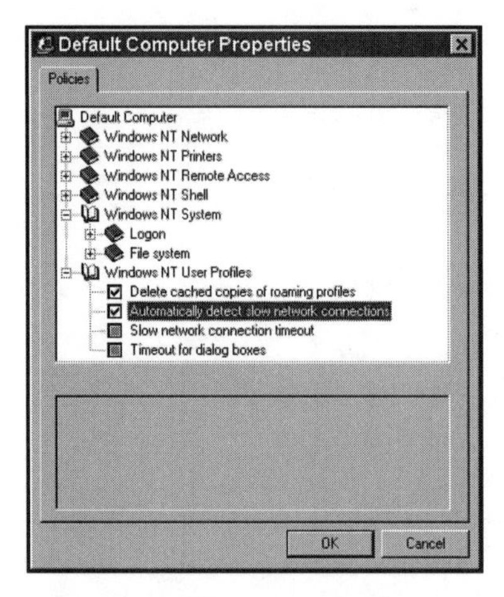

Figure 31.28.
Change the detection of slow network connections.

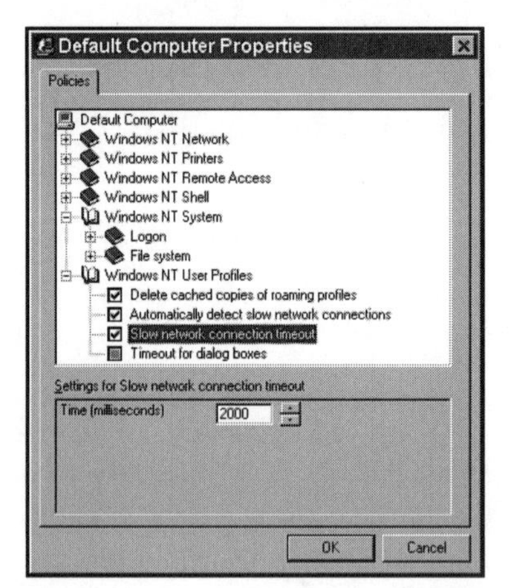

Figure 31.29.
Setting the threshold for slow network connections.

Windows NT System/Windows NT User Profiles/Timeout for Dialog Boxes

Some dialog boxes, such as the one that allows you to use a cached profile instead of downloading the profile from the server, are set to activate themselves if you do not respond to them in a specified period of time. If you set one such dialog box for a longer time, it waits for you. Set it for a shorter time and it goes on without you even if you are not there. (See Figure 31.30.)

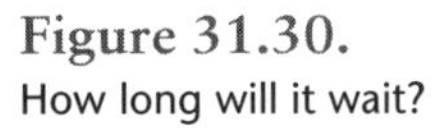

Figure 31.30.
How long will it wait?

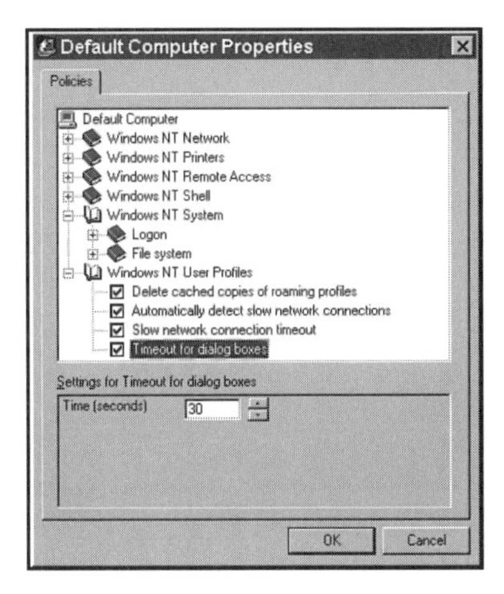

The Short Lists

To enhance security, set the entries in Table 31.1.

Table 31.1. Entries that can be configured to enhance security.

ADM File	*Policy*
`WINNT.ADM`	Windows NT Network/Sharing/Create hidden drive shares
`WINNT.ADM`	Windows NT Printers/Disable browse thread on this computer
`WINNT.ADM`	Windows NT Remote Access/Max number of unsuccessful authentication retries
`WINNT.ADM`	Windows NT Remote Access/Max time limit for authentication
`WINNT.ADM`	Windows NT System/Logon/Enable shutdown from Authentication dialog box
`WINNT.ADM`	Windows NT System/Logon/Do not display last logged-on user name
`WINNT.ADM`	Windows NT System/File System/Do not create 8.3 filenames for long file names

To enhance performance, set the entries in Table 31.2.

Table 31.2. Performance is enhanced by configuring these entries.

ADM File	*Policy*
WINNT.ADM	Windows NT Printers/Scheduler priority
WINNT.ADM	Windows NT System/Logon/Run logon scripts synchronously
WINNT.ADM	Windows NT System/File System/Do not create 8.3 filenames for long filenames
WINNT.ADM	Windows NT System/File System/Do not update last access time
WINNT.ADM	Windows NT User Profiles/Timeout for dialog boxes

Default Computer versus Named Computer

System Policy Editor creates two policies by default. One policy is created for the Default Computer, and another is created for the default user. (See Figure 31.31.)

Figure 31.31. System Policy Editor creates two default policies.

Setting system policies can be done either for all computers or for individual computers. To name a specific computer and associate a policy with it, select Edit | Add Computer. Type or browse for the NetBIOS name of the computer, and click OK. (See Figure 31.32.)

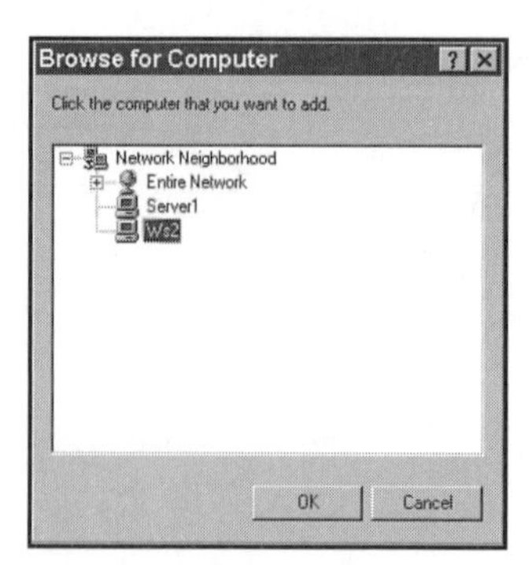

Figure 31.32. Choosing a computer for a specific policy.

If your computer isn't specifically named, you get the settings associated with the Default Computer. With a policy in place for the named computer, as shown in Figure 31.33, any policy specified will overwrite the Registry. Any policy settings for the named computer cannot affect any other systems, but the Default Computer policy may still affect the named one if there is no setting in the named computer policy.

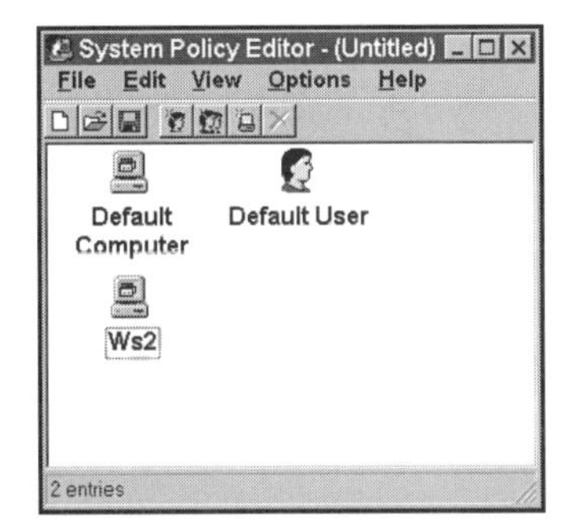

Figure 31.33.
WS2 can have specific policies associated with it.

Policies in Conflict

When policies are written into the Registry, the active policies (whether the policy is activated or deactivated) from the Default Computer are written first. (See Figure 31.34.) Then, active policies at each named computer get written.

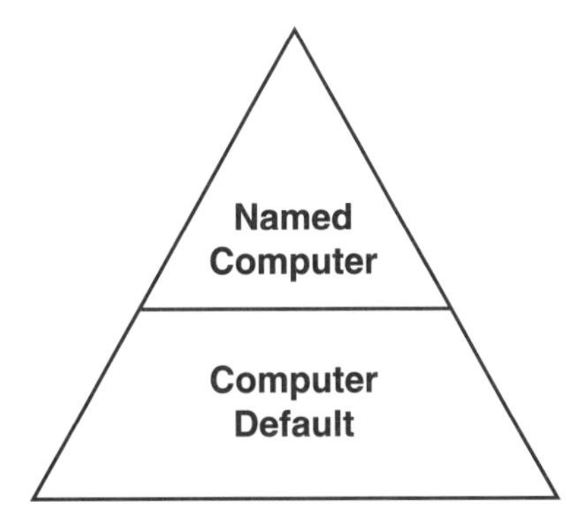

Figure 31.34.
Default Computer policies get written to the Registry first, followed by named computer policies.

This is particularly important when the policies are in conflict with each other. If the policy of the named computer is set to activate or deactivate, it makes no difference what the setting is at the Default Computer. As an example, in Figure 31.35, the computer named WS2 is set to create hidden drive shares. As shown in Figure 31.36, the Default Computer is set not to create them. The policy for WS2 is the one that will take effect.

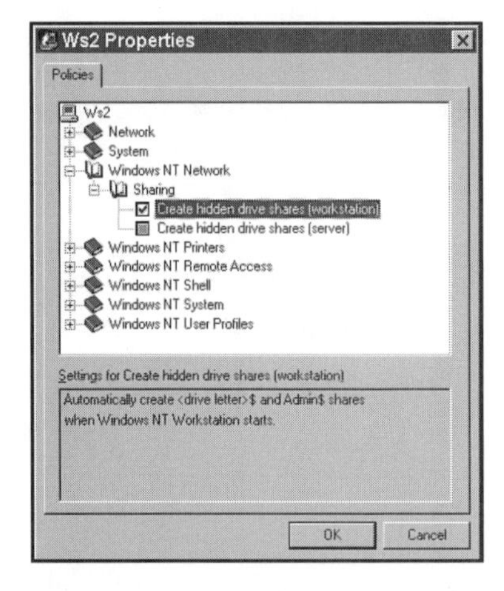

Figure 31.35.
WS2 policy.

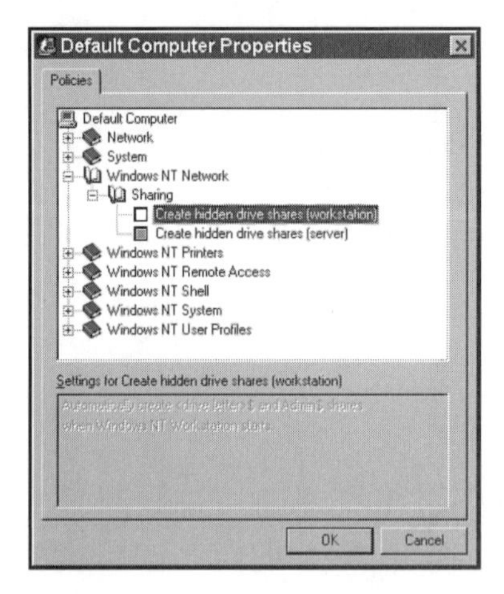

Figure 31.36.
Default Computer policy, which is overridden by the WS2 policy.

In another instance, the policy associated with WS2 is ignored, and the policy associated with Default Computer is implemented. In Figure 31.37, the policy for WS2 is set to ignore the NT Printer setting. As shown in Figure 31.38, the Default Computer has the policy set to disable the browse thread. Because the WS2 policy is set to use whatever is already there, it also disables the browse thread.

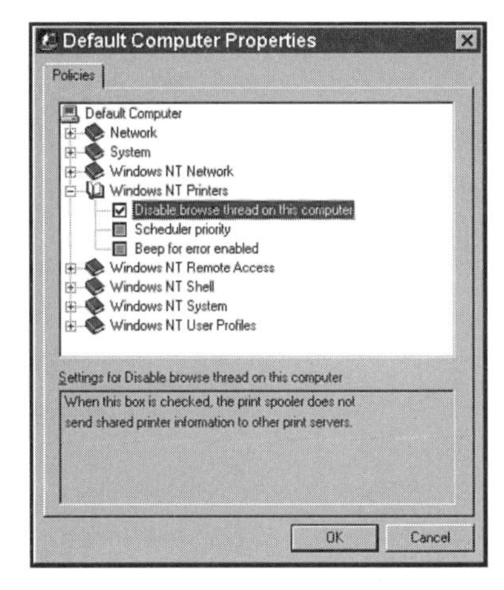

Figure 31.37.
WS2 policy.

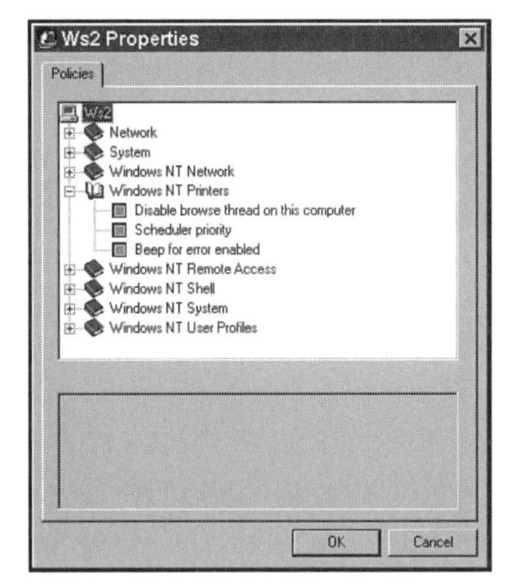

Figure 31.38.
Default Computer policy, which is not overridden by the WS2 policy in this case.

Summary

You can set any or all of these settings for individual computers or for every computer in your network. By choosing to use these settings, you can manage the computers in your network from a single NT server, and the policies can affect any computer in the network.

CHAPTER 32

Managing Domain Users with System Policy Editor

Just as there are many options for policies for computers, there are many options for policies for users. However, the types of settings are different, and they follow the user, regardless of which Windows NT 4.0 system he logs onto.

Most of these settings restrict the user. The more challenges the user has and the more recurrent errors he makes, the more appropriate restrictions are.

Note

Do I like my users making mistakes? Absolutely! If they never made mistakes, they would never learn anything. I just want my users to always make *new* mistakes. If a user makes a new mistake, that means he is progressing.

The problem I have is when users make the same mistakes over and over and over. If users continually make the same mistakes, it normally means they haven't learned from them. Your job as an administrator is to train users and help them recover from mistakes. I only restrict my users when they haven't learned from their mistakes, and when those mistakes are preventing them, and me, from being productive.

Restrictions can be very powerful tools for augmenting your training process. Your users, just like you, had to start at the beginning. The point at which you are now is just a function of training.

If a user continually makes the same mistakes, it shows that your training isn't working. It's possible that the user cannot be trained, but that is highly unlikely. It's more likely that you haven't done enough to help him learn.

However, you'll occasionally find users who simply refuse to learn, or who are malicious. Those are the two cases in which restrictions are particularly important.

Policies for Users and Groups

The default user is the unnamed user in the policy. Figure 32.1 shows the System Policy Editor screen for the Default User and Default Computer. Additionally, you can select individuals for whom you will assign a policy, or you can assign a policy to a group of users as designated in User Manager for Domains.

To add an individual policy, select Edit | Add User. Type the name of the user (it must be a user in User Manager for Domains) and click OK. (See Figure 32.2.) Alternatively, you can click Browse to see the list of users, and select one. That user will then have his own policy.

To add a group policy, select Edit | Add Group. Choose from a list of global groups from User Manager for Domains, or type the name of the group. You can add a group name that is not in User Manager for Domains, but it will have no effect, and none of the users will be affected by any change made to the policy of that group. (See Figure 32.3.)

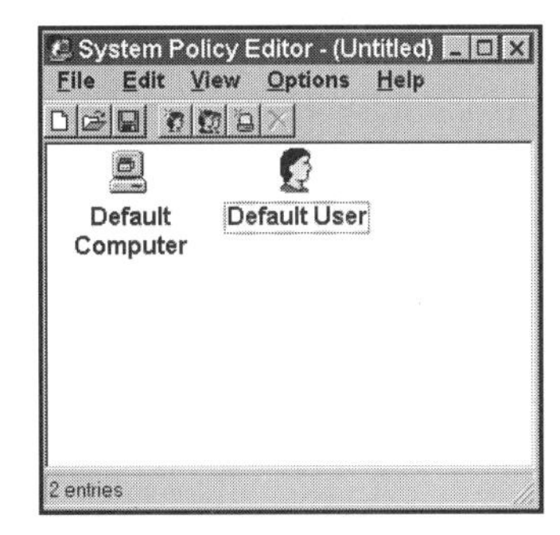

Figure 32.1. Default user policies in System Policy Editor.

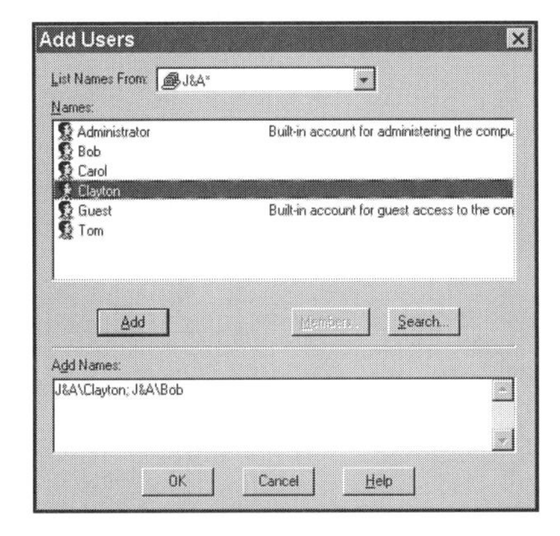

Figure 32.2. Adding a user policy.

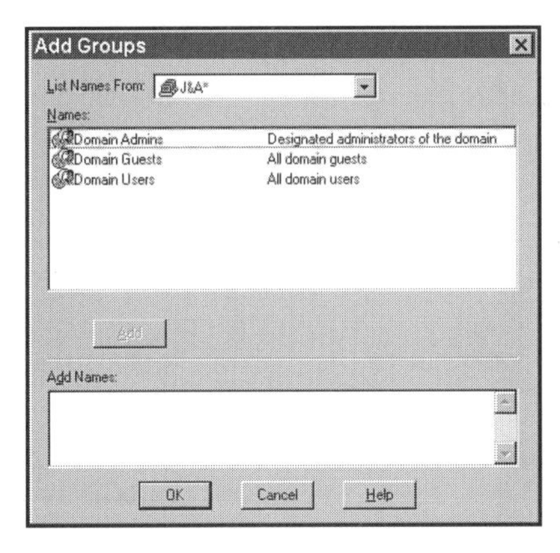

Figure 32.3. Adding a group policy.

Tip

In User Manager for Domains, add groups and group your users according to job function, skill, and security demands. Rather than just an Accounting Users global group, you might have Accounting Users-Novice, Accounting Users-Intermediate, and Accounting Users-Expert groups. Assign the policies and security functions to the global group. Then, when a user advances in skill and reliability, you can move him from one group to another, and he will inherit the policies and security rights from the new group.

With the individual user and group policies created (as shown in Figure 32.4), you can give each user the specific settings as required, balancing the individuality with administrative shortcuts.

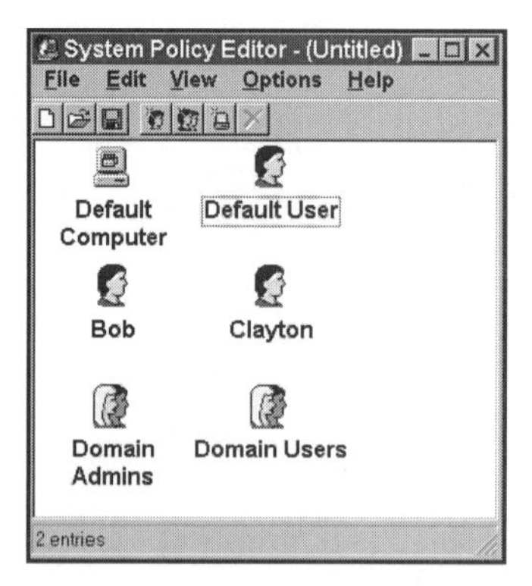

Figure 32.4. Setting policies for users and groups.

Conflicts Between Default User, Named User, and Group Policies

If there are different settings for the default user, the named users, and the groups, there will inevitably be conflict between the policies. To get the exact results you want, you must understand how System Policy Editor resolves these conflicts.

First, the default user policy gets loaded. Then come the group policies in order of priority. Finally, the individual user policy gets loaded, overwriting the Registry changes that have been made. (See Figure 32.5.)

Policy priority is very straightforward, except in the case of multiple groups. If a named user is a member of multiple groups, and each group has a policy, which of the policies takes effect?

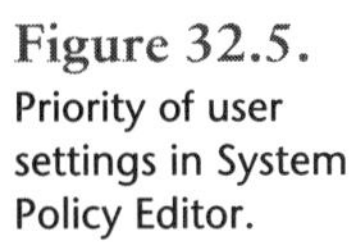

Figure 32.5.
Priority of user settings in System Policy Editor.

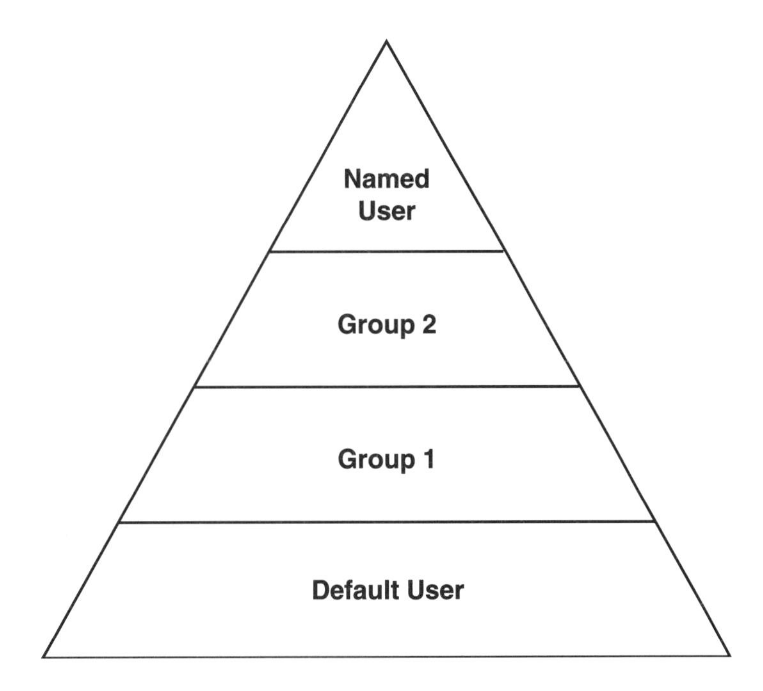

In the example of Figure 32.6, the named user, Jennie, who is a member of both the Domain Admins group and the Domain Users group, has a policy that overwrites all of the others. In that case, the priority of the groups has no effect.

In the example in Figure 32.7, Jennie's policy is to use whatever setting is currently in place. That means that the priority of the groups is critical in determining whether Jennie can edit the Registry. With Jennie in the Domain Admins group, you would assume that she should have that right.

The policy Jennie uses depends on which of the two groups (Domain Admins and Domain Users) has priority. Normally, the Domain Admins group would have priority, but System Policy Editor chooses priority in a different way. It sets priority in the order of creation of the groups in System Policy Editor. If the Domain Users group was created first, it has priority, and Jennie does not get to edit the Registry. Unfortunately, that is not a very good way to determine priority.

Figure 32.6.
Multiple policies all affect the user.

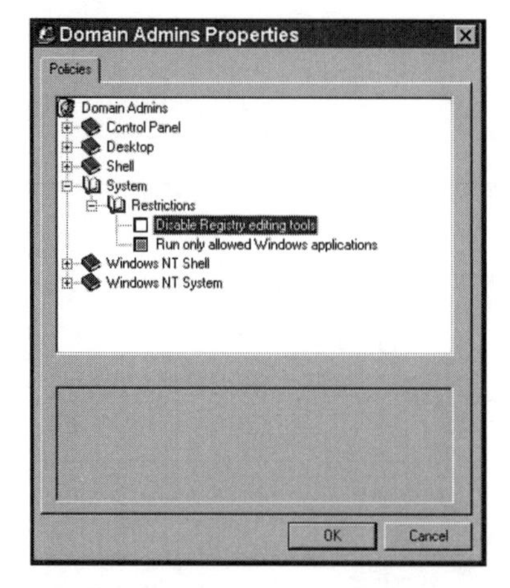

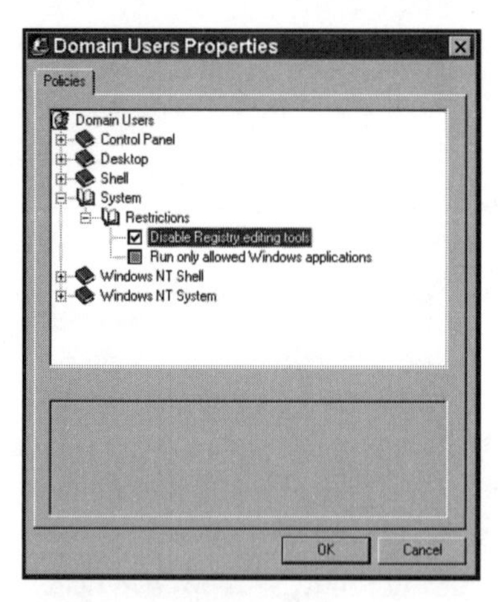

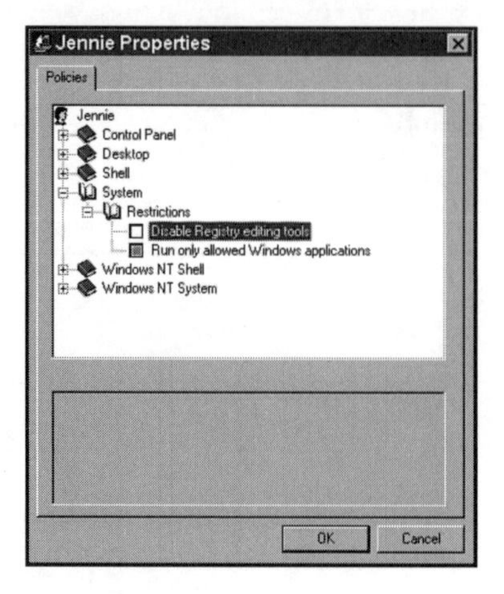

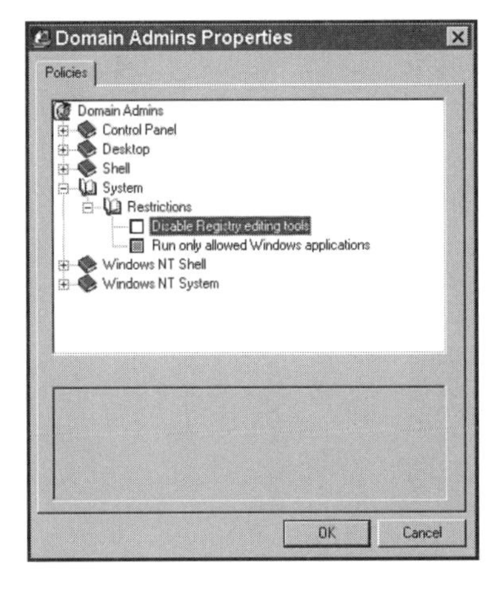

Figure 32.7. Group policy priority determines the effect on the user.

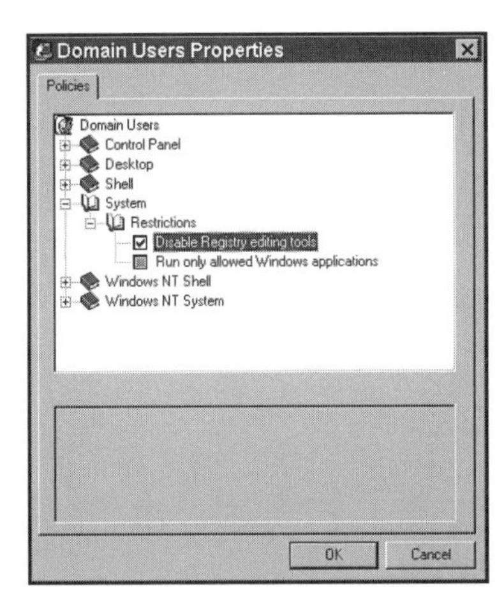

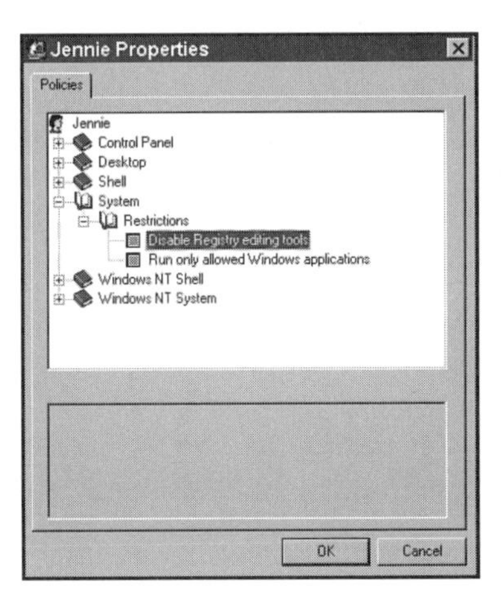

Manually Setting the Priority of Groups

To select the priority of group policies, click any group icon, and choose Options | Group Priority. The dialog box shown in Figure 32.8 appears, giving you the option of setting the priority of the groups.

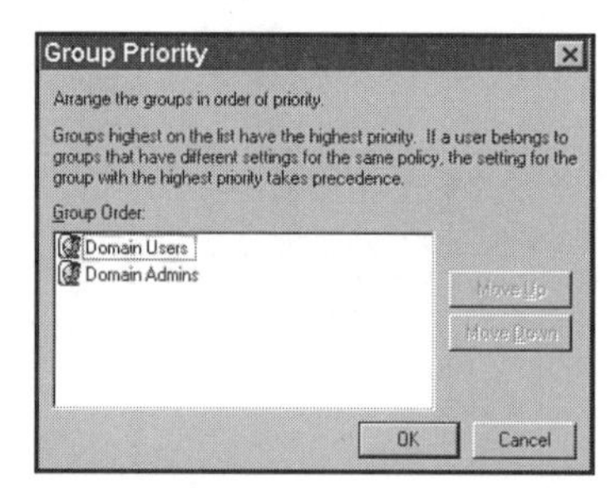

Figure 32.8.
Group priority settings in System Policy Editor.

To change the priority, highlight the group and select Move Up or Move Down. When the order of priority is correct, select OK. The policies will then be implemented as expected.

With the group policy priority applied as it is in Figure 32.9, Disable Registry editing tools will be turned off, giving Jennie the ability to edit her Registry.

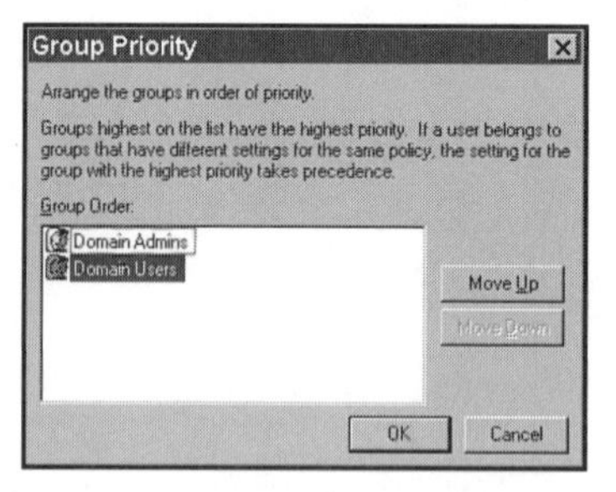

Figure 32.9.
Changing the group priority settings.

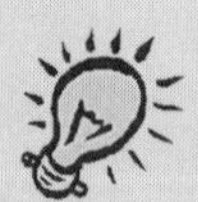

Tip

Open the policy for Administrator and ensure that the selection is made to allow Administrator to edit the Registry. If Administrator is denied that right, the results could be disastrous. The Administrator would not have the ability to edit the Registry, and would have to restore a backup of the Registry to gain access. Any other settings added since the backup would be lost.

User Policies in COMMON.ADM

Most of the restrictions for users are in COMMON.ADM and work for both Windows NT and Windows 95. This is because nearly all of them are associated with the Explorer interface. It is also why they do not work with NT 3.5*x*. Some of the settings are outstanding, but some are just plain silly. Pick and choose carefully.

The settings are listed with the categories, policies, and parts for each separated by a forward slash like so: Network/System Policies Update/Remote Update.

Control Panel/Display/Restrict Display/ Deny Access to Display Icon

Beginning users should probably be restricted from using the Control Panel | Display function, but it makes sense to restrict only a few others. If you restrict the Control Panel | Display function here, it will still show in the Control Panel folder. However, when you try to access the function, it will not let you. (See Figure 32.10.)

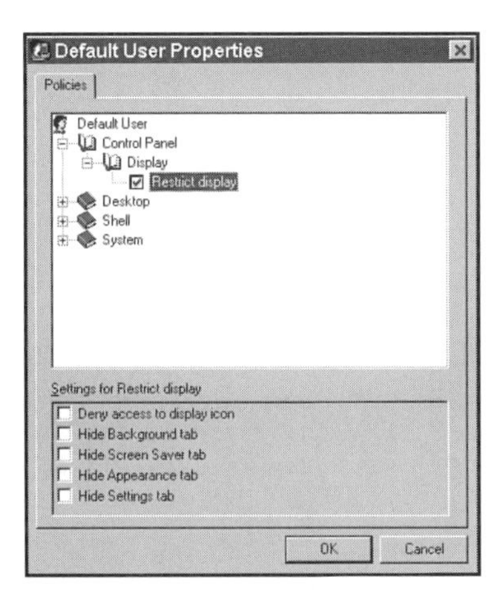

Figure 32.10.
Control Panel display restrictions.

Control Panel/Display/Restrict Display/ Hide Background Tab

You can restrict the user's use of patterns and wallpapers with the Hide Background tab. The user would have no opportunity then to change the pattern or wallpaper. Figure 32.11 shows the Background tab from Control Panel | Display.

Note

I have no idea why Microsoft even bothered with restrictions like Hide Background tab. Pornographic photographs aside, choosing a different pattern or wallpaper has no impact on performance or security.

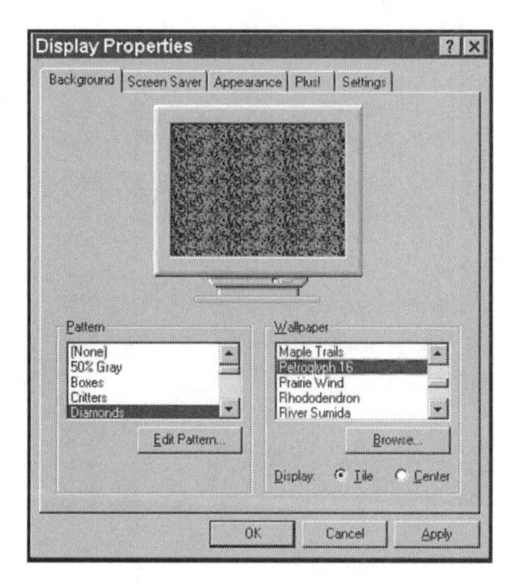

Figure 32.11.
The Background tab in Control Panel | Display.

Control Panel/Display/Restrict Display/ Hide Screen Saver Tab

Screen savers seem harmless enough. Unfortunately, if you use one (particularly one of the OpenGL screen savers shown in Figure 32.12), you may use all available CPU time. Access to your computer for file and printer sharing will be horribly slow. So, you should *never ever* put a screen saver on a server!

Tip

If you want to keep prying eyes away from your system, lock the workstation with Ctrl+Alt+Del, and click the Lock Workstation button. It will require your password or the Administrator to log on to get back, but it requires no CPU time.

Most screen savers in NT use the user's password. If you have a screen saver that uses a different password and the user forgets that password, you will have to restart the system to get back in.

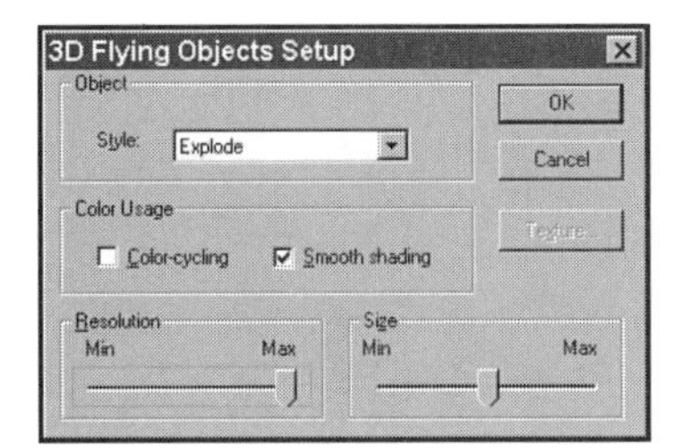

Figure 32.12. Activating an OpenGL screen saver in Control Panel | Display | Screen Saver.

Control Panel/Display/Restrict Display/ Hide Appearance Tab

What are you in the mood for today? A purple screen with pink letters? Who cares, as long as you are getting your work done. If you find your chosen colors distracting, change them. If you are obsessive in your desire for control, you can restrict your users with this setting, as shown in Figure 32.13.

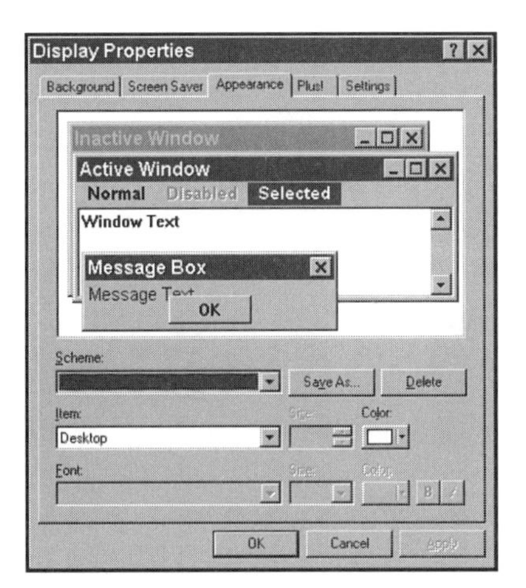

Figure 32.13. The Appearance tab in Control Panel | Display.

Control Panel/Display/Restrict Display/ Hide Settings Tab

Why would an ordinary user need access to the Settings tab in Control Panel | Display? He doesn't. Access to the Settings tab allows the user to change the screen resolution, the number of colors, and the display driver. If the user tries to change the display driver and sets it incorrectly, you will have to repair it, and in the worst case, you might have to reinstall Windows NT. Absolutely, without question, hide the Settings tab for users who like to tinker with their systems. (See Figure 32.14.)

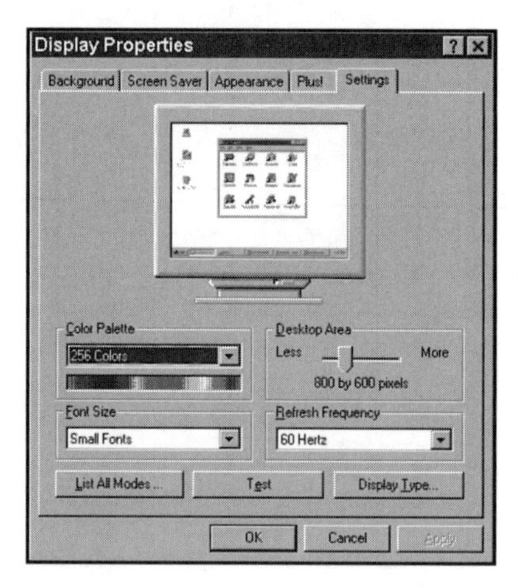

Figure 32.14.
The Settings tab in Control Panel | Display.

Desktop/Wallpaper

If you want your company logo to grace the screens of all the systems in your organization, you can set that with the Wallpaper option (as shown in Figure 32.15). If the user changes the wallpaper during a session, the user's choice will be overridden after he logs off and back on.

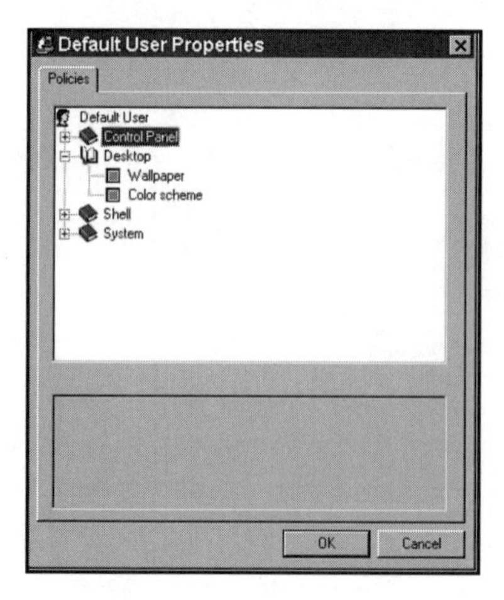

Figure 32.15.
Desktop settings.

To ensure that everyone has equal access to the wallpaper, put it in the `NETLOGON` share. Everyone always has access to the `NETLOGON` share.

Desktop/Color Scheme

Setting the Color Scheme changes all the user's colors on the desktop. It's a fast and easy way to set the colors; simply select from the list of color schemes.

It seems a little too restrictive, forcing a specific color scheme on users. Of course, if you are a practical joker, you could recreate "Hot Dog Stand" and force your co-workers to use it. Simply set it as a policy.

Shell/Restrictions/Remove Run Command from Start Menu

This is an outstanding option. You can effectively curtail the use of outside applications or applications that users should not use by removing the Run command from the Start menu. (See Figure 32.16.)

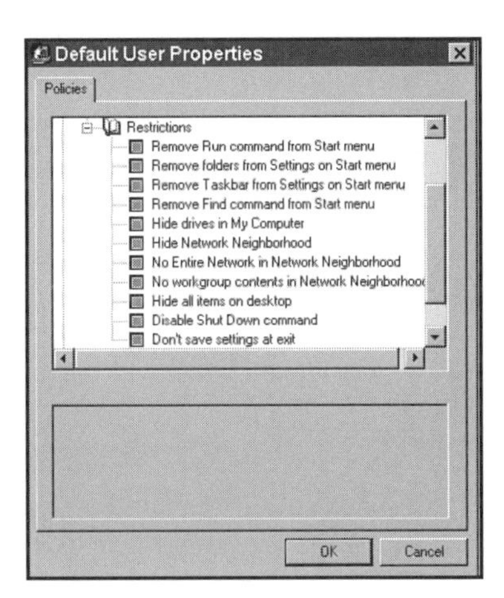

Figure 32.16.
Shell restrictions.

Of course, applications can still be started from Explorer.

Shell/Restrictions/Remove Folders from Settings on Start Menu

If you don't want your users to change settings on their systems, you can remove all the folders from the Start menu Settings function.

Shell/Restrictions/Remove Taskbar from Settings on Start Menu

Deny users the ability to change the Taskbar by removing access to it through the settings on the Start menu. (See Figure 32.17.) Doing so restricts the user's ability to change the properties of the Taskbar; the user cannot set the Taskbar to hide, or to always be visible. When access is denied, the user cannot customize the Start menu or remove the contents of the Document menu through Start | Settings.

However, even if this setting is imposed on a user, he can still change the contents of the Start menu and Document menu through Explorer. The Start menu contents are stored in the `\WINNT\Profiles\`*`username`*`\Start Menu` folder, and the Document menu contents are stored in the `\WINNT\Profiles\`*`username`*`\Recent` folder.

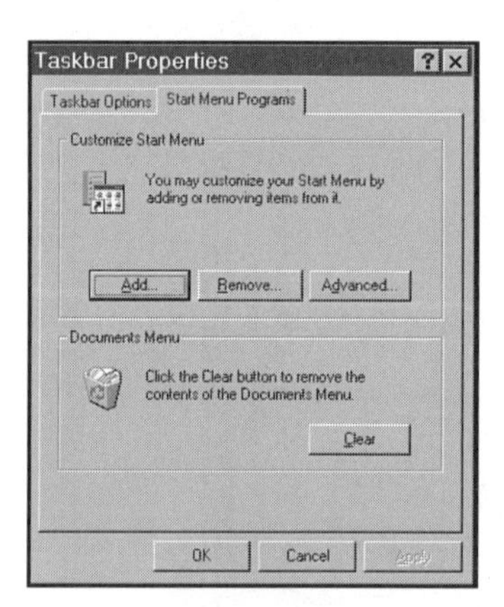

Figure 32.17. Changing the Start menu with the Taskbar settings.

With access to the Taskbar functions, users can add or remove items from the Start menu, and they may lose the ability to easily launch some applications if they delete the wrong items.

Shell/Restrictions/Remove Find Command from Start Menu

When you remove the Find command from the Start menu, the command is also removed from Explorer. In that case, users cannot browse their own hard disk. If they do not have a shortcut or know exactly where to find the application or data file, they cannot access it without looking in every directory.

Shell/Restrictions/Hide Drives in My Computer

Setting this essentially disables My Computer and Explorer. If you can't see any drives or look at any files in My Computer or Explorer, it is pretty tough to use them. Hiding the drives is the only way to restrict access because it is not possible to remove My Computer from the desktop.

The only files that a user can use when this setting is enabled are those that had a shortcut added to the Start menu or desktop or those for which he knows the complete path and filename.

Shell/Restrictions/Hide Network Neighborhood

If you have set up logon scripts correctly (using mapped drives for all the connections your user normally needs), the need to browse the network using Network Neighborhood is almost nonexistent. The icon is removed from the desktop and from all Explorer functions, including saving and opening files.

The user can still make all necessary connections; he just cannot browse to do it. That saves a lot of traffic on the network.

Shell/Restrictions/No Entire Network in Network Neighborhood

If you don't want to remove the whole Network Neighborhood, consider limiting what the user can see. Without the Entire Network icon, the user can only see the computers on his own physical segment. He cannot browse beyond that. He would still have the opportunity to map drives directly, but he would need to know the path.

Shell/Restrictions/No Workgroup Contents in Network Neighborhood

If some computers are not members of the domain but are still on the physical network, they will show up in the browse list. It's doubtful that any security is attached to their folders or printers. Allowing simple access to those systems may compromise the security of your network. Restricting the user so he must know the name of the system and the name of the share increases security.

Shell/Restrictions/Hide All Items on the Desktop

The only time it's useful to be able to hide all the items on a desktop is in the case of a single-use, highly public machine. You don't want anyone walking up and messing with the settings on the system, or running anything other than the designated program.

Tip

Want a great April Fool's Day trick? Get a screen shot of Windows NT 3.51 or Windows for Workgroups. Use the setting listed previously to specify it as the wallpaper. Hide all the items on the desktop, and your user will be clicking for days.

Shell/Restrictions/Disable Shut Down Command

With this option enabled, you cannot restart the system or prepare it to be turned off with the software. The only way to protect Windows NT if you use this setting is to ensure that the user cannot get to the power or reset buttons.

Warning

Windows NT has a specific routine that it uses to prepare files for shutdown. In the case of power failure, reset, or manual power-down, files may be damaged. Windows NT can fix the files, in most cases, but it takes resources and time, potentially hurting performance. You also may lose unsaved data, requiring re-entry.

Shell/Restrictions/Don't Save Settings at Exit

This outstanding setting changes the way Explorer works. Normally, NT remembers where you put things if you had any system-level programs (like Control Panel or Explorer) open every time you log off. The next time you log on, NT restarts those system-level programs and all of your icons will be where you left them.

If you don't save the settings at exit, NT always retains exactly the same starting point for you. I call it the "maid" feature. When you leave, the maid comes in and cleans up for you.

Warning

If this setting is not activated and you have Explorer in your Startup group, you may end up with multiple instances of it loading. If you left Explorer open when you logged off, you will have two instances of Explorer when you log on again.

System/Restrictions/Disable Registry Editing Tools

Disabling the use of Registry tools is very important. As mentioned earlier, every user has the ability to edit his own Registry, and some may be able to edit others. Figure 32.18 shows the System Restrictions.

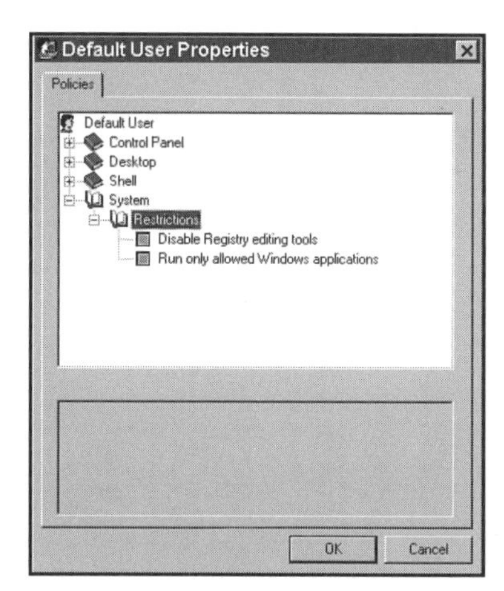

Figure 32.18.
System Restrictions in COMMON.ADM.

Setting this option restricts the user from running REGEDT32.EXE or REGEDIT.EXE regardless of where the file is run. Whether from the Run command, an icon, the DOS prompt, Explorer, or File Manager, the user cannot edit the Registry. Even if you change the name of REGEDT32.EXE or REGEDIT.EXE, the user cannot activate the file.

Warning

Even though the user cannot use a manual Registry editing tool, this does not restrict him from running System Policy Editor.

System/Restrictions/Run Only Allowed Windows Applications

Caution! Caution! Caution! The most restrictive of all policies is the restriction to run only allowed Windows applications.

If you set this policy, the user can only run the actual programs listed in the dialog box as shown in Figure 32.19. To add items to the list, click the Add button and type the name of the application. Do not type the path, just the executable filename. That way, regardless of the location of the file, the program will still run.

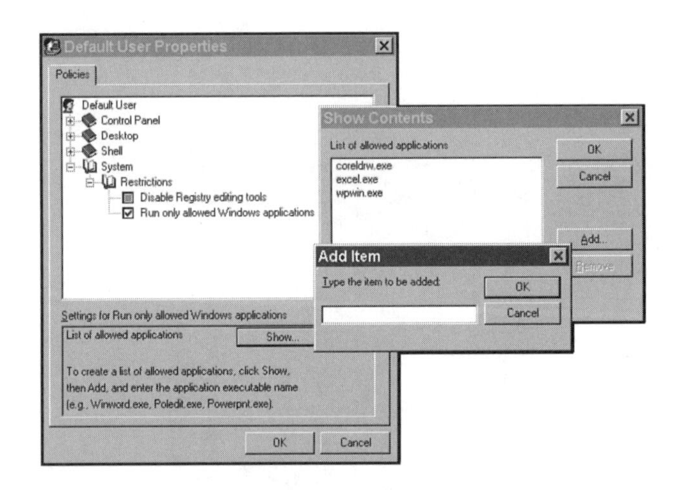

Figure 32.19. Listing only the applications available for use.

If the application is not listed here, it cannot be activated.

Tip

When you use this tip in conjunction with the option to hide all items on the desktop and the option to restrict Start menu items, a public machine can be very secure. For example, a system that runs a time-clock program for all employees could qualify for these settings. A user who has been playing too many games and fiddling too much with NT could be another candidate for the settings.

Be very careful, though. It is very easy to over-restrict with this setting. If an application is not listed here, you can't run it.

Note

There is no need to worry about complex applications not working correctly if they are listed here. When an application calls another executable, the executable is being called by the system, not by the user. Therefore, the application will still work, even without the additional executable files listed in the dialog box.

User Policies in `WINNT.ADM`

Most of the policies for users are found in `COMMON.ADM`. Many of the ones listed are even similar to the computer-based policies listed in Chapter 31, "Managing Domain Computers with System Policy Editor." The main difference is that these are associated with a user name or group instead of a blanket policy for all users. The real tip-off to that is in the location of the files. In the computer-based policies, the file is set in `all users`; here, they are set for individual user profiles.

Windows NT Shell/Custom Folders/ Custom Programs Folder

Members of the Accounting group would probably need the same shortcuts available to them. Setting the Custom Programs folder for everyone in the group is the fastest way to accomplish that. (See Figure 32.20.)

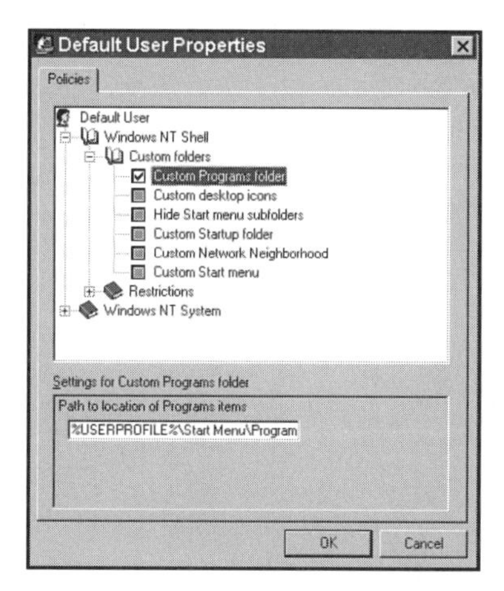

Figure 32.20. Setting the Custom Programs folder.

Windows NT Shell/Custom Folders/Custom Desktop Icons

Members of the Accounting group would probably need the same icons available to them. Setting the Custom desktop icons for everyone in the group is the fastest way to accomplish that. (See Figure 32.21.)

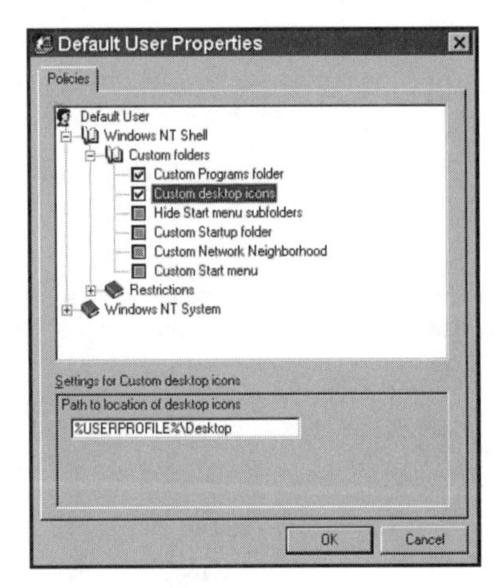

Figure 32.21.
Setting the Custom desktop icons.

Windows NT Shell/Custom Folders/Hide Start Menu Subfolders

Only shortcuts to applications show in the Start menu. This minimizes clutter and removes most of the pop-up menus that appear. (See Figure 32.22.)

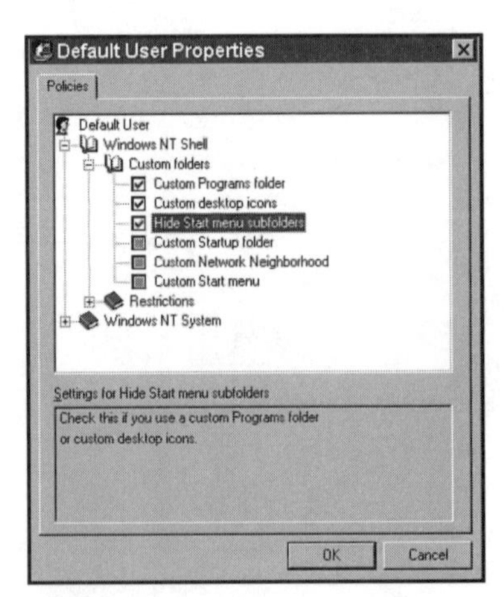

Figure 32.22.
Minimizing clutter in the Start menu.

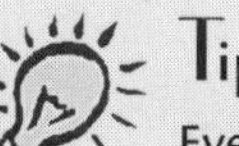

Tip

Everything in the menus in Windows NT is alphabetical. If you want to specify the order of items, you will need to be creative. You may want to put a number in front of the name to specify the order, or you could move the Accounting shortcut to the bottom of the list by renaming the shortcut `X-Accounting`.

Windows NT Shell/Custom Folders/ Custom Startup Folder

This setting gives you the ability to create a separate startup process for every user. Depending on the user or group, specific applications may be needed every time. This setting allows them to load automatically. (See Figure 32.23.)

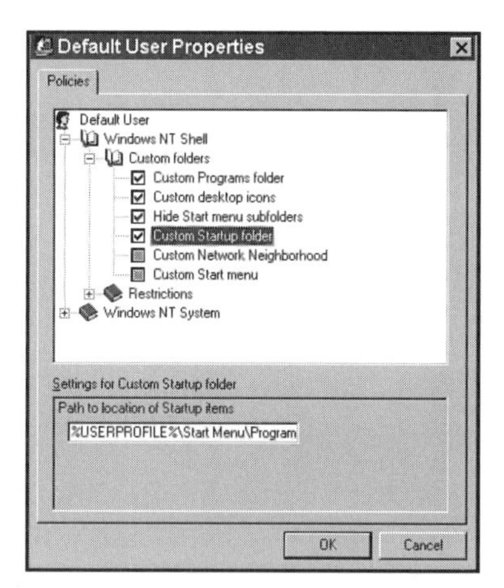

Figure 32.23. Creating a separate startup process for every user.

Windows NT Shell/Custom Folders/ Custom Network Neighborhood

With this tip, you can create a set of shortcuts to shared folders across the network, and use it as your Network Neighborhood. Multiple users can all use the same list, thus improving your performance because shortcuts would already be in place instead of relying on the browser. (See Figure 32.24.)

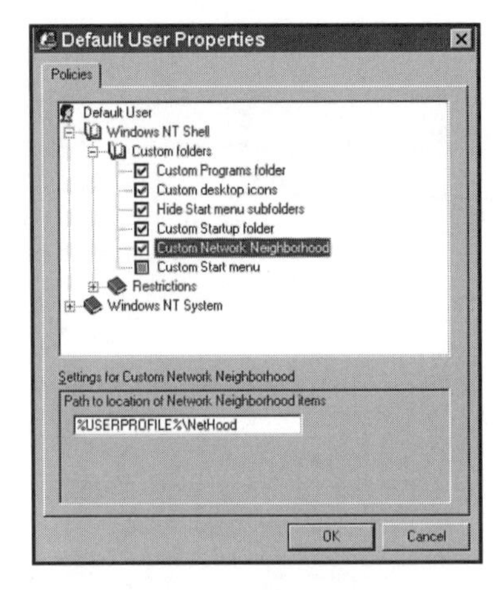

Figure 32.24. Create a set of shortcuts to shared folders across the network and use it as your Network Neighborhood.

Windows NT Shell/Custom Folders/ Custom Start Menu

This setting allows you to create a customized Start menu for every user or group, which is simple enough. (See Figure 32.25.)

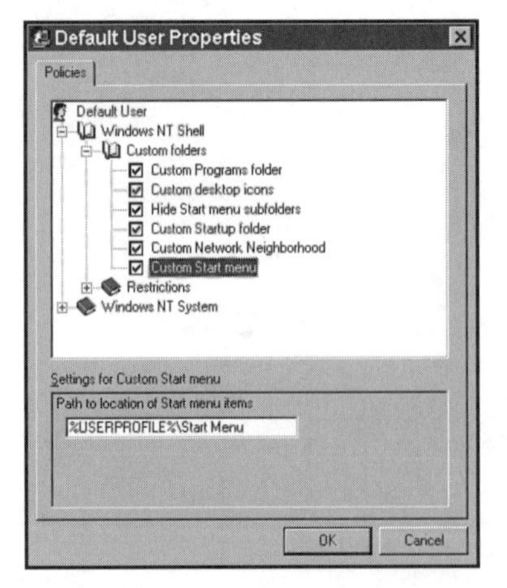

Figure 32.25. Create a customized Start menu for every user or group.

Windows NT Shell/Restrictions/Only Use Approved Shell Extensions

If this setting is turned on, any files in the folders for menus or the desktop must have an extension listed in `HKEY_CLASSES_ROOT` for them to be used. Generally, you would only put shortcuts to executable files, batch files, and documents associated with an application there anyway. This setting forces you to do so. (See Figure 32.26.)

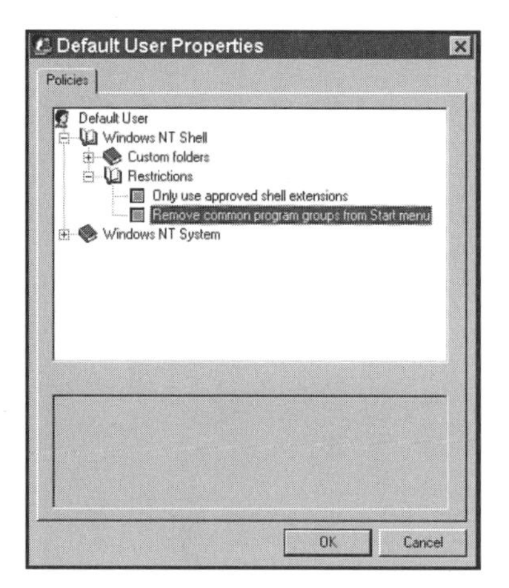

Figure 32.26.
All files in the folders for menus or the desktop must have an extension listed in `HKEY_CLASSES_ROOT`.

Windows NT Shell/Restrictions/Remove Common Program Groups from Start Menu

If you remove access to the common program groups from the Start menu, the user cannot be prevented from using the applications that were there. However, they would be required to have another shortcut or find the executable file in Explorer.

Warning

If you remove access to the common groups, you may lose more than access to administrative programs. Common groups are often created when the application is going to be used by multiple people who use the computer. Add shortcuts to necessary applications to the shell-restriction options, and the users will retain access.

Tip

An alternative to removing access to all the common groups is to simply remove the Administrative Tools folder from the All Users profile. Copy the shortcuts to the profiles where necessary, and then remove the Administrative Tools folder.

Windows NT System/Parse AUTOEXEC.BAT

Parsing the AUTOEXEC.BAT file removes all unnecessary lines from the system. For example, parsing this file would remove drivers for a CD-ROM drive if NT had drivers that could be used. AUTOEXEC.BAT is parsed when Windows NT is installed, and this may need to be done again if the file gets cluttered with extraneous information. (See Figure 32.27.)

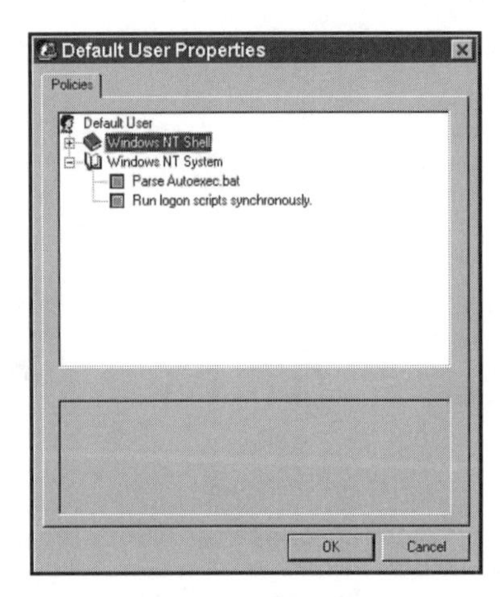

Figure 32.27. Parse AUTOEXEC.BAT to remove unnecessary lines from the system.

Windows NT System/Run Logon Scripts Synchronously

The setting in WINNT.ADM activated as a computer-based option in System Policy Editor will override this setting. If you have a particular user who roams the network, and that user has a complex logon script, you may need to order the shell to wait for the logon script to finish before loading.

Recommendations

It is always easier to start with restrictions than impose them later. It is always easier to ease restrictions than tighten them. Start with restrictions, and loosen them as the users prove their abilities. You may even choose to use them as a carrot when training and testing is completed.

Tip

How would you feel if restrictions were to be imposed upon you? That's exactly the way your users feel. Be judicious in your restrictions and follow up with additional training and support.

When an irate user calls you about a restriction imposed on him, how you respond determines the rest of the conversation, and possibly the rest of your relationship. Someone may call you, yelling or not, and ask, "Jim can change desktop settings, why can't I?" Respond calmly, without getting angry and without condescending, "What was it that you wanted to do?" and sit back and listen. If it is a valid request, they always tell you.

Asking that one simple question always starts a dialog that allows you to discover what the user is thinking, what he really needs, and how you can help him.

Talk to your users. Setting restrictions is a training issue. Your users will appreciate your help.

Top 10 Lists

Here are lists of the best and the worst in user settings in System Policy Editor.

The most valuable players in user settings, arranged in order of priority, are as follows:

1. Control Panel/Display/Restrict Display/Hide Settings Tab
2. Shell/Restrictions/Remove Run Command from Start Menu
3. Shell/Restrictions/Remove Taskbar from Settings on Start Menu
4. Shell/Restrictions/Hide Network Neighborhood
5. Shell/Restrictions/No Entire Network in Network Neighborhood
6. Shell/Restrictions/Don't Save Settings at Exit
7. System/Restrictions/Disable Registry Editing Tools
8. System/Restrictions/Run Only Allowed Windows Applications
9. Windows NT Shell/Restrictions/Remove Common Program Groups from Start Menu
10. Windows NT System/Run Logon Scripts Synchronously

In the author's opinion, the silliest settings are these:

1. Control Panel/Display/Restrict Display/Hide Background Tab
2. Control Panel/Display/Restrict Display/Hide Screen Saver Tab
3. Control Panel/Display/Restrict Display/Hide Appearance Tab
4. Desktop/Wallpaper
5. Desktop/Color Scheme
6. Shell/Restrictions/Remove Find Command from Start Menu

7. Shell/Restrictions/Hide Drives in My Computer
8. Shell/Restrictions/Hide All Items on the Desktop
9. Shell/Restrictions/Disable Shut Down Command
10. Windows NT System/Parse `Autoexec.bat`

Summary

User settings and restrictions are the most powerful management and training tools I have ever seen. Users who change critical settings incorrectly (whether accidentally or maliciously) hurt the entire organization. The amount of time that is spent fixing silly problems and bailing out users who are technically over their heads is phenomenal. Imagine the increases in productivity if the technical support staff could focus on helping users improve their skills.

System Policy Editor is the tool to change the focus of support in your organization. It will literally change the way you do business.

CHAPTER 33

Managing Windows 95 Users with System Policy Editor

Windows 95 was the first of the Windows operating systems with System Policy Editor. It is an outstanding program that gives a tremendous amount of capabilities to administrators, who can now control Windows 95 systems across the network. The System Policy Editor in Windows NT Server 4.0 has a few extra features, but, unfortunately, it will not create policy files that are compatible with Windows 95. The only way to create compatible policy files is to use the Windows 95 System Policy Editor.

Warning

Even if you copy all the files from the Windows 95 CD for its version of System Policy Editor, you cannot use the 95 Editor inside NT 4.0. The program will launch, and you can make all the necessary settings, but the policy file cannot be saved. If you try, you will get an error: "An error occurred writing the Registry. The file cannot be saved."

Using Template Files for Windows 95 with System Policy Editor

The template files for Windows NT and Windows 95 have exactly the same format and syntax. The main differences are based on the differences in the Registry. Windows 95 has some entries that NT doesn't, and the number of entries found in NT that are not in Windows 95 is astounding. Because of the similarities between the two, and the common Explorer interface, there are also many common entries.

The Win95 System Policy Editor allows only one template file, `ADMIN.ADM`. If you ever want to add to the template, you need to edit that file. Figure 33.1 illustrates the fact that the files are compatible, and `ADMIN.ADM` (without modifications) will load, and could even be used, in the System Policy Editor for Windows NT.

Figure 33.1.
`ADMIN.ADM` will also load into the Windows NT System Policy Editor.

If there is a problem loading the template, you would get an error similar to the one shown in Figure 33.2. The error dialog box lists the line number and the type of problem. The challenge is simply in the size of the file. Without any additions, ADMIN.ADM already has 1122 lines (951 lines for the policy, and the rest for text strings).

Tip

If you open ADMIN.ADM into Notepad, there is no line numbering feature. If you open it into Word or WordPerfect or WordPro, you can set line numbering. Unfortunately, it will number every line, whether it is the start of a new paragraph (following a hard return) or wrapped text. There is no way to turn off text wrap, as there is in Notepad.

To solve that problem, change the layout of the page to Landscape, and the margins will be wide enough to allow the entire line of text on one line, without wrapping the text to the next line. Line numbering will then work very well for this purpose.

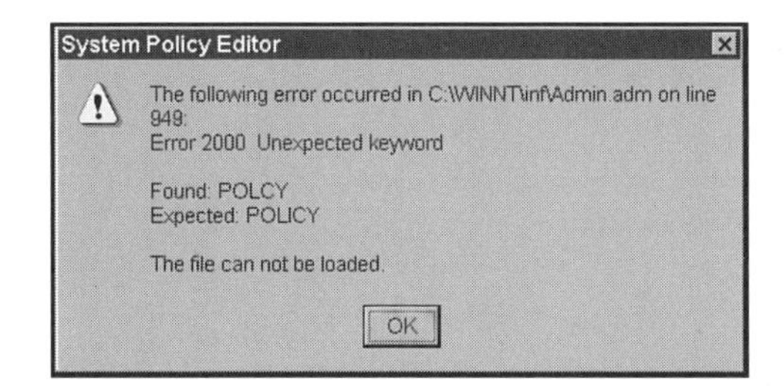

Figure 33.2. Error dialog when opening an edited ADMIN.ADM.

Imagine having to find the error by the line number. In this case, it wouldn't be that hard to fix in a word processor, searching for the word "Polcy" and replacing it with "Policy." Other errors may not be so simple.

Note

One of the major advantages of the System Policy Editor in Windows NT is that it allows multiple .ADM files. Each of the files is independently loaded, and so they are smaller. If there is an error, it is easier to find and correct. If the policy files were compatible between NT and 95, for Windows 95 users on your network, you would load COMMON.ADM and WINDOWS.ADM. They are almost exactly the same as ADMIN.ADM, with only two minor differences, both regarding automated logon to a network.

The Run Once command and the Run Services commands are in ADMIN.ADM but not in COMMON.ADM or WINDOWS.ADM. If they are particularly important to you, you

continues

continued

can edit the files and add them. The Run Once command could launch functions like an application installation, or a request for data. The Run Services command starts services that are set in the Control Panel to Manual instead of Automatic.

Other than these examples, all of the rest of the entries that are in `ADMIN.ADM` are also in the System Policy Editor for Windows NT.

Which Policy File Do I Use?

Windows NT systems look, by default, to `NTCONFIG.POL` in the `NETLOGON` share for their policies. Windows 95 systems also look in the `NETLOGON` share for `CONFIG.POL`. There are no differences in the content of the file, just in the file structure. Both policy files may exist in the `NETLOGON` share at the same time, and each will be accessed by its respective systems.

Tip

Windows 95 systems connected to a NetWare network automatically look for the `CONFIG.POL` file in the `PUBLIC` share on the server. There are no settings required; it is automatic.

If you would like to have the policy file in a different location, you can change the location by changing the Registry through System Policy Editor. On a workgroup network, where there is no central server, this setting would be required to implement policies.

To change the location and/or the name of the file to look to for policies, use the following steps. If you have not yet installed the System Policy Editor files from the Windows 95 CD-ROM, see Chapter 28, "System Policy Editor: Understanding Policy Files."

1. Open the Windows 95 System Policy Editor.
2. Open the local Registry with File | Open Registry.
3. Double-click on the Local Computer.
4. As shown in Figure 33.3, expand the Network and System policies update entries.
5. Select Remote update.
6. Choose Manual from the drop-down list for the Update mode.

Note

The setting is a little deceptive, in that it says "Manual" in the Update mode. There is nothing manual about the update. The Registry is automatically updated at logon, but it just uses a different path.

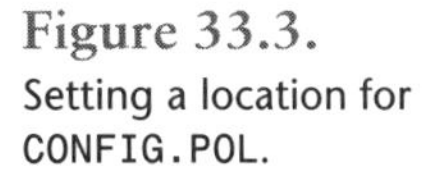

Figure 33.3.
Setting a location for CONFIG.POL.

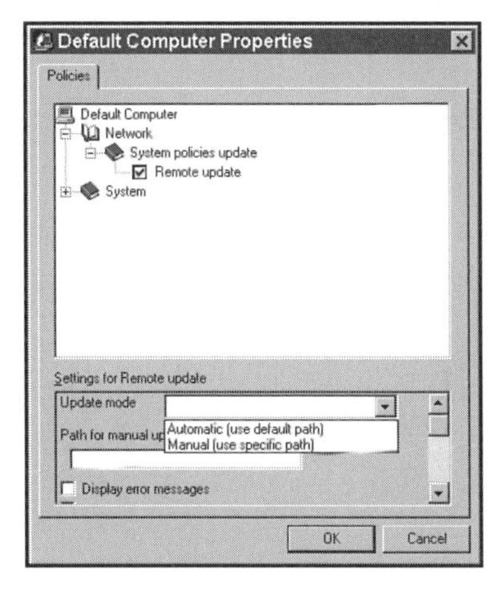

7. Enter the path for the policy file in the `\\systemname\share\CONFIG.POL` format.

Warning

Unless you insert the name of the file, the system will not recognize it. Be very specific.

8. Select OK.
9. Save the changes.

In turn, open the Registry of every machine with File | Connect and repeat steps 3 through 9 for each one.

Allowing Policies to Update Windows 95 Systems

In order for a Windows 95 system's Registry to be updated by System Policy Editor, that system must have Remote Administration enabled, and it must be running the Remote Registry Service.

Add the Remote Registry Service

Remote Registry Service does not automatically get installed with Windows 95. To install the service, which is available only on the CD-ROM, do the following:

1. Go to Control Panel | Network and choose Add.
2. Select Service and click Add.

3. Instead of using any of the services listed, choose Have Disk and browse for the `\Admin\Nettools\Remotreg directory`.
4. Confirm the location and choose OK to select the Remote Registry Service. (See Figure 33.4.)
5. Restart your system.

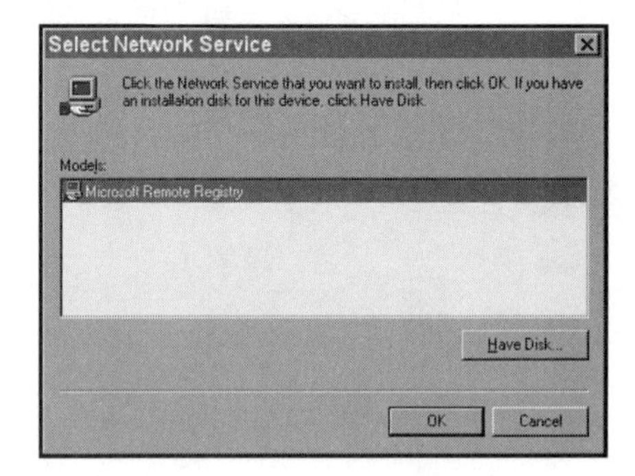

Figure 33.4. Setting up the Remote Registry Service.

Set the System to User-Level Access Control

After you install the Remote Registry Service, User-level access control must be enabled. Open the Network section of Control Panel. On the Access Control tab, select User-level access control, as shown in Figure 33.5, and supply the name of the domain where the administrators are. (This is where the list of groups and users are for the Remote Administration Service.)

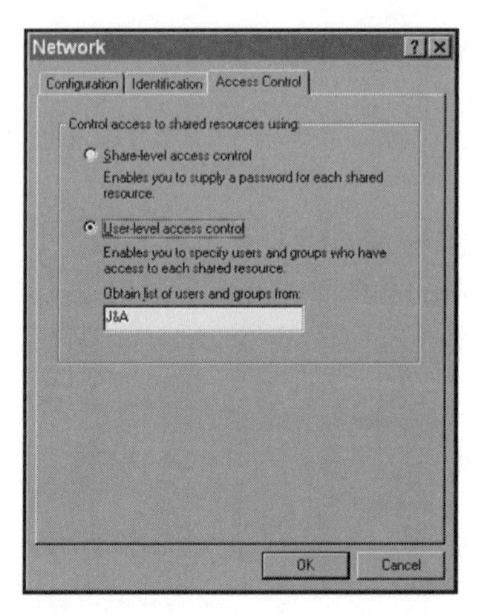

Figure 33.5. Setting User-level access control.

Start the Remote Administration Service

In order to start the Remote Administration Service on the Windows 95 system, go to the Passwords section of the Control Panel. Select the Remote Administration tab and click Enable Remote Administration on this server. (See Figure 33.6.)

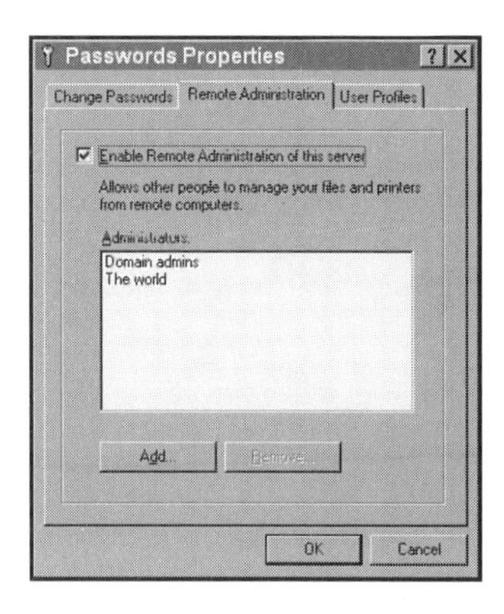

Figure 33.6.
Setting up Remote Administration on a Windows 95 system.

Note

Even though it says "server," any Windows 95 system can be edited this way. When remote functions are allowed, the system is its server processes.

Add the users and groups who will be allowed to edit the Registry. The ones that are the most critical are the Administrators group and Administrator. After confirmation, the system will need to be restarted, and then it will allow remote editing and the Windows 95 Registry can be updated across the network by System Policy Editor.

Solutions

Why is it so difficult to set up Windows 95 machines for use with System Policy Editor, and so easy for Windows NT systems?

Windows NT was designed from the ground up to be a networked system, allowing network access, management, and control. Windows 95 was designed as a stand-alone system, with networking as an add-on. If you run NT as a stand-alone system, the extra networking functions and procedures can be cumbersome. If you run the NT system on a network, the seamless nature of the networking is a great benefit.

Windows 95 appears to have been designed as a stand-alone machine, and the processes streamlined for optimum performance in that environment. Adding

continues

continued

networking is very easy, but allowing network management is quite cumbersome, with no automated way of changing all the systems on a network at one time. Each must be changed manually.

If you are setting up several new systems, consider adding the remote management functions on one system, and then clone it, as shown in Chapter 36, "Cloning Windows 95 Systems."

Computer-Based Settings in ADMIN.ADM

Many of the settings for Windows 95 systems are different than those of Windows NT. There are controllable features that NT simply doesn't have. Most of the entries in ADMIN.ADM are based on those unique features. The features that are the same as Windows NT, and share the same Registry setting, are in the NT template called COMMON.ADM. The entries that are the same in Windows 95's ADMIN.ADM and Windows NT's COMMON.ADM are listed in Listing 33.1 (for computer-based settings) and Listing 33.2 (for user-based settings), and are discussed in detail in Chapters 31 and 32. Detailed descriptions are presented here for the unique settings only.

Listing 33.1. Computer settings in ADMIN.ADM that are also in COMMON.ADM.

```
Default Computer/Network/Logon/Logon banner
Default Computer/Network/SNMP/Communities
Default Computer/Network/SNMP/Permitted Managers
Default Computer/Network/SNMP/Traps for 'Public' Community
Default Computer/Network/Update/Remote Update
Default Computer/System/Run
```

Listing 33.2. User settings in ADMIN.ADM that are also in COMMON.ADM.

```
Default User/Control Panel/Display/Restrict Display Control Panel
Default User/Desktop/Wallpaper
Default User/Desktop/Color Scheme
Default User/Shell/Custom Folders
Default User/Shell/Restrictions
Default User/System/Restrictions/Disable Registry Editing Tools
Default User/System/Restrictions/Run only allowed Windows applications
```

For more details on these entries, see the corresponding entries in Chapters 31 and 32. The balance of the settings in this chapter are unique to ADMIN.ADM and Windows 95 systems and users.

Network/Access Control/User-Level Access Control

With this setting, Windows 95 systems will look for logon validation from a Windows NT server or NetWare server, as shown in Figure 33.7. A single password would then allow the user access to shares on the network based on user rights assigned at the server. The default is share-level access control, where a password is assigned to every share.

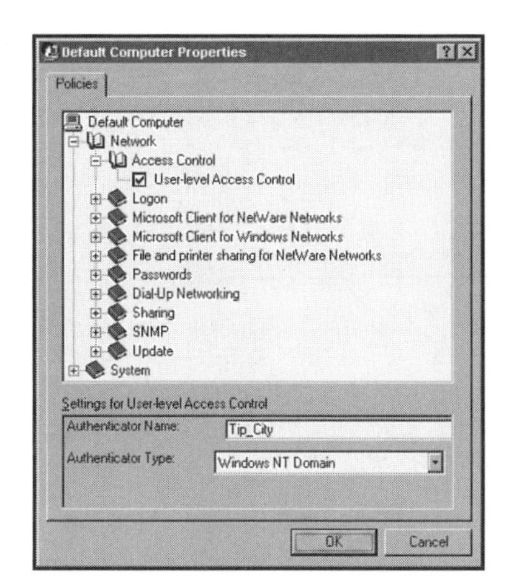

Figure 33.7.
Setting access to the network based on user-level rights.

Network/Logon/Require Validation by Network for Windows Access

Without this setting shown in Figure 33.8 turned on, users could press Esc at the logon dialog box and enter Windows NT, even though they could not access network resources.

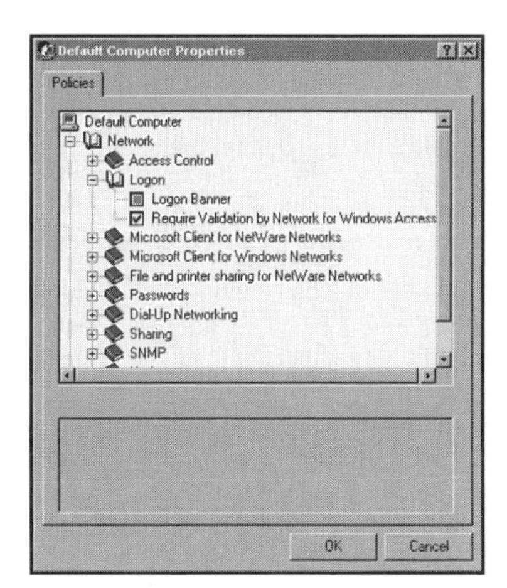

Figure 33.8.
Preventing the circumvention of network logon.

Network/Microsoft Client Service for NetWare Networks/Preferred Server

A preferred server in a NetWare environment is the one that the client wants to log in to. If a preferred server is not specified, the client will log in to the nearest login NetWare server. That may affect the login scripts, shares, and much more. Set this, and the network connections to the NetWare network will be much more consistent and stable. Enter the name of the preferred server in the entry box as shown in Figure 33.9.

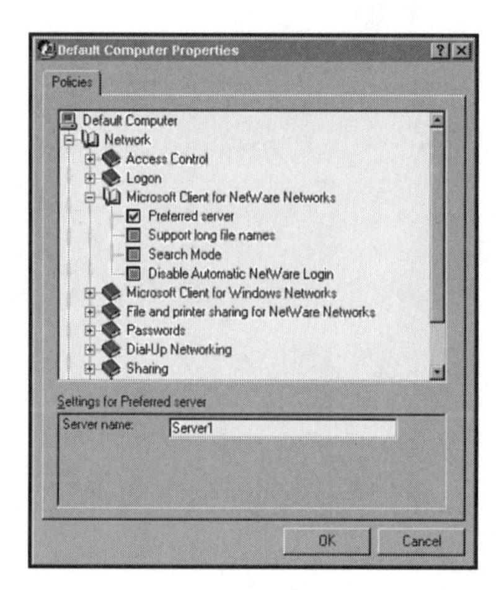

Figure 33.9.
Choose your preferred server.

Network/Microsoft Client Service for NetWare Networks/Support Long Filenames

Long filenames are supported with a Namespace in Netware 3.12, and they are supported natively in NetWare 4.*x*. As shown in Figure 33.10, you can choose on which type of server to support them. If the Windows 95 system is not set to support long filenames, even with name space installed, it will not be allowed to use them on files saved on the server.

Network/Microsoft Client Service for NetWare Networks/Disable Automatic NetWare Login

With the Client for Windows networks installed along with the Client Service for NetWare, passwords are passed between them. The password used at the Windows logon would then be used as the NetWare password, and if the password is correct, you would also be logged into NetWare. Turning this off, as shown in Figure 33.11, will force the user to log into NetWare independently.

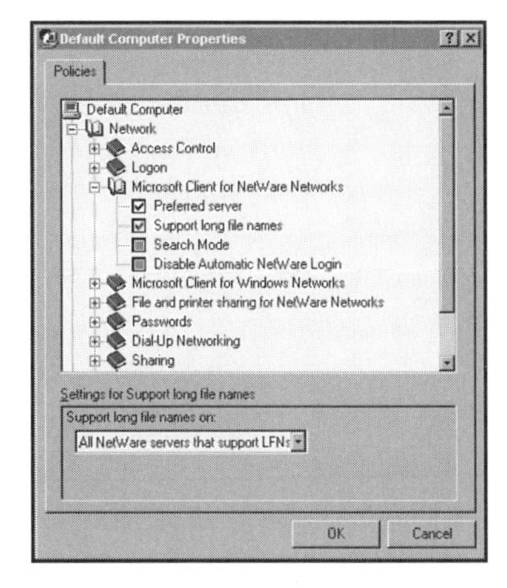

Figure 33.10. Setting up long filename support in Windows 95 for NetWare servers.

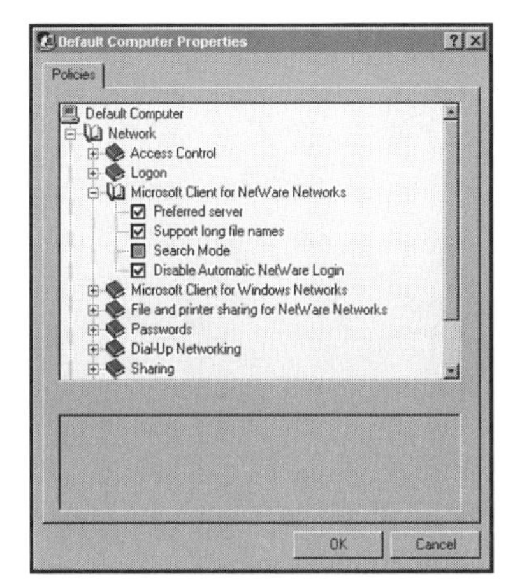

Figure 33.11. Turning off the password pass-through.

Windows 95 Network/Microsoft Client for Windows Networks/Log on to Windows NT

Be part of the Windows NT domain with the setting shown in Figure 33.12. Combined with the setting for user-level validation, logging onto a Windows NT server will provide premium security.

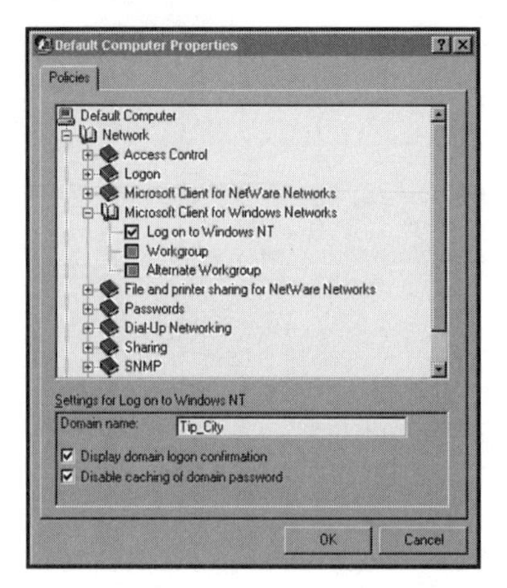

Figure 33.12.
Forced logon to NT domain.

Windows 95 Network/Microsoft Client for Windows Networks/Workgroup

This setting allows you to specify the workgroup name for the Windows 95 system. Usually set during installation, workgroup names on the network may end up being very different. This setting, shown in Figure 33.13, makes it easy to standardize the names across the network, and reduce browsing time and confusion.

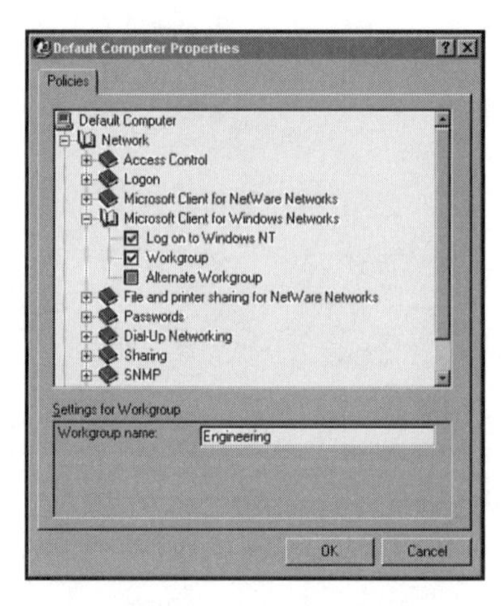

Figure 33.13.
Setting the standard workgroup name.

Windows 95 Network/Microsoft Client for Windows Networks/Alternate Workgroup

If you are the only one on the network with a particular workgroup name, usually it is added as a workgroup of one. If this setting is turned on, as shown in Figure 33.14, you will simply join the alternate workgroup specified. This is particularly helpful for notebook users who regularly connect to more than one network.

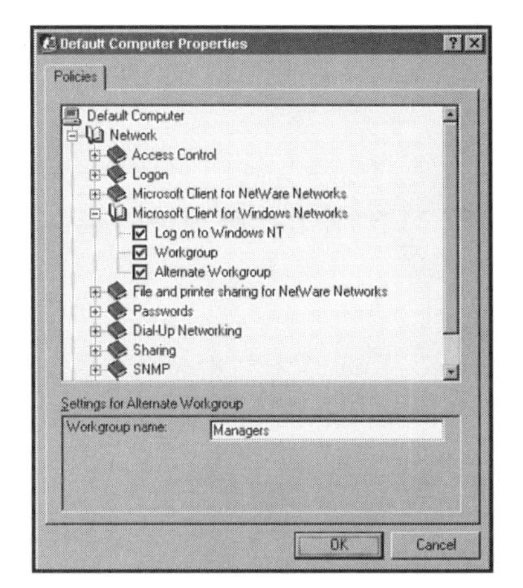

Figure 33.14. Add an alternate network to smooth network communications.

Windows 95 Network/File and Printer Sharing for NetWare Networks/Disable SAP Advertising

SAP (Server Advertising Protocol) advertising tells other clients that you are a NetWare server, or that you have shares for NetWare clients to use. You would then show up in server lists. Turning off the advertising, as shown in Figure 33.15, will keep you from that advertisement. Advertising yourself to the rest of the network as a NetWare compatible server is the default. Hiding yourself from the network would deter most others from using your shares. Because there is little security in Windows 95, you may consider using this as a deterrence from unauthorized people connecting to your shares.

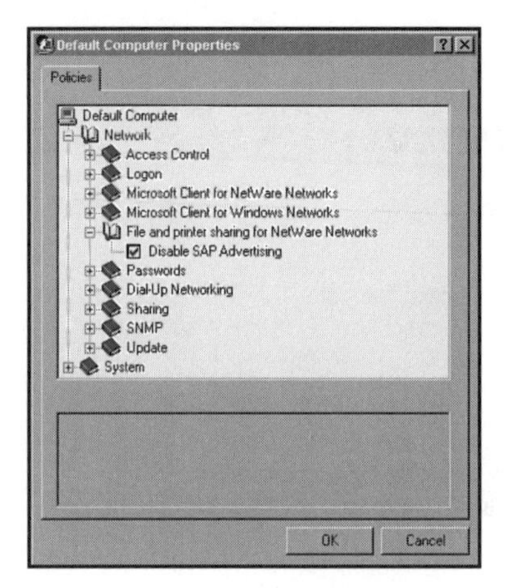

Figure 33.15.
Turn off NetWare server advertising.

Network/Passwords/Hide Share Passwords with Asterisks

If this setting is turned on, share passwords that include an asterisks will be hidden to others. Figure 33.16 illustrates this setting, as it does the next three settings.

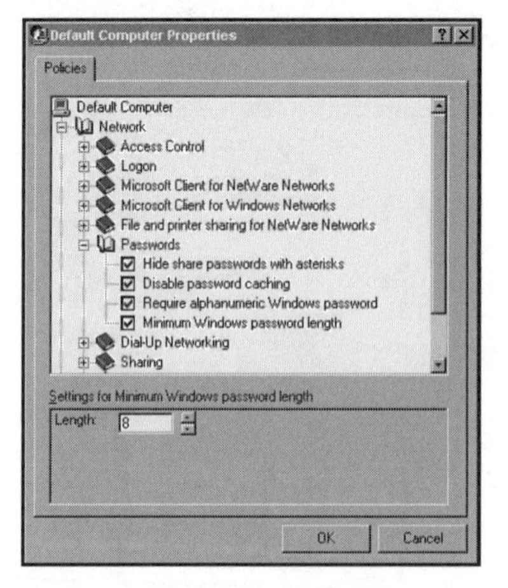

Figure 33.16.
Password settings in `ADMIN.ADM`.

Network/Passwords/Disable Password Caching

Normally, Windows 95 will cache passwords, so the logon performance will be enhanced. It presents a potential security breach because it is possible to crack that file and read information from it. It also can allow a user to bypass the real validation from the server. Turn this option on to increase security on your network.

Network/Passwords/Require Alphanumeric Windows Password

This setting, in combination with the next one, strengthens your password policy. With this setting turned on, a blank password is not a valid password. It will not be accepted. Of course, this is a sound security choice.

Network/Passwords/Min Windows Password Length

You can ensure that the password is of a specific length or greater. If you specified 6 characters, the potential combinations are staggering to comprehend at 26 to the sixth power or nearly 309 million.

Network/Dial-Up Networking/Disable Dial-in

With Dial-up networking enabled, you can also have people dial into your system. Turn it off with this choice, shown in Figure 33.17.

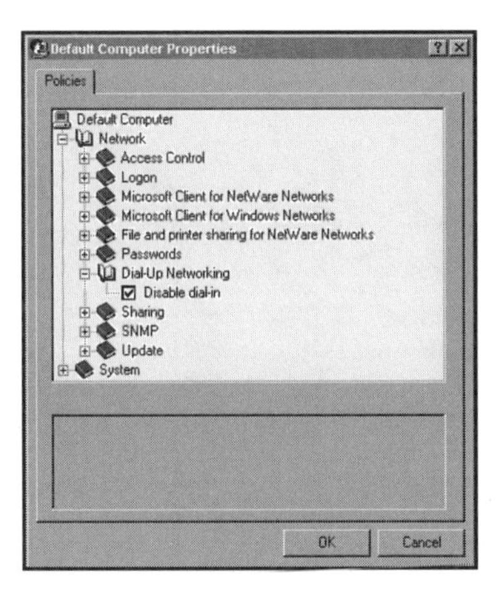

Figure 33.17.
Don't answer when someone calls.

Network/Sharing/Disable File Sharing

With this setting, you will not share any files and folders with others on your network. It also means you will not hold a browse list of other shares on the network. Figure 33.18 shows the disabling of file and printer sharing.

Network/Sharing/Disable Printer Sharing

No other users on the network can share your printers with this option turned on. It improves your performance because the system does not have to share its resources with anyone else.

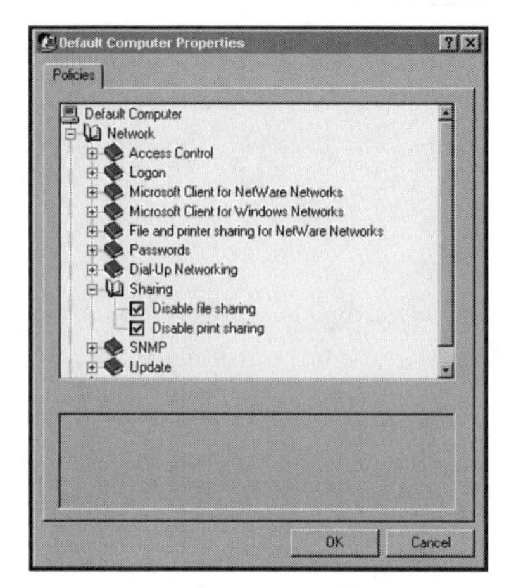

Figure 33.18. Disable file and printer sharing on Windows 95.

System/Profiles/Enable User Profiles

User profiles keep user information about every user that logs onto a particular system. The information is held in `\Windows\Profiles\username\USER.DAT`. If set correctly, you can use the same profile, or desktop settings on any Windows 95 system on the network. Figure 33.19 shows you where to enable it.

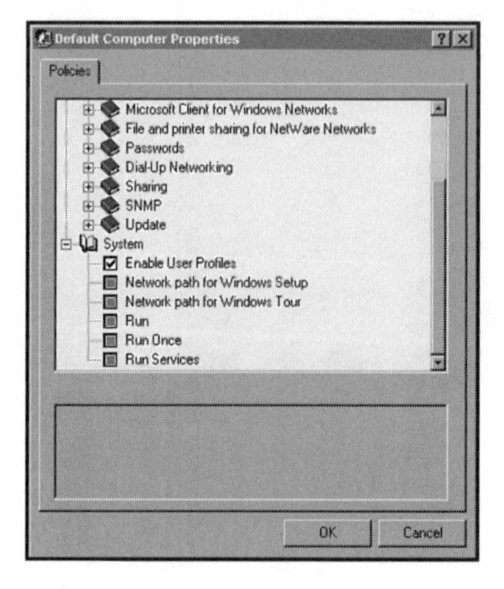

Figure 33.19. Consistent desktop settings are available with user profiles.

System/Network Path for Windows Setup

For subsequent installation of features for Windows 95, the system normally looks to the same location from which it was installed. That means that every user needs access to the original files. If you set this, as shown in Figure 33.20, you can have one set of files for all users to access. That will make administration much easier. It will also override the request to look at the local floppy disk drive or CD-ROM drive.

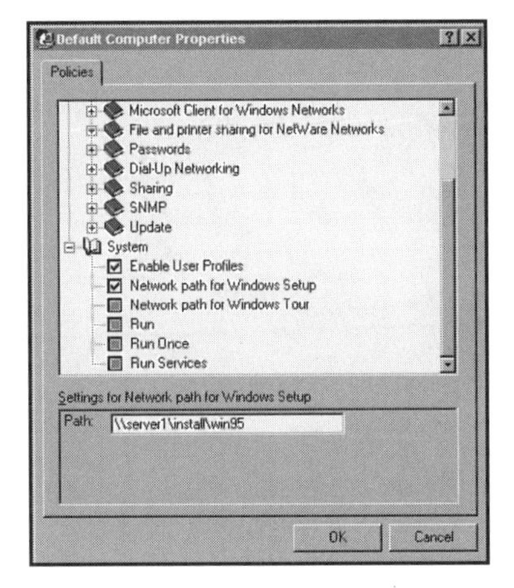

Figure 33.20.
Where are the Windows 95 cabinet files?

System/Network Path for Windows Tour

Windows 95 will look for the Tour (the tutorial) at the same location as the Windows 95 operating system files. Set this to a network path, as illustrated in Figure 33.21; there only needs to be one copy on the entire network. It will save a few megabytes on every system, and is well worth it because it usually only gets used once per user anyway.

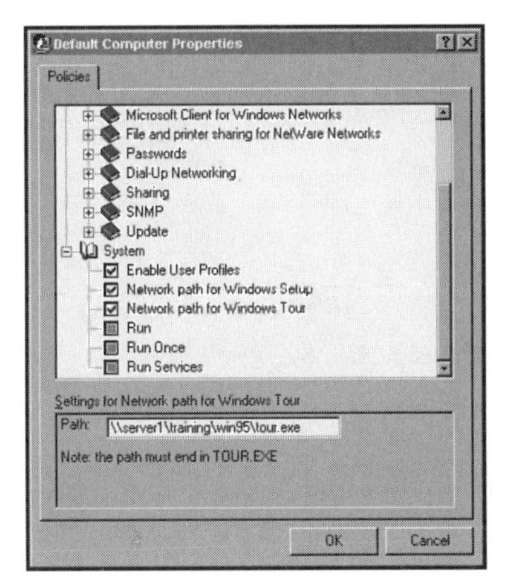

Figure 33.21.
Setting the central location of the Tour files.

System/Run Once

Similar to the Run function that is available in both Windows 95 and NT, the Run Once command allows the system administrator to add applications that will be run, but when completed will never be run again. This is particularly helpful in upgrading applications, adding a service pack (OS update), or polling the user for input. Figure 33.22 shows the options available.

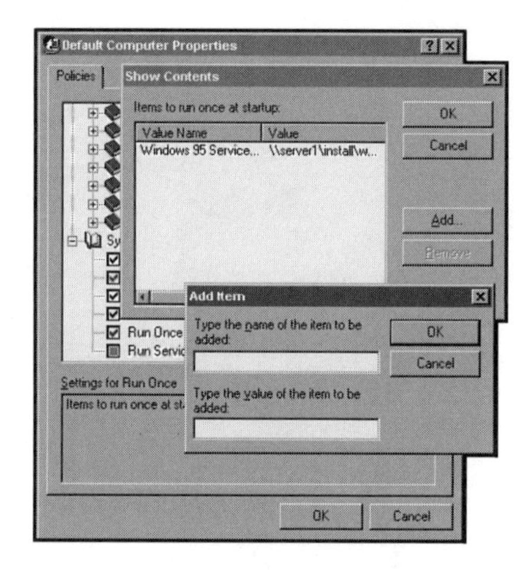

Figure 33.22. Items to be run only once on the system.

System/Run Services

Run Services allows services such as Dial-up Networking Server service to be activated at startup. No user intervention is required, making the management of the system easier. See Figure 33.23 and the dialog boxes for making the setting.

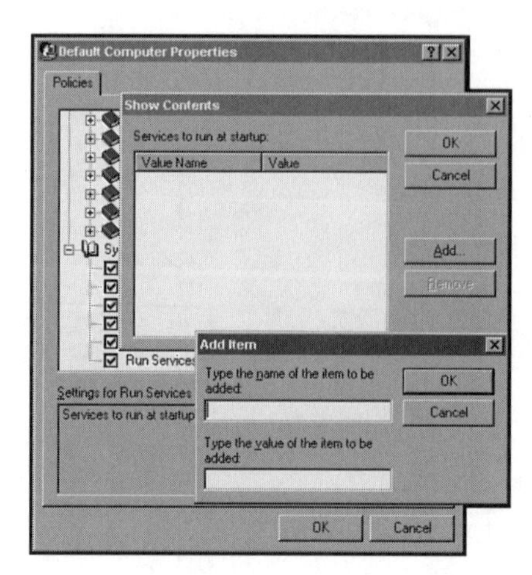

Figure 33.23. Setting services to run at startup.

User-Based Settings in ADMIN.ADM

There is much more control available for users in Windows 95 than in Windows NT 4.0. Maybe that is because Microsoft expected more novice users to use 95 than NT. Whatever the reason, if all the user restrictions in `ADMIN.ADM` were implemented, the user would probably quit and go elsewhere, somewhere that offered him some personal choice.

These settings allow the administrator to restrict access to features to improve security, stability, and reliability of the system.

Tip

Some people say the only stable Windows 95 system is the one that nobody touches. Much of the alleged instability comes from users playing with options. Use the System Policy Editor to restrict the users, and fewer problems with the operating system will occur.

However, the downside of the restrictions are that you, as the administrator, will have to make more of the changes.

Control Panel/Network/Restrict Network Control Panel

With this setting, you can disable the entire Network Control Panel, hide the Identification tab, or hide the Access Control tab. Figure 33.24 illustrates the options. The Identification tab allows you to change the name of the system and workgroup, and the Access Control tab allows you to choose between share-level and user-level access control.

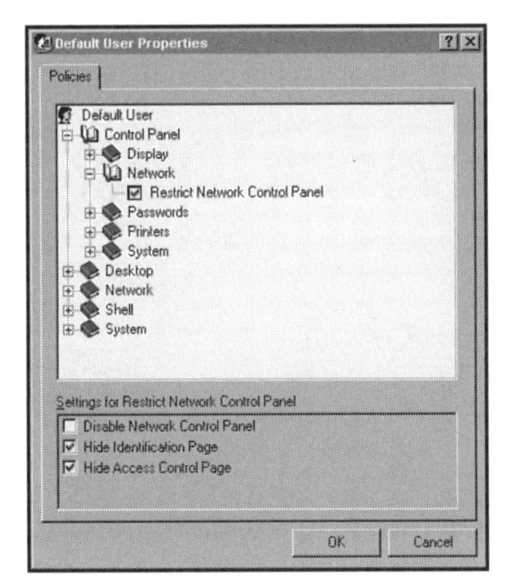

Figure 33.24.
Setting levels of access to the Network Control Panel.

Control Panel/Passwords/Restrict Passwords Control Panel

If you want to restrict how users can work with the Passwords section of the Control Panel, select this option, as shown in Figure 33.25. Several levels of restriction are available, including restricting access to the User Profiles tab, the Remote Administration tab, and the Change Passwords tab. Alternatively, you can completely restrict access to this entire section of the Control Panel.

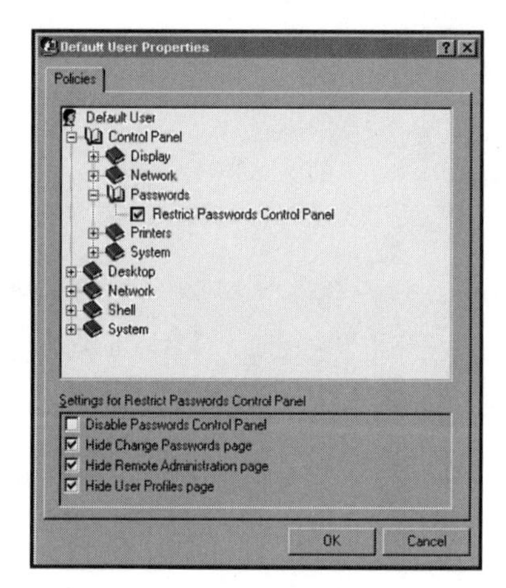

Figure 33.25. Password Control Panel restrictions.

Control Panel/Printers/Restrict Printer Settings

Figure 33.26 shows the options for restriction of access to the Printers Control Panel applet. It can be fully restricted, or limited to changing the properties, or adding or deleting printers.

Control Panel/System/Restrict System Control Panel

Changing the settings of hardware in your system is done through the System section of the Control Panel. To ensure that your users do not change critical settings, invoke all of these options, as shown in Figure 33.27.

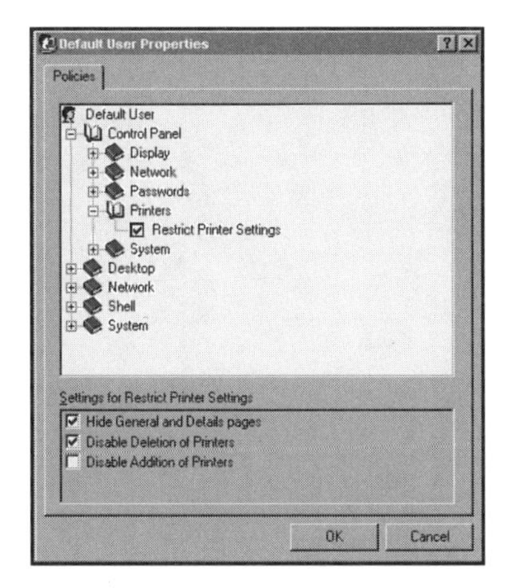

Figure 33.26. Restricting access to Printer settings.

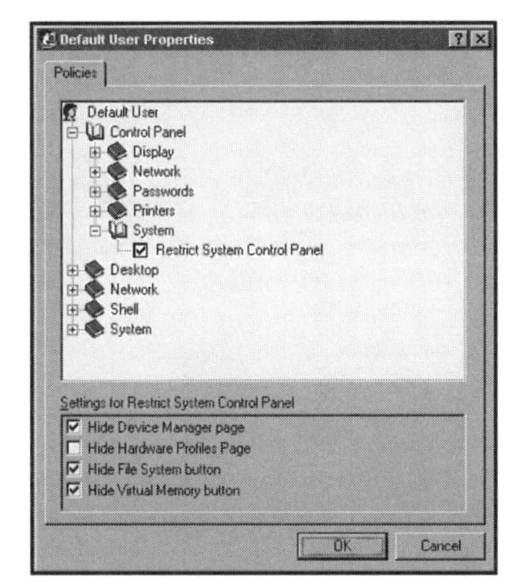

Figure 33.27. System settings in the Control Panel.

Network/Sharing/Disable File Sharing and Disable Print Sharing Controls

These settings do exactly the same thing as the settings in the computer-based restrictions. The only difference is that the computer-based restrictions limit any user who is logged on the machine. These settings restrict the user, wherever he logs onto the network.

Disabling the sharing, as shown in Figure 33.28, in whichever setting, takes precedence. For example, if the system is not restricted but the user is, the restrictions will be in place. If the system is restricted, the user will be restricted, regardless of the user settings.

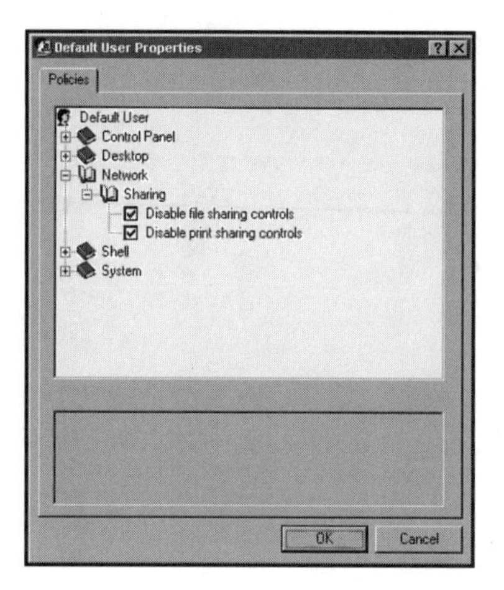

Figure 33.28.
Disabling file and print sharing controls.

System/Restrictions/Disable MS-DOS Prompt

If your user can get to a DOS prompt, he could run DOS applications and commands that may not be permitted in your organization. This policy restricts it, according to the graphic in Figure 33.29. Select it, and the MS-DOS prompt will be disabled.

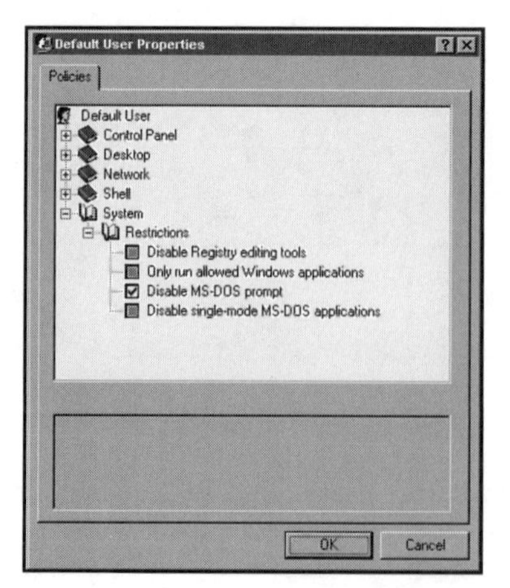

Figure 33.29.
Removing the MS-DOS prompt option from Windows 95.

Windows 95/System/Restrictions/Disable Single-Mode MS-DOS Apps

Certain MS-DOS apps require different MS-DOS environments, including different settings for the path, files, buffers, and drivers. Most of these applications would not work if you disabled this option as shown in Figure 33.30. The most common instance of single-mode MS-DOS apps is games. Many will not work unless special settings are made.

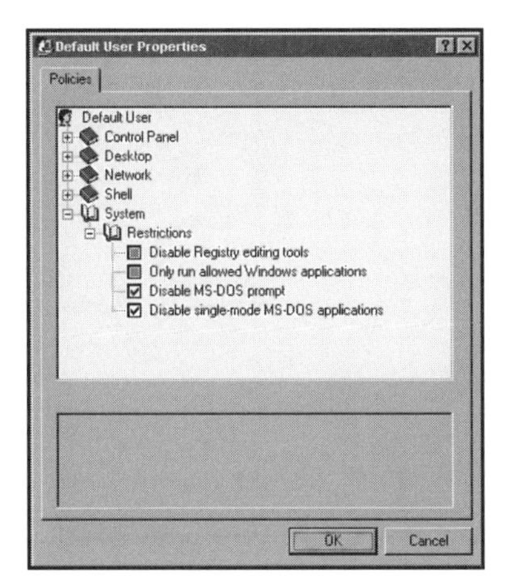

Figure 33.30. Restricting access to single-mode MS-DOS application settings.

Summary

The settings in `WINDOWS.ADM` in conjunction with `COMMON.ADM` would give you roughly the same capabilities as `ADMIN.ADM`, while allowing you to have a consolidated policy for all users, if only it worked. It doesn't, so you will have to use System Policy Editor in Windows 95 and `ADMIN.ADM`. The main point of all of System Policy Editor is to make necessary changes on the system, and feed them automatically to the system as a user logs on. The available changes are incredible, allowing centralized management of Windows 95 systems from a single location.

CHAPTER 34

Creating Custom Policies

One of the best things about System Policy Editor is its capability to add policies and Registry changes to the ones already present. The current template files include many options and restrictions, but much more is possible. Many of the Registry changes discussed in Chapters 13 through 25 are perfect for implementation as custom policies because of their universal application to all users on the network.

Any Registry change can be implemented across the network, given to computers, individuals, or groups. There is actually no faster way to manage and update Registries than this.

This chapter explains the file structure, what items affect which parts of the policy file, and walks through some examples. The most important part of this chapter is how to create a usable .ADM template file. Because the template file structure is the same for both Windows 95 and Windows NT, as long as the Registry change will work, the template will work for both.

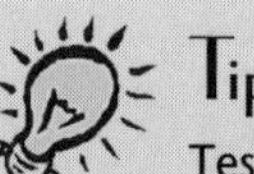

Tip

Test your Registry change as a manual change before creating a policy for it. If it doesn't work as a manual change, it won't work as a policy.

.ADM File Structure

Knowing the required syntax for a template file is critical for understanding current files and for creating new files. Any mistakes in the template file result in errors and require changes before the file can be loaded as a template. Figure 34.1 illustrates the structure of a simple policy file.

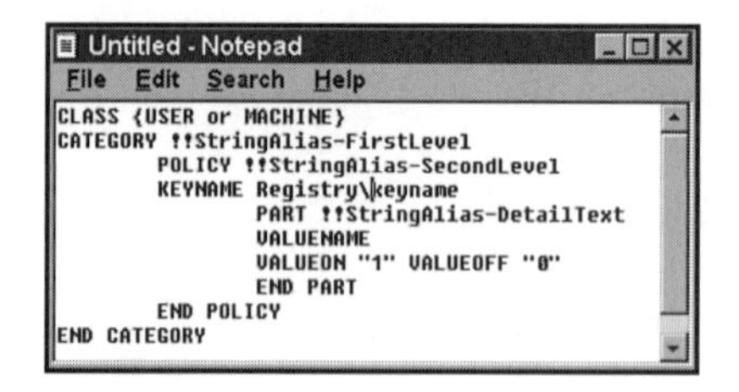

Figure 34.1.
Policy file structure.

CLASS

Because you are only going to be changing HKEY_LOCAL_MACHINE or HKEY_CURRENT_USER, your only options for the CLASS setting are

- CLASS MACHINE
- CLASS USER

The CLASS entry determines whether the entry will affect the computer or the user functions. It is possible to have CLASS entries for both user and computer in the same template file. Group all policies under these headings according to type of change, as shown in Figure 34.2.

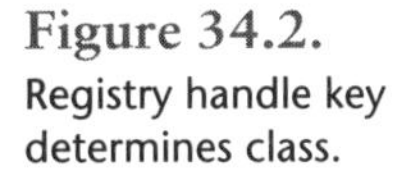

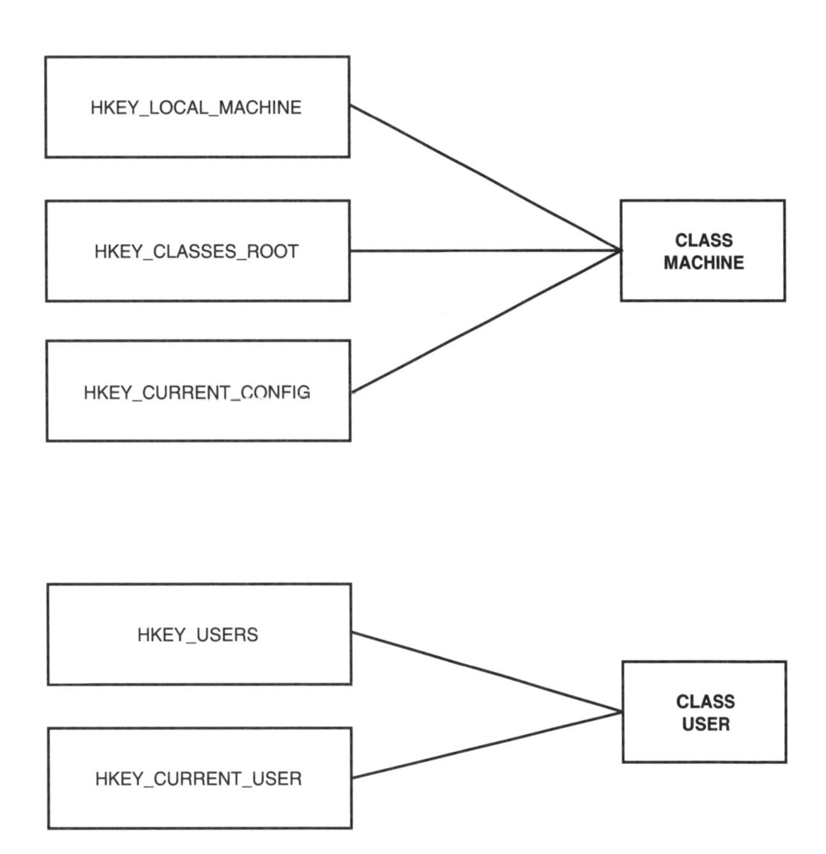

Registry handle key determines class.

CATEGORY

The `CATEGORY` setting sets the text for initial headings. It also groups multiple policies for ease of use and editing. You can have as many categories under a heading as you want. You can also put additional subcategories under a category to create a more detailed hierarchical structure.

Close the `CATEGORY` section with an `END CATEGORY` command.

POLICY

The `POLICY` section is where you actually make the choice to implement the change. It puts a check box before the text, allowing you to set it for Ignore, Activate, or Deactivate.

Close the `POLICY` section with an `END POLICY` command.

KEYNAME

For each policy, there must be a `KEYNAME` and at least one value. The `KEYNAME` entry must start at the level below the handle key.

Tip

Do not start the KEYNAME with a backslash (\). Start with the key below the handle key. If you start with a backslash, the file will be imported without error, but the setting will not work.

VALUENAME

The VALUENAME is the same as in the Registry. Ensure that there are no spaces in the value name in the policy file if there are none in the Registry change.

PART

The data for the values and the type of System Policy Editor entry desired are listed in PART.

Close the PART section with an END PART command.

Strings

Strings are shown in the .ADM file starting with a double exclamation (!!). The text following the double exclamation cannot include a space. The text listed in the [Strings] section replaces the STRING entry in System Policy Editor. An alternative is to simply put the text in quotation marks (as shown in Figure 34.3).

```
Untitled - Notepad
File Edit Search Help
CLASS MACHINE
CATEGORY  !!Network
  CATEGORY !!Sharing
    KEYNAME System\CurrentControlSet\Services\LanManServer\Parameters
      POLICY !!WorkstationShareAutoCreate
        VALUENAME "AutoShareWks"
                VALUEOFF NUMERIC 0
                        PART !!ShareWks_Tip1    TEXT    END PART
                        PART !!ShareWks_Tip2    TEXT    END PART
      END POLICY

      POLICY !!ServerShareAutoCreate
        VALUENAME "AutoShareServer"
                VALUEOFF NUMERIC 0
                        PART !!ShareServer_Tip1 TEXT    END PART
                        PART !!ShareServer_Tip2 TEXT    END PART
      END POLICY
  END CATEGORY    ; Sharing
END CATEGORY    ; Network

[Strings]
Network="Windows NT Network"
Sharing="Sharing"
WorkstationShareAutoCreate="Create hidden drive shares (workstation)"
ServerShareAutoCreate="Create hidden drive shares (server)"
ShareWks_Tip1=Automatically create <drive letter>$ and Admin$ shares
ShareWks_Tip2=when Windows NT Workstation starts.
ShareServer_Tip1=Automatically create <drive letter>$ and Admin$ shares
ShareServer_Tip2=when Windows NT Server starts.
```

Figure 34.3.
Text in the [Strings] section.

Each of the corresponding parts of the System Policy Editor screen is generated by the `.ADM` file. An example from the `WINNT.ADM` file is shown in Figure 34.4.

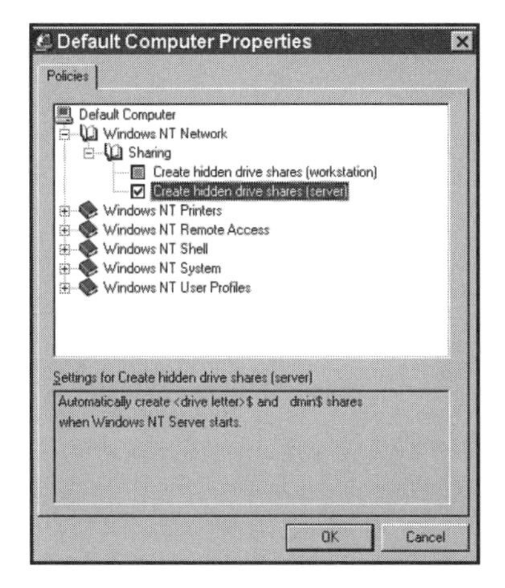

Figure 34.4.
Each section of the `.ADM` file affects the System Policy Editor screen.

Tip

One of the most common mistakes by creators of template files is the omission of the closing entry. For every `CATEGORY`, there must be an `END CATEGORY`. For every `POLICY`, there must be an `END POLICY`. For every `PART`, there must be an `END PART`.

Creating a Custom Policy: MenuShowDelay

`MenuShowDelay` is a Registry change that makes the system feel faster because the menus respond to mouse movement more quickly. It uses the `Control Panel\Desktop` key. Because it affects the user, make it a `CLASS USER` entry. Use Notepad, WordPad, or any text editor or word processor to create the file. When you finish, save it as a text-only file with an `.ADM` extension.

Note

For more details on the `MenuShowDelay` Registry change, see the section titled "Boost the Speed of Your Menus" in Chapter 23, "Windows NT 4 Users and the Registry," and Chapter 25, "Windows 95 Users and the Registry."

Tip

The text for CATEGORY and POLICY can be any text. You can use the actual text in brackets or use the text-string options (!!) for a reusable string.

Listing 34.1 contains the text for this .ADM file that will provide the MenuShowDelay option in System Policy Editor.

Listing 34.1. MenuShowDelay template file.

```
CLASS USER
    CATEGORY !!SPEED
        POLICY "Boost Menu Speed"
        KEYNAME "Control Panel\Desktop"
            PART "Enter menu speed (1-10000, lower is faster)" EDITTEXT
            VALUENAME MenuShowDelay
            END PART
        END POLICY
    END CATEGORY
[STRINGS]
SPEED="Enhance Interface Performance"
```

Note

The entries in an .ADM file are not case-sensitive. They are shown here and in the standard template files with upper- and lowercase to make them easier to read. The tabs are also not required, but are used to make the file more readable. Each entry must be separated by one of three characters: a hard return, a tab, or a space. If there is a space in text between two words that are supposed to stay together, use quotes around them to indicate the text as one entry.

Note

This template file uses EDITTEXT as the type of PART entry. It allows the administrator to type in a value. For more details on the type of parts available, see Appendix I, "System Policy Editor Keyword Reference."

Save the file as a text file with an .ADM extension. It does not have to be in \WINNT\INF with the rest of the template files, but it makes it easier to find.

Tip

Initially, save all your Windows 95 templates separately from your `ADMIN.ADM` file. Import the file into System Policy Editor, test it, and then append it on the end of your `ADMIN.ADM` file.

This `.ADM` creates the policy (as shown in Figure 34.5).

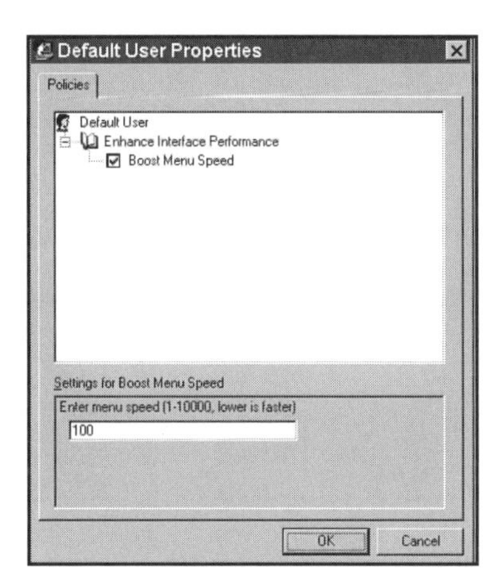

Figure 34.5.
Boost the menu speed with a policy.

Tip

`MenuShowDelay` will also work with Windows 95, and the value name will be added by System Policy Editor.

Tip

If you save the file and type the name as `MENU.ADM` in Notepad, the actual result will be `MENU.ADM.TXT`. Notepad always puts a `.TXT` extension on anything you type in the File Name entry box. To create the file without a `.TXT` extension, put the name in quotes (`"MENU.ADM"`).

Creating a Custom Policy: MinAnimate

MinAnimate boosts the speed of your interface by eliminating the animation shown when a window is minimized or maximized. The MinAnimate value is not in the Registry, so System Policy Editor adds it for you automatically based on the entries shown in Listing 34.2.

Here is the listing of the text for this .ADM file.

Listing 34.2. MinAnimate template file.

```
CLASS USER
    CATEGORY !!SPEED
        POLICY "Boost Window Speed"
        KEYNAME "Control Panel\Desktop\WindowMetrics"
            PART "I want faster windows" CHECKBOX
            VALUENAME MinAnimate
                VALUEON "0" VALUEOFF "1"
            END PART
        END POLICY
    END CATEGORY
[STRINGS]
SPEED="Enhance Interface Performance"
```

The two things to notice in this template file are the change in the type of PART and the addition of the VALUEON/VALUEOFF entries. The check box allows you to enable or disable a selection. The VALUEON/VALUEOFF entries determine what happens when you make your selection.

Note

Notice that the normal entries for VALUEON and VALUEOFF have been reversed. The default is on, meaning that the animation is executed. However, in the dialog box presented to users, users choose whether they want faster windows. To get the faster windows (a YES selection), MinAnimate must be turned off.

Set the template file so it is easy to read and understand, and then make the entries comply with the text.

The results of this template file are shown in Figure 34.6.

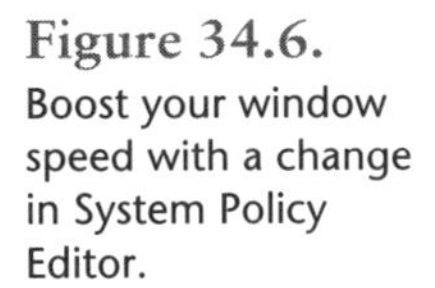

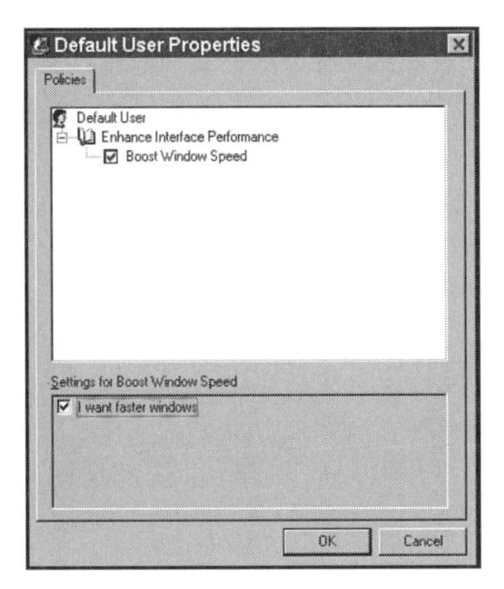

Figure 34.6.
Boost your window speed with a change in System Policy Editor.

Consolidate Your Template Files

Even though it is easy to manage multiple small template files, it is occasionally better to consolidate them. If you add both of the templates you just created to System Policy Editor, the category listing is duplicated, as illustrated in Figure 34.7.

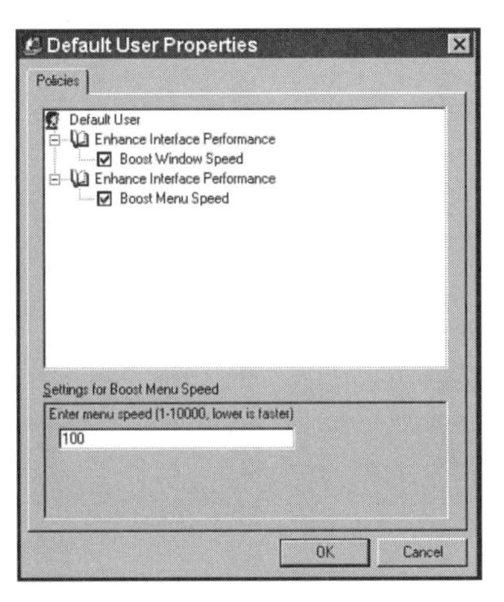

Figure 34.7.
Multiple template files with the same `CATEGORY` name.

Even if Listing 34.1 and Listing 34.2 are in the same `.ADM` file, if two first-level categories are listed, they both show in System Policy Editor. To consolidate the categories, copy and add the `POLICY` section from one into the other, as shown in Listing 34.3. Figure 34.8 shows the result of the consolidation.

Listing 34.3. Consolidated template file.

```
CLASS USER
    CATEGORY !!SPEED
        POLICY "Boost Menu Speed"
        KEYNAME "Control Panel\Desktop"
            PART "Enter menu speed (1-10000, lower is faster)" EDITTEXT
            VALUENAME MenuShowDelay
            END PART
        END POLICY
        POLICY "Boost Window Speed"
        KEYNAME "Control Panel\Desktop\WindowMetrics"
            PART "I want faster windows" CHECKBOX
            VALUENAME MinAnimate
                VALUEON "0" VALUEOFF "1"
            END PART
        END POLICY
    END CATEGORY
[STRINGS]
SPEED="Enhance Interface Performance"
```

Obviously, consolidating the entries makes the whole process easier, cleaner, and more professional. You may want to group whole sections of policies together for ease of use.

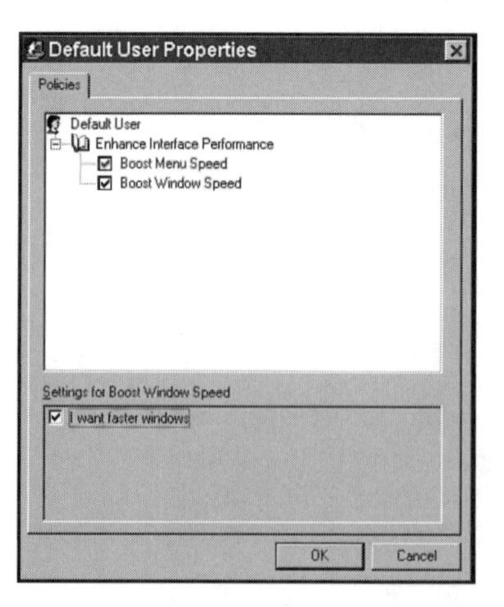

Figure 34.8.
Consolidated entries make a clean, concise policy.

Creating a Custom Policy: Network Install

Installation of software can be a challenging thing for an administrator. The Network Installation routine using a Registry change shown in Chapter 18, "Windows NT Networking and the Registry," greatly simplifies the task without the expense of buying and implementing something like SMS (Systems Management Server) from Microsoft.

To make the Registry change work, create a share and copy the installation files to it. For example, create a share named `Install` and create subdirectories for Excel, Collage for Windows, and PageMaker.

At the server, edit `\WINNT\APPS.INF` (for Windows NT) or `\WINDOWS\APPS.INF` (for Windows 95) and add the `[AppInstallList]` section, followed by a line for each of the applications, in the format *`Label=path to SETUP.EXE`*. This would look like the information in Figure 34.9.

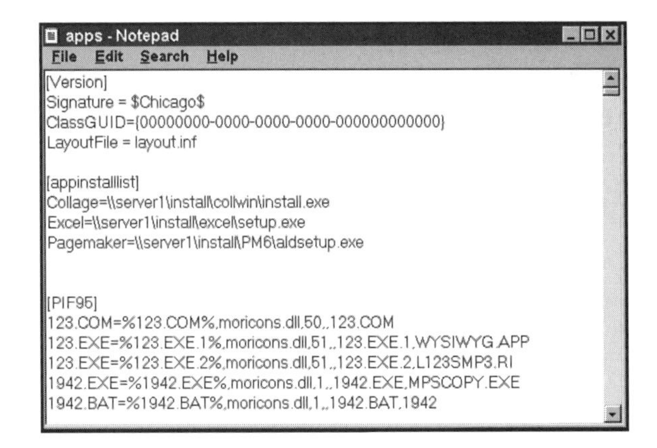

Figure 34.9.
Revised `APPS.INF` shows applications available for installation.

Next, create a policy for all systems that will allow the users to access the server directly for installing the applications. The template for the policy is shown in Listing 34.4.

Listing 34.4. Template file for network installation of software.

```
CLASS MACHINE
    CATEGORY "Installation"
        POLICY !!INSTALL
        KEYNAME SOFTWARE\Microsoft\Windows\CurrentVersion
            VALUENAME AppInstallPath
            VALUEON "\\SERVER1\WINNT\INF\APPS.INF" VALUEOFF ""
        END POLICY
    END CATEGORY
[STRINGS]
INSTALL="Allow network installation of applications"
```

Note

Without a `PART` entry, no part type need be listed. `VALUEON` and `VALUEOFF` automatically set the interface to use a check box for the `POLICY`, and allow the selection at the second level instead of the third.

After the policy is activated at a workstation, the new Network Install tab is available in Control Panel | Add/Remove Software. Choose from the list and click Install to start the installation. The installation will then proceed the same as a normal installation, and you will need to answer all the questions.

Note

During a normal installation of Microsoft software, a CD-KEY is required. Though the installation files copied to the server are exactly the same as on the installation CD-ROM, the user will not be prompted for a CD-KEY.

Figure 34.10 shows the results of this new policy. It can be activated for individual systems or for all of the systems with default computer.

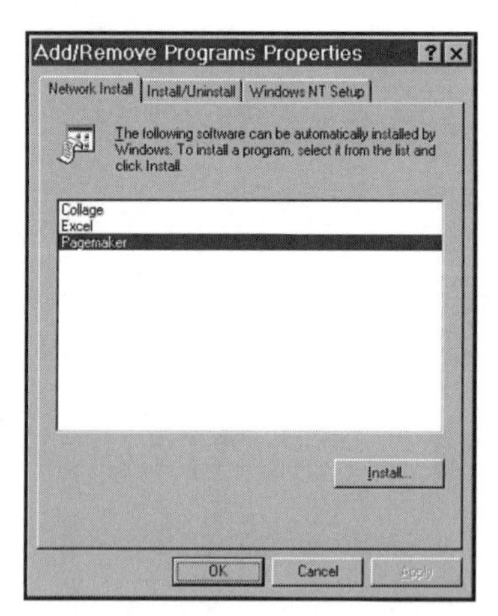

Figure 34.10. Application installation simplified.

Effectively Implementing Custom Policies

Establish a procedure for implementing your policies, and *always* test your custom policy before rolling it out to all of your users. If you make a disastrous mistake in changing the Registries of all of the computers on the network, you might find it takes too much time to undo it. Most of the time, you can simply reverse the procedure in System Policy Editor, but you might find yourself in a real bind.

Tip

Create a new group in User Manager for Domains for testing purposes. I have five users in mine. Before I roll out any policy for all of the users on my network, I always test it on my "guinea pig" group. If it works for them, I can roll it out to others. All the users in the guinea pig group are fairly advanced, and can usually recover from any mistakes I make.

One of the biggest challenges is making a sweeping, universal change to every system in the network after you have several systems, users, and groups specified in System Policy Editor. To make a change for all the users or all the systems, even if there are system, users, or groups specified, make the change only to the default. Even if there is a specified computer in System Policy Editor, the original setting for any policy is to ignore it. If you don't change that, and you add a new policy and set it for the default computer, it will still be activated on the specified system.

If your current policy has already updated the Registries of all the systems on your network, and if the policies invoked do not require constant resetting, you can simply remove the policy file you have and replace it with another. Obviously, if you have set a policy to restrict a user with a setting that can easily be changed with Control Panel, you may want to leave your current policy in place. A set policy is only good as long as it does not get changed by the user.

An Alternative Implementation Procedure

Alternatively, you can create a temporary policy. Use the following steps to leave your previous policy intact for the long term, and create a temporary policy for the short term.

1. Copy your current policy file to another directory.
2. Remove the templates normally used.
3. Add a template or templates for your temporary policy.
4. Make the settings for Default Computer, Default User, or specified computers, individuals, or groups.
5. Save the file as `NTCONFIG.POL` (for Windows NT) or `CONFIG.POL` (for Windows 95) in the `NETLOGON` or `PUBLIC` share.
6. Instruct everyone to log off the network and back on again.
7. When users log back on to the network, the policy updates the Registry.
8. Copy the original file back to the `NETLOGON` or `PUBLIC` share.

The next time the users log on to the network, they will get the old policy file, but their Registries will have been changed.

Summary

Custom policies are relatively easy, and allow additional changes that the Microsoft programmers didn't include in System Policy Editor. Many of the changes listed in Chapters 13 through 25 make excellent options for custom policies. Of course, if you receive a Registry change from Microsoft in response to a support request, you might also want to implement that through a custom policy.

Creating custom policies doesn't take any programming skill or experience. It just requires you to be meticulous in your work. Use the steps shown here, and you will be able to easily and quickly update your system with any Registry setting you like.

CHAPTER 35

Cloning Windows NT Systems

You might be wondering what installing software and cloning systems has to do with the Registry. After all, most 32-bit application developers use Registry changes to control the application and its functions. If you were to simply copy the application's files to another system, it probably wouldn't work because the required corresponding Registry changes for the application's initialization and control would not have been implemented.

Say you need to set up 15 new systems for new employees, each system identical, each containing 10 applications. Plus, imagine having to implement the necessary modifications to the Registry for the Explorer interface and security. Setting that up manually would be costly in terms of time and productivity. Allowing users to install NT and applications for you wastes their productive time and leads to installation errors. Cloning is the answer.

Cloning Limitations and Requirements

The goal of cloning is to create a system that duplicates another, with all its interface changes, tweaks, installed software, and options, and to do it with these caveats:

- Every system has to be considered a unique system on the network. Merely copying all the files with `XCOPY.EXE` won't work. A copied system would have exactly the same security identifiers (SID) for the operating system, the machine name, and the shares. The real problem is the SID associated with the machine name. Even if you change the name, the SID is retained so that connectivity with the servers can be maintained. Every cloned system needs to have unique SIDs.
- The cloning process must be fast. If it isn't fast, cloning won't be worth it. You could go to each machine and make all the changes to the Registry, or even use System Policy Editor to make the changes. Then you could install all the applications one by one and make the modifications to the toolbars, and so on. But that's too slow, and it's very tedious.

The best option is to take a currently setup system, get everything exactly as you would like it, and clone it (except for the SIDs discussed previously). Then you could use that procedure over and over to make your installation work more easily, faster, and error-free. What you want to achieve is shown in Figure 35.1.

In the past, Computer Profile Setup was included with the Windows NT 3.51 Resource Kit. Unfortunately, even though it did a passable job, it had too many limitations, particularly in relation to long filenames and hardware differences. It was difficult to use, and didn't always create unique SIDs for the systems. The complexity and undependable results made it unusable for most organizations. Now, however, `SYSDIFF.EXE` is available to help you clone your system.

Figure 35.1.
A fully installed system.

SYSDIFF.EXE

NT 4.0 Server offers a new deployment tool called `SYSDIFF.EXE`, which is designed to allow quick and easy system cloning. `SYSDIFF.EXE` does not install or help install the operating system—just all of the modifications, applications, and changes. It can help make the necessary interface changes and connections to the network and shares. It can also help install the application files and implement the necessary Registry changes associated with those files.

`SYSDIFF.EXE` allows you to perform these tasks in two ways. You can combine the changes to the Registry with the binary files required to run the applications into one item called a *difference file* (it is the difference between the original system and the system after all modifications), then copy the difference file to the new system. That process is outlined in the section titled "Cloning Step by Step." An illustration of this method is shown in Figure 35.2.

Alternatively, you can use the cloning tool to make only Registry changes, which will create an `.INF` file. You then copy the actual files another way, by performing a backup-and-restore or by recording the files on a CD-recordable drive, and copy them to the target system. That option is outlined in the section titled "An Alternative Procedure for Installing Files on the Target System." Figure 35.3 illustrates this type of installation. Whether you include all the actual programs and auxiliary files or not, when you decide to clone your system, the most critical part is the Registry.

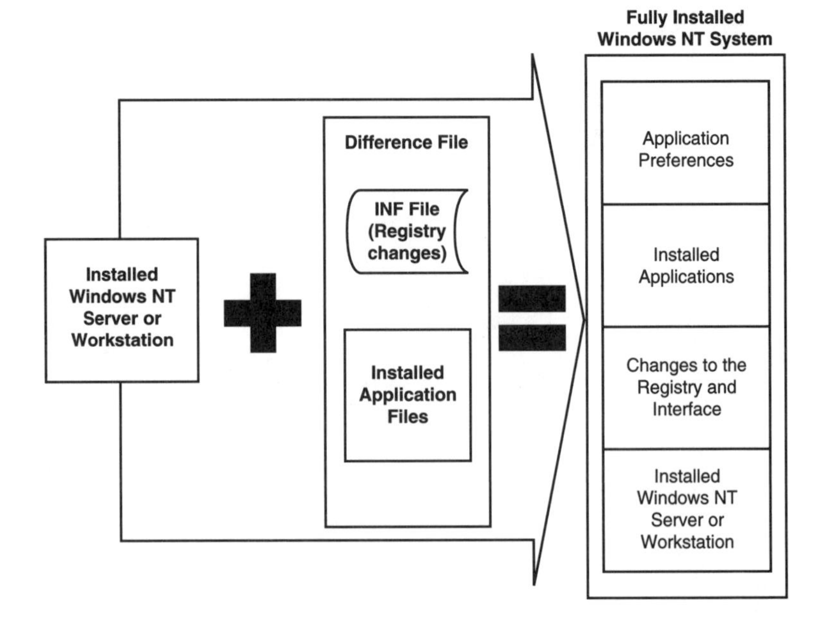

Figure 35.2.
Easy installation with a difference file.

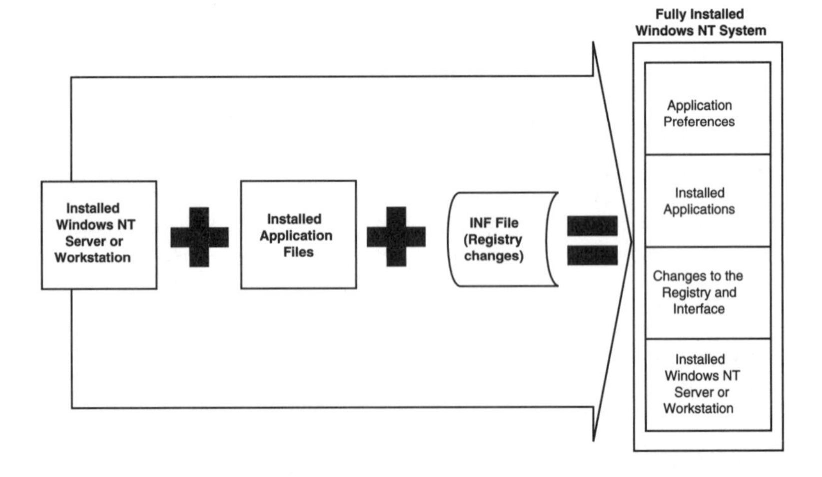

Figure 35.3.
Using separate application and `.INF` files for a clone installation.

Note

The `.INF` file includes only the Registry changes that were made. Separating the `.INF` file from the difference file will be discussed later.

Solutions

Why not just use something like GHOST, a third-party product?

GHOST is a very good program, and it does cloning very well on systems like Windows 3.x and Windows 95. The limitations of the product make it more of a challenge working with NT, and it does not have as many options as the tools in this chapter do. The biggest limitation is the requirement to have unique computer names and IP addresses, plus the possibility of differences in hardware, drivers, and settings. All of those are compensated for with the Setup Manager.

SYSDIFF.EXE Parts and Pieces

For SYSDIFF.EXE to work correctly, several things are required, including

- A master system with Windows NT Server or Workstation 4.0 installed, on which you will make necessary changes and add applications.
- A share on the server for the SYSDIFF.EXE application and auxiliary files with sufficient space for all the applications to be installed on the master system.
- SYSDIFF.EXE, which creates and applies the files necessary for cloning. This application is on the NT 4.0 Server CD-ROM in the \Support\Deptools\platform directory. It should be copied into the share on the server.
- SYSDIFF.INF, which controls what SYSDIFF.EXE looks for when it creates its snapshot and difference files.
- The snapshot file, which is created by SYSDIFF.EXE to determine the current system, or the *before* picture.
- The difference file, which is created by SYSDIFF.EXE and includes the changes made to the Registry, the application files, and the files associated with them. This file is also referred to as the *after* picture. Figure 35.4 illustrates the contents of the difference file.
- The target systems, which have Windows NT installed. These systems get the changes in the difference file.

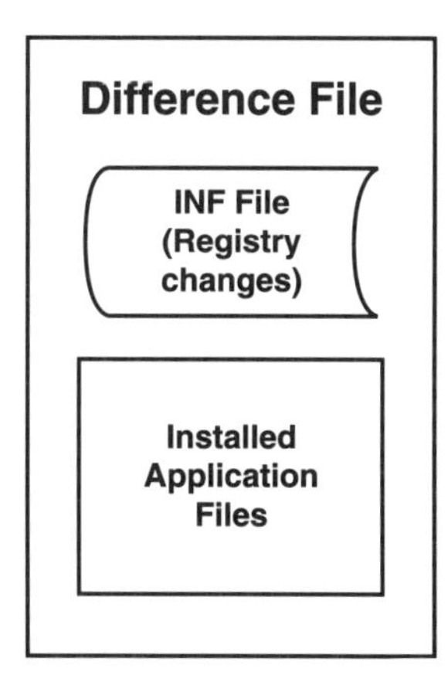

Figure 35.4.
The difference file includes the Registry changes and the application files.

If any of these parts are missing, preparing and implementing the clone installations will not work.

Cloning Step by Step

Follow these steps for fast, error-free cloning of Windows NT systems:

1. Install Windows NT Workstation or Server 4.0 on the master system.
2. At the master system, map a drive letter to a share on the server (for example, `X:\` is mapped to `D:\BIN`).
3. At the server, copy the `SYSDIFF.EXE` and the `SYSDIFF.INF` files from the NT 4.0 Server CD-ROM in the `\Support\Deptools\platform` directory to `D:\BIN`.

Tip

Run the `SYSDIFF.EXE` application from the server's shared directory. Store the snapshot and difference files in this directory as well. You might get a little more performance by running `SYSDIFF.EXE` from your local drive, but it requires more manual copying of files.

Warning

Putting the difference file on your local drive on the master system may cause `SYSDIFF.EXE` to create a monstrous file, or even hang the process. It may get caught in a loop, trying to copy the file it is copying to. To use your local drive for the storage of the difference file for more performance, add the path where it will be stored to the `SYSDIFF.INF` file under the `[ExcludeDirectoryTrees]` section. `SYSDIFF.EXE` will ignore and exclude it from the snapshot and difference file.

4. At the master system, run `SYSDIFF /SNAP X:\before.img` (any 32-bit valid filename may be used). This will take a snapshot of the current Windows NT installation and of all installed files and settings. The snapshot includes the directories and files, the Registry, and the `.INI` files. Figure 35.5 shows the concept, and Figure 35.6 shows the `SYSDIFF` procedure in process. When finished with the process, `SYSDIFF` notifies you with the dialog box shown in Figure 35.7.

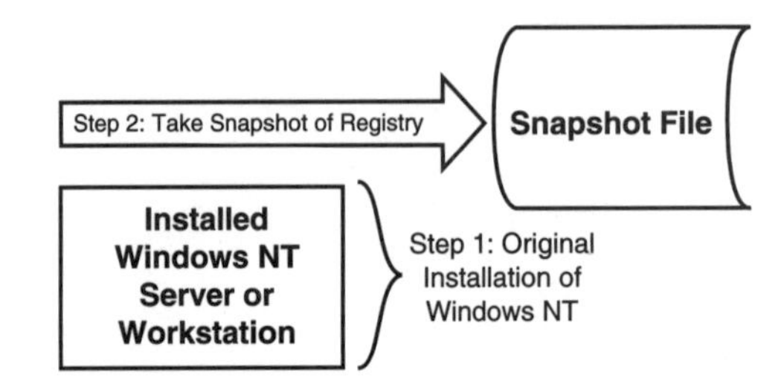

Figure 35.5.
Creating the snapshot file.

Note

You can also use the procedures listed here to add software to an installed system. When you run the snapshot, it takes a current picture. From that point on, adding other items produces a difference file.

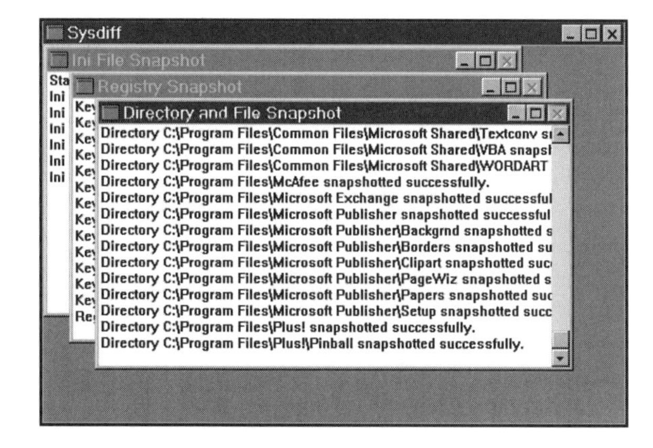

Figure 35.6.
The snapshot procedure in progress.

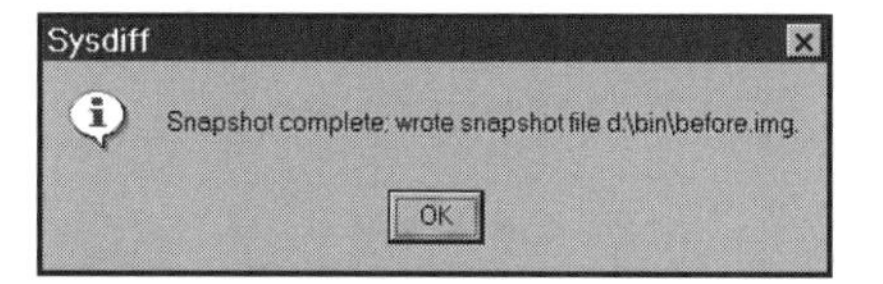

Figure 35.7.
The snapshot is finished, and the file is written to disk.

5. Set up Windows NT on the master system however you want, including (but not limited to) shares, printers, and network connections.
6. Make changes to Registry on the master system through direct editing of the Registry or through the Control Panel.
7. Add software applications to the master system.
8. Set up the software according to your preferences, including default directories, toolbars, preferences, and other settings.

Warning

Before running the next step to create the difference file, restart the system to ensure all functions relating to the application installation are completed and all files have been closed.

9. Run `SYSDIFF /DIFF X:\before.img X:\after.img` at the master system, with `X:\before.img` being the snapshot file and path, and `X:\after.img` being the difference file and path. `SYSDIFF.EXE` takes a snapshot of the entire system again, compares the

new snapshot to the old one, as illustrated in Figure 35.8, and writes the difference file to the hard disk. The difference file includes all changes, directories, and files, and may be an extremely large file.

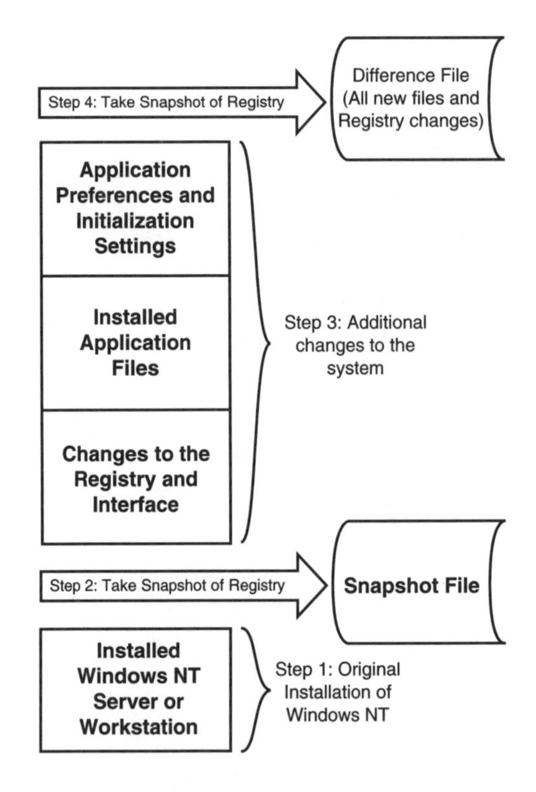

Figure 35.8.
The difference file compares the original snapshot to the current installation.

Note

For the results shown in Figure 35.9, I took a snapshot of my current system (three hard drives, 2.2GB total space with 220MB free), and the snapshot file was 4.5MB. Then I added a program that used 8.25MB of space. When the difference file was created, it was 7.5MB, indicating significant compression in the writing of the difference file to disk.

The difference file includes the directories and files, as shown in Figure 35.9; the Registry changes, as shown in Figure 35.10; and the `.INI` files, as shown in Figure 35.11.

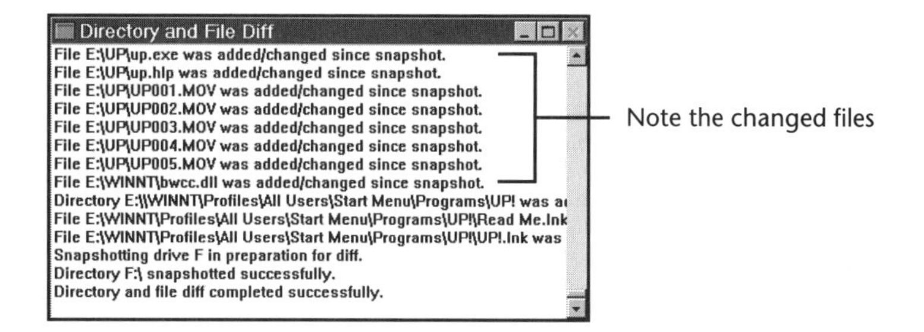

Figure 35.9. The directories and files are examined and compared against the original snapshot file.

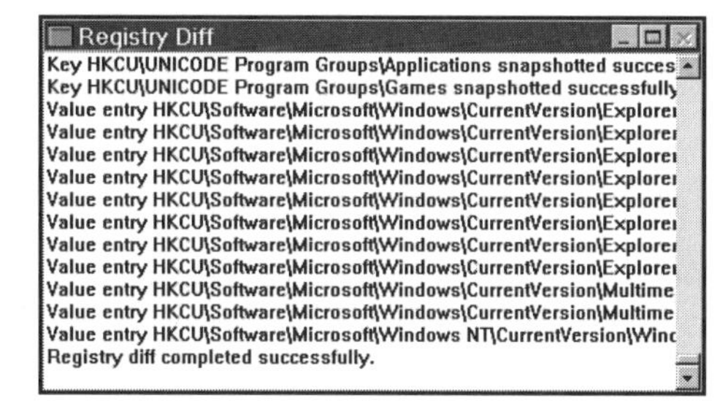

Figure 35.10. The current Registry is compared with the past Registry and differences noted.

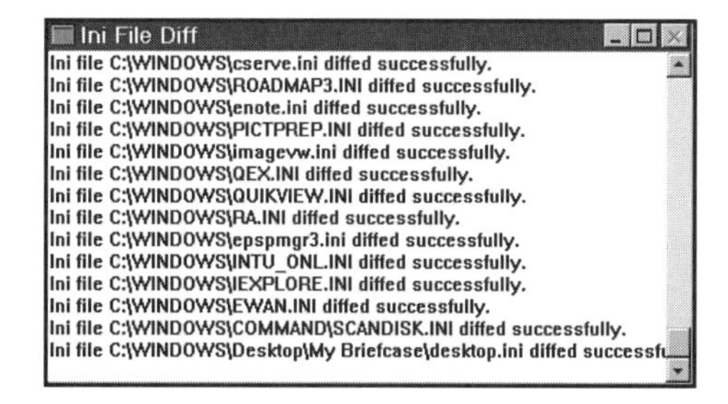

Figure 35.11. `.INI` files are compared for differences from the original `.INI` files.

The dialog box indicating the completion of the process is shown in Figure 35.12.

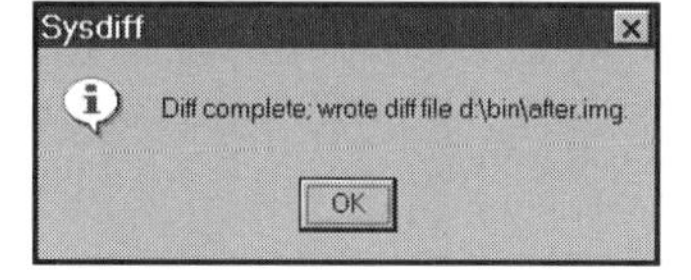

Figure 35.12. After the differences are calculated, they are written to the hard disk.

10. Install Windows NT on the target system.

Warning

Windows NT must be in the same directory for all systems receiving the difference file.

11. On the target system, map a drive letter to the snapshot/difference file location, such as `X:\` mapped to the server's `D:\BIN`.
12. Apply the difference file to the target system using `SYSDIFF /m /apply X:\after.img` with `X:\after.img` being the difference file and path. (See Figure 35.13.) When `SYSDIFF.EXE` starts, it launches the Setup function of the installation of the software, as shown in Figure 35.14.

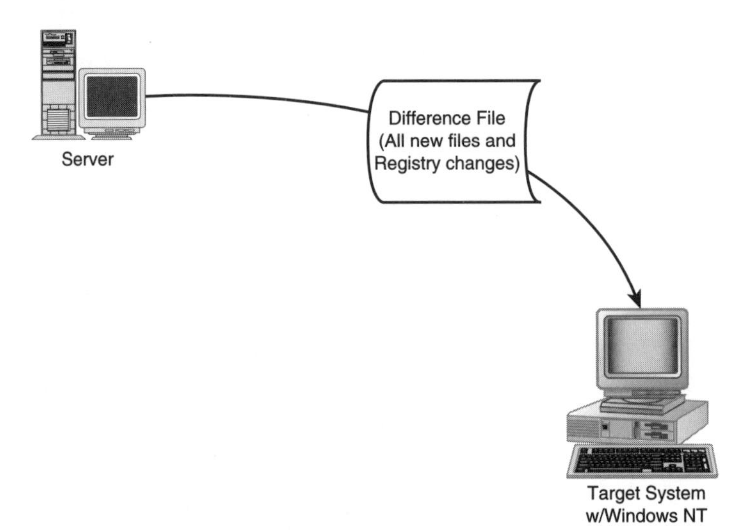

Figure 35.13.
Using the difference file to update the target systems.

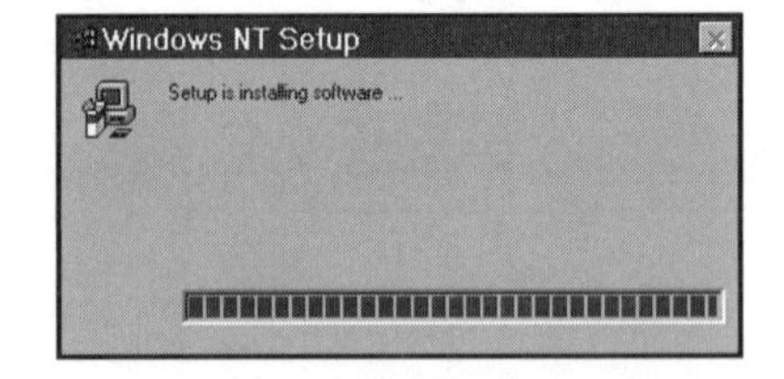

Figure 35.14.
The /APPLY option installs the applications on the new system using the Setup function.

As soon as you get one system started in the cloning process, you can start another. Windows NT networking allows multiple systems to access the same file. The only disadvantage to having multiple systems access the server is the amount of traffic each system generates.

Tip

At this point, you can apply the difference file to as many systems at one time as you can connect to the network. However, test it on one first to ensure that the procedure works exactly as planned. Then, attach to the network and clone away.

Combining the Installation and Cloning Processes

A great shortcut to increase performance when working with cloning is to combine the installation process and the cloning process into one command by using SYSDIFF.EXE. The entire process is controlled by the answer file created by SETUPMGR.EXE, as shown in Figure 35.15, for unattended installation. Using SETUPMGR.EXE to create a text file with all the answers you normally have to give during the Windows NT installation routine can be a great time-saver.

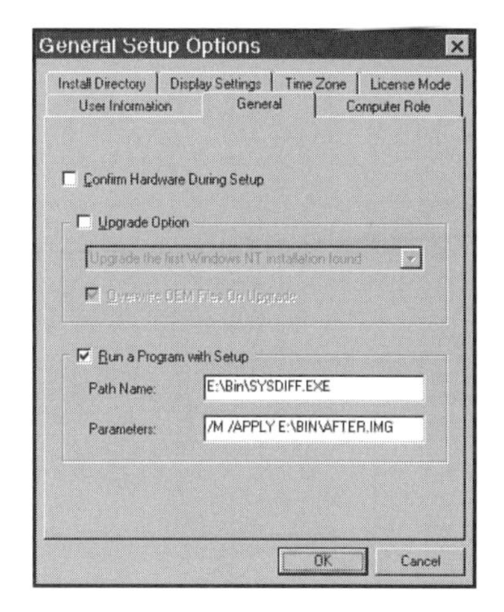

Figure 35.15.
The unattended answer file launches SYSDIFF.EXE to complete the installation.

With all the setup information you supply to SETUPMGR.EXE, plus the difference file you created, you will have the necessary files to help you do a complete installation with NT, services, applications, Registry settings, and all preferences set. After you boot the system and use a client to connect to the server, start the installation of NT and the difference file. The command line you use, assuming you named the answer file UNATTEND.TXT in E:\BIN, is WINNT /U:E:\BIN\UNATTEND.TXT.

Streamlining the SYSDIFF Process

The SYSDIFF process is controlled by the SYSDIFF.INF file included with SYSDIFF.EXE on the CD-ROM. By editing the SYSDIFF.INF file, you can make the cloning process smoother, faster, and more space-efficient. The SYSDIFF.INF file is basically an inclusion/exclusion file that determines what will or will not be reviewed.

The file on the CD-ROM has nine sections:

```
[Version]
[ExcludeDrives]
[ExcludeDirectoryTrees]
[ExcludeSingleDirectories]
[ExcludeFiles]
[IncludeFilesInDir]
```

```
[ExcludeRegistryKeys]
[ExcludeRegistryTrees]
[ExcludeRegistryValues]
```

Entries in the `SYSDIFF.INF` file (as long as the file is in the same directory as `SYSDIFF.EXE`) will direct the cloning process. For example, if you chose to add the drive letter "E" to the `[ExcludeDrives]` section, it would not even look there for the snapshot or the difference file. That could save a lot of time in the process if there was nothing there to be used.

Be very careful about removing any of the default entries in the `SYSDIFF.INF` file. Doing so may make the cloning process unsuccessful.

An Alternative Procedure for Installing Files on the Target System

The difference file contains all the Registry changes, the `.INI` file changes, and the actual files that are new since the first snapshot. One of the side effects of using `SYSDIFF.EXE` and the difference file to install applications is that files inherit the date of the installation instead of retaining their original date when they are written to the hard drive, as shown in Figure 35.16.

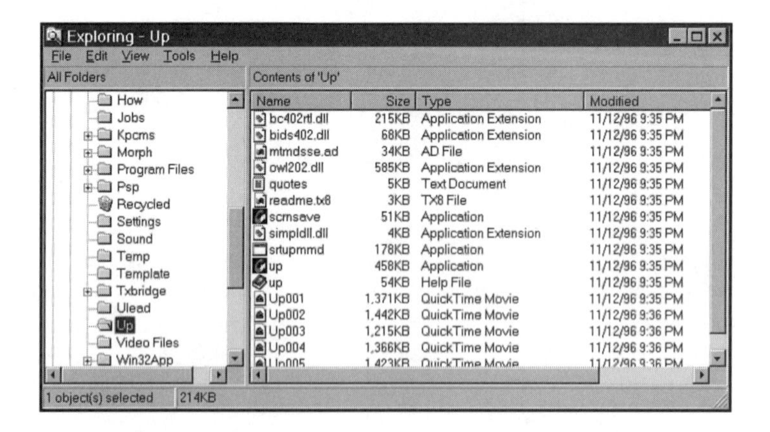

Figure 35.16. The file dates reflect the date they were installed with `SYSDIFF.EXE`.

Alternatively, you can split the Registry and `.INI` file changes from the files and copy the files another way to retain the original dates of the files.

To use this alternate procedure, perform steps 1 through 11 to create the difference file and prepare the target system for file installation. Instead of using the difference file to install the software, split the file between the `.INF` file (which will update Registry and `.INI` files) and the actual program and data files.

Create an .INF File

To create the `.INF` file, use the Start | Run function and type `D:\Bin\SYSDIFF.EXE /inf d:\bin\after.img d:\bin2`. `D:\bin\after.img` is the path and name of the difference file, and `d:\bin2` is the location for the `.INF` file and the changes to the system.

The .INF file is given the same name as the difference file, except that the .INF file has an .INF extension (in this case, AFTER.INF). The contents of the .INF file are readable in Notepad or in any other text editor or word processor, and are shown in Figure 35.17.

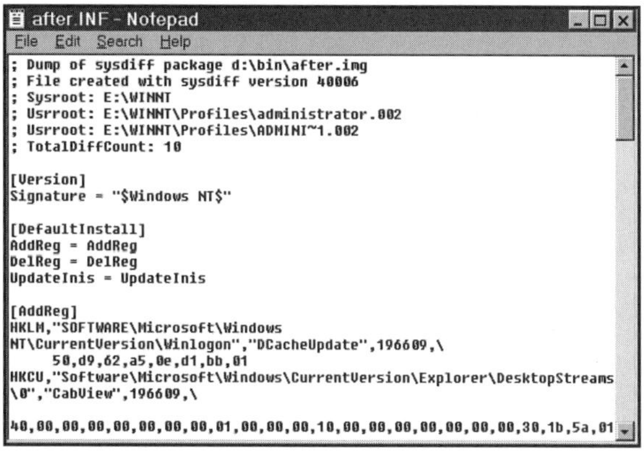
after.INF - Notepad
File Edit Search Help
; Dump of sysdiff package d:\bin\after.img
; File created with sysdiff version 40006
; Sysroot: E:\WINNT
; Usrroot: E:\WINNT\Profiles\administrator.002
; Usrroot: E:\WINNT\Profiles\ADMINI~1.002
; TotalDiffCount: 10
[Version]
Signature = "$Windows NT$"
[DefaultInstall]
AddReg = AddReg
DelReg = DelReg
UpdateInis = UpdateInis
[AddReg]
HKLM,"SOFTWARE\Microsoft\Windows
NT\CurrentVersion\Winlogon","DCacheUpdate",196609,\
50,d9,62,a5,0e,d1,bb,01
HKCU,"Software\Microsoft\Windows\CurrentVersion\Explorer\DesktopStreams
\0","CabView",196609,\
40,00,00,00,00,00,00,00,01,00,00,00,10,00,00,00,00,00,00,00,30,1b,5a,01

Figure 35.17. Text listing of the .INF file.

Use the .INF File to Change the Registry

Make changes to Registry and .INI files on the target system by adding the .INF file to the list of files to use at installation. SETUPMGR.EXE has an easy way of including it, as shown in Figure 35.18. Start SETUPMGR.EXE and choose Advanced Options. Select the Boot Files tab. Add the path and name of the file. When Windows NT is installed using the answer file, the Registry and .INI file changes are made automatically.

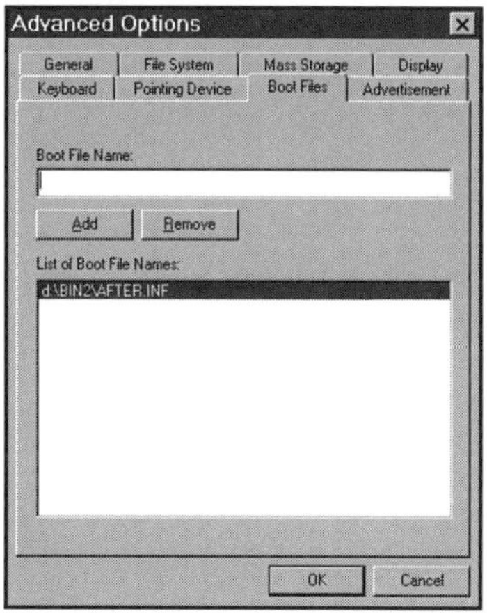
Advanced Options
General
File System
Mass Storage
Display
Keyboard
Pointing Device
Boot Files
Advertisement
Boot File Name:
Add
Remove
List of Boot File Names:
d:\BIN2\AFTER.INF
OK
Cancel

Figure 35.18. Adding the .INF file to the answer file in SETUPMGR.EXE.

Copy the Directories and Files to Complete the Installation

For your convenience, the `.INF` file-creation procedure also copies all files included in the difference file into subdirectories (as shown in Figure 35.19). When the files are copied into the `$OEM$` subdirectory, the date on the files changes to the current date. Using the files in the `$OEM$` directory may compromise your security if you are using any date-stamping for your files.

Even though the files have been copied into the `$OEM$` directory, you don't need to include them in the installation process. Instead of copying and using the files in the `$OEM$` directory, install NT with an answer file, then copy the originals with `XCOPY.EXE`, and the dates and times will be preserved.

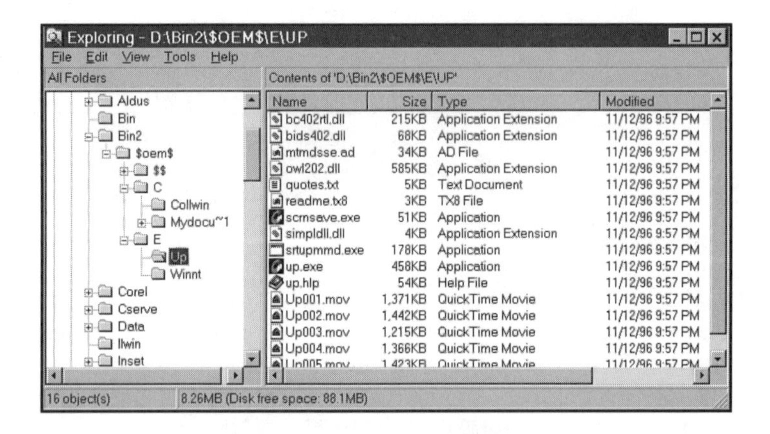

Figure 35.19. All files from the difference file are copied into directory structures for easy copying to the target system.

Use the `.INF` File for Backup of Software Registry Entries

The `.INF` file can also be used in the event of a Registry problem with an application. Normally, you would need to reinstall, then make the necessary changes to the menus, toolbars, and preferences. However, if you could have a list of every change the installation and modification made to the Registry and `.INI` files, it would save a tremendous amount of time.

If you create a difference file after you install an application, you have the information you need. Create a loadable `.INF` file from the difference file. With that file, you can repair the Registry. If the application's Registry entries become corrupted, load the `.INF` file back into the system.

Instead of reinstalling the current Windows NT, choose to do an update, including the `.INF` file in the Advanced Options | Boot Files section of `SETUPMGR.EXE`. The Registry will be updated with the `.INF` file information.

Possible Error Messages

Of course, something could go wrong, and, unfortunately, there is very little documentation on this process. Here are some of the more common problems and their solutions.

Computer Hangs During the SYSDIFF/APPLY Operation

This will usually happen because of a lack of disk space or there is a problem with the difference file (either corrupted, or a part of the application or data files is bad). Check for disk space on the target system (where the applications will go). If it is insufficient, you will have this problem. If there is plenty of disk space, try manually installing the difference file from the local system instead of across the network. If that doesn't work, re-create the difference file.

Error Message: System Error 5

When SYSDIFF.EXE attempts to enter restricted areas of the Registry, you may get this message. Edit the SYSDIFF.INF file to exclude sections of the Registry that are off limits.

Error Message: Diff Failed (Error 2)

This is a syntax error on the command line when the /DIFF option is used. Check the step-by-step instructions and try again.

Error Message: Diff Failed (Error 32)

Error 32 indicates an open file error. The files could be open because applications are in use, or the system has opened other applications.

1. Restart the system, and run the SYSDIFF /DIFF procedure before running any other applications.
2. Turn off virus checking or system monitoring.
3. Exclude directories on a domain controller.

   \WINNT\SYSTEM32\WINS (used by system for WINS management)

   \WINNT\SYSTEM32\DHCP (used by system for DHCP management)

   \WINNT\SYSTEM32\SYNCAGNT (used by system for domain synchronization)
4. Exclude location of the difference file.
5. Exclude all .LOG files.

Error Message: Access Denied

When you create one image in the installation location with the `SYSDIFF /INF` option, and then run the function again to add another difference file to it, you may get this error.

The easiest way to get around the problem is to use the first image crated with the `SYSDIFF /INF` option for the installation, and apply the second difference file manually with the `SYSDIFF /APPLY` option.

Summary

Use `SYSDIFF.EXE` to update the Registry during installation. It will greatly enhance your installation and cloning procedures, plus give you opportunities to create loadable `.INF` files for Registry repair.

CHAPTER 36

Cloning Windows 95 Systems

When it comes to creating duplicate Windows 95 systems, there are two main ways that you can go. You can do it with several steps, a little imagination, and no extra software, or you can do it with a little money and a lot less effort using a commercial software package called GHOST.

Regardless of the way you choose, you will need a source machine and a target machine. The source machine is generally one that is set up exactly the way you want the second or subsequent machines. The target machine is the one where you want the operating system, applications, and data to end up. Optionally, you may want a distribution machine to hold the clone image so you can quickly replicate 95 to many machines at once.

Even though Windows 95 is a DOS-based operating system, normal tools such as XCOPY will not work. The Registry and system files are the challenges here. If you want to back up the system and restore it, you can do it, as long as you use the tips in the next section.

Cloning with Windows 95

Inside Windows 95, there are features that will allow you to make a clone of a machine, making the installation easy. In Chapter 6, "Protecting the Windows 95 Registry," I discussed some tools to protect the system. As always, make sure you have a good copy of the Registry before trying to clone the system.

At the source system

- Set up the operating system, applications, and data.
- Create an Emergency Recovery Disk (a bootable disk with `FORMAT.COM` on it).
- Run `LFNBK.EXE` to back up the long filenames.
- Back up the system from Real Mode DOS with a backup utility.

At the target system

- Format the hard drive with the Windows 95 bootable disk.
- Reboot the system from the hard drive.
- Restore the backup to the system.
- Using your Emergency Recovery Disk, run ERU to replace all the system files.
- Reboot the system into Windows 95.
- Run `LFNBK.EXE` to replace all the long filenames.

Using GHOST to Clone Windows 95 Systems

GHOST is an acronym for General Hardware Oriented System Transfer, a software package from Innovative Software in Milwaukee, Wisconsin. There are several ways to use GHOST, but cloning Windows 95 systems is probably the best. You can also use it to clone Windows NT systems, but domains, SIDs, and hardware differences sometimes cause problems. When you are cloning a Windows 95 system, GHOST copies the entire partition structure of the source PC to the target PC. There is no need to partition the drive with FDISK. The current version of GHOST doesn't even require the target hard disk to be the same size and physical geometry (heads, sectors, and cylinders) as the original.

You have options to do the transfer in three ways: You can connect the two computers together via the parallel ports and do a direct copy; you can insert the second disk into the same machine and do a disk-to-disk copy; or, you can create an image on a distribution disk for later transfer. That distribution disk could easily be a CD, a JAZ disk, or a network disk.

In this chapter, we are going to do the most popular option, creating an image and then using it to create a new system as fast as possible.

Step-by-Step Creation of the Image

The following numbered list gives detailed instructions for creating a duplicate image of your hard drive on another drive (either connected to the same system or connected to the network):

1. Create a bootable disk with the drivers to hit your distribution source. If you are going to copy the image to a JAZ drive, you would need the drivers for DOS on your disk. Similarly, if you were going to send the image to a network drive, you would need network drivers on the disk to create the connection. Copy the GHOST files to that disk, also.
2. Restart your system with the disk.

Warning

You can run GHOST from within Windows 95, but its reliability is significantly diminished. Windows 95 always has some files open, which may cause problems to the system. Use GHOST to clone Windows 95 hard disk drives, but use DOS drivers booted from a DOS disk whenever possible. Then, at the DOS prompt, run the GHOST application. The reliability of the process will be much better.

3. Connect to the distribution disk.
4. Run GHOST from the floppy disk.
5. When GHOST starts, you get options to choose which type of connection you would like.

   Most of the time you would use the Local/Server option. It assumes you have a disk connection or a network connection to a system that has a large enough disk. The NetBIOS option allows you to connect two systems together with network cards and cabling, but no networking software is required. The LPT Slave/Master option allows a similar connection, except it is through the parallel port and uses a LapLink or FastLynx cable. Local/Server is the fastest option, followed by NetBIOS, and then, trailing way behind, is the parallel option.

6. After choosing the type of transfer, you need to select the type of copy you will make. You can create an immediate image on another disk with the Clone disk to disk function. If you want to create an image for later downloading, use Dump disk image to file. Figure 36.1 shows the transfer options.

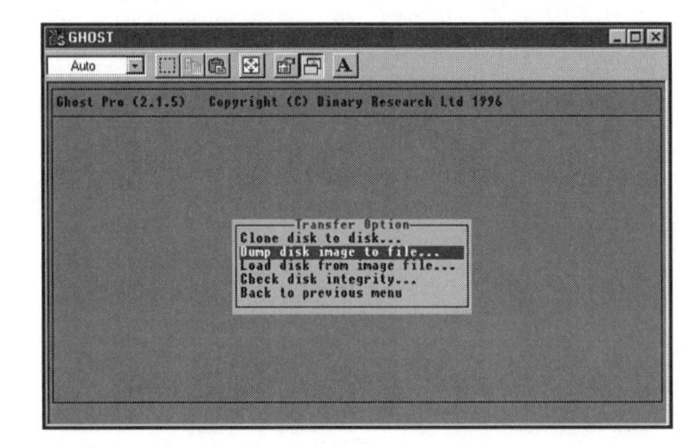

Figure 36.1. Transfer options in GHOST.

7. The next step is to choose which drive you will copy, if you have multiple drives in your system, as shown in Figure 36.2.

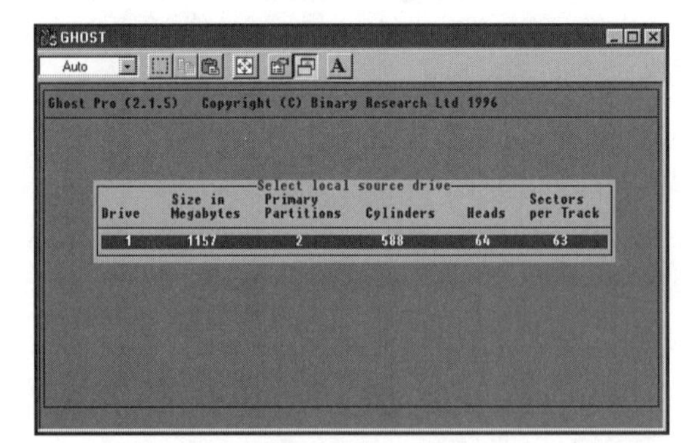

Figure 36.2. Choose the drive to copy.

Note

GHOST will not allow you to independently copy logical drives. For example, if you have C: and D: on the same physical drive, it will copy both to the image or drive. If they are on separate physical drives, you will be able to work with them separately.

Enter the target location. If you are using a network and you try to use an UNC as your target, you may experience an error that says you have no space available. Instead, map the network drive to a letter, and then use that. Figure 36.3 shows the distribution disk location.

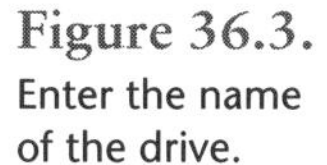

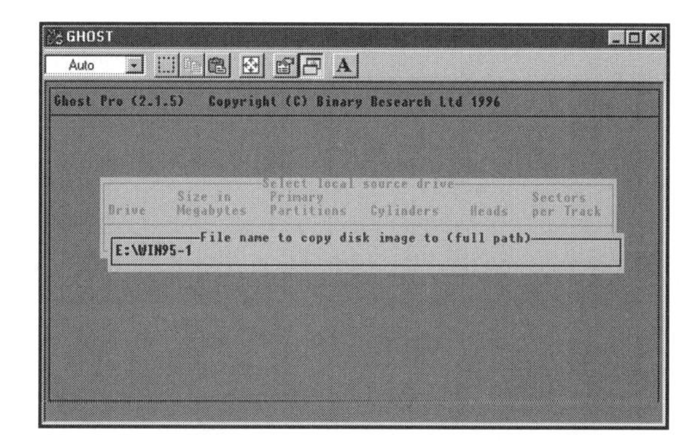

Figure 36.3.
Enter the name of the drive.

GHOST will provide you with the status of the image creation, including size, elapsed time, time to finish, and the filenames and directories copied. Figure 36.4 shows the status screen.

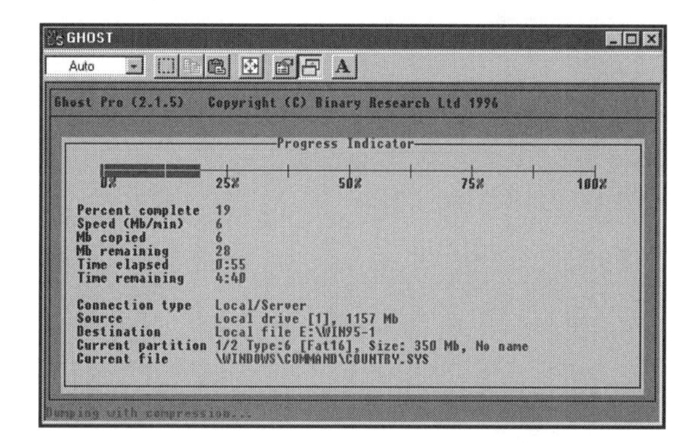

Figure 36.4.
The status of the image creation is constantly updated.

Once the entire image has been created, the file will be closed, and GHOST is finished. You may then transport and store that image via hard disk, network, CD-Recordable, or backup. You cannot go directly to backup or CD-Recordable, but once the file is created, you can easily move it there.

Step-by-Step Transfer of the Image to a Target Computer

Now that you have the image ready, you can easily recreate the partitions and drives. The disk at the target system does not need to be partitioned or formatted. GHOST will do that during the process.

The following list gives detailed instructions for using the stored image to create a Windows 95–based system on a new computer.

1. Boot with driver disk created in Step 1 of the Image Creation.
2. Connect to the distribution disk.

3. Run GHOST from the floppy disk.
4. Choose the connection type. You do not have to use the same connection type you used to create the image.
5. If you created an image, you will need to choose Load disk from image file, shown in Figure 36.5.

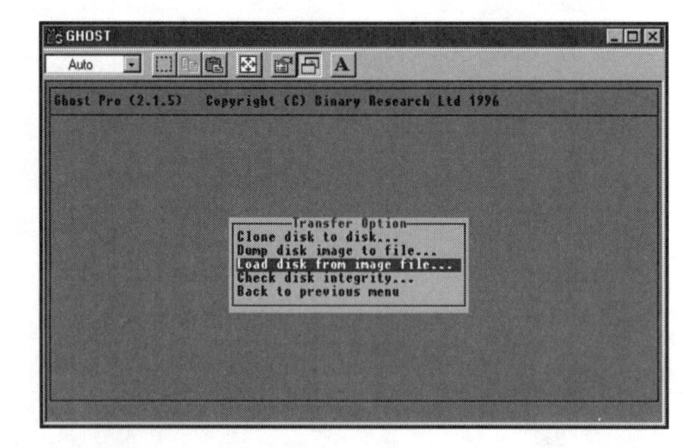

Figure 36.5.
Choose the transfer option.

6. Enter the path and the filename of the image.
7. Select the local destination drive.

Warning

GHOST will write over all the partitions on the physical drive. None of the data that is currently on the target system will be retained.

GHOST will examine the source image file, determine the number and size of the partitions, and recommend the partition sizes. If there is additional room on the disk that is not partitioned, GHOST will recommend putting that space in the first partition, as shown in Figure 36.6.

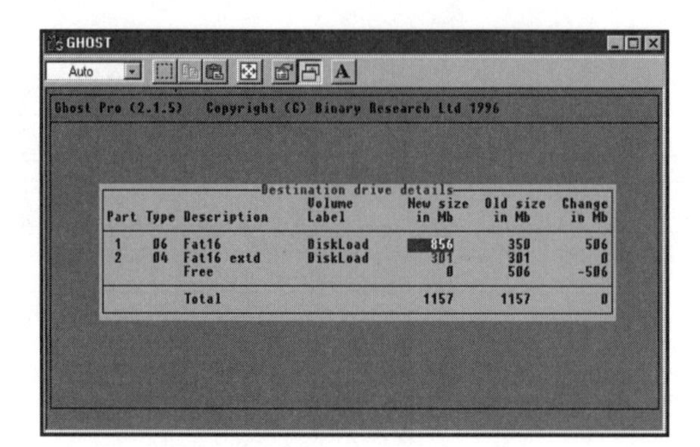

Figure 36.6.
Destination drive details.

8. Select the new partition size, and press Enter. GHOST will re-allocate the space on the drive, as shown in Figure 36.7. You will be given the option of selecting the capacity of the second partition as well.

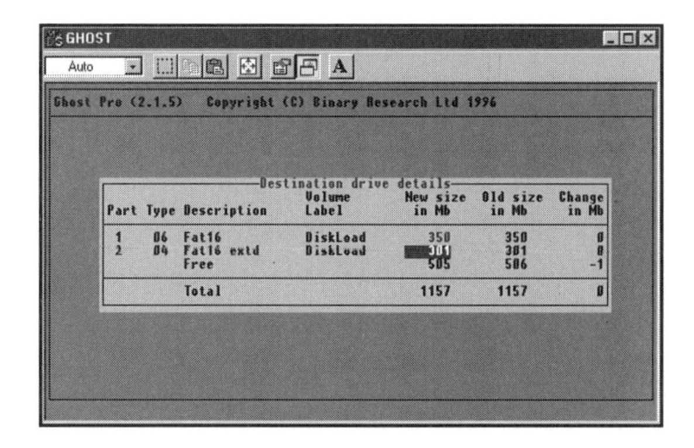

Figure 36.7.
Allocate partition sizes in GHOST.

9. Select Yes to continue with the transfer of the image.

Warning

Once you start the transfer of the GHOST image to the target system, there is no turning back. As soon as it starts, the current partitions will be destroyed.

10. Once the transfer process is complete, restart the system. Any hardware changes will be recognized at startup, and the system will boot directly into Windows 95.

Summary

The cloning process is very fast and easy with GHOST, and it allows you to create new systems very fast. Each system is a mirror image of the original system, so if you plan well, you can make the process work very well for you. Whichever way you choose to create the clone, you will need to change the system name if it is going to be connected to a network. Other than that, it's as close to a perfect cloning process as it can get.

Part VIII

Part VIII
Part VIII
Part VIII
Part VIII
Part VIII
Part VIII
Part VIII
Part VIII
Part VIII
Part VIII
Part VIII

Using Shareware Registry Tools

CHAPTER 37

Increasing the Utility of REGEDT32.EXE with Additional Searching Tools

The Registry is full of opportunities for improvement, and the real trick is in finding the information you want. Unfortunately, in `REGEDT32.EXE` for Windows NT, the only thing you can search for is a key. The search capability is a little better in `REGEDIT.EXE` for Windows 95 or Windows NT, but you give up a lot of security and features just to get the better searching. Neither `REGEDIT.EXE` or `REGEDT32.EXE` will allow you to do a search and replace.

Enter Registry Search and Replace, from Steven J. Hoek Software, a $20.00 shareware program. It can be used with Windows 95, Windows NT 3.51, and Windows NT 4.0. It works best with 95 and NT 4.0 because of the Explorer interface. Prior to installation of Registry Search and Replace, in order to do any searching in the Registry, you had to open the Registry editor and use the Find function. After you install the Registry Search and Replace program and restart your system, when you look in your Start menu under Find, you will see a new option to search the Registry. Figure 37.1 shows the Find Menu prior to the installation, and Figure 37.2 shows the menu after the new option is installed.

One of the best parts about the Registry Search and Replace is that it doesn't require the opening of a Registry editor. It is fast and easy, and well worth the $20.00.

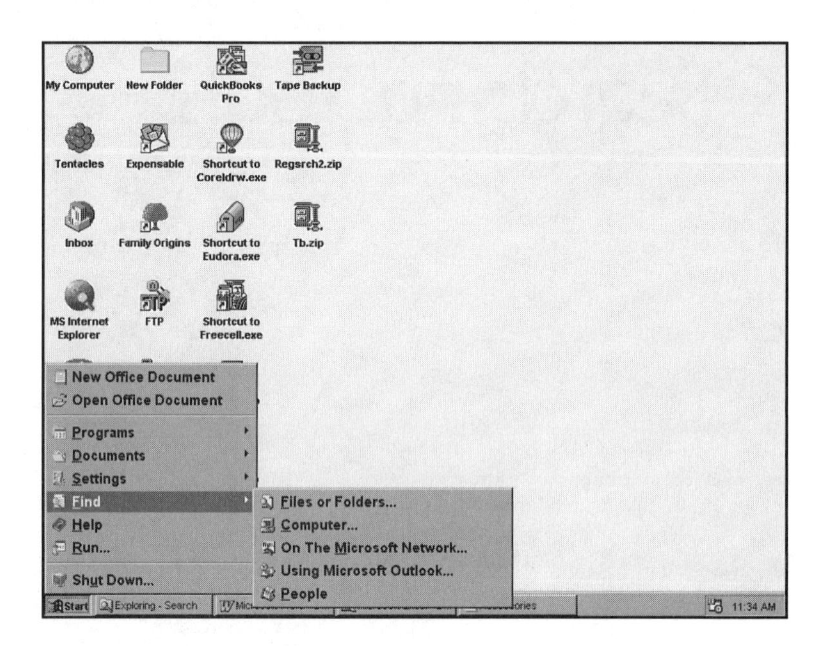

Figure 37.1.
The Windows 95 Start | Find menu.

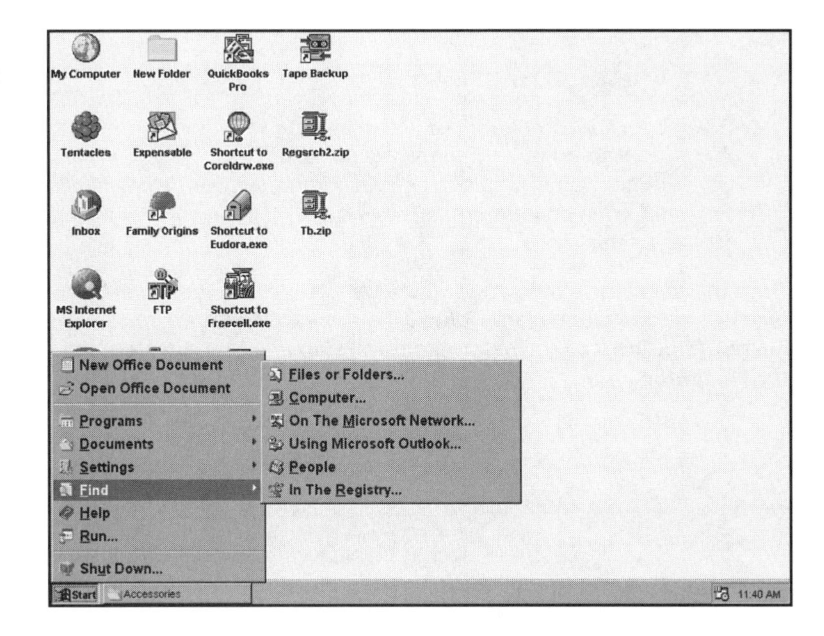

Figure 37.2.
The Windows 95 Start | Find menu including Registry Search and Replace.

Finding Registry Entries

To find any entry in the Registry, go to Start | Find | In the Registry...and enter your search criteria, as shown in Figure 37.3. Type in the data, select the precision of the matching, and choose whether you will replace the found information or not. Select Search to finish the criteria and start the search.

Any restriction of the type of search will speed the search by quickly eliminating alternatives. On the other hand, if you think you know the data you are looking for, entering a partial match will still work, and give you more possible matches to review.

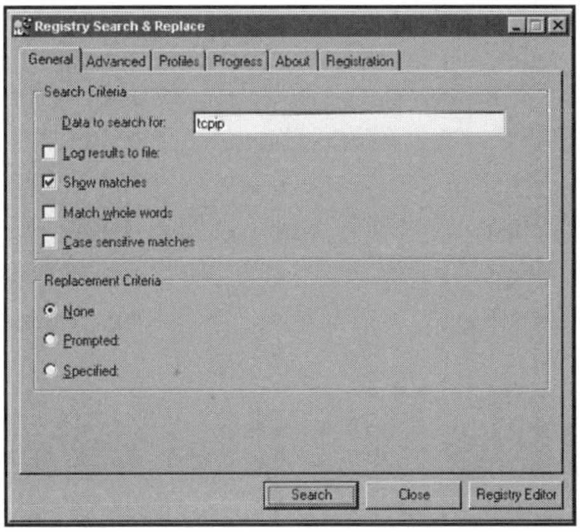

Figure 37.3.
Search criteria in Registry Search and Replace.

Note

Registry entries are not normally case-sensitive for functionality, but you may still want to use the option. For example, if a user typed his name in lowercase during installation of a product, you may want to search to find where that information is being stored.

Once the search is started, you will see the progress of the search as the program automatically switches to the Progress tab. Figure 37.4 shows a search in progress, and Figure 37.5 shows the results of the search. The program will stop at a found match, waiting for you to choose the OK button.

Note

Notice the button to start the Registry Editor in the lower right corner of Figure 37.5. Registry Search and Replace will start the editor, but unfortunately will not take you to the location you found automatically. You'll still have to navigate the Registry manually.

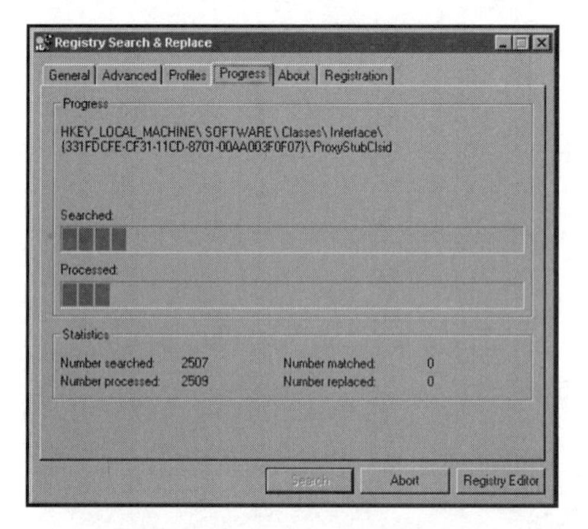

Figure 37.4.
High-speed searching of the Registry.

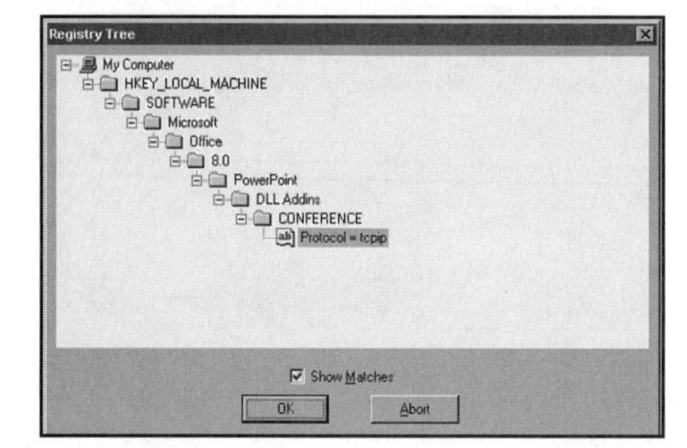

Figure 37.5.
Search results in Registry Search and Replace.

Search Locations

The Advanced tab allows you to select the handles keys to search through, and the types of data to look at. Figure 37.6 shows the Registry Criteria for the search. You can select whether to search for a value name or a data string. If you choose a data string, you can choose what type of data strings to look in. For example, if you knew that IP addresses assigned to your network card in Windows NT were listed in a `REG_MULTI_SZ` entry, you could select that and search using your IP address. You would select only the `HKEY_LOCAL_MACHINE` hive, in your local machine. The results would show you the exact location where those IP addresses are held. The search would be very fast, and focused on the specific item.

Alternatively, you can search for the same kind of information on a remote system as well, as shown in Figure 37.7.

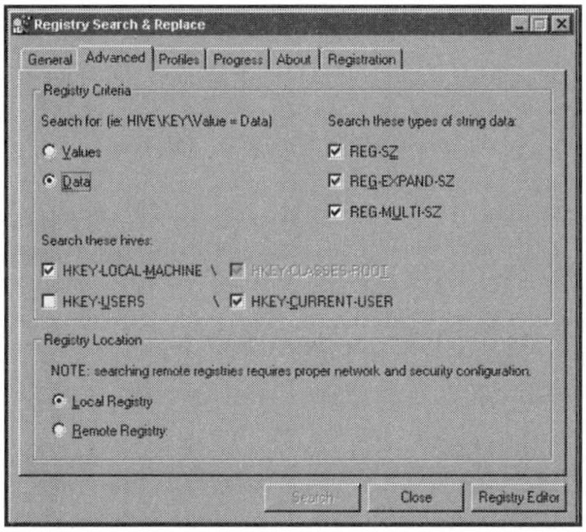

Figure 37.6.
Selecting the Registry Criteria for a search.

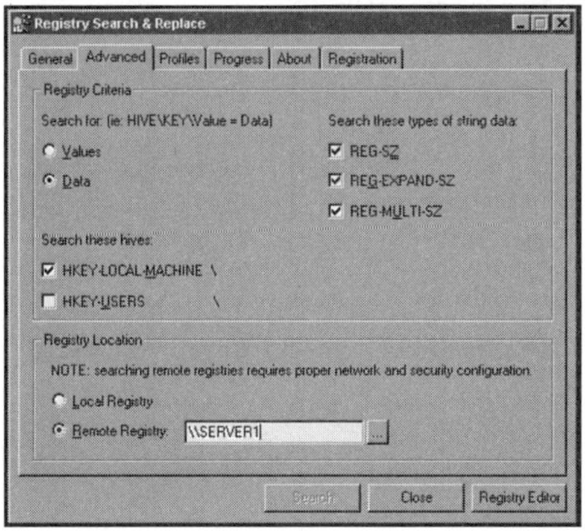

Figure 37.7.
Remote searching of a Registry.

Creating a Search Profile

Once you have selected exactly the settings you want to use to do the searching, you can create a profile, so you would not have to manually make the settings again. The only thing you would have to enter is the data you want to search for.

Select the items in your search, click the Profiles tab, and select Save As. Enter the desired name of the profile, and click Save. The next time you want to use the same profile for a search, select the Profiles tab, click Open, and choose the name of the profile. Figure 37.8 shows the Open Profile dialog box.

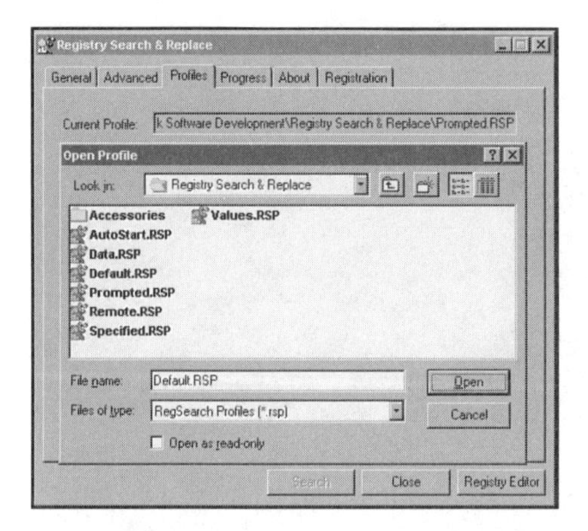

Figure 37.8. Opening a profile for use in searching the Registry.

Search and Replace

The previous features are certainly an improvement on the similar searching features found in `REGEDIT.EXE` and `REGEDT32.EXE`. There is no automatic replacement function in the Registry editors. The availability of a fast, easy, and ultimately powerful search and replace function is something of a two-edged sword. What cuts one way may also cut the other, causing as much or more damage than the initial cut.

Warning

The search and replace functions used improperly or overzealously may make the Registry completely unusable and cause the system to crash. Be extremely careful. One good way to ensure better protection is to use only the prompted replacement. It may save you a lot of time in the long run.

Most people have made an error like searching and replacing "won" with "lost," only to find themselves with words like "lostderful." In addition to selecting Prompted for the Replacement criteria, select Match whole words, restricting the type of replacements.

Prompted Replacements

To ensure that the only changes made are the ones you really want, you can choose Prompted in the Replacement Criteria in the General tab. Figure 37.9 shows the location of the choice.

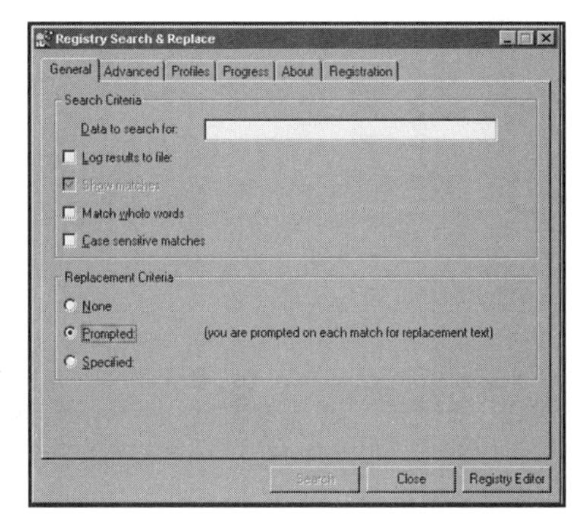

Figure 37.9.
Selecting a prompted replacement.

When the search finds a match, you are given a choice to replace the string, skip this instance, or abort the process, as shown in Figure 37.10.

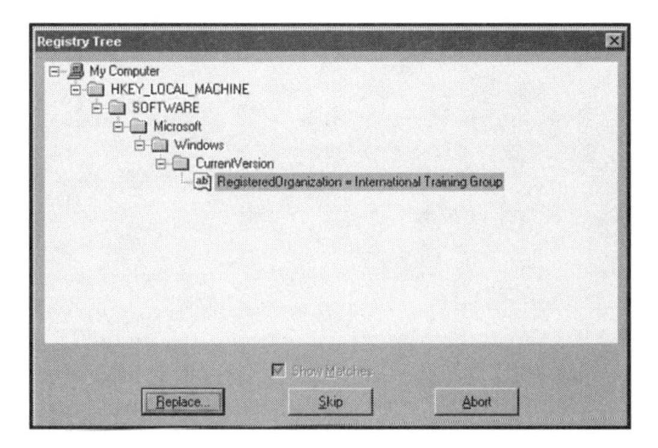

Figure 37.10.
The search is successful; the replacement is optional.

Choose to replace, and you will be prompted for the replacement string for each match. Figure 37.11 shows the replacement text dialog box. Notice that you can force it to all upper- or lowercase also.

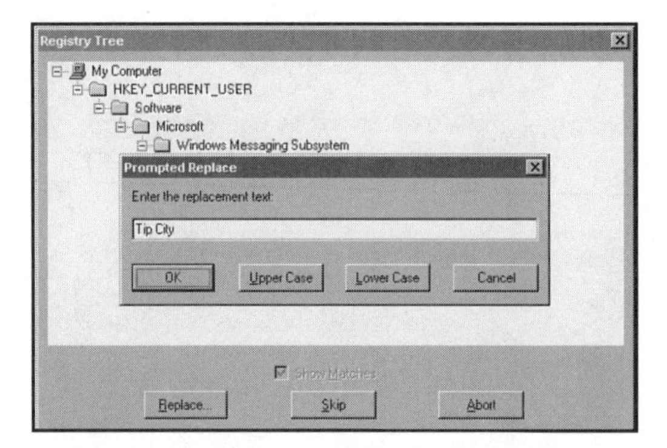

Figure 37.11.
Enter the replacement string data.

Specified Replacements

An automatic replacement for all found instances of the string is called a Specified Replacement. Enter the data to search for and the replacement string. When you select Search, all instances found will be replaced, without opportunity to choose. Figure 37.12 shows the option to set a Specified replacement.

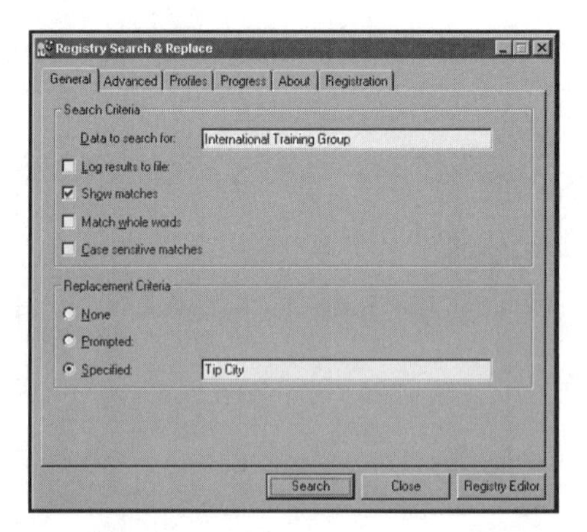

Figure 37.12.
Automatic replacement of string data.

Tip

Whenever you choose to do a Specified replacement, also choose to log the results to a file (at the General tab). If there is a problem, you can at least look back to the file for the locations.

Be sure to make a backup of the Registry before doing a Specified Replacement. There is no undo feature.

Warning

If you replace all the instances of a data string with another, you cannot undo it. Likewise, it is not smart to reverse the process.

Imagine changing every instance of "ABC" with "XYZ." Later you find that you were mistaken, and not every one should have been changed. If you replace every "XYZ" with "ABC," you may make the problem worse. There may have been other instances of "XYZ" that were not a result of the replacement. It could have disastrous results.

Back it up!

Summary

Registry Search and Replace is an outstanding program to augment your Registry tools. It is a bargain at $20.00, and should be in every troubleshooter's software toolbox. For more information and a live tutorial, visit `http://ourworld.compuserve.com/homepages/shoek` and run the tutorial there.

CHAPTER 38

Offline Search and Replace

The ability to search the Registry is one of the most important functions you can have. With REGEDIT.EXE in both Windows 95 and Windows NT, you can search for string data in the keys, value names, and the actual data. With REGEDT32.EXE in Windows NT, you can only search for the key names. There's room, therefore, for a third-party search tool that will enhance the search process. Registry Surfer (RegSurf) is one of those tools.

RegSurf 1.01 is a shareware tool included on the CD-ROM with this book, and is produced by ISES. It is an excellent example of a Visual Basic add-on to improve current functions and increase the capabilities of a program.

Using RegSurf

RegSurf is an application independent from either Registry editor included with Windows NT or 95. Launch it from the Start menu or from the program's directory, and you will get the opening dialog box, as pictured in Figure 38.1.

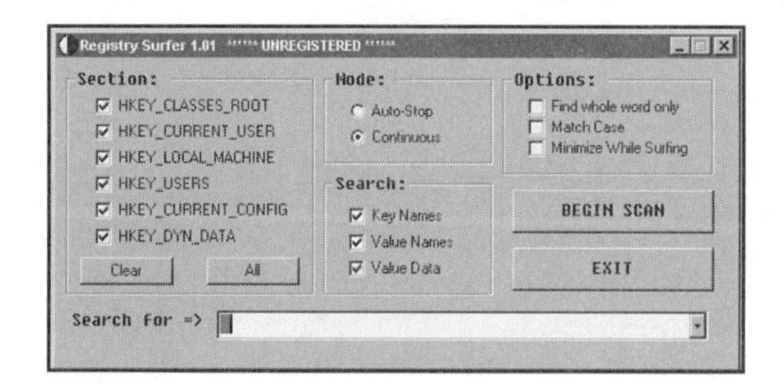

Figure 38.1. The RegSurf opening dialog box.

Selecting the handle keys that you want to search through is the first step. You can search through any of the handle keys for information. Registry Search and Replace, covered in Chapter 37, "Increasing the Utility of REGEDT32.EXE with Additional Searching Tools," only allows you to search in some of the keys. Searching in all the handle keys is useful so you can work with the data in the format that you want. Obviously, if it is in HKEY_CLASSES_ROOT, it will also be in HKEY_LOCAL_MACHINE. One of the best parts of selecting all of the handle keys is that you will quickly see the relationship between the different keys.

The next step is to choose the mode that RegSurf will run in. Auto-Stop mode pauses after each successful search of a string. Continuous mode shows each time the data is found, and then continues. If you are looking for a specific location with your search, you would probably use the Auto-Stop mode. If you wanted to find all the instances of a particular entry, it would make more sense to use Continuous mode.

Select what type of data to search, and then set the data-specific options of Find whole word, Match Case, and Minimize While Surfing. If you set it to minimize while surfing, it will run about twice as fast as it would in full screen. It also has a cool animated logo going during the search.

Type in the data that you will search for, and click Begin Scan. The drop-down list will display the last 10 values you searched for, so if you are recreating a search, find it in this list.

Figure 38.2 shows a search in Auto-Stop mode, looking for "shutdown." The ET is the elapsed time of the search, and you can see running statistics of the number of keys, values, and data strings that have been examined.

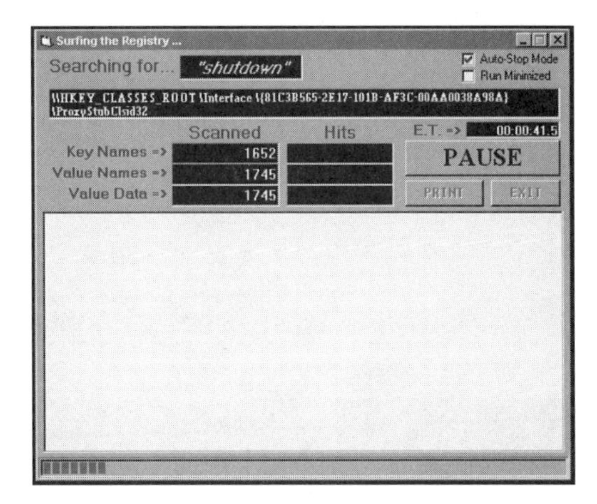

Figure 38.2.
RegSurf search in progress.

When a match is found, the path to the match is shown on screen, as pictured in Figure 38.3.

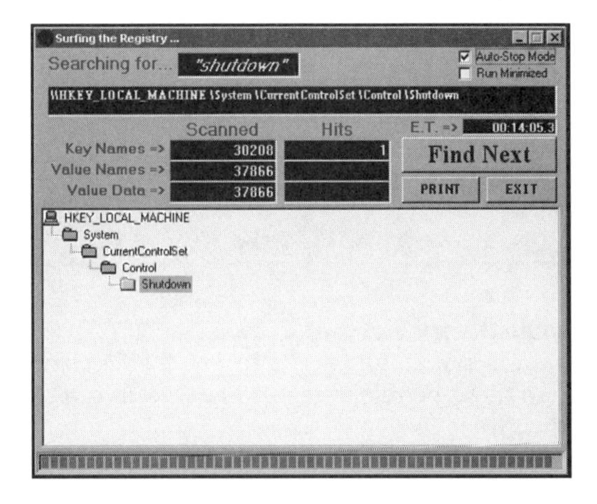

Figure 38.3.
A RegSurf successful search.

With a search in RegSurf, it is easier to see the results and the key location than it is in `REGEDIT.EXE` or `REGEDT32.EXE`. Select Find Next to continue the search. If there are additional entries, they will show in the results window. If not, the program will tell you it is done, as shown in Figure 38.4. Notice the number of Registry entries on this Windows 95 machine. It took just under 15 minutes to search through over 31,000 keys and 43,000 values.

The ability to print the results is also a nice touch, and the lack of the ability to jump to the key makes printing particularly important.

If you choose to run the search in minimized mode, it will take only one-third to one-half as long. Figure 38.5 shows the results of the search if you select the Minimize While Surfing option on the opening screen.

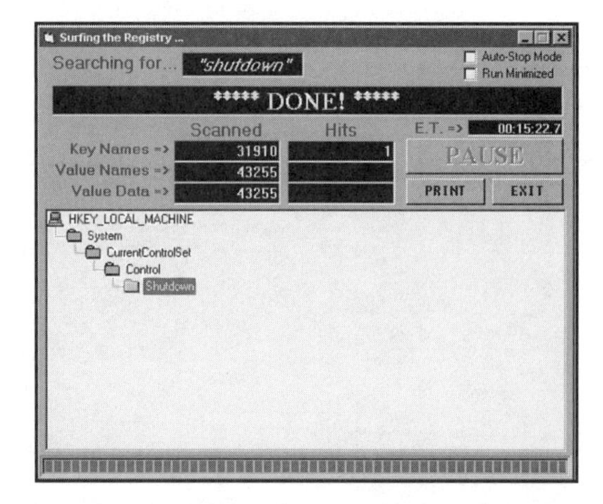

Figure 38.4. The search is complete.

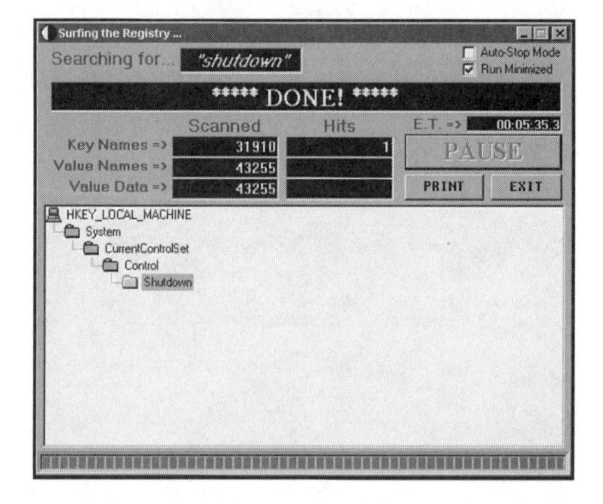

Figure 38.5. Optimum search speed attained while application is minimized.

It took only about five minutes for the search to complete when While Minimize Surfing is chosen. That's different, however, than simply minimizing it after starting. If you do not select Minimize While Surfing, and then you minimize it later, it will interrupt you and your screen by bringing RegSurf to the front to notify you.

Summary

The Registry Surfer is a nice tool for doing extra searches in the Registry. The search tool is quite fast, it gives you a lot of options, and the ability to print the results is particularly nice. Its biggest drawbacks are the requirement to have Visual Basic 4.0 available and the lack of a feature to jump to the location you just found.

The Registry Surfer is fast, easy, and works very well. Use it to expand your searching capabilities in the Registry.

CHAPTER 39

PowerToys

Another shareware tool available for both Windows 95 and Windows NT is PowerToys. It was written by the Windows 95 shell team, and then modified slightly to make it work for both 95 and NT 4.0. The current version, version 1.1 (11/17/96), supports NT 4.0 and adds more features.

PowerToys is a collection of applications that actually should have been included directly with 95 and NT. There are applications to change the Registry, some to add extra shortcuts to the system tray, and others to change how the menus work. Many of the settings are in the Registry changes in this book, and others are in the System Policy Editor.

Table 39.1 lists the components of PowerToys and the operating systems that it will work with.

Table 39.1. Applications in PowerToys.

Application	*Type*	*Windows 95*	*Windows NT*
`Quickres.exe`	Tray tool	Yes	No
TweakUI	Control Panel	Yes	Yes
FlexiCD	Tray Tool	Yes	Yes
DeskMenu	Tray Tool	Yes	Yes
DOS Prompt Here	Context Menu	Yes	Yes
TapiTNA	Tray Tool	Yes	Yes
Fast Folder Contents	Context Menu	Yes	Yes
Round Clock	Application	Yes	Yes
Explore from here	Context Menu	Yes	Yes
Shortcut target menu	Context Menu	Yes	Yes
Xmouse	Control Panel	Yes	Yes
CAB file Viewer	Context Menu	Yes	No
Send to X	Context Menu	Yes	Yes
Find X	Context Menu	Yes	Yes

Installing PowerToys

Copy the file from the CD that accompanies this book into the `\Windows\System` directory on a Windows 95 system, or the `\WINNT\SYSTEM32` directory on an NT system. Double-click on the `POWERTOYS.EXE` file. It is a self-extracting file, so all the functions will be present immediately in Windows 95, and in Windows NT, they will be available upon logoff and logon.

If you have extracted the file into another location, most of the functions will not work. All of the context menu items and the Control Panel items will not work correctly. Their files need to be in a specific location in order to work.

Because PowerToys is free, you do not need to register it, nor pay any fees to use it. However, because you are going to change how the system is going to work, you should make a backup of your Registry before installing it.

The most powerful part of PowerToys is TweakUI, and it has the most applicability to this book, because it makes changes to the Registry. The balance of the chapter is devoted to the use of TweakUI.

Using TweakUI

TweakUI is an automated way to make Registry changes to the interface without having to edit the Registry directly. Many of the slickest interface changes have been incorporated into a Control Panel applet, making the changes easy, secure, and faster.

When you launch TweakUI from the Control Panel, you get the dialog box shown in Figure 39.1.

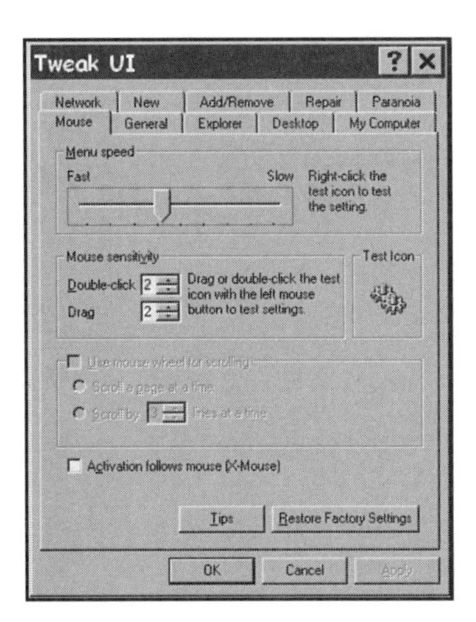

Figure 39.1.
The opening dialog box from TweakUI.

Before doing anything else, notice the two buttons at the bottom of the screen. The Tips button will take you to a nice help file that you should read before doing anything. The Restore Factory Settings button will undo all of the settings you have changed on that page. There is no option to just change one or two items back to the default settings. If you need to change just a single item, select the tab for that item and change the individual item. Also, selecting the Restore Factory Settings does not change all the Registry settings back; it just changes those on the same page as the button.

Another benefit of using TweakUI is that the changes are immediately made to the Registry, and most of them take effect immediately, without requiring a reboot or logoff to activate.

Mouse Settings

The four settings on the Mouse page can make your work faster and easier. The Menu speed options affect the `MenuShowDelay` value in the `HKEY_CURRENT_USER\Control Panel\Desktop` key. Instead of using a number-based system, as done in the Control Panel, you get a slider bar with which you can set the relative speed and test it before activating it.

The second section, Mouse sensitivity, is similar to functions already in the Control Panel. The Double-click option is the same as in the Mouse applet in Control Panel, and it's included here for ease of use. Drag sensitivity specifies how far (in pixels) the mouse must move with the button held down before the system decides that you are dragging the object. If you regularly get errors that you cannot copy an item onto itself in Explorer, then you might want to increase this value.

The next two settings are for Windows NT only; they do not appear in the Windows 95 program even though the files are the same. Figure 39.1 shows the Mouse tab when PowerToys is installed in NT 4.0, and Figure 39.2 shows it in Windows 95.

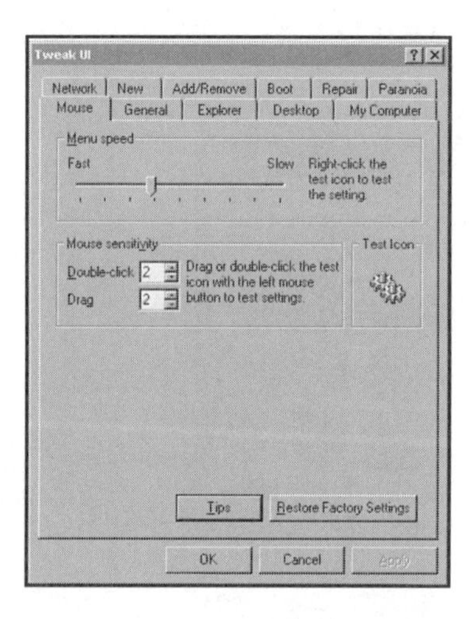

Figure 39.2.
TweakUI in Windows 95 has fewer options.

If you have the new Microsoft Intellimouse (the mouse with the scrolling wheel), you can use TweakUI in NT to adjust how the scrolling will work. With this setting, you can easily get the extra performance you want.

The last option is to make the window selection the same as in X Window. X Window is an implementation of a GUI on UNIX. When your mouse moves over a window, that window automatically becomes the chosen one. When your mouse moves over another, that window is selected. This option is particularly nice when you are using a very large screen and have the windows arranged so they are not overlapping. When using a small screen and overlapping windows, it is not nearly as effective.

General Options

The General tab includes options that didn't really fit anywhere else, but were still desirable enough to put in the program. Figure 39.3 shows the options available.

The Window animation effect is the `MinAnimate` value in the `HKEY_CURRENT_USER\Control Panel\Desktop\WindowMetrics` key, as discussed in Chapter 27, "Questions and Answers for Users and the Registry." Smooth scrolling changes the way the windows scroll. With it turned off, the windows jump a page at a time when you click in the slider bar. With the scrolling option turned on, it will scroll the page much more smoothly.

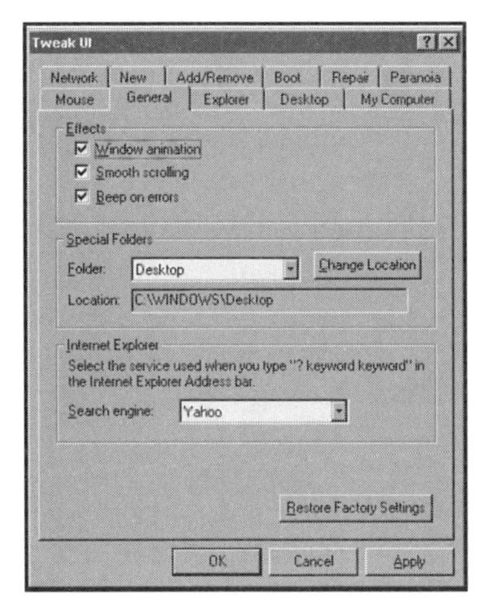

Figure 39.3. The General tab dialog in TweakUI.

The special folders allow you to select different locations for the items shown in Figure 39.4. By selecting a different location, you can easily customize the folders, including or excluding exactly what you need.

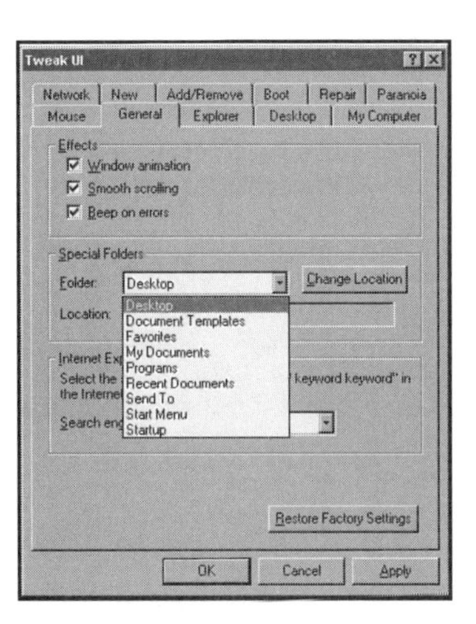

Figure 39.4. Special folder options in TweakUI.

You can also choose the default search engine for Internet Explorer 3.0 or higher. Figure 39.5 gives you an extensive list of options available.

This option will also determine which search engine will be used when you search with the address line in your browser. It will save you a significant amount of time to search with the address line instead of opening the search engine Web page or clicking on the Search button. To search at the address line, type **`go request`** and press Enter. If you have an earlier version of Internet Explorer or another browser, this option will not be available.

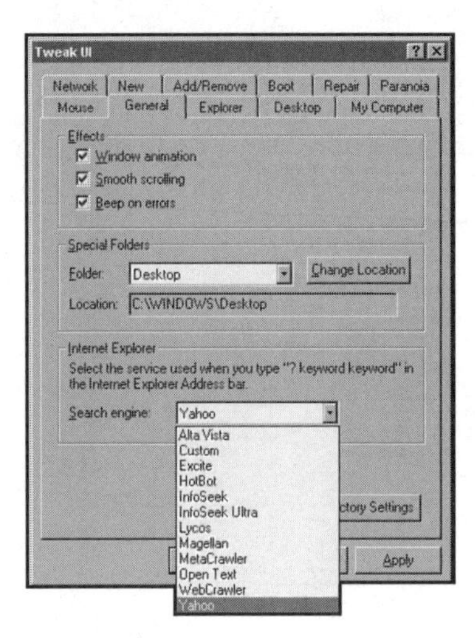

Figure 39.5.
Search engine designation for Internet Explorer.

Options for Explorer

The Explorer options enable you to change how some of the features in the Explorer interface operate. You can change the arrows on the shortcuts, change some of the startup options, and change specific settings.

Removing the "Shortcut to..." text is a popular option. Most people delete the text anyway, so this makes life a little easier, and your desktop look better.

The Save Windows settings option is the same as in System Policy Editor, so that if a user changes the size and location of open windows, the system will accept them. If the box is cleared, no changes to the location and size of the windows will be saved.

The final two options, Adjust the case of 8.3 filenames and the setting of the color for compressed files, are not in Windows 95, so they also will not appear in the TweakUI options when the applet is run under Windows 95.

Desktop Options in TweakUI

The Desktop options allow you to choose which icons will be displayed on the desktop. This list of items, shown in Figure 39.6, is much easier to use than editing the Registry directly.

These changes are actually in `HKEY_CLASSES_ROOT`, and the individual icon information is shown with `CLASS_ID` numbers, instead of names, and the finding of the parts is very difficult.

With many of the items, you also have the option to make the icon into a file, so you can move and copy it anywhere. That gives you extra flexibility.

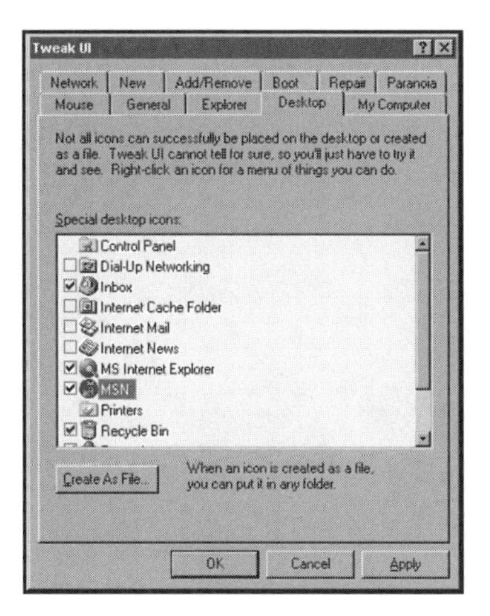

Figure 39.6.
Select icons to show on the desktop.

My Computer Options in TweakUI

The My Computer options in TweakUI are limited to the visibility of the drives in My Computer, Explorer, and the Load File/Save File functions of applications. Any that are checked, as shown in Figure 39.7, will be visible. Any that are cleared will not be visible.

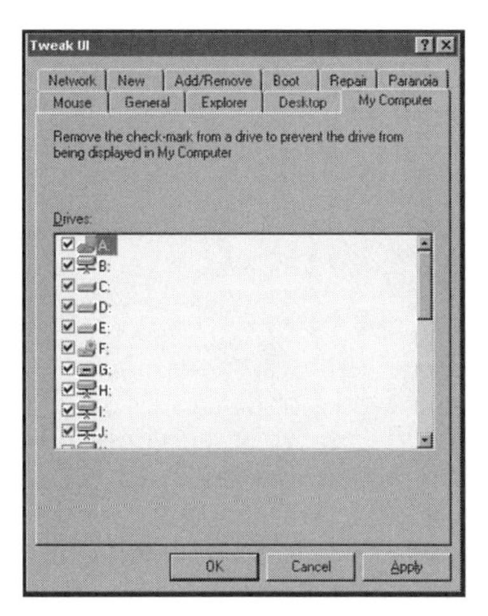

Figure 39.7.
Drive selection in TweakUI.

Just because the drive is not selected does not mean that it cannot be accessed. It means that it will not show and cannot be browsed. If you want to use it, you can still enter the drive letter name and filename to access files, but you cannot browse for them.

Network Tab

The Network options in the TweakUI applet are exclusively for automatic logon to the network. With the checkbox selected as shown in Figure 39.8, the network will log you on without any user input.

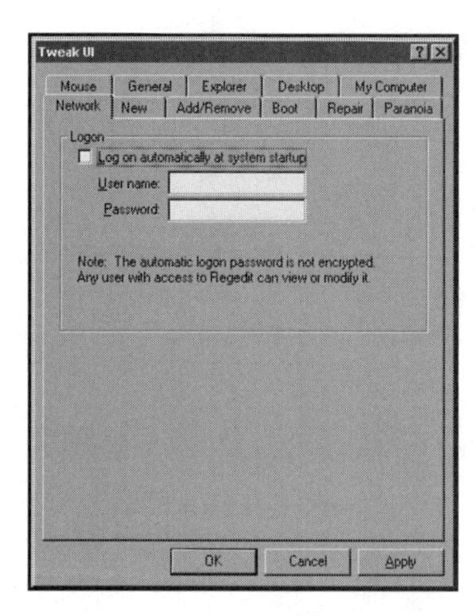

Figure 39.8.
Set the automatic logon to the network.

To override the automatic logon, log off from the network and hold the Shift key down until the logon screen comes up. Enter the other user name, and you will log on as the different user. You will need to change the logon information in TweakUI back to resume correct automatic logons in the future.

Changing Context-Sensitive Document Creation

When you right-click on the Desktop, in Explorer, or in My Computer, you are given the option to create a New item. Your choices are Folder, Shortcut, and documents for currently installed applications. Most new applications that create documents add an option there, making it very easy to use. As part of Microsoft's document-centric concept, it works very well. Most people, though, simply open the application and create the document. If you want to streamline the New menu, select the New tab, as shown in Figure 39.9.

Deselect the items you want to remove from the menu. It will streamline your menus and make them easier to use.

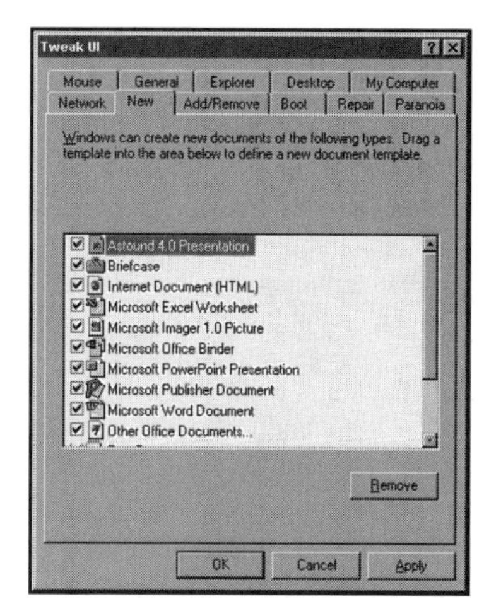

Figure 39.9.
Changing the context-sensitive menus.

Add/Remove Program Options

The Add/Remove applet in the Control Panel gives you options to easily access application setup. Occasionally, you might like to change the information that is in the list. Either you have already removed the application, and it wasn't removed from the list, or you don't want someone playing around with the setup functions of the application. Whatever the case, you could use the Add/Remove options in TweakUI, shown in Figure 39.10, to remove items from the list.

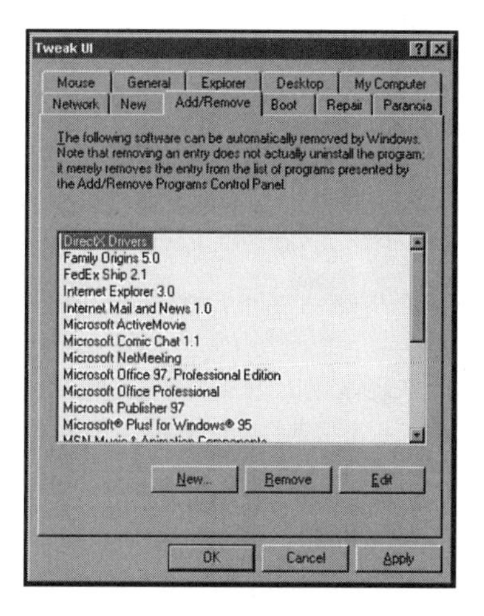

Figure 39.10.
List management for the Add/Remove Programs function in Control Panel.

As indicated on the screen, this does not remove programs; it simply modifies the list.

Boot Options

The Boot options shown in Figure 39.11 are available only in Windows 95. In fact, the tab is not even present in NT. These options determine how 95 will behave at startup, and they also give you extra choices not normally available.

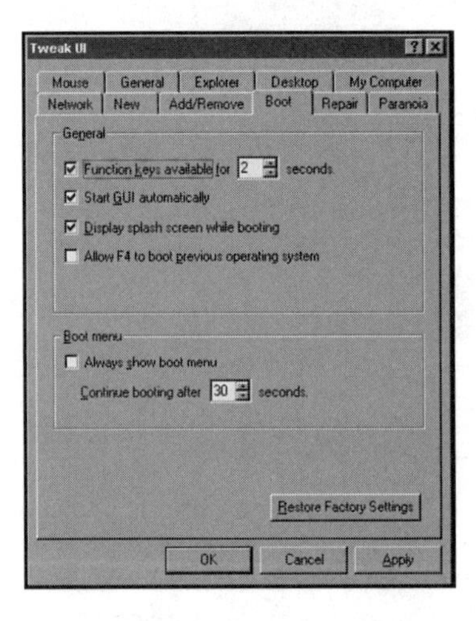

Figure 39.11.
Extra options for booting Windows 95.

These options are particularly useful for those who have a dual-boot configuration with Windows 95 and another DOS environment. You can extend the time, change the defaults, and make working with dual-boot much more forgiving time-wise, and much more friendly.

Repair Options

If you have icons in Explorer that are not pointing to valid programs, you can select the Repair tab, as shown in Figure 39.12. Click the Rebuild Icons button and it will examine all of your icons in Explorer and try to match them with the correct applications.

When you choose the Repair Font Folder button, it will re-establish the folder with its special attributes, and make sure all the fonts are set correctly with their correct IDs.

The Repair System Files button does not do anything for the boot sector, the `BOOT.INI` file (in Windows NT), or the DOS files necessary for Windows 95 to start. It does repair the files that are commonly used for Windows startup, such as `COMMDLG32.DLL`. If an application has mistakenly copied an unacceptable file over the top of the correct file, this will fix it. It checks for version compatibility as well.

There are two buttons that are in TweakUI in Windows 95 that are not available for NT. Figure 39.13 shows the Repair tab in Windows 95 TweakUI.

In Windows 95, you can reset all the Regedit options with the Repair Regedit button. It resets the windows, the columns, and completely closes all the menu trees. The Repair Associations button resets all the default associations between data files and applications, checks in `HKEY_CLASSES_ROOT` for all listed data file types, and confirms associations to currently installed applications. If the application is no longer installed, the association will be reset to its default, or the association will be lost. If the association is lost, you will need to re-establish it after activating the data file.

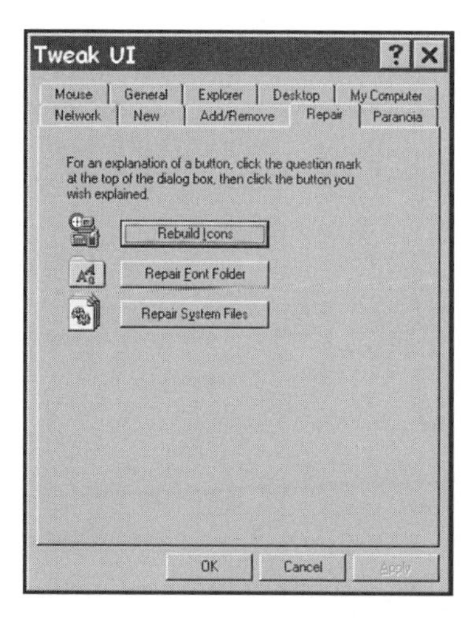

Figure 39.12. Repair your Explorer icons, your Font folder, or your System files for Windows NT.

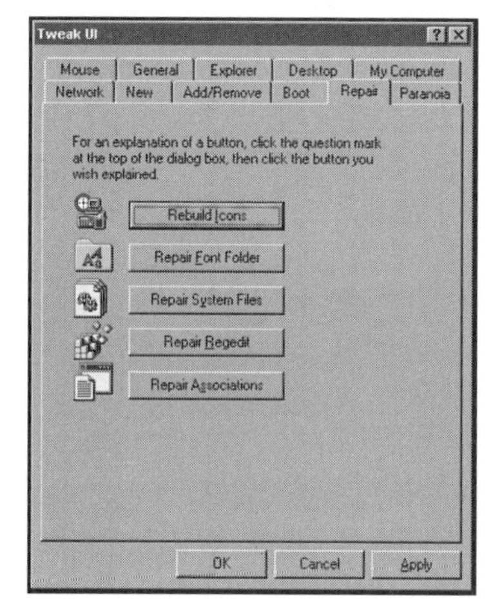

Figure 39.13. Extra options in TweakUI in Windows 95.

Paranoia

Paranoia runs rampant in many organizations, particularly the one that created this application, Microsoft. Actually, it is not all bad. As a security function, the more you can make a potential hacker guess, the harder it will be to infiltrate your system. Figure 39.14 shows the Paranoia page for Windows NT, with its many options.

Each of the six options in Covering Your Tracks has information held in the Registry as an MRU (Most Recently Used) list. Selecting these options simply clears the lists from the Registry at logon. If somebody needed information about server names or application names, they might be able to get it easily from the MRU lists.

You can also choose not to play CDs automatically, and choose between audio and data formats. By doing this, you can get rid of the annoying startup of all the CDs in your tower when you insert a new CD.

There is an extra option in TweakUI in Windows 95 that is not in Windows NT. Figure 39.15 shows the option to log all errors to `FAULTLOG.TXT`. Windows NT does not use that file, and does not need the function, because the function is already built into Dr. Watson and the `BOOTLOG.TXT` files.

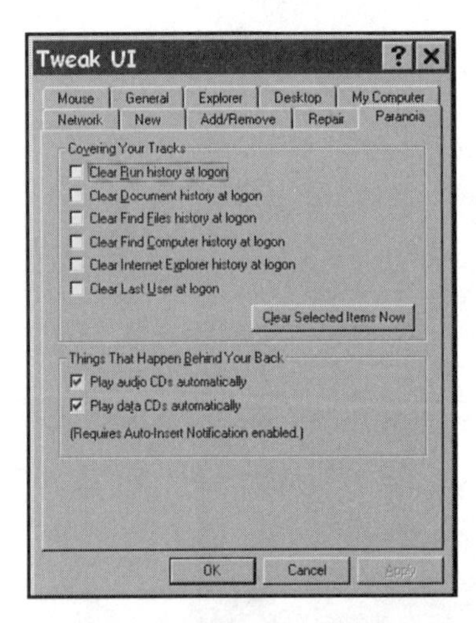

Figure 39.14. Extra choices for security in Windows NT.

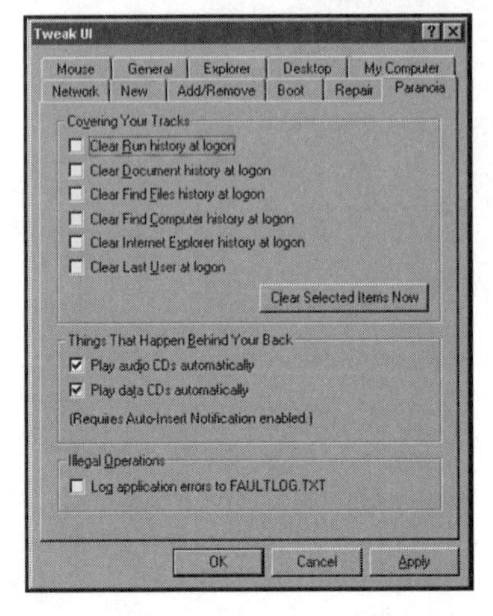

Figure 39.15. TweakUI Paranoia in Windows 95.

Summary

PowerToys is one of the best ways for users to change how their system will work, and one of the safest ways for them to change the Registry. Now that it works for Windows NT as well, it is a tool that every organization should have.

CHAPTER 40

Using Somarsoft DumpReg

People ask me every day where I find my Registry tips; I make them up.

But when that doesn't work, I need to get into the Registry to see the changes that might have happened so I can make these same changes on another system. For example, if you have an application that changes how your system works, and you would like to implement that change on another system, without installing the software, you have to get very creative. You need to know what the changes were, so you can duplicate them. It takes quite a bit of patience, a lot of investigative testing, and some luck. (That's why you have to back it up first!) Plus, you need a tool to let you see what changed and when. DumpReg is the best tool there is for that.

DumpReg is a utility to show the contents of the Registry in a list format, which can be sorted in several ways. It works for both Windows NT (any version) and Windows 95. Options include finding all the Registry keys or values matching a specific string and filtering so only the matching items are shown. It also allows you to copy the information to the clipboard, or to print the report. Printing is not available until the software is registered, for only $10. Register the software. It is a steal for what you get.

Installation

Installation is as simple as copying the files into any directory. As soon as you launch `DUMPREG.EXE` the first time, it will put an entry into the Registry in `HKEY_CURRENT_USER\SOFTWARE\Somarsoft\DumpReg`, but it will make no other changes to the system.

Note

Isn't it refreshing to know what a program is going to do to the Registry before it happens? I love it!

Limitations of DumpReg and Windows 95

Windows 95 does not support the time of the last modification, so the Show Time and Sort By Time options are disabled on Windows 95. Other than that, the program works exactly the same for Windows 95 and Windows NT. This chapter shows DumpReg on Windows NT, so you can see all of the options.

Using DumpReg

To start using DumpReg, launch the application, and go to Report | Dump Registry. It will prompt you for the Registry Hive you would like to list, as shown in Figure 40.1.

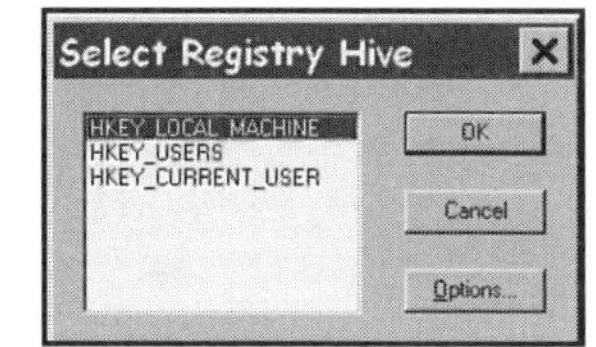

Figure 40.1.
Choose the Handle Key to view.

The options allow you to filter the entries based on the amount of data to be shown, and also to filter by date. Figure 40.2 shows you the options.

Figure 40.2.
Optional filtering for the report.

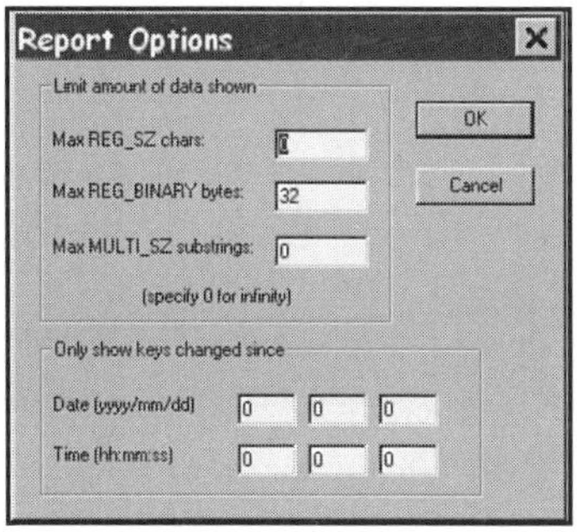

When you press OK to confirm the filtering and again to launch the report, DumpReg will pull all of the Registry information in the selected key and list it by time, with the most recent changes first. Figure 40.3 shows a sample report from my Primary Domain Controller (PDC).

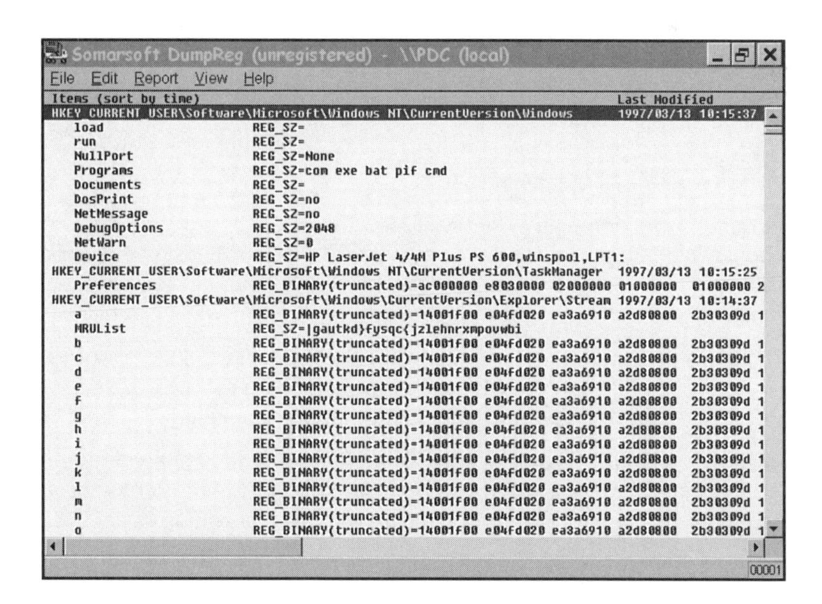

Figure 40.3.
HKEY_CURRENT_USER from the PDC.

DumpReg is an extremely powerful way to determine what changes have been made to your system. Simply filter the output by date, and you can see what last happened to your system. For example, many people are concerned about what will happen to the Registry when they install Microsoft Office 97. If you have DumpReg on your system, you could make the installation, and then look at each of the Handle Keys to see the changes. Set the time limits for only that day and the report will be quite short.

Note

You may be amazed at the number of changes made to the Registry every day. It is a very dynamic, ever-changing database of entries.

Though the time-sorted format is the most beneficial for determining what changes took place, you may want to see only the current status of different keys. You can quickly sort the report by key instead of by time.

You can also save the report, for later review or comparisons in a word processor. Finding the difference can be a little difficult, but using a compare document function could save you a lot of time.

Inspecting a Remote Computer's Registry

You can also use DumpReg to examine the Registry of a remote computer, by selecting Report | Select Computer, and typing in the name in a UNC format (that is, `\\server1`). There is no browse option, so you will have to know the name of the system. Imagine if something happened to a computer on your network and you found out right away; you could check to see if it was a Registry problem by looking at that system's Registry, sorting it by time, and looking for the changes.

Performance Tips

Printing is disabled on the shareware version until it is registered. Once it is enabled, you can choose many options for printing. One of the best options is to change the format for printing, setting it to landscape. Then, you can expand the size of the entries to get more data in the report. If you don't expand the size, some of the text will be truncated.

You also have an option to search inside the report for a specific string of text, so you won't have to wade through the whole report. That string can be in a key, value, or in the data in the value. The report is now just text, so it will look everywhere.

Another option is to filter the report contents. Instead of showing the complete Registry and searching through one string at a time, you can tell the report to show only the items that contain a specific string. Figure 40.4 shows the Filter option ready for a text string.

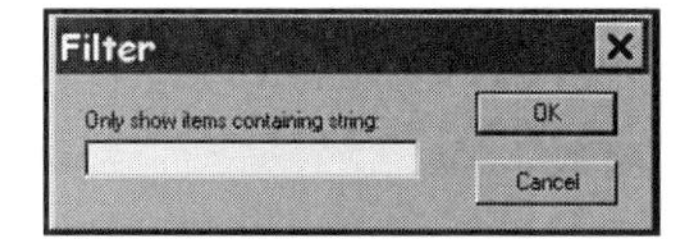

Figure 40.4.
Filtering to reduce the size of the report.

Summary

DumpReg is a great tool, and every administrator or technical support person should have it. It is fast, easy, and extremely helpful. The Registry is a dynamic, ever-changing database of information. Because it changes so much, you and I need all the information we can get. DumpReg helps us wade through the masses of data and pull out exactly what will help us the most.

As you work through your challenges with the Registry, use all the functions and tools shown in this book. Understanding the Registry is very much like gaining wisdom. No matter how much you have, there is always more, and part of the wisdom you have is knowing that there will always be more.

Good luck in your quest. I hope this book will be of great help. Let me know how you do.

APPENDIX A

A Closer Look at HKEY_LOCAL_MACHINE for Windows NT

HKEY_LOCAL_MACHINE is the handle key that represents the hives that control the system and software. It is independent of the user, and settings made are for all users who log on to the system. Figure A.1 shows the five main keys in HKEY_LOCAL_MACHINE, three of which you have access to.

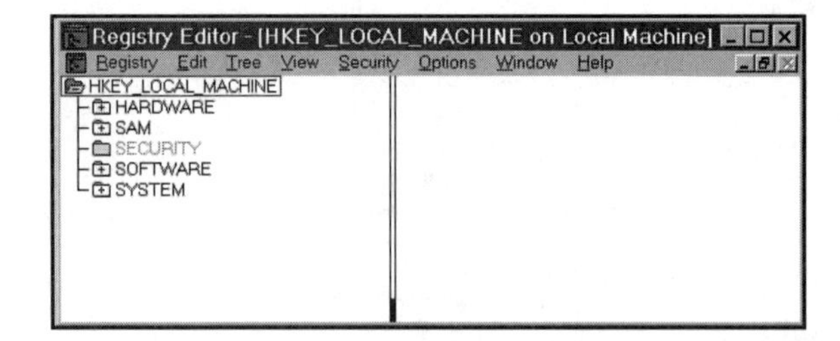

Figure A.1. HKEY_LOCAL_MACHINE and its five first-level keys.

SAM (Security Accounts Manager) and SECURITY are part of HKEY_LOCAL_MACHINE, but they are not available for modification by users in the Registry editors. The changes for SAM and SECURITY are made through User Manager for Domains, Explorer, and File Manager.

All of the settings in this appendix appear in the following format.

Key Name

Full path=*Handle Key\Keyname*

Description, specific information, values

Second-Level Key Name

Full path=*Handle Key\Keyname\Keyname*

Description, specific information, values

Third-Level Key Name

Full path=*Handle Key\Keyname\Keyname\Keyname*

Description, specific information, values

Additional Level Key Names

Full path=*Handle Key\Keyname\Keyname\Keyname\Keyname(\Keyname)*

Description, specific information, values

Hardware

HKEY_LOCAL_MACHINE\HARDWARE

This key holds all the keys, subkeys, and values to control all hardware devices with Windows NT. NT does not allow applications to control these devices directly, so the application must know all the information about each device. Also, NT only reads the BIOS information at startup, so that BIOS information must be loaded, too.

Description

HKEY_LOCAL_MACHINE\HARDWARE\DESCRIPTION

This key holds the descriptions for all the devices on the system. In the other parts of the Registry, the devices are listed by device names, driver names, or codes. All of the translations are listed in this key, making it easier for you to use and understand.

System

HKEY_LOCAL_MACHINE\HARDWARE\DESCRIPTION\System

This key holds specifications and information about the system board, system BIOS, and video BIOS, plus subkeys for the processors and bus controllers.

CentralProcessor

HKEY_LOCAL_MACHINE\HARDWARE\DESCRIPTION\System\CentralProcessor

If your system has multiple processors, they are all listed as subkeys under this key. If your system has only one processor, it is listed as processor 0.

HKEY_LOCAL_MACHINE\HARDWARE\DESCRIPTION\System\CentralProcessor\0

This key holds information about the processor, including its manufacturer, description, and rated speed. (And no, you cannot boost the speed of the processor by changing the value!)

FloatingPointProcessor

HKEY_LOCAL_MACHINE\HARDWARE\DESCRIPTION\System\FloatingPointProcessor

A floating-point processor is what is commonly known as a math co-processor. This key holds information regarding it.

HKEY_LOCAL_MACHINE\HARDWARE\DESCRIPTION\System\FloatingPointProcessor\0

Identification and configuration information about the floating-point processor is found in this key.

MultifunctionAdapter

```
HKEY_LOCAL_MACHINE\HARDWARE\DESCRIPTION\System\MultifunctionAdapter
```

This key holds information about the BIOS-controlled adapters in the system.

```
HKEY_LOCAL_MACHINE\HARDWARE\DESCRIPTION\System\MultifunctionAdapter\0 (PCI)
```

This key holds information for the configuration of the PCI bus. 32- and 64-bit PCI cards are plugged into this bus. BIOS-supported PCI devices are listed under this key.

```
HKEY_LOCAL_MACHINE\HARDWARE\DESCRIPTION\System\MultifunctionAdapter\1 (PNP BIOS)
```

This key holds the information for the Plug and Play BIOS. Currently, NT does not fully support Plug and Play devices, so no devices are listed under this key.

```
HKEY_LOCAL_MACHINE\HARDWARE\DESCRIPTION\System\MultifunctionAdapter\2 (ISA)
```

This key holds the information for the ISA (legacy) bus. 16- and 32-bit ISA and VESA cards are plugged into this bus and are listed under this key.

```
HKEY_LOCAL_MACHINE\HARDWARE\DESCRIPTION\System\MultifunctionAdapter\2\DiskController
```

This key holds the settings for the hard- and floppy-disk controllers.

```
HKEY_LOCAL_MACHINE\HARDWARE\DESCRIPTION\System\MultifunctionAdapter\2\KeyboardController
```

This key holds the settings for the standard keyboard controller.

```
HKEY_LOCAL_MACHINE\HARDWARE\DESCRIPTION\System\MultifunctionAdapter\2\ParallelController
```

This key holds the settings for the parallel port controller and installed parallel ports.

```
HKEY_LOCAL_MACHINE\HARDWARE\DESCRIPTION\System\MultifunctionAdapter\2\PointerController
```

This key holds the settings for the mouse port controller.

```
HKEY_LOCAL_MACHINE\HARDWARE\DESCRIPTION\System\MultifunctionAdapter\2\SerialController
```

This key holds the settings for the serial port controller and installed serial ports.

DEVICEMAP

```
HKEY_LOCAL_MACHINE\HARDWARE\DEVICEMAP
```

This key holds the pointers to all the hardware device drivers and settings on the system. It usually points to the control set that is currently on the system.

KeyboardClass

```
HKEY_LOCAL_MACHINE\HARDWARE\DEVICEMAP\KeyboardClass
```

This key points to the control set and the driver information listed there, as a map would to a traveler.

KeyboardPort

```
HKEY_LOCAL_MACHINE\HARDWARE\DEVICEMAP\KeyboardPort
```

This key points to the control set and the driver information listed there.

PARALLEL PORTS

```
HKEY_LOCAL_MACHINE\HARDWARE\DEVICEMAP\PARALLEL PORTS
```

This key points to the control set and the driver information listed there.

PointerClass

```
HKEY_LOCAL_MACHINE\HARDWARE\DEVICEMAP\PointerClass
```

This key points to the control set and the driver information listed there.

PointerPort

```
HKEY_LOCAL_MACHINE\HARDWARE\DEVICEMAP\PointerPort
```

This key points to the control set and the driver information listed there.

SCSI

```
HKEY_LOCAL_MACHINE\HARDWARE\DEVICEMAP\SCSI
```

SCSI (Small Computer Systems Interface) is an adapter/device combination that allows tremendous growth and outstanding speed. The settings for all host adapters and devices are listed under this key.

SCSI Port 0 (ATAPI Hard Disk Controller)

```
HKEY_LOCAL_MACHINE\HARDWARE\DEVICEMAP\SCSI\SCSI Port 0
```

SCSI Port 0 is the first SCSI host device found in the system, and this key holds the identification and configuration information for it.

```
HKEY_LOCAL_MACHINE\HARDWARE\DEVICEMAP\SCSI\SCSI Port 0\SCSI Bus 0
HKEY_LOCAL_MACHINE\HARDWARE\DEVICEMAP\SCSI\SCSI Port 0\SCSI Bus 0\Initiator Id
➥255
HKEY_LOCAL_MACHINE\HARDWARE\DEVICEMAP\SCSI\SCSI Port 0\SCSI Bus 0\Target Id 0
```

There are no configurable devices connected to this adapter, so no settings are listed in this key.

```
HKEY_LOCAL_MACHINE\HARDWARE\DEVICEMAP\SCSI\SCSI Port 0\SCSI Bus 0\Target Id
➥0\Logical Unit Id 0
```

This key holds the settings for the SCSI ID number of the devices attached to the host adapter, and the description of the device.

SCSI Port 1 (ATAPI Floppy-Disk Controller)

```
HKEY_LOCAL_MACHINE\HARDWARE\DEVICEMAP\SCSI\SCSI Port 1
```

The floppy-disk controller is also considered a nonconfigurable SCSI device to Windows NT, using an IDE-to-SCSI conversion driver called ATAPI. This key holds all the settings for devices attached to the floppy controller.

```
HKEY_LOCAL_MACHINE\HARDWARE\DEVICEMAP\SCSI\SCSI Port 1\SCSI Bus 0
HKEY_LOCAL_MACHINE\HARDWARE\DEVICEMAP\SCSI\SCSI Port 1\SCSI Bus 0\Initiator Id
➥255
HKEY_LOCAL_MACHINE\HARDWARE\DEVICEMAP\SCSI\SCSI Port 1\SCSI Bus 0\Target Id 0
HKEY_LOCAL_MACHINE\HARDWARE\DEVICEMAP\SCSI\SCSI Port 1\SCSI Bus 0\Target Id
➥0\Logical Unit Id 0
```

SCSI Port 2 (AHA154x)

```
HKEY_LOCAL_MACHINE\HARDWARE\DEVICEMAP\SCSI\SCSI Port 2
```

This key is for the settings for the Adaptec 1542c SCSI host adapter, and all the devices connected to it. Figure A.2 shows that there are three devices connected to this host adapter, and each has its own Target ID key below this key.

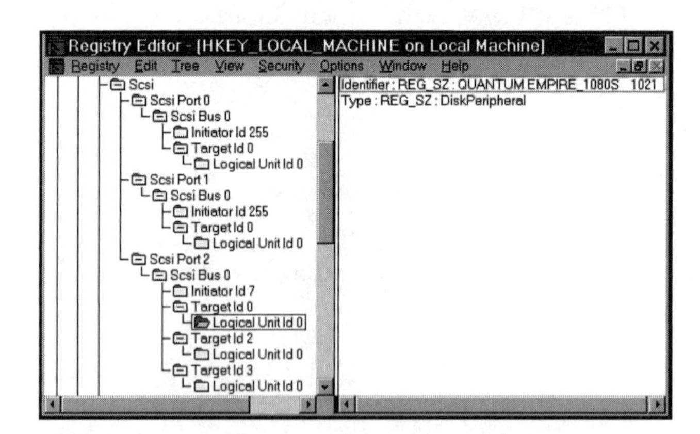

Figure A.2. Device connections to SCSI adapters.

```
HKEY_LOCAL_MACHINE\HARDWARE\DEVICEMAP\SCSI\SCSI Port 2\SCSI Bus 0
HKEY_LOCAL_MACHINE\HARDWARE\DEVICEMAP\SCSI\SCSI Port 2\SCSI Bus 0\Initiator Id 7
HKEY_LOCAL_MACHINE\HARDWARE\DEVICEMAP\SCSI\SCSI Port 2\SCSI Bus 0\Target Id 0
```

This is the key for the description and settings for the connected hard drive.

```
HKEY_LOCAL_MACHINE\HARDWARE\DEVICEMAP\SCSI\SCSI Port 2\SCSI Bus 0\Target Id 2
```

This is the key for the description and settings for the connected scanner.

```
HKEY_LOCAL_MACHINE\HARDWARE\DEVICEMAP\SCSI\SCSI Port 2\SCSI Bus 0\Target Id 3
```

This is the key for the description and settings for the connected Syquest removable media drive.

SERIALCOMM

HKEY_LOCAL_MACHINE\HARDWARE\DEVICEMAP\SERIALCOMM

This key lists the names of the installed serial ports.

VIDEO

HKEY_LOCAL_MACHINE\HARDWARE\DEVICEMAP\VIDEO

This key points to the control set and the driver information listed there.

OWNERMAP

HKEY_LOCAL_MACHINE\HARDWARE\OWNERMAP

When a device gives up all control to another, it is said to be *owned*. Those devices and their owners are listed in this key.

RESOURCEMAP

HKEY_LOCAL_MACHINE\HARDWARE\RESOURCEMAP

This key holds all the basic connection settings for devices on the system, such as IRQ, DMA, and I/O port addresses. They are separated into subkeys, depending on the type of control.

Hardware Abstraction Layer

HKEY_LOCAL_MACHINE\HARDWARE\RESOURCEMAP\Hardware Abstraction Layer

The Hardware Abstraction Layer (HAL) separates the system devices from the software and operating system, ensuring that even in the worst application crashes, the operating system and base hardware continue to run.

The HAL is the way the standard devices are controlled, including parallel and serial ports, disk controllers, and others.

HKEY_LOCAL_MACHINE\HARDWARE\RESOURCEMAP\Hardware Abstraction Layer\PC Compatible Eisa/Isa HAL

This key is the actual type of HAL for the system. There are several types, including PC compatible Eisa/Isa, DEC, MIPS, PowerPC, and Compaq. The values for this key are the actual settings for all the devices.

KeyboardPort/PointerPort

HKEY_LOCAL_MACHINE\HARDWARE\RESOURCEMAP\KeyboardPort/PointerPort

The settings for the keyboard and pointer (PS/2 mouse) port are in this key.

i8042prt

HKEY_LOCAL_MACHINE\HARDWARE\RESOURCEMAP\KeyboardPort/PointerPort\i8042prt

Standard keyboards use an 8042 controller chip. This key holds information about the chip, so the system does not have to read it off the keyboard BIOS.

LOADED PARALLEL DRIVER RESOURCES

HKEY_LOCAL_MACHINE\HARDWARE\RESOURCEMAP\LOADED PARALLEL DRIVER RESOURCES

The parallel port drivers in use are listed here.

Parport

HKEY_LOCAL_MACHINE\HARDWARE\RESOURCEMAP\LOADED PARALLEL DRIVER RESOURCES\Parport

Settings for the currently active parallel ports are listed in the values in this key. Settings made in Control Panel to change the parallel port name (LPT1, LPT2, and so on) or resources are listed here.

LOADED SERIAL DRIVER RESOURCES

HKEY_LOCAL_MACHINE\HARDWARE\RESOURCEMAP\LOADED SERIAL DRIVER RESOURCES

The serial port drivers in use are listed here.

Serial

HKEY_LOCAL_MACHINE\HARDWARE\RESOURCEMAP\LOADED SERIAL DRIVER RESOURCES\Serial

Settings for the currently active serial ports are listed in the values in this key. Settings made in Control Panel to change the serial port name (COM1, COM2, and so on) or resources are listed here.

OtherDrivers

HKEY_LOCAL_MACHINE\HARDWARE\RESOURCEMAP\OtherDrivers

Other drivers that are not standard for system operations are listed here, so they can be recognized by the system.

Floppy

HKEY_LOCAL_MACHINE\HARDWARE\RESOURCEMAP\OtherDrivers\Floppy

The floppy-drive controller driver settings are listed in this key.

PCI3210

HKEY_LOCAL_MACHINE\HARDWARE\RESOURCEMAP\OtherDrivers\PCI3210

This key lists the settings for a PCI network card.

SCSIAdapter

HKEY_LOCAL_MACHINE\HARDWARE\RESOURCEMAP\SCSIAdapter

SCSI adapters are listed in this key, so specific settings can be made for each one.

Aha154x

HKEY_LOCAL_MACHINE\HARDWARE\RESOURCEMAP\SCSIAdapter\Aha154x

The Adaptec 1542C SCSI host adapter settings are listed in this key.

atapi

HKEY_LOCAL_MACHINE\HARDWARE\RESOURCEMAP\SCSIAdapter\atapi

ATAPI is a driver that translates SCSI-level information for IDE and Enhanced IDE interface cards.

System Resources

HKEY_LOCAL_MACHINE\HARDWARE\RESOURCEMAP\System Resources

Memory and virtual memory settings are listed in this key.

Physical Memory

HKEY_LOCAL_MACHINE\HARDWARE\RESOURCEMAP\System Resources\Physical Memory

Memory that is reserved in the Reserved memory area is listed here.

VIDEO

HKEY_LOCAL_MACHINE\HARDWARE\RESOURCEMAP\VIDEO

Video driver information for current drivers is listed in this key.

s3

HKEY_LOCAL_MACHINE\HARDWARE\RESOURCEMAP\VIDEO\s3

The s3 video driver is the one to be used when the system boots. This key holds the settings for the video card.

VgaSave

`HKEY_LOCAL_MACHINE\HARDWARE\RESOURCEMAP\VIDEO\VgaSave`

If the video driver is not able to work with the installed video card, the system switches to the driver listed here. The system also uses it if VGA mode is chosen during startup.

VgaStart

`HKEY_LOCAL_MACHINE\HARDWARE\RESOURCEMAP\VIDEO\VgaStart`

The video driver information actually used during startup is listed here.

SAM

`HKEY_LOCAL_MACHINE\SAM`

This key is inaccessible from the Registry editors, and it points to information about all the users on the domain.

SECURITY

`HKEY_LOCAL_MACHINE\SECURITY`

All rights and privileges are included in this Registry setting, but it is inaccessible from the Registry editors.

SOFTWARE

`HKEY_LOCAL_MACHINE\SOFTWARE`

The settings for all installed 32-bit software and `.INI` files for applications are listed in this key. The items included vary, depending on the software installed. Control functions for those applications are listed in the many subkeys located here.

SYSTEM

`HKEY_LOCAL_MACHINE\SYSTEM`

This key stores all information required for the system to start, and for the recovery of the system in case of failure.

Clone

HKEY_LOCAL_MACHINE\SYSTEM\Clone

This subkey is a non-accessible section that holds duplicate information for use by the system in case of failure. This key is saved with RDISK.EXE and activated by Last Known Good, and points to the *%SYSTEMROOT%*\Repair directory.

ControlSet001

HKEY_LOCAL_MACHINE\SYSTEM\ControlSct001

This subkey contains descriptions and controls for device drivers and other services. Multiple sets are created when drivers are changed in the system, and are labeled ControlSet001, ControlSet002, and so on.

Control

HKEY_LOCAL_MACHINE\SYSTEM\ControlSet001\Control

This subkey holds the information that is set in the Control Panel applets in Windows NT. Do not edit this information through the Registry editor because some applets make changes in more than one Registry location. A missing entry may cause the system to be unstable. The following list holds the subkeys under the Control key:

```
BootverificationProgram
Class
ComputerName
CrashControl
FileSystem
GraphicsDrivers
GroupOrderList
hivelist
IDConfigDB
Keyboard Layout
Keyboard Layouts
Lsa
MediaProperties
MediaResources
NetworkProvider
Nls
Print
PriorityControl
ProductOptions
RegistrySizeLimit
SecurePipeServers
SecurityProviders
ServiceGroupOrder
```

```
ServiceProvider
Session Manager
Setup
SystemBesources
TimeZoneInformation
Update
VirtualDeviceDrivers
Windows
WOW
```

Enum

`HKEY_LOCAL_MACHINE\SYSTEM\ControlSet001\Enum`

Bus enumerator information for Windows NT is added to the Registry during installation of the devices and Windows NT. It is not dynamic, and does not get changed. All the information is required to make NT and its devices start up.

HTREE

`HKEY_LOCAL_MACHINE\SYSTEM\ControlSet001\Enum\HTREE`

This subkey holds information and pointers to details about devices, including the driver names, based on bus connections. Devices are split between Legacy (ISA) and Plug and Play bus functions.

`HKEY_LOCAL_MACHINE\SYSTEM\ControlSet001\Enum\HTREE\ROOT`

This subkey simply holds the next subkey.

`HKEY_LOCAL_MACHINE\SYSTEM\ControlSet001\Enum\HTREE\ROOT\0`

The actual locations of the bus-connected devices and their driver information are listed here.

Root

`HKEY_LOCAL_MACHINE\SYSTEM\ControlSet001\Enum\Root`

This key contains control information for ISA and PNP bus connections, using the drivers listed next. The information contained in the subkeys in the `Root` key (shown in the following list) is specifically related to the connection settings and resources:

```
*PNP030b
*PNP0F03
LEGACY_AFD
LEGACY_AHAl 54X
LEGACY_ASYNCMAC
LEGACY_ATAPI
LEGACY_BEEP
LEGACY_BROWSER
LEGACY_CDFS
```

```
LEGACY_CDROM
LEGACY_DISK
LEGACY_EE16
LEGACY_FASTFAT
LEGACY_FLOPPY
LEGACY_FS_REC
LEGACY_KBDCLASS
LEGACY_KSECDD
LEGACY_LANMANSERVER
LEGACY_LANMANWORKSTATION
LEGACY_LMHOSTS
LEGACY_MESSENGER
LEGACY_MOUCLASS
LEGACY_MSFS
LEGACY_MUP
LEGACY_NBF
LEGACY_NDIS
LEGACY_NDISTAPI
LEGACY_NDISWAN
LEGACY_NETBIOS
LEGACY_NETBT
LEGACY_NETDETECT
LEGACY_NETLOGON
LEGACY_NPFS
LEGACY_NULL
LEGACY_NWLNKIPX
LEGACY_NWLNKNB
LEGACY_NWLNKSPX
LEGACY_PARALLEL
LEGACY_PARPORT
LEGACY_PARVDM
LEGACY_PCI3210
LEGACY_RASACD
LEGACY_RASARP
LEGACY_RASAUTO
LEGACY_RASMAN
LEGACY_RDR
LEGACY_RPCSS
LEGACY_S3
LEGACY_SCSISCAN
LEGACY_SERIAL
LEGACY_SNDBLST
LEGACY_SPOOLER
LEGACY_SRV
LEGACY_TAPISRV
LEGACY_TCPIP
LEGACY_VGASAVE
UNIMODEM5DC8F5BA
```

Hardware Profiles

```
HKEY_LOCAL_MACHINE\SYSTEM\ControlSet001\Hardware Profiles
```

Hardware profiles allow the user to select what hardware will be active after boot. Hardware profiles are normally used for notebooks or other portable systems, where the active/installed hardware may be different. For example, a notebook connected at the office might have a docking station with a network card, a SCSI tape drive, and external monitor and mouse. Different drivers would be required to run that system than when the notebook was detached from these features. Hardware profiles also prevent the system from trying to load all of those drivers when the system is not connected. All controls for hardware profiles are under this key.

0001

```
HKEY_LOCAL_MACHINE\SYSTEM\ControlSet001\Hardware Profiles\0001
```

The first set of drivers, shown at startup as the Original Configuration, is listed as profile 0001.

```
HKEY_LOCAL_MACHINE\SYSTEM\ControlSet001\Hardware Profiles\0001\Software
```

Software associated with specific devices that may not be connected with another profile is listed here. Software is only listed here if it is affected by another profile.

```
HKEY_LOCAL_MACHINE\SYSTEM\ControlSet001\Hardware Profiles\0001\System
```

System information that is unique to profile 0001 is listed here.

```
HKEY_LOCAL_MACHINE\SYSTEM\ControlSet001\Hardware
Profiles\0001\System\CurrentControlSet
HKEY_LOCAL_MACHINE\SYSTEM\ControlSet001\Hardware
Profiles\0001\System\CurrentControlSet\Control
HKEY_LOCAL_MACHINE\SYSTEM\ControlSet001\Hardware
Profiles\0001\System\CurrentControlSet\Enum
HKEY_LOCAL_MACHINE\SYSTEM\ControlSet001\Hardware
Profiles\0001\System\CurrentControlSet\Services
```

0002

```
HKEY_LOCAL_MACHINE\SYSTEM\ControlSet001\Hardware Profiles\0002
```

Profile 0002 is the second profile created for NT. The first (0001) was done during installation. This second profile uses different drivers and settings required for a different hardware setup. The type of information in the following keys mirrors the information that is in hardware profile 0001.

```
HKEY_LOCAL_MACHINE\SYSTEM\ControlSet001\Hardware Profiles\0002\Software
HKEY_LOCAL_MACHINE\SYSTEM\ControlSet001\Hardware Profiles\0002\System
HKEY_LOCAL_MACHINE\SYSTEM\ControlSet001\Hardware
Profiles\0002\System\CurrentControlSet
HKEY_LOCAL_MACHINE\SYSTEM\ControlSet001\Hardware
Profiles\0002\System\CurrentControlSet\Control
HKEY_LOCAL_MACHINE\SYSTEM\ControlSet001\Hardware
Profiles\0002\System\CurrentControlSet\Enum
HKEY_LOCAL_MACHINE\SYSTEM\ControlSet001\Hardware
Profiles\0002\System\CurrentControlSet\Services
```

Current

```
HKEY_LOCAL_MACHINE\SYSTEM\ControlSet001\Hardware Profiles\Current
```

This key contains the profiles that are actually current in the system. The choice made during startup affects which of the two (or more) hardware profiles is current. For example, if Profile 0002 is chosen, all of the Profile 0002 information will be mapped into these keys.

```
HKEY_LOCAL_MACHINE\SYSTEM\ControlSet001\Hardware Profiles\Current\Software
HKEY_LOCAL_MACHINE\SYSTEM\ControlSet001\Hardware Profiles\Current\System
HKEY_LOCAL_MACHINE\SYSTEM\ControlSet001\Hardware
Profiles\Current\System\CurrentControlSet
HKEY_LOCAL_MACHINE\SYSTEM\ControlSet001\Hardware
Profiles\Current\System\CurrentControlSet\Control
HKEY_LOCAL_MACHINE\SYSTEM\ControlSet001\Hardware
Profiles\Current\System\CurrentControlSet\Enum
HKEY_LOCAL_MACHINE\SYSTEM\ControlSet001\Hardware
Profiles\Current\System\CurrentControlSet\Services
```

Services

```
HKEY_LOCAL_MACHINE\SYSTEM\ControlSet001\Services
```

This key contains all the standard services that come with Windows NT, plus any that have been added through the installation of services or devices. Each standard Services key (shown in the following list) contains configuration and identification settings.

```
Abiosdsk        ClipSrv      Jazzg300
Afd             Cpqarray     Jazzg364
Aha154x         cpqfws2e     Jzvxl484
Aha174x         dac960nt     Kbdclass
aic78xx         dce376nt     KSecDD
Alerter         Dell_DGX     LanmanServer
Always          Delldsa      LanmanWorkstation
ami0nt          DHCP         LmHosts
amsint          Disk         Messenger
Arrow           Diskperf     mga
AsyncMac        DptSCSI      mga_mil
AsyncMac3       dtc329x      mitsumi
atapi           et4000       mkecr5xx
Atdisk          EventLog     Modem
ati             Fastfat      Mouclass
Beep            Fd16_700     Msfs
Browser         Fd7000ex     Mup
BusLogic        Fd8xx        Nbf
Busmouse        flashpnt     Ncr53c9x
Cdaudio         Floppy       ncr77c22
Cdfs            Fs_Rec       Ncrc700
Cdrom           Ftdisk       Ncrc710
Changer         i8042prt     NDIS
cirrus          Inport       NdisTapi
```

NdisWan
NdisWan2
NdisWan4
NdisWan5
NdisWan6
NetBIOS
NetBIOSInformation
NetBT
NetDDE
NetDDEdsdm
NetDetect
Netlogon
Npfs
Ntfs
NtLmSsp
Null
NwlnkIpx
NwlnkNb
NwlnkSpx
Oliscsi
Parallel
Parport
ParVdm
PCI3210
PCI32101
PCIDump
Pcmcia
PlugPlay
pnpisa
psidisp
0I10wnt
qv
RasAcd
RasArp
RasAuto
RasMan
Rdr
RemoteAccess
Replictor
RPCLOCATOR
RpcSs
s3
Schedule
SCSIprnt
SCSIscan
Serial
Sermouse
Sfloppy
Simbad
slcd32
sndblst
SNMP
Sparrow
Spock
Spooler
symc810
T128
T13B
TapiSrv
Tcpip
tga
tmv1
Ultral24
Ultra14f
Ultra24f
UPS
v7vrarn
VgaSave
VgaStart
Wd33c93
wd90c24a
wdvga
weitekp9
WinSock
WinSock2
WinTrust
Xga

ControlSet002

HKEY_LOCAL_MACHINE\SYSTEM\ControlSet002

When drivers are changed, if no other control set has the same drivers and information, an additional one is created with an incremental number such as `ControlSet002`. If a control set with the same drivers exists, that one is used instead.

CurrentControlSet

HKEY_LOCAL_MACHINE\SYSTEM\CurrentControlSet

The control set (listed previously) currently in use is mapped into all the keys listed next at startup. See Figure A.3 for an example.

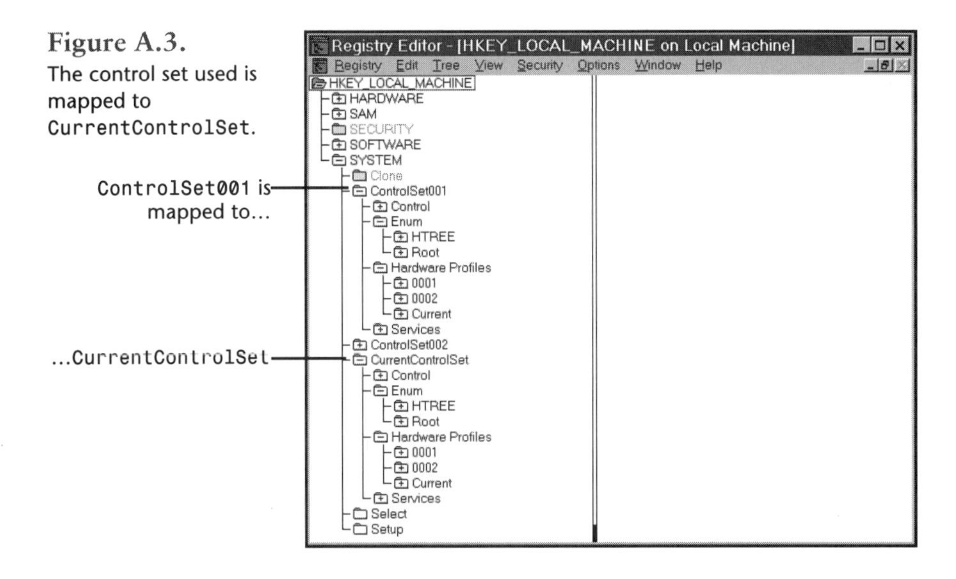

Figure A.3.
The control set used is mapped to `CurrentControlSet`.

Control

`HKEY_LOCAL_MACHINE\SYSTEM\CurrentControlSet\Control`

This is mapped information from a specific control set (such as `ControlSet001`).

Enum

`HKEY_LOCAL_MACHINE\SYSTEM\CurrentControlSet\Enum`

This is mapped information from a specific control set (such as `ControlSet001`).

Hardware Profiles

`HKEY_LOCAL_MACHINE\SYSTEM\CurrentControlSet\Hardware Profiles`

This is mapped information from a specific control set (such as `ControlSet001`).

Services

`HKEY_LOCAL_MACHINE\SYSTEM\CurrentControlSet\Services`

This is mapped information from a specific control set (such as `ControlSet001`).

Select

```
HKEY_LOCAL_MACHINE\SYSTEM\Select
```

This key lists the current control set, which is saved as Last Known Good. This key also lists which control sets, if any, failed during startup.

Setup

```
HKEY_LOCAL_MACHINE\SYSTEM\Setup
```

This key lists the system partition, the setup status, and other information about the setup process for the system.

Summary

HKEY_LOCAL_MACHINE holds all the filename, file-location, and setting information for the entire system, and all its attached devices. It is updated by the Control Panel, by the installation of devices, and through utilities such as Windows NT Diagnostics. HKEY_LOCAL_MACHINE is protected by Last Known Good and the Emergency Repair Disk because of the critical nature of the contained Registry settings.

APPENDIX B

A Closer Look at HKEY_LOCAL_MACHINE for Windows 95

HKEY_LOCAL_MACHINE is the handle key that represents the hives that control the system and software. The settings are independent of the user, because they are made for all users who will use the system. Figure B.1 shows the eight main keys in HKEY_LOCAL_MACHINE inside REGEDIT.EXE, the Registry editor for Windows 95.

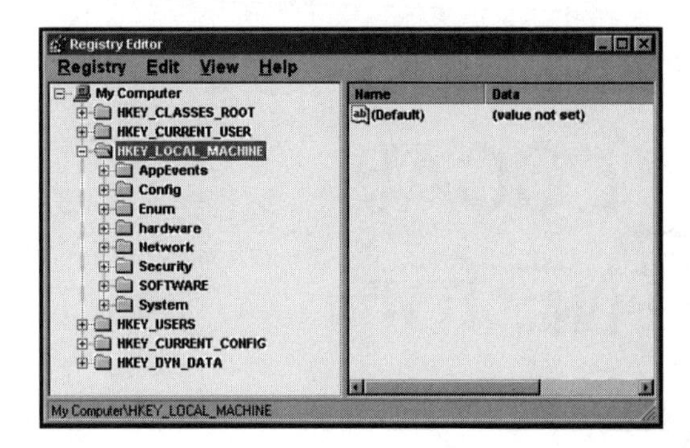

Figure B.1.
HKEY_LOCAL_MACHINE and its eight first-level keys.

All of the settings in this chapter appear in the following format.

Key Name

Full path=*Handle Key\Keyname*

Description, specific information, values

Second-Level Key Name

Full path=*Handle Key\Keyname\Keyname*

Description, specific information, values

Third-Level Key Name

Full path=*Handle Key\Keyname\Keyname\Keyname*

Description, specific information, values

Additional Level Key Names

Full path=*Handle Key\Keyname\Keyname\Keyname\Keyname(\Keyname)*

Description, specific information, values

AppEvents

HKEY_LOCAL_MACHINE\AppEvents

The AppEvents key in Windows 95 is empty, for future use with client/server applications in thin clients. The application will actually reside on the network server, and this key will hold the pointers to the parts and pieces.

Config

HKEY_LOCAL_MACHINE\Config

The Config key holds display and printer configurations. Each configuration will be stored in a key called 0001 or 0002 and so on, one for every configuration. If you only have a single hardware configuration, you will only have the key 0001.

0001

HKEY_LOCAL_MACHINE\Config\0001

This is the only key under Config if you have only one hardware profile. The value ProfileFlags shows whether hardware profiles are used on the system. The default is 00 00 00 00, which means they are turned off.

Display

HKEY_LOCAL_MACHINE\Config\0001\Display

This shows the display settings for the screen font, window sizing, and window positioning.

System

HKEY_LOCAL_MACHINE\Config\0001\System

This key holds information about the printers on the system.

CurrentControlSet\Control\Print\Printers

HKEY_LOCAL_MACHINE\Config\0001\System\CurrentControlSet\Control\Print\Printers

Under this key, there is a key for each printer on the system.

Figure B.2 shows the printers in my system.

Adding and removing printers through Control Panel will adjust this list.

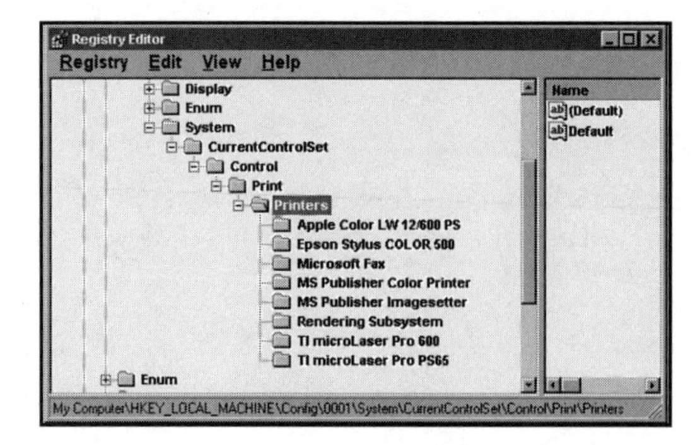

Figure B.2.
Installed printers.

Enum

`HKEY_LOCAL_MACHINE\Enum`

The `Enum` key holds the information about hardware devices that are found during startup. Windows 95 uses "bus enumerators" to detect hardware during setup and pull information form various `.INF` files. The devices shown here are those that were installed and have been detected at startup. Figure B.3 shows the keys under the `Enum` key.

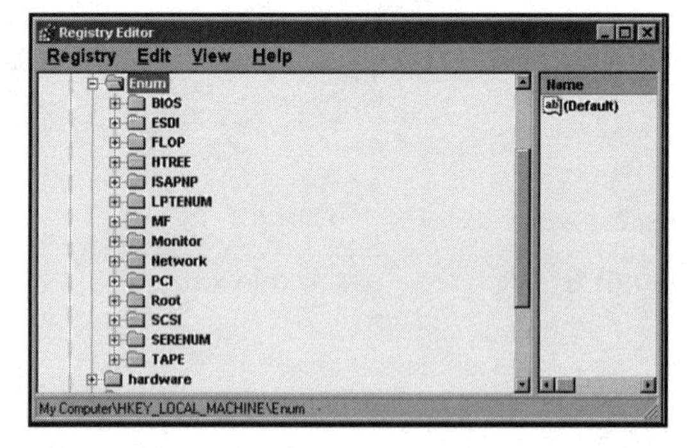

Figure B.3.
All of the hardware settings in Windows 95 are referenced in the `Enum` key.

Listed in this section will only be devices that are unique and require special explanation.

BIOS

`HKEY_LOCAL_MACHINE\Enum\BIOS`

The BIOS key stores information on all the Plug and Play devices in the system. They are listed as a set of code numbers, with specifications for each in the values. For example, `*PNP0400` is the key for the parallel port LPT1. If LPT1 didn't respond to the Plug and Play functions, instead of being listed here, it would have been listed in the `Root` key under `Enum`.

Root

HKEY_LOCAL_MACHINE\Enum\Root

The Root key holds all the information for the non-Plug and Play BIOS devices. Looking here, we can quickly determine which devices have responded to Plug and Play functions, and which haven't. Figure B.4 illustrates that, and lists the devices in my system that are not compatible with Plug and Play.

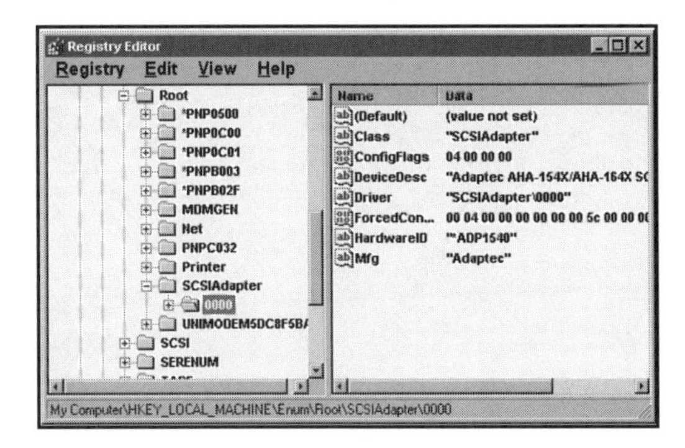

Figure B.4.
Devices incompatible with Plug and Play.

An example is the SCSI adapter, my Adaptec 1542C host adapter. A device that must match the configuration in Windows 95 with the hardware settings has a value named ForcedConfig, which the system will not try to change.

Network

HKEY_LOCAL_MACHINE\Enum\Network

The networking functions for Windows 95 are detailed in this key. Subkeys are included for each major service and protocol that is installed. Table B.1 shows the key and its corresponding service.

Table B.1. Network services in the Registry.

Key name	*Description*
MSTCP	TCP/IP protocol
NETBEUI	NetBEUI protocol
NWLINK	NWLink protocol
NWNBLINK	NWLink protocol with NetBIOS support
NWREDIR	Microsoft client for NetWare networks
REMOTEREG	Remote Registry Editing service
VREDIR	Client for Microsoft networks
VSERVER	File and Printer sharing for Microsoft networks

Inside of each of the keys is details about how Windows 95 will use the service.

Hardware

HKEY_LOCAL_MACHINE\HARDWARE

A little deceptive, the Hardware key only holds information for the HyperTerminal program, relative to the math co-processor and the serial ports. It appears that it would hold much more and be a major key, but all of the settings and specifics are in the Enum key.

Network

HKEY_LOCAL_MACHINE\Network

This key holds information only about the primary network logon. The details of all the network services are held in the HKEY_LOCAL_MACHINE\Enum\Network key.

SECURITY

HKEY_LOCAL_MACHINE\SECURITY

This key is reserved for future use with higher security functions and compatibility with Windows NT.

SOFTWARE

HKEY_LOCAL_MACHINE\SOFTWARE

The settings for all installed 32-bit software and .INI files for applications are listed in this key. The items included vary, depending on the software installed. Control functions for those applications are listed in the many subkeys located here.

SYSTEM

HKEY_LOCAL_MACHINE\SYSTEM

This key stores all information required for the system to start, and for the recovery of the system in case of failure. It includes the control sets describing the device drivers, their settings, and other services.

CurrentControlSet

HKEY_LOCAL_MACHINE\SYSTEM\CurrentControlSet

This subkey contains descriptions and controls for device drivers and other services. Unlike Windows NT, Windows 95 only holds information on the current control set of drivers.

Control

`HKEY_LOCAL_MACHINE\SYSTEM\CurrentControlSet\Control`

This subkey holds the information that is set in the Control Panel applets in Windows 95. Do not edit this information through the Registry editor because some applets make changes in more than one Registry location. A missing entry may cause the system to be unstable. The following list holds the subkeys under the `Control` key:

```
ComputerName
FileSystem
IDConfigDB
InstalledFiles
Keyboard Layouts
MediaProperties
MediaResources
NetworkProvider
Nls
PerfStats
Print
PwdProvider
SecurityProviders
ServiceProvider
Session Manager
Shutdown
TimeZoneInformation
Update
VMM32Files
WebPost
```

Services

`HKEY_LOCAL_MACHINE\SYSTEM\CurrentControlSet\Services`

This key contains all the standard services that come with Windows 95, plus any that have been added through the installation of services or devices. Each standard service key contains configuration and identification settings.

Arbitrators

`HKEY_LOCAL_MACHINE\SYSTEM\CurrentControlSet\Services\Arbitrators`

The arbitrators keys hold the information required to resolve conflicts between two devices when they are competing for the same settings. The four subkeys hold information about RAM address conflicts, DMA, I/O port conflicts, and IRQ conflicts.

Class

HKEY_LOCAL_MACHINE\SYSTEM\CurrentControlSet\Services\Class

The class key holds all the subkeys for control of all the classes of devices that Windows 95 supports. These are similar to the groupings of devices you see in the Add New Hardware wizard, and holds information as to how the devices will be installed.

inetaccs

HKEY_LOCAL_MACHINE\SYSTEM\CurrentControlSet\Services\inetaccs

This key holds information about the various Internet Explorer accessories available in the system. It is only installed when you have installed Internet Explorer 2.0 or above.

MSNP32

HKEY_LOCAL_MACHINE\SYSTEM\CurrentControlSet\Services\MSNP32

The MSNP32 key describes how the Client for Microsoft Networks is going to function. It holds information about the authentication process and the authenticator.

NWNP32

HKEY_LOCAL_MACHINE\SYSTEM\CurrentControlSet\Services\NWNP32

The NWNP32 key describes how the Microsoft Client for NetWare Networks is going to function. It holds information about the authentication process and the authenticator.

RemoteAccess

HKEY_LOCAL_MACHINE\SYSTEM\CurrentControlSet\Services\RemoteAccess

Inside this key is the information required for Remote Access to work on the Windows 95 system. It includes authentication parameters, host information, and protocol information in order to create a dial-up environment that will work.

SNMP

HKEY_LOCAL_MACHINE\SYSTEM\CurrentControlSet\Services\SNMP

This key holds all the parameters for SNMP (Simple Network Management Protocol). That includes the permitted managers, the trap configuration, and the valid communities.

VxD

HKEY_LOCAL_MACHINE\SYSTEM\CurrentControlSet\Services\VxD

The VxD key holds information on all the 32-bit virtual device drivers in Windows 95. Windows 95 automatically manages them, so there is no reason to edit them with a Registry editor. All the static VxDs are listed with a subkey under this key.

WebPost

HKEY_LOCAL_MACHINE\SYSTEM\CurrentControlSet\Services\WebPost

The WebPost key holds settings and pointers for all loaded Internet Mail post offices. If you connect to a service provider, and it is listed here, you will poll the server for any mail that is to be delivered to you.

Winsock

HKEY_LOCAL_MACHINE\SYSTEM\CurrentControlSet\Services\Winsock

Information about the Winsock file to be used when connecting to the Internet is listed in this key. If the incorrect file is listed, you will not be able to get onto the Internet.

WinTrust

HKEY_LOCAL_MACHINE\SYSTEM\CurrentControlSet\Services\WinTrust

The WinTrust function is set in the Registry as part of the process of checking every file downloaded from the Internet for viruses. It will ensure you get only clean files.

Summary

HKEY_LOCAL_MACHINE holds all the filename, file-location, and setting information for the entire system, and all its attached devices. It is updated by the Control Panel, by the installation of devices, and through utilities.

APPENDIX C

A Closer Look at HKEY_CLASSES_ROOT

HKEY_CLASSES_ROOT is the section of the Registry that controls all the data files on the system. It is nearly identical on both Windows NT and Windows 95. For that reason, there is only one appendix concerning it. The HKEY_CLASSES_ROOT handle key includes all the file extensions and associations with executable files, as shown in Figure C.1. It also determines how an application will react when a document file is double-clicked.

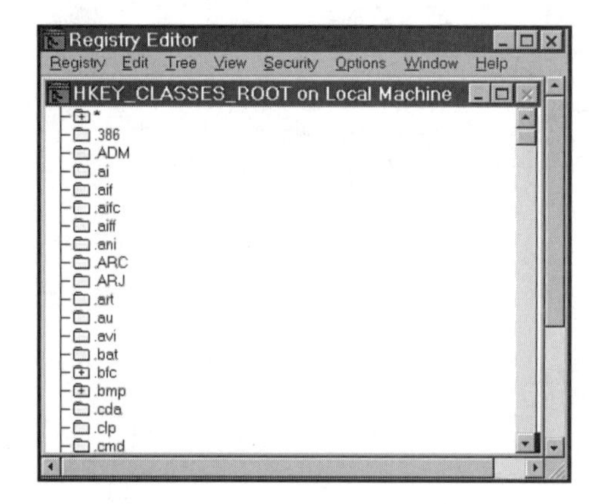

Figure C.1.
HKEY_CLASSES_ROOT controls data files and their extensions.

HKEY_CLASSES_ROOT is really just a portion of HKEY_LOCAL_COMPUTER, and settings can be edited in either location, as shown in Figure C.2. As soon as one is changed, the other is also changed. HKEY_CLASSES_ROOT is used, however, to make it easy for programmers to send information during an installation. In Windows NT and Windows 95, HKEY_CLASSES_ROOT is the same as HKEY_LOCAL_MACHINE\Software\Classes. Programmers need not worry about the actual location when developing their startup routines. Instead, they can just send data to HKEY_CLASSES_ROOT.

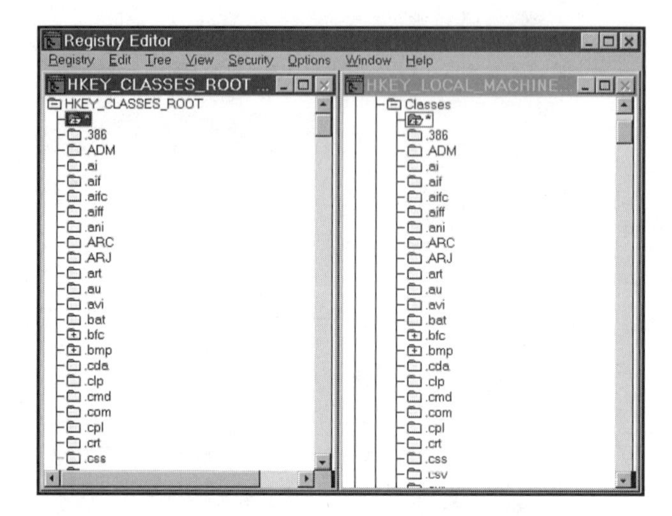

Figure C.2.
HKEY_CLASSES_ROOT and HKEY_LOCAL_MACHINE\Software\Classes are the same.

Table C.1 lists extensions from HKEY_CLASSES_ROOT in the first column, and their corresponding file types in the second column. These file types are also entries in HKEY_CLASSES_ROOT and give more detail about the function of the files, including their locations and the launching characteristics.

Table C.1. HKEY_CLASSES_ROOT **extensions.**

Extension	*File Type*
.ADM	ADM_auto_file
.aif	aifffile
.aifc	aifffile
.aiff	aifffile
.ani	anifile
.art	artfile
.au	aufile
.snd	aufile
.avi	AVIFile
.bat	batfile
.bfc	Briefcase
.cda	cdafile
.crt	certificatefile
.der	certificatefile
.clp	clpfile
.cmd	cmdfile
.com	comfile
.cpl	cplfile
.cur	curfile
.dat	DAT_auto_file
.dcx	DCXImage.Document
.dll	dllfile
.shb	DocShortcut
.drv	drvfile
.xla	EXCEL.Addin
.xlk	Excel.Backup
.xlc	Excel.Chart.5
.csv	Excel.CSV
.xld	Excel.Dialog
.dif	Excel.DIF

continues

Table C.1. continued

Extension	*File Type*
.xlb	Excel.Sheet.5
.xls	Excel.Sheet.5
.slk	Excel.SLK
.xlt	Excel.Template
.xlv	Excel.VBAModule
.xlw	Excel.Workspace
.xll	Excel.XLL
.xlm	ExcelMacrosheet
.exe	exefile
.fnd	fndfile
.fon	fonfile
.gif	giffile
.goc	gocserve
.hlp	helpfile
.ht	htfile
.htm	htmlfile
.html	htmlfile
.ico	icofile
.inf	inffile
.ini	inifile
.url	InternetShortcut
.job	JobObject
.jfif	jpegfile
.jpe	jpegfile
.jpeg	jpegfile
.jpg	jpegfile
.lnk	lnkfile
.mid	MIDFile
.mmm	MPlayer
.rmi	MPlayer
.gra	MSGraph.Chart.5
.grp	MSProgramGroup
.obd	Office.Binder.95
.obt	Office.Binder.Template
.obz	Office.Binder.Wizard

Extension	*File Type*
.ofn	Office.FileNew
.bmp	Paint.Picture
.pbk	pbkfile
.pcx	PCXImage.Document
.pma	PerfFile
.pmc	PerfFile
.pml	PerfFile
.pmr	PerfFile
.pmw	PerfFile
.pfm	pfmfile
.pif	piffile
.mov	PlayerFrameClass
.pnf	pnffile
.que	QueueObject
.ra	RealAudio File
.ram	RealAudio File
.reg	regfile
.rnk	rnkfile
.scr	scrfile
.shs	ShellScrap
.sys	sysfile
.tif	TIFImage.Document
.tiff	TIFImage.Document
.ttf	ttffile
.DIC	txtfile
.EXC	txtfile
.log	txtfile
.scp	txtfile
.txt	txtfile
.pic	ViewerFrameClass
.vir	virfile
.vsd	Visio.Drawing.4
.vss	Visio.Drawing.4
.vst	Visio.Drawing.4
.vsw	Visio.Drawing.4

continues

Table C.1. continued

Extension	File Type
.386	vxdfile
.wav	WAVFiles
.ARC	WinZip
.ARJ	WinZip
.gz	WinZip
.LZH	WinZip
.tar	WinZip
.taz	WinZip
.tgz	WinZip
.z	WinZip
.zip	WinZip
.wll	Word.Addin
.wbk	Word.Backup
.rtf	Word.RTF
.DOT	Word.Template
.wiz	Word.Wizard
.doc	WordDocument
.wri	wrifile
.xbm	xbmfile
.xif	XIfImage.Document

Other extensions listed in HKEY_CLASSES_ROOT can be found in Table C.2. They have no corresponding entries in the Registry because they have not yet been associated with an application. The descriptions listed here do not have specific Registry entries.

Table C.2. Unassociated extensions.

Extension	Description
.ai	postscript file
.css	text/css file
.eps	postscript file
.fif	fractal file
.hqx	Macintosh binary file

Extension	*Description*
.latex	x-latex file
.man	x-troff-man file
.movie	x-sgi-movie file
.mpe	video/mpeg file
.mpeg	video/mpeg file
.mpg	video/mpeg file
.PS	postscript file
.qt	video/quicktime file
.rpm	real audio plug-in
.sit	x-stuffit file
.wrl	x-world/x-vrml file

CLSID

Everything in Windows NT is dealt with as a number instead of as a name. People, however, tend to deal with things by name. CLSID is where all the numbers are listed for icons, applications, directories, file types, and more. Each one must be unique, and is assigned to the manufacturer by Microsoft. The manufacturer then puts the CLSID into the installation program files so it can update the Registry upon installation.

The Registry is the database that applications turn to when they need instructions about what to do. For example, assume you have a Microsoft Word 7 document with an embedded Excel 7 spreadsheet. When you double-click the spreadsheet inside Word, the application menus change to Excel menus and the spreadsheet is ready to edit, just as if you were in Excel. How does it know to do that? Every file created by Excel 7 has Excel's CLSID attached. Word reads the CLSID, goes to the Registry for instructions, and launches .DLL files or the application, depending on the data under the CLSID.

If the embedded spreadsheet is from Excel 5 (and a later version is not on the system), the reaction to the double-click is different. Each version of each software has a different CLSID.

The CLSID key also includes information about other properties of the application or function. For example, the CLSID key for a .BMP (Paintbrush picture) extension lists the file type, the default applications used for editing, running, or printing the document, the default icons, and other information required for correct use of the file. Figure C.3 shows the type of numbers used for a CLSID. Although the number types may all look the same in the graphic, they are actually quite different. Each is a 128-bit unsigned integer, and has a combination of letters and numbers assigned to each specific item.

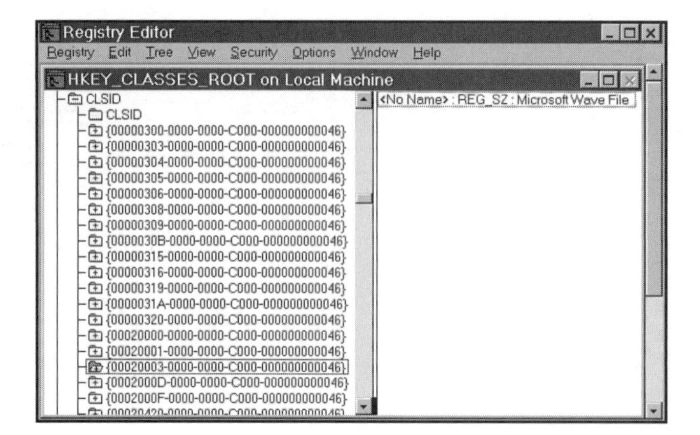

Figure C.3.
`CLSID` numbers in `HKEY_CLASSES_ROOT`.

Streamlining Your Context-Sensitive Menus with HKEY_CLASSES_ROOT

One way to improve performance using the Explorer interface is to set the menus to your preference. When you right-click just about anything in NT or Windows 95, you get a menu of choices on the screen (as shown in Figure C.4). Because the function is part of Explorer, you get a drop-down context-sensitive menu when you click anything that uses the Explorer functions. Included are the desktop, icons, anything in the Explorer application (see Figure C.5), My Computer, and the Open and Save functions in 32-bit applications.

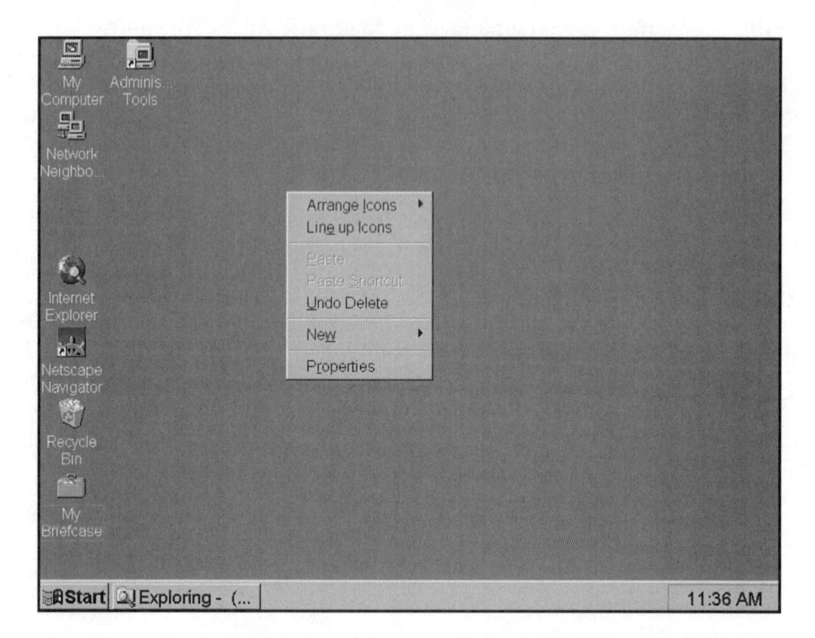

Figure C.4.
Context-sensitive menu at the desktop.

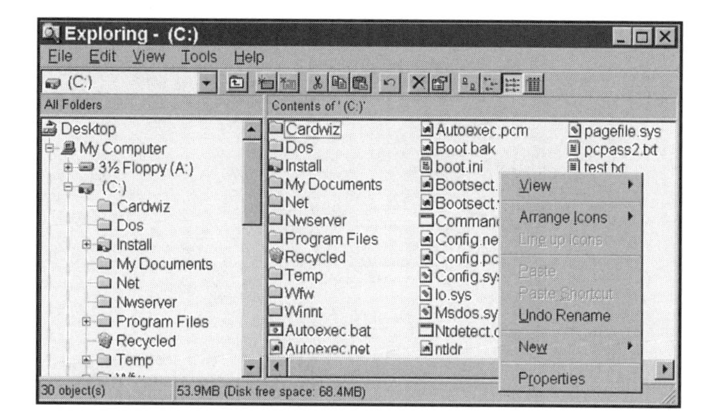

Figure C.5.
Context-sensitive menu in Explorer.

Tip

To learn more about something you see on the desktop, right-click it and select Properties from the menu. You can then see the settings and details for the item, and you may even be able to change the nature of the item directly from there. Right-clicking the My Computer icon takes you to the SYSTEM functions of the Control Panel. Right-clicking the Network Neighborhood icon takes you to the NETWORK applet in the Control Panel.

Selecting the new option pops up an additional menu of choices, as shown in Figure C.6. The choices above the line (Folder and Shortcut) are set by Explorer and cannot be changed. The items below the line are added when an application is installed. Some applications are installed with Windows NT, and others are installed by the user.

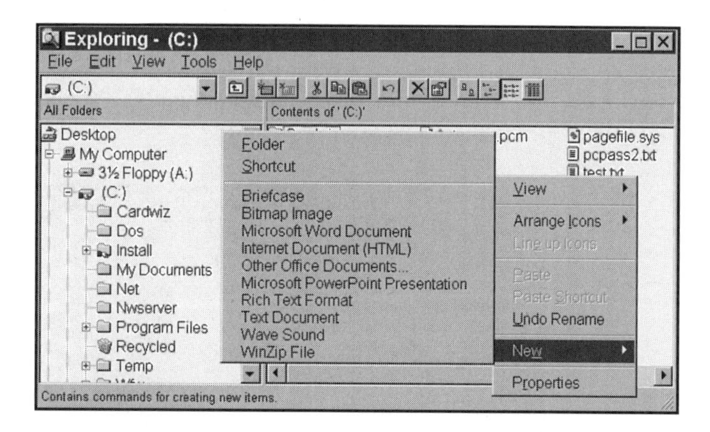

Figure C.6.
Pop-up menu for creating new items.

To create a text document, right-click, select New, then click Text Document. If you are at the desktop, a new document is created on the desktop. If you are in another folder, a new text document is created in that folder (as shown in Figure C.7).

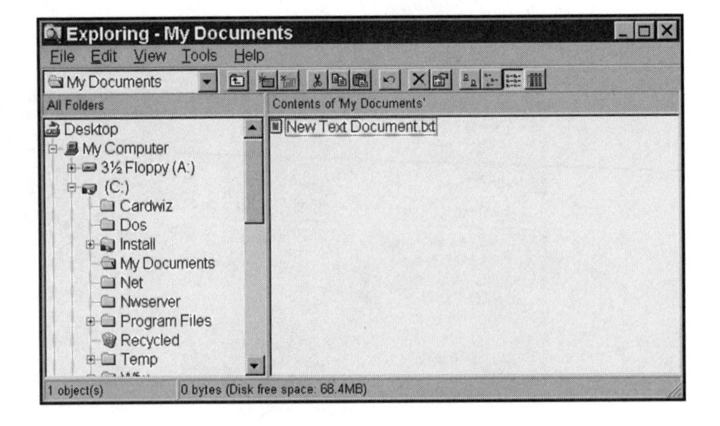

Figure C.7.
A new text document in the `My Documents` folder.

Most of the file types are helpful, but what about Briefcase or Wave Sound? If you do not find a file type to be useful, you can remove it from your menu, thus streamlining your menus and saving you time. Wave Sound is on the menu because of a key in `HKEY_CLASSES_ROOT`. In `HKEY_CLASSES_ROOT`, the extension for a wave sound is listed as `.WAV`. Notice the plus sign (+) in the folder icon next to the listing (as shown in Figure C.8).

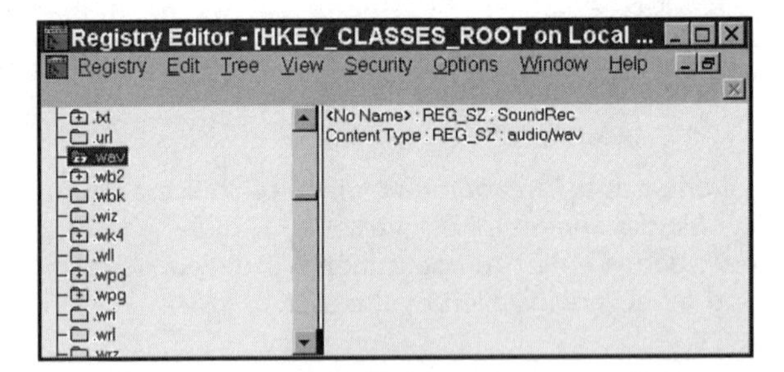

Figure C.8.
The `.WAV` extension in `HKEY_CLASSES_ROOT`.

When the tree is expanded to show the contents of the `.WAV` key, the `ShellNew` subkey is shown. (See Figure C.9.) Delete the `ShellNew` key to see the menu shown in Figure C.10 (note that there is no option for creating a new Wave Sound).

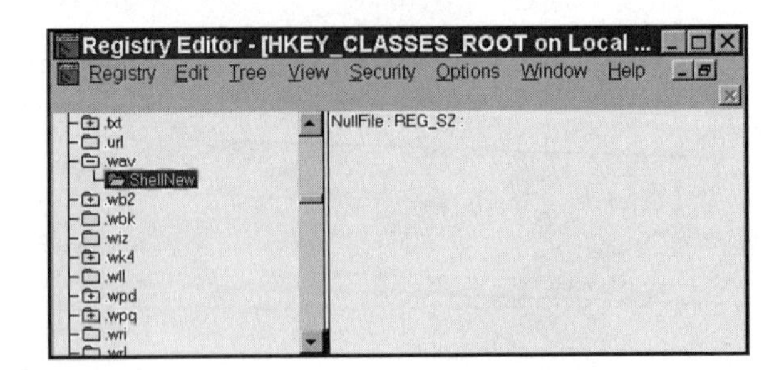

Figure C.9.
The `ShellNew` key under `.WAV` in `HKEY_CLASSES_ROOT`.

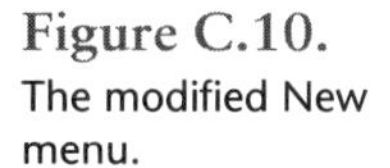

Figure C.10.
The modified New menu.

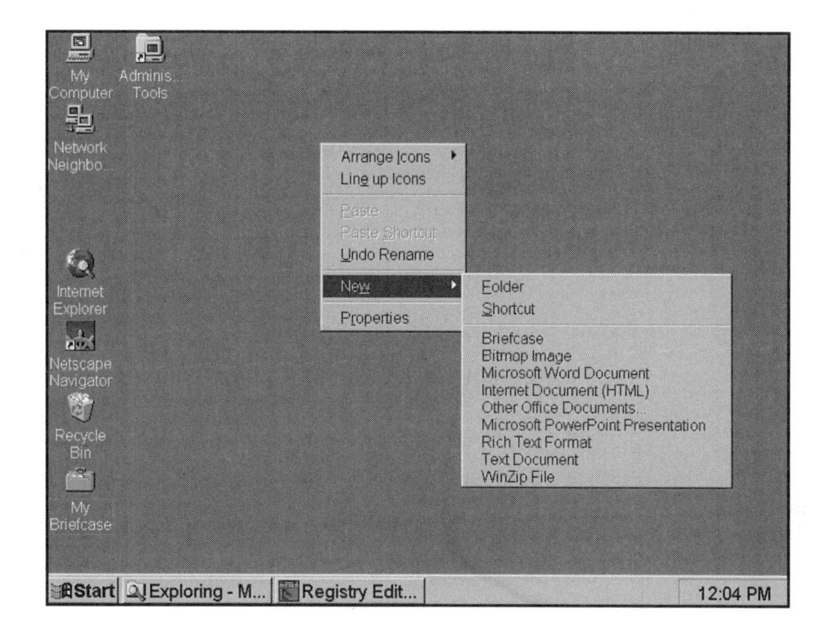

Use this procedure to remove any items in the context-sensitive New menu, thus streamlining your menus and improving your performance.

Adding to Your Context-Sensitive Menus with HKEY_CLASSES_ROOT

The opposite function, adding to context-sensitive menus, is also available by editing `HKEY_CLASSES_ROOT`. For any item you want to create, find the file extension in the list. Add a key called `ShellNew`; in it, add a `REG_SZ` value called `NullFile`. When it asks for the string, do not add anything. Simply click OK to continue. The context menu pulls the name of the data file from the Registry and lists it with the others in the menu. The new file will be blank.

Associating a Data File with an Application

To associate a data file with a particular application, double-click the data file. If the data file is not already associated with an application, NT opens the dialog box shown in Figure C.11. Choose the application to be associated with the extension, select the Always use this program to open this file check box, and click OK. Every time a file with the same extension in activated, NT runs the associated application.

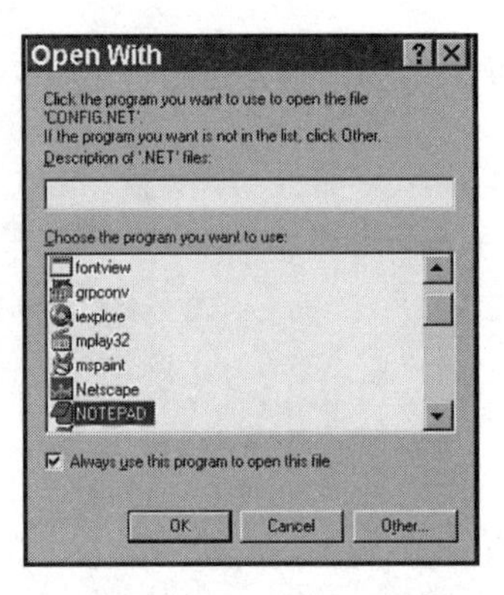

Figure C.11.
Associating a data file with an application.

What if you accidentally select the wrong application? Every time you double-click the file, it runs the wrong program. What if you change text editors, and you don't want all your text files to be edited with NOTEPAD.EXE? You could edit the HKEY_CLASSES_ROOT handle key in the Registry, or use a feature in Explorer. Hold the Shift key down and right-click the data file. Select Open With, and then scroll to the correct application to be associated with the data file.

Summary

Besides extensions and file types associated with those extensions, there are many more items in HKEY_CLASSES_ROOT. All of these items are details for NT, the interface, and applications to be run. You would normally edit only a very few of these items. Everything but the context menu tips included here is changed only by installing applications, by setting modifications inside applications, or by creating associations.

You couldn't run the system without HKEY_CLASSES_ROOT; you just hardly ever edit it manually. HKEY_CLASSES_ROOT is one of the main reasons you need the Registry: for the control of applications and the operating system. Given the sheer size and complexity of this handle key, it is no wonder that SYSTEM.INI and WIN.INI were no longer sufficient.

APPENDIX D

A Closer Look at HKEY_CURRENT_CONFIG for Windows NT

At startup, when multiple profiles are used in NT, the Last Known Good menu is automatically engaged, giving you the option of selecting which profile you would like to use. `HKEY_CURRENT_CONFIG` is the handle key representing the current hardware profile chosen at startup.

Depending on the choice of profiles, one of the Registry hardware profile entries will be chosen. When that profile is loaded into the system, it will be loaded into both `HKEY_LOCAL_MACHINE\SYSTEM\ControlSet001\Hardware Profiles\Current` and also into `HKEY_CURRENT_CONFIG`. Figure D.1 shows the results of the mapping.

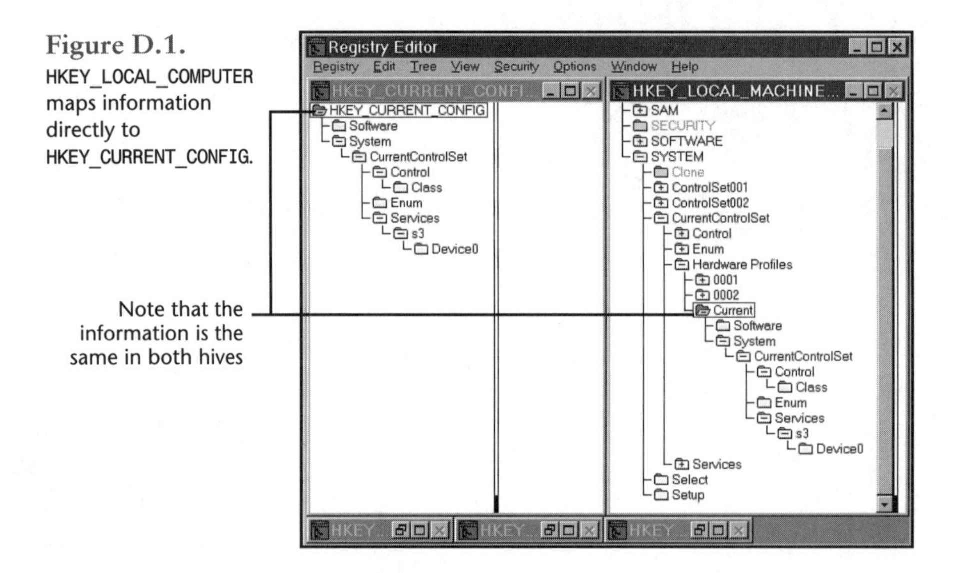

Figure D.1. `HKEY_LOCAL_COMPUTER` maps information directly to `HKEY_CURRENT_CONFIG`.

After the system is started, any change to either location automatically updates the other. `HKEY_CURRENT_CONFIG` is used to make access to the configuration information easier for programmers.

`HKEY_CURRENT_CONFIG` includes all of the details of the profile that is actually current in the system. The choice made during startup affects which of the two (or more) hardware profiles is current. For example, if Profile 0002 had been chosen, all of the Profile 0002 information would have been mapped into these keys.

All of the settings in this appendix appear in the following format:

Key Name

Full path=*`Handle Key\Keyname`*

Description, specific information, values

Second-Level Key Name

Full path=*Handle Key\Keyname\Keyname*

Description, specific information, values

Third-Level Key Name

Full path=*Handle Key\Keyname\Keyname\Keyname*

Description, specific information, values

Additional Level Key Names

Full path=*Handle Key\Keyname\Keyname\Keyname\Keyname(\Keyname)*

Description, specific information, values

Software

```
HKEY_CURRENT_CONFIG\Software
```

Without any software difference between the available profiles, there is nothing listed here. If the selected profile included software specific to hardware that was only present during this profile, it would be listed here. That is extremely rare. In nearly all cases, the `Software` entry is here for future expansion possibilities, particularly when full Plug and Play is implemented in Windows NT.

System

```
HKEY_CURRENT_CONFIG\System
```

This key holds all the subkeys for settings that are unique to the currently installed profile.

CurrentControlSet

```
HKEY_CURRENT_CONFIG\System\CurrentControlSet
```

This key holds subkeys for `Control`, `Enum`, and `Services`.

Control

```
HKEY_CURRENT_CONFIG\System\CurrentControlSet\Control
```

Availability of the Control Panel functions might be different depending on the hardware activated. If there is a difference, it is listed here.

Class

```
HKEY_CURRENT_CONFIG\System\CurrentControlSet\Control\Class
```

Different icons for the Control Panel are listed here if necessary.

Enum

```
HKEY_CURRENT_CONFIG\System\CurrentControlSet\Enum
```

This key holds information about additional buses that might be available in a hardware profile. For example, a docking station that includes a separate bus would be listed and configured here.

Services

```
HKEY_CURRENT_CONFIG\System\CurrentControlSet\Services
```

Any differences in loaded drivers based on the hardware profile are listed as subkeys to this key.

s3

```
HKEY_CURRENT_CONFIG\System\CurrentControlSet\Services\s3
```

This video driver is different because it can run a higher default resolution with a different monitor. Those settings are in the following key:

```
HKEY_CURRENT_CONFIG\System\CurrentControlSet\Services\s3\Device0
```

Summary

HKEY_CURRENT_CONFIG allows software and device-driver programmers to easily update the Registry, without concern for multiple profile information. The same data is in HKEY_LOCAL_MACHINE, and any Registry change will update both locations simultaneously.

APPENDIX E

A Closer Look at HKEY_CURRENT_CONFIG for Windows 95

Windows 95 normally uses only one hardware profile. If there is more than one profile, an additional set of keys is added to HKEY_LOCAL_MACHINE\Config.

At startup, you can choose which profile you would like to use, if there is more than one setup. Every time the system is restarted, you must choose. HKEY_CURRENT_CONFIG is the handle key representing the current hardware profile chosen at startup.

After the system is started, any change to either location automatically updates the other. HKEY_CURRENT_CONFIG is used to make access to the configuration information easier for programmers.

HKEY_CURRENT_CONFIG includes all of the details of the profile that are actually current in the system. The choice made during startup affects which of the two (or more) hardware profiles is current. For example, if Profile 0002 had been chosen, all of the Profile 0002 information would have been mapped into these keys.

All of the settings in this appendix appear in the following format.

Key Name

Full path=*Handle Key\Keyname*

Description, specific information, values

Second-Level Key Name

Full path=*Handle Key\Keyname\Keyname*

Description, specific information, values

Third-Level Key Name

Full path=*Handle Key\Keyname\Keyname\Keyname*

Description, specific information, values

Additional Level Key Names

Full path=*Handle Key\Keyname\Keyname\Keyname\Keyname(\Keyname)*

Description, specific information, values

Display

HKEY_CURRENT_CONFIG\Display

The same information is listed here as in HKEY_LOCAL_MACHINE\Config\0001\Display, if there is only one profile. It will match the Display key from whichever profile is used.

Enum

HKEY_CURRENT_CONFIG\Enum

The same information is listed here as in HKEY_LOCAL_MACHINE\Config\0001\Enum, if there is only one profile. It will match the Enum key from whichever profile is used.

System

HKEY_CURRENT_CONFIG\System

The same information is listed here as in HKEY_LOCAL_MACHINE\Config\0001\Enum, if there is only one profile. It will match the Enum key from whichever profile is used.

Summary

HKEY_CURRENT_CONFIG allows software and device-driver programmers to easily update the Registry, without concern for multiple profile information. The same data is in HKEY_LOCAL_MACHINE and any Registry change will update both locations simultaneously.

APPENDIX F

A Closer Look at HKEY_DYN_DATA

All of the information in HKEY_DYN_DATA is written to the key at startup. It represents the dynamic data that Windows 95 uses to control the hardware in the system. There are only three keys, and they hold very simple information that the system needs for current status monitoring.

None of the data in HKEY_DYN_DATA is written to the hard disk, except in a temporary file. All of the data gets rewritten every time the system restarts. Additionally, with Plug and Play, some of the data may get written over when the status of a device changes (for example, inserting a network card into a PCMCIA slot while the system is running).

Config Manager

The Config Manager contains startup information about every device installed in Windows 95. It gets its list from HKEY_CURRENT_CONFIG and checks each item at startup. If a device is found that is not on this list, it reports that information to the system for installation. If a device is listed that is no longer in the system, it will indicate that in the values in this key.

Enum

Startup status of every device that has been installed on the system is listed in this key. If the device is not ready, it will show here. If it is ready, that will also show. Pointers are also listed for each device to show which Registry the device uses for its control.

PerfStats

The performance characteristics of all of the devices in the system are stored in this key. It is difficult to read here, but very simple to read and understand with System Monitor.

Security

The security key shows which authenticator the logged-on user used to get validated on the machine and on the network.

APPENDIX G

A Closer Look at HKEY_USERS

HKEY_USERS pulls user information into the Registry editor for the default user and the currently logged-on user. For Windows 95, it only uses the logged-on user if there are user profiles activated. In the case of Windows NT, it always uses both.

Windows 95 gets its information from USER.DAT (in the Windows directory), and Windows NT gets its information from NTUSER.DAT from the WINNT\PROFILES*username*\NTUSER.DAT directory.

The .DAT file holds all user-based Registry settings and allows you to configure the user's environment. If you make changes to the default user settings, all new users inherit the same settings. However, the users who have already been created are not affected. To make changes for all users, use System Policy Editor as discussed in previous chapters.

The logged-on user is listed by SID (Security Identifier) in Windows NT rather than by name, and any changes made update that user's NTUSER.DAT. Figure G.1 shows the HKEY_USERS options. In Windows 95, the user is shown as the default user, if no profiles are used, and by name if they are.

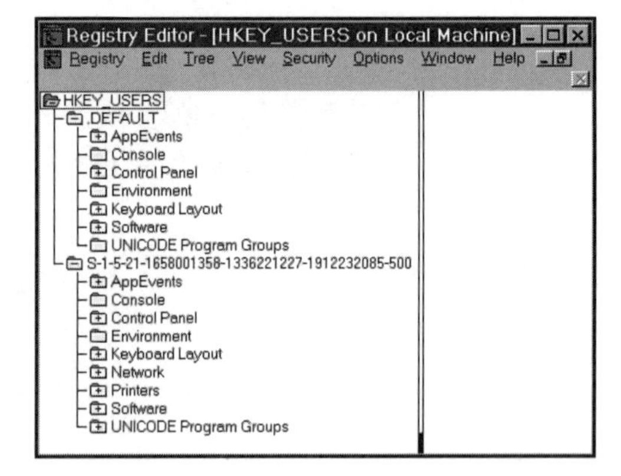

Figure G.1. HKEY_USERS allows direct editing of the default user's and the logged-on user's environment.

The logged-on user has two additional keys, for network connections and for printers. These settings are not automatically set up for every user, and they are therefore not in the default user section.

All of the settings in this chapter appear in the following format.

Key Name

```
Full path=Handle Key\Keyname
```

Description, specific information, values

Second-Level Key Name

```
Full path=Handle Key\Keyname\Keyname
```

Description, specific information, values

Third-Level Key Name

```
Full path=Handle Key\Keyname\Keyname\Keyname
```

Description, specific information, values

Additional Level Key Names

```
Full path=Handle Key\Keyname\Keyname\Keyname\Keyname(\Keyname)
```

Description, specific information, values

.DEFAULT

```
HKEY_USERS\.DEFAULT
```

The settings in this key apply to all new users; their user profiles are created from this profile. It includes all environment, screen, sound, and other user-related functions.

AppEvents

```
HKEY_USERS\.DEFAULT\AppEvents
```

This key lists the event labels, descriptions, and sounds for system functions.

EventLabels

```
HKEY_USERS\.DEFAULT\AppEvents\EventLabels
```

This key lists strings and corresponding full descriptions for the following Windows functions. In the operating system, the string is used, and then translated with the data in the Registry to make it more readable. The following list shows the event labels:

```
AppGPFault
Close
EmptyRecycleBin
Maximize
MenuCommand
MenuPopup
Minimize
Open
RestoreDown
RestoreUp
SystemAsterisk
SystemDefault
SystemExclamation
SystemExit
SystemHand
SystemQuestion
SystemStart
```

Schemes

`HKEY_USERS\.DEFAULT\AppEvents\Schemes`

The default and current sound schemes are listed in this key and its subkeys. The system plays whatever sound is listed at the time of the event.

Apps

`HKEY_USERS\.DEFAULT\AppEvents\Schemes\Apps`

This key lists the sounds and descriptions of default Windows functions, plus the settings for Explorer, Media Player, and Sound Recorder.

`HKEY_USERS\.DEFAULT\AppEvents\Schemes\Apps\.Default`

The default and current sound settings are listed for each of the following Windows events. These settings, as shown in the following list, can be changed here, but are normally changed in Control Panel:

```
AppGPFault
Close
EmptyRecycleBin
Maximize
MenuCommand
MenuPopup
Minimize
Open
RestoreDown
RestoreUp
SystemAsterisk
SystemDefault
SystemExclamation
SystemExit
SystemHand
SystemQuestion
SystemStart
```

`HKEY_USERS\.DEFAULT\AppEvents\Schemes\Apps\Explorer`

The sound settings for Explorer are set in this key. The only item listed for the default user is the setting for `EmptyRecycleBin`.

`HKEY_USERS\.DEFAULT\AppEvents\Schemes\Apps\MPlay32`

This key contains the default and current sound settings for the opening and closing of Media Player.

`HKEY_USERS\.DEFAULT\AppEvents\Schemes\Apps\SndRec32`

This key contains the current sound settings for the opening and closing of Sound Recorder.

Names

HKEY_USERS\.DEFAULT\AppEvents\Schemes\Names

This key holds the descriptions for two strings: `.Default` and `.None`. When the operating system sees these two strings in relation to sounds, it replaces them onscreen with `Windows NT Default` and `No Sounds`, respectively.

Console

HKEY_USERS\.DEFAULT\Console

This key holds the options, layout, screen color, and font settings for MS-DOS windows.

Control Panel

HKEY_USERS\.DEFAULT\Control Panel

All the settings configured in the Control Panel are held in this key and its subkeys.

Accessibility

HKEY_USERS\.DEFAULT\Control Panel\Accessibility

This key holds all the settings for the Accessibility applet in the Control Panel. These subkeys are shown in the following list, but are normally set in the Control Panel, not in a Registry editor:

```
Keyboard Response
MouseKeys
ShowSounds
SoundSentry
StickyKeys
TimeOut
ToggleKeys
```

Appearance

HKEY_USERS\.DEFAULT\Control Panel\Appearance

This key holds all the settings for the Appearance tab in the Display applet in the Control Panel. These are normally set in the Control Panel, not in a Registry editor.

Schemes

HKEY_USERS\.DEFAULT\Control Panel\Appearance\Schemes

This key lists the schemes available by default, and what each scheme includes as colors and fonts.

Colors

```
HKEY_USERS\.DEFAULT\Control Panel\Colors
```

This key holds the settings for each default color in Windows. Each value (the color name) is listed as an RGB (red, green, blue) value. For example, black is `0 0 0`, which means the red value is set to `0`, the green value is set to `0`, and the blue value is set to `0`. White is on the opposite end of the spectrum at `255 255 255`. Every other color is a combination of those RGB values.

Current

```
HKEY_USERS\.DEFAULT\Control Panel\Current
```

This key holds the setting for the current color scheme for the default user.

Cursors

```
HKEY_USERS\.DEFAULT\Control Panel\Cursors
```

This key holds the cursor schemes available to the system by default.

Schemes

```
HKEY_USERS\.DEFAULT\Control Panel\Cursors\Schemes
```

This key holds the file locations and names that make up the cursor schemes. The schemes listed in the key are shown in the following list:

3D-Bronze
3D-White
Conductor
Dinosaur
Hands 1
Hands 2
Magnified
Old Fashioned
Variations
Windows Animated
Windows Default

Custom Colors

```
HKEY_USERS\.DEFAULT\Control Panel\Custom Colors
```

This key holds the settings for up to 16 possible custom colors that can be created in Control Panel. The colors are created by selecting Display | Appearance with Other Colors.

Desktop

HKEY_USERS\.DEFAULT\Control Panel\Desktop

This key holds all the settings for the desktop, its appearance, and how the windows and menus react to user input.

WindowMetrics

HKEY_USERS\.DEFAULT\Control Panel\Desktop\WindowMetrics

Specifics about the windows that appear onscreen are held in this key.

International

HKEY_USERS\.DEFAULT\Control Panel\International

The Control Panel options for International settings are held in this key. These are normally set in Control Panel, not in a Registry editor.

Keyboard

HKEY_USERS\.DEFAULT\Control Panel\Keyboard

This key controls the keyboard options for lock activation, repeat delay, and repeat speed.

MMCPL

HKEY_USERS\.DEFAULT\Control Panel\MMCPL

This is a nonfunctional key relating to the Multimedia Control Panel applet.

Mouse

HKEY_USERS\.DEFAULT\Control Panel\Mouse

This key holds the mouse settings in the corresponding Control Panel applet.

Patterns

HKEY_USERS\.DEFAULT\Control Panel\Patterns

This key holds the default and custom pattern settings from Control Panel | Display | Background—Pattern.

Screen Saver.3DFlyingObj

```
HKEY_USERS\.DEFAULT\Control Panel\Screen Saver.3DFlyingObj
```

This key holds the settings for the 3D Flying Objects screen saver as set in Control Panel | Screen Saver | Settings.

Screen Saver.3Dpipes

```
HKEY_USERS\.DEFAULT\Control Panel\Screen Saver.3Dpipes
```

This key holds the settings for the 3D Pipes screen saver as set in Control Panel | Screen Saver | Settings.

Screen Saver.Bezier

```
HKEY_USERS\.DEFAULT\Control Panel\Screen Saver.Bezier
```

This key holds the settings for the Bezier screen saver as set in Control Panel | Screen Saver | Settings.

Screen Saver.Marquee

```
HKEY_USERS\.DEFAULT\Control Panel\Screen Saver.Marquee
```

This key holds the settings for the Marquee screen saver as set in Control Panel | Screen Saver | Settings.

Screen Saver.Mystify

```
HKEY_USERS\.DEFAULT\Control Panel\Screen Saver.Mystify
```

This key holds the settings for the Mystify screen saver as set in Control Panel | Screen Saver | Settings.

Screen Saver.Stars

```
HKEY_USERS\.DEFAULT\Control Panel\Screen Saver.Stars
```

This key holds the settings for the Stars screen saver as set in Control Panel | Screen Saver | Settings.

Sound

```
HKEY_USERS\.DEFAULT\Control Panel\Sound
```

This key determines whether the system beeps at errors.

Environment

```
HKEY_USERS\.DEFAULT\Environment
```

This key holds the environment settings, specifically the temporary file locations.

Keyboard Layout

```
HKEY_USERS\.DEFAULT\Keyboard Layout
```

The keyboard layout settings are set for the standard U.S. English QWERTY layout. If you choose to use an alternative layout, such as Dvorak or International, the number listed is different.

Warning

Do not change the `Keyboard Layout` setting in the Registry editor.

Software

```
HKEY_USERS\.DEFAULT\Software
```

Software settings for installed applications are held in this setting. The default user has only the settings for Microsoft applications.

Microsoft

```
HKEY_USERS\.DEFAULT\Software\Microsoft
```

The settings for the Microsoft Windows applications are set in this key. If other Microsoft applications are installed, they update the user's `Microsoft` key. Items controlled by default are shown in the following list:

Clock
Command Processor
File Manager
Internet Explorer
NetDDE
Ntbackup
RegEdt32
Schedule+
Windows
Windows Help
Windows NT

Windows

```
HKEY_USERS\.DEFAULT\Software\Microsoft\Windows
```

This key holds settings that are independent of Windows NT, but are related to Windows. These settings are the same as in Windows 95, using the same drivers and functions.

```
HKEY_USERS\.DEFAULT\Software\Microsoft\Windows\CurrentVersion
```

This key holds settings for the following items:

Explorer
GrpConv
Internet Settings
Multimedia
Policies
Telephony

Windows NT

```
HKEY_USERS\.DEFAULT\Software\Microsoft\Windows NT
```

The Windows NT settings in this key are based on NT functions. Windows NT could not function without these settings, which establish the environment and the procedures for networking, user access, printers, fonts, and much more.

```
HKEY_USERS\.DEFAULT\Software\Microsoft\Windows NT\CurrentVersion
```

This key holds specific information for the control of the Windows NT 4.0 functions. The following subkeys hold the settings for NT and its properties:

Devices
Extensions
Network
PrinterPorts
Program Manager
TrueType
Windows
Winlogon

Network

```
HKEY_USERS\.DEFAULT\Software\Microsoft\Windows NT\CurrentVersion\Network
```

This key determines whether settings made on the network are saved for the following items:

Event Viewer
Persistent Connections
Server Manager
User Manager
User Manager for Domains

Program Manager

`HKEY_USERS\.DEFAULT\Software\Microsoft\Windows NT\CurrentVersion\Program Manager`

This key holds the settings for several items for the 32-bit Program Manager included with Windows NT. The subkeys under Program Manager are listed next:

Common Groups
Restrictions
Settings
Unicode Groups

Winlogon

`HKEY_USERS\.DEFAULT\Software\Microsoft\Windows NT\CurrentVersion\Winlogon`

This setting controls the logon functions for Windows NT.

Unicode Program Groups

`HKEY_USERS\.DEFAULT\UNICODE Program Groups`

The default Unicode program groups are only available when using Program Manager. Explorer does not use them.

S-1-5-21-1658001358-1336221227-1912232085-500 (*SID*)

`HKEY_USERS\S-1-5-21-1658001358-1336221227-1912232085-500`

This is the SID for the currently logged-on user. Every user on the network is assigned a SID by User Manager for Domains, and each SID is unique, so depending on who is logged on, this information changes. It is pulled from the `NTUSER.DAT` file in the user's profile. Generally, the subkeys are more extensive, based on the software installed, the choices made, and the resulting settings.

Note

Rather than list a SID for user, the rest of this section will use the placeholder *SID*.

The main areas of change are in the addition of the `Network` and `Printers` keys, and in the `Software` key and its subkeys. All other settings perform the same functions, though the settings may differ greatly from the default user's settings. Figure G.2 shows the similarity between the default user's options and those for the logged-on user.

Figure G.2.
The logged-on user has two additional keys.

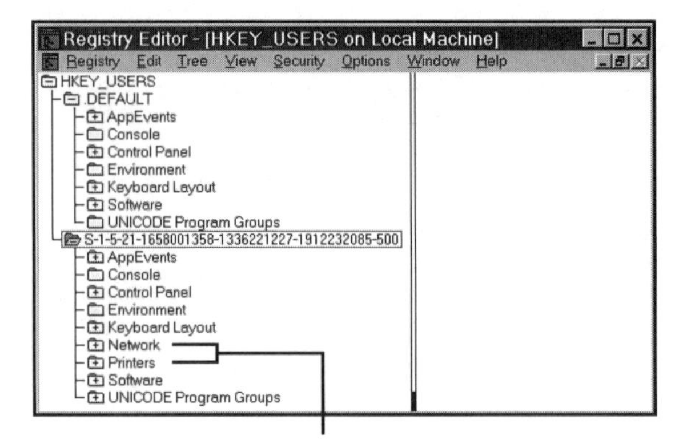

These settings are not in the `.DEFAULT` key

Network

`HKEY_USERS\SID\Network`

This key shows the mapped connections to other systems. For example, if you map drive `H:` to `\\SERVER1\DOCS`, it would be shown in a subkey.

Printers

`HKEY_USERS\SID\Printers`

This key shows all the installed, shared, and connected printers for this user.

Tip

If you save the keys from a logged-on user, you can add them to the default user's Registry using Registry | Save Key. To add the `Network` key so all new users have the same network connections at startup, perform the following steps.

1. Use Edit | Add Key to add a key to the default user called `Network`.
2. Highlight the `Network` key for the default user, and select Registry | Restore.
3. In the `Network` key, go to each connection and change `UserName` to `%username%`.
4. Save the `Network` key at the logged-on user with Registry | Save Key.

As shown in Figure G.3, the default user and all new users created from the default will have the same connections automatically. The same tip works with Printer | Connections, but not necessarily with the other portions of the key.

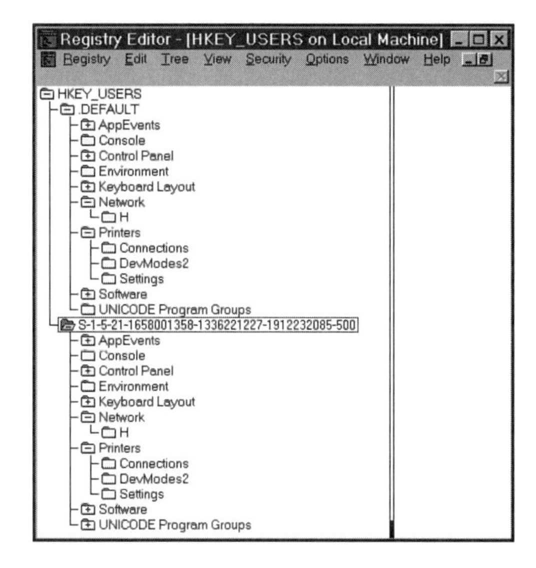

Figure G.3.
The logged-on user's SID and settings in the Registry.

Software

```
HKEY_USERS\SID\Software
```

This key is expanded for the individual user, based on the additional software installed by or for that user.

Summary

HKEY_USERS holds all the settings for the currently logged-on user and the default user. The information for the logged-on user changes as different users use the system. The user information is represented by the SID. Using the procedure to retrieve any user's NTUSER.DAT file and bring it into the Registry for viewing and editing (as shown in Chapter 9, "Making Manual Changes to the Registry Using REGEDT32.EXE") simplifies the editing of a specific user's data.

APPENDIX H

A Closer Look at HKEY_CURRENT_USER

`HKEY_CURRENT_USER` contains the same information as that listed by the security identifier in `HKEY_USERS`, as shown in Figure H.1. Any change made to `HKEY_CURRENT_USER` is immediately made to `HKEY_USERS` also. The opposite is also true.

Note

All of the settings in `HKEY_CURRENT_USER` are the same in both Windows NT and Windows 95. There is a minor difference in location, but the actual keys are the same. For that reason, only the Windows NT information will be shown, and the descriptions of all the keys are the same for Windows 95.

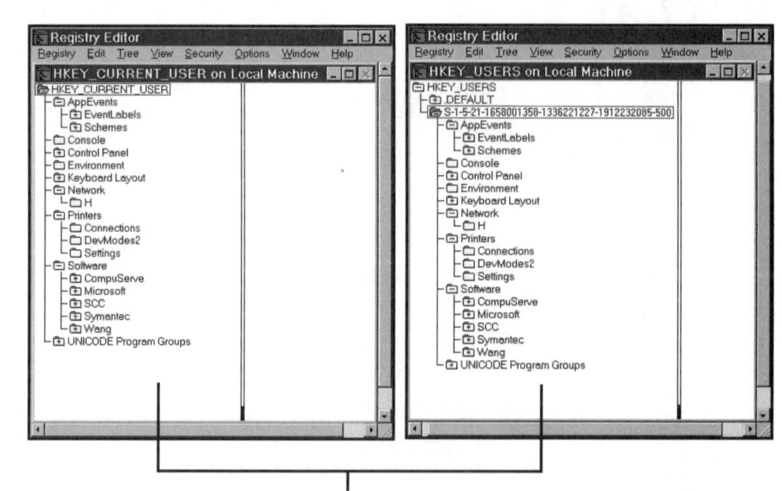

Figure H.1. `HKEY_CURRENT_USER` and the currently logged-on user in `HKEY_USERS` are both mapped from `NTUSER.DAT`.

All of the settings in this chapter appear in the following format:

Key Name

```
Full path=Handle Key\Keyname
```

Description, specific information, values

Second-Level Key Name

```
Full path=Handle Key\Keyname\Keyname
```

Description, specific information, values

Third-Level Key Name

```
Full path=Handle Key\Keyname\Keyname\Keyname
```

Description, specific information, values

Additional Level Key Names

```
Full path=Handle Key\Keyname\Keyname\Keyname\Keyname(\Keyname)
```

Description, specific information, values

AppEvents

```
HKEY_CURRENT_USER\AppEvents
```

This key lists the event labels, descriptions, and sounds for system functions.

EventLabels

```
HKEY_CURRENT_USER\AppEvents\EventLabels
```

This key lists strings and corresponding full descriptions for the following Windows functions. In the operating system, the string is used and then translated with the data in the Registry to make it more readable. The different event labels are shown in the following list:

```
AppGPFault
Close
EmptyRecycleBin
Maximize
MenuCommand
MenuPopup
Minimize
Open
RestoreDown
RestoreUp
SystemAsterisk
SystemDefault
SystemExclamation
SystemExit
SystemHand
SystemQuestion
SystemStart
```

Schemes

```
HKEY_CURRENT_USER\AppEvents\Schemes
```

The default and current sound schemes are listed in this key and its subkeys. The system plays whatever sound is listed at the time of the event.

Apps

`HKEY_CURRENT_USER\AppEvents\Schemes\Apps`

This key lists the sounds and descriptions of default Windows NT functions, plus the settings for Explorer, Media Player, and Sound Recorder.

`HKEY_CURRENT_USER\AppEvents\Schemes\Apps\.Default`

The default and current sound settings are listed for each of the following Windows NT events. These settings, as shown in the following list, could be changed here, but normally they are changed in Control Panel:

```
AppGPFault
Close
EmptyRecycleBin
Maximize
MenuCommand
MenuPopup
Minimize
Open
RestoreDown
RestoreUp
SystemAsterisk
SystemDefault
SystemExclamation
SystemExit
SystemHand
SystemQuestion
SystemStart
```

`HKEY_CURRENT_USER\AppEvents\Schemes\Apps\Explorer`

The sound settings for Explorer are set in this key. The only item listed for the user is the setting for `EmptyRecycleBin`.

`HKEY_CURRENT_USER\AppEvents\Schemes\Apps\MPlay32`

This key contains the default and current sound settings for the opening and closing of Media Player.

`HKEY_CURRENT_USER\AppEvents\Schemes\Apps\SndRec32`

This key contains the current sound settings for the opening and closing of Sound Recorder.

Names

`HKEY_CURRENT_USER\AppEvents\Schemes\Names`

This key holds the descriptions for two strings: `.Default` and `.None`. When the operating system sees these strings in relation to sounds, it replaces them on-screen with `NT Default` and `No Sounds`, respectively.

Console

```
HKEY_CURRENT_USER\Console
```

This key holds the options, layout, screen color, and font settings for MS-DOS windows.

Control Panel

```
HKEY_CURRENT_USER\Control Panel
```

All the settings that are made in the Control Panel are held in this key and its subkeys.

Accessibility

```
HKEY_CURRENT_USER\Control Panel\Accessibility
```

This key holds all the settings for the Accessibility applet in the Control Panel. These are normally set in the Control Panel, not in a Registry editor. The following lists the Registry keys corresponding to the accessibility options:

```
Keyboard Response
MouseKeys
ShowSounds
SoundSentry
StickyKeys
TimeOut
ToggleKeys
```

Appearance

```
HKEY_CURRENT_USER\Control Panel\Appearance
```

This key holds all the settings for the Appearance tab in the Display applet in the Control Panel. These are normally set in the Control Panel, not in a Registry editor.

Schemes

```
HKEY_CURRENT_USER\Control Panel\Appearance\Schemes
```

This key lists the schemes available by default, plus any created by the user, and what each scheme includes as colors and fonts.

Colors

```
HKEY_CURRENT_USER\Control Panel\Colors
```

This key holds the settings for each default color in Windows NT. Each value (the color name) is listed as an RGB (Red, Green, Blue) value. For example, Black is `0 0 0`, which means the red value is set to `0`, the green value is set to `0`, and the blue value is set to `0`. White is on the opposite end of the spectrum at `255 255 255`. Every other color is a combination of those RGB values. This setting also holds colors created by the user.

Current

```
HKEY_CURRENT_USER\Control Panel\Current
```

This key holds the setting for the current color scheme for the current user.

Cursors

```
HKEY_CURRENT_USER\Control Panel\Cursors
```

This key holds the cursor schemes available to the system by default, plus any that have been added by the user.

Schemes

```
HKEY_CURRENT_USER\Control Panel\Cursors\Schemes
```

This key holds the file locations and names that make up the cursor schemes. The following schemes are in the key:

3D-Bronze
3D-White
Conductor
Dinosaur
Hands 1
Hands 2
Magnified
Old Fashioned
Variations
Windows Animated
Windows Default

Custom Colors

```
HKEY_CURRENT_USER\Control Panel\Custom Colors
```

This key holds the settings for up to 16 custom colors that can be created in Control Panel. The colors are created in the Display | Appearance with Other Colors.

Desktop

HKEY_CURRENT_USER\Control Panel\Desktop

This key holds all the settings for the desktop, its appearance, and how the windows and menus will react to user input.

WindowMetrics

HKEY_CURRENT_USER\Control Panel\Desktop\WindowMetrics

Specifics about the windows that appear onscreen are held in this key. It includes sizes and border widths and minimize/maximize properties.

International

HKEY_CURRENT_USER\Control Panel\International

The Control Panel options for International settings are held in this key. These are normally set in the Control Panel, not in a Registry editor.

Keyboard

HKEY_CURRENT_USER\Control Panel\Keyboard

This key controls the keyboard options for lock activation, repeat delay, and repeat speed.

MMCPL

HKEY_CURRENT_USER\Control Panel\MMCPL

This is a nonfunctional key relating to the Multimedia Control Panel applet.

Mouse

HKEY_CURRENT_USER\Control Panel\Mouse

This key holds the mouse settings in the corresponding Control Panel applet.

Patterns

HKEY_CURRENT_USER\Control Panel\Patterns

This key holds the default and custom pattern settings from Control Panel | Display | Background | Pattern.

Screen Saver.3DFlyingObj

```
HKEY_CURRENT_USER\Control Panel\Screen Saver.3DFlyingObj
```

This key holds the settings for the 3D Flying Objects screen saver as set in Control Panel | Screen Saver | Settings.

Screen Saver.3Dpipes

```
HKEY_CURRENT_USER\Control Panel\Screen Saver.3Dpipes
```

This key holds the settings for the 3D Pipes screen saver as set in Control Panel | Screen Saver | Settings.

Screen Saver.Bezier

```
HKEY_CURRENT_USER\Control Panel\Screen Saver.Bezier
```

This key holds the settings for the Bezier screen saver as set in Control Panel | Screen Saver | Settings.

Screen Saver.Marquee

```
HKEY_CURRENT_USER\Control Panel\Screen Saver.Marquee
```

This key holds the settings for the Marquee screen saver as set in Control Panel | Screen Saver | Settings.

Screen Saver.Mystify

```
HKEY_CURRENT_USER\Control Panel\Screen Saver.Mystify
```

This key holds the settings for the Mystify screen saver as set in Control Panel | Screen Saver | Settings.

Screen Saver.Stars

```
HKEY_CURRENT_USER\Control Panel\Screen Saver.Stars
```

This key holds the settings for the Stars screen saver as set in Control Panel | Screen Saver | Settings.

Sound

```
HKEY_CURRENT_USER\Control Panel\Sound
```

This key determines whether the system will beep on errors.

Environment

`HKEY_CURRENT_USER\Environment`

This key holds the environment settings, specifically the temporary file locations.

Keyboard Layout

`HKEY_CURRENT_USER\Keyboard Layout`

The keyboard layout settings are set for the standard U.S. English QWERTY layout. If you choose to use an alternative layout, such as Dvorak, the number listed is different.

Warning

Do not change the `Keyboard Layout` setting in the Registry Editor. It will make your keyboard respond incorrectly. Use only the Keyboard Control Panel applet to make keyboard changes.

Software

`HKEY_CURRENT_USER\Software`

Software settings for installed applications are held in this setting. The current user has the settings for Microsoft NT applications, plus any other applications added to the system.

Microsoft

`HKEY_CURRENT_USER\Software\Microsoft`

The settings for the Microsoft Windows NT and Windows 95 applications (32-bit) are set in this key, and shown in the following list. If other Microsoft applications are installed, they update the specific user's `Microsoft` key. The Microsoft items that are controlled by default are listed next:

Clock
Command Processor
File Manager
Internet Explorer
NetDDE
Ntbackup
RegEdt32
Schedule+
Windows
Windows Help
Windows NT

On my system, CompuServe 3.0 has been added, so a subkey was created for it. Every 32-bit application creates a subkey here.

Windows

```
HKEY_CURRENT_USER\Software\Microsoft\Windows
```

The `Windows` key holds settings that are independent of Windows NT, but that are related to Windows. These settings are the same as in Windows 95, using the same drivers and functions.

```
HKEY_CURRENT_USER\Software\Microsoft\Windows\CurrentVersion
```

This key holds settings for the following items:

Explorer
GrpConv
Internet Settings
Multimedia
Policies
Telephony

Windows NT

```
HKEY_CURRENT_USER\Software\Microsoft\Windows NT
```

The Windows NT settings in this key are based on NT functions. Windows NT could not function without these settings, which establish the environment and the procedures for networking, user access, printers, fonts, and much more.

```
HKEY_CURRENT_USER\Software\Microsoft\Windows NT\CurrentVersion
```

This key holds specific information for the control of the Windows NT 4.0 functions. Inside this key, the subkeys listed next hold the settings for NT and its properties:

Devices
Extensions
Network
PrinterPorts
Program Manager
Shutdown
TaskManager
TrueType
Windows
Winlogon

Network

```
HKEY_CURRENT_USER\Software\Microsoft\Windows NT\CurrentVersion\Network
```

This key determines whether settings made on the network are saved for the following items:

Event Viewer
Persistent Connections
Server Manager
User Manager
User Manager for Domains

Program Manager

```
HKEY_CURRENT_USER\Software\Microsoft\Windows NT\CurrentVersion\Program Manager
```

This key holds the settings for several items for the 32-bit Program Manager included with Windows NT. The subkeys under Program Manager are listed next:

Common Groups
Restrictions
Settings
Unicode Groups

Winlogon

```
HKEY_CURRENT_USER\Software\Microsoft\Windows NT\CurrentVersion\Winlogon
```

This setting controls the logon functions specific to this user for Windows NT.

Unicode Program Groups

```
HKEY_CURRENT_USER\UNICODE Program Groups
```

The Unicode program groups are available only when using Program Manager. Explorer does not use them.

Summary

HKEY_CURRENT_USER allows programmers and developers easy access to the currently logged-on user's settings. By establishing this key, Microsoft made it very easy to make changes, additions, and settings without concern for the user's SID.

Each handle key has a purpose. The more you understand their contents, the better you can understand how NT works, how applications and hardware interface with the operating system, and how you can troubleshoot and fix problems that happen on your systems.

APPENDIX I

System Policy Editor Keyword Reference

Understanding current System Policy Editor template files can be difficult if you don't understand the syntax used. Creating custom policies is virtually impossible without that understanding. This appendix focuses on the individual keywords used in System Policy Editor to facilitate the understanding and creation of template files. The concepts and the procedures will work equally well for Windows NT and Windows 95. The structure of the `.ADM` files and types of options for them are exactly the same for both operating systems. In this reference, simply replace `COMMON.ADM` with `ADMIN.ADM` for Windows 95.

Figure I.1 illustrates the relationship of `CATEGORY`, `POLICY`, and `PART` components of a template file.

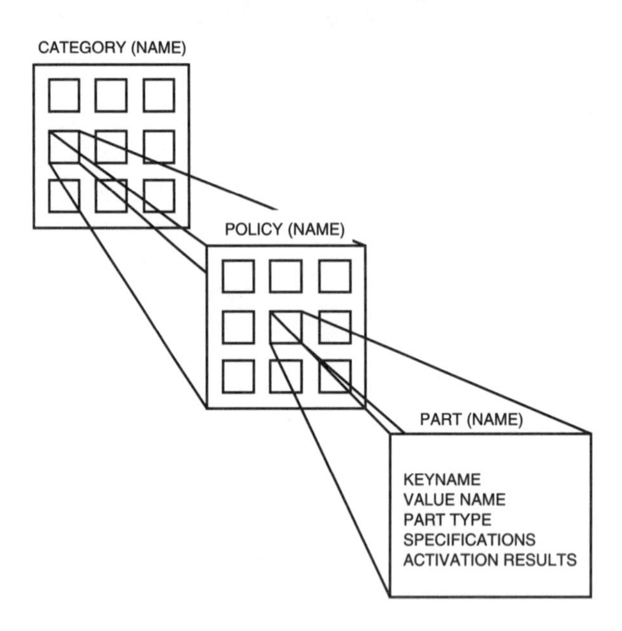

Figure I.1. The hierarchical structure of template files.

Template files are text files with `.ADM` extensions. They can be edited by any word processor or text editor. All entries in the file must be separated by a space, a tab, or a hard return. Multiple spaces, tabs, or hard returns are still considered a single separator.

Note

`.ADM` file entries are not case-sensitive. In this appendix, however, the part of the file is listed in UPPERCASE, to distinguish it from simple text.

CLASS

CLASS determines whether the change is for the computer or the user. The only valid entries are MACHINE and USER. These also determine which handle key gets updated. MACHINE updates HKEY_LOCAL_MACHINE, and USER updates HKEY_USERS.

CATEGORY/END CATEGORY

The CATEGORY listing is the first level of choices in System Policy Editor. It allows the grouping of policies for simplification, consolidation, and categorization of entries, as shown in Figure I.2. It does not allow the user to make specific selections, only to group other selections. A KEYNAME may be specified here if all entries in CATEGORY use the same one.

END CATEGORY is required for closure. Without it, System Policy Editor does not accept the template. Each category listing creates a book icon in the System Policy Editor, and the categories from COMMON.ADM are shown in Figure I.2.

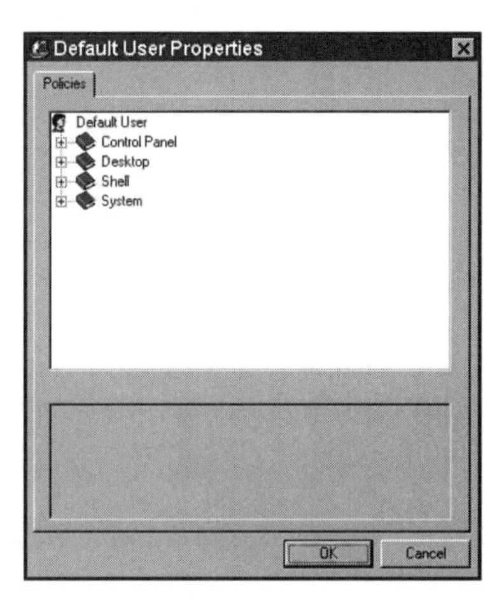

Figure I.2.
Listed categories in COMMON.ADM.

POLICY/END POLICY

The POLICY entry allows you to further classify the entries in System Policy Editor, or to implement an individual policy. For further classification, add POLICY or PART entries. The additional PART entries create a deeper hierarchical list.

The POLICY entry creates a check box for selection that allows you turn the POLICY on or off. The POLICY listings shown in Figure I.3 are for Wallpaper and Color scheme.

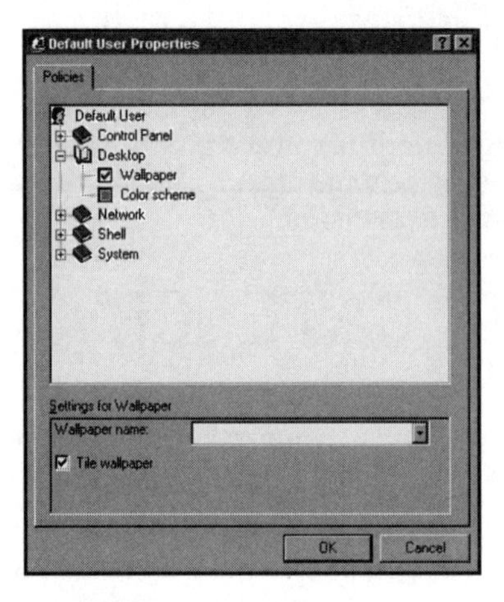

Figure I.3. Policies from `COMMON.ADM` in System Policy Editor.

For policy implementation, add a `KEYNAME` (if not already done in `CATEGORY`), `VALUENAME`, and other required entries for implementation (part type and data).

`END POLICY` is required for closure. Without it, System Policy Editor will not accept the template.

PART/END PART

The `PART` entry allows for multiple settings inside a single `POLICY`. Each `PART` entry must include a `KEYNAME`, `VALUENAME`, and entries. The `KEYNAME` may be specified at higher levels, thus inherited by the `PART`.

The `PART` may also include a part type. The default type is a `CHECKBOX`, so if another is not listed in the `PART`, System Policy Editor creates a check box. Figure I.4 shows several `PART`s under one `POLICY`.

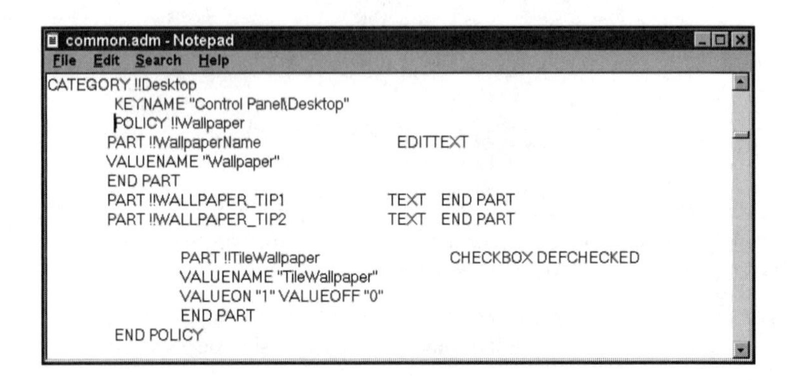

Figure I.4. Listed parts in `COMMON.ADM`.

`END PART` is required for closure. Without it, System Policy Editor does not accept the template.

KEYNAME

The KEYNAME is a critical function that determines where the change in the Registry occurs. It can be listed in the PART, the POLICY, or the CATEGORY, depending on the scope of the changes. For example, if a single KEYNAME is used for all items in a CATEGORY, KEYNAME is listed in CATEGORY. If different POLICY entries use different KEYNAMEs, the KEYNAMEs are listed under POLICY instead of CATEGORY. The same holds true for PART. It is quite rare, though, for the KEYNAME to be listed under PART, but it can be.

When you list the KEYNAME, start at the key below the handle key but do not include the backslash. The correct listing in the .ADM file for HKEY_LOCAL_MACHINE\HARDWARE\DESCRIPTION\System\CentralProcessor\0 is HARDWARE\DESCRIPTION\System\CentralProcessor\0. Figure I.5 shows a similar KEYNAME.

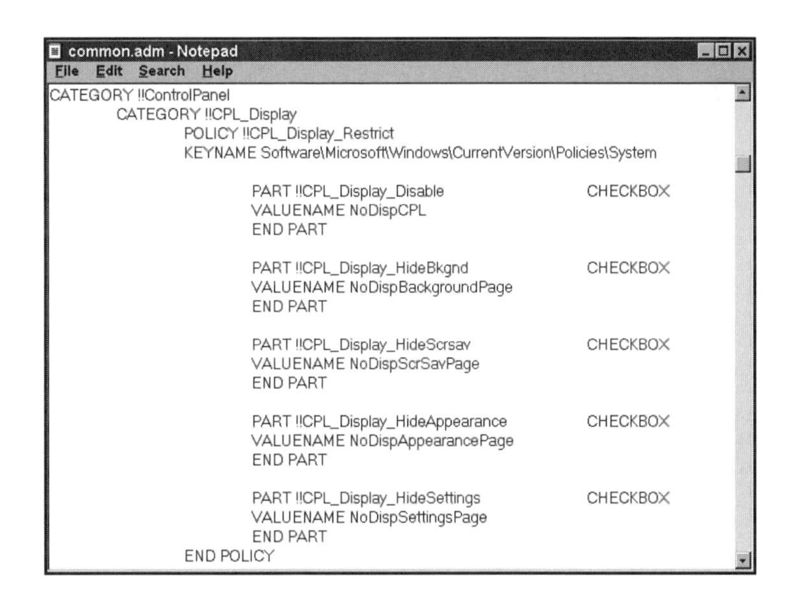

Figure I.5. Using a KEYNAME in COMMON.ADM.

If the KEYNAME does not exist, System Policy Editor creates it.

If the KEYNAME entered does not work in the Registry, no error is recorded. It simply does not work.

VALUENAME

VALUENAME is the actual location where the data is entered. If it is not present, it is added by System Policy Editor upon implementation of the policy. A VALUENAME has been highlighted in Figure I.6.

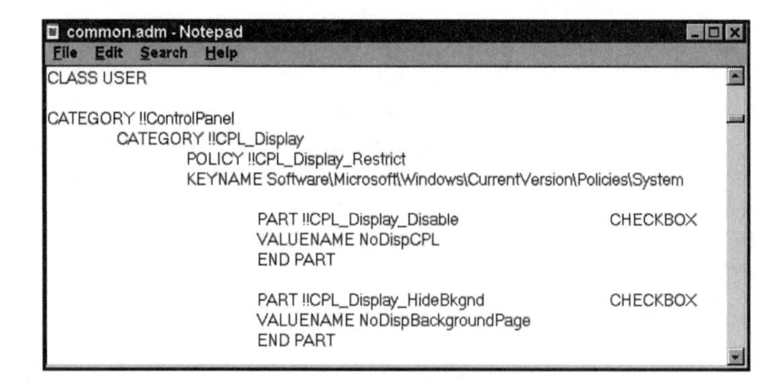
```
CLASS USER

CATEGORY !!ControlPanel
        CATEGORY !!CPL_Display
                POLICY !!CPL_Display_Restrict
                KEYNAME Software\Microsoft\Windows\CurrentVersion\Policies\System

                        PART !!CPL_Display_Disable              CHECKBOX
                        VALUENAME NoDispCPL
                        END PART

                        PART !!CPL_Display_HideBkgnd            CHECKBOX
                        VALUENAME NoDispBackgroundPage
                        END PART
```

Figure I.6. Using VALUENAME in COMMON.ADM.

If the VALUENAME entered does not work in the Registry, no error is recorded. It simply does not work.

The default value type is REG_SZ. To enter data as binary, use the NUMERIC designation with VALUE.

NUMERIC

The addition of the NUMERIC modifier after VALUE forces the data to be entered as a number rather than text. It changes the value type in the Registry to binary and converts the number automatically from decimal to binary values.

; (Comment)

The semicolon (;) allows the writer of the template file to include remarks or comments in the .ADM file without them showing in the System Policy Editor. A hard return at the end of a line ends the remark.

STRINGS

Labels for CATEGORY, POLICY, and PART entries may be made with text in quotation marks, or by the addition of STRINGS. The STRINGS listing in the policy is shown with double exclamation marks (!!). STRINGS cannot contain spaces, but can be as long as desired.

An example of a string entry would be POLICY !!RemoteUpdate in COMMON.ADM. Rather than list the text as "Remote Update" on the POLICY line, Microsoft chose to use the double exclamation (!!) and list the actual text in the [STRINGS] section of COMMON.ADM. Figure I.7 shows text from [STRINGS] as it will appear in the System Policy Editor user interface.

The replacement for the STRINGS is listed at the bottom of the template file under the [STRINGS] heading. Doing this allows the multiple use of strings, and reduces the typing required at each CATEGORY, POLICY, or PART.

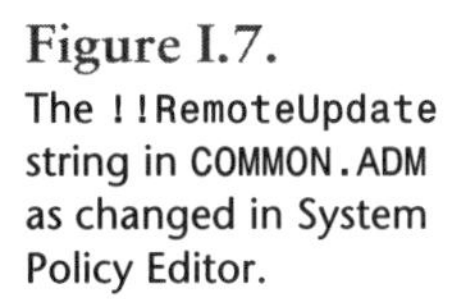

Figure I.7.
The `!!RemoteUpdate` string in `COMMON.ADM` as changed in System Policy Editor.

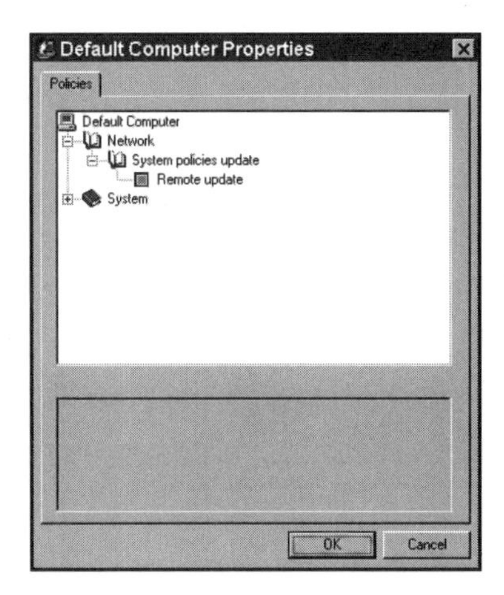

PART Types

Inside a `POLICY` or `PART`, several different types of entries are available. Each has specific limitations, and each gives a different type of entry for the value.

CHECKBOX

A `CHECKBOX` part type allows the activation or deactivation of policies. If the box is checked, the `VALUEON` value is entered. If the box is empty, the `VALUEOFF` value is entered. If the box is grayed, the entry is ignored. Whatever is currently in the Registry remains.

`CHECKBOX` is the most common type of `PART`, and is shown in Figure I.8.

Figure I.8.
`CHECKBOX` entries from `COMMON.ADM`, as displayed in the System Policy Editor.

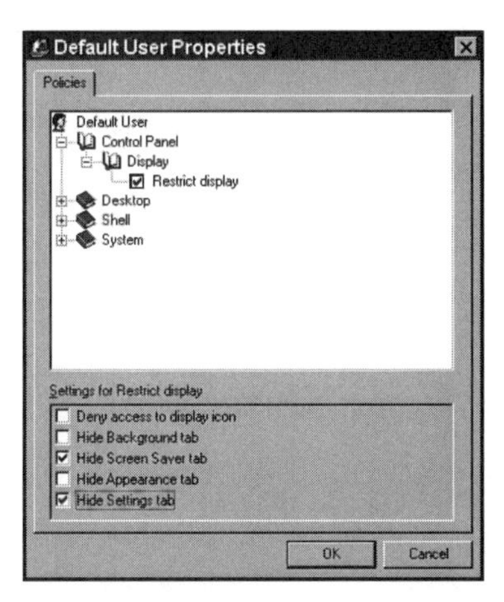

VALUEON

When CHECKBOX is selected, the string immediately following VALUEON is entered in the value.

VALUEOFF

When CHECKBOX is deselected, the string immediately following VALUEOFF is entered in the value.

EDITTEXT

Choosing an EDITTEXT type of PART allows the entry of alphanumeric text strings for the Registry. Figure I.9 shows a text box waiting for an entry.

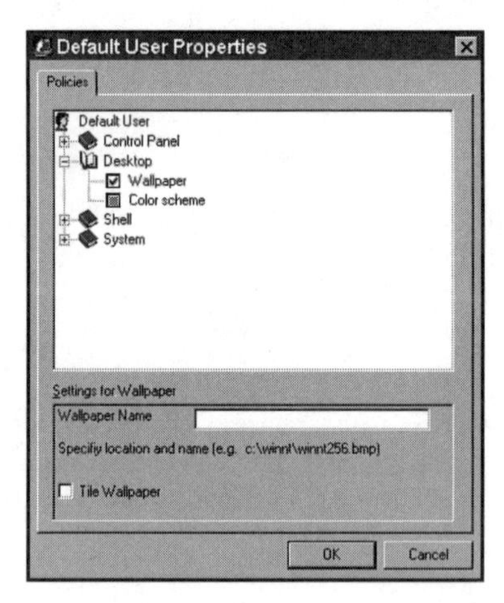

Figure I.9. An EDITTEXT entry from COMMON.ADM, as displayed in the System Policy Editor.

DEFAULT

Using a DEFAULT setting fills the text box with the default entry, but it can be typed over at any time. The syntax for this setting is DEFAULT *data*. If you do not have a DEFAULT entry, the text box is initially empty.

MAXLEN

Set the maximum length of the string with MAXLEN. The syntax is MAXLEN *value*, with the limits of 1–255 characters. For example, if you set MAXLEN 128, the maximum length of the string would be 128 characters.

REQUIRED

REQUIRED specifies that an entry is mandatory for the part to be enabled.

LISTBOX

You can add a series of entries with a LISTBOX. A LISTBOX entry will create multiple REG_SZ entries in the Registry. With no modifier, LISTBOX replaces all the current entries in the key. With the modifier ADDITIVE used, new entries from the System Policy Editor will be displayed in addition to the current entries in the key. The complex entry box created by LISTBOX is shown in Figure I.10.

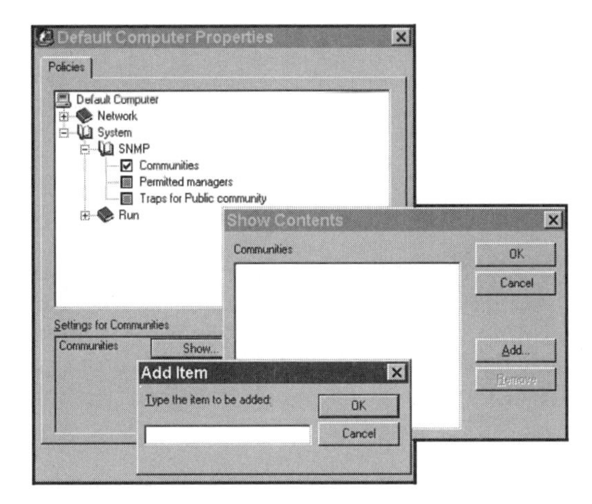

Figure I.10. An LISTBOX entry from COMMON.ADM, as displayed in the System Policy Editor.

VALUENAME

This VALUENAME is different than the one that determines where data is entered. This entry gives a name to the LISTBOX.

ADDITIVE

LISTBOX entries override current data in the Registry. If you add this modifier, entries are appended onto the end of whatever is currently in the value.

EXPLICITVALUE

Two columns of data are created with EXPLICITVALUE. The first column holds the item name; the second holds the item data. Without this modifier, the VALUENAME and the value data are the same.

DROPDOWNLIST

A DROPDOWNLIST gives the user a list of entries from which to choose. It eliminates typing errors and allows only specific entries, as shown in Figure I.11.

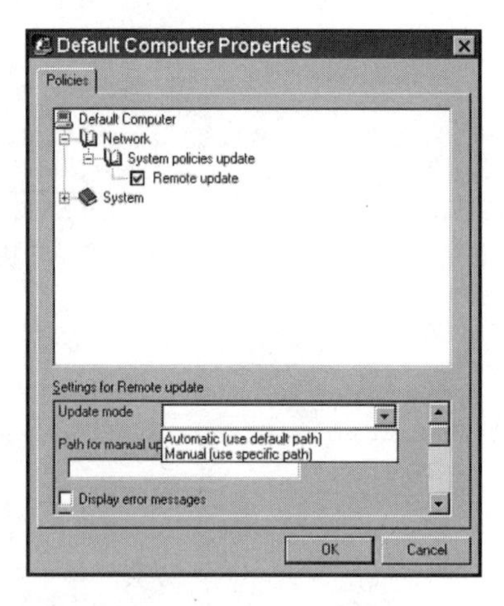

Figure I.11.
A DROPDOWNLIST entry from COMMON.ADM, as displayed in the System Policy Editor.

ITEMLIST/END ITEMLIST

ITEMLIST contains all the entries that appear in the DROPDOWNLIST. After all items have been listed, use END ITEMLIST to close the list (required). Each item consists of a NAME and a VALUE or ACTIONLIST.

NAME

The NAME is the text that appears in the DROPDOWNLIST.

VALUE

Use the VALUE parameter for the actual entry if the name is chosen in the list. Remember, if it is a binary or numeric value, use VALUE NUMERIC.

ACTIONLIST/END ACTIONLIST

ACTIONLIST is an alternative to a single-entry list. ACTIONLIST starts a list of actions if the selection is made. ACTIONLIST is used with the NAME entry. If NAME is chosen, ACTIONLIST is activated.

This requires an END ACTIONLIST to conclude the list.

REQUIRED

REQUIRED specifies that an entry is mandatory for the part to be enabled.

COMBOBOX

A COMBOBOX works like a combination of a DROPDOWNLIST and an EDITTEXT box. The items show in a list, and the user can choose one, or can add one of his own. It is more flexible than DROPDOWNLIST. If additional entries are required in the future, using a COMBOBOX means you are not required to edit the template file. Figure I.12 shows a COMBOBOX.

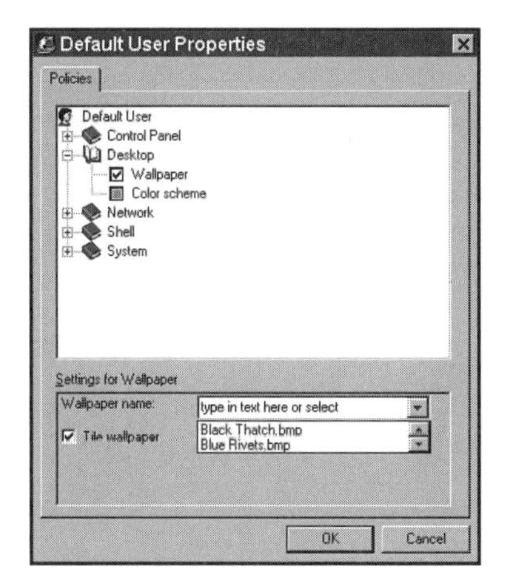

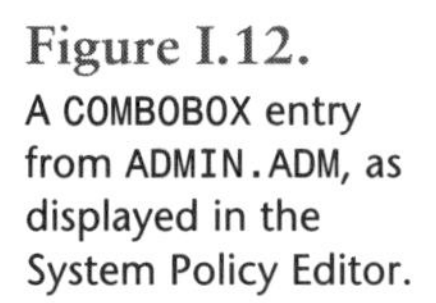
Figure I.12.
A COMBOBOX entry from ADMIN.ADM, as displayed in the System Policy Editor.

ITEMLIST/END ITEMLIST

The ITEMLIST contains all the entries that appear in the COMBOBOX. After all the items have been listed, use END ITEMLIST to close the list (required). Each item consists of a NAME and a VALUE or ACTIONLIST.

NAME

The NAME is the text that appears in the COMBOBOX.

VALUE

Use the VALUE parameter for the actual entry if the name is chosen in the list. Remember, if it is a binary or numeric value, use VALUE NUMERIC.

ACTIONLIST/END ACTIONLIST

ACTIONLIST is an alternative to a single-entry list. ACTIONLIST starts a list of actions if the selection is made. ACTIONLIST is used with the NAME entry. If NAME is chosen, ACTIONLIST is activated.

This requires an END ACTIONLIST to conclude the list.

DEFAULT

Using a DEFAULT setting fills in the text box with the default entry, but it can be typed over at any time. The syntax for this setting is DEFAULT *data*. If you do not have a DEFAULT entry, the text box is initially empty.

MAXLEN

Set the maximum length of the string with `MAXLEN`. The syntax is `MAXLEN` *`value`*, with the limits of 1–255 characters. For example, if you set `MAXLEN 128`, the maximum length of the string would be 128 characters.

REQUIRED

`REQUIRED` specifies that an entry is mandatory for the part to be enabled.

SUGGESTIONS/END SUGGESTIONS

You can specify a list of `SUGGESTIONS` in the `COMBOBOX`. All items in the list are separated only by a space. If a single item has a space in it, enclose it in quotes.

End the list with `END SUGGESTIONS`.

NUMERIC

The `NUMERIC` entry is very similar to `EDITTEXT` in that the user types a specific value. However, it is always a number instead of text.

DEFAULT

Using a `DEFAULT` setting fills in the entry box with the default entry, but it can be typed over at any time. The syntax for this setting is `DEFAULT` *`data`*. If you do not have a `DEFAULT` entry, the box is initially empty.

MAX

This setting sets the maximum length of the entry (not the maximum value). The syntax is `MAX` *`value`* (with the default of `9999` characters).

MIN

This setting sets the minimum length of the entry (not the minimum value). The syntax is `MIN` *`value`* (with the default of `0` characters).

REQUIRED

`REQUIRED` specifies that an entry is mandatory for the part to be enabled. This overrides a `MIN` value of `0`.

SPIN

Using this modifier increments the entry to the Registry every time a user makes an entry. The syntax is `SPIN` *`value`* (which increments the amount by the *`value`*). For example, `SPIN 5` increments the value by 5 for every entry; `SPIN 1` increments it by 1; `SPIN 0` turns it off.

TXTCONVERT

If you want to enter a value as text instead of a number, use `TXTCONVERT`.

ACTIONLISTON/END ACTIONLISTON

This setting allows you to set a list of items to occur simultaneously when an option is turned `ON`. Make one setting in the System Policy Editor, and it makes a number of settings for you.

ACTIONLISTOFF/END ACTIONLISTOFF

The direct opposite of `ACTIONLISTON`, `ACTIONLISTOFF` allows you to set a list of items to occur simultaneously when an option is turned `OFF`. Make one setting in the System Policy Editor, and it makes a number of settings for you. Figure I.13 illustrates the use of `ACTIONLISTON` and `ACTIONLISTOFF`.

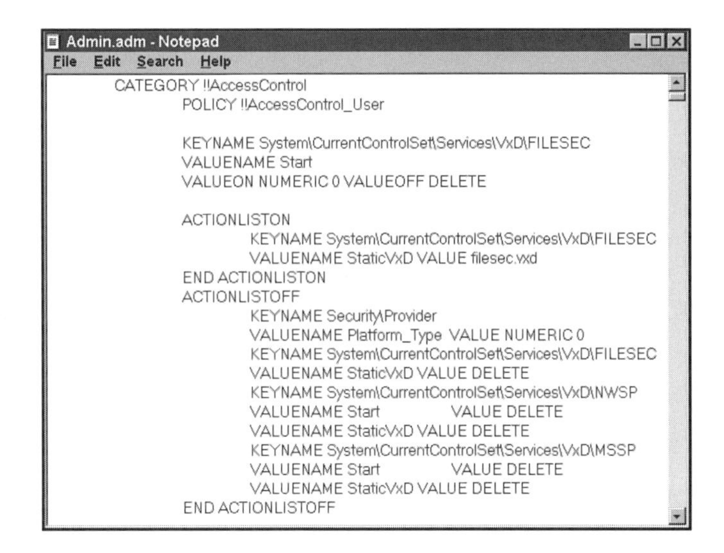

```
Admin.adm - Notepad
File Edit Search Help
CATEGORY !!AccessControl
    POLICY !!AccessControl_User

    KEYNAME System\CurrentControlSet\Services\VxD\FILESEC
    VALUENAME Start
    VALUEON NUMERIC 0 VALUEOFF DELETE

    ACTIONLISTON
        KEYNAME System\CurrentControlSet\Services\VxD\FILESEC
        VALUENAME StaticVxD VALUE filesec.vxd
    END ACTIONLISTON
    ACTIONLISTOFF
        KEYNAME Security\Provider
        VALUENAME Platform_Type VALUE NUMERIC 0
        KEYNAME System\CurrentControlSet\Services\VxD\FILESEC
        VALUENAME StaticVxD VALUE DELETE
        KEYNAME System\CurrentControlSet\Services\VxD\NWSP
        VALUENAME Start         VALUE DELETE
        VALUENAME StaticVxD VALUE DELETE
        KEYNAME System\CurrentControlSet\Services\VxD\MSSP
        VALUENAME Start         VALUE DELETE
        VALUENAME StaticVxD VALUE DELETE
    END ACTIONLISTOFF
```

Figure I.13. `ACTIONLISTON` and `ACTIONLISTOFF` allow for sweeping updates of the Registry.

APPENDIX J

Sample .ADM Files

Template files allow you to add options to System Policy Editor quickly and easily. Writing the template files can be a little difficult, so I have included template files for most of the Registry changes made in the rest of the book. You will find each of these files in the CD-ROM kit that accompanies this book. Feel free to modify them to your needs and to use them to help manage your organization better.

In Windows NT, you can simply add extra template files to the System Policy Editor. In Windows 95, you will either need to append these files on the end of `ADMIN.ADM` or use them separately. I recommend testing them by using them separately first. Then, if you are satisfied with the results, you could append them onto the end of the `ADMIN.ADM` file.

Interface Changes for the Registry

Some of the settings regarding the interface changes do not lend themselves to be policies in System Policy Editor. Two examples are Force the Windows NT Screen Saver to Start During Logon and Change the Wallpaper that Appears at the Logon Screen. They are settings that apply to every user, and all the settings made in System Policy Editor configure settings to individual users. The Default User function in System Policy Editor applies the policy to each user individually, not the All Users Registry. Logon functions apply only to All Users. This template will work equally well for Windows 95 and Windows NT.

The filename on the CD-ROM that accompanies this book for the `.ADM` file created from the interface Registry entries is `INTERFACE.ADM`. Listing J.1 shows the contents of `INTERFACE.ADM`.

Listing J.1. Template file with interface Registry changes.

```
CLASS USER
    CATEGORY !!SPEED
        POLICY "Boost Menu Speed"
        KEYNAME "Control Panel\Desktop"
            PART "Enter menu speed (1-10000, lower is faster)" EDITTEXT
            VALUENAME MenuShowDelay
            END PART
        END POLICY
        POLICY "Boost Window Speed"
        KEYNAME "Control Panel\Desktop\WindowMetrics"
            PART "I want faster windows" CHECKBOX
            VALUENAME MinAnimate
                VALUEON "0" VALUEOFF "1"
            END PART
        END POLICY
    END CATEGORY
    CATEGORY !!LOOK
        POLICY !!MOVE
        KEYNAME "Control Panel\Desktop"
            PART "Horizontal Value (from left edge, in pixels)"  EDITTEXT
                VALUENAME WallPaperOriginX
            END PART
            PART "Vertical Value (from top edge, in pixels)"  EDITTEXT
                VALUENAME WallPaperOriginY
            END PART
        END POLICY
        POLICY !!PRESERVE
```

```
        KEYNAME Software\Microsoft\Windows\CurrentVersion\Policies\Explorer
            VALUENAME NoSaveSettings
            VALUEON "0" VALUEOFF "1"
        END POLICY
    END CATEGORY
    CATEGORY !!SHUTDOWN
        POLICY "Specify Shutdown Setting"
        KEYNAME Software\Microsoft\Windows\CurrentVersion\Explorer
            PART "Select preferred shutdown option" DROPDOWNLIST
            VALUENAME "Shutdown Setting"
                ITEMLIST
                    NAME "Shut down the computer?" VALUE NUMERIC 1
                    NAME "Restart the computer?" VALUE NUMERIC 2
                    NAME "Close all programs and log on
                    ➥as a different user?" VALUE NUMERIC 3
                END ITEMLIST
            END PART
        END POLICY
    END CATEGORY
CLASS MACHINE
    CATEGORY !!ICON
        POLICY "Remove shortcut arrows from icons"
            KEYNAME SOFTWARE\Classes\Lnkfile
            ACTIONLISTON
                VALUENAME IsShortcut VALUE NUMERIC 0
            END ACTIONLISTON
        END POLICY
    END CATEGORY
    CATEGORY !!SHELL
        POLICY "Use Program Manager as the Shell"
            KEYNAME "SOFTWARE\Microsoft\Windows NT\CurrentVersion\Winlogon"
                VALUENAME Shell
                VALUEON "progman.exe" VALUEOFF "explorer.exe"
        END POLICY
        POLICY "Use the old Task List"
            KEYNAME "SOFTWARE\Microsoft\Windows NT\CurrentVersion\Winlogon"
                VALUENAME TaskMan
                VALUEON "taskman.exe" VALUEOFF "taskmgr.exe"
        END POLICY
    END CATEGORY
[STRINGS]
SPEED="Enhance Interface Performance"
LOOK="Change Desktop Appearance"
MOVE="Move the wallpaper from the center of the screen"
PRESERVE="Preserve Desktop Settings at Exit"
SHUTDOWN="Shutdown Settings"
ICON="Desktop Icons"
SHELL="Shell"
```

The resulting System Policy Editor entries are shown in Figures J.1 through J.5.

Figure J.1 shows the result of the `MenuShowDelay` function in Listing J.1. The `!!Speed` string (as a category name) is replaced by the Enhance Interface Performance text in Figure J.1.

Improving performance is also the goal of the `MinAnimate` portion of the template in Listing J.1. Figure J.2 shows the result of the template in the System Policy Editor screen.

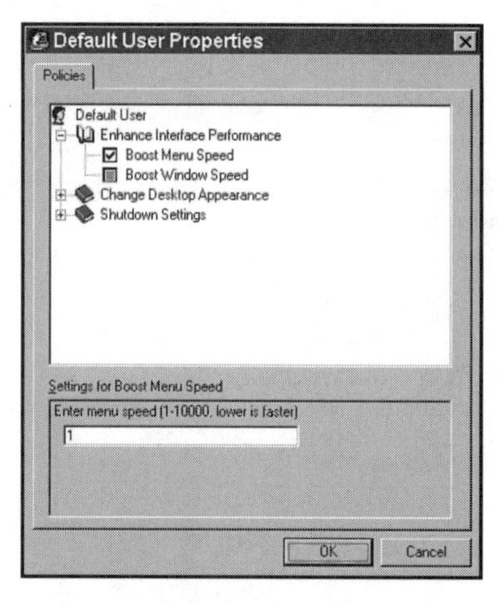

Figure J.1. Boosting the menu speed with System Policy Editor.

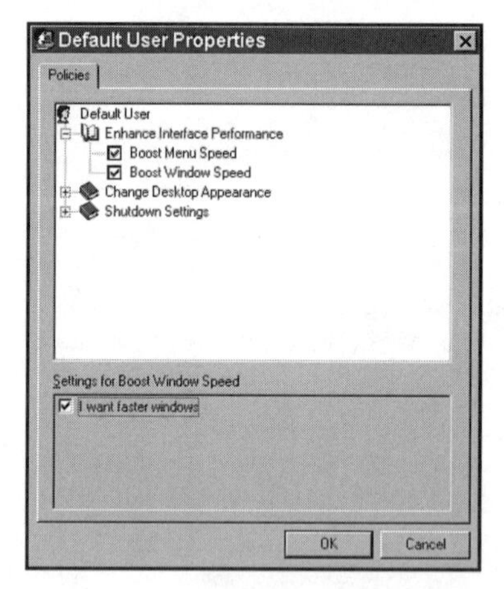

Figure J.2. Removing the window animation with System Policy Editor.

If your icons get in the way of your wallpaper, you can move the wallpaper with `WallpaperOriginX` and `WallpaperOriginY` Registry settings. The settings are included in Listing J.1, and the resulting policy is shown in Figure J.3.

Every time you exit Windows, you can set it to the same option with the Shutdown setting in the System Policy Editor. The `ITEMLIST` entry in Listing J.1 produces the lists shown at the bottom of Figure J.4.

The `CLASS MACHINE` settings in `INTERFACE.ADM` create the settings for the computer, as shown in Figure J.5.

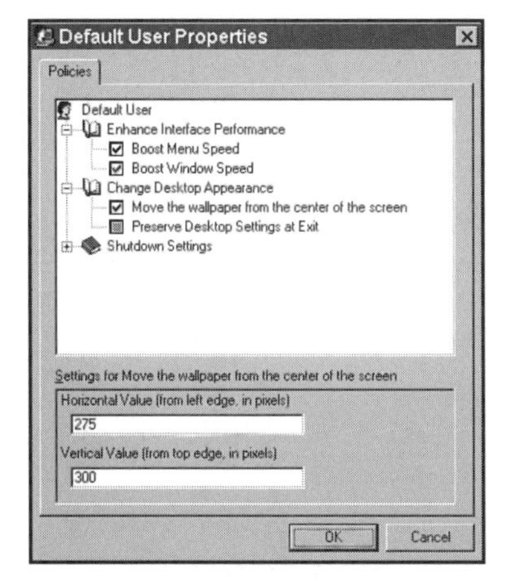

Figure J.3. Offset the wallpaper for better viewing.

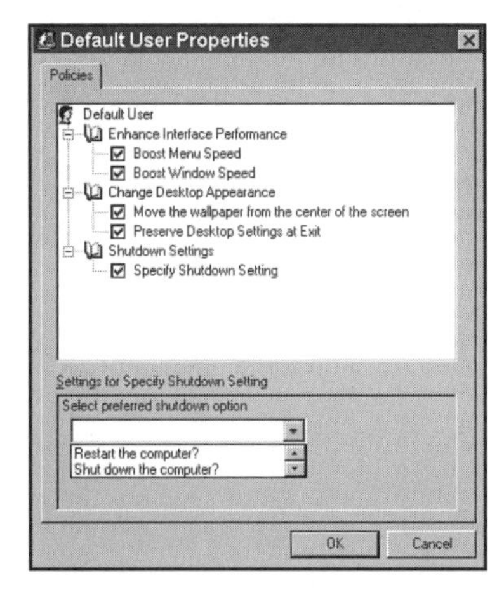

Figure J.4. Set the shut-down settings for consistency.

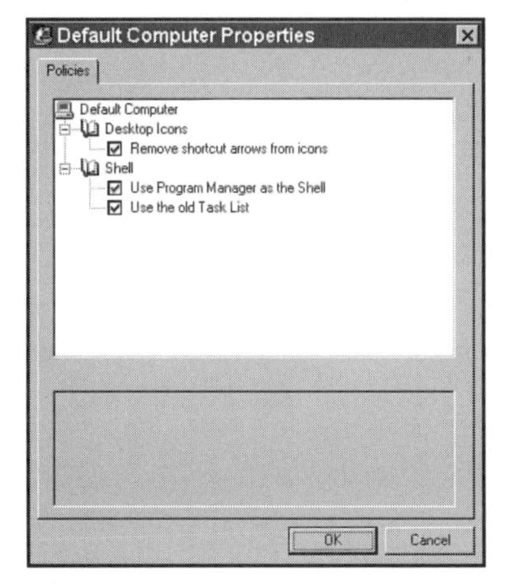

Figure J.5. Computer-based settings allow system customization.

Changes for NT Workstation

The usable changes for NT Workstation are listed in this file, called WS.ADM on the CD-ROM that accompanies this book. With that information, you can effectively create additional template files that configure NWLink and TCP/IP settings across the network.

There are no settings for CLASS USER in this template, only for the computer. Default user is blank unless you add other templates that have user settings. The Registry changes for the NT Workstation are included in the WS.ADM file, as shown in Listing J.2.

Listing J.2. Template file with Workstation Registry changes.

```
CLASS MACHINE
    CATEGORY "Registry"
        POLICY "Restrict Access to Registry"
            KEYNAME SYSTEM\CurrentControlSet\Control\SecurePipeServers\WinReg
                VALUENAME Description
                VALUEON "Registry Server" VALUEOFF ""
        END POLICY
    END CATEGORY
    CATEGORY "Browsing"
        POLICY "Master Browser"
            KEYNAME SYSTEM\CurrentControlSet\Services\Browser\Parameters
                PART "This system should:" DROPDOWNLIST
                VALUENAME MaintainServerList
                ITEMLIST
                    NAME "Be automatically selected" VALUE "Auto"
                    NAME "NEVER be a Master Browser" VALUE "No"
                    NAME "ALWAYS be the Master" VALUE "Yes"
                END ITEMLIST
                END PART
        END POLICY
    END CATEGORY
    CATEGORY "TCP/IP"
        POLICY "Domain Name Service"
            KEYNAME SYSTEM\CurrentControlSet\Services\Tcpip\Parameters
                PART "DNS Domain Name" EDITTEXT
                    VALUENAME Domain
                END PART
        END POLICY
    END CATEGORY
```

In System Policy Editor, the WS.ADM file creates policies that are easy to understand and set, as shown in Figures J.6 and J.7.

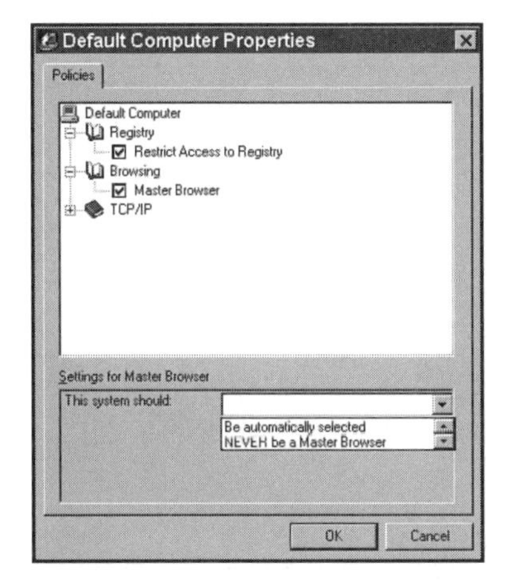

Figure J.6. Registry access and browse list restrictions for the Workstation.

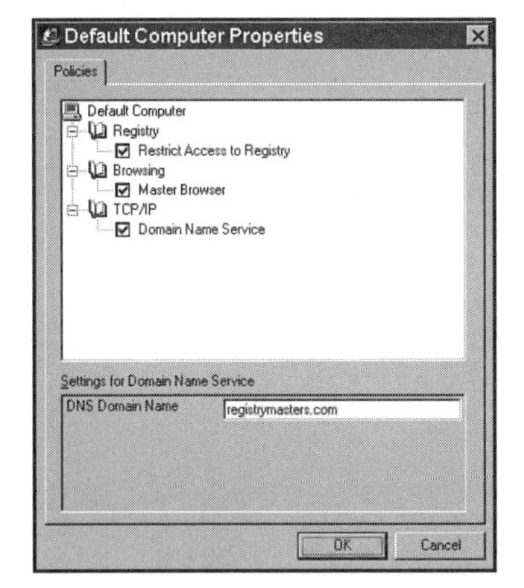

Figure J.7. Changing the DNS domain name for systems on the network quickly and easily.

Changes for NT Server

These computer-based settings are for servers and server functions on Workstation. In your system, you can also add other settings if you know your network card and drivers. Listing J.3 lists the contents of the SERVER.ADM file.

Listing J.3. Template file with server Registry changes.

```
CLASS MACHINE
    CATEGORY "Performance"
        POLICY "Server Thread Priority"
            KEYNAME SYSTEM\CurrentControlSet\Services\LanmanServer\Parameters
            PART "Server Thread priority:" DROPDOWNLIST
                VALUENAME Threadpriority
                ITEMLIST
```

continues

Listing J.3. continued

```
                        NAME "same as background" VALUE NUMERIC 0
                        NAME "same as foreground" VALUE NUMERIC 1
                        NAME "one above foreground" VALUE NUMERIC 2
                    END ITEMLIST
                END PART
            END POLICY
        END CATEGORY
        CATEGORY "Printing"
            POLICY "Disable Print Notification"
                KEYNAME SYSTEM\CurrentControlSet\Control\Print\Providers
                    VALUENAME NetPopup
                    VALUEON NUMERIC 0 VALUEOFF NUMERIC 1
            END POLICY
        END CATEGORY
        CATEGORY "Browsing"
            POLICY "Hide system from browse list"
                KEYNAME SYSTEM\CurrentControlSet\Services\LanmanServer\Parameters
                    VALUENAME Hidden
                    VALUEON NUMERIC 1 VALUEOFF NUMERIC 0
            END POLICY
        END CATEGORY
```

The settings from SERVER.ADM are shown in Figures J.8 and J.9. There are no user settings because a server is always a server, regardless of which user logs on to the system.

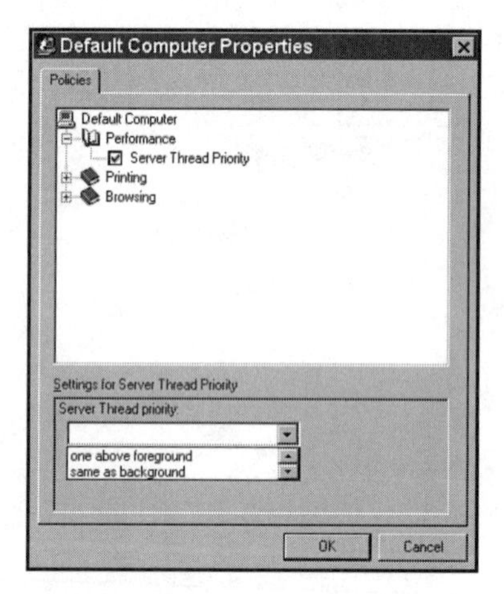

Figure J.8. Changing the thread priority for the Server service.

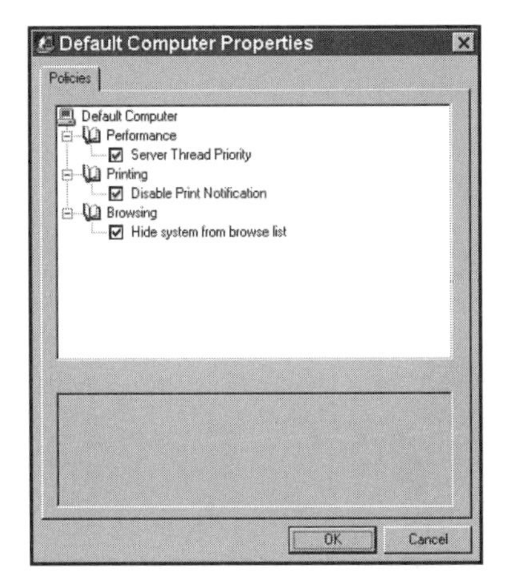

Figure J.9.
Printing and browsing optional settings for servers.

Changes for General Networking in the Registry

General networking settings allow access to different networking functions across all protocols. The biggest challenge with settings in relation to the network is the requirement to know the network card. Without that information, NETWORK.ADM has only a few, but very powerful, settings. Listing J.4 shows the contents of NETWORK.ADM.

Listing J.4. Template file with networking Registry changes.

```
CLASS MACHINE
    CATEGORY "Connection"
        POLICY "Allow Ghosted Connections"
            KEYNAME "SYSTEM\CurrentControlSet\Control\NetworkProvider"
                VALUENAME RestoreConnection
                VALUEON NUMERIC 0 VALUEOFF NUMERIC 1
        END POLICY
    END CATEGORY
    CATEGORY "Installation"
        POLICY !!INSTALL
        KEYNAME SOFTWARE\Microsoft\Windows\CurrentVersion
            VALUENAME AppInstallPath
            VALUEON "\\SERVER1\WINNT\INF\APPS.INF" VALUEOFF ""
        END POLICY
    END CATEGORY
[STRINGS]
INSTALL="Allow network installation of applications"
```

Figure J.10 shows the settings in System Policy Editor from NETWORK.ADM that allow you to enhance networking functions.

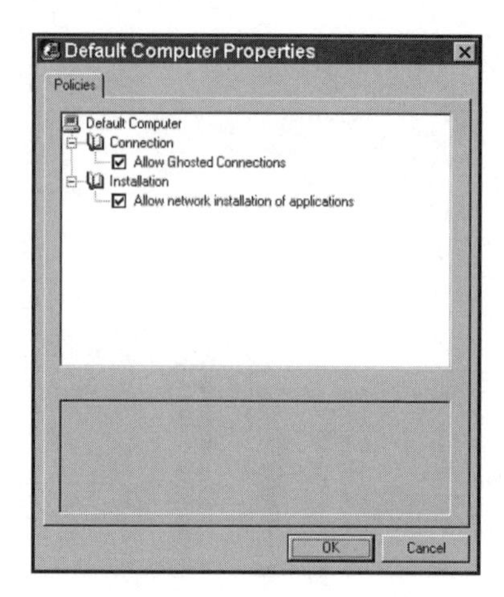

Figure J.10.
Networking options with `NETWORK.ADM`.

Use these files, modify them for your own use, and use them to learn more about creating your own custom policy files. Good luck!

APPENDIX K

CD-ROM Contents

The CD-ROM included with this book includes Windows NT/95 Registry utilities and tools, as well as system tools, scripts, productivity shareware, and more. Here's a quick run-down of the directories on the CD-ROM, and a sampling of what they contain:

`\Registry`

- `\FAQ`—Windows 95 Registry FAQ
- `\Tools`
  - `\95only`
    - `\RegClass`—Shareware Registry class browser
    - `\Rescue`—Restore your Windows 95 Registry after a crash
    - `\SmallReg`—Tool to compress Windows 95 Registry files
  - `\Both`
    - `\Ini2reg`—Loads the contents of any INI file into the Registry
    - `\RegMon`—32-bit Registry monitor tool
    - `\RegSurf`—Search tool for Windows NT or 95 Registry
  - `\NTonly`
    - `\NTDure`—Allows an NT administrator to change various default settings
    - `\Somar`—Includes DumpEVT, DumpREG, DumpACL, and ACTS
    - `\RegAdmin`—Windows NT Registry administration tool
    - `\Search`—Registry search editing tool

`\Utils`

- `\ExecSW`
  - `\Diskeep`—Lite version of the popular NT server defragmentation
  - `\Fraganal`—Fragmentation analysis tools
- `\Command`—A compilation of various disk utilties for Windows NT
- `\Instant`—Gives you access to all your drives by the click of an icon in the traybar
- `\More`—Customization tool for Windows 95 standard interface
- `\Remote32`—Remote access utility for Windows NT/95

`\Misc`

- `\Iexplore`—Version 3.02 of Microsoft's Web browser for Windows NT and 95
- `\GHOST`—(General Hardware Oriented Software Transfer) Disk copying tool

INDEX

SYMBOLS

A

B

C

D

E

F

G

H

I

K

L

M

N

O

P

Q–R

S

T

U

V

W

X–Y–Z

Technical Support:

If you need assistance with the information in this book or with a CD/Disk accompanying the book, please access the Knowledge Base on our Web site at **http://www.superlibrary.com/general/support**. Our most Frequently Asked Questions are answered there. If you do not find the answer to your questions on our Web site, you may contact Macmillan Technical Support at **(317) 581-3833** or e-mail us at **support@mcp.com**.

Robert Cowart's Windows NT 4 Unleashed, Professional Reference Edition

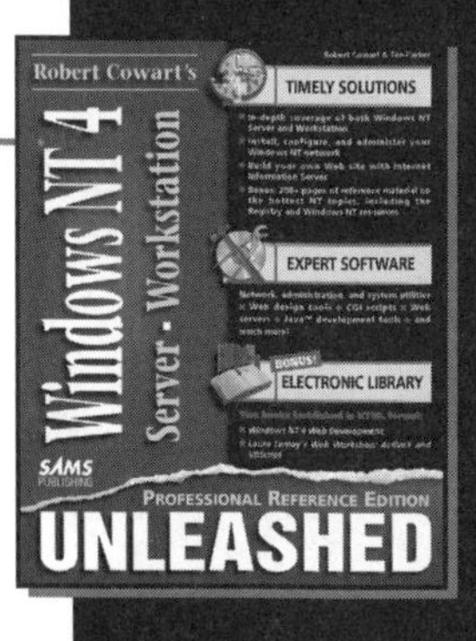

Robert Cowart

The only reference Windows NT administrators need to learn in order to configure their NT systems for maximum performance, security, and reliability. This comprehensive reference explains how to install, maintain, and configure an individual workstation, as well as connecting computers to peer-to-peer networking. This book includes comprehensive advice for setting up and administering an NT server network, and focuses on the new and improved administration and connectivity features of version 4.0.

CD-ROM includes source code, utilities, and sample applications from the book.

Covers Windows NT 4 Server and Workstation.

$59.99 USA/$84.95 CDN *0-672-31001-5* *1,400 pp.*
User Level: Intermediate—Expert *Operating System* *03/01/97*

Building an Intranet with Windows NT 4

Scott Zimmerman and Tim Evans

This hands-on guide teaches readers how to set up and maintain an efficient intranet with Windows NT. It comes complete with a selection of the best software for setting up a server, creating content, and for developing intranet applications.

CD-ROM includes a complete Windows NT intranet toolkit with a full-featured Web server, Web content development tools, and ready-to-use intranet applications.

Includes complete specifications for several of the most popular intranet applications—group scheduling, discussions, database access, and more. Covers Windows NT 4.0.

$49.99 USA/$70.95 CDN *1-57521-137-8* *600 pp.*
User Level: Casual—Accomplished *Internet—Intranets* *07/01/96*

Programming Windows NT 4 Unleashed

David Hamilton, Mickey Williams, and Griffith Kadnier

Readers get a clear understanding of the modes of operation and architecture for Windows NT. Everything—including execution models, processes, threads, DLLs, memory, controls, security, and more—is covered with precise detail.

CD-ROM contains source code and completed sample programs from the book.

Teaches OLE, DDE, Drag and Drop, OCX development, and the component gallery. Explores Microsoft BackOffice programming.

$59.99 USA/$84.95 CDN *0-672-30905-X* *1,200 pp.*
User Level: Accomplished—Expert *Programming* *07/01/96*

Peter Norton's Complete Guide to Windows 95, Second Edition

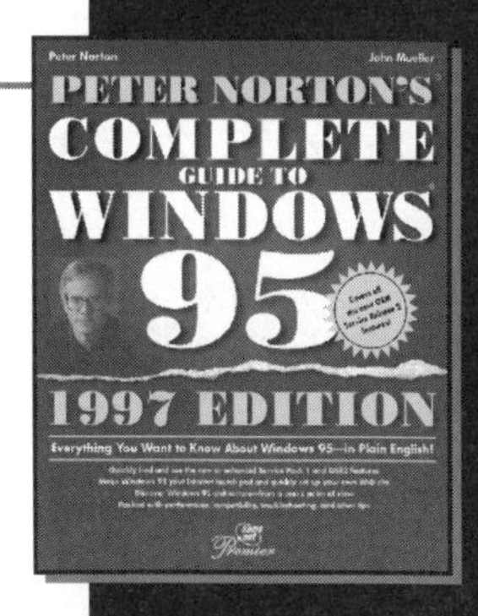

Peter Norton and John Mueller

Following the success of the best-selling Peter Norton Premier series, this complete reference provides users with in-depth, detailed insights into this powerful operating system. Users will master all the tricks of the trade as well as learn how to create a Web page.

Covers the new Internet Explorer interface, DSD, OEM Service Pack 2.1 enhancements, and more. Provides advanced tips, optimization techniques, and detailed architectural information. Extensive coverage of the Microsoft Plus! Pack. Peter's Principles, quick reference, and tear-out survival guide makes learning easy. Covers Windows 95.

$35.00 USA/$49.95 CDN *0-672-31040-6* *1,000 pp.*
User Level: Accomplished—Expert *Operating Systems* *02/01/97*

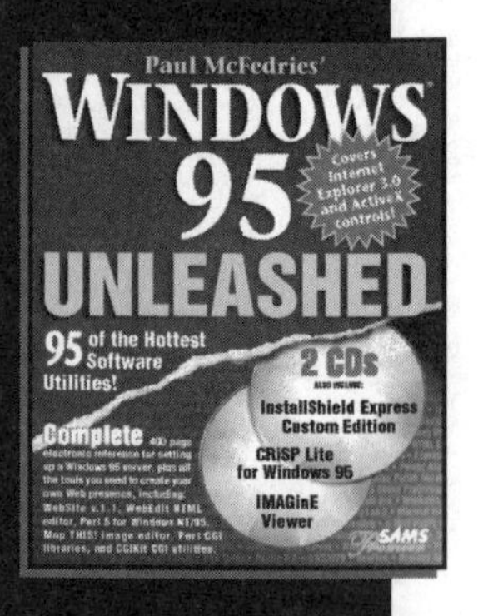

Paul McFedries' Windows 95 Unleashed, Premier Edition

Paul McFedries

Best-selling author Paul McFedries has created a completely updated and revised Windows 95 user's masterpiece. And, in the traditional style of the Unleashed series, every new feature is discussed in detail, leaving the reader fully informed and completely functional within the new operating system. It also includes coverage of soon-to-be-released Microsoft Internet products, such as Visual Basic Script, Internet Studio, and Microsoft Exchange—coverage not found anywhere else.

CD-ROM contains an easy-to-search online chapter on troubleshooting for Windows 96.

Covers Internet topics, including the Microsoft Network. Discusses multimedia topics, Internetworking, and communication issues.

$59.99 USA/$84.95 CDN *0-672-30932-7* *1,376 pp.*
User Level: Accomplished—Expert *Programming* *07/01/96*

Peter Norton
Rob McGregor
PETER NORTON'S GUIDE TO
WINDOWS
95/NT 4
PROGRAMMING WITH
MFC
SAMS Premier

Peter Norton's Guide to Windows 95/NT 4 Programming with MFC

Peter Norton and Rob McGregor

Following in the wake of the best-selling Peter Norton series, this book gives the reader a rapid tour of programming Windows 95 applications. The reader will learn to use, change, and augment the functions of the MFC library.

Readers will use the Microsoft Foundation Class libraries to get the information they need to begin programming immediately. Covers the latest version of MFC for Windows 95 and Windows NT 4.

$49.99 USA/$70.95 CDN *0-672-30900-9* *1,200 pp.*
User Level: New—Casual *Programming* *10/01/96*

Windows NT 4 Server Unleashed

Jason Garms, et al.

The Windows NT server has been gaining tremendous market share over Novell and the new upgrade—which includes a Windows 95 interface—is sure to add momentum to its market drive. To that end, *Windows NT 4 Server Unleashed* is written to meet that growing market. It provides information on disk and file management, integrated networking, BackOffice integration, and TCP/IP protocols.

CD-ROM includes source code from the book and valuable utilities.

Focuses on using Windows NT as an Internet server. Covers security issues and Macintosh support.

$59.99 USA/$84.95 CDN *0-672-30933-5* *1,100 pp.*
User Level: Accomplished—Expert *Networking* *07/01/96*

Windows NT Workstation 4 Unleashed

Sean Mathias, Eric Osborne, et al.

NT Workstation is expected to become the platform of choice for corporate America! This new edition focuses on NT Workstation's new and improved features as a high-end graphics workstation and scaleable development platform. Provides in-depth advice on installing, configuring, and managing Windows NT Workstation. Features comprehensive, detailed advice for NT.

CD-ROM includes Windows NT Utilities, demos, and more.

Covers Windows NT Workstation 4.

$39.99 USA/$56.95 CDN *0-672-30972-6* *696 pp.*
User Level: Accomplished—Expert *Operating Systems* *11/01/96*

Book ISBN 0-672-31066-X

What's on the Disc

The companion CD-ROM contains an assortment of third-party tools and product demos. The disc creates a new program group for this book and utilizes Windows Explorer. Using the icons in the program group and Windows Explorer, you can view information concerning products and companies, and install programs with just a few clicks of the mouse.

Some of the utilities and programs mentioned in this book are included on this CD-ROM. If they are not, a reference to a Web site or FTP location is usually provided in the body of the reference. If a reference is missing, up-to-date information can almost always be obtained from a comprehensive shareware site such as Beverly Hills Software (`www.bhs.com`), TUCOWS (`www.tucows.com`), or ClNet (`www.shareware.com`) for third-party Windows NT products.

To create the program group for this book, follow these steps.

Windows NT Installation Instructions

1. Insert the CD-ROM disc into your CD-ROM drive.
2. With Windows NT installed on your computer and the AutoPlay feature enabled, a Program Group for this book is automatically created whenever you insert the disc into your CD-ROM drive. Follow the directions provided in the installation program.
3. If Autoplay is not enabled, using Windows Explorer, choose `Setup.exe` from the root level of the CD-ROM to create the Program Group for this book.
4. Double-click the Browse the CD-ROM icon in the newly created Program Group to access the installation programs of the software or reference material included on this CD-ROM.
5. To review the latest information about this CD-ROM, double-click the icon About this CD-ROM.

Note

For best results, set your monitor to display between 256 and 64,000 colors. A screen resolution of 640×480 pixels is also recommended. If necessary, adjust your monitor settings before using the CD-ROM.

Technical Support

If you need assistance with the information in this book or with the CD-ROM accompanying this book, please access the Knowledge Base on our Web site at

`http://www.superlibrary.com/general/support`

Our most Frequently Asked Questions are answered there. If you do not find the answer to your questions on our Web site, you may contact Macmillan Technical Support at (317) 581-3833 or e-mail us at `support@mcp.com`.